John L. Mackay's commentary on Jeremiah is a first class explanation of the prophet from a staunchly and well-argued conservative and grammatico-historical perspective. It is certain to become the first 'port of call' in my studies of the book. A thorough and helpful presentation of introductory issues (which includes some fine work on historical context) is followed by an excellent verse-by-verse explanation which does not lose sight of the broader literary canvas. While engaging helpfully and competently with the Hebrew text, the style and format is accessible to the non-specialist. Mackay does not look to major on contemporary application. However, in addition to the various hints offered he has the ability to uncover the significance of the original message in such a way as to leave the application (almost) transparent.

Stephen Dray

John L. Mackay's commentary on Jeremiah is trebly welcome. First, from his earlier work on Exodus in this series we know that he will take the highest view of Scripture as the Word of God, and do so as one fully conversant with the wide literature on Jeremiah. His workmanlike approach and marvellous attention to detail forbid him to take shortcuts, fudge issues, or misrepresent those who take a different view from his own.

Second, he argues cogently for Jeremiah as author of the whole, contending that the book as we have it represents written records contemporary with the prophet's preaching. He rejects the unsubstantiated idea of an ongoing 'school' of interpreters, adaptors and supplemetarists of a Jeremianic 'core'.

Thirdly, from the start he is unfolding a unified message. Lovers of Hebrew will find a kindred spirit in the author. Those without Hebrew will find a patient teacher leaving no stone unturned to make the Word of God plain.

Alec Motyer

This eagerly awaited commentary on one of the longest and most taxing books of the Old Testament fulfills every expectation. Professor Mackay has already demonstrated his erudition and scholarship in previous commentaries, and this work is a landmark in Jeremiah studies as well as in conservative evangelical exposition of the Old Testament text. The message of Jeremiah's forty-year ministry is here firmly rooted in the Old Testament as a message from the Lord to his ancient people; but its abiding relevance is also brought out in Professor Mackay's careful application of the material. This will quickly become an indispensible tool for anyone wishing to study and preach from the Book of Jeremiah.

Iain D. Campbell

This commentary is refreshing—it actually explains the text of Jeremiah. John L. Mackay knows the critical speculations about the text but doesn't bore us with them. He avoids nothing; he ploughs through every bit of the text and gives a lucid explanation of it. Mackay will not write your sermon for you but gives you what you need to write your sermon—a clear understanding of what the text says.

Dale Ralph Davis

JEREMIAH

An Introduction and Commentary

Volume 2: Chapters 21–52

John L. Mackay

MENTOR

Jeremiah Volume 1: Chapters 1–20
ISBN 1 85792 937 3

Scripture quotations, unless otherwise indicated, are taken from the
HOLY BIBLE, NEW INTERNATIONAL VERSION
Copyright © 1973, 1978, 1984 by International Bible Society.
Used by permission of Hodder & Stoughton Publishers.

Copyright © John L. Mackay 2004

ISBN 1 85792 938 1

Published in 2004
in the Mentor imprint
by Christian Focus Publications, Geanies House,
Fearn, Ross-shire, IV20 1TW, Scotland.

www.christianfocus.com

Cover design by Alister MacInnes

Printed and bound by
WS Bookwell, Finland

CONTENTS

Volume 2

Abbreviations 7

Maps 9

COMMENTARY

VIII.   Kings and Prophets Denounced (21:1–24:10) 11

IX.   Judgment on the Nations (25:1-31) 87

X.   Controversy with False Prophets (26:1–29:32) 113

XI.   The Restoration of Israel and Judah (30:1–33:26) 179

XII.   The Need for Faithfulness (34:1–36:32) 285

XIII.   The Siege and Fall of Jerusalem (37:1–39:18) 331

XIV.   Jeremiah after the Fall of Jerusalem (40:1–45:5) 375

XV.   The LORD's Words against the Nations (46:1–51:64) 435

XVI.   A Supplement: Prophecy Fulfilled (52:1-34) 583

APPENDIX

The Chronology of the Period 603

Works Cited 617

Subject Index 625

Scripture Index 632

Index of Hebrew Words 635

ABBREVIATIONS

ABD   *Anchor Bible Dictionary.* D. N. Freedman (ed.). 6 volumes. New York: Doubleday, 1992.

ANET   *Ancient Near Eastern Texts Relating to the Old Testament.* J. B. Pritchard (ed.) 3rd edition. Princeton: Princeton University Press, 1969.

AV   Authorised Version (King James) (1611).

BDB   F. Brown, S. R. Driver and C. A. Briggs (eds.), *A Hebrew and English Lexicon of the Old Testament.* Oxford: Clarendon Press, 1907.

BHS   *Biblica Hebraica Stuttgartensia.* K. Elliger and W. Rudolph (eds.). Stuttgart: Deutsche Bibelstiftung, 1977.

GKC   W. Gesenius, E. Kautzsch and A. E. Cowley, *Gesenius Hebrew Grammar.* Oxford: Clarendon Press, 1910 (second edition). (cited by section.)

GNB   Good News Bible (= Today's English Version). Glasgow: Collins/Fontana, 1976.

HALOT   *The Hebrew and Aramaic Lexicon of the Old Testament.* L. Koehler, W. Baumgartner and J. J. Stamm. 5 volumes. Brill: Leiden, 1994-1999. (cited by page.)

IBHS   *An Introduction to Biblical Hebrew Syntax.* B. K. Waltke and M. O'Connor. Winona Lake, Indiana: Eisenbrauns, 1990. (cited by section.)

ISBE   *International Standard Bible Encyclopedia.* G. W. Bromiley (ed.). 4 volumes. Grand Rapids: Eerdmans, 1979-1988.

Joüon   Joüon, P. *A Grammar of Biblical Hebrew.* Translated and revised by T. Muraoka. Rome: Editrice Pontificio Istituto Biblico, 1991.

LXX   Septuagint, according to *Septuaginta II*, ed. A. Rahlfs. Deutsche Bibelgesellschaft: Stuttgart, 1982.

MT   Massoretic Text (as in *BHS* above).

NASB   New American Standard Bible. LaHabra, California: The Lockman Foundation, 1995.

NIDOTTE   *New International Dictionary of Old Testament Theology and Exegesis.* W. A. VanGemeren (ed.). 5 volumes. Grand Rapids: Zondervan, 1997. (cited by volume and page.)

NIV   New International Version. London: Hodder and Stoughton, 1988.

NJPS   *Tanakh: The Holy Scriptures: The New JPS Translation according to the Traditional Hebrew Text.* Philadelphia: The

Jewish Publication Society, 1985.

NKJV   New King James Version. Nashville: Thomas Nelson, 1982.

NLT   New Living Translation. Wheaton, Illinois: Tyndale House, 1997.

NRSV   New Revised Standard Version. New York and Oxford: Oxford University Press, 1989.

REB   Revised English Bible. Oxford University Press and Cambridge University Press, 1989.

RSV   Revised Standard Version. London: Oxford University Press, 1963.

TDOT   *Theological Dictionary of the Old Testament.* G. J. Botterweck, H. Ringgren and H-J. Fabry (eds.) 11 volumes, continuing. Grand Rapids: Eerdmans, 1974-.

TWOT   *Theological Wordbook of the Old Testament.* R. L. Harris and G. L. Archer (eds.). 2 volumes. Chicago: Moody Press, 1980. (cited by entry number.)

Map 1 Syria - Palestine

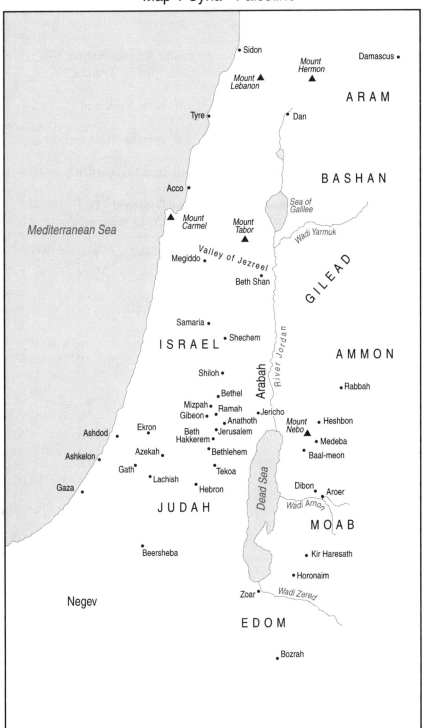

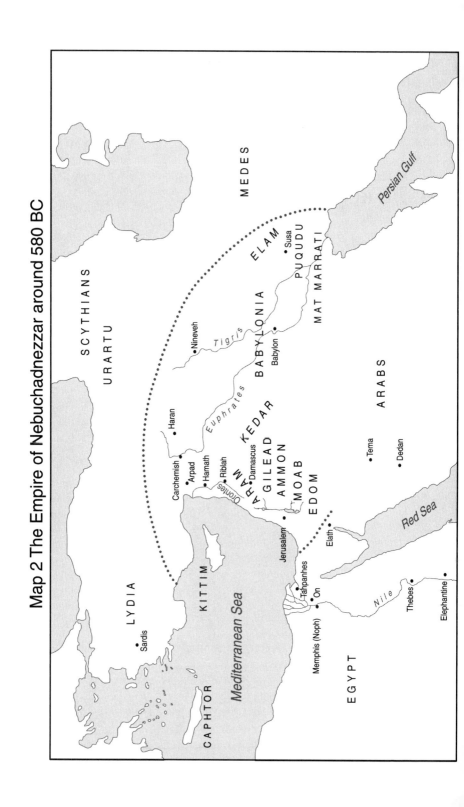

Map 2 The Empire of Nebuchadnezzar around 580 BC

VIII. KINGS AND PROPHETS DENOUNCED

(21:1–24:10)

OUTLINE

A. A Royal Inquiry (21:1-14)
  1. The Request (21:1-2)
  2. A Bleak Response (21:3-7)
  3. A Message for the People (21:8-10)
  4. A Message for the Royal House (21:11-14)
B. The Kings of Judah (22:1–23:8)
  1. Warning to the King of Judah (22:1-9)
  2. Concerning Shallum (22:10-12)
  3. Concerning Jehoiakim (22:13-19)
  4. Complacency Overturned (22:20-23)
  5. Concerning Jehoiachin (22:24-30)
  6. The Righteous Branch (23:1-8)
C. Concerning the Prophets (23:9-40)
  1. Condemnation of the Evil Prophets (23:9-15)
  2. Do Not Listen (23:16-24)
  3. The Fire and the Hammer (23:25-32)
  4. The 'Burden' of the LORD (23:33-40)
D. Baskets of Figs (24:1-10)
  1. The Two Baskets (24:1-3)
  2. The Good Figs (24:4-7)
  3. The Bad Figs (24:8-10)

At the beginning of chapter 21 there is a decided break in Jeremiah, and the following material has a higher proportion of prose, often located in specific historical contexts. More than that, the clock at first moves significantly forwards and we are brought to the closing years of Zedekiah. The change of style has suggested to many that there is an alteration in the way the book was composed. The most reasonable hypothesis regarding this is that Baruch began to take a more active role in assembling the material that Jeremiah gave to him, and that it is Baruch and Jeremiah who are jointly the narrators responsible for this presentation. The interrupted chronological sequence shows that there is a deliberate contrast being made between the earlier ministry of Jeremiah holding out repentance as the way to avert catastrophe coming on the nation and his later ministry when the nation's doom was sealed but the possibility of mitigating the disaster was present if, belatedly, they paid heed to the prophet's exhortation.

This part of the prophecy begins with a formal introductory formula that indicates Jeremiah's warrant for speaking (21:1). Commentators are not agreed as to whether 21:11 marks the start of a new section of material, or not. The view is taken here that it does not, and that the whole of chapter 21 was brought together as a unit during the closing years of Zedekiah's reign. It is followed in chapter 22 by denunciations made of recent kings of Judah, culminating in 23:1-8 with a vision of the Righteous Branch who will be a true and blessed ruler of the covenant people. It is interesting that Zedekiah (the name means, 'The LORD is my righteousness') is not explicitly mentioned among the kings who are criticised, and that Righteous Branch (23:5) is a play on his name. It seems probable that this section of the prophecy was brought together by Baruch in the closing months of the siege to constitute an appeal to Zedekiah to act responsibly as regards the welfare of his people—and as regards his own future. It incorporates a plea for repentance, but not of the sort that Jeremiah gave earlier in his ministry when a return to the LORD would have averted the catastrophe coming upon the land. Now the nation's fate is sealed, but it is possible to lessen their punishment if only they are obedient to Jeremiah's word to surrender to the Babylonians rather than resist them. That was the challenge given to Zedekiah and the people. Submission was considered an act of treason, which at a political level it undoubtedly was, and advocating it brought Jeremiah much suffering in the period leading up to the fall of Jerusalem. It does, however, explain why this section came to be gathered together, and the function it might well have performed. This message would have continued to be of vital relevance to the survivors of the collapse of Judah: Babylon was the

LORD's appointed means of punishing his people. To acquiesce in Babylonian rule was to recognise the divine mandate that lay behind it—for the moment.

The remaining two sections in this part of the prophecy focus on other groups in the land. The pernicious influence of the false prophets is exposed in 23:9-40, and in a concluding postscript chapter 24 relates a vision that sets out the fate of the people in general under the imagery of two baskets of figs. Together these provide a background which reinforces the folly of existing policy in Jerusalem and sets out the future as the LORD sees it. In his earlier messages Jeremiah had not subjected the monarchy to the detailed and personal critique which is built up in this division of his prophecy.

A. A ROYAL INQUIRY (21:1-14)

The view taken here is that the phrase at the beginning of v. 11 does not mark the start of a new section running through to 23:8, but that there is a threefold response to the royal inquiry made in vv. 1-2. Jeremiah first responds directly to the king with an uncompromising word of warning regarding the destruction that awaits the city (vv. 3-7). But the fate of Jerusalem is not something that concerns the king alone. It is equally a matter for the whole of the nation, who are given advice as to how to mitigate the sentence that has been passed against them (vv. 8-10). There is then a word for the royal household (king and courtiers) regarding the justice of what was to befall them (vv. 11-12) and also of the certainty of the LORD putting into effect the sentence he had uttered against those who had a false sense of their impregnability (vv. 13-14).

1. The Request (21:1-2)

1. The introductory formula, **The word came to Jeremiah from the LORD**, is identical in Hebrew to that found at 7:1 where it is translated, 'This is the word that came to Jeremiah from the LORD'. It marks a major transition in the book by reminding the reader of the source of the prophet's authority. The content of the message is not made clear until v. 4, because first of all further details are provided regarding the occasion on which it was uttered: **when King Zedekiah sent to him Pashhur son of Malkijah and the priest Zephaniah son of Maaseiah. They said.** The request itself is stated in v. 2. Zedekiah was a weak figure with an insecure power base. For further information regarding his character and situation, see on 37:1. When a new pharaoh, Hophra (also known as Apries, 589–570 BC), came to the throne in Egypt and seemed to favour making trouble for the Babylonians, Zedekiah was induced to break his oath of allegiance to Nebuchadnezzar. The Babylonians did not let such action pass unnoticed, not merely because any rebellion against their dominion was viewed as serious, but because Judah was a key buffer state against Egyptian encroachment northwards and it was a major feature of Babylonian policy to prevent that. So the situation came about where Zedekiah was left in Jerusalem with the Babylonian army encircling the city while no help seemed to be forthcoming from Egypt. Here we find him casting about in any and every direction to work out what to do next, and this is the first of a number of occasions on which he turned to Jeremiah. (For an overview of the sequence of events during the final siege of Jerusalem, see Volume 1, Introduction §4.6.) Zedekiah obviously recognised that the oracles of the peace prophets had been flawed, as had the hopes of his counsellors that Egypt would come to their assistance. Like many before and since, he turned to God as a last resort.

In sending this deputation Zedekiah was unconsciously fulfilling the prophecy of 15:11 that Jeremiah's enemies would plead with him when divine judgment fell on them. In approaching the prophet Zedekiah was showing greater acceptance of his credentials and fidelity than Ahab had been prepared to do in the case of the prophet Micaiah (1 Kgs. 22). Furthermore it was a high level group that Zedekiah sent to the prophet. The Pashhur mentioned here is not the same person as Pashhur the son of Immer (20:1), though it might well be the case that the double occurrence of this name led to this section being placed after chapter 20 when Jeremiah and Baruch brought together the accounts of various episodes in Jeremiah's ministry. The contrast between the two men with the same name, one punishing the prophet and the other coming to seek his help, stressed the extent to which the prophet's credibility had risen in Jerusalem now that the disaster he had long predicted had come upon the nation. Pashhur son of Malkijah was a senior royal counsellor, one of those who at a later stage in the siege were responsible for treating Jeremiah harshly (38:1-6). His descendants are mentioned in Neh. 11:12 and 1 Chron. 9:12.

Zephaniah the priest was also an influential figure in Jerusalem at the time (29:25; 37:3; 52:24). He was 'the priest next in rank' to the chief priest (52:24), and was thus the overseer of the Temple, a successor in that post to the Pashhur of chapter 20. After the fall of the city he was executed by the Babylonians (52:27). He does, however, seem to have been favourably disposed to Jeremiah. At least he had earlier been accused of not taking the prophet to task and punishing him when he ought to have (29:24-29). He also formed part of a second deputation from Zedekiah to Jeremiah on a somewhat later occasion (37:3). Here he represents the religious leadership of the day, as Pashhur represents the civil leadership.

2. The deputation's task is to petition the prophet that he **inquire now of the LORD for us.** 'Now' (*nāʿ*, 'please' NKJV, NRSV) renders the precative particle, here used to emphasise that the request is made with due respect to the prophet. 'Inquire' (<√*dāraš*, 10:21) is a somewhat different request from 'intercede' (<√*pālal* hithpael, 7:16; 37:3). Of the 165 Old Testament instances of the root *dāraš*, 100 involve seeking or inquiring of God (Balentine 1984:167), often as an expression of general faithfulness or a request for help (Pss. 34:4; 77:2). However, twenty of these occurrences involve approaching a prophet with a request to 'inquire of God'. Other examples include Jehoshaphat asking for a word as to whether he and the king of Israel should engage in battle (1 Kgs. 22:7-8); Josiah sending a group of officials, including Hilkiah the priest, to inquire from Huldah regarding the meaning of the book of the law (2 Kgs. 22:13, 18); the elders of Israel coming to Ezekiel to inquire about the fate of the exiles (Ezek. 20:1, 3). In these instances the prophet acted as a channel of divine communication so that the mind of the LORD for the king and the people in their current situation might be ascertained. So here the thrust of the request is for information regarding what was going to happen next and advice from the LORD as to what they should do.

The reason they were seeking advice was clear enough: it was **because** (*kî*) **Nebuchadnezzar king of Babylon is attacking us.** For the significance and spelling of the name Nebuchadnezzar see on 27:6. It is not totally clear what is indicated by 'attacking us'/'making war against us'. The chronology of the final siege of Jerusalem presents several difficulties, but it would appear that late in 589 BC the Babylonian forces moved south against Judah and began their blockade of the city on the tenth day of the tenth month of Zedekiah's ninth year (2 Kgs. 25:1), that is, 15th January 588 BC. Verse 4 indicates that the enemy has arrived in Judah, and the siege may well have begun. Now the siege probably lasted for two and a half years, interrupted in the early months of 587 BC by belated Egyptian intervention (see Appendix §12). At that point Jeremiah was arrested (37:13) and he was imprisoned. However, there is no suggestion in this passage that Jeremiah is in detention, and so it may be dated just before or during (depending on one's interpretation of v. 4) the early stages of the siege, probably not long after January 588 BC. When the prophet is approached here, the strength of the army from the north is all too evident, and Egyptian assistance has not yet materialised.

The king through his emissaries puts before the prophet the possibility: **perhaps the LORD will perform wonders for us**[1] **as in times past so that he will withdraw from us.**[2] 'Wonders' (*niplaʾôt*) refers to God's acts of astounding power that display his sovereign control of all things. The term is frequently used in the book of Psalms, e.g. Ps. 86:10. It looks back to the redemption the LORD provided at the time of the Exodus when he struck the Egyptians with all the wonders he performed among them (Exod. 3:20). No doubt what was in the mind of the king and his advisers was more especially the way in which the Assyrian siege had been lifted miraculously through the LORD's intervention in the days of Hezekiah in 701 BC (2 Kgs. 19:2). Perhaps they also considered that previous Babylonian approaches to the city in 605 BC and 597 BC had not been as completely disastrous as they might have been. While they do not presume to dictate ('perhaps'), a repeat performance, particularly of 701 BC, was exactly what they really wanted to see. Would Babylon be dealt with in the same way as Egypt and Assyria before that? Would the LORD prove a reliable source of deliverance in the impending crisis? But the request makes clear that the lesson Jeremiah had been trying to teach for nearly forty years had fallen on deaf ears. There was no mention of repentance; there was no acknowledgment that what was happening was the just consequence of their sin. They are still in effect endorsing the one-sided theology of the peace prophets and expecting the LORD to act without any change on their part.

2. A Bleak Response (21:3-7)

3-4. Jeremiah's reply is uncompromising. **But Jeremiah said to them, 'Tell (masc. pl.) Zedekiah, "This is what the LORD, the God of Israel, says: I am about to turn against you the weapons of war that are in your hands, which you are using to fight the king of**

---

1. *ʿôtānû*, the object marker, for *ʿittānû*, 'with us'. The expression is literally 'do with us according to all his wonderful acts'. It is omitted in the LXX and the REB.

2. *wayaʿăleh* (<√ʿālâ, 'to go up') has a simple *waw*, and so the clause probably expresses intention or consequence. The NIV takes the verb as a qal, but the form might equally well be a hiphil, 'so that he (the LORD) will make him (Nebuchadnezzar) to go up from upon us (*mēʿālênû*)'.

Babylon and the Babylonians who are outside the wall besieging you".' The LORD's response is a categoric declaration of divine initiative and control, but it offers the people no support. There are two ways of understanding the statement depending upon whether the phrase 'outside the wall'/'from outside with respect to the wall' is taken to refer to the Babylonians (as in the NIV), or to the weapons of war. It would have been obvious to the original hearers which was intended. If it is the Babylonians who are outside the walls, then the siege is already tightly in place and the weapons of war referred to are those that the defenders of the city are using against those outside it. The last clause, **and I will gather them inside this city**, would then, as NLT makes explicit, refer to the Babylonian troops who are envisaged as victorious inside the captured city.

However, it is also possible to read the Hebrew so that it is the defenders' weapons of war that were located outside the city. If so, the time is an earlier stage of the Babylonian campaign when the blockade of the city was not as tightly enforced as it was later to become. It was still possible for the forces of Judah to make sorties outside the walls. The LORD declares that the weapons they are using outside the city walls in fighting the Babylonians are by his decree going to be brought inside the walls (perhaps the usage is a metonymy for the soldiers who use the weapons), and there they will be used in internal strife: 'against you'. The last clause of the verse then refers to the arms/soldiers being assembled inside the city. 'I will pile your soldiers' weapons in the centre of the city' (GNB).

'Babylonians' here and throughout Jeremiah is literally 'Chaldeans' (*kaśdîm*; cf. NKJV, NRSV). The Chaldeans were originally a semi-nomadic people inhabiting the area south of Babylon, particularly the marshy zone between the north of Arabia and the Persian Gulf. Over the centuries they mingled with the Aramean tribes of the area, and by the time of Jeremiah Chaldea was used to refer to the whole area around Babylon where there was a common language and writing. People of Chaldean descent were still identifiable as such. They were generally wealthier, being more involved in trade and politics, and were influential in the religion (Dan. 3:8) and administration (Dan. 5:7) of the region in both the neo-Babylonian and Persian eras.

5. The plight of the people of Judah will become intense because they will have to face the opposition not only of the might of Babylon but of the LORD himself. **I myself** (emphatic *'ănî*) **will fight** (the same word is used of the Babylonians in v. 4) **against you with an outstretched hand and a mighty arm**. The phrase 'with mighty hand and with outstretched arm' was traditionally associated with the LORD's deliverance from Egypt (Deut. 4:34; 5:15; 26:8), with 'hand' and 'arm' being used of exertion and labour, applied anthropomorphically to God. Here, however, the words in the phrase are unusually reversed to 'with outstretched hand and with mighty arm' (compare 27:5; 32:17) and there is a corresponding reversal of what the LORD is going to do. There will be 'wonders' (v. 2), extraordinary acts of power, but they will not benefit the people because the LORD will not be fighting for them, but against them. This will be done **in anger** (ʿap, 2:35) **and fury** (ḥēmâ, 4:4) **and great wrath.** This triplet (32:37; Deut. 29:28) builds in intensity, culminating not merely in wrath (qeṣep, 10:10), itself a strong word, but in 'great wrath'. The mighty power of the LORD will be made known not in deliverance but in the punishment he brings on his people.

6. The detail of what will be involved is spelled out. **I will strike down** (<√nākâ, 2:30; here obviously a fatal blow) **those who live in this city—both men and animals—and they will die of a terrible plague.** Pestilence or plague (deber, 14:12) was always one of the possibilities in an overcrowded city undergoing protracted siege, and particularly when the water supply became contaminated or failed entirely. The animals would have been livestock that the people would have brought into the city before the advancing army.

7. **'After that,' declares the LORD** refers to what would happen in the city after it had been taken and the ordeals of the siege had come to an end. The survivors, particularly the king and his advisers, would not be spared by the enemy. **I will hand over Zedekiah king of Judah, his officials and the people in this city who survive[3] the plague, sword and famine, to Nebuchadnezzar king of Babylon and to their enemies who seek their lives.** 'Officials' is here ʿăbādîm, 'servants', a wider designation than the higher echelons of advisers (śārîm). Again we find the triplet 'plague, sword and famine' (14:12) categorising the horrors of siege warfare. These did not end when a city capitulated because surrender was frequently followed by major slaughter. Zedekiah and some of his men tried unsuccessfully to escape from this (39:4-5). 'To seek the life/soul' (bāqaš [piel] nepeš) expresses a desire to kill someone (19:7, 9; 22:35; 34:20; 38:16; 46:26;

---

3. The Massoretic Text has waʾet before 'survivors'/'those surviving', as if to indicate four categories of people, but there is no group who could be called survivors, apart from the king, his officials and the people. The phrase is therefore epexegetic and treated as such in English translations. 'Who survive' probably refers to the three groups and not just the people.

49:37). The same expression also occurs frequently in the Psalms (Pss. 35:4; 38:12; 40:14; 54:3; 63:9; 70:2; 86:14). Possibly in this passage which uses triplets for emphasis another is to be found in Nebuchadnezzar, their enemies, and those who seek their lives. **He will put them to the sword**/'to the mouth of the sword' denotes merciless killing (Gen. 34:26). **He will show no mercy or pity or compassion.** Another triplet emphasises the unsparing attitude of Nebuchadnezzar. The same three terms, with the order of the first two switched, are used in 13:14 regarding God's attitude towards his disobedient people.[4] Nebuchadnezzar is going to be the instrument through whom this relentless judgment will be imposed. He too will allow nothing to deflect him from the course of action he has embarked on (52:10, 24-27). What we have here are general statements about the fate of the group as a whole, and they are not necessarily in conflict with what happened to Zedekiah who was not in fact slain. His eyes were put out and he died in exile (39:7; 2 Kgs. 25:6-7; Ezek. 12:13).

It was an act of extraordinary fortitude for Jeremiah to proclaim such a message to Zedekiah and his officials when they were desperately trying to devise some stratagem whereby the invading Babylonian forces would be prevented from bringing their action to such a conclusion.

3. A Message for the People (21:8-10)

Jeremiah's proclamation was not confined to a response to the royal inquiries. Verses 8-10 present a message for the people, which, while it may not have been part of the response given to the royal delegation at that moment, was uttered around the same time. These words are particularly significant in that they advise the people how they may ameliorate the impact of the impending catastrophe by submitting to the Babylonians.

8. Jeremiah is instructed to present the people with a choice. **Furthermore[5], tell** (masc. sing.) **the people, 'This is what the LORD says: See, I am setting before you the way of life and the way of death.'** They were being told that there was a stark choice to be made. The

---

4. Indeed, in this passage the LXX has a doublet, 'I will not show them mercy and I will not show them compassion', omitting the second term found in the Massoretic Text. The change of person is probably a scribal confusion with 13:14, though undoubtedly this reading too make a suitable climax here.

5. 'But' rather than 'and' is the appropriate translation of the conjunction here because it is deliberately followed by a non-verb to indicate a contrast.

language is reminiscent of Deut. 30:15, 'See, I set before you today life
and prosperity, death and destruction' (cf. also Deut. 11:26; 30:19).
'Way' refers to their course of life and conduct in general. Is it going
to be one that acknowledges the LORD and submits to him, or are they
going to continue their wilful disobedience? The people are again
being tested because the LORD sets before them a genuine choice, but
it is a grimly ironic one. The way of life is no longer one in which the
obedient enjoy the blessings of the land. It now consists of submission
to Babylon, and the life set before them is one of exile, poverty and
enslavement. However, the participial form 'am setting' indicates that
it is an offer that will remain open until the final catastrophe closes it
for the inhabitants of the city.

9. On the one hand, **whoever stays in this city will die by the sword,
famine or plague.** Again (v. 7) mention is made of the triad of
disasters that would occur in the siege. While the siege could not be
averted, mitigation of its impact would occur if they were prepared to
trust the advice given by the LORD. **But whoever goes out and
surrenders to[6] the Babylonians who are besieging you will live.[7]**
'Go out' ($<\sqrt{y\bar{a}\d{s}\bar{a}^{c}}$) was a term often associated with the Israelites'
departure from Egypt (Exod. 11:8; 13:3; 20:2; Ps. 114:1), but now
'departure' has inverted implications; it is not to freedom but to
bondage. 'Surrender to'/'fall to' ($<\sqrt{n\bar{a}pal}$) is the idiom used for going
over to the other side (37:14; 39:9; 52:15; 2 Kgs. 25:11), including
deserting to an opposing army. The policy of submission to Babylon
was one that Jeremiah consistently brought before the people and the
king (38:1; 38:17; see also 27:11). It appears that many acted on it
(38:19; 39:9; 52:15) in a way that was considered to be treason (37:13;
38:4) by the Jerusalem establishment. But the first loyalty of the people
ought to have been to their divine Overlord, and he had told them that
Nebuchadnezzar was officially recognised as his agent. Furthermore,
even at the level of worldly politics, Zedekiah had rebelled against
Nebuchadnezzar, and those defecting to the Babylonians might be
construed as acting in accordance with the oath of fealty which
Zedekiah himself had reneged on. If an individual acted in accordance
with the prophetic advice, **he will escape with his life**/'shall have his

---

6. ʿal is used for ʾel. Waw-consecutive perfect after a participle is here used
with simple chronological force (IBHS §32.2.5b).

7. The kethibh yiḥyeh, 'he will live', is correct corresponding to the earlier
yāmût, 'he will die'. The qere wəḥāyâ, 'and he will live' (a waw consecutive
perfect) is unnecessary, probably due to a misunderstanding of wənāpal, 'and
he surrenders'.

life (*nepeš*, 2:34) as booty'. The origins of this idiom, which is found
only in Jeremiah (38:2; 39:18; 45:5), are obscure. It may have begun as
a sarcastic comment on a defeated army which rather than returning
home as victors carrying the spoils of war had to be content with the
fact that the only booty they are able to bring back with them was their
own lives. In that case the idiom would imply his life but nothing
more. Those who surrendered would remain the subjects of Babylon,
probably losing all their possessions but remaining alive. It was for
promoting this policy that Jeremiah was labelled a traitor.

10. The LORD then shows why this advice was the only way in which
individuals could escape the impending disaster. 'For' (*kî*) **I have
determined**/'set my face at' (44:11) **to do this city harm and not
good, declares the LORD. It will be given into the hands of the king
of Babylon, and he will destroy it with fire.** The fact of the LORD's
irrevocable intention to destroy the city meant that the only choice
open to the people was to surrender, or to face inevitable siege and
capture. The city was divinely designated for destruction by fire
(52:13). This was not an inevitable outcome to the capture of a
besieged city, though it did occur frequently, especially in circumstances such as that of Jerusalem where the Babylonian aim was not
merely to capture the city but to punish it for its rebellion. Any
possibility of mitigation is ruled out if the people adhere to current
policy.

4. A Message for the Royal House (21:11-14)

This section develops the theme of the royal responsibility for the
situation that is going to come upon the land. Verses 11 and 12 are
addressed to the 'house of the king of Judah', not so much the royal
dynasty, as to the courtiers around the king. They had responsibilities
under the covenant for the way the land was administered. Their failure
had led to the present catastrophe.

As the threatened judgment is presented in conditional form in
v. 12, it is often argued that these words were originally uttered at an
earlier, more hopeful period, possibly early in the reign of Jehoiakim.
Even if that is so, their repetition here serves to underscore the persis-
tence with which the court had evaded its responsibilities, and this is
traced back to the prevailing attitude of arrogance in Jerusalem
(vv. 13-14).

11. Moreover, say to the royal house of Judah, 'Hear (masc. pl.)
the word of the LORD.' 'The royal house'/'house of the king' does
not refer to just the royal family, but to the whole royal establishment.

It is difficult to be certain how the transition to v. 11 should be understood. Many interpreters point to the parallel that exists between 'and concerning the house of the king of Judah' (*ŭləbêt melek yəhûdâ*) in this verse and 'concerning the prophets' (*lannəbī'îm*) in 23:9, though there is no conjunction there, and argue that both function as headings to collections of prophetic sayings about kings and prophets respectively. They identify a section that comprises 21:11–23:8. On the other hand, it is possible to take this as a third section of Jeremiah's response to the inquiry made in v. 2. Having used 'and to the people' in v. 8 makes it probable that 'and to the house of the king' in v. 11 follows the same sequence, even though a different preposition is used. This line of interpretation is represented by the NIV expansion of the simple conjunction 'and', used disjunctively, to 'furthermore' in v. 8 and 'moreover' in v. 11. On that basis the NIV also adds the supplement 'say' in v. 11.

12. O house of David reminds the sorry royal house of Judah of the ideal and standard that was encapsulated in David, the founder of the dynasty. Looking to such a figure from the past set the criterion for assessing the conduct of his descendants, and also reminded them of the Messianic figure who would be the culmination of the LORD's purposes for the house of David. But here the thought is principally of the gap between their conduct and what was expected of them. The thought is not introduced to suggest that if they reform their civil administration, then even at that late stage there would be divine intervention to avert the peril at their gates, but rather to show them that it was their failure to rule properly that had brought this judgment on them. They should not expect a wonder (v. 2) from the LORD in the light of their flagrant breaches of covenant protocol.

This is what the LORD says: 'Administer justice every morning.'[8] It was the duty of the king and his officials (both 'administer' and 'rescue' are masculine plural imperatives) to ensure that justice was maintained throughout the land. This was a standard requirement throughout the ancient Near East, because the king was perceived as the one in whose hands justice ultimately lay. In the Old Testament there is the further aspect that this justice is seen as supremely

---

8. 'Every morning' renders the expression *labbōqer*, 'to the morning', possibly a distributive expression as in Amos 4:4. The same sense is conveyed in 1 Chron. 9:27 by repeating the phrase (*NIDOTTE* 1:712). The REB rendering 'betimes' is a curiosity, reflecting the fact that this obsolete expression which meant 'early' could also imply 'speedily', and thus caught the two ideas which were felt to lie behind the Hebrew idiom.

achieved in the coming Messianic king (23:5-6; Pss. 45:4-8; 72:1-4, 12-14; Isa. 9:6-7; 11:1-4). 'Every morning' points to the time when law courts usually convened, thus avoiding the heat of the day (2 Sam. 4:5; 15:1-6; Amos 4:4; Ps. 59:16). The idea is that justice should be administered regularly and diligently, so that no sense of grievance would exist in the land and the people would be content with the king's rule. In fact it was David's neglect of this duty that gave Absalom the opportunity to foment rebellion (2 Sam. 15:2), though Solomon, at least in the early part of his reign, acted more responsibly (1 Kgs. 3:18).

Rescue from the hand of his oppressor the one who has been robbed. 'Rescue'/'deliver' (<√*nāṣal*, 1:8) implies taking action to snatch back from danger. The justice system was intended not merely to give a verdict in favour of those who had been wronged, but also to take effective action to ensure the enforcement of that verdict. The oppressor (<√*ʿāšaq*, 7:6) was one who used economic pressure and physical force to achieve his ends. 'One who has been robbed' (<√*gāzal*) points to the open seizure of property (Judg. 21:23; 2 Sam. 23:21; Mic. 2:2; Isa. 10:2, NKJV) in contrast to the root *gānab*, which emphasises the stealth with which goods are taken (7:9). The justice administered by the king was not to be merely passive, responding to cases brought to his attention, but also to be active, seeking out and rectifying wrongs, particularly if committed against those who were of the lower classes, whose cases might not otherwise ever come for due legal hearing. This responsibility rested with the king who, of course, exercised it through his officials.

The threatened alternative is then set out in words that reflect 4:4b. **Or** (*pen*, 'lest') **my wrath will break out and burn like fire because of the evil you**[9] **have done—burn with no one to quench it.** The question arises as to how this fits in with the present context where the enemy was already at the city gates. It may be that the passage comes from earlier in Jeremiah's ministry when it had truly functioned as a warning, but in this context the logic is reversed. It is not a case of, 'Do this lest a certain outcome eventuate', but 'The outcome is staring you in the face. Can you not see where you have gone wrong?' Acknowledging that their past conduct had been grievously deficient would have opened the way towards accepting the message Jeremiah was now bringing them. It was not that judgment could be averted, but that its worst consequences might be avoided (v. 10).

---

9. The kethibh is *maʿalalêhem*, 'their doings', a scribal error for the qere, which is also the reading of many manuscripts, *maʿalalêkem*, 'your doings'.

13. There is then a change in the person addressed. The subject of the next section is not stated but the feminine references are probably to Jerusalem. The LORD identifies her arrogant self-assurance as that which has given rise to his determination to destroy her (v. 14). The connection is probably that the proud attitude of the royal household typified that of the city as a whole. **I am against you, ⌐Jerusalem⌐** has undoubtedly got the right addition, in that 'you' is feminine singular, the normal Hebrew gender for addressing a city, and reverts to the practice found earlier of personifying the city as Daughter Zion. Here we have the LORD's word of challenge to those who were not inclined to obey him, notifying them of his opposition. The city is described as **you who live above this valley on the rocky plateau**/'sitting one of the valley, rock of the plain'. The charge against them is their defiant pride, and this may be brought out in the two descriptive phrases used of the city as well as in their attitude. The NKJV takes the first phrase as 'O inhabitant of the valley', which might be understood as coming from the way Jerusalem is said to be surrounded by hills (Ps. 125:2), and so by comparison being in a valley. However, it is more probable that the phrase is similar to that used to describe the LORD 'enthroned between the cherubim'/'sitting one of the cherubim' (1 Sam. 4:4; 2 Sam. 6:2 = 1 Chron. 13:6; Pss. 80:1; 99:1). The NIV supplement 'above' captures Jerusalem's sense of inviolability, almost an attitude of deifying herself. Surrounded on every side but the north by deep valleys, she sat, almost like God, enthroned above the valleys that she thought of as her defence. It was a similar attitude to that which the Jebusites of old had displayed due to the naturally impregnable position of the city, when they taunted David, saying, 'You will not get in here' (2 Sam. 5:6).

Similarly the description **on the rocky plateau** is suitable to her physical location as a hill standing out of a high plateau. But 'rock' (*ṣûr*) was also a frequent description of God. It occurs early, particularly in Deuteronomy (Deut. 32:4, 15, 18, 30, 31; and in reference to pagan gods in Deut. 32:31, 37) and there may well be overtones here of the arrogance which Jerusalem viewed her position. Certainly that is what is found in their thinking. **You who say, 'Who can come against us? Who can enter our refuge?'** These are rhetorical questions, emphatically refuting these possibilities. There is a switch here to thinking of people, perhaps more particularly the king and his advisers ('you' is masculine plural). The verb 'come'[10] (<√*nāḥat*) is rendered 'come down' (NRSV, REB, NASB, NKJV), a somewhat surprising

10. The form *yēḥat* arises by assimilation from *yinḥat*.

choice of word given the height of Jerusalem, which would have led us to expect 'come up'. Either the verb is being used in a different sense of 'to overwhelm defences', or else the thought is directed against divine intervention. 'Refuge' is literally 'refuges' (*mə'ônôt*, cf. 9:10 *mā'ôn*), and is a word used both for the lairs of animals and for the dwelling place of God. Its use here may well reflect the Zion theology that assured the citizens of Jerusalem that they were secure because Jerusalem was the dwelling place of God (7:4; 8:19). These questions vividly depict the complacent self-assurance that was the downfall of the city. It resembles that expressed by Edom (Obad. 3-4) which also underrated the power of God.

14. But to assurance divorced from obedience, the LORD has only one response. The strength of their city will be no barrier to the execution of the LORD's judgment. **'I will punish** (<√*pāqad*) **you** (masc. pl.) **as your deeds deserve,' declares the LORD**. It is not 'punish with your deeds' as though the direct consequences of their evil would be their punishment, but 'according to the fruit of your deeds', in proportion to the outcome of the evil they had done (6:19; 17:10). The LORD is not arbitrary, and there will be a correlation between what they have done and what will be done to them. **I will kindle a fire in your forests that will consume everything around you.** 'Your' and 'you' are literally 'her', the feminine singular reference going back to the beginning of v. 13. Such switching of the person used in speech is not uncommon in Hebrew style, though it is quite unnatural in English. Some have found in the reference to 'forests' (literally, 'forest', possibly a collective use), either a picture of the royal dwellings (22:6; 1 Kgs. 7:2; 10:21), or else to the city as a whole referred to as a forest (22:6). But probably there is here no other picture than forests which then existed around Jerusalem being engulfed in fire. All around her was burnt, and the unstated implication of it is left threateningly obvious. Who can escape when surrounded by a forest fire?

B. THE KINGS OF JUDAH (22:1–23:8)

This section contains a number of messages regarding kings of Judah and shows the extent to which Jeremiah's ministry subjected them to detailed criticism in the years preceding the fall of Jerusalem. If the first section (vv. 1-9) was addressed to Zedekiah and if the last section also reflects indirectly on him (23:1-8), then this forms a neat inclusion. Although the material regarding the three previous kings was originally delivered earlier, by reproducing these words of warning

Jeremiah challenged Zedekiah not to repeat the errors of his predecessors, who had ignored what was said to them and had suffered as a consequence.

1. Warning to the King of Judah (22:1-9)

There is no information given as to when this message was originally received by Jeremiah. It may have been early in Jehoiakim's reign, not long after Josiah's death because there was already a general appreciation of what the new king's character was like. After all, initially the people themselves had deliberately bypassed him and chosen Jehoahaz as their king (see Volume 1, Introduction §§3.7, 3.8). Jeremiah's message would then have served to remind Jehoiakim of his covenant responsibilities as king before he became so set in his ways that he could not change. It is also probable that Jeremiah repeated this message early in Zedekiah's reign with a view to recalling him to the standards required of a king ruling under covenant with the LORD. Such repeated use might explain the anonymous way in which it has been preserved in a division of the prophecy where the setting of most material is evident.

1-2. This is what the LORD says marks the beginning of a new section of material. Although Jeremiah is not named as the recipient of the message, there can be no doubt about who is intended. **Go down** (masc. sing.) **to the palace of the king of Judah and proclaim this message there.** 'Go down' indicates that Jeremiah was in the Temple at the time, because the palace lay to the south of the Temple, and was lower than it (36:12; cf. 26:10). The message is in the first instance directed to the king. **Hear** (masc. sing.) **the word of the LORD, O king of Judah, you who sit on David's throne.** 'Throne of David' is used to refer to David's God-given rule over Israel (7:13, 16; 14:9; 2 Sam. 3:10), and sitting on his throne refers to David and his descendants exercising this royal power (cf. 13:13). It reminds the king of the privilege that is his and of the standards which he should observe in carrying out his task, as well as the example David himself had given in these matters. Possibly the king was sitting in the gate, and the message is not delivered privately to him but is to be heard by others also: **you, your officials and your people who come through these gates.** The designation 'your people' may not be those of the nation who approached the king's palace either for justice or in the course of administration; it may be the royal household in an extended sense. The 'gates' are obviously those of the palace complex (v. 4).

3. The word which is addressed to them all concerns the maintenance of covenant standards in the areas of public administration. **This is what the LORD says: Do** (masc. pl.) **what is just and right**/'justice and righteousness' (5:1; 7:5; 23:5). 'Do' is broader than 'administer' (21:12), covering policy formulation and general attitudes as well as the specifics of government. This formula encapsulates the basic covenant demands on the king which require that he does not act autonomously but rules in accordance with the principles of divine law. 'What is just'/'justice' (*mišpāṭ*, 5:4) is one component of righteousness, relating to the societal mechanisms by which public policy seeks to enunciate and enforce the norms of righteousness. If the laws of the land are equitable and they are justly administered within the court system, this promotes righteousness throughout the community. But there is more than social justice involved in 'what is right'/'righteousness' (*ṣədāqâ*, 4:2), which extends to all aspects of living and requires action in a way appropriate to a relationship, in this instance, the covenant bond between the LORD and his people. There are many areas of life that are not under judicial scrutiny but which are still vital aspects of righteous living before God.

The general requirement is then illustrated with specific instances. **Rescue from the hand of the oppressor** (<√*āšaq*) **the one who has been robbed** (<√*gāzal*). For this command, see 21:12.[11] It was the rich and powerful within the community who were acting oppressively towards their neighbours. **Do no wrong or violence to the alien, the fatherless or the widow.** 'Do no wrong' (<√*yānâ*, 'to oppress, be violent') is closely related to *āšaq*, and relates to economic exploitation and extortion, particularly the social injustice by which the wealthy misused their dominant position in society to exploit the poor. The three groups mentioned constituted the exposed groups in Israelite society (see on 7:6; also on 5:28). Special provision was made for them in the covenant, and a curse was called down on any who deprived them of justice. 'Cursed is the man who withholds justice from the alien, the fatherless or the widow' (Deut. 27:19). This is followed by another requirement of the covenant that was also mentioned in Jeremiah's Temple Sermon (7:6). **Do not shed innocent blood in this place.** 'In this place' refers to the city of Jerusalem and more particularly the royal palace. For 'innocent', see 2:34. There was to be no return to the malpractice of Manasseh's reign (2 Kgs. 21:16).

4. In language reminiscent of 17:25, v. 4 sets out the reason for acting in accordance with the divine commands. It will ensure that blessing

---

11. The only difference is that the noun *ašôq*, 'oppressor', is used instead of the participle *ōšēq*, 'one who is oppressing', found in 21:12.

will come upon the dynasty. **For (*kî*) if you are careful to carry out these commands, then kings who sit on David's throne will come through the gates of this palace, riding in chariots and on horses, accompanied by their officials**[12] **and their people.** The procession with horses and chariots is a display of royal status and kingly authority. This is a land enjoying security and prosperity, but the focus is on the dynasty rather than the city. Note the change from 'gates of this city' (17:25) to 'gates of this palace', and the omission of references to the men of Judah and the inhabitants of Jerusalem.

5. On the other hand there is the possibility of rejection of the LORD's covenant standards, and then there will follow disaster (cf. 17:27). **But if you do not obey these commands, declares the LORD, I swear**[13] **by myself that this palace will become a ruin.** Oaths were guaranteed by naming a god who would punish the oath-taker if what he said was untrue or if he did not keep any promise he had made. As there is no being or power higher than the LORD, he had to swear by himself. 'I lift up my hand to heaven and declare: As surely as I live for ever' (Deut. 32:40; cf. Heb. 6:13). Such language conveys a very solemn assurance, here a warning of impending disaster (49:13; 51:14; Gen. 22:16; Isa. 45:23; Amos 6:8). 'Ruin' (*ḥorbâ*, 7:34) pictures the palace as a desolation, 'a pile of rubble' (NLT), and what happened to the palace indicated the fate which would befall the regime, because *bayit*, 'house', may refer to either (as well as to the Temple [cf. 7:10], but it is not under consideration here).

6. Such a destiny would inevitably come on the disobedient in accordance with the threats the LORD had already issued. **For (*kî*) this is what the LORD says about the palace of the king of Judah: 'Though you are like Gilead to me, like the summit**[14] **of Lebanon.'** These poetic lines use metaphor ('You are Gilead to me, the head of Lebanon'; cf. NKJV) to convey the extent of the ruin the LORD will bring on the palace and the city. The northern limit of Gilead (8:22) is not explicitly determined in Scripture, so that the term often included Bashan as well, which was well known for its oak trees (Isa. 2:13;

---

12.   The kethibh is *wəʿabdô*, 'his servant', whereas the qere rightly reads *waʿăbādāw,* 'his servants'.

13.   The perfect may be used to represent an action already accomplished in the conception of the speaker (GKC §106i), or more probably it is a performative perfect in which the action referred to is actually accomplished through the speech that is uttered.

14.   *rōʾš*, 'head', may not indicate the summit of the mountains. If the focus is on the forests, then it may convey the idea of 'best, highest quality'.

Zech. 11:1-2). Gilead as a whole was renowned for its pastures and
livestock, and was a symbol of productivity and plenty (Num. 32:1;
Mic. 7:14). But in combination with Lebanon the emphasis is probably
on trees and forests. Lebanon with its tall and stately cedars was a
symbol of the lofty and splendid (Isa. 2:13; Hos. 14:5-7). The timber
they provided had been a favourite building material for the kings in
Jerusalem from the time of David (2 Sam. 7:2, 7), and particularly in
Solomon's day when a part of the royal complex was known as the
House of the Forest of Lebanon because of the amount of cedar used in
its construction and finish (1 Kgs. 7:2-5). Whether the reference is
primarily to the forests found in these areas or the grand buildings in
Jerusalem constructed from their timber, the LORD compares the
people to them as his chosen and choice possession. But even so, he
would not spare them. Though such grand buildings were a source of
pleasure and delight, they too would fall because of the LORD's anger
against what took place within them. **I will surely**[15] **make you** is a
solemn undertaking that the LORD gives regarding the palace which he
will transform so that what had been forests would become **like a
desert, like towns not inhabited.**[16] 'Desert'/'wilderness' (2:2) is the
arid waste where no stately trees are to be found; at best there is just
low-growing scrub. The plural phrase 'towns not inhabited' may arise
from the complex of palace buildings that are involved, or the double
nature of the comparison.

7. The way in which the LORD intends to effect this demolition is then
detailed. **I shall send destroyers against you.** 'Send' (<√qādaš piel,
'to sanctify', 6:4) or 'prepare' (NKJV, NRSV) may be a weakened use
of a root that originally indicated an act of consecration, but it is more
probable that there was a continuing awareness of the wars of the
LORD in which God himself fought on behalf of his people. That tradition is now turned on its head because the LORD is instituting a war in
which he will back the enemies of his people. He is the one who serves
notices on them: 'I am against you' (21:13). 'Destroyers' (<√šāḥat,

---

15. ʿim-lōʾ ('surely'; literally 'if not') is taken by the NIV as a particle of
asseveration (15:11; cf. GKC §149a). This idiom arises from its use as an
introductory particle for a positive oath, and this is brought out in the REB and
NRSV renderings, 'I swear that I shall turn you' (GKC §149b).

16. The kethibh nôšābâ, 'she is inhabited', is usually taken to be a scribal
slip which is emended by the qere to nôšābû, 'they are inhabited'. The NRSV
assumes it is the plural ʿārîm, 'cities', that is at fault and changes it to a
singular, but Hebrew manuscripts and the early versions support reading a
plural here.

5:10; cf. also 'a destroyer of nations' 4:7) will function as those through whom the LORD will execute his purposes. **Each man with his weapons** points to the destroyers as constituting an army, but 'weapons' (*kēlîm*) is a fairly general word, and so the NLT considers it is 'tools to dismantle you' which are brought by this demolition team. **And they will cut up your fine**[17] **cedar beams and throw them into the fire.** The amount of wood used in construction and panelling of ancient palaces made it easy to burn them down, but this was preceded by an orgy of destruction (Ps. 74:4-8).

8. Verse 8 reverts to prose and records what will happen after the destruction of the city. **People from many nations will pass by this city and will ask one another, 'Why has the LORD done such a thing to this great city?'** This reflects back on Deut. 29:24 which envisaged that after the LORD's judgment had fallen on Israel, 'All the nations will ask: "Why has the LORD done this to this land? Why this fierce, burning anger?" ' (cf. also 1 Kgs. 9:8). The city will become a thing of horror and an object lesson to other nations. The thinking found here and in Deuteronomy is analogous to that of secular treaties in which kings bound their subject peoples to themselves. For instance there is a passage in the annals of the last great Assyrian king Ashurbanipal (668–627 BC):

> Whenever the inhabitants of Arabia asked each other: 'On account of what have these calamities befallen Arabia?' (they answered themselves:) 'Because we did not keep the solemn oaths (sworn by) Ashur, because we offended the friendliness of Ashurbanipal, the king, beloved by Ellil!' (*ANET* 300)

9. The response that is envisaged is also modelled on Deuteronomy. **And the answer will be: 'Because they have forsaken** (<√*'āzab*, 2:13) **the covenant of the LORD their God and have worshipped and served other gods.'** These ancient words were still as determinative of the destiny of the covenant people as they had ever been, because the covenant Overlord had not changed his purposes. 'And the answer will be: "It is because this people abandoned the covenant of the LORD, the God of their fathers, the covenant he made with them when he brought them out of Egypt. They went off and worshipped other gods and bowed down to them, gods they did not know, gods he had not given them' (Deut. 29:25-26; cf. also 1 Kgs. 9:9). It had always been foreseen that Israel's disloyalty would strike at the very heart of the covenant if they turned from the LORD and worshipped pagan gods,

---

17. *mibḥār*, 'select place, choicest element', and so 'choicest element of your cedars' expresses the outstanding quality of the wood that is destroyed.

so breaching the first commandment (Exod. 20:3; Deut. 5:7). Such an affront to the majesty of their king and great benefactor could not be ignored and would certainly result in punishment.

2. Concerning Shallum (22:10-12)

The language of v. 10 is not specific and some translations (NKJV, NRSV) prefer to take it as a general statement. However, the context seems to favour treating vv. 10-12 as a unit which focuses on Shallum, the son of Josiah, who was also known as Jehoahaz (1 Chron. 3:15; 2 Kgs. 23:30, 33-34). Josiah had met an unexpected death when he tried to stop the forces of Pharaoh Neco who was going to assist the remnants of the Assyrian army against Babylon. At Megiddo in 609 BC (probably about May/June), Josiah was seriously wounded and died (2 Kgs. 23:30; 2 Chron. 35:23-24). Shallum is listed last in the genealogy of 1 Chron. 3:15 and this supports the inference that he was Josiah's youngest son. Even so, his popularity or his political leanings (he probably continued his father's anti-Egyptian policies) were such that the 'people of the land' (often understood to be the influential landowners in Judah) put this twenty-three year old on the throne (2 Kgs. 23:30-31; 2 Chron. 36:1-2). Jehoahaz, 'The LORD sustains/ holds' (also found as Joahaz in Chronicles), seems to have been his throne name, but he was not loyal to the LORD (2 Kgs. 23:32). At any rate, once Neco established his control over the area, he summoned Jehoahaz to Riblah, where he deposed him in August/September 609 BC after a brief reign of three months, and exiled him to Egypt where he died (2 Kgs. 23:33-34; 2 Chron. 36:2-3). In these verses Jeremiah does not condemn Jehoahaz but stresses that he was not going to return. Given that Jehoahaz had enjoyed a considerable measure of popular support, Jeremiah's saying served notice on the people that they should not focus their thoughts on the exiled king, hoping that he would be restored. This passage evidently originated at the time when Jehoahaz was at Riblah or shortly thereafter.

10.   When Josiah was killed, there had been widespread mourning in the land in which Jeremiah played a prominent role (2 Chron. 35:24-25). Josiah's death when about forty years old was a national tragedy, and the sorrow it occasioned was remembered a century later (Zech. 12:11). Jeremiah tells the people that their changed circumstances necessitate that they desist from grief over Josiah. **Do not weep for the dead ⌊king⌋ or mourn his loss.** 'Mourn' (√*nûd*, 4:1) relates to the conventional swaying of the head in expressing condolence. The name of the one who has died is not given. From the context of the poem it is assumed to be a king, namely Josiah, but he is just referred to as 'ᴛtheᴊ dead one'. Josiah is not to be mourned, not because his loss was not great to the country (for Jeremiah's attitude to Josiah see vv. 15-16 below), but because there was a still greater tragedy in that their young king who had left them was never going to return. This was the first time a king of Judah had been deported to die in exile, and it presaged the fate that would shortly encompass the people themselves. They were entering the age of exile and death.

Rather, weep bitterly[18] **for him who is exiled, because** (*kî*) **he will never return nor see his native land again.** 'Him who is exiled' refers to Jehoahaz as 'the going one', a phrase which could convey going into exile (1 Chron. 5:41; Ezek. 37:21). The participle 'the going one' might well be used of the immediate future, 'the one who is about to go'. 'His native land' ('*ereṣ môledet*, 46:16) is rendered more literally by the REB as 'the land of his birth'.

11-12. Verses 11 and 12 are a prose addition, explaining the unnamed references of v. 10, perhaps in the context of a later audience, because by Zedekiah's day Jehoiachin had also been taken into exile. While it may be unusual for a poet to add a prose commentary to his verse, Jeremiah was primarily a prophet, and could easily have clarified what he had previously said when the passage of time made references unclear.

For (*kî*) **this is what the LORD says about Shallum son of Josiah who succeeded his father as king of Judah but has gone from this place: 'He will never return.'** 'About' is literally 'to' ('*el*), cf. v. 18. This may be an instance of '*el* being used instead of '*al*, 'concerning', but it is just as likely that the message delivered in Jerusalem was communicated to wherever Shallum was. 'Has gone'/'departed' is not a reference to Josiah's last exit from 'this place', that is, Jerusalem, but to the circumstances of Shallum's exile, as what follows makes clear. His departure would not be reversed. 'For' (*kî*, though after the preceding negative 'but' introducing a contrast is also possible, NKJV, NRSV) **he will die in the place where they have led him captive; he will not see this land again.** This came true, as 2 Kgs. 23:34 makes clear.

---

18. In *bǝkû bākô*, the infinitive absolute follows the imperative, and so it is undecided whether it is emphatic or indicates long continuance (GKC §113r; *IBHS* §35.3.1i). It may denote extended weeping, 'weep continually' (NASB), or the extent of weeping 'weep bitterly' (NKJV), or be an emphatic contrast 'weep rather' (REB, NRSV). The NIV rendering, 'rather, weep bitterly', combines the last two options.

3. Concerning Jehoiakim (22:13-19)

Though there is no formal indication in the text, there follows a section
in which the focus switches to Jehoiakim (October 609 BC–9th December 598 BC, McFall 1991:39) who succeeded Jehoahaz (Shallum). He
was in fact his elder brother Eliakim who, aged 25 years, was placed
on the throne by Pharaoh Neco and given the throne name Jehoiakim
(2 Kgs. 23:35-36). Such renaming was an exercise of an overlord's
authority, and a very clear indication of the subordinate status of
Jehoiakim. The fact that the name was based on the tetragrammaton
YHWH was probably a propaganda attempt to curry favour with the
people, or a superstitious attempt to placate the gods. Jeremiah had
nothing good to say about Jehoiakim, and the fact that the people had
initially passed him over may well indicate that they did not hold a
high opinion of him either.

The section has a chiastic structure. The oracle of vv. 13-15a
exposes and criticises the actions of the unnamed king, and is followed
by a positive statement of his father's conduct (vv. 15b-16). This is
completed by further criticism of the king in v. 17 before a sentence of
condemnation in vv. 18-19 is explicitly uttered against Jehoiakim.

13. **Woe** (*hôy*) was originally a particle used to introduce laments for
the dead ('alas' v. 18; 34:5; 1 Kgs. 13:30), but the prophets developed
it to begin an indictment against someone on whom severe judgment is
pronounced (e.g., 23:1; Isa. 5:8, 11). In this case the focus of attention
is an individual who is not named until v. 18. **Woe to him who builds
his palace by unrighteousness, his** (possibly 'its') **upper rooms by
injustice.** Since 'palace' is simply *bayit*, 'house', it is not evident in
vv. 13-14 that a king is in view, though it is obviously someone who is
in a position to exploit others. 'Justice' and 'righteousness' (cf. v. 3)
were the required characteristics of the covenant king—and also of all
who were living in terms of the covenant. Here Jeremiah characterises
the builder's activity as being 'not righteousness' and 'not justice'.
Palace building was a clear mark of success for an Eastern potentate,
and Jehoiakim was determined to have all the trappings of a king.
'Upper rooms' (also in v. 14) probably refers to sleeping quarters
above the main floor. A small citadel built by Jehoiakim has been
located at Ramat Raḥel, halfway between the Old City of Jerusalem
and Bethlehem. It was fortified with a casement wall constructed with
regular masonry, and within the wall were a large courtyard, storehouse and palace (*NIDOTTE* 1:1027). The reference may be to this
structure or to other, perhaps grander, building work of Jehoiakim.

But unlike successful emperors who could finance extravagant public works by the booty they had seized on their military campaigns and through taxation of subject people, Jehoiakim did not have the resources to match his grandiose pretensions. Indeed he had to pay tribute to Egypt (2 Kgs. 23:35). He therefore employed other means to further his plans. Consequently the charges laid against him are specified as **making his countrymen work for nothing, not paying them for their labour.** 'Labour' (*pōʿal*) may refer to their work or the wages due for it: 'giving them no wage for their labour' (REB). The citizens of Judah and Judah are called his 'countrymen'/'fellows, neighbours' (9:3, 4, 7), emphasising the covenant solidarity that ought to exist between the king and his people (Deut. 17:20). But he violated this bond by forcing them to work for him without payment (Deut. 24:14-15). In using forced labour (which while not enslavement was equivalent to additional taxation) Jehoiakim was emulating Solomon (1 Kgs. 5:27-28; 11:28). This no doubt added to his unpopularity, because he had already agreed to pay considerable tribute to Pharaoh as a condition of becoming king and had passed the burden on to the people (2 Kgs. 23:35).

14. But Jehoiakim had ostentatious ideas. **He says,**[19] **'I will build myself a great palace** (*bêt middôt*, 'a house of measurements', that is, of a grand size, a mansion) **with spacious**[20] **upper rooms.'** If only he had built it himself! Instead he is forcing others to do the work for him. 'Spacious' (<√*rûḥ*) is a difficult term to translate. Lexicographers (*HALOT* 1195-96) are uncertain whether the basic thought is 'made broad', referring to the dimensions of the apartments in the palace, or whether it is related to *rûaḥ*, 'wind', and so has the sense 'airy' (REB), which would be a very desirable feature in hot climates. Either thought fits this context where the upper rooms were probably the royal sleeping quarters and private apartments. **So he makes**[21] **large windows in**

---

19. The REB rendering 'Woe to him who says, …' by repeating the 'Woe' of v. 13 brings out the significance of the participle *hāʿōmēr*, 'the one who says' as parallel to *bōneh*, 'who builds' (cf. NKJV, NRSV).

20. *məruwwāḥîm*, 'spacious', constitutes a problem in that it is a *masculine* plural pual participle, following the feminine plural 'upper rooms'. Perhaps it is to be understood as a phrase in apposition, 'upper rooms, ones that are spacious' (Craigie et al. 1991:308).

21. *qāraʿ lô*, 'cuts for it', or possibly 'for himself'. *ḥallōnāy*, 'my windows', is a form that is difficult to explain. English versions read it as a plural 'windows' without the suffix. GKC §88c suggests it may be a dual form describing a 'double window'. Possibly a *waw* has been omitted in error to give a third person singular suffix, 'his (or its) windows'.

it, panels[22] it with cedar and decorates (<√*māšaḥ*, 'to spread,
smear') it in red. Windows were not glazed but fitted with latticework
or covered internally with curtains. Cedar panelling was the ultimate in
royal distinction (v. 7), and red or vermilion, a metal oxide which
yielded a bright red pigment unsuitable for dyeing fabric but used for
painting walls, was the dearest and grandest colour scheme available
(Ezek. 23:14).

15. Verses 15-17 are divine speech addressed to Jehoiakim. Does it
make you a king to have more and more cedar?/'Are you a king
because (*kî*) you compete in cedar?' (NRSV). 'To have more and
more'/'to compete' (a tiphel form <√*ḥārâ*, 12:4) presents a picture of
striving to outshine others, or getting very hot through one's exertions
in rivalling others. Jehoiakim tried to establish himself as a second
Solomon through becoming renowned for his building projects in Jerusalem. By such ostentatious public works he would prove that he was
really a king. (Was this a reaction to his insecurity when he was
initially rejected by the people? to his subordinate status to Egypt?)
But building projects were not at all of the essence of kingship, and to
point this out the example of his father Josiah is used. Did not your
father have food and drink? The rhetorical question has 'your father'
fronted for emphasis, as if to say, 'Think of your father. You must
agree he ate and drank.' This does not mean that Josiah had just
enough to get by on, but indicates he lived a full and comfortable life
(Eccl. 2:24; 3:13). That was not inconsistent with the true ideals of
kingship, but more was needed. He did[23] what was right and just.
The NIV inverts the order of the terms 'justice' (*mišpāṭ*) and
'righteousness' (*ṣədāqâ*), which are the standards for kingly conduct
(v. 3; 21:12). Josiah's behaviour complied with the requirements of the
covenant, and so all went well with him. Covenant blessing followed
on from covenant obedience as the graciously bestowed gift God was
pleased to disburse to those who were loyal to him.

16. More is said to show how Josiah conformed to the kingly ideal.
He defended the cause of the poor and needy. 'Defended the cause'
(*dān dîn*, a verb with a cognate accusative, <√*dîn*, 5:28) uses a root
which overlaps in meaning with the more common *šāpaṭ*, 'to judge'.
However, *dîn* does not focus on the broader tasks of establishing and

---

22. *sāpûn*, 'being panelled', is a passive participle but *māšôaḥ*,
'decorates'/'anoints', is an infinitive absolute. Many repoint to *sāpôn*, an
infinitive absolute.

23. Here, as often, the series of *waw* + perfects beginning with a perfect has
merely copulative force (*IBHS* §32.1.1a).

maintaining order through efficient and fair administration, but primarily refers to procedure in cases brought to trial (*NIDOTTE* 1:940). 'Poor' (*ʿānî*, 'one suffering through disability or distress') and 'needy' (*ʿebyôn*, 5:28) are used in hendiadys to describe one group of people, the worst off and victimised in the community. Josiah cared for their welfare, which was true to the paradigm for a covenant king: 'He will defend the afflicted among the people and save the children of the needy; he will crush the oppressor' (Ps. 72:4). The consequence of such obedience is again spelled out: **and so all went well.** This time the blessing is expressed absolutely, without the addition of 'with him', probably implying the prosperity of the nation as well as that of the king. Although his death at the early age of 39 or 40 overshadows subsequent perception of Josiah's reign, it was in fact a time when, with Assyrian control weakening, territory was regained, religious reforms were carried through, and there was a generally optimistic outlook for the land.

'Is that[24] not what it means to know me?' declares the LORD. This knowledge is not simply acquisition of facts, but comes from a heart regard for the LORD and a desire to fulfil his requirements (compare the argument in Isa. 58:6-9). The question expects a positive answer to the effect that Josiah was a genuine instance of covenant loyalty and devotion; he was a king who lived with due regard for the LORD. His lasting fame did not derive from Temple renovation or outward religious reform through suppression of idolatry and pagan cults, but from his faithfulness in carrying out his kingly responsibilities. He acknowledged the LORD as his sovereign and the one who defined his conduct and duty.

17. Jehoiakim, however, did not share his father's outlook. **But** (*kî* of contrast after preceding negative) **your eyes and your heart are set only** (*kî ʿim*, 'but rather') **on dishonest gain, on shedding innocent blood and on oppression and extortion.** Jehoiakim did not aim to please the LORD but to get as much as he could for himself. 'Dishonest gain' (*beṣaʿ*, 'gain', 6:13; 8:10) was a particular temptation for those in leadership, and any inclination towards abusing their post for personal profit rendered individuals unfit for office (Exod. 18:21; Ezek. 22:27). 'Innocent blood' (v. 3; 2:34; 7:6; 19:4; Deut. 19:10; 2 Kgs. 24:4) is a standard expression for those whose lives have been unlawfully taken or threatened. Jehoiakim is known to have put to death the prophet Uriah who had rebuked him (26:20-23). In this way his reign continued

---

24. 'That' is feminine *hîʾ* agreeing with *daʿat*, 'knowledge': 'Is not that knowledge of me?'

characteristics found in that of Manasseh (2 Kgs. 24:3-4). Jehoiakim
also permitted pagan rites to flourish again, including those of Egypt
(Ezek. 8:5-17), but that is not mentioned here. The focus is on the
public administration of the land where 'oppression' (<√'āšaq, 6:6) and
'extortion' (<√rāṣaṣ, 'to crush, oppress') were prevalent.

18. Therefore (lākēn of judgment) **this is what the LORD says about
Jehoiakim son of Josiah king of Judah** delivers the LORD's verdict
upon Jehoiakim. The accusations made against him were true and so
he is judged as one who cared little for the well-being of his citizens
and ruthlessly pursued his own ambitions. Just as his life had been
different from his father's, so too would be the circumstances of his
death: there would be no widespread lamentation at the death of such
an oppressive and unpopular monarch. **They will not mourn for
him:**[25] **'Alas, my brother! Alas, my sister!'** 'Mourn' (<√sāpad) refers
to wailing where the cries were less formal than in a lament. For 'alas!'
see 'woe!' (v. 13). To cry out, 'My sister', over the departed king
seemed so odd that the early Greek translators of the Septuagint
omitted it entirely. It has also seemed odd to more modern interpreters,
and one of their attempts to ease the difficulty is seen in the REB turning 'āḥôt, 'sister', into a word to be rendered 'brother'. The expression
may be explained either along the lines proposed by Calvin, that this is
what the mourners say to each other (1850, 3:107), or else as simply
stating that conventional expressions of grief will be absent from his
funeral. The second aspect of the situation is that **they will not mourn
for him: 'Alas, my master! Alas, his splendour!'**[26] 'Master' ('ādôn,
'lord') refers to a leader, one with authority, and 'his splendour' may
be equivalent to 'his majesty'. It is foretold that when Jehoiakim died,
his subjects will express no grief at his departure, and there would be
no opportunity for the ostentatious displays of a state funeral.

19. Jehoiakim's ignominious end was also foretold in different words
in 36:30. **He will have the burial**[27] **of a donkey—dragged away**[28]
(<√sāḥab, 15:3) **and thrown outside the gates of Jerusalem.** It was a

---

25. The NRSV addition 'saying' here and in the next colon is unnecessary.

26. The kethibh hdh might be read as hōdāh, 'her splendour', which does
not fit the context at all, but was probably intended to be hōdōh, 'his
splendour' (GKC §91e). The qere has the regular form of the suffix in hōdô,
'his splendour/majesty'.

27. In ⌐with⌐ the burial of a donkey he will be buried' the cognate accusative institutes a comparison (IBHS §10.2.1g).

28. The infinitives absolute are used adverbially (GKC §113h; IBHS
§4.6.2b; 35.5.2d).

great curse not to have a proper burial, and here Jehoiakim is being
treated like a dead ass, taken to the rubbish tip outside the city walls
and left there. In the light of 2 Kgs. 24:6 which tells us that Jehoiakim
'rested/slept with his fathers', a problem arises as to the fulfilment of
this prophecy. But the tension only exists if we understand the phrase
in Kings to mean 'met with a peaceful end and was buried'. That it
does not mean a peaceful end is indicated by its use in connection with
Ahab (1 Kgs. 22:40), and that it is not the same as buried is shown by
the careful note regarding Manasseh, 'So Manasseh slept with his
fathers and was buried' (2 Kgs. 21:18). There are, however, obscurities
regarding Jehoiakim's death. According to 2 Chron. 36:6 he was
bound over to be taken captive to Babylon, but apparently he was not
taken there. This, however, seems to have happened earlier in his reign
and not around the time of his death. According to the Jewish historian
Josephus, Nebuchadnezzar ordered his body thrown outside the wall
(*Ant.*10.6.3). The Bible itself, however, does not tell us that. However,
the fact that this prediction is repeated in substance in 36:30 indicates
that it is to be taken as literally intended and not just a graphic idiom
for an ignominious end.

The scathing criticism of Jehoiakim and his corruption that Jeremiah
here records goes a long way towards explaining the unrelenting
opposition of that despot to the prophet. Jehoiakim may well have been
the most bitter enemy Jeremiah had to face.

4. Complacency Overturned (22:20-23)

Verses 20-23 follow up the implications for the land of having kings of
the calibre of Jehoiakim. Divine speech is addressed in the feminine
singular to Daughter Zion, the people of Jerusalem and Judah. Their
conduct is shown not to have changed since the days of Jeremiah's
early ministry, with the obstinate defiance of v. 21 reminding one of
their earlier responses in 2:20, 23, 25, 31, 35.

20. Go up to Lebanon and cry out is the first of three commands to
the people to go to mountainous areas on the border of the land. The
first of these, Lebanon, was situated to the north-west, and from there it
is envisaged that their cry would be heard far and wide. However, 'cry
out' ($<\sqrt{ṣ\bar{a}^caq}$)[29] usually denotes a cry for help, rather than one of
mourning. **Let your voice be heard in Bashan** turns to the north-east,
where the broad, fertile plateau of Bashan was located at a height of
about 2000 feet (610 m), east of the Sea of Galilee. 'Let your voice be

---

29. For the form $ṣ\partial^c\bar{a}q\hat{\imath}$, see GKC §§10h, 46d.

heard'/'Give, or raise, your voice' may refer to expressing grief (48:34), or simply to speaking loudly. Thirdly, the verb of the first injunction is repeated in relation to the south-east: **cry out from Abarim**. Abarim refers to the northernmost mountains of Moab on the east of the Dead Sea. It was here that Mount Nebo was located from which Moses had viewed the Promised Land (Num. 27:12; Deut. 32:49).

To whom are these commands given, and precisely what did they entail? The four imperatives are feminine singular, and it seems clear that it is Jerusalem that is again being addressed. The orders are therefore given to the people of Judah in general. One possibility is that they are to direct their cries outwards, away from Judah, **for** (*kî*) **all your allies are crushed.** 'Allies'/'lovers' (30:14; a similar term is found in 4:30) refers to those with whom they had engaged in political intrigues, including Egypt (2:36) and various neighbouring small states (27:3; 46:2-12; 47:2-7; 2 Kgs. 24:1-4). Previously these allies were viewed as deserting Judah (2:36), but now they themselves are destroyed. However, rather than personified Jerusalem speaking outwards in lament over her fallen allies, it is more probable that she is envisaged acting as a messenger speaking inwards towards the land of Judah itself and announcing that it is now left isolated and alone.

21. Despite previous warnings given by the LORD to his people, Judah had fallen into a desperate state. **I warned you when you felt secure, but you said, 'I will not listen!'** 'Warned'/'spoke' indicates what the LORD had done by his servants the prophets by way of warning the people of the danger of their situation. But it was a time when they felt secure/'in their prosperities' (<*šalwâ*). The form here is plural and may indicate the completeness of their feelings/situation: 'days of prosperous ease' (REB). In itself that is not condemned, but it can be a time of spiritual danger because it is liable to lead to carelessness about the need for principled living, moulded by the LORD's requirements, and so may degenerate into complacency, ignoring warnings because they could see no threat to their security on the horizon (cf. the related adjective in 49:31; and also Prov. 1:32; Ezek. 16:49; Dan. 8:25; 11:21, 24). Such an unresponsive attitude had emerged during the days of Josiah when the Assyrian empire was in eclipse and a measure of prosperity and territorial expansion was possible for Judah.

But it was not only in the recent past that this characteristic had been found. The events after Josiah's death were the last act in a drama that had been played out ever since the Exodus. **This has been your way** (*derek*) **from your youth;** 'for' (*kî*) **you have not obeyed me.**

The 'youth' of the nation (2:2; Hos. 2:17) refers to the period in the wilderness and during the settlement in the land. Even then disobedience had been characteristic of the nation, particularly at a time when they were enjoying divine favour.

22. But the peace and prosperity of the land will be shattered with the coming of Nebuchadnezzar. The land will suffer internally in that **the wind will drive all your shepherds away.** 'Wind' refers to God's judgment in the form of invading armies (4:11-12; 13:24; 18:17). 'Shepherds'[30] relates principally to the rulers of the nation (2:8; 10:21; 23:1-4), who are no longer going to be around to provide pasture for the people where they can feel secure. 'Drive away' is literally 'shepherd': the wind[31] is going to act as shepherd for these shepherds, rounding them up and sweeping them away. In the event in 597 BC Nebuchadnezzar took away not only King Jehoiachin but also the most experienced statesmen and administrators of Judah, so that under Zedekiah the land had to put up with third-rate politicians. Externally too, Judah would be affected in that she will be without friends. **And your allies**/'lovers' (v. 20) **will go into exile.** The nations from which they had expected support will themselves be overcome and deported by the Babylonians. Neither friends abroad nor leaders at home will be there to help them in their distress. The conjunction *kî* which introduces the next line seems to be intensive or asseverative in force, 'surely' (NKJV). **Then you shall be ashamed and disgraced because of all your wickedness** (*rā'â*). 'Be ashamed' (<√*bôš*, 2:26) may indicate that they will be made to feel ashamed by the discovery of the reality of their situation. 'Disgraced' (<√*kālam*, 3:3) reinforces the picture of the people utterly embarrassed by their situation, which will have arisen because of their sinful conduct.

23. The use of 'you', feminine singular, continues, indicating that Zion/Jerusalem is being addressed. **You who live**[32] **in 'Lebanon', who are nestled in cedar buildings.** This refers particularly to the

---

30. The REB translation 'friends' involves changing *rō'ayik* to *rē'ayik*, but this is not supported by the versions which identify the play between the verb and the noun 'shepherds'.

31. There is alliteration in the Hebrew, *rō'ayik tir'eh-rûaḥ*, where the gutturals and *resh* reinforce the idea of gusts of wind.

32. The kethibh *yšbty* could be vocalised as *yāšabtî* with the old second feminine ending, 'you lived', but the following kethibh *mqnnty* demands a participial rendering. The qere offers segolate feminine singular participial forms, *yōšabt* and *məqunnant* (cf. 10:17; GKC §90n), but the spelling of the kethibh might be explained as using *hireq campaginis* (GKC §90m).

king, but probably also to the upper classes in Jerusalem who had built
for themselves grand houses clad in cedar (v. 6). Lebanon is here
evocative both of the opulence of the lifestyle affected in Jerusalem
and of the sense of security that the people had. 'Nestled' (√qānan, 'to
build a nest') refers to her comfort and protection in nests high in the
cedars (vv. 6-7; 21:13). But this is going to be completely changed.
**How you will groan[33] when pangs come upon you, pain like that of
a woman in labour!** Jeremiah frequently uses this metaphor for
sudden and commanding distress to refer to divine judgment that is to
come upon the people, here appropriately personified as daughter Zion
(4:31; 6:24; 13:21).

5. Concerning Jehoiachin (22:24-30)

Jehoiachin's reign lasted for three months and 10 days (2 Chron. 26:9),
and it ended with the capture of Jerusalem on 16th March 597 BC (see
Appendix §2). He was only 18 years old at the time (2 Kgs. 24:8; for
the 'eight years old' of 2 Chron. 26:9 as marking the beginning of a co-
regency with his father right from the start of his reign in 608, see
McFall 1991:39). His name is found in no less than five forms in
Hebrew, and there are three variants in English translations. Probably
Jehoiachin (52:31, 33) was his throne name, in which two components
of his original name (Jeconiah) are reversed. Coniah, the found form
here and also in 22:28 and 37:1, is a shortened version of Jeconiah
(24:1; 27:20; 28:4; 29:2). All the forms seem to mean, 'The LORD will
establish'.

There are two oracles regarding Jehoiachin. The first in prose (vv.
24-27) is addressed to him and predicts that he will be taken by the
Babylonians into exile, never to return. We know he was released from
prison in Babylon on 2nd April 561 BC (52:31), but we do not know
how long he lived after that. The second oracle is in poetic form
(vv. 28-30) and predicts that with Jehoiachin the line of Judah's kings
will come to an end. Nothing is said here about his character or deeds,
though the verdict elsewhere is unfavourable (2 Kgs. 24:9; 2 Chron.
36:9; Ezek. 19:5-9).

---

33. The Massoretic *mah-nēḥant*, 'how you will be pitied' (NRSV footnote;
cf. NKJV, NJPS), derives from the Hebrew root *ḥanan*, 'to be gracious, show
favour'. The LXX suggests another root is to be found here *ʿānaḥ*, 'to groan',
and this is followed by the NIV, REB, NRSV and NASB. It involves a
complicated transformation of a niphal form *neʿĕnaḥt* into *nēnaḥt* and then
metathesis to give *nēḥant* (cf. GKC §23f).

a. A Ring Pulled Off (22:24-27)

24. The LORD solemnly notifies Jehoiachin that he is going to disown him. **'As surely as I live,' declares the LORD** is an oath formula, in which the LORD swears by himself because there is none higher to whom appeal might be made (v. 5). **Even if** (*kî ʿim*) **you, Jehoiachin son of Jehoiakim king of Judah, were a signet ring on my right hand,** 'yet' (*kî* emphatic, *NIDOTTE* 4:1030) **I would still pull you off.**[34] A signet ring (the same imagery is developed in a different way in Hag. 2:23) was used to impress a mark of ownership or to endorse documents, much like a signature in more modern times. Although some signet rings were highly ornate, its value derived not from its material worth but through what it could effect (Gen. 41:42; 1 Kgs. 21:8; Est. 3:10; 8:2). As such it was not something an individual would usually let out of his possession, often being tied by a piece of cord round the neck (cf. Song of S. 8:6). Such a close link between a person and his signet ring was an illustration of the relationship that should exist between the LORD and the king who acted as his representative. But even if that close relationship had existed, and the expression used assumes that it did not, the LORD will have nothing more to do with him. The signet ring will be pulled off.

25. I will hand you over to those who seek your life, those you fear—to Nebuchadnezzar king of Babylon and to the Babylonians. Throughout his brief reign the Babylonians were besieging the city, and here the LORD indicates that they are going to be successful. 'Seek your life' (21:7) usually denotes a desire to kill someone, though in fact the Babylonians spared Jehoiachin. 'Dread' (<√*yāgar*) occurs seven times in the Old Testament (cf. 39:17) for the fear resulting from divine wrath or punishment. Perhaps this term was used here because the enemy threat was the result of covenant disobedience ('dreaded', Deut. 28:60).

26. I will hurl you and the mother who gave you birth into

---

34. In Hebrew the protasis is in the third person, 'Even if Coniah son of Jehoiakim king of Judah were a signet ring …' (NKJV, NRSV), and then there is a switch to a second person reference in the apodosis, 'I would pull you off.' Such a change of person is awkward in English style; hence the change found in the NIV. The verb *ʾettəqenkā*, 'I would pull you off' (<√*nātaq*) is unusual in that it has an unassimilated energic nun (*IBHS* §31.7.2a). Holladay (1986, 1:606) suggests this may have arisen because the form is in pause, or to underscore the wordplay with *ûnətattîkā*, 'I will give', with which the next verse begins.

another country[35], **where neither of you was born,**[36] **and there you
both will die.** 'Hurl' (<√ṭûl, 16:13) is used both here and in v. 28 for
the forceful exile of Jehoiachin and his mother. The queen mother
played a significant role in the political life of Judah, and it may be that
Jehoiachin's mother, Nehusta, had a higher profile than usual because
of Jehoiachin's comparative youth at his ascension to the throne
(13:18; 2 Kgs. 24:8). She was to suffer the same fate as him, when the
Babylonians took the ruling classes off into exile (24:1; 29:2; 2 Kgs.
24:12, 15).

27. The verse begins with the disjunctive construction, *waw* followed
by a non-verb: 'but' (NKJV, NRSV). **You will never come back to
the land you long to return to.** The exile imposed on them would not
be reversed. In the event there were still people in Judah who remained
loyal to Jehoiachin and expected his return (28:4, 10), but theirs was a
vain hope. The Babylonians allowed a steward to maintain the royal
estates on his behalf (cf. 28:4), and he was eventually liberated from
captivity in Babylon (52:31-34), but he and his mother would not be
permitted to fulfil their deeply felt desire. 'Long' is a participle,
denoting the continuance of the action in their future exile as they were
'lifting up their desire (<*nepeš*, 2:34)' towards the land, that is, yearning for it (44:14; Deut. 24:15; Hos. 4:8).

b. ... And Hurled Away (22:28-30)
This section presents a further reflection on Jehoiachin's destiny from
about the same period, possibly after he had been taken away by
Nebuchadnezzar. It has a sad note about it, looking in dismay at the
end of the Davidic line of kings in Judah. Jeremiah's concern is not so
much for Jehoiachin and what is happening to him personally, but for
what it all means in terms of the LORD's relationship with the people.

**28. Is this man Jehoiachin a despised, broken pot, an object no
one wants?** The word rendered 'pot' (*'eṣeb*) occurs only here, but the
verb from which it is derived means 'to form' and the same root is
used in Job 10:8 to refer to shaping or fashioning an article. Two views
prevail as to the type of article that is in view. One takes Jehoiachin to
be viewed as an 'idol' (NKJV), something made but without
substance, and thus the metaphor is one for a 'mere puppet' (REB).
The other view seeks to elucidate the meaning of the word here by the

---

35. Unusually the article occurs with land; GKC §126z suggests it should be
omitted.
36. This verb and the next are plural referring both to the king and his
mother as is brought out by the NIV additions, 'neither of' and 'both'.

parallelism with the second question where mention of 'vessel' suggests a piece of pottery. Certainly the picture of him being taken off into exile was a pathetic one, and the questions expect the answer 'Yes', he is something that no one wants, as useless as a broken earthenware jar. The third question **Why will**[37] **he and his children be hurled out, cast into a land they do not know?** picks up the word 'hurl' from v. 26. Although young at the time of his accession, his wives are mentioned among those taken captive (2 Kgs. 24:15), and so he might already have had children. The tense used to translate the verb depends on the view taken of when these words were uttered in relation to the events of 597 BC. The perfect may imply that they have already been hurled out. The question challenges Jeremiah's hearers to think deeply about what has gone on to bring their new king so swiftly into such a position of insecurity and oblivion in a foreign land. No answer is given because what is facing the nation is one of the unresolved aspects of a hopeless situation into which their sin has plunged the land.

29. The prophet's dismay at the slow and inadequate response of the people to what is going on around them is brought out in the pathetic words, **O land, land, land! hear the word of the LORD!** Although the NKJV translation 'earth' is a possible rendering of ʿ*eres*, 'land', it does not fit this context, where the focus is not on the attitude of the nations in general but on the intransigence of Judah. The emphatic threefold repetition of the word shows the prophet expressing his anguish, bewilderment and exasperation at the spiritual hardness of the people. Will they never listen and learn?

30. The final message regarding Jehoiachin uses the imagery of conducting a census, or preparing an official genealogy. **This is what the LORD says: 'Record this man as if childless,**[38] **a man who will not prosper in his lifetime.'** 'Record'/'write' is used in relation to drawing up an official register of citizens (Num. 11:26; 1 Chron. 4:41; Ps. 87:6; cf. Ezra 2:2-62; Neh. 7:5-64). However, it is no ordinary citizen list that is in view here but the royal genealogy of the kings of Judah. The NIV adds 'as if' because Jehoiachin had in fact seven sons (1 Chron. 3:17-18), and five of them at any rate survived in Babylon as a cuneiform document from there proves (*ANET* 308). But for the purposes of an heir to the throne he would be as if he had no children. There would be no entry descending from him in the royal genealogy;

---

37. For the pointing of the verb, see GKC §10g.

38. The REB 'stripped of all honour' represents an attempt to find another meaning for this word, but it is highly speculative (*HALOT* 884).

his line would become extinct. Although his grandson Zerubbabel (1 Chron. 3:19) was ruler in post-exilic Jerusalem, it was as a governor, part of the Persian provincial administration, not as a king. Furthermore Jehoiachin would not know good fortune during his life. He would in fact live out his life in Babylon, in prison certainly until he was 54 years old.

It was also the case that their father's misfortune would be reflected also in the lives of his descendants. **For** (*kî*) **none of his offspring will prosper, none will sit on the throne of David or rule any more in Judah.** Jehoiachin's name is, however, included in the genealogy of Christ (Matt. 1:12). His uncle ruled after him but died before him. His grandson Zerubbabel was never king. He was the last survivor of the kingly line.

6. The Righteous Branch (23:1-8)

This section brings to a conclusion this collection of material about the kings of Judah. We might then have expected something about Zedekiah since the collection as a whole dates from his reign and had begun with the king sending a delegation to the prophet (21:1). Instead Jeremiah ends with an oracle that condemns those rulers who have been deficient carrying out their duty (vv. 1-2) and promises divine action to provide appropriate rulers for the people of the LORD (vv. 3-4). However, the prophet was permitted to see beyond the provision of adequate rulers in general to the coming of one specific ruler, the Righteous Branch (vv. 5-6). The section ends by recording the response that will be given to the LORD's intervention in the affairs of his people (vv. 7-8).

a. The Failed Shepherds (23:1-2)
1. The message begins with a general announcement of doom on the shepherds. **'Woe to the shepherds who are destroying and scatter- ing the sheep of my pasture!' declares the LORD.** 'Woe' (*hôy*, 22:13) points to the judgment that the LORD is going to bring on the shepherds (2:8). The metaphor of shepherd is frequently used of the king in Israel as the one whose duty it was to guide, protect and provide for the people and to set them an example to follow. We do not know of any king of Israel or Judah who used this as an official title, but ancient Near Eastern records show that many rulers did designate themselves in this way. As the context focuses on the administration of justice and public policy in the land, the term shepherds here does not include religious leaders, either the priests or the prophets. It probably

also excludes those officials who were the chief administrators in the kingdom. Though they had leadership roles in the community, it was the king who was ultimately responsible for the conduct and character of the affairs of the nation. The plural term 'shepherds' probably encompasses the final four final kings of Judah whose mismanagement and misgovernment disqualified them from being worthy holders of the office.

'Destroying' (<√ʿābad[39]) may also mean 'to lose, allow to go astray', 'let ... be lost' (REB). A participle is used in the expression to bring out the fact that it was characteristic of these kings that they did not provide the leadership that would have kept the people together as a flock dedicated to the service of the LORD. Instead the nation was left without the political and spiritual guidance it required. In this way the shepherds also kept on 'scattering' the people. 'Scatter' (<pûṣ hiphil, 9:16) views the sheep not as gradually straying apart as they graze, but as spreading panic-stricken before some external threat from which the shepherd has made no attempt to protect them. 'The sheep of my pasture' (marʿît, 10:21) were those the LORD had committed to their care, and regarding whose welfare he himself was concerned (Pss. 74:1; 79:13; 100:3). The phrase makes clear the role of the kings as under-shepherds and the LORD himself as the true Shepherd. It was the failure of the under-shepherds that led to their own downfall and that of the people.

2. After the indictment against the shepherds there follows the divine sentence on them. **Therefore** (lākēn, of judgment) **this is what the LORD, the God of Israel, says to[40] the shepherds who tend[41] my people.** 'God of Israel' emphasises the special relationship that existed between him and the people, which is also brought out by the expression 'my people'. The kings/shepherds were answerable to the LORD for the way in which they discharged their duties because the people they ruled over were his.

'Because you have scattered my flock and driven them away

---

39. It is the piel of ʿābad that is found here. It also occurs in Eccl. 3:6, 'a time to seek, and a time to lose' (NRSV), where the contrast makes the idea of 'to lose' clear.

40. 'To' is ʿal, which might be translated 'concerning' (NASB, NRSV) or even 'against' (NKJV), but since they are directly addressed in what follows, taking it as the equivalent of ʿel, 'to', seems more appropriate.

41. The word hārōʿîm is repeated, as is brought out by the NRSV rendering 'the shepherds who shepherd'. The active participle is first used as a substantive and then as a relative (IBHS §37.1c).

and have not bestowed care on them, I will bestow punishment on you for the evil you have done,' declares the LORD. The initial 'You' (*'attem*) is emphatic: 'It is you who have scattered' (NRSV). It contrasts with 'But I myself' (*wa'ănî*, v. 3). There are three aspects to their improper conduct. (1) Scattering (cf. v. 1) the flock is the opposite action to that expected of a shepherd, who would keep the flock together as a means of protecting and superintending it. This brings out the divisive consequences for the nation of current social and political behaviour sanctioned by the king. Consequently the people were no longer able to function with cohesion and effectiveness in the face of an external threat. (2) 'Driven them away' (<√*nādaḥ*, 8:3) goes beyond 'destroy'/'lose' in v. 1 by making clear that the kings were not simply passive in his process. Royal misgovernment not only prevented the people obtaining justice in the courts, but was also responsible for their exile from the land. (3) 'Have not bestowed care' (<√*pāqad*) denotes the action of a superior towards those under him, both in providing for them, and in monitoring and appropriately rewarding their performance. Ezekiel gives a more detailed picture of the way in which the kings had failed in their role as shepherds (Ezek. 34:2-6). Now because the shepherds have not cared appropriately, the LORD will 'care' for them, bringing punishment (<√*pāqad*) on them for the evil of their actions. The wordplay on *pāqad* brought out by the use of 'bestow' in the NIV is found in most English translations: 'You have not watched over them; but I am watching over you to punish you' (REB); 'You have not attended to them. So I will attend to you' (NRSV).

b. The Gathered Flock (23:3-4)
3. The message of vv. 1-2 about the shepherds who failed is followed in vv. 3-4 by an oracle in which the LORD promises to reverse the consequences of their failure (v. 3) and take action to provide appropriate rulers for his people in future (v. 4). The inclusion of this material suggests that Jeremiah compiled this section with more than the current king, Zedekiah, in mind. This is a word to comfort and sustain those who were loyal to the LORD but who had been engulfed by the tragedy that had come upon their nation. They were already struggling with the dark words of doom that the prophet delivered, but this brighter prospect, albeit a distant one, served to indicate that all was not completely lost. This perspective can also be seen in chapters 30–31 which date from the same period late in Zedekiah's reign.

The LORD's behaviour towards his flock will be quite different from that of the unworthy shepherds. He begins 'But I' to distinguish emphatically his conduct from theirs (v. 2). **I myself will gather the**

remnant[42] **of my flock out of all the countries where I have driven them.** 'Gather' (<√$qābaṣ$, the opposite of $pûṣ$ found in vv. 1-2) is a natural word to describe the action of a shepherd bringing together his scattered flock, and it is also used of God's action in bringing together the people from exile (29:14; 31:8, 10; Isa. 43:5; 56:8; Ezek. 11:17; 20:34). Such a return had already been envisaged in 3:15-18, but still it will only be of a 'remnant' ($šəʾērît$, 31:7; 42:2) who have survived the judgment that will come on the nation.

'Driven' (<√$nādaḥ$, v. 2) is now used by the LORD of his own action. The description of God as the shepherd of his people is found at the time of the Exodus (Exod. 15:13, 17); he was the powerful leader who drove out other nations and made room for his own flock (Ps. 78:52-55, 70-72). However, as a consequence of the lack of proper oversight on the part of the under-shepherds, he had to intervene in judgment and drive the people from the land into exile. But that is not to be the LORD's last word on the destiny of Israel. The shepherd will ensure the return of the people (31:8-14; Isa. 40:11; 49:9-13). 'Out of all the countries' is a comprehensive expression: no matter where they have gone, the LORD knows where they are and will restore them.

The LORD further promises that he **will bring them**[43] **back to their pasture, where they will be fruitful and increase in number.** The 'pasture' ($nāweh$, not the same word as in v. 1) is not merely the land, but the land as the LORD's covenant inheritance for his people, a place of beauty and security, where they can stay well-nourished and contented (10:25). When they are 'brought back' (<√$šûb$, hiphil) by the LORD's sovereign and effective action, they are not merely restored but enabled to fulfil the creation mandate of God to 'be fruitful and increase in number' (Gen. 1:26) and also the terms of the Abrahamic covenant (Gen. 17:6; 22:17). It will be a time of covenant blessing and fulfilment (Amos 9:11-15; Hos. 2:21-23; Ezek. 3:6; Zech. 8:9-13).

4. But a regathered flock raises the question of how they were to be governed. Would there merely be a reinstitution of the structures that had previously existed? The first answer to that question involves an assurance that new provision will be made for proper guidance of the

---

42. Jeremiah generally uses $šəʾērît$ to refer to those left in the land, but here (and also 31:7; 50:20) it is used of the exiles.

43. 'Them' and 'their' are feminine plurals, the feminine reflecting the collective $ṣōʾn$, 'flock', though a masculine plural might have been expected in line with $ʾōtām$ in 'I have driven *them*'. The change to plural forms possibly brings out the numbers that will be involved in the return.

people. 'I will place[44] shepherds over them who will tend them, and
they will no longer be afraid or terrified ($<\sqrt{}$ḥātat qal, 1:17), nor
will any be missing,' declares the LORD. The shepherds will 'tend
them'/'shepherd them' not just in name but in reality. This will lead to
a decisive break with the past, marked by the use of 'no longer'. As a
result of the new regime provided by God the people will be freed
from living in fear ($<\sqrt{}$yārē‘, 'to fear), unable to function properly
through terror. They will enjoy outward prosperity and inward psychological and spiritual stability. What is more there will be none
'missing'. This word constitutes a play on yet a third meaning of the
root pāqad in the niphal, 'to be lacking' (3:16; 1 Sam. 25:7; Num.
31:49). The fulfilment of this prophecy may be seen in part in the
rulers of the restored nation in post-exilic times, such as Zerubbabel, or
Ezra and Nehemiah. But at best they were able to realise only to a very
limited extent what the LORD intended for his people. They were
precursors of the full provision the LORD would give, as the further
prophecy in the following verses shows.

c. The Messianic Shepherd (23:5-6)
The rulers to be provided by the LORD would anticipate the one final
king who would completely embody all that a ruler of the LORD's
people ought to be. Jeremiah is therefore given this further message
about the royal deliverer to come.

5. '**The days are coming,' declares the LORD** is a phrase that looks
forward to a time in the future which is not definitely located, but is
viewed as arising already as a logical consequence of what God has
promised in his covenant commitment and has begun to provide (7:32).
When I will raise up (wahăqimōtî, the same word as is translated 'I
will place' in v. 4, linking the verses together) **to David a righteous
Branch** (ṣemaḥ $<\sqrt{}$ṣāmaḥ, 'to sprout, spring up'). The root ṣāmaḥ is
part of the vocabulary of plant growth, including growth out of the
ground (Gen. 2:9), growth of leaves (Ezek. 17:9) and growth of the
plant itself (Exod. 10:5). It evokes a picture of the unfolding of life in
its fruitfulness and vitality. Here the term is used metaphorically of the
Messiah, the prophesied ruler of Davidic descent ('up from David's
line', NIV margin), who would fulfil all that was required of him. The
special Messianic employment of ṣāmaḥ may be traced back to
David's last words where he reflected on the LORD's covenant

---

44. It may be that 'I will place' ($<\sqrt{}$qûm hiphil) reflects on the name
Jehoiakim, 'the LORD will place/cause to stand', incorporating the same root.
Since the verb is a common one, it is not possible to be certain of this.

promises to him: 'Is not my house like this with God? For he has made with me an everlasting covenant, ordered in all things and secure. Will he not cause to prosper (<√*ṣāmaḥ* hiphil 'cause to sprout') all my help and my desire?' (2 Sam. 23:5 NRSV). This association with the Davidic covenant and its fulfilment is also found in the divine promise recorded in Ps. 132:17, 'There I will cause a horn to sprout up (<√*ṣāmaḥ* hiphil) for David; I have prepared a lamp for my anointed one' (NRSV). The associated noun, 'branch' (*ṣemaḥ*), is used as a Messianic term in 33:15; Zech. 3:8; 6:12. A similar word *nēṣer*, 'branch', is used in Isa. 11:1, and *ṣemaḥ* itself may possibly be employed Messianically in Isa. 4:2 (Baldwin 1964). The New Testament does not seem to employ the title, Branch, in relation to the Messiah. However, Kaiser (*TWOT* #1928a) notes that *ṣāmaḥ* is regularly translated in the LXX by *anatellō*, which is found used in messianic contexts in Luke 1:78 and Heb. 7:14. He suggests that 'by which the rising sun (*anatolē*) will come to us from heaven' might well be rendered 'by which the Branch will come to us from heaven'. However, it is more probable that the LXX altered the image suggested by *ṣāmaḥ* to that of the appearance of light, and it is that image which is developed in the New Testament (*NIDOTTE* 3:816-17).

But what is 'a *righteous* Branch'? A Phoenician inscription from Lapethos in Cyprus, dated 3rd century BC, refers to Ptolemy II Philadelphus as *ṣemaḥ ṣedeq*, 'righteous branch'/'legitimate ruler', that is, all that a ruler should be, and that is reflected in the REB margin, 'legitimate shoot'. While the idea of the Branch being the true and legitimate occupant of David's throne may well be present to some extent, the references in the context to doing what is right (*ṣədāqâ*) and the LORD our Righteousness (*ṣedeq*) indicate that 'a righteous (*ṣaddîq*) branch' looks beyond the status of the ruler, and is to be understood primarily of his behaviour. In either sense the Messianic ruler will qualify for the description 'righteous', and in this he would be quite unlike the sorry occupants of David's throne in the years leading up to the fall of Jerusalem. First, Jehoiakim had been put on the throne by Pharaoh Neco, and later Zedekiah was Nebuchadnezzar's appointee: neither really qualifying for the epithet 'legitimate', and as regards their behaviour neither the despotic Jehoiakim nor the vacillating Zedekiah were shining examples of kings who were right with God. In contrast to the existing state of the Davidic dynasty, the ruler who will be the LORD's ultimate provision for his people will conform to all that is expected of him by the LORD and set out in the covenant. Though there will be continuity with the past, he will represent new growth sprouting directly from the ground.

The royal behaviour displayed by the one who will be divinely raised up to be Israel's shepherd is then described. **A King who will reign wisely** brings together two thoughts: 'he will reign ⌐as⌐ king', probably in the sense of being truly a king and not just a puppet figure such as Zedekiah (cf. 37:1); and 'he will act wisely' (<√*śākal* hiphil, 3:15; 9:24), combining the idea of understanding/insight with the prosperity that should accompany the application of such insight in practical situations. The policies he will implement will be effective and successful. He will **do what is just and right in the land.** Here is the true descendant of David, who in his day had done 'what was just and right for all his people' (2 Sam. 8:15). That was what was held out before David's successors as the mark of the ideal king: 'He will judge your people in righteousness, your afflicted ones with justice' (Ps. 72:2). However, their conduct often fell far short of what was desired and they had to be challenged to do what was just and right (22:3). The Messianic ruler will require no such prophetic remonstrance because he will live true to the divine requirements.

6. In his days Judah will be saved and Israel will live in safety (33:16). This fulfils the covenant blessing, 'So Israel will live in safety alone' (Deut. 33:28), which was prophesied as the outcome of the LORD's intervention on behalf of his people. It is still expected that divine action will be required to render the promise effective, but the addition of 'in his days' suggests that that action is realised in conjunction with the anticipated king. 'Be saved' (<√*yāša'* niphal, 4:14) is a broad term for deliverance from difficulty and danger. The following expression 'live/reside (*šākan*) in safety' suggests the vision is principally one of return from the Exile, the deliverance being from the punishment imposed on them as a consequence of their breaches of the covenant. When the LORD intervenes in the days of the Messiah, the people will be able to enter once more into the privileges of the covenant and enjoy them without interference or disruption. The joint mention of Judah and Israel envisages that it will be a time of reunion of the two parts of the divided nation (3:18). This promise was partially fulfilled in the return from the Exile, but it awaited the coming of the Messiah before it began to be realised in a deeper sense. Even now, though the new age has been inaugurated, the full blessing described here has not yet arrived, but will be found in the new heavens and the new earth where the LORD's purpose for his creation and his people will be finally realised (Rev. 21:1-4).

'In safety'/'in security' (*lābeṭaḥ*) is a phrase that depicts a multi-dimensional situation. In Lev. 25:18-19 the primary emphasis is on security from famine as the land yields its produce to those who are obedient to the LORD. In the following chapter (Lev. 26:4-8) this thought is expanded to include security from attack by wild animals and from human aggression. This leads to a situation of total well-being (*šālôm*; Lev. 26:6). Clustering round the concept of *beṭaḥ*, 'safety', there are also social and political factors, including adequate provision even for the poorest of the poor (Isa. 14:30) and equitable administration of justice as here (see also Isa. 32:16-17 where *beṭaḥ* is rendered 'confidence'). The ultimate provision of security and safety is in the eschatological covenant of peace which was only partially anticipated in the return from the Exile (Ezek. 34:25-29).

This is the name by which he will be called:[45] **The LORD Our Righteousness.**[46] The name (traditionally transliterated as Jehovah Tsidkenu) sums up all that he truly is. It is unlikely that Jeremiah considered this name to involve an ascription of deity to the coming king. The same title is later (33:17) applied to the city of Jerusalem. Equally, it is improbable that Jeremiah understood righteousness in the Pauline sense of a forensic declaration of the standing of the people of God provided by their identification with the Messiah as their Saviour. This is not at variance with the name, but in its Old Testament context it has a much broader application. The thought encapsulated in such names was typically a sentence (Gen. 33:20; Exod. 17:15), and here it is a descriptive title that may be translated, 'The LORD is our righteousness' (NRSV). The Messianic king is the very embodiment of the truth that the LORD is the one who provides and constitutes all that is embodied in righteousness for his people. The name could then apply equally to Jerusalem, because it is the city which is a pledge of the LORD's presence with his people and of his provision for them. The focus is not on the nature of the Messiah, but on what the LORD will accomplish through him, in contrast to what the human endeavours of previous kings had failed to achieve. An expansion of how this promise would initially be realised is provided in Ezek. 34:25-31.

---

45. *yqr'w* is a *forma mixta* (GKC §60c) of *yiqrā'ô*, 'he will call him' and *yiqrə'û*, 'they will call'. In the first case, the third person singular verb is used impersonally.

46. The words *YHWH* and *ṣidqēnû* are separated by the vertical divider paseq to indicate that the Massoretes did not want the words read as 'the LORD our righteousness', but rather as 'the LORD is our righteousness'. On the other hand, the disjunctive accent tipḥa under *yiqrə'ô* and the conjunctive accent merka under *YHWH* oppose the translation, 'The LORD will call him, our righteousness'.

What then is the 'righteousness' that is here referred to? The Old Testament concept of righteousness refers to attitudes and actions that are in conformity with what is required in a relationship. Here what is being talked about is the action of the LORD as the covenant king in relation to his people. He had committed himself to defend them, and so at a national level occasions of deliverance or military victory were described as displays of the righteousness of the LORD (Judg. 5:11; Isa. 41:2; 45:8; 46:13). In this way the LORD is 'a righteous God and a Saviour' (Isa. 45:11). In this context the term is applied to the envisaged situation where the people will be suffering in exile as a consequence of their rebellion against their king. His wrath against them was fully justified and had led to their punishment, but the purpose of God does not stop there. He will recall and reclaim his own. His commitment to the eventual consummation of the covenant leads to him providing deliverance once the purpose that was involved in his discipline of his people is realised. God's covenant love and commitment is to be found in, and lasts through, the punishment he imposes. He always acts righteously/appropriately in his dealings even with the rebellious, and through his restoring mercy will show himself as *our* righteousness.

The name probably involves a sideways glance at King Zedekiah, whose own name *ṣidqiyāhû*, 'my righteousness is the LORD', had the same two elements in reverse order. Zedekiah had failed to live up to that title, but the Messiah will not.

After indicating the expectation that in the day of God's ultimate intervention to establish his justice, there would be the combination of righteousness and salvation described here, Wright comments: 'In the event, they called his name Jesus; that is, in Hebrew, Joshua, which means "The LORD is salvation". One can picture Jeremiah happily nodding his assent to what he would have regarded as a perfectly satisfactory, indeed equivalent, fulfilment of his prophecy' (1983:139).

d. Restoration Accomplished (23:7-8)

7-8. 'So then, the days are coming,' (cf. v. 5) **declares the LORD, 'when people will no longer say, "As surely as the LORD lives, who brought the Israelites up out of Egypt," but** (*kî 'im*, 'but rather') **they will say, "As surely as the LORD lives, who brought the descendants of Israel up out of the land of the north and out of all the countries where he had banished them."**[47] **Then they will live**

---

47. The Massoretic Text has *hiddaḥtîm*, 'I had driven them', but the LXX reads *hiddîḥām*, 'he had driven them' (followed by the NIV and NRSV).

in their own land.' The message of vv. 7-8 has already been substantially given in 16:14-15,[48] [49] but here the stress is not so much on the fact of the Exile as on the certainty of return from it, with the theme of restoration to the land being resumed from v. 3. The Exodus from Egypt will pale into insignificance with this new Exodus. The imagery of a second Exodus had already been used by Isaiah (Isa. 11:11-12, 15-16; 43:16-21; 49:8-13; 51:91-11). It is wrong to limit this just to the northern kingdom; Israel here refers to the whole covenant people who will be brought back from the captivity in Babylon or wherever their captors had taken them. This new act of deliverance will become the confession heard on the lips of the restored people. They will no longer be under the jurisdiction of the ominous foe from the north, but will leave his country and 'they will live (<√*yāšab*, 'to dwell, inhabit') in their own land': the opposite of being uprooted and carried away to a foreign land.

C. CONCERNING THE PROPHETS (23:9-40)

From the preceding section the impression might readily be gained that the problems facing Jeremiah had to do with the political institutions of Judah and its civil leadership. That unfortunately was true, but they were by no means the exclusive source of opposition to him. Both church and state were corrupt in Judah, and in this section the focus is on the religious degeneracy of the land. The central figures in the worship of Israel were the priests, many of whom seem to have been largely passive figures, more concerned with survival and continuing to enjoy the perquisites of their office than maintaining a testimony for the truth. But though there was widespread corruption in the priesthood, the real source of religious decline was actually the behaviour of

---

48. The NIV varies its translation of the introductory *lākēn* ('therefore', often introducing a saying of judgment, but here used more generally) from 'however' to 'so then'. 'People will no longer say' renders *yoʼmərû*, 'they will say' with an indefinite subject, whereas in 16:14 there was a niphal *yēʼāmēr*, 'it will be said'. This passage adds in v. 8 to 'who brought up' the additional clause 'and who brought' (not represented in the NIV). Rather than 'Israelites'/'sons of Israel' (16:15) there is now found 'descendants of the house of Israel'. The concluding clause is different in the two places.

49. The LXX places vv. 7-8 at the end of the chapter after v. 40. Perhaps this reflects the inclination of the translators to omit duplicate passages, and the insertion of these verses is a later correction within the Septuagintal tradition.

the prophets. Nominally they were under the control of the priesthood, but in fact they were the opinion formers of the day, and it was what they proclaimed in the name of the LORD that set the tone for church and state in Judah, as well as reflecting prevailing sentiment.

Prophecy was a divine institution in Israel, and it is not obvious how it came to be corrupted in the way that it was in Jeremiah's time. The prophet of the LORD was one who was called by him, and the prophets of Jerusalem considered that they had received a divine call. Part of the problem was, of course, that the experience of a call was subjective. An individual might well be personally certain that he had received a divine call and yet be deluded in that belief, and that would seem to have been the case with the Jerusalem prophets.

It is significant that the Old Testament does not itself use the term 'false prophet'. It originated several centuries after Jeremiah when the Septuagint, the Greek translation of the Old Testament, was made. By then, with the benefit of hindsight, it was abundantly clear who had been the true prophet and who had been false. The devastation threatened by Jeremiah against Jerusalem had come to pass, and the visions of the false prophets had evaporated. But the matter was far from easy for the people of Jeremiah's day. If the test for false prophecy is to wait and see which word comes true, then it can really only apply retrospectively.

But there were other tests for false prophecy. One was the name of the god by whose authority the prophet claimed to speak. There is no suggestion that the prophets of Jerusalem claimed to speak by Baal, though the message they proclaimed and the view that they had of religion and of their own role was probably significantly influenced by heathen thought. Furthermore the language used by the Jerusalem prophets was not such that it provided a simple test for identifying them. They too could speak of the 'burden of the LORD' (v. 34) and use the same phrases as the true prophet: 'The LORD declares' (v. 31); 'This is what the LORD Almighty, the God of Israel says' (28:2). Little wonder people were confused!

Another test for the genuineness of a prophet was the consonance of his message with what had been spoken previously by the LORD through those who were acknowledged to be prophets. That was a test that could be applied contemporaneously, and it was. It forms the basis of the argument of the elders in chapter 26. However, even that test was not without its difficulties. There were undoubtedly prophets with a range of beliefs and practices, but the best of the Jerusalem prophets claimed to be speaking in accordance with the word of the LORD. The most delusive heresy is not that which blatantly opposes Scripture, but that which quotes Scripture while subtly distorting it. The ideology of the false prophets was one which quoted the Scripture promises of blessing to Zion while omitting the balancing truth of the need for covenant obedience. They argued that the mere presence of the Temple in Jerusalem guaranteed that God would act for her. They could quote Scripture and the precedent of history to reinforce their point. They proclaimed an unequivocal state of *šālôm*, 'peace', would hold for Jerusalem (4:10; 6:14; 8:11; 14:13; 23:17).

There are several lines of thought which suggest how this state of affairs came to prevail. It is possible that the Temple prophets represent an institutionalisation of the 'schools of the prophets', more properly, the 'sons of the prophets', groups of men who had attached themselves to a prophetic figure such as Elijah or Elisha, who had lived at various sites in the land, and who had devoted themselves to divine service and proclamation of the prophetic word (2 Kgs. 2:3, 5). At first it is evident that they practised communal living, which was frequently on the poverty line (2 Kgs. 4:38-44). It is supposed that when they lacked a true prophetic leader, these communities rapidly degenerated from their first ideal in a way not dissimilar to that whereby the mendicant orders in the medieval church developed into corrupt and ambitious popularity seekers. Micah had spoken out against this tendency a century earlier (Mic. 3:8-11), and Ezekiel was to do so later also (Ezek. 13:1-23).

That these groups clustered round the Temple seems to have arisen through conformity with the practices of surrounding pagan religions. It was customary for prophetic figures and soothsayers to be found at pagan shrines, and as Judah's perception of what constituted covenant religion became increasingly corrupt there was no sense of incongruity in having many prophets at the Temple in Jerusalem. If prophets had first become an accepted feature of local sanctuaries throughout the land, then, after worship there was suppressed by Josiah, they might have made their way to Jerusalem and supplemented the groups Micah had previously criticised.

That these prophets were essentially Temple prophets points to another factor in the situation. Prophets of the LORD had always been found at the royal court, acting as advisers to, and fearless critics of, the king. Now the prophets are part of the Jerusalem establishment. The Temple was seen as a royal chapel, and those who wished to fit in there had to adopt the consensus belief system and to support the policies of the king and his courtiers. Prophets were part of the accepted procedures of government in the ancient East, and Judah was not going to be left out of that. The prophet's loyalty was primarily to the system and not to the LORD. The false prophet was not necessarily morally degenerate or politically corrupt, but he was an institution-alised figure, a professional adviser to the king, who was concerned with keeping his job by saying what it was prudent to say.

These prophets caused Jeremiah no end of trouble. Their message was contrary to his, and particularly during the reign of Zedekiah there was a battle between them for the mind and heart of the king and people. It is probable that many of the prophecies found in this section date from that time.

A comparison of various translations shows that there is divergence of viewpoint over how to treat the middle verses of this section. Verses 9-15 are acknowledged to be verse and vv. 33-40 are taken as prose, but in between decisions about what is verse and what is prose are varied. In itself this shows that it can be difficult to discriminate between elegant Hebrew prose and poetry. While those who view the difference between prose and poetry as a key consideration in estab-lishing the origin and authenticity of a passage find great significance in the difference, if Jeremiah is considered as having delivered messages in both prose and poetry, the matter is one of literary form rather than of great exegetical importance.

1. Condemnation of the Evil Prophets (23:9-15)

Jeremiah begins this section by recording his personal distress at the religious situation in the land (vv. 9-10). He does not specifically name the prophets as the cause of this distress, but in the context it is clear that it is their influence that he has in mind. There then follow two judgment speeches of the LORD (vv. 11-12; 13-15) in which he first states the grounds of his dissatisfaction with the religious establish-ment of Judah and follows this up with his sentence of condemnation.

9. Although the NKJV integrates the phrase **concerning the prophets** into the first sentence, 'My heart within me is broken because of the prophets', it is generally acknowledged to be a title for what follows down to v. 40 (cf. 46:2; 48:1; 49:1, 7, 23, 28). The prophets who are referred to here are not genuine prophets of the LORD who were Jere-miah's contemporaries, such as Zephaniah during the early part of his ministry or Ezekiel in Babylon during his later ministry. Rather these prophets are part of the Jerusalem religious establishment, who func-tioned as the opinion formers of the day. They prophesied in the name of the LORD, but they did so without warrant. Their message was gen-erally one of peace (šālôm), regardless of the moral condition of those addressed, so that 'peace-prophets' is a reasonable characterisation of them. It may be that some of them exhibited low standards of personal morality, but the main problem was with the spiritual havoc they were causing in the land. People were only too ready to hear an easy message assuring them that all was well with them no matter what their conduct was really like, but Jeremiah knew from the LORD that the spiritual condition of the nation urgently required not complacency but repentance if disaster was to be averted.

My heart is broken (<√*šābar*, 4:7) **within me** is probably misleading in that the reference is not to the emotionally distraught state we would call being heart-broken, nor is it a reaction to sin as in Pss. 34:19; 51:19. 'Heart' here refers to whole consciousness of the prophet, particularly his mind. 'Within me' (*bəqirbî*, 'in the midst of me') reinforces the reference to his inner reaction. It was not just a matter of saying that he was inconsolably sad, but that his whole being was in such turmoil that he did not know what to think or how to react to the situation that he was confronted with. 'My reason is staggered' (Bright 1965:151). **All my bones tremble.** This is the only place in the Old Testament that *rāḥap*, 'tremble', occurs in the qal, though the piel is found in Gen. 1:2; Deut. 32:11 to denote an action like that of a bird hovering over its nest. The qal may have a meaning similar to this: 'to shake, quiver'. Others, on the basis of an etymology from an Arabic root, suggest the meaning is 'to grow soft': 'There is no strength in my bones' (REB). This may also be supported by the parallelism of Ps. 22:15. 'Bones' were considered to be the seat of one's physical health and strength, and also the subject of joy, distress, and sorrow. The bones gave structure to one's being, and by saying they are trembling or without strength, Jeremiah describes himself as being in a state of agitation, distress and inability to settle. **I am like a drunken man, like a man overcome by wine.** The figure conveys the thought of being unable to control one's reactions and to think clearly; so Jeremiah cannot work out a co-ordinated response to the situation that he is confronted with. 'The total picture is one of a prophet who is extremely agitated and unsettled by what he sees in the land' (Overholt 1970:60). **Because of the LORD and his holy words.** It does not appear that Jeremiah's perplexity principally arises from the temerity of the peace prophets in claiming that they have been divinely commissioned to speak. As the one to whom the LORD has spoken, Jeremiah's concern focuses on the implications of what the LORD has said about the land. It is not an undemanding or comfortable message that he has been given, and the prophet is at a loss to know how to counter the endeavours of the peace prophets who with their words of easy salvation sought to undermine the message of repentance. The LORD's words express the holiness of conduct that he expects to find in his people, but the peace prophets were assuring them that it was all right to continue as they were, behaving as they wished.

10. Jeremiah further elaborates on the reasons for his reaction. There seem to be three lines of thought presented.

(1) 'For' (*kî*) **the land is full of adulterers** (<√*nāʿap*, 3:8). The question arises whether this is marital infidelity (5:7; 29:23) or a reference to spiritual adultery, Baal worship (3:8; 9:2). It is probably the latter, though there is the possibility that both sorts of misbehaviour were involved, both alike being opposed to the holiness of the LORD, and therefore bringing judgment on the land.

(2) A second aspect of Jeremiah's perplexity is that the LORD has already responded to the rebellion of the people. The land is already suffering as a consequence of the chastisement of the covenant. 'For' (*kî*, introducing another reason for Jeremiah's turmoil) **because of the curse[50] the land lies parched** (<√ʿ*ābal*, 4:28) **and the pastures in the desert are withered.** The curse (*ālâ*) is the judicial pronouncement of the LORD because of the broken covenant (11:3, 8; Deut. 28:15-68; 29:19-21) whereby drought (12:4; 14:1) had been brought on the land since the people were unwilling to amend their behaviour. The LORD was therefore chastising them to bring them to their senses. For 'pastures in the desert/wilderness' see on 9:10. 'Pasture' (*nāwâ*, cf. the masculine form of the word in v. 3[51]) is frequently used, not in a literal sense but in connection with the LORD's action vis-à-vis the land, whether destructive (9:10; 10:25) or constructive (31:23; 33:12; 50:19).

(3) Reverting to the misconduct in the land, Jeremiah brings out another aspect of the situation: **The ⌐prophets⌐ follow an evil course** (*mərûṣâ*, 'style of running', 8:6; 2 Sam. 18:27; <√*rûṣ*, 'to run', cf. v. 21). This a general statement about an unspecified 'they'. Since the verse is discussing the land as a whole, it might refer to the people in general, who are not getting the spiritual leadership they need, and therefore the leaders who are falling down in their responsibilities will be punished (v. 12). The NIV takes the unspecified reference as being to the prophets mentioned in the title to the section, and links

---

50. 'Curse' is ʿ*ālâ*, but a few manuscripts, the LXX and Vulgate read the same consonants differently as ʿ*ēlleh*, 'these'. This is found in the NIV footnote and the REB. Given ʿ*ālâ* is a more difficult reading than the more common ʿ*ēlleh*, it should be retained.

51. The NKJV translation 'pleasant places' links the plural of *nāwâ* where there is an intrusive aleph, *nəʾôt*, with the root *nāʾâ*, 'to be pleasing/delightful'.

Jeremiah's third reason closely to the following divine declaration regarding the religious leaders of the day. They **use their power unjustly** lends itself to the English wordplay, 'Their might is not right' (NKJV, NRSV). The power they exercise is the strength of man guided by a merely human wisdom, and it is not employed for proper ends.

11. There is then a transition from the prophet's speech about himself to the word of the LORD which he cites beginning with *kî*, 'for', not to give the reason for the misconduct of those spoken about, but to introduce the evidence that supports the description he has given. It is equivalent to saying, 'I am justified in making these statements because this is what the LORD declares'. The messenger and the one who sent him are at one in their diagnosis of the spiritual ailment affecting the land. **Both prophet and priest are godless.** The verb (<√*ḥānap*, 'to be defiled', cf. 3:2) in the first instance denotes pollution (hence NASB) and then develops the idea of those who are polluted in God's sight and consequently have to live apart from him. They are in effect heathen, infidels. The pollution or profanation may occur involuntarily (Mic. 4:11), but it is most often the result of one's own actions. **'Even in my temple I find their wickedness,' declares the LORD.** Although Josiah had reformed the worship of the Temple, the situation did not continue long after his death. Their wickedness could then refer to the heathen worship that had been reintroduced there (more extensively described in Ezek. 8:1-18). This God had discovered, and it forms the basis of the characterisation of them as polluted and pagan.

12. Their judgment is then proclaimed. **Therefore** (*lākēn* of judgment) **their path will become slippery; they will be banished[52] to darkness and there they will fall.** The Hebrew accents support the idea of taking 'in darkness' with the first part of the verse, 'Therefore their way shall be to them like slippery paths in the darkness, into which they shall be driven and fall' (NRSV). In that way there is only one picture combining two images. (1) Slippery paths (<√*ḥālaq* I, 'to be smooth, slippery, deceptive', in the sense of flattery and so easily accepted by their hearers) are situations in this life where it is difficult

---

52. *yiddaḥû* (<√*dāḥaḥ*). A few manuscripts read *yiddāḥû* <√*dāḥâ*. *dāḥaḥ* occurs only in the niphal (2 Sam. 14:14 and here) and has the same meaning as the niphal of *dāḥâ*, qal 'to push, overthrow', niphal 'to be cast down'. The imagery is that of a wall that is pushed so hard that it falls over (Pss. 36:12; 62:3; 118:13; Prov. 14:32; *NIDOTTE* 1:933). 'Dispersed' (REB) seems to understand the root as *nādaḥ*, niphal 'to be scattered'.

to maintain one's footing (Pss. 35:6; 73:18). By way of judgment God
will bring on the people times when outside pressures and the course
of events will threaten their ability to survive. (2) Darkness (*ʾăpēlâ*,
'darkness, gloominess, calamity') may refer to the darkness of night
which naturally follows day, but it is often used metaphorically of
God's judgment on the wicked and disobedient (13:16; Prov. 4:19;
Zeph. 1:15) which brings gloom and despair. When such darkness
comes on the unrighteous, they are unable to stay upright, no matter
how successfully they had negotiated the slippery paths in the daytime.
This outcome will come upon them 'for' (*kî*) **'I will bring disaster on
them in the year they are punished** (<√*pāqad*),**' declares the LORD**
is the same doom as is described in 6:15; 11:23. 'Year' refers to the
time of divine action. The precise form the judgment will take is not
yet clear; but it will undoubtedly be from the LORD himself, and 'year'
(rather than 'day') probably implies that it is going to be prolonged.

13. Another judgment speech follows with the grounds of condemnation set out in vv. 13-14 and the sentence imposed in v. 15. Verses 13
and 14 present two balanced scenes, each beginning, 'And among the
prophets of …' First there is a look back to the northern kingdom
before 722 BC. **Among the prophets of Samaria I saw this repulsive
thing: they prophesied**[53] **by Baal and led my people Israel astray.**
The downfall of the north could be traced back to the activities of the
Baal prophets (7:15; 1 Kgs. 18:16-40), who openly repudiated the
LORD and claimed Baal as the source of the message they proclaimed.
This is categorised as 'repulsive' (<√*tāpal*). A related word is used in
Lam. 3:14 for the 'worthless' visions of the false prophets in Jerusalem
and in Job 6:6 for 'tasteless' food which had to be rejected because it
could not be eaten. So too prophesying in the name of Baal was a
breach of Mosaic law and punishable by death (Deut. 13:1-5), and it
was something that the LORD could not stomach. It only served to lead
Israel astray (<√*tāʿâ* 'to go astray', hiphil 'to lead astray'), that is, away
from the covenant requirements of the LORD.

14. 'But' (NRSV) finds a contrast here: 'But in the prophets of Jerusalem …'—they are even worse. However, the construction seems
merely to involve co-ordination with v. 13. Having set the scene by
describing the past, the LORD then brings matters up to date. Use of the
north to bring home to Judah the nature of their own conduct is also
employed in 3:6-13. **And among the prophets of Jerusalem I have**

seen[54] **something horrible.** 'Something horrible' (*ša'ărûrâ*, 5:30) is a stronger term than 'repulsive' (cf. 18:13; 'as strong a term as Jeremiah can find', Jones 1992:307), occurring only here and 5:30, both times in connection with prophets who walk in *šeqer*, 'a lie'. **They commit adultery and live a lie.**[55] These expressions may possibly denote pagan worship. 'Adultery' (v. 10) is used to describe engaging in the rituals of pagan worship, and the word 'lie' may be an oblique reference to Baal (13:25; 5:31; 20:6). But these features on their own do not seem to warrant the intensified condemnation of the Jerusalem prophets. The translations tend to take the reference to be to literal adultery and living a lie (that is, 'walking' in it, conducting one's life that way) as indicating a life that is not up to what it claims to be ('adulterers and hypocrites', REB). The more shocking thing still would then be that they claimed to be prophets of the LORD (not Baal as in the north) while their actions and words ran counter to the stipulations of his covenant, either in terms of the moral standards they condoned, or the lives they lived. **They strengthen**[56] **the hands of evildoers, so that no one turns** ($<\sqrt{\check{s}\hat{u}b}$)[57] **from his wickedness.** 'Strengthen the hands of' is an idiom expressing encouragement (Judg. 9:24; Ezek. 13:22). But McKane (1986, 1:575) argues that here it is not aiding and abetting, but failing to show impartiality and even-handedness in the exercise of prophetic ministry. Their lives were no standard to encourage the people, and the message of prosperity they uttered failed to alert their contemporaries to the shocking nature of their deeds. No one turned (cf. Ezek. 13:22). **They are all like Sodom to me; the people of Jerusalem are like Gomorrah.** The point of this comparison is not that they are going to experience a similar destruction from heaven—at least not directly. The focus seems to be rather on the nature of their conduct. It was as perverted as that of the cities of the plain had been—and so the implicit thought is their end will match theirs (Deut. 32:32; Isa. 1:10).

---

54. 'I have seen' renders the same word *rā'îtî* as does 'I saw' in v. 13. The same variation is found also in the NRSV and NASB to indicate that the first action is in the more remote past, whereas the second is more recent, indeed still continuing, 'I see' (REB).

55. The two verbs are infinitives absolute, probably to place greater emphasis on the nature of the action (*IBHS* §35.5.2)

56. The *waw*-consecutive perfect after the infinitives absolute functioning as replacements for finite verbs may be taken as the apodosis for which the infinitives provide the condition (*IBHS* §32.2.5d).

57. An unusual construction: *ləbiltî* + perfect, rather than infinitive construct or an imperfect. GKC §152x suggests that the text should be emended.

15. The conduct of the peace prophets had led to an intolerable situation existing in Judah, and the prophets are accordingly condemned.
Therefore (*lākēn* of judgment)**, this is what the LORD Almighty says
concerning the prophets: 'I will make them eat bitter food and
drink poisoned water, because** (*kî*) **from the prophets of Jerusalem
ungodliness has spread throughout the land.'** The description of
how the prophets are to be punished is vague as to the means that will
give it effect. For 'eat bitter food and drink poisoned water', see on
9:15 where is describes the fate of the people, which the false prophets
are going to share. 'Ungodliness' (*ḥănuppâ*) comes from the same root
as 'godless' (v. 11). Not only were the prophets themselves polluted in
God's sight and effectively heathen; they had contaminated the whole
land by their teaching and example.

2. Do Not Listen (23:16-24)

The next section constitutes a divine appeal to the people to ignore
what the peace prophets are saying. Their vision is false (vv. 16-17)
because they have not been admitted to the council of the LORD (v.
18). In reality the word from the LORD is not one of peace but wrath
(vv. 19-20), and so those with another message have not been divinely
commissioned (vv. 21-22). The section concludes with three questions
(vv. 23-24) which press home the impossibility of escaping divine
scrutiny.

16. The section begins with an exhortation to the people. 'You' in
vv. 16-20 is masculine plural. **This is what the LORD Almighty says:
'Do not listen to what the prophets are prophesying to you; they
fill you with false hopes'.** 'Fill with false hopes'/'buoy you up with
false hopes' (REB) is a hiphil participle from the root *hābal*, from
which also comes the noun *hebel*, 'breath, insubstantial thing', which
Jeremiah uses to refer to the lack of substantive reality behind idols
(2:5). Here the words of the prophets are as transient as a puff of air:
there is nothing to them. Consequently those who listened to them
were being hoaxed, taken in by what was fraudulent. Possibly there is
also the thought (Lee 1999:105) that by their deceptive words the
prophets are acting the part of Cain, leading the people astray and
making them become like Abel (*hebel*).

The proclamation of the peace prophets was turning the people
away from the living, powerful and effective God and causing them to
place their confidence in beliefs (and possibly other deities) which
were without a substantial basis. **They speak visions from their own
minds** (<*lēb*, 'heart', 5:21; 7:31)**, not from the mouth of the LORD.**

The source of their message was wrong, and therefore it could not convey genuine revelation. Such a declaration, of course, presented the people with a choice: would they listen to those who had simply thought up for themselves what they were going to say, or would they heed Jeremiah who was relaying what he had heard from the mouth of God? Since vision was a legitimate mode of prophetic reception of their message (1 Sam. 3:1; Ps. 89:20; Hos. 12:11), the objection is not to visions as such, but to their source. It is their human origin that makes them false (14:14).

17. There is then cited a typical oracle of these prophets. **They keep saying**[58] **to those who despise me, 'The LORD says: You will have peace.'**[59] 'Despise' ($<\sqrt{nā'aṣ}$, 'to reject as having no value', 14:21) reveals the inner attitude of the people as one of dissociation from the LORD, and therefore lacking commitment to his covenant. But even though this mind-set was evident, the Jerusalem prophets continued to promise them welfare and prosperity from the LORD (4:10; 6:14; 14:13). 'Peace' (*šālôm*, 6:14) is a wider concept than merely the absence of war, though that no doubt figured largely in it in the upheavals of Jeremiah's time (8:14-16). 'In the troubled political situation of Jeremiah's day it is no wonder that the major connotation of peace is that of security from warfare' (Overholt 1970:59). The peace prophets considered that the Temple as the symbol of the LORD's presence provided Jerusalem with cast-iron security. The LORD was there and so no one would be permitted to overwhelm the city. **And to all who follow the stubbornness of their hearts they say, 'No harm will come to you.'** 'The stubbornness of their hearts' (3:17) refers to the fact that they had made up their own minds as to how they would live and what they would do. This was not submission to the LORD but rebellion against him. Nonetheless the Jerusalem prophets encouraged them by saying that 'harm' (*rā'â*, 'evil, disaster', 5:12; 14:13) would not befall them. They were therefore presenting a message that the people would be only too ready to receive, for it merely endorsed what they had already decided to do anyway. But the underlying theology was not that of the covenant because it embodied the characteristic

---

58. The infinitive absolute has to follow the participle, and here has the sense of continued activity (GKC §113r).

59. The formula *dibber YHWH*, 'the LORD says', introducing divine speech is not found elsewhere, though such an unusual phrase might here be used in a mocking fashion. The LXX repointed *məna'aṣay dibber YHWH*, 'to those who despise me, The LORD says', to give *limna'ăṣê dəbar YHWH*, 'to those who despise ('spurn', REB) the word of the LORD' (NRSV).

pagan disjunction between obedience to the LORD's commands and enjoyment of the blessings he provides.

18. The people are challenged to consider the qualifications of those who present them with messages purportedly from the LORD. **But (*kî*) which of them has stood in the council of the LORD to see[60] or to hear his word?**[61] The NIV and the REB add 'of them' so as to yield a question that requires the answer, No. The Hebrew is much more open: 'Who has stood?' It is a invitation to assess the messengers by asking which of the messages has come from the council of the LORD. 'Stood' refers to trusted servants who have the privilege of access to the king (15:1; 1 Kgs. 17:1; 18:15). Here the LORD is viewed as a king who has summoned his council (*sôd*), his confidential advisers. They are gathered in his throne room to hear what the king has to say and to respond if required (Pss. 89:8; 89:6; 82:1; Isa. 6:1-8; 2 Kgs. 22:19-22.) Into this gathering the true prophet was elevated by the Spirit so that he would have first-hand knowledge of the LORD's intentions which he then reported to the people. It was such a situation that the prophet Micaiah described when he said, 'I saw the LORD sitting on his throne with all the host of heaven standing on his right and on his left' (2 Chron. 18:18). The idea of a divine assembly composed of gods and goddesses was well known in Canaan and Mesopotamia where it had been incorporated into their myths, possibly derived from the council of elders who would have constituted a set of advisers to an earthly king. 'See his word' refers to the vision the LORD would give to them concerning his purposes (2:31). **Who has listened and heard his word?** Which type of prophet has had the access that would enable him to hear the LORD's decrees and respond to them? The only message the people should concern themselves with was one that originated with the LORD himself, and if the messenger had not received his message from him, then he had no authority to speak and nothing worthwhile to say. Whatever the Jerusalem prophets had experienced was just an illusion, and their message could therefore be nothing other than a delusion.

19. The words of this and the following verse might be an example of the divine 'word' (v. 18) which has not been heard. In contrast to the

---

60. *Waw*-conjunctive plus imperfect apocopated (jussive), expressing design or consequence, 'so as to see' (NRSV), (GKC §109f).
61. The kethibh is *dəbārî*, 'my word'; the qere *dəbārô*, 'his word'. The switch between third person and first person references in divine speech occurs elsewhere and so the kethibh may stand, but English idiom prefers 'his'.

easy optimism of the peace prophets, those who have truly stood in the
divine council have a different message to relate, namely, the impending execution of the LORD's judgment on the people of that generation,
who are described as the wicked. These verses are substantially
repeated in 30:23-24. **See, the storm** (*sə'ārâ*, a feminine variant of the
word used later) **of the LORD will burst out in wrath**, 'even'
(epexegetic *waw*) **a whirlwind** (*sa'ar*) **swirling**[62] **down on the heads
of the wicked.** 'Storm' may apply to a literal tempest (Jonah 1:4, 12;
feminine form Pss. 107:25, 29; 148:8), or to outbursts of divine anger
as here, where it leads to overwhelming devastation coming on the
land as it experiences the outpouring of the LORD's wrath (*hēmâ*, 4:4).
This is a message that contrasts completely with the easy optimism of
the peace-prophets. Alternatively, 'the wicked' may refer to false
prophets, and the vision of judgment may be principally directed
against them. This seems less likely in that the purposes of the LORD
(v. 20) are much broader than the destiny he has decreed for the false
prophets.

20.   The anger (*'ap*, 4:8) **of the LORD will not turn back until he
fully accomplishes the purposes of his heart**. 'Heart' refers to
thought and decisions as well as emotions (4:4). 'Purposes'
(<*məzimmâ*) is an ethically neutral word, which at times is used pejora-
tively (11:15). Here it refers to the LORD's capacity to devise a policy
which can be effectively carried out ('executed and accomplished'
NRSV; cf. 30:24). McKane (1965:84) argues 'the context (vv. 20-23)
deals with Yahweh's effective interventions in the history of Israel in
salvation and judgment, and so it is Yahweh (and not the statesmen)
who plans and directs Israel's life, and the prophet, contrary to what
the *śārîm* ['officials'] represent, is a key political figure.' This is in
contrast to the 'visions of their own hearts' (v. 16) which is all that the
false prophets can present. What the LORD thinks and intends is
announced by the true prophet, and it is a prospect of doom.

In days to come, though often a phrase which looks forward to the
consummation of all things, here refers to the time after the immediately impending judgment has been exhausted. Even after the events of
597 BC, which one might have thought would have brought the nation
to its senses religiously, the prophets in Babylon were still resting their
hopes upon a speedy turn around in the situation (29:21-23). But after
586 BC advocacy of such a scenario was no longer feasible. **You will
understand it clearly**/'You will understand it ⌐with⌐ understanding', a

---

62. The hithpolel participle of *hûl* I, 'to whirl around', 'a whirling storm
wind', is followed by the imperfect qal of the same verb.

cognate accusative being used to express the completeness of the insight that will prevail after the execution of the LORD's judgment. Matters will then be so clear that assessment of what has led up to them will be obvious.

21. Then the test of v. 18 regarding the qualifications and commission of the peace prophets is taken up. **I did not send these prophets, yet they** (wəhēm, an emphatic contrast) **have run with their message.** The formal sending of the messenger by the LORD was a vital part of his prophetic calling (1:6; Isa. 6:8; Ezek. 3:5; Amos 7:14). The image is that of a messenger sent with news from a king (cf. v. 10; 51:31; 2 Sam. 18:19-24; Isa. 40:9; 52:7; Hab. 2:2), though 'run' may also suggest the eagerness of the prophets to fulfil their self-appointed task. Overholt (1970:61) argues that Jeremiah is not denying the validity of his opponents' call but is centring his attack on their message. But it is more likely given the parallelism with 'yet they have prophesied', that it is being emphasised not just that their message is unreliable, but that is unreliable precisely because they are doing what they have not been authorised to do. Whatever status they may have been accorded in the Jerusalem Temple, these spokesmen were not those who had made some mistake in transmitting a message. They had no message. **I did not speak to them, yet they** (wəhēm, again an emphatic contrast) **have prophesied.** It took not only the call of the prophet, but also a specific message to deliver before he could be qualified to speak as the LORD's messenger. These two elements were crucial in Jeremiah's own experience of being called.

22. The matter is now put in the form of a supposition. **But if they had stood in my council, they would have proclaimed my words to my people.** Those who were truly acknowledged by the king and privileged with access to his throne room would have been able to act as his heralds with his message. Does, however, the second aspect **and would have turned them from their evil ways and from their evil deeds** not set too high a test? Would Jeremiah himself have been able to pass this test? His ministry did not meet with any great success. The NKJV is an attempt to get round that: 'But if they had stood in my counsel and had caused my people to hear my words, then they would have turned them.' But even on the NIV rendering it could be taken of a desire to achieve this purpose, which was something the false prophets did not have.

23. Verses 23 and 24 consist of three brief divine sayings, each of them a question, and each pressing home the same truth, the inescapability of divine scrutiny (cf. Ps. 139:7-10). Each question is

authenticated by the phrase, 'declares the LORD', which possibly opens
the way for the later discussion of how this phrase should be used
(v. 31). **'Am I only a God nearby[63],' declares the LORD, 'and not a
God far away?'**[64] Zion theology emphasised the indwelling of the
LORD in the Temple and tended to limit God and restrict divine freedom. The LORD simply had to act on behalf of Jerusalem because he
had presenced himself there. Over against such a comfortable theology
with a narrow and localised conception of the divine, the question
denies the possibility of restricting God to any physical locality. He is
transcendent, and his lofty majesty must ever be kept in mind. His
sovereign power is a function of his exalted status. His power is not
limited by his transcendence as though God was removed to a distance
and so rendered impotent. Divine exaltation does not impair God's
ability to see into the hearts of all people (Ps. 33:13-15) and to judge
what they do (Pss. 11:4-5; 113:5-6).

24. The LORD is also omniscient. The question, **'Can anyone hide in
secret places so that I cannot see him?' declares the LORD**, denies
the possibility of finding a place of concealment that is impenetrable to
divine searching. Though he is transcendent, nothing they can do
remains hidden from him (16:17). To think that he is incapable of spot-
ting them wherever they hide is to trivialise him and to have a
diminished sense of the reality of God.

The LORD is omnipresent. **'Do not I fill heaven and earth?'
declares the LORD** is perhaps the most profound of the three questions. The concept of Yahweh's universal sovereignty can be
expressed by saying that his glory fills, or is over, the whole earth (Pss.
57:5, 11; 72:19), which implies that all around bears testimony to his
power and nature. But the expression here, that the LORD fills heaven
and earth, goes further than that. It expresses his effective presence
throughout the created realm. How then can these prophets expect to
get away with behaviour such as that which they have been perpetrat-
ing? How can Israel expect to do so? How can anyone?

---

63. For the construct before a prepositional phrase, cf. GKC §130a; *IBHS*
§9.6b.

64. The LXX vocalises *ha'ĕlōhê* as *hā'ĕlōhê* with the article rather than the
interrogative, and so translates, 'I am ⌊the⌋ God nearby, says the Lord, and not
⌊the⌋ God far off.' This was done, presumably, to show that the LORD is at
hand in Jeremiah's word. The passage is, however, emphasising the transcendence, and therefore the omniscience, of the LORD (cf. 'from afar', Ps.
139:2; Job 36:3).

3. The Fire and the Hammer (23:25-32)

After declaring his omnipresence and inescapability, the LORD
proceeds to make them the basis for the word of condemnation that
will come upon the false prophets. What they are doing is known to the
LORD and inevitably attracts his censure.

25. Because the LORD is inescapably present, he is aware of what has
been going on in Jerusalem. **I have heard what the prophets say who
prophesy lies in my name.** The LORD disowns these prophets by
categorising their message as a lie (*šeqer*). The prophets presented
themselves as genuine, dispatched by LORD and so able to claim that
what they proclaimed originated with God. But the LORD dissociates
himself from these men and their messages, branding both as
inauthentic. **They say, 'I had a dream! I had a dream!'** Scripture
views ordinary human dreams as transient and insubstantial (Job 20:8;
Ps. 73:20; Isa. 29:7-8), but it was always recognised that God had
revealed himself in this way in earlier ages (for instance, to Jacob in
Gen. 28:10-17 and 31:10-13, and to Joseph, Gen. 37:5-10) and had
also indicated that this mode of communication would be used in the
future (Num. 12:6; Joel 2:28). So when the prophets claimed that the
message of God had been revealed to them in a dream which they have
been able to interpret and so can come to the people with a message,
there was nothing that would immediately indicate the falsity of what
was going on. It is even the case that the prophets may have convinced
themselves that their dream was divinely given, and by viewing it
through the prism of their own beliefs and expectations they would no
doubt find little difficulty in turning it into a message that was
consonant with their overall philosophy. A dream was not in and of
itself inherently false. The test that had to be applied was whether it
was conveying a message that diverged from previous divine revelation (Deut. 13:2-6). Jeremiah also reflects unfavourably on dreams at
27:9 and 29:8. For an intertestamental view of dreams, see Ecclus.
34:1-7.

26. There are two questions in v. 26 (NRSV, NASB), which the NIV
runs together: **How long will this continue in the hearts of these
lying prophets, who prophesy the delusions of their own minds?**
The first question, 'How long?', asks if the current state of affairs will
continue. This may be viewing matters from the divine point of view,
as if to ask how long the LORD will permit this imposture to continue,
or, in view of the next question, it is more probable that what is being
asked is how long will the prophets be able to maintain this imposture
in the light of mounting evidence that their messages were not coming

true. The second question lacks a subject, 'Will this exist in the heart of the prophets who prophesy the lie and prophets of delusion of their own heart?'[65] The prophets are characterised in two ways: (1) they prophesy the lie (14:14); (2) they are 'prophets of the deception of their own heart'. The second statement clearly indicates that they have wittingly deceived themselves.

27. They think the dreams they tell one another[66] will make my people forget my name. The outcome they intend or plan ('think' <√$ḥāšab$, 'to reckon', 18:8; often used of harmful projects, 1 Sam. 18:25; Est. 9:24; Neh. 6:2, 6; Ps. 140:5) is not one in which the people are no longer familiar with the sound of the LORD's name, but one in which they will lose sight of who the LORD really is and what he had revealed his true character to be (Exod. 3:13-14; Isa. 9:6). How did the prophets intend to achieve this? By reiterating their false messages until they became part of the accepted way of thinking about things. Those who have their perception of God moulded by falsehood can then be persuaded to accept any message at all, especially one of a God who says, 'Peace!' ($šālôm$), to those who are intent on breaking his covenant. 'Tell one another' indicates that the propagation of false ideas begins within the circle of the false prophets themselves. They engage in mutual encouragement by a conference in which they share and expound their dreams. Having secured the approval of their fellows that their proposed message conforms to acceptable norms, they set out to delude the people. **Just as their fathers forgot my name through Baal worship** recalls that a similar process of forgetting the facts regarding the character and requirements of the LORD had taken place earlier in the history of the people in the face of the cultural and spiritual aggression of Canaan (Judg. 3:7; 1 Sam. 12:9).

28. But there is a clear distinction between the dreams of the false prophets and the message that has been sent by God. **Let the prophet who has a dream tell his dream.** Tell it, that is, for what it is, the product of his own mind, and not making any unwarranted claims for it. This does not deny that dreams had been, and would still be, given by God. But the dreams of these men have no divine authorisation. **But let the one who has my word speak it faithfully.** The true prophet is

---

65. Yet another solution is reflected in the NRSV, 'Will the hearts of the prophets ever turn back?' which involves taking $hāyēš$ $baleb$ as $hăyāšub$ $lēb$.

66. The phrase here is '$îš$ $lərē'hû$, 'a man to his fellow', which might convey the idea of 'everyone to his neighbour' (NKJV) outside the prophetic circles, but it is usually a reciprocal phrase, as in the corresponding expression '$îš$ $mē'ēt$ $rē'ēhû$ in v. 30.

required to proclaim the message he has been given by God without addition or diminution ('faithfully', ʾĕmet, in a conscientious manner which can be relied on). **'For what[67] has straw to do with grain?' declares the LORD?** 'Straw' refers to the chopped stalks of plants, used for feeding oxen (Isa. 11:7), as binding material in making bricks (Exod. 5:10), or as bedding for horses (1 Kgs. 4:28). This seems to cite a proverbial saying which compares what is valuable to what is of little or no worth. The word of God is compared to what is able to give spiritual nourishment, whereas the straw (compare 'chaff' in 13:25) cannot provide any real food for man. The point of the metaphor is the relative worthlessness of the straw.

29. **'Is not my word like fire?' declares the LORD** brings out the irresistible power of the word of the LORD (5:14; 20:9). It does not leave an individual unaffected by what he hears, but works according to its own latent potential. 'Fire' highlights the destructive potential of the dynamic word of God when it expresses his impending judgment (Nah. 1:6). When the word of the LORD is received by an individual, it burns in his heart and is not capable of being restrained (Ps. 39:3) The LORD's word is also **like a hammer that breaks a rock in pieces.** In 51:20 'hammer' (paṭṭiš) refers to a tool used as a sledgehammer, though in Isa. 41:7 it possibly refers to a device for smoothing. The divine word is an implement that is able to accomplish much, demolishing obstacles and all that stands in its way (2 Cor. 10:4; Heb. 4:12). This fits in with the prevailing thrust of Jeremiah's message which was to break the current behaviour patterns of the people. The LORD's word has power to deal with those who proclaim another message than the one God wishes.

30. **Therefore** (lākēn) introduces a word of judgment which looks back to the whole section from v. 25 on. Three times the LORD announces his implacable hostility to the false prophets using the phrase, **I am against the prophets who ...** (cf. Ezek. 5:8). Each time a different aspect of their procedure is singled out for condemnation. It can hardly be that three distinct groups of prophets are in view. Firstly, there is the fact that they **steal from one another words supposedly from me.** The Hebrew is concise and ironic, 'my words', which the NIV expands, because it obviously does not refer to a true message from the LORD, but one that is merely presented as such. Here we see

---

67. 'For what?' has 'for' as a supplement. For the idiom, 'What with respect to straw with grain?', that is, 'What do they have in common?', see *IBHS* §18.3b.

one way in which the false prophets generated their messages: prophetic plagiarism. They pilfered from one another what they were going to say! This may also possibly refer to the prophets divorcing divine words from their original context and passing them on to one another to use, no longer conveying truth but subverting it to conform to their own ideology. How unlike Jeremiah when the word came to him: even though he would rather not proclaim it, its impact left him unable to keep it in (20:9).

31. Secondly, the LORD declares his opposition to the peace prophets in that they make false claims as to the origin of their message. **'Yes,' declares the LORD, 'I am against the prophets who wag their own tongues and yet declare,**[68] **"The LORD declares".'** 'Wag their own tongues/'take (<√*lāqaḥ*) their tongues' at their own initiative, and with the hint that they like to hear the sound of their own voices. They then make an imposing presentation using the formula that the true prophets used, 'The LORD declares'. In fact 'the LORD' is not expressed in Hebrew; it is simply, 'They declare, 'It is declared'." However, the repeated use of *nəʾum*, 'declare', 'declaration', makes it clear that they are using this as a formula to claim a divine origin for their own words. The omission of 'the LORD' points out the lack of a true basis for what they claim. It was not possible to tell from their speech that they were impostors, because they mimicked the real thing so closely.

32. The third feature mentioned regarding the behaviour of the false prophets is that they relate dreams. **'Indeed, I am against those who prophesy**[69] **false dreams,' declares the LORD. 'They tell them and lead my people astray with their reckless lies** (plural of *šeqer*)**'.** This looks back to the description in vv. 25-27, with the dreams being explicitly characterised as lying (*šeqer*). Their recounting of their dreams is said to lead the people astray. 'Reckless' (*paḥăzût* is a hapax <√*pāḥaz*, 'to be reckless, arrogant') points to the fact that they do not take into consideration the full consequences of the devastation that will come upon the nation as a result of the imposture made on them (Zeph. 3:4).

The concluding part of v. 32 is a general statement of their imposture. **Yet I did not send or appoint them.** They were unauthorised

---

68. This is the only instance of the root *nāʾam* being used as a finite verb. The root seems to point to an authoritative utterance. It serves to authenticate the prophetic speech as coming from Yahweh himself, whether it be a word of threat (13:25) or promise (31:32).

69. For the form of this participle without the initial mem usual in a piel cf. GKC §52s.

messengers (14:14; 23:21). **'They do not benefit these people in the least,'**[70] **declares the** LORD. 'Benefit' ($<\sqrt{y\bar{a}^c al}$, 2:8) is an ironic understatement of the fact that they were doing great harm.

4. The 'Burden' of the LORD (23:33-40)

Problems of translation and interpretation occur in the following section. One concerns who it is that is being addressed. In vv. 33-34 'you' is masculine singular, and it would seem to be the prophet who is being spoken to. 'You' in vv. 35-36 and vv. 38-40 is plural and seems to cover prophets, priests and people, and probably that applies also to the singular 'you' in v. 37.

Throughout the passage there is a play on the word *maśśā*᷄, which may be translated 'burden' or 'oracle'. Much scholarly energy has been taken up with the question of whether we are dealing with two identically spelled words, or one word with two ranges of meaning. In either case the root is *nāśā*᷄, 'to lift up', 'to carry'. It is certain that the word is used of a load carried by man or beast, occurring four times in this sense in 17:21-27 (see also Exod. 23:5; Num. 4:27; 2 Sam. 15:33; Ps. 38:4). If this sense of 'burden' was carried over to the use in prophetic contexts, it might indicate that the word of the LORD was a heavy responsibility on the prophet to whom it was given, or that it was a weight on the people who were condemned by it (Isa. 15:1; Nah. 1:1). However, the word is not always used of a condemnatory message (Zech. 12:1), and so it is argued that it originated in the idea of the prophet lifting up his voice to make himself clearly heard as he delivered the divine message that had been entrusted to him. Nonetheless, even if the word may have originated as a designation for a prophetic speech, it is clear that its association with the sense 'burden' was obvious to Hebrew speakers so that it readily acquired ominous overtones in many contexts.

While v. 33 is generally assigned by commentators to Jeremiah himself, vv. 34-40 are felt to be written in a later, careless style which might be dated around 450 BC (Holladay 1986, 1:649). Lindblom considered that this passage was one of the longest glosses to be found in the prophets, being a specimen of Talmudic learning, incorporated as an interpretative addition long after the time of Jeremiah (1962:290).

33. When (*kî*) **these people, or a prophet or a priest, ask you,**

---

70. Representing a hiphil infinitive absolute, written with *ê* rather than *ē* (GKC §53k).

'What is the oracle of the LORD?' envisages a set of circumstances which might have arisen during the reign of Zedekiah. At that time the message of doom that Jeremiah had been proclaiming had been at least partly vindicated by events, and there was a measure of openness towards the prophet, with even the king consulting him (21:1). Here the LORD directs Jeremiah how to respond if one of the people or a religious official, such as a prophet or priest, consults him to see if he has received a word from the LORD regarding the current situation. But was their inquiry genuine, or was it a piece of mockery they were engaging in? The answer to this depends on the interpretation given to the word that is rendered 'oracle' or 'burden'. The latter sense seems more appropriate here so that the inquiry may be taken as uttered in mockery: 'What gloomy word from the LORD do you have today, Jeremiah? What burden do you have to weigh us down?' It is note-worthy that Jeremiah himself did not use the word 'burden' to describe his own sayings, possibly because the word was misused in con-temporary speech.

The answer he is told to give such an inquiry is variously translated. **Say to them, 'What oracle? I will forsake you, declares the LORD'** renders the Hebrew closely. Their question is to receive the same reply as Jeremiah had been giving for nearly forty years, and it is to be uttered with the traditional mark of divine authentication, 'declares the LORD' (*nəᶜum YHWH*). The NIV footnote indicates another rendering found in the Septuagint and the Vulgate, which keeps the consonants of the Hebrew but divides them differently, and gives the answer, 'You are the burden; I will forsake you, declares the LORD.'[71] In that case, the burdensome thing is not the word of the LORD to the people, but the people's behaviour in the LORD's estimation, which results in a message of judgment being relayed to them. 'Forsake' (<√*nāṭaš*) often functions as a synonym for 'abandon' (√*ᶜāzab*) as in 7:29; 12:7, but here and in v. 39 it is translated in the LXX and Vulgate by 'throw off', and that may also be the thought in Ezek. 29:5; 31:12; 32:4. The imagery is more than easing a burden off one's shoulders and leaving it lying on the ground. There is a degree of vigour in the rejection: the burden is cast aside.

34. This verse is closely linked to the preceding one as the repetition

---

71. The LXX reads *ᶜt-mh-mś*ᶜ as *ᶜtm hmś*ᶜ, that is, *ᶜattem hammaśśāᶜ*, 'You are the burden'. This has the additional strength of disposing of the awkward initial *ᶜet*, which can hardly function to mark an accusative, but might serve to indicate a quotation of the people's words: 'As for your question, "What is the oracle?", the oracle is "I will forsake you".'

of prophet, priest and people shows, and it obviously declares the
LORD's judgment on those who speak ill-advisedly. **If a prophet or a
priest or anyone else[72] claims, 'This is the oracle of the LORD,' I
will punish that man and his household.** The NIV translation considers the offence to be a continuation of what had been condemned
before (vv. 30-31), namely, unwarrantably claiming to have received
revelation from God. The LORD will take note of and act appropriately
against (<√*pāqad*) any individual behaving in that way, whoever they
are. However, the words may also be translated as a continuation of
v. 33: 'If a prophet or a priest or anyone else says, "A burden from the
LORD", I will punish that man and his household.' In that case, what is
being condemned is a view of God that claims he has only hard and
burdensome things to utter. It reflects a self-justifying attitude that
cannot see why God is condemning the people, and rather than repenting, casts aspersions on the character of God instead. Perhaps the
divine punishment is here extended to the individual's household
because it was their duty to monitor and correct the public behaviour of
one of their number. If he is allowed to behave in this way unchecked,
then responsibility for his conduct extends to them also.

35. This verse is also capable of being understood in two ways. It may
present a picture of intense interest in what God was saying to them.
**This is what each of you keeps on saying to his friend or relative:
'What is the LORD's answer?' or 'What has the LORD spoken?'**
Alternatively, this may be understood as a divinely given instruction:
'This is what each of you is to say to his friend or relative'. In either
event the behaviour described is viewed positively.

36. But you must not mention[73] 'the oracle of the LORD' again.
This does not set up a blanket ban of the use of the term *maśśāʿ* for the
future. It was in fact used by later prophets (Zech. 9:1; 12:1; Mal. 1:1).
What was being forbidden was the negative slant being given to the
term. They were being forbidden to characterise the LORD's message
as a burden, as if he had quite unreasonably nothing but judgment to
offer them.

   **Because (*kî*) every man's own word becomes his oracle and so
you distort the words of the living God, the LORD Almighty, our
God.** The first clause here is difficult to understand. Literally it reads,
'for/because the burden/oracle to a man his word'. The NIV translation

---

72. 'Anyone else' here renders *hāʿām*, 'the people', which may mean the
general population (21:7; 22:4).
73. 'Mention' renders *tzkrw* pointed as a hiphil, *tazkirû*, following the LXX.
The Massoretic Text reads *tizkərû*, a qal, 'you are to remember'.

proceeds on the basis that what is being condemned are false messages which each has dreamed up for himself and which they are presenting as genuine oracles even though they are merely human words. Obviously messages that did not come from God would distort (<√*hāpak*, 'to turn, overturn, transform, change', 13:23) what he had to say, and the heinous nature of the offence is emphasised by the titles given to him. 'The living God' (10:10) reminds them that this is one who is active and able to take action, not one of the lifeless heathen gods. The LORD Almighty declares that he is the one who has the hosts of creation under his command (2:19). The additional term 'our God' makes this threefold characterisation unique in the Old Testament, and serves to focus on the reason for the LORD's interest in what is being said among them: he is in covenant relationship with them.

Equally, the reason given may be understood in terms of *maśśāʿ* as 'burden'. They were not to talk of the LORD's word as a burden since what really constitutes the burden that each has to bear is what he has himself said: 'because every man's word will be his burden' (so the Vulgate). By characterising God as the problem and not recognising the part their own conduct has played in the situation they are distorting the true significance of the words that God had addressed to them.

37. This is what you keep saying to a prophet is structured similarly to the beginning of v. 35, but here 'you' is masculine singular, not seemingly in reference to Jeremiah, but to any individual among the people (GKC §144h). Again, they are viewed as asking proper questions: **'What is the LORD's answer to you?'**[74] or **'What has the LORD spoken?'** The people are coming to a prophet (whether a genuine one or one of the peace prophets is not clear from the context) as someone who can provide them with information from the LORD.

38. Although you (plural) **claim, 'This is the oracle of the LORD,'** 'therefore' (*lākēn*) **this is what the LORD says: You used**[75] **the words, 'This is the oracle of the LORD,' even though I told you that you must not claim, 'This is the oracle of the LORD.'** This sets out the grounds on which they were to be condemned, either as in the NIV because they falsely claimed to have divine revelation, or because they persisted in characterising the LORD's message as a burden. The presence here of 'therefore' would seem to indicate the verdict reached regarding them, though this is not in fact stated till v. 39. There is first

---

74. *ʿānāk*, 'he has answered you'; for the form of the pronominal suffix see GKC §58g, 75ll.

75. *yaʿan*, 'because/because of' is followed by an infinitive construct, *ʿămorəkem*, 'your saying' (*IBHS* §38.4a).

a restatement of their offence.

39. Therefore (*lākēn* of judgment)**, I will surely**[76] **forget you and cast you out of my presence along with the city I gave to you and your fathers.** 'Utterly forget' (<√*nāšâ/nāšā*ʿ) involves another word play on *maśśāʿ*, 'burden/oracle' through the similarity of the sounds of the words involved. The translation found in the NRSV, 'I will surely lift you up', follows a few Hebrew manuscripts and many of the early versions by identifying the root as *nāšāʿ*, 'to lift up/carry' (it differs in only one letter), from which *maśśāʿ*, 'burden/oracle', is derived. It is felt that lifting up and casting away presents a more obvious sequence of thought, though 'forgetting' is by no means impossible either as regards its meaning or the assonance it provides. 'Cast' (<√*nāṭaš* 'forsake', v. 33) refers to the banishment that the LORD will bring on them. Unusually it is not the land but the city which is viewed here as the inheritance that had been divinely allotted to them.

40. I will bring upon you everlasting disgrace—everlasting shame that will not be forgotten. This is what the LORD assigns to the people who mistreat his word. 'Disgrace' (*ḥerpâ*, 6:10) relates to what is evaluated as of no worth and treated accordingly. 'Shame' (*kəlimmût*) points to public humiliation and dishonour. 'Everlasting' (*ʿôlām*) need not point to the verdict of the final day of judgment. It may point to what is perpetual or permanent ('for all time' NJPS). Though the NRSV and other translations (going back to the Vulgate) use different words 'everlasting ... perpetual', in fact it is the same word that occurs twice. The second phrase is virtually identical to that found in 20:11.[77] It is not stated by whom this shame will not be forgotten: is it by the survivors of the people or by others?

In Jerusalem before its destruction truth and error were confused, particularly as regards what it was that the LORD was saying to the people. The establishment prophets, basing their message on only part of divine revelation, promised the people that prosperity lay ahead

---

76. For *nāšōʿ* as the form of the infinitive absolute rather than *nāšōh*, see GKC §23l. The Massoretic Text reads *wənāšîtî ... nāšōʿ*, the first form being from *nāšâ*, but the second being a final-*aleph* verb form, though there is often confusion between final-*aleph* and final-*he* forms (GKC §75qq). A few manuscripts make the play more direct (as does LXX, Syriac and Vulgate) by reading *wənāšîtî*, as if from *nāśâ*, treated as a final *aleph* verb; hence the NRSV rendering 'I will surely lift you up'.

77. In 20:11 the noun is *kəlimmâ*, whereas here the hapax *kəlimmût* is used with substantially the same meaning.

because the LORD was committed to Jerusalem through his presence in the Temple. They clothed their message in the language used by true prophets and effectively deceived the people, who consequently looked on Jeremiah's message as unwarrantably gloomy and forbidding. But Jeremiah was right and his message was genuine. The peace prophets were the ones whose words were specious and whose ministry was an imposture. With the passage of time and the fulfilment of what Jeremiah had said this was incontrovertible. 'The visions of your prophets were false and worthless; they did not expose your sin to ward off your captivity. The oracles they gave you were false and misleading' (Lam. 2:14). But by then it was too late.

D. BASKETS OF FIGS (24:1-10)

Chapter 24 presents a vision whose authenticity has often been questioned. Because it presents in a very favourable light those who went into captivity in 597 BC and reflects unfavourably on those who remained behind, it is argued that its present form is late, being written to justify the status of those returning to Palestine from the captivity. This in itself is not without problems, because with a date from just after 597 BC the vision does not directly refer to the status of the main group of exiles who were deported in 586 BC. By implication at least they are to be included in the group described as unfavoured in vv. 9-10. It is also argued that the attitudes revealed here do not reflect what we know of Jeremiah elsewhere. In chapter 22 Jeremiah views Jehoiachin dismissively (22:24-30). Further, it was in 597 BC that Pashhur of chapter 20 would have been taken captive, and yet here Jeremiah presents those exiles favourably. Equally, the view given of Zedekiah (v. 8) contrasts with what we see of Jeremiah's portrayal of him elsewhere as weak rather than bad. However, the prophet's assessment of the character of those included in the groups is really irrelevant because the groups are not being rewarded on the grounds of some intrinsic merit they personally possessed. The whole point of the vision is that the LORD's purposes are not going to be worked out as human thinking would consider probable, but according to his grace. It is a warning not to engage in too facile a reading of his providence: God does not automatically take the side of the rejected or displaced.

This vision brings this division of the prophecy to a conclusion by returning to the question Zedekiah had raised in 21:2: 'Is there going to be a miraculous intervention to save Jerusalem?' The answer is still unequivocal: 'No. There will be no escape.' Exile had already occurred and it would come again. Repentance was no longer a possible way of averting doom, but surprisingly there was a message of restoration beyond judgment. What is more, the focus for the future was to be found among the exiles, not those who seemed to be more favoured by being left in the land.

1. The Two Baskets (24:1-3)

1. The NIV in common with a number of English translations (RSV, NASB) reverses the order of the Hebrew clauses and begins with the temporal clause: **After Jehoiachin son of Jehoiakim king of Judah and the officials, the craftsmen, and the artisans of Judah were carried into exile from Jerusalem to Babylon by Nebuchadnezzar king of Babylon.** This locates the vision in the aftermath of the events of March 597 BC. If the deportation took place in April after the turn of the year (2 Chron. 36:10), then assuming it is real figs that are seen, this incident would have occurred a few months later in August when figs became ripe. There is no need to suppose that a longer period is required so that the attitude of the king and his court might become evident. What is presented here is prophecy regarding how the LORD has decided to shape the future of his people.

Further details regarding the deportation are given in 2 Kgs. 24. Jehoiachin had only been on the throne for three months when he surrendered to Babylon. The 'officials' (*śārîm*) would include all those associated with the king's council of state. They were the people who had been instrumental in stirring up the rebellion against Nebuchadnezzar, and he obviously did not want to leave them in a position to cause further trouble. The term would cover both military and civilian officials, if that is not too modern a distinction, and possibly the leading members of the priesthood as well. The other groups were taken for their usefulness in Nebuchadnezzar's various building projects. The craftsmen (*ḥārāš*, a collective noun, 10:3) were skilled workers in wood, stone or metal. 'Artisans' (*masgēr*) is another collective term, but of uncertain meaning. The root *sāgar* conveys the idea of 'shut up'[78] and is used in connection with sieges. This has generated the idea that these men were skilled as military engineers, but others suggest it is skilled locksmiths that are in view, while yet another view is that the word is a synonym of the 'craftsmen'. The list of those deported is more abbreviated than that in 29:2, and figures for the numbers involved are given in 2 Kgs. 24:14-16. Not only did such a loss

---

78. This root also gives rise to the suggestion found in the REB footnote: 'harem'. The word order in this clause makes that proposal improbable in this context.

weaken the land militarily and economically; it also meant that those left to guide Zechariah, Nebuchadnezzar's appointee to rule Judah, lacked experience.

It was a few months into the new administration in Jerusalem that the LORD took the initiative and revealed his purpose to Jeremiah by means of a vision. **The LORD showed me** is a formula that is used elsewhere for divine disclosure through a vision (Amos 7:1, 4, 7; 8:1; Zech. 1:20; 3:1). The vision involved **two baskets**[79] **of figs placed in front of the temple of the LORD.** It resembles in form and substance that of Amos 8:1-3 where the prophet saw a basket of ripe fruit, where a question was posed and an answer given, and where a message of impending judgment on Israel was pronounced. Here, however, there are two baskets, and the fact that one is of poor figs indicates that this vision is not a case of symbolic perception (cf. 1:11; *contra* Lindblom 1962:140). A basket of bad figs would never have been allowed near the Temple as an offering. However, the use of figs in the vision may well indicate that this occurred shortly after the harvest.

The word rendered 'placed' (the hophal participle of *yāʿad*, 'to appoint, assign') is significant here.[80] It is used of the LORD meeting with his people at the Tabernacle (Exod. 25:22; 29:42; 30:6), and so here what is symbolically represented is a meeting of the LORD with his people as represented by the two baskets and their contents. They have been called by divine appointment 'in front of the temple', to the place he has designated as the one where he will meet his people, and where they are subject to his scrutiny and approval.

2. But the contents of the two baskets were of different quality. **One**[81] **basket had very good figs, like those that ripen early.** They were not first-ripe figs, but 'like' them, that is, of the same high quality. Those figs ripened in June on the wood of the previous year, before the second crop which came in late August at the same time as the rest of the fruit harvest. They were particularly juicy and considered to be a prize delicacy (Isa. 28:4; Hos. 9:10). The fruit in the first basket was obviously of prime quality.

---

79. 'Baskets' renders *dūdāʾē* from a form which would normally be taken to indicate the fruit of the mandrake plant. By translating 'basket' it is assumed that the spelling is corrupt or that the plural is a by-form of *dûd*, 'basket'.

80. The hophal participle is also found in Ezek. 21:16, 'wherever your blade is turned' (NIV), but note 'is ordered' (NKJV), 'is directed' (NRSV).

81. That the definite noun *hadûd* is followed by *ʾeḥād* without the article may be explained by the numeral being regarded as definite in itself (GKC §134l).

The other basket had very poor figs, so bad that they could not be eaten. 'Poor' and 'bad' are both from the root *ra'*, 'evil'. The word had an extensive range of meaning, but that it was used to refer to moral evil opened up the way for the application of the vision. In the first instance, however, it refers to the quality of the fruit. The damaged and rotten fruit was unfit for human consumption and should not have been presented to the LORD.

3. The significance of the vision was not immediately apparent to Jeremiah, and the question of v. 3 is part of a divine technique that was often used on such occasions to focus attention on the specific significant aspect of the scene and to explain it (1:11, 13; Amos 8:2). **Then the LORD asked me, 'What do you see, Jeremiah?'** In his reply Jeremiah restates the description he has already given of the content of the vision. **'Figs,' I answered. 'The good ones are very good, but the poor ones are so bad that they cannot be eaten.'**

2. The Good Figs (24:4-7)

There then follows the divine explanation of the vision in two parts: vv. 4-7 regarding the good figs, and vv. 8-10 regarding the bad ones. The two types of fig represent the two groups to be found in the people of Judah: some deported by the Babylonians, some both at home and in Egypt enjoying freedom. The surprising application of the vision is that the good figs represent the deportees, and the poor quality figs the others.

4-5. 'Again' (NKJV) is simply 'and', and there is no reason to suppose that there was a lapse of time before the explanation was given. **Then the word of the LORD came to me: 'This is what the LORD, the God of Israel, says: "Like these good figs, I regard as good the exiles from Judah, whom I sent away from this place to the land of the Babylonians".'** The use of this introductory formula shows clearly that Jeremiah did not receive this vision and its explanation in a purely private capacity, but as a prophet of the LORD, charged to bring this message to the people. It presents a divine evaluation of the situation that would not have been obvious to Jeremiah's contemporaries. 'Regard' (<√*nākar* I hiphil) can have special reference to God's care for his own (Pss. 103:16; 142:4). 'Exiles' may not be the best translation into English because exile may sometimes occur voluntarily, whereas the Hebrew root *gālâ* always signifies forced deportation to a foreign land. The natural conclusion would have been that those who remained in the land were fortunate to have escaped deportation, and that the unfortunates were those who had been deported. However, all has taken place under the LORD's supervision. 'For good' does not signify the character of those who were exiled. The prophet says nothing about their religious character or their social standing. The transformation that they are going to experience derives from the role they have been sovereignly assigned in the outworking of God's purpose. Through the Babylonians acting as his agents, the LORD had sent this group from 'this place' (Judah/Jerusalem, 7:3) which he had selected as his own. Though now in a foreign land, they did not fall outwith God's purpose for his people. Indeed it was with them that that purpose would in fact be forwarded. This would not have been a welcome thought to those left in Jerusalem who considered that the future of the people lay with them.

6. My eyes[82] **will watch/'I will set my eye' over them for their good.** The phrase 'for good' is identical to that in the previous verse. God promises that even though they are in a distant land he will take care of them, and in fact the exiles did prosper in Babylon (29:4-7; 2 Kgs. 25:27-30). But it is not just their economic well-being while in exile that is in view. **And I will bring them back to this land. I will build them up and not tear them down; I will plant them and not uproot them.** Return from exile for those from the north and the south had already been promised (Hos. 6:11; Amos 9:14). These words look back to the commission given Jeremiah at his call (1:10, but here NIV translates *hāras* as 'tear down' whereas it used 'overthrow' for the same root in 1:10). The use of negated opposites renders even more emphatic the promise that beyond the judgment of God on the nation there will be a time of restoration and rebuilding which is scheduled in the divine plan. His way forward involves using the dispossessed, those despised by their fellows, as the ones round whom he will form his new community.

7. Although there is no mention here of repentance on the part of the people, it is clear that this is not going to happen automatically, nor is this restoration going to be primarily a political concern. The emphasis is on the divine initiative in the matter. **I will give them a heart to know me,**[83] **that** (*kî* introducing noun clause, or perhaps = 'for', introducing the reason why he will act in this way) **I am the LORD.** (29:13; 31:33; Ezek. 36:26-27; 37:13-14, 27-28; Zech. 13:9). Because of the

---

82. A few manuscripts, the LXX and Vulgate read *'ênay*, 'my eyes', but most manuscripts have the singular *'ênî*, 'my eye', which is idiomatic Hebrew.

83. This is expressed by the object marker with a first person singular suffix, *'ōtî*, rather than a pronominal suffix to avoid ambiguity with 'that I might know' (*IBHS* §36.1.1e).

change God will sovereignly bestow they will be given a new inner capacity of mind and will to know, that is, to commit themselves totally to the LORD in his capacity as the God of the covenant. The need for heart change is part of Jeremiah's vision for the future of the people (31:33; 32:39; Ps. 51:12), and provides the remedy for their condition previously diagnosed as being of a stubborn heart (3:17). There then follows the standard formula of the covenant relationship (31:33; 7:23; 11:4; 31:1; 30:22; 32:28). **They will be my people, and I will be their God**, but the reality of this will only be achieved because they will be those who have been given a heart to know the LORD: **for ($k\hat{\imath}$[84]) they will return ($<\sqrt{}\check{s}\hat{u}b$) to me with all their heart** (3:10; Deut. 30:10). This is the response that Jeremiah had always wished to see in the people. It is now proclaimed as a result of a saving change they will experience in their exile, when there will come a total commitment to the LORD so that a true relationship with him will prevail. Throughout vv. 5-7 the subject of the verbs is predominantly 'I' referring to the LORD and emphasising his initiative and control in the process by which the new community will come into existence.

3. The Bad Figs (24:8-10)

8. Verse 8 turns to consider the other side of the coin: those who had escaped deportation. In the thinking of the establishment prophets in Jerusalem the worst had now passed for the city and its remaining inhabitants were fortunate in being left in the land. This air of optimism was countered by the message of this vision. **'But** (*waw*-disjunctive) **like the poor figs, which are so bad that they cannot be eaten,' says the LORD.** 'For (*$k\hat{\imath}$*) thus says the LORD' indicates that this exposition is in parallel with what has preceded regarding the good figs.[85] **So I will deal with Zedekiah king of Judah, his officials and the survivors from Jerusalem, whether they remain in this land or live in Egypt.** It is not immediately stated how they will be dealt with, but the details are given in the next verse. The thought seems to be, 'Just as an individual will deal with poor, uneatable figs, so I will deal with those remaining in the land.' In both cases they are thrown away.

84. Craigie et al. (1991:360) argue that *$k\hat{\imath}$* here should be translated 'if'. The promise is not unconditional but contingent upon repentance. However, the LORD is promising that he will take action to ensure that this change of heart does occur.

85. *$k\hat{\imath}$* is frequently treated here as asseverative, 'surely' (NKJV), 'indeed' (NASB). The clause, 'thus says the LORD', is unusually inserted as a parenthesis, though the NRSV places it first.

So the complacent in Jerusalem are warned of further judgment ahead. In this way the LORD declares himself against the rule of Zedekiah and the policies he put into effect.

The addition of 'live in Egypt' constitutes a problem. The presence of this phrase leads critics such as Nicholson (1970:27) to conclude that 'this already presupposes the period *after* 586 BC and the flight to Egypt of the community set up by the Babylonians under Gedaliah. ... In view of this it seems more plausible to see in the present sermon the development of something which Jeremiah had said and its adaptation to a later situation than that in which he spoke.' But while there has not been up to this point any mention of a group from Judah residing in Egypt, there are various possibilities as to when people may have gone to Egypt in significant numbers: with Jehoahaz in 609 BC (22:10-12), or around 605 when Nebuchadnezzar first made his presence felt in Syria–Palestine, or possibly at the time of the invasion in 597. Equally plausible is the existence of an expatriate community in Egypt for commercial purposes, whose numbers may have been augmented at times of crisis further north. We do know that a considerable number of refugees fled south around 586 BC, but the text does not have them in view at this point. The Egyptian party are not the focus of the following two verses as the phrase 'until they are destroyed from the land' (v. 10) indicates. 'In Egypt' as an expression denotes both a punishment and the worst lack of faith on the part of those who have gone there voluntarily.

9. I will make them abhorrent[86] and an offence to all the kingdoms of the earth, a reproach and a byword, an object of ridicule and cursing. 'I will make them' (<√*nātan*) picks up and expands 'I will deal' (<√*nātan*, v. 8). Some of the phrases that are used draw on the language of covenant curse found in Deuteronomy, but there are other expressions not found there. It is not possible to set up an adequate model to explain this use of language except to view the Jeremiah passage as couched in already traditional vocabulary, but by no means limited to it. 'Abhorrent' refers to an 'object that causes trembling or fright' (15:4; see there also for the NKJV 'to trouble'; Deut. 28:25). 'Offence' (*rā'â*, 'evil') does not occur in the similar expressions using 'to all the kingdoms of the earth' that are found in 15:4, 29:18 and 34:17. Perhaps it is added here because it has been used of the bad figs (vv. 2, 3, 8). Not only will the LORD view this portion of Judah with disgust; they will be treated in the same way by the nations. Four

---

86. The kethibh is *lzw'h*; the qere transposes *waw* and *ayin*, *ləza'ăwâ* < √*zāwa'*, 'to tremble, quake' (cf. 15:4)..

further terms are added to indicate the attitude with which the people will be viewed. 'A reproach' (*ḥerpâ*; 'offensive, 6:10; Deut. 28:37) describes the people as being despised and treated as of no account. 'Byword' renders *māšāl*, which is often used neutrally in the sense of a proverb or wisdom saying, but here it takes on negative overtones, 'an unfavourable comparison', pointing out conduct or a condition that is to be avoided. It is not simply a taunt or reproach. 'An object of ridicule' (*šənînâ* < *šēn*, 'tooth') describes a sharp, biting word, which occurs elsewhere three times (Deut. 28:37; 1 Kgs. 9:7; 2 Chron. 7:20) always in parallel with *māšāl*. 'An object of cursing' (*qəlālâ*, 25:18) points to something treated as valueless and worthy of scorn.

Wherever I banish them points to another aspect of the situation. Those in view here are not those who had been deported in 597 BC, but those who at that stage had already fled to Egypt and those who had been left in the land by Nebuchadnezzar. They were the poor quality figs, but they were not going to be exempt from the LORD's punishment and would also be driven from the land. 'Banish' (<√*nādaḥ*, 8:3) refers to their enforced removal, in which they will go to many foreign parts as both the mention of 'all the kingdoms of the earth' and 'wherever' ('in all the places where I banish them') indicate.

10. The fate of the people will not just be deportation, but will involve the horrors of warfare and conquest which Jeremiah had announced to them throughout his ministry. **I will send the sword, famine and plague against them until they are destroyed from the land I gave to them and their fathers.** The deadly trio (14:12) again signal the outpouring of the LORD's wrath on the people. This will continue until their existence as a nation comes to an end ('destroyed' <√*tāmam*, 14:15). No prospect of alleviation or deflection is offered.

The divine choice of the community in exile as the ones through whom the LORD will forward his purposes ran counter to the thinking of Jeremiah's day where it was treated as self-evident that those who had escaped deportation were the ones favoured by God. But the divine purpose was to be promoted through those whom the world reckoned as written off, written out of the pages of history. 'Brothers, think of what you were when you were called. Not many of you were wise by human standards; not many were influential; not many were of noble birth. But God chose the foolish things of the world to shame the wise; God chose the weak things of the world to shame the strong' (1 Cor. 1:26-27). Supremely this mode of acting was revealed when the stone that the builders rejected became the headstone of the corner (Ps. 118:22-23; Mark 12:10-11).

IX. JUDGMENT ON THE NATIONS

(25:1-38)

OUTLINE

A. Judah (25:1-14)
    1. Spurned Warnings (25:1-7)
    2. Seventy Years (25:8-14)
B. The Cup of the LORD's Wrath (25:15-38)
    1. The Wine of Wrath (25:15-26)
    2. You Must Drink It! (25:27-29)
    3. The Storm of Judgment (25:30-38)

The fact that the events of chapter 25 took place several years before those recorded in chapter 24 again reminds us that at this point the material has been gathered thematically rather than chronologically. Discussions of the original form of this chapter have to take into account the fact that in the Septuagint the material is found in a different form. The principal difference is that in the LXX text towards the end of v. 13 there are placed the Oracles against the Nations, which are found in chapters 46–51 of the Massoretic Text (see introduction to chap. 46). There are also many differences between the LXX and the Massoretic Text in the first thirteen verses. Scholarly opinion generally supposes that the LXX (or rather the Hebrew text that underlies it) represents the original text and the Massoretic Text is a later expansion. Even if this verdict is accepted, it does not necessarily follow that the Massoretic Text is non-Jeremianic. The most plausible hypothesis would seem to be that prior to the fall of Jerusalem Jeremiah did issue his Oracles against the Nations in the context of the material now found in chapter 25, but when after the fall of Jerusalem he instructed Baruch regarding the final form of his prophecy, he ordered the material in a different way and significantly modified this chapter so that it could stand separately. In particular it was made much clearer than originally that the foe from the north was in fact Babylon.

In the first part of the chapter (vv. 1-14) the focus is primarily on how unreceptive the people had been to the warnings given them by the prophets and on the judgment that would inevitably come upon them and last for a period of seventy years. After that time has elapsed, the Babylonians, who will be the instruments of the LORD's judgment, will themselves be subject to judgment. There is then a section that describes the LORD's judgment on the nations in terms of the cup of his wrath which he will make all nations drink (vv. 15-29), which is followed by further statements regarding the impact of divine judgment (vv. 30-38).

A. JUDAH (25:1-14)

The first part of the chapter deals with the conduct and destiny of Judah. For years they had ignored the warnings the LORD had sent through the prophets (vv. 4-7), and especially those that Jeremiah had given during the preceding twenty-three years (v. 3). It was therefore inevitable that the LORD would unleash his judgment on them, and it would take the form of an invasion led by Babylon (vv. 8-11). This was how the foe from the north would become a reality, not just another prophetic warning to be disregarded in the light of the exhortations of the peace prophets. But the LORD's sovereign control extended beyond Judah, and in due course Babylon too would be judged (vv. 12-14).

1. Spurned Warnings (25:1-7)

1. The word came to[1] **Jeremiah concerning all the people of Judah in the fourth year of Jehoiakim son of Josiah king of Judah, which was the first year of Nebuchadnezzar king of Babylon.** The NIV smoothes out the Hebrew construction of vv. 1-2, where there is no verb: 'The word which came to Jeremiah ... which Jeremiah the prophet spoke to all the people of Judah ...'. The expression is also unusual in that after 'word', referring obviously to a word of the LORD, it is natural to expect there to be a divine oracle, whereas in vv. 3-5 it is Jeremiah himself who speaks. The heading is similar to that found in 7:1; 11:1; 18:1; 21:1; 30:1.

The historical settings for Jeremiah's ministry found in 21:1 and 24:1 are continued here with the first of four references in the book to Jehoiakim's fourth year (also 36:1; 45:1; 46:2), which, based on an autumn calendar and assuming Jehoiakim's reign began with a lengthy accession year, would be from autumn 605 BC to autumn 604 BC (Appendix §§5-8). May 605 BC had witnessed the Battle of Carchemish at which Babylon under Nebuchadnezzar redrew the political map of the whole region (see Volume 1, Introduction §3.8). Babylonian practice too used accession years to cover the period up to the first New Year's Day in a king's reign, but official years were calculated from the spring so that Babylonian style Nebuchadnezzar's first regnal year was from spring 604 BC to spring 603 BC. However, it was common practice for scribes in one country to translate dates of other kingdoms into the pattern that they used for their own. In Judahite reckoning Nebuchadnezzar's accession year was a matter of a few weeks until autumn 605 BC which saw the start of his first regnal year, lasting until autumn 604 BC. It would then be the year beginning in autumn 605 BC that is referred to in this verse.

It is not, however, calendrical considerations that are uppermost here. The dual dating is employed to emphasise that from this point onwards the real power in the land is Nebuchadnezzar (cf. 32:1, the only other text in the book to employ dual dating). Jeremiah is

---

1. 'To' and 'concerning' both translate *ʿal*. Presumably the first has to be rendered as the equivalent of *ʿel*, 'to'. That may well be true of the second occurrence also, 'the word which to Jeremiah to all the people', indicating it was to be presented to them.

speaking against a background when the power of Babylon has already impinged upon the small kingdom of Judah. Jehoiakim is no longer free to do as he pleases in Judah, and the long-threatened judgment of the LORD has begun to be implemented.

2. So Jeremiah the prophet said to[2] all the people of Judah and to all those living in Jerusalem. Towards the end of Jehoiakim's fourth regnal year or at the beginning of his fifth Jeremiah was unable to speak to the people because of restrictions imposed on him (36:1-5); so what is recorded in this chapter occurred late in 605 BC or in the earlier months of 604 BC.

3. Jeremiah first challenged the people with the warnings he had brought to them over many years. **For twenty-three years—from the thirteenth year of Josiah son of Amon king of Judah until this very day—the word of the LORD has come to me and I have spoken to you again and again[3], but you have not listened.[4]** There is a sharp contrast here between the assiduous activity ('persistently' NRSV, cf. 7:13) of the prophet and the unresponsiveness of the people. The twenty-three years, starting from 627 BC, are made up of nineteen under Josiah, and four under Jehoiakim, as well as the intervening three months of Jehoahaz' reign which is not mentioned. The total figure is consistent with what is stated in 1:2. Jeremiah was able to persevere in his mission because he had no doubt that the LORD himself had originated the message that he was proclaiming to them. Even so, the lack of interest and response weighed heavily upon him. A similar statement regarding Jeremiah's ministry is found in 36:2, written shortly after this chapter. Despite all that he had said and done, he admits that the nation's response had been, 'You have not listened'.

4. Jeremiah then emphasises how over a long period the LORD had repeatedly given warnings to the people. **And though the LORD has sent[5] all his servants the prophets to you again and again, you have not listened or paid any attention.** The prophets referred to here

---

2. The first 'to' is ʿal and the second ʾel, indicating their equivalence.

3. The Massoretic Text has ʾaškēm, which may be an Aramaic form for the expected haškēm, as in v. 4 and repeatedly elsewhere (e.g. 7:13, 25; GKC §113k), rather than a hiphil imperfect, 'I kept rising early and to speak' which does not fit the grammar (GKC §53k).

4. For 'the word of the LORD ... have not listened' the LXX has simply 'I spoke to you, rising early and speaking', where 'I' is understood to be the LORD himself, who also continues to speak to the end of v. 7.

5. wəšālaḥ, 'and he sent', is a waw-consecutive perfect expressing frequently repeated action in the past (GKC §112dd).

might be those that were contemporary with Jeremiah such as Uriah, Zephaniah and Habakkuk, but more probably this is the line of prophetic ministry stretching back to much earlier times, by which the LORD sought to recall his errant subjects, and which received in general the same response, or rather non-response (7:25-26; 11:7; 26:4-5; 32:33; 35:14-15; 44:4-5).

5. The message that the prophets had brought over the centuries had remained essentially the same so that what Jeremiah proclaimed was no novelty. **They said, 'Turn now, each of you, from your evil ways and your evil practices,[6] and you can stay[7] in the land which the LORD gave to you and your fathers for ever and ever.'** Their 'ways' (18:11) refers to their lifestyle in general, whereas 'practices' refers to more specific actions that arise from the prevailing consensus (4:18). Both are characterised as 'evil' ($<\sqrt{r\bar{a}'a}$), contrary to what the LORD required. Therefore there was a need for turning/repentance ($<\sqrt{\check{s}\hat{u}b}$, cf. 23:22) which Jeremiah so often emphasised. If they turned, then they could stay/dwell ($<\sqrt{y\bar{a}\check{s}ab}$) in the land, a wordplay bringing out the assonance with 'turn'. 'For ever and ever'/'with respect to from perpetuity and as far as perpetuity' repeats '$\hat{o}l\bar{a}m$ (cf. v. 9) for emphasis. Possession of the land without limit of time was part of the covenant promise made to Abraham (Gen. 13:15; 17:8), but enjoyment of the promised blessings of the covenant was conditional on obedience to their Overlord's stipulations.

6. The charge against the people is not simply rebellion against the commands of God or worshipping him in an unauthorised fashion, but engaging in pagan, idolatrous worship. **Do not follow other gods to serve and worship them.** They are urged to avoid the inevitable consequence of such unfaithful behaviour. **Do not[8] provoke me to anger with what your hands have made.** 'Provoke' ($<\sqrt{k\bar{a}'as}$ hiphil) is frequently found in Jeremiah for the impact that deliberate flouting of the LORD's commands has on him. 'The work of your hands' (here

---

6. The use of '$\hat{\imath}\check{s}$, 'man', as a distributive 'each' has resulted in Hebrew in the use of 'from his evil way' (cf. NASB) before reverting to the second person plural in 'from your evil practices'.

7. $\check{s}\hat{u}b\hat{u}$ ... $\hat{u}\check{s}\partial b\hat{u}$, 'turn ... and ... stay/dwell', is an instance of a construction where an imperative, expressing a virtual condition, is followed by *waw* with another imperative which indicates the consequence which will follow on fulfilment of the condition. The use of the imperative indicates that this is the outcome that is desired by the speaker (GKC §110f).

8. GKC §109g treats $w\partial l\bar{o}'-tak'\hat{\imath}s\hat{u}$ as a negative final clause, which would be equivalent to, 'lest you provoke me'.

and in the following verse) probably refers specifically to idolatry
(1:16; Isa. 2:8; 37:19), though the phrase may also describe conduct
more generally (25:14; 32:30). If they gave heed to these warnings and
desisted from idolatry, **then** the LORD assures them, **I will not harm
you** (1:16; 7:6, 18; 13:10), but if not, they would stir up his wrath
against them.

7. The people, however, simply did not believe the caution the
prophets issued to them. As far as they and their religious leaders were
concerned, it was inconceivable that the LORD would act against his
people. Consequently Jeremiah switches from his own résumé of the
message brought by the prophets, including himself, to citing the very
words of the LORD against their spiritual intransigence. **'But you did
not listen to me,'** declares the LORD, **'and you have provoked me**[9]
**with what your hands have made, and you have brought harm to
yourselves.'** 'Harm' is from the same root as 'evil' back in v. 5 and as
the verb 'I will not harm' at the end of v. 6. They had been clearly
notified of the consequences of their conduct and how to avert them.
Though they had heard the words, they had not acknowledged the
truthfulness of the message. If they did not turn/repent, they had only
themselves to blame for what would happen next.

2. Seventy Years (25:8-14)

The divine sentence of seventy years of subjugation to Babylon is
issued in vv. 8-11. But, surprisingly, the period of seventy years is then
used to indicate how long it will be before the mighty Babylonian
empire is itself swept away (vv. 12-14).

8. **Therefore** (*lākēn*) **the LORD Almighty says this: 'Because you
have not listened to my words'.** The reason for the sentence against
them resumes what has been said in v. 7. This continuing lack of
response to the warnings repeatedly given by the LORD through the
prophets is clearly indicated as the precipitating factor in the divine
judgment (7:13).

9. **'I will summon**[10] **all the peoples of the north and my servant**

---

9. The kethibh is a perfect *hik'isûnî* which following *ləma'an* reads more
roughly than the qere *hak'îsēnî*, which is an infinitive. The sense is unaltered.
ləma'an appears to be used to indicate result rather than purpose (cf. 7:18, 19).

10. Literally, 'Behold me summoning!', an idiom Jeremiah frequently uses
to express what is about to occur in the immediate future (cf. 1:15). It is then
followed by a *waw*-consecutive perfect, 'and I will take to (*'el*) Nebuchadnezzar', an elliptical expression for 'calling to and taking'.

Nebuchadnezzar king of Babylon,' declares the LORD.[11] 'Will summon' is literally 'am sending and will take'. It is the LORD as the supreme ruler of the nations of earth who is going to determine how events unfold and how his agents in history respond to them. 'Peoples'/'clans' or 'tribes' (1:15) indicates either the composite nature of the Babylonian empire and therefore of the troops which are going to come, or it may just be a way of asserting that the whole might of Babylon was involved in that every clan would come. It seems to be here that Jeremiah for the first time confirmed that the long awaited foe from the north was in fact the Babylonians. 21:2, 7 and 24:1, though coming earlier in the book, date from Zedekiah's reign. If we are right in taking Pashhur's action against Jeremiah as leading to his being debarred from the Temple, then the mention of Babylon in 20:4, 6 also comes after this address which was presumably given in the Temple precincts.

But even more threatening for Judah than the revelation of Babylon is the designation of Nebuchadnezzar as 'my servant'. This is not to say that he would worship the LORD. No intimate relationship or faith commitment is implied.

> Nebuchadnezzar thought he was making war with the God of Israel when he invaded Judah; and only ambition, and avarice, and cruelty impelled him to undertake so many wars. When, therefore, we think of him, of his designs and his projects, we cannot say that he was God's servant; but this is to be referred to God only, who governs by his hidden and incomprehensible power both the devil and the ungodly, so that they execute, though unwittingly, whatever he determines. There is a great difference between these and God's servants, who, when anything is commanded them, seek to render that obedience which they ought—all such are faithful servants. (Calvin 1850, 3:252)

The occurrence of the phrase 'my servant' here and in 27:6 and 43:10 is not supported by the LXX, probably being omitted because its implications were considered offensive (compare 'Cyrus, my shepherd' and his 'anointed', Isa. 44:28; 45:1). The LORD had previously sent his servants the prophets to see if suasion would turn the people back to him (v. 4), but they had ignored them. Now, he is sending a servant of another sort, and they will not be able to ignore him as he fulfils the role the LORD has assigned him. The idea that foreign rulers would be recognised by the LORD and used by him against his people would

---

11. In Hebrew the phrase 'declares the LORD' is placed between 'all the peoples of the north' and 'Nebuchadnezzar', intensifying the dramatic nature of the disclosure of the agent through whom the LORD will work.

have seemed far-fetched, indeed blasphemous, to those brought up under the shalom theology of the establishment prophets.

It is through Nebuchadnezzar and the forces he commands that the LORD is going to punish the people for their rebellion. **I will bring them against this land and its inhabitants and against all the surrounding nations.** 'This land' where Jeremiah is speaking is in contrast to 'that land' (v. 13). The Babylonian invasion will also engulf nations adjacent to Judah, whose ways they had copied. Those involved are listed later in the chapter (vv. 19-25). Judah and the nations will be completely devastated by the action taken against them. Their immediate aggressors will be the Babylonians and their allies, but the ultimate enemy is the LORD himself. **I will completely destroy them** (<√$hāram$) uses a term that is found earlier in the Old Testament to describe the wholesale destruction of the peoples and their property which the LORD enjoined upon Israel when he brought them into Canaan. As his agents they were to devote the existing inhabitants to the LORD by destroying them. The reason for such a policy is set out in Deut. 7:1-6. Israel was chosen by the LORD and dedicated to him, but the heathen in the land would be liable to corrupt Israel (Deut. 20:17-18; Josh. 6:18). Some commentators suggest that the significance of the root had been weakened by Jeremiah's day to 'total extermination' (certainly the ancient versions of Jeremiah show no awareness of sacral overtones in the word), but the term seems to be specially selected here. Now it is Judah that is the source of pollution in the land, and they are the ones who are going to be devoted to the ban and the role the Israelites had previously been charged with has now been transferred to the Babylonians. Though the focus is on Judah, neighbouring peoples are also involved (the same verb is used also in 50:21, 26; 51:3).

By declaring war against his people, the LORD sovereignly imposes on them the curses of the broken covenant. He will **make them an object of horror and scorn, and an everlasting ruin.**[12] 'Horror' (*šammâ*, 2:15, involves assonance with *śîm*, 'to set/make') and 'scorn' (*šarēqâ*, 19:8) convey the reaction of others as they look at the fate that has overtaken Judah. 'Everlasting' (*ʿôlām*), though often translated 'eternal', does in fact denote time stretching throughout a specified period, which may be as short as an individual's lifetime, e.g. in reference to a slave bound in 'perpetual', i.e. lifelong, service to his master (Exod. 21:6; Deut. 15:17). Here the reference to Judah and

---

12. 'An everlasting disgrace' (NRSV) reads *ḥerpat* with the LXX for the Massoretic *ḥorəbôt*, 'desolations'. For 'disgrace' see 23:40; 24:9.

Jerusalem has to be interpreted in the light of the subsequent mention
of seventy years (v. 11; 29:10-14). There is no mitigation of the impact
of judgment when its consequences will remain for so long, but still
there is the hope of something eventually emerging from the ruin of the
nation.

10. Silence will descend on the devastated land because of the absence
of community life in the aftermath of the coming invasion. **I will
banish from them the sounds of joy and gladness, the voices of
bride and bridegroom, the sound of millstones and the light of the
lamp.** Five times the word *qôl*, 'sound'/'voice', is repeated to emphasise the comprehensiveness of the picture. Such repetition is a feature of
Jeremiah's style (8:1, 2; 51:20-23). The description is hyperbolic,
because there were still groups and settlements in Judah throughout the
period of the Exile. 'Banish' may be too specific a rendering of 'cause
to perish'. The thought is 'bring to an end' rather than 'send them off'
somewhere else. Similar descriptions of the end of rejoicing and
celebration in the land are found in 7:34 and 16:9, but the closing two
phrases are additional aspects of the curse of the broken covenant. Not
only special occasions but also the routines of daily life were going to
be affected by the tragedy that would come upon the land. The
millstones would typically be heard soon after dawn as corn was
ground to bake the day's bread. The light of the lamp points to the
evening when, after the day's work was done, artificial lighting was
required. The 'lamp' (*nēr*) was the small domestic lamp, generally
bowl shaped, filled with oil and with a pinched spout through which a
fabric wick was placed. Now both phenomena would be absent either
because grain and oil will be in short supply, or else because there will
be no one left to grind corn or light lamps. A bleak and grim silence
descends on the land under divine judgment.

11. This whole country will become a desolate wasteland again
describes the impact of the invasion on Judah, with 'desolate' echoing
'horror' (v. 9) and 'wasteland', the singular form of 'ruin' (v. 9). There
is then added, **and these nations will serve the king of Babylon for
seventy years.** The expression is no doubt to be understood in a
distributed sense, as implying also that Judah will serve Babylon and
the surrounding nations will become desolate. This is the only place in
this chapter of judgment where there might be found any possibility of
limitation in the sentence to be imposed. What would happen to the
nations after the seventy years? In the prevailing conditions Jeremiah
did not explore that possibility (but see 29:10-14); the lesson that had
to be taught was the inescapable outpouring of divine wrath.

But what period is to be reckoned as comprising the seventy years? One possibility is to take the figure as a conventional expression for an extended period. Some backing for this has been given by an earlier inscription dated in the reign of the Assyrian emperor Esarhaddon which talks of a seventy-year period of subjugation for Babylon. 'Seventy years' might then in such a context denotes a substantial but not permanent period of domination. However, the biblical use of the phrase does not readily fit in with such an imprecise expression, and it is repeated again in various later contexts with chronological overtones (2 Chron. 36:21; Dan. 9:2; Zech. 1:12; 7:5).[13] It might seem from the present passage that this period of Babylon domination begins once the land has been destroyed. However, the Babylonian empire fell in 539 BC, and even if one argues that the seventy-year period has to be extended to include the years in the 530s before the exiles returned to Jerusalem (Harrison 1973:126), it seems probable that the starting point for the seventy years ought to begin earlier. It might be extended back to 597 BC, the year Jerusalem first came into Babylonian hands, or possibly to 605 BC, when the battle of Carchemish established Babylonian hegemony over Syria–Palestine. Even so, the time that elapsed amounts to 66 years. More probably the seventy years here is a measure of the length of the Babylonian empire as the dominant power in Mesopotamia, and that this ought to be calculated from the final collapse of Assyrian power in 609 BC. Seventy years was also the expected life span of an individual (Ps. 90:10), and its length indicated that the period of Babylonian domination would not be some passing phenomenon. No adult then living could expect to return from the Exile. In Chronicles the seventy years is connected with the land enjoying its Sabbaths so that the long desolation came as retribution for the people's neglect of the law of the Sabbatical year (2 Chron. 36:21).

12. The previous verses have already shown that the LORD's judgment extended beyond the covenant people to include neighbouring nations. The following verses (vv. 12-14) bring Babylon itself within the scope of divine examination and retribution. The nations and empires of the world are under the scrutiny of God and liable to his judgment just as much as the people who acknowledge his name and who have been given special revelational privileges. There are no exemptions when it comes to having to give an account to the judge of all the earth.

---

13. In Zech. 1:12 mention is made of the LORD's anger against Judah and Jerusalem lasting for seventy years, that is, from the destruction of the Temple in 586 BC until its reopening in 516 BC, but it is unlikely that this is the same seventy-year period as the one mentioned in this passage.

At the end of the seventy-year period not only will there be a change in the fortunes of the lands that have been subjugated by Babylon; the fortunes of Babylon itself will be turned around. No other ancient empire of comparable magnitude collapsed as quickly as the neo-Babylonian empire, and this prophecy therefore ran counter to what the informed commentators of the day would have expected. **'But when the seventy years are fulfilled,**[14] **I will punish the king of Babylon and his nation, the land of the Babylonians, for their guilt,' declares the LORD.** The LORD who is the God of the nations, will subject Babylon to scrutiny and assign appropriate rewards (*pāqad*, 10:15; 11:22). It will not turn out well for Babylon and her king. 'I will punish' is omitted in the LXX. If v. 26 is a veiled prediction of the destruction of the king of Babylon, it is possible that this oracle originally delivered at the same period was similarly non-specific, and only clarified by Jeremiah at a later period of his ministry. Their guilt (*'awôn*) has arisen not from what they had done to the nations—in that they had been used by God—but from the wrong way in which they had acted (50:11-13; Isa. 47:5-7). Therefore the LORD says that he **will make it**[15] **desolate for ever.** 'Desolate' renders an intensive plural of *šəmāmâ* (4:7), 'utter desolations'.

13. I will bring[16] **upon that land all the things I have spoken against it** concludes the divine sentence of judgment upon Babylon. 'All' brings out how completely the LORD will act in judgment. **All that are written in this book and prophesied by Jeremiah against all the nations** obviously does not come from the original delivery of this oracle by Jeremiah. When they were added by him depends on what 'this book/scroll' refers to. It could well be that this refers to either the First or Second Scroll written shortly after this time in Jehoiakim's reign. This raises the question of whether or not these scrolls contained sufficient material against Babylon to warrant this reference. Two possibilities emerge. Either the Scroll had the material which is contained to the end of the chapter, and the reference is then particularly to that. Or else, we have to take into account the fact that at this point the Septuagint introduced the Oracles against the Nations

---

14. The qal infinitive construct of *mālē'* here occurs with the ending *-ôt* found in final-*he* verbs (GKC §74h).

15. 'It', *'ōtô*, is masculine, referring not to the land (*'ereṣ* is feminine) but to the nation.

16. The kethibh *hăbi'ōtî* is changed by the qere to *hēbē'tî*, an alternative hiphil form with the same meaning, which occurs elsewhere in Jeremiah (3:14; 36:31; 49:36) (GKC §76h).

(now contained in chapters 46–51 of the book, though in a different order) and took the final clause of the verse as a title for the prophecies. It may well be that those oracles originally did come in here, and that this marks the ending of the prophecy at some stage in Jeremiah's composition of it, and that when subsequently he enlarged it what is now found in the rest of chapter 25 was incorporated here and the Oracles retained as an appendix. On the other hand vv. 15-38 coming after the oracles as in the LXX is distinctly odd. These verses do not read naturally as a conclusion.

14. The verse begins *kî*, 'for', explaining how what is said in v. 12 will come to pass. **They themselves will be enslaved**[17] **by many nations and great kings** refers to the subjugation of Babylon by the Medes and Persians ('many nations') under Cyrus in 539 BC. **I will repay them according to their deeds and the work of their hands.** Divine justice for the nations is retributive. It is not arbitrary but reflects the misconduct they have exhibited (50:29; 51:24), but there is still no hint that judgment on Babylon will bring relief and restoration to Judah.

B. THE CUP OF THE LORD'S WRATH (25:15-38)

This section of the chapter is not so exclusively focused on Judah as the earlier part had been. Judah is still mentioned as one of the nations, but now the scope of the LORD's judgment reaches out and includes other peoples also.

1. The Wine of Wrath (25:15-26)

In vv. 15-29 the dominant figure is the cup of God's wrath, which is used to illustrate more fully the judgment that would come on the nations. 'Cup' is used throughout Scripture as a metaphor for what God designates as the portion of each. It can be used in a positive way, referring to his blessings (Pss. 16:5; 23:5; 116:13). But it frequently points to God's wrath and judgment upon those who have sinned against him ('portion of their cup' Ps. 11:6, NKJV, NRSV; Ps. 75:9; Isa. 51:17, 22; Lam. 4:21; Ezek. 23:31-34; Hab. 2:16). The same metaphor underlies Mark 10:38; Luke 22:42; John 18:11. Various

---

17. *gam-ḥēmmâ* emphasises the pronominal suffix on *bām* (GKC §135g). The NIV renders *ʿābədû*, 'they will impose slavery on' (for this sense of the verb see 22:13), passively whereas 'many nations and great kings' are the subject of the verb in Hebrew. The verb is generally acknowledged to be a prophetic perfect.

attempts have been made to find a background for this expression. One suggestion is that it reflects the rites used to ratify an international treaty. There is evidence that drinking from a cup might be employed on such an occasion. If the act involved an element of self-malediction, then 'one is left to wonder whether the drinking of the cup as a treaty rite could also have contained the curse that would have turned it into a cup of staggering and madness' (Keown et al. 1995:279).

Another suggestion has been the cup of ordeal found in Num. 5:11-31, but then a problem arises in that no one here passes unscathed through the ordeal, and the cup is not one of wormwood or poison, but of wine. A further possibility is that this was some sort of banqueting metaphor, but instead of God playing the part of the welcoming host, this was an anti-banquet of death. But such a supposition can quickly become far-fetched. It seems best to regard it as an ancient metaphor that symbolises God's dealing out to each their portion. Some have argued that the transaction may have been carried through symbolically by Jeremiah approaching a representative from these nations—perhaps one attending an ambassadors' conference such as that in 27:3. However, someone trying to approach Nebuchadnezzar or Pharaoh with a cup to drink would have done so at hazard of his life, and their representatives probably enjoyed similar security arrangements. It is best to take the language here as metaphorical, and Jeremiah's involvement through either a visionary experience or some less hazardous symbolic enactment. Usually the cup is described as coming directly from the hand of God, but the traditional implications of this metaphor are developed here at least to the extent that Jeremiah is represented as the cupbearer, a role which fits in well with him acting as the LORD's servant.

15. 'For' (*kî*) at the beginning of v. 15 links what follows back to v. 11 and adds further explanatory details about the fate of the nations mentioned there. **This is what the LORD, the God of Israel, said to me,**[18] **'Take** (masc. sing.) **from my hand this cup filled with the wine of my wrath.'**[19] Jeremiah records the message that was given to him regarding the LORD's prerogative to determine what is going to

---

18. Although 'to me' is omitted by the LXX, this seems to be a mistake in that v. 17 makes it clear that this report comes from Jeremiah himself.

19. *kôs hayyayin haḥēmâ hazzō't* is an unusual expression in that the article with *yayin*, 'wine', indicates the end of the construct chain, 'the cup of wine'. 'Wrath' is to be taken as in apposition to 'wine', that is, 'wine ⌊even⌋ this wrath'. The feminine demonstrative might agree with either 'cup' or 'wrath', but not 'wine' which is a masculine noun.

happen. **Make all the nations to whom I send you drink it.**[20]
Jeremiah is not just sent with a cup of wine; he is given the word of the
LORD. Making the nations drink it involves stating the word of the
LORD to them. It is not clear how Jeremiah carried this out, but we
need suppose no more than that he spoke these words in the Temple
while facing in the direction of the nation involved. None were to be
exempt.

16. As the prophet announces the divine sentence, it is viewed as
coming into effect. The cup does not seem to contain poison, but to
induce drunkenness, or possibly illness. **When they drink it, they will
stagger and go mad**[21] **because of the sword I will send among
them.** 'Stagger' $<\sqrt{g\bar{a}\,\dot{s}}$, 'to rise and fall noisily',[22] is used in 5:22 and
46:7 to refer to the surging of water. The REB renders it 'vomit' on the
basis of the LXX, but a different word for 'vomit' is used in v. 27 and
that possibly indicates that is not the intended meaning here. After
Jeremiah has announced their sentence, the LORD will act to bring
about the judgment that has been pronounced. The impact of what
happens to them is pictured as that of men becoming drunk and losing
control of their capacity to co-ordinate action, indeed control of their
reason. The mention of the sword eclipses the metaphor of the cup by
introducing more vividly the reality of the invasion the LORD will bring
upon them through the Babylonians. 'Am sending' (NRSV) is
preferable as a translation to 'will send'; a participle is used to indicate
that action has already been initiated.

17. Having received the LORD's command, Jeremiah reports that he
carried out the commission given to him. **So I took the cup from the
LORD's hand and made all the nations to which he sent me drink
it.** Jeremiah is not to be thought of as making a tour of various capitals,
or even as presenting a cup to ambassadors in Jerusalem. Possibly as
Jeremiah declared the LORD's judgment against each nation, he
symbolically extended a cup of wine in their direction.

18. The judgment begins with the LORD's people (Amos 3:2; Mal.
3:1-5). Judah no longer had any special status, and is not exempt from
divine punishment. **Jerusalem and the towns of Judah, its kings and
its officials, to make them a ruin and an object of horror and scorn
and cursing.** By prophesying the LORD's word Jeremiah set in train

20. 'It' ('ōtô) is masculine agreeing with 'wine'.
21. Hithpolel of hālal III, 'to pretend to be mad, behave as if mad'.
22. The form is a unique instance of a hithpoel, a minor variant of the hithpael (GKC §55b; IBHS §26.1.1c).

the course of events that the LORD had determined would fulfil his word. For the plural 'kings', see on 19:3; they and their courtiers are particularly mentioned as being responsible for the attitude displayed by the nation. The impact on the land and its leaders is such as to turn them into a source of horrified revulsion for others. For 'ruin' (*ḥorbâ*) and 'horror' (*šammâ*) see vv. 9, 11; for 'scorn' see v. 9. 'Cursing' (*qəlālâ*, 24:9) denotes the absence (or reversal) of blessing, a state of insignificance and divine disapproval, part of the curse of the broken covenant. **As they are today** presents a problem in that the description obviously refers to conditions after 605 BC, and most probably after the Babylonian capture of the city. On the other hand, since it would no longer be so applicable after the return from the Exile when Jerusalem began to be rebuilt, it is unlikely to be a post-exilic addition. Because the phrase is not found in the LXX, it is probably best to take it as added by Jeremiah in a later edition of his prophecy after the fall of Jerusalem in that what started in 605 BC was in reality one with what occurred in 586 BC. Keil's explanation of the expression as equivalent to 'as is now about to happen' (1873, 1:380) seems contrived.

19. Having begun with the family of God (cf. 1 Pet. 4:17), the focus of judgment then moves outward. The list of the foreign nations that will be subject to the LORD's judgment begins in the south and moves in a generally northward direction. There are considerable differences from the list found in the LXX, which omits 'cursing as they are today' (v. 18), 'all the kings of Uz', 'all the kings of the Philistines' (v. 20), 'of the coastlands' (v. 22), 'all the kings of Arabia' (v. 24), 'all the kings of Zimri' (v. 25; the phrase 'all the kings of' is repeated in Hebrew before the following two places), and 'after all of them, the king of Sheshach will drink it too' (v. 26). It would seem that when Jeremiah reordered the material in his prophecy he expanded the list, and brought it to a significant conclusion. All the nations mentioned in chapters 46–51 are included here with the exception of Damascus (49:23-27). **Pharaoh king of Egypt, his attendants, his officials and all his people.** Pharaoh (literally 'great house') was the title, not the name, of the Egyptian king. In connection with 'officials', that is government advisers and administrators, 'attendants'/'servants' probably refers to 'courtiers' (REB), his personal entourage. See 46:2-28 for further details regarding the judgment against Egypt.

20. **All the foreign people there**/'all the mixed peoples' (*'ereb*, people of different races, Exod. 12:38; Neh. 13:3) is an expression of uncertain reference. It may apply to non-Egyptian peoples under their control, or to foreign communities resident in the Nile valley, possibly including exiles from Judah (24:8). **All the kings of** 'the land of' **Uz** might at first seem to refer to the homeland of Job (Job 1:1). Traditionally this has been located in the east of Syria, south of Damascus (so Josephus *Ant.* 1.6.4), but that seems out of place here. Either the traditional identification is wrong or there were two areas known as Uz. Uz is associated with Edom in Lam. 4:21, and if it lay to the south of Edom towards the north of Arabia, that would fit in with the northward movement in this list. But its precise location remains speculative.

Switching to the coastal zone of the Mediterranean, mention is next made of **all the kings of** 'the land of' **the Philistines (those of Ashkelon, Gaza, Ekron, and the people left at Ashdod)**. For further details regarding the LORD's judgment on the Philistines, see 47:1-7. There is no mention of the fifth member of the Philistine pentapolis, Gath, which seems to have been destroyed by this date. It is similarly omitted in Amos 1:7; Zeph. 2:4; 2 Chron. 26:6, probably having been overthrown by Hazael (2 Kgs. 12:17). 'The people left at/remnant of Ashdod' fits in with the record preserved in Herodotus (*Hist.* 2.157) of a twenty-nine year siege of Ashdod by Psammetichus I of Egypt (663–609 BC), so that the city would have been in ruins at the time of this prophecy. It was later rebuilt. The mention of Ashkelon would then seem to date the prophecy prior to its sack by Nebuchadnezzar in November/December 604 BC.

21. Returning to the east of the Jordan valley, the list continues with **Edom, Moab and Ammon.** The third term refers to the people, the Ammonites/'sons of Ammon', rather than their land. Their territories were contiguous, to the east of the Dead Sea, and are listed from south to north. Further details of the divine judgment against them are given in 49:7-22 (Edom), 48:1-47 (Moab), and 49:1-6 (Ammon).

22. All the kings of Tyre and Sidon; the kings of the coastlands across the sea. Tyre and Sidon were the two major Phoenician cities on the coast of Lebanon. 'Kings' as previously (vv. 18, 20) are mentioned in the plural. The judgment that came on these cities is referred to in 47:4 along with the destruction of the Philistines. The 'coastlands' (the plural form is used in 2:10) refers to Phoenician settlements around the Mediterranean sea, particularly in Cyprus and Asia Minor.

23. Dedan, Tema, Buz and all who are in distant places. Dedan (49:8; Isa. 21:13-14) was a major oasis and trading centre in north-west Arabia, whose inhabitants were descended from Abraham by Keturah (Gen. 25:3). Tema too was an oasis city in north-west Arabia whose connections were with Ishmael (Gen. 25:15). Judgment against Dedan and Tema is mentioned in conjunction with the judgment on Edom in 47:7-8. Buz is mentioned in Job 32:2, 6 as Elihu's country or tribe of origin, and it may have been connected with Nahor, Abraham's brother (Gen. 22:21). Presumably it too was in the same area of the Arabian peninsula. 'All who are in distant places' seems to be a catch-all description of the remaining inhabitants of Arabia, certainly those in northern and western areas. For the NIV marginal reading, 'who clip the hair by their foreheads', see on 9:26.

24. All the kings of Arabia and all the kings of the foreign people who live in the desert.[23] This refers to the area east and south-east of the Jordan. 'Foreign people' is again 'mixed multitude' (v. 20), referring to small groups of diverse ethnic origins, each with their own leader. See 49:28-33 for judgment against some of these Arabian peoples.

25. With **all the kings of Zimri, Elam and Media**, the focus moves further north. Zimri is a location otherwise unknown. Bright suggested that it might be an error for Zimki, which in turn would be an *athbash* (cf. v. 26) for Elam (1965:161). Elam and Media are east of the Tigris, with Media the more northerly of the two. See 49:34-39 for judgment against Elam.

26. And all the kings of the north, near and far, one after the other—all the kingdoms on the face of the earth.[24] 'Near ... far' is a typical Semitic merism, a figure of speech which lists the extremes in a series to indicate that all that falls within is also included. Indeed throughout vv. 19-26 the repetition of 'all' (cf. vv. 13, 15) emphasises the comprehensiveness of the divine action.

The list then reaches its climax (omitted in the LXX). **And after all of them, the king of Sheshach will drink it too**. 'After all of them' referring to the fact that the judgment of God is going to come upon the others by means of the Babylonians. Sheshach is a cryptic reference to Babylon (51:41; cf. also 51:1). The device is known as *athbash* (*ʿatbāš*), an elementary code which wrote the consonants of a Hebrew word by reversing the letters of the alphabet (the first letter *aleph* for the last letter *tau* and vice-versa; the second letter *beth* for the

23. The REB footnote indicating that Hebrew adds 'and all the kings of the Arabs' results from pointing the second occurrence of *ʿrb* in the same way as the first, i.e. as *ʿărab* rather than *ʿereb*, 'mixed multitude', cf. v. 20.

24. The article with the construct 'kingdoms' is anomalous. GKC §127g suggests that 'the earth' is a later insertion.

penultimate letter *shin* and vice-versa; etc.). Why it should be employed here is uncertain. It may reflect an earlier stage in Jeremiah's ministry where it was imprudent to speak openly against Babylon. Certainly in the final version of the prophecy its use does not arise out of the need for secrecy, in that Babylon is openly mentioned earlier. However, it is possible that this device transformed the name Babylon into a noun which might have other meanings associated with it, such as 'sinking down' or 'humiliation', and this feature perpetuated its use. But the main point of the message is the inclusiveness of the scene of judgment, which has as its obverse the inclusiveness of the LORD's dominion: none is exempt from his scrutiny and judgment.

2. You Must Drink It! (25:27-29)

After the list of the nations to whom the cup of wine was brought vv. 27-29 resume the earlier metaphor and Jeremiah is instructed to present the message of impending judgment.

27. Then tell them, 'This is what the LORD Almighty, the God of Israel, says: "Drink, get drunk and vomit,[25] **and fall to rise no more because of the sword I will be sending among you".'** The sequence of masculine plural commands concerns the nations. They are presented as being overcome by drink and stumbling so as not being able to get up again. The mention of the sword, the military might of Babylon, again moves from metaphor to reality (v. 16). Before the power of Babylon all the nations would be helpless. 'Vomit' may be part of the picture of drunkenness, but it does also suggest disgorging of booty taken earlier.

28. But if (*kî*) **they refuse to take the cup from your hand and drink, tell them, 'This what the LORD Almighty says: You must drink it!**[26] Presumably this is a refusal to accept that the message of impending judgment is true and/or refers to them. In that case Jeremiah has no option but to repeat the message more peremptorily. The nations have no option in the matter. This might well have been accompanied by appropriate gestures in a symbolic act of presentation.

29. 'For' (*kî*) introduces the reason why they cannot escape the LORD's judgment. **See, I am beginning to bring disaster on the city that bears my name.** The stress is on 'beginning'. Something has

---

25. Various forms of verb are found. GKC §76h relates *qəyû* to a secondary stem *qāyâ*, or else the text is a slip for *qîʿû* from the regular stem *qîʿ*.

26. The infinitive absolute precedes the finite verb to reinforce the idea of obligation conveyed by the imperfect (*IBHS* §31.4g; 35.3.1h).

started, but the scale of the disaster is not yet completely evident. 'To
bring disaster' is not the usual expression (the hiphil of *bô*ᶜ) but a
stronger one, 'to do evil/disaster' (the hiphil of *rā*ᶜ*a*ᶜ). The city that
bears my name is an evident reference to Jerusalem, though the usual
phrase in Jeremiah is 'the house that bears my name' (7:10-11, 14, 30).
The phrase is more accurately rendered 'over which my name is called', and is a formula denoting ownership, and consequently also protection. What the LORD has started to do with his own city gives added
emphasis to the question: **and will you indeed go unpunished?** There
is no expressed interrogative in the Hebrew (GKC §150a). The nations
who are not in covenant relationship with the LORD have no reason to
think that they are immune from judgment because of their sin. 'For it
is time for judgment to begin with the family of God; and if it begins
with us, what will the outcome be for those who do not obey the gospel
of God?' (1 Pet. 4:17). **'You will not go unpunished, for** (*kî*) **I am
calling down a sword upon all who live on the earth,' declares the
LORD Almighty.** There are 25 occurrences in the Old Testament of
*nə*ᶜ*um*, declaration/ 'declares', with LORD Almighty (*TDOT* IX:112). It
is an expression of God's sovereign intention as king of all the earth.
He takes note of all that offends him and when he announces his purpose, there should be no doubt that he will carry it through.

3. The Storm of Judgment (25:30-38)

Verses 30-38 reinforce the previous message of divine judgment on
Judah and the nations. Though Jeremiah's message was couched as a
prophetic warning to all those involved, it presumably was particularly
addressed to Judah. Castellino (1980) persuasively analyses vv. 30-38
as consisting of (a) vv. 30-31 setting the stage. God roars thundering
on high against the nations, intent on punishment. His roar reaches the
end of the earth. (b) vv. 32-33: in v. 32 the direct quotation solemnly
and mysteriously announces the sweep of the hurricane while v. 33 is a
prophetic description of the ensuing ruin. (c) vv. 34-38: God's reproof
reaches directly the shepherds and leaders responsible for the ruin of
their flocks.

a. The Roar of the LORD (25:30-31)
30. Now prophesy (masc. sing.) **all these words against them and
say to them.** 'Now' may be temporal or logical; here it is probably the
latter. In the light of the judgment that has been pronounced Jeremiah
is to reinforce the message with a further warning to the nations. What
follows is then in poetry apart from the prose explanation of v. 33.

Although the LORD is referred to in the third person, the conclusion to
v. 31 makes clear that what precedes is divine speech.

The LORD will roar from on high. The lion imagery had been
previously used in Amos 1:2 and Joel 4:16. It indicates a fierce and
threatening message: judgment is about to be executed. Does this indicate that the lion has its prey in sight? But unlike Amos, where the
LORD threatens from Jerusalem and Zion, he now does so from 'on
high', that is, from heaven, because his voice of threatening is as much
against his own land as against the nations. **He will thunder from his
holy dwelling.** 'Dwelling' (*mā'on*) is used elsewhere to describe the
return of the land to an uninhabited state ('haunt' 9:11; 10:22) and to a
remote refuge (21:13). It is the latter idea that is emphasised here. The
divine residence in heaven is infinitely removed from the created realm
inhabited by mankind. **And roar mightily against his land**/'his
pasture' (*nāweh*), a reference to Judah (10:25). This word was used to
refer to Canaan as the place the LORD chose to dwell with his people
(Exod. 15:13) and which was given to them as their inheritance
(10:25). Now in his anger he is like a lion ready to devour it.

The remainder of the verse is difficult to translate. **He will shout
like those who tread the grapes.** 'Shout' is 'answer' or possibly 'sing
out'[27] ⌐with a⌐ shout (*hêdād*), possibly a war cry, but it occurs most
often in harvest contexts and seems rather to be a cry of well-being
(48:33; Isa. 16:9-10; *HALOT* 243). The picture here is of the time of
grape harvest. As the harvesters tread the grapes ('grapes' is not
expressed but is derived from the context) in the winepress, they tramp
their feet and cry out to mark the rhythm of their action. It may be that
the point of the comparison is the noise and vigour of those treading
grapes rather than their joyfulness. On the other hand, their cries would
not be those of misery or alarm, but of those engaging in a welcome
duty, gathering in the harvest. So there may be the implication that the
task of judgment is one that the LORD does not shrink back from, or
engage in unwillingly, so gross have the violations of his law become.
Mirroring the movement in 25:8-11, 18, the horizon then widens
beyond the LORD's own people because he will **shout against all who
live on the earth**, although possibly *'ereṣ* here is simply 'land', with
the extension to the whole earth not occurring until the next verse.

31. The tumult will resound to the ends of the earth. 'Tumult'
(*šā'ôn*) reflects the loud noise of a crowd, possibly gathered together

---

27. There is a variety of meanings for the root *'ānâ*. *'ānâ* I means 'to answer', but there may also exist a root *'ānâ* IV, 'to sing', particularly used for
antiphonal singing.

for battle (48:45; 51:55; Ps. 74:23; Isa. 13:4; 17:12, 13; Hos. 10:14; Amos 2:2). The noise of the action that the LORD takes will not be held within bounds. **For (*kî*) the LORD will bring charges against the nations.** He is entering a legal case with them (*rîb*, 2:9, 35). But it goes further than notification of a complaint against them. **'He will bring judgment on all mankind and put the wicked to the sword,' declares the LORD.** The LORD concludes the description he has been giving of his own activity by pointing to the universal nature of his action. 'Mankind'/'flesh' points to the inherent weakness of mankind before the power of God.

b. The Sweep of the Hurricane (25:32-33)
32. Another picture is presented in a second poem, which reinforces the message of the preceding one. **This is what the LORD Almighty says: 'Look! Disaster (*rā'â*) is spreading from nation to nation; a mighty storm is rising from the ends of the earth.'** 'Spreading' envisages it as 'going out' from a starting point until it affects all nations. The storm (*sa'ar*, 23:19) refers to the impact of the invading troops as they come in accordance with the divine decree.

33. Verse 33 is generally recognised as prose. In it the prophet brings out the extent of the calamity. **At that time those slain by the LORD will be everywhere—from one end of the earth to the other. They will not be mourned or gathered up or buried, but will be like refuse lying on the ground.** 'At that time'/'on that day' (in contrast to 'this day' in v. 18) gives the passage eschatological overtones. The impending scene will presage the final judgment of God. Previous descriptions of the slain had focused on the environs of Jerusalem (7:32-33; 19:11), but now the impact of the judgment is evident on all sides. There will be so many slaughtered on that day that it will be impossible to carry out the traditional mourning rites, and the corpses will be left untended where they have fallen (8:2; 9:22; 12:2; 16:4).

c. The Overthrow of the Shepherds (25:34-38)
34. Then in vv. 34-38 we have words presented, probably as Jeremiah's own, in address to the rulers of the nations (and not just those of Judah). **Weep and wail, you shepherds; roll in the dust, you leaders (*'addîr*, 14:3) of the flock.** 'Weep' (*hêlîlû*) picks up 'those slain' (*helalê*) from the previous verse. 'Wail' (<√*zā'aq*, 'to cry out') refers to shouts due to distress. There will be no exemption from the judgment. 'Shepherds' here, as previously (10:21; 22:22), refers to kings. 'Leaders' emphasises their dignity and status; the term is used of

the LORD himself in Pss. 76:5; 93:4. In a reversal of their status, they
are called upon to 'roll ⸤in dust⸥', an ellipsis of the idea expressed in
full in 6:26. Those whose rank had made them immune from many
other discomforts of life will not be able to escape the misery and
calamity that will come upon their people. **For** (*kî*) **your time to be
slaughtered has come**/'your days with respect to slaughter (<√*ṭābaḥ*,
the ordinary word for butchering an animal, 11:19) are full.' This is
sarcasm: it is usually the sheep that are slaughtered, not the shepherds.
But now there would be no more delay in bringing disaster (Lam.
4:18). There then follows a word that has caused problems over the
centuries. Some take the word to be a verb, perhaps with the meaning
'to shatter'; hence the NIV translation, **You will fall and be shattered
like fine pottery.** This has the drawback that it has to reverse the order
of the verbs, because 'be shattered and fall' seems to put things the
wrong way round, but 'fall' may indicate the state of lying fallen rather
than the action of falling down. The word is translated literally 'your
dispersions'[28] in the NKJV and NRSV, and treated as a description of
the nature of the period that has arrived. It will be a time when rulers
will be displaced from their thrones and exiled from their lands. The
REB pursues another approach: by deleting the word, and understanding the word for 'pottery' (*kiklî*) as 'rams' (*kǝʿêlê*, following LXX; so
also RSV), it renders 'you will fall like fine rams', continuing the
imagery of slaughter. However, it is doubtful if 'fine' (*ḥemdâ*, 'what is
desirable or precious') was a natural choice to describe livestock. The
REB footnote, 'Hebrew a fine instrument', makes the text seem more
obscure than it need be. *kǝlî* often refers to pottery. But here what is in
view is not an ordinary clay vessel which might possibly have
remained intact after being knocked over, but rather a delicate vase that
has fallen and now inevitably lies in pieces.

**35. The shepherds will have nowhere to flee, the leaders of the
flock no place to escape.** It is emphasised that even the leaders of the
community will be unable to devise a successful plan to get away from
the impending destruction. Literally, it is, 'flight (*mānôs*,
'place of escape, refuge', 16:19) will vanish from the shepherds'.
'Escape'/'deliverance' (<√*pālaṭ*, 'to save'; piel, 'to bring to safety')
will not be possible.

---

28. *ûtǝpôṣôtîkem*, could be understood as a regular noun formation if the
first *ô* is replaced by *û*, from *tǝpûṣâ*, 'dispersion, scattering', only found here.
It is not translated in the LXX. It may be a verbal form, possibly a mixed form
of the qal, *tāpûṣû*, and niphal, *hăpîṣôtîkem*, of *pûṣ*, 'to scatter, disperse' (GKC
§91 l; *HALOT* 1775).

36. Jeremiah then refers not just to what he has seen in the vision
granted to him, but to what he has heard. The scene had been vividly
before his senses, and he tries to communicate that to his hearers. This
was not just an exercise in effective literary artistry, but an attempt to
penetrate their defences and present an urgent spiritual warning. **Hear
the cry of the shepherds, the wailing of the leaders of the flock, for**
(*kî*) **the LORD is destroying their pasture.** 'Cry' is *ṣǝ'āqâ* (cf. 'wail'
v. 34) and 'wailing' ('howling in distress'). It is the LORD who is
acting to destroy (*šādad*, 4:13). Jeremiah often uses this word to indicate the process of judgment (6:26; 15:8), and it occurs frequently in
the Oracles against the Nations (47:4; 48:8; 48:18; 48:32; 49:28;
51:48, 55, 56). For 'pasture', see on 10:21; 23:1.

37. The imagery of the shepherds and pastures is maintained. **The
peaceful meadows/'meadows** (9:10; 23:10) of peace (*šālôm*)' **will be
laid waste because of the fierce anger of the LORD.** Where the
LORD's blessing should have been seen in the increase and well-being
of their livestock (that is, the subjects of the rulers), there will instead
be devastation. 'Will be laid waste' understands the verb to be from
dāmam III, 'to perish' (niphal 'to be devastated'). Alternatively, the
root may be *dāmam* I, 'to stand still, be silent' and refer to the silence
that results from destruction (NASB; 48:2; 49:26; 50:30; 51:6). There
are neither shepherds nor sheep in sight or within earshot, just emptiness and ruin because of the 'fierce anger' (*ḥărôn 'ap*, 4:8).

38. The section ends with an inclusion, reverting to the imagery of the
lion found in v. 30. It is not clear whether the reference here is
primarily to the LORD or to the one he will use as his instrument of
judgment. In that the section has focused on the LORD himself as exec-
uting judgment, the former seems more probable and avoids the abrupt
introduction of another character. **Like a lion he will leave his lair,**[29]
and (*kî* may be emphatic here rather than causal) **their land will
become desolate because of the sword of the oppressor and
because of the LORD's fierce anger** (v. 37). There are problems with
the text here in the phrase 'anger of the oppressor' (*ḥărôn hayyônâ*),
which is rendered 'sword of the oppressor' in the NIV and REB, based
on the parallel found in 46:16; 50:16, and a supposed confusion with
the beginning of the following line. The NKJV retains 'because of the

---

29. The REB rendering 'They flee like a young lion abandoning his lair' has
no textual support, nor any merit. It takes *kǝ* as of comparison, gives 'has left'
as the sense of *'azab* and takes a general, impersonal subject to the verb, 'like
the people have left their lair'. Others consider *kǝ* a dittography and omit it:
'the lion leaves its lair because (*kî*) the land has become desolate'.

fierceness of the Oppressor', whereas the NRSV has 'the cruel sword', and the NASB favours a conflation 'because of the fierceness of the oppressing *sword*'.[30]

---

30. The Hebrew is *mippənê ḥărôn hayyônâ*, 'because of the anger of the oppressing one (fem.)'. 'Anger' is masculine, and 'oppressing' has the article and is feminine. The usual expression is 'the oppressing sword' and this is found in some Hebrew manuscripts, the feminine being a collective. See also 46:16; 50:16 regarding the conduct of the Babylonian armies.

X. CONTROVERSY WITH FALSE PROPHETS

(26:1–29:32)

OUTLINE

A. On Trial in the Temple (26:1-24)
  1. The Temple Sermon (26:1-6)
  2. Accusations Levelled (26:7-9)
  3. The Court in Session (26:10-16)
  4. The Precedent of Micah (26:17-19)
  5. The Martyrdom of Uriah (26:20-23)
  6. The Intervention of Ahikam (26:24)
B. Zedekiah's Conspiracy (27:1-22)
  1. The LORD's Message to the Nations (27:1-11)
  2. The LORD's Message to King Zedekiah (27:12-15)
  3. The LORD's Message to the Priests and People (27:16-22)
C. Confrontation with Hananiah (28:1-17)
  1. Hananiah's Hopeful Message (28:1-4)
  2. Jeremiah's Rejection of Hananiah's Message (28:5-9)
  3. Jeremiah's Silence (28:10-11)
  4. Jeremiah's Return (28:12-17)
D. Correspondence with the Exiles (29:1-32)
  1. Jeremiah's Letter (29:1-23)
  2. Controversy with Shemaiah (29:24-32)

Chapter 25 is, as we have noted, a hinge chapter in the ordering of the material in Jeremiah. After it there are placed three major collections: chapters 26–36, which explore the ideological clashes that occurred in the years before the fall of Jerusalem, and chapters 37–45, which set out the events connected with the fall of the city, particularly as they impacted on the life of Jeremiah. There then follow the Oracles against the Nations in chapters 46–51. While there is no good reason to doubt that Jeremiah himself was the source of the material in these chapters, it is customary to suppose that others, particularly Baruch, played a significant role in preparing the record we now have.

Chapters 26 and 36 delimit this first collection, both being dated about the same time, with the former setting out the rejection of God's messenger and the latter focusing on the rejection of God's message. Throughout the collection the theme moves on from urging the community to repent in time and so avert the impending disaster. What is recorded is increasingly dominated by the thought that catastrophe is irrevocable, and so the presentation is oriented towards limiting the impact of that calamity and towards how the remanent community may cope with its aftermath. Chapters 26–29 are thematically linked in terms of the open opposition that Jeremiah had to face. During Josiah's reign opposition seems to have been furtive and not officially sponsored, but during the reigns of Jehoiakim and Zedekiah it became outspoken and virulent. The incident narrated in chapter 26 occurred about fourteen years before chapters 27–29. It was followed by the events of chapter 36, after which Jeremiah stayed out of public view during most of the remainder of Jehoiakim's reign.

Chapter 26 seems to be placed before the more detailed account of the confrontation with the peace prophets, and particularly with Hananiah (chap. 28), to give a feel for the background against which such incidents took place. When chapters 1–25 had been written up in their present form, it would seem that Baruch added the material in chapters 26–36, arranging it thematically to explore the theme of the destiny of God's people both in terms of the controversy between Jeremiah who brought the ominous, but true, message from God and the Jerusalem establishment, the priests, prophets and kings, but particularly the peace prophets who originated and promoted the optimistic, but false, message that all would inevitably be well with the city. The inclusion of the Book of Consolation in chapters 30–33 is to be seen as deliberately positioned to counter the prevailing consensus of what the future held for the people of God in a way that did not undermine the reality of their accountability before God, but also provided a vision that would sustain hope through difficult times.

A. ON TRIAL IN THE TEMPLE (26:1-24)

The address of Jeremiah that is summarised in chapter 26 is generally
identified with that recorded in greater detail in chapter 7. As with
many of Jeremiah's sermons it was proclaimed in the Temple. There
are linguistic similarities between the two records, such as 'reform
your ways and your actions' (v. 13; 7:3, 5; 18:11) and 'walk in my law'
(v. 4; 9:12). There are also many standard Jeremianic phrases in chapter 26, for instance, 'each will turn from his evil way' (v. 3), 'because
of the evil they have done' (v. 3); 'my servants the prophets, whom I
have sent to you again and again' (v. 5), 'an object of cursing among
all the nations of the earth' (v. 6). Also, when the distinctive reference
to Shiloh (v. 6; 7:12-14) is taken into account, the identity of the two
addresses seems fairly certain. Furthermore, there is the argument that
if on this occasion such a sermon aroused so critical a response, then it
is improbable that the proclamation of chapter 7 would have occurred
without a similar reaction, and it is unlikely that there were two such
incidents.

It should also be recognised that the two accounts of the sermon are
presented for different purposes. The first account in chapter 7 is set in
the context of Jeremiah's preaching, warning the community that they
must reform their behaviour or the city will be destroyed. The second
account in chapter 26 is placed at the beginning of the story of how the
destruction of the city came about. It sets out the personal danger that
had to be faced by Jeremiah, whose message sets him at odds with the
ecclesiastical leaders of Judah. Here we have a portrait of the spiritual
confusion and imperceptivity that held sway at the religious centre of
the land.

1. The Temple Sermon (26:1-6)

**1. Early in the reign of Jehoiakim son of Josiah king of Judah, this
word came from the LORD.** Surprisingly there is no statement as to
whom the word came. Whoever was writing this expected that it would
be automatically taken to be Jeremiah, an assumption that makes it all
the more plausible that even though this section begins without any
verbal link to what precedes, it was in fact written as a continuation of
previously existing material about the prophet, and not as a separate
work. The phrase 'early in the reign of' (*bərē'šît mamləkût*, 'in the
beginning of the reign of') is now generally accepted as equivalent to
the Akkadian technical term *reš šarruti*, 'accession year', that is, the
period between a king's accession to the throne and the following New

Year's Day, when reckoning of regnal years conventionally began. If that is so, then in the case of Jehoiakim the period would begin in September 609 BC when he was placed on the throne by Pharaoh Neco (2 Kgs. 23:34-35) and would last either until the following month or until the following Nisan (March/April) 608 BC, depending upon which calendar was in use (see Appendix §3). However, it is far from certain that this technical use of the phrase is found here (or in 27:1 and 28:1). If this address is identified with the one recorded in chapter 7, it is difficult to see how the malpractices that are listed there became widespread within a period as short as six months (perhaps less if those coming to the Temple were doing so in connection with the autumn festivals in the month Tishri, September/October). It may have been the case that many heathen practices continued underground during Josiah's reforms, but it is improbable that he tolerated open defiance of royal edicts regarding what modes of worship were permitted. It is therefore more probable that, with older commentators, this phrase refers generally to the early period of Jehoiakim's reign. Since there is no mention of the Babylonians and since Jehoiakim is still on good terms with Egypt (v. 22), a date late in 606 BC or early in 605 BC is likely.

2. This is what the LORD says: Stand in the courtyard of the LORD's house and speak to all the people of the towns of Judah[1] who come to worship in the house of the LORD. Jeremiah is told where to go, when to speak, and in the following verse what response is sought. The reference to the worshippers coming to the Temple probably relates to the occasion of some pilgrim festival when a large section of the population, and not just people from the capital, would gather at the Temple (cf. 11:12). There is a similar command in 7:2 with respect to the gate of the Temple, and this probably describes the same location from a different perspective, standing at the Temple gate and facing into the outer court of the Temple (19:14). Jeremiah's place for delivering his message seems to have been a customary site for prophets to speak.

Tell them everything I command; do not omit a word. This recalls the message given to Jeremiah at his call (1:7). Perhaps it was needed on this occasion because the changed circumstances under the new regime made open hostility more likely. It would be only natural

---

1. Literally, 'speak to all the towns of Judah, those coming to worship', where the reference is obviously to people from these towns. 'Coming' is a masculine plural participle (cities is feminine), which amply warrants the expansion in the NIV.

for Jeremiah to shrink back from the commission the LORD was giving him. 'Omit' ($<\sqrt{g\bar{a}ra^c}$, 'to cut out, reduce') is also used of clipping a beard in 48:37. But Jeremiah is not to 'trim' what he has been told to say to make it more attractive to his hearers. A prophet's mission was not to court personal popularity, but to act as a faithful messenger. In any event, as many texts from the ancient Near East also bear witness, it was treasonable to modify the words of the king, and that was certainly true when the king was the LORD (Deut. 4:2; 12:32). Here there was the additional consideration that those being addressed had placed themselves in great danger by their rebellious behaviour, and it would intensify their peril if they did not hear the whole message that the LORD had sent to them.

3. A private explanation is offered to Jeremiah as to why the message was being delivered. **Perhaps they will listen and each will turn from his evil way.** So far the response to the prophet's message had not been encouraging, but 'perhaps' (*'ûlay*, 36:3) still leaves a door open. Listening (*šāmaʿ*) and turning (*šûb*) are viewed as two parts of the one act of acceptance of what is said. 'Each' emphasises the need for an individual response to the LORD's message. Although the divine reaction will depend on the people as a whole repenting, this is not something that they can do collectively; the communal response is the aggregate of individual responses.

Then I will relent and not bring on them the disaster I was planning because of the evil they have done. 'Relent'/'repent' (*nāham* niphal, 4:28) relates to the conditional element in prophetic presentation. Initially their task was not to announce a doom sealed beforehand, but to point to the inevitable outcome of the people continuing on their present course of behaviour. It might be that the warnings relayed of the horrific consequences of rejection would unsettle their complacency and induce them to repent.

4. Verses 4-6 present the message Jeremiah had to deliver. If this is the same incident as that in chapter 7, then this is obviously an abbreviated form of his address. The present narrative focuses on the response to the prophet's message rather than its content. **Say to them, 'This is what the LORD says: If you do not listen to me and follow my law, which I have set before you'** implies that there has been a lack of obedience. The law comprises all the requirements of the Sinaitic covenant which had been given to the people by Moses and republished extensively by Josiah during his reign, so that Jeremiah's hearers knew what was required of them. The 'and' before 'follow my law' is not expressed in Hebrew, and similarly at the beginning of v. 5

there is no 'and'. 'If you do not listen to me' is the main thought which is further specified as 'so as to follow my law', and that in turn is further specified by, 'so as to listen to the words of my servants the prophets'. Listening to the LORD necessarily involves being prepared to listen to his authorised messengers.

5. The law was the theological and covenantal basis for the prophetic message. **And if you do not listen to the words of my servants the prophets, whom I have sent to you again and again (though you have not listened).** This is not a secondary insertion (*contra* Holladay 1989, 2:104), but a significant Jeremianic theme. What was being said to the people was no novelty, but reiterated what the LORD had often said to them. Their rejection of it was therefore all the more culpable. Even though in long-suffering the LORD had repeatedly and earnestly ('again and again'/'rising early and sending', 7:25[2]) warned them, they still continued recalcitrant, treating the message as outmoded and no longer relevant. But it was not just disembodied words that the LORD sent. He had spoken through faithful prophetic messengers, and Jeremiah is here associated with those who had previously been given a similar commission by the LORD. Even so, faithful warnings continued to go unheeded as the nation's treatment of Jeremiah and Uriah (vv. 20-23) will show.

6. The LORD then warns that if the lack of response portrayed in vv. 4-5 continues, there will be inevitable consequences. **Then I will make this house like Shiloh and[3] this[4] city an object of cursing among all the nations of the earth.** It was the example of Shiloh that seems to have aroused the hostility of the audience as it so obviously struck at the theological underpinnings of the prevailing Zion theology. Mention of the overthrow of Shiloh occurs here and in 7:12, and also in Ps. 78:60-61. Centuries before, Shiloh had not escaped destruction even though the ark had been located at a sanctuary there and Shiloh had been the centre for the worship of the LORD in the land. In the same way one of the principal points of confidence in the false religion

---

2. Cf. 25:3, though here with an extra *waw* before the first infinitive absolute. GKC §113k suggests the *waw* should be omitted (cf. also *IBHS* §35.3.2c).

3. There are two clauses in the Hebrew with the second introduced by *waw* plus a non-verb and so in apposition to the first. The NIV deals with this by not translating the second occurrence of 'I will make' (*ʿettēn*).

4. The kethibh *hazzōʿtâ* is most probably an error for the qere *hazzōʿt* (GKC §109b), though it has also been supposed it might be a colloquial form that is preserved here (*IBHS* p307, note 5).

of the people was the inviolability of the sanctuary and the holy city, but Jerusalem too was under threat of having her special privileges annulled and becoming a deserted ruin. An 'object of cursing' refers to the reaction that other people will have towards the city, treating it as a thing of contempt, and referring to it as a standard of malediction upon their enemies (7:12; 24:9), in effect saying, 'May all the curses that came on Jerusalem come upon you'.

There is a danger in all religious circles that what is traditional but non-essential supplants the essence of a living relationship with God. Jesus was later to warn of the impending destruction of the Temple that stood in Jerusalem in his day (Mark 13:2; Luke 19:44-48), and that too was misinterpreted by those who identified the form of religion with its substance (Matt. 26:61). That Jeremiah's message was principally concerned with the religious, rather than the political, outlook of the city can be clearly seen from those who united in opposition to him on this occasion.

2. Accusations Levelled (26:7-9)

7. As is often the case in prophetic records, it is the message of the LORD to the prophet that is given in full, not that of the prophet to the people, so that, like Jeremiah's original audience, we are confronted with the word of the LORD. It is taken as evident that Jeremiah fulfilled his commission, and the narrative moves directly to the response given to his proclamation. This involves the most detailed account that we have of a trial in the Old Testament, but given the emotionally intensity of the proceedings we should not necessarily assume that everything was done by the letter of the law. **The priests, the prophets and all the people heard** (<√*šāmaʿ*, cf. v. 3) **Jeremiah speak these words in the house of the LORD** indicates that Jeremiah was permitted to utter all that he had to say. Throughout his address, of which only a synopsis is given here, there must have been a growing feeling of indignation and fury among his audience. They were indeed hearing his words, but not turning from their rebellious conduct as had been hoped (v. 3). For the significance of 'all the people' see v. 8.

8. But as soon as Jeremiah had finished telling all the people everything that the LORD had commanded him to say, the priests, the prophets and all the people seized him and said, 'You must die!' The moment the prophet stopped speaking, the fury of the crowd erupted. 'Seize' (<√*tāpaś*, 'to handle' 2:8, but 'arrest' in 37:13, 14) indicates that Jeremiah was taken into custody by his audience. 'You must die!'/'You shall surely die!' is an emphatic construction with the infinitive absolute preceding the finite verb. The chant of the enraged crowd demands that the death sentence be judicially imposed (1 Sam. 14:44; 1 Kgs. 2:37, 42). In their frenzied agitation they know what they want the outcome to be before they state the charges they are lodging against Jeremiah.

The principal accusers of Jeremiah were the priests and the prophets, who considered they now had unequivocal evidence on which to base proceedings against him. The main interest of the priests and prophets was the maintenance of the cult. They might have acknowledged that there was an element of truth in some of Jeremiah's accusations against public life in Jerusalem. But they saw the way ahead not as that of radical critique, but as one of gradually influencing the ethos of the nation and certainly not offending the political authorities. They were happy with a policy of accommodation because they felt so much had already been achieved by Josiah's Temple reforms. Their response to the sermon therefore was not contrived but reflected a genuine conviction that the LORD could not desert his people because of the presence of the (recently renovated) Temple. Jeremiah's message was so obviously contrary to their views and the current consensus that it would not take arguments of great theological subtlety to establish that he was guilty of blasphemy and that his claim to speak in the name of the LORD was self-evidently presumptuous (Deut. 18:20).

The third group mentioned are 'all the people'. They had constituted Jeremiah's audience, but a problem arises with their changed role in v. 10 following, where they are associated with the princes, as opposed to the priests and prophets. It is possible to argue that a different group is in mind in the later verses. As regards the repeated phrase 'all the people' Nicholson (1970:53) characterises an attempt to delete it in v. 8b as 'hypercritical' because 'there is no difficulty in understanding the people referred to in vv. 11, 16 as having belonged to the court as distinct from those who formed the mob which assailed the prophet in the Temple.' He further claims that the elders of v. 17 along with the officials belong to the court and constitute the 'people' referred to in vv. 11 and 16. Another feature might be a technical use of the phrase. Matthews and Benjamin argue: 'The official and legal character of the trial of Jeremiah is indicated by the phrase "all the people", which does not mean that every last household in the state is present. "All the people" is a technical legal term for a quorum, which means that enough people are present for the trial to be official. Whenever the Bible notes that all the people are present, an action is official, legal and binding (Gen. 19:4). Any other assembly is illegal' (Matthews and Benjamin 1993:236).

9. The specification of their accusation against Jeremiah is interesting. **Why do you prophesy in the LORD's name that this house will be like Shiloh and this city shall be desolate and deserted?** They omit the conditional aspect of the threatening, transforming Jeremiah's message from a word of covenant warning into an absolute prophecy. The focus of their thinking was the destruction of the Temple whose inviolability was at the core of their theology. They were so incensed by Jeremiah's attack on it that they did not really hear his call for covenant obedience. They challenged Jeremiah's right to preach such a message in the name of the LORD when it was so contrary to what they considered the LORD's message to be—and no doubt the fact that he had done so in the Temple itself would have enraged them even further, particularly if it was disrupting the proceedings of a festival. The rhetorical question is not a request for information, but an indignant rebuke of Jeremiah's presumption in claiming that he spoke in the name of the LORD.

And all the people crowded around Jeremiah in the house of the LORD. 'Crowded round' (<√*qāhal*) is used for any sort of gathering, the precise connotation to be gathered from context as here. But the associated noun is employed of the congregation or assembly of Israel, and here in the Temple it is not a mere mob that is found, but an official gathering of the people, their feelings aroused and demanding that Jeremiah be tried for his life because what he had said against the Temple and the city was enough to prove that he did not speak for the LORD who had chosen Jerusalem as his sanctuary for ever (Ps. 132:14). The prophet was therefore liable to the death penalty (Exod. 22:28; Lev. 24:10-16; Deut. 18:20).

3. The Court in Session (26:10-16)

10. When the officials of Judah heard these things. The officials (*śārîm*) were royal advisers of the highest rank. 'Princes' (NKJV) is misleading in that it suggests they were members of the royal family, which they need not have been, but they were drawn from the upper classes in Jerusalem. The king's house, i.e. the palace, was not far from the Temple, and no doubt news of the near riot conditions quickly spread from the Temple to the officials who were at work close by. It need not be that all the king's officials were present or involved, but those who were decided as the king's representatives they had to act immediately. **They went up from the royal palace to the house of the LORD.** The temple was of course at the highest point on Zion, and so any movement to it was upwards. Then they **took their places at**

the entrance of the New Gate of the LORD's house[5]. On the basis of
36:10 the New Gate has traditionally been identified with the gate into
the Inner Court built by Jotham (2 Kgs. 15:35), perhaps being the same
as the Benjamin Gate (20:2). It would have offered a suitable place for
holding court with a courtyard before it. It may have been the normal
place for administering justice (38:7), or just used for convenience on
this occasion because the matter had obviously to be dealt with
summarily. There is no doubt that 'they sat' indicates that a court had
formally been convened. In general at this point in the middle of
Jehoiakim's reign the officials seem less hostile towards Jeremiah than
the religious community.

11. The priests and prophets are paired elsewhere as Jeremiah's
antagonists (4:9; 5:31; 6:13; 14:18). **Then the priests and the
prophets said to the officials and all the people** raises the problem of
the role of the people. They were not merely spectators at the trial;
their presence was needed to give validity to the proceedings as public
administration of justice. The prosecution consists of the priests and
the prophets, and the judges are the officials. The charges against
Jeremiah are ideological, arising from his teaching regarding the
Temple. Presumably what is recorded is a digest of the accusations.
This man should be sentenced to death because (*kî*, 'for') **he has
prophesied against this city.** They use a technical term ('verdict of
death', *mišpaṭ* in its sense of 'judicial decision', cf. v. 16) to call for
the imposition of the death sentence. The main thrust of their case has
political overtones: Jeremiah has spoken against the good of the city.
While the fortunes of the Temple and city were undoubtedly intertwined, the mention of the city rather than the Temple suggests that
Jeremiah's accusers deliberately focused on that aspect of the situation
that affected everyone and might more readily sway the civil leaders. It
was not, however, for seditious talk that they wanted Jeremiah
condemned, but as a false prophet whose utterance against the city was
so obviously contrary to what the LORD had declared that it made him
liable to the death penalty. They cite as evidence to prove their charge
the fact that the substance of his speech was common knowledge. **You
have heard it with your own ears**! 'You', of course, refers to the
people, rather than the officials who had been in the palace at the time.
There was no need to prove the charge since the facts were public.

---

5. 'House' is lacking here in a majority of Hebrew manuscripts, though
many do in fact include it. It is obviously implied in the expression 'the New
Gate of the LORD', and is found in many manuscripts of the LXX and in early
versions.

12. Jeremiah's defence is straightforward and bold. **Then Jeremiah said to all the officials and all the people: 'The LORD sent me to prophesy.'** He does not retract anything he has said or claim not to have said it, but the charge of prophesying presumptuously is rebutted. Jeremiah's warrant for his action was God's command. The LORD is emphatically brought forward before the verb in the Hebrew. And it was not just to events twenty years before when he had been called to the prophetic ministry that he is referring. It relates to the specific circumstances of that day: **against** ('el, 'to', in the sense of 'al, 'against') **this house and this city all the things you have heard.** Notice that Jeremiah here restores the original agenda of his message, which had been abbreviated to just the city in v. 11. He does not deny any of the matters he had spoken. As the divine spokesman, he had conveyed God's verdict on the nation. 'All the things you have heard' constitute not just the evidence in his trial, but the LORD's verdict on the nation's conduct and his challenge to them to repent. Will what they have heard provide grounds for persecuting the authorised messenger or become the basis for returning to the LORD?

13. Jeremiah did not permit his personal vulnerability to divert him from the main thrust of the proclamation he had to deliver. **Now reform your ways and your actions and obey the LORD your God.** For 'reform your ways', see on 7:3, 5: it evidently derives from the fuller form of his address. Jeremiah had called for recognition of their wrongdoing and for a sincere return in obedience to the LORD. This substantially altered the evidence before the court as to what he had said. Perhaps it also made an impression on the officials. They were men who had been trained under Josiah, and who presumably had a measure of sympathy with the aims of Josiah's reformation. They seem to have recognised the genuineness of Jeremiah's commission.

The theme of conditional repentance would have been well understood, both as it had been proclaimed by the LORD's prophets, and from the examples of Eastern diplomacy. The kings of the empires did not always come with massive armies against recalcitrant peoples, but offered first the possibility of reforming their ways. **Then the LORD will relent and not bring the disaster he has pronounced against you.** This is the public statement corresponding to the private explanation given in v. 3. What had to be settled was not the case of the priests and the prophets against Jeremiah, but the LORD's case against his rebellious people, Jeremiah's accusers and judges included! Jeremiah's message was not one of unconditional doom, but was in fact a message of hope if only those to whom it came would accept the LORD's evaluation of their situation and conduct.

14. Having set out the substance of his message as it concerned the relationship between the LORD and the people, Jeremiah then refers to the predicament he found himself in. **As for me, I am in your hands; do with me whatever you think is good and right.** He acknowledges the jurisdiction of the court, and humbly places himself in its hands. He pleads that they act according to what is 'good and right'. 'Good' (*ṭôb*) re-echoes 'reform' (<√*yāṭab* hiphil, 'make good'). As always in a trial, the judges are as much under scrutiny as to their motives and ideology as is the accused, and Jeremiah's statement implicitly reminded them of their higher accountability.

15. But there is a warning given, because Jeremiah is not acting on his own recognisance, but at the LORD's command. The prophet addresses not his accusers but the royal officials who are his judges. **Be assured** ('know' with the infinitive absolute for emphasis)**, however** (*ʿak*)**, that if you put me to death, you will bring the guilt of innocent blood on yourselves and on this city and on those who live in it.** 'Innocent blood' (2:34; 22:17) refers to undeserved death, which if judicially imposed by the representatives of the people brings guilt upon the whole community (Deut. 19:10-13; 21:8). This will occur **for** (*kî*) **in truth the LORD has sent me to you to speak all these words in your hearing.** Again Jeremiah protests the genuineness of his prophetic commission, not just in general, but also specifically relating to the message he had just delivered. The challenge that Jeremiah's accusers and judges have to meet is that of recognising truth when they hear it (John 18:37-38).

16. The outcome of the trial is then recorded as the negative of what the accusers had requested in v. 11. **Then the officials and all the people said to the priests and the prophets, 'This man should not be sentenced to death!'** That the officials in their capacity as the king's representatives should render a verdict is not surprising, but what role did 'all the people' play? Had they to ratify the verdict by popular acclaim, or was it the case that the defence Jeremiah had brought forward had so impressed them also that they showed their approval of the judgment? The verdict of acquittal was accompanied by a statement of the thinking on which it was based. 'For' (*kî*) **he has spoken to us in the name of the LORD our God.** That is, the officials and the people recognised Jeremiah's standing as a prophet of the LORD. They make no comment on his message, but grant that he has the right to speak and to be heard. As vv. 17-19 reveal, the elders of the land took a view regarding Jeremiah diametrically opposed to that of the prophets and priests. It is likely that the views of the king's officials fell somewhere between them. They did not consider it appropriate or necessary to silence the prophet. On the other hand they did not feel inclined to accept the advice that Jeremiah brought and urge any change in public policy.

4. The Precedent of Micah (26:17-19)

It is not clear at what stage in the proceedings vv. 17-19 occurred. Two views are possible. (1) Although vv. 17-19 are related after the giving of the verdict, there is much to be said for taking them as occurring during the course of the trial. What stronger case for the defence can be given than citing precedent? (2) It may, however, be that the elders speak to explain the decision and to persuade the people regarding it. 'It is uncertain whether what is here recited was spoken before the acquittal of Jeremiah or not; for the Scripture does not always exactly preserve order in narrating things. It is yet probable, that while they were still deliberating and the minds of the people were not sufficiently pacified, the elders interposed, in order to calm the multitude and soften their irritated minds' (Calvin 1850, 3:331). However, v. 16 has presented the people as in favour of the verdict when it is given, and the closing words of v. 19, 'We are about to bring a terrible disaster on ourselves!', seem out of place after the matter has been decided. So it is unlikely that the trial is presented as continuing here.

If the chapter ended at v. 16 with the verdict of acquittal, it would primarily be a record of a key incident in Jeremiah's life. But the two further sections point to the theological motivation for its inclusion. The speech for the defence is recorded after the verdict has been given because it sets out the manner in which the word of the LORD has been rejected by Judah. Nicholson (1970:54) argues that 'although Jehoiakim is not mentioned in these verses the whole force of the reference to Hezekiah is surely ... to contrast that king's humble and penitent response to the Word of Yahweh spoken by Micah with Jehoiakim's rejection of the words of Jeremiah.' Indeed, one of the puzzling silences of the chapter is Jehoiakim's role in the matter. Was he out of Jerusalem when all this took place? The next section (vv. 20-23) makes it abundantly clear where the king's sympathies lay in such affairs.

17. Some of the elders of the land stepped forward and said to the entire assembly of people. 'Assembly' comes from the same root as 'crowded around' (v. 9), and may just denote a crowd, or gathering. However, the presence of the officials did give the gathering formal status. 'Elders' literally denotes old men, but it is not their age that is being emphasised here, as if some would personally be able to recall the events of Micah's ministry a century before. The elders are rather those who held a semi-official position in communities throughout the country. It was to them that cases would be ordinarily brought for decision in the local courts (Prov. 31:23), as distinct from the royal courts in Jerusalem or a religious court. The elders presumably represented their villages on major public occasions and were in the capital for the feast at which Jeremiah spoke. Some of them (either of those present or of the total number in the land) spoke out at what was going on and reminded the assembled people (<*qāhāl*, the assembled congregation of worshippers) of what had happened in the past.

18. The elders refer to the prophet Micah who came from Moresheth, a country town twenty-five miles (40 km) to the south-west of Jerusalem. **Micah**[6] **of Moresheth prophesied**[7] **in the days of Hezekiah king of Judah.** This information is to be found in Mic. 1:1 where it is said that he prophesied a century earlier during the reigns of Jotham, Ahaz and Hezekiah so that his ministry was contemporary with the earlier part of Isaiah's. Here the elders pin the reference down more particularly to the reign of Hezekiah, presumably soon after the death of his father around March 715 BC (McFall 1991:36).

He told all the people of Judah, 'This is what the LORD Almighty says: "Zion will be ploughed like a field, Jerusalem will become a heap of rubble, the temple hill a mound overgrown with thickets".' The prophecy quoted here is from Mic. 3:12,[8] and is the only case of an attributed citation from a writing prophet within another Old Testament book. There is no good reason to doubt that the elders had in their possession a written copy of Micah's prophecy. This saying was originally addressed to the leaders of the house of Jacob and the rulers of the house of Israel (Mic. 3:9), but the elders rightly appreciated that its message was not confined to them and had been addressed to all the people of Judah (not to be identified with the technical expression 'all the people', but nonetheless being used as a

---

6. The kethibh *mykyh* reflects the fuller form of the name *mîkāyâ*, whereas the qere gives the normal short form *mîkâ*.

7. The compound expression *hāyâ nibbāʿ*, 'was prophesying'/'used to prophesy', may denote ongoing past action or it may be an Aramaic idiom equivalent to a simple past tense (*IBHS* §37.7.1).

8. The only change in the form of the quotation from that found in Micah is in the spelling of *ʿayyîm*, 'heaps of rubble', where an Aramaic form of plural, *ʿiyyîn*, is found in Mic. 3:12.

catchphrase to link the passage together). The elders also use the
prophetic attribution formula, 'This is what the LORD Almighty says',
though it is not used by Micah himself. They had no doubt that his
message came from God, and that it had been one of destruction both
for the city and for the Temple. Zion (3:14) is here in poetic parallelism with Jerusalem, referring to the city as a whole rather than just
the Temple area mentioned subsequently. 'A mound overgrown with
thickets'/'high places of a thicket' is probably ironic. High places
(7:31) were the sites of pagan worship, often with trees, and Jerusalem
and the Temple would only be fit for that once they had undergone the
LORD's judgment.

19. Though Micah's prophecy was expressed as one of unconditional
judgment, the elders argued that Hezekiah understood its true
significance and responded appropriately. **Did Hezekiah king of
Judah or anyone else in Judah put him to death?**[9] The answer
implied is 'No'. **Did not Hezekiah fear the LORD and seek his
favour?** The answer implied is 'Yes'. It is only from this passage that
we know of the influential role that Micah played in the affairs of
Judah, alongside his more illustrious contemporary Isaiah. For 'fear the
LORD' see on 5:22. 'Seek his favour' is literally 'stroke the face of the
LORD', but the expression is only found in a metaphorical sense. The
custom that lies behind this idiom is unknown; suggestions include the
ceremonies of eastern courts and pagan idol worship. In 2 Kgs.
19:14-19 Hezekiah's prayer is recorded (though without mention of
Micah), and the LORD granted deliverance from the Assyrians who
were surrounding Jerusalem. He did not bring about the doom that had
been forecast—at least not in Hezekiah's day. **And did not the LORD
relent** (<*nāḥam* niphal, v. 3)**, so that he did not bring the disaster he
pronounced against them?** That being so, the elders' third question
presses home the conclusion that should be arrived at in the present
case. The precedent of history should allow them to acquit Jeremiah.
His message was one that had been brought before, no matter what
the current theological consensus was. Ignoring his message and not
learning from the example of Hezekiah would be liable to have fearful
consequences. **We**[10] **are about to bring a terrible disaster on ourselves** (<*nepeš*, 2:34)**!** Like the prophet himself, the elders refocused

---

9. 'Ever' (NKJV) and 'actually' (NRSV) are attempts to render the infinitive
absolute *hāmēt*. Holladay (1989, 2:108) suggests that its force here is that of
representing an extreme, 'Did they go so far as to put him to death?'

10. After the series of questions, the speakers continue with a *waw*-
disjunctive.

the people's attention from the specific charge against the prophet, that he had spoken presumptuously in bringing the message he had delivered and claiming it was from the LORD, onto the content and challenge of the message. Would they respond as Hezekiah had done?

Here we see how easy it is for a community that has turned from the LORD to be forgetful of its own history and so to misinterpret the present. Our evaluation of history is not neutral but depends crucially on the frame of reference with which we approach it. History can teach lessons, but only if we are mindful of the role of the Lord of history. This is greatly aided by studying the incidents recorded for us in Scripture (1 Cor. 10:11).

5. The Martyrdom of Uriah (26:20-23)

In the previous narrative there has been one absentee and that is the king himself, Jehoiakim. Perhaps he had not been at home at the time the incident took place; or possibly he had felt it beneath his dignity to intervene in disposing of a squabble in the Temple. But when this section came to be written up, Baruch added this postscript to point out the very real danger Jeremiah was in at that time because of the attitude of the king. Unlike his pious ancestor Hezekiah, Jehoiakim had no respect for the LORD or for his prophets. To deliver a message that he disapproved of was to put one's life at stake. But through his contempt for the LORD Jehoiakim was in fact imperilling the life of the whole nation.

20. Verses 20-23 are not part of the previous incident, as indicated by the NIV's brackets. It is, however, closely related to it as 'also' (*gam*, NKJV, NASB, NJPS) signifies. **Now Uriah son of Shemaiah from Kiriath Jearim was another man who prophesied[11] in the name of the LORD; he prophesied against this city and this land as Jeremiah did.** We know nothing more about Uriah than what is told us here. Like Jeremiah (and Micah too for that matter) he did not come

---

11. The construction is again the somewhat uncommon one of the perfect of *hāyâ* followed by a participle (cf. v. 18). This, as well as 'also', emphasises the parallel with Micah. In this case the participle is the hithpael of *nābāʿ* rather than the niphal as in v. 18 and later in this verse. Lexicons are not quite sure if the difference is significant. If there is one, this passage makes it clear that the hithpael does not denote the behaviour of false prophets (though it is used of them in 14:14 and 23:13, and in a disparaging way in 29:26). The hithpael might indicate behaviour like that of a prophet, whereas the niphal would focus more on the content of the message conveyed.

from the capital itself, but from some distance out of town. Kiriath-
Jearim had been a Gibeonite city (Josh. 9:17) and was located in the
hill country of Judah probably nine miles (14 km) west of Jerusalem on
the road to Jaffa. Uriah was also authorised by the LORD to act as a
prophet and he presented the same message to the people as Jeremiah
did. The mention of 'the land', which is not the subject of Jeremiah's
Temple sermon but is mentioned extensively in earlier chapters of the
prophecy, indicates that Uriah's message reflected themes found
throughout Jeremiah's ministry. Just as the LORD had once used Micah
and Isaiah to testify to the people, so now he was using both Jeremiah
and Uriah. They were instances of how he sent prophets again and
again to the people (v. 5). However, the reaction to their message was
not repentance and prayer, but outright hostility.

**21. When King Jehoiakim and all his officers and officials heard
his words, the king sought to put him to death.** The 'officers' were
the king's highest military advisers (or an elite corps of personal
guards), just as the 'officials' (*śārîm*, v. 10) were his highest civil
advisers. The mention of Egypt shows that this incident occurred
during the early part of Jehoiakim's reign when he was a vassal of
Pharaoh. It is not clear why the officials' attitude towards Uriah was
different from that towards Jeremiah. Perhaps their private views
diverged from those of the king (as chapter 36 indicates), and on this
occasion the king was present and dictated what happened. Notice that
when the message that Uriah presented became widely known throughout the ruling classes of Judah, it was the king who sought to have him
arrested and executed (not the officials). However, the king's intention
became known (where did the leak come from?). **But Uriah heard of
it and fled in fear to Egypt.** 'Fled' (<√*bārah*, 4:29) is used to describe
secret, unobserved flight, often that of a refugee seeking safety elsewhere. If he had been under suspicion of sedition, his flight would
have increased the evidence against him. Although the route to Egypt
was a common one for those fleeing from Palestine, it did not make
much sense at this time, because early in Jehoiakim's reign Judah was
a vassal of Egypt and there were diplomatic relations between them
(2 Kgs. 23:34-35). A standard clause in such arrangements was for the
repatriation of those fleeing one domain for another. No doubt it was
this possibility of extradition that Jehoiakim resolved to invoke. This
dates the incident before Jehoiakim became a vassal to Babylon in
605 BC, and before Jeremiah's Temple Sermon if a later dating for it is
accepted (cf. v. 1).

22. King Jehoiakim, however, sent Elnathan son of Acbor men to

Egypt, along with some other men.[12] Elnathan was an official of considerable significance (36:12, 25). His father Acbor (more commonly transliterated as Achbor) is mentioned in 2 Kgs. 22:12-14 as an official of Josiah. Elnathan might even have been the man whose daughter Nehusta was Jehoiachin's mother (2 Kgs. 24:8), and so the king's father-in-law. He is listed among those who hear Baruch reading Jeremiah's scroll (36:12). So it was a very high-ranking deputation that went to Egypt to invoke the extradition clause that would no doubt have been present in Neco's treaty with Jehoiakim.

23. They brought Uriah out of Egypt and took him to King Jehoiakim, who had him struck down with a sword and his body thrown into the burial place of the common people. There is no hint that Uriah was given a trial. It is presented as the king's summary execution of justice. The prophet was not granted a customary burial in the tomb of his fathers, but was unceremoniously and contemptuously dumped in the Kidron Valley to the east of Jerusalem (2 Kgs. 23:6). 'The common people'/'sons of the people' (an idiom indicating membership of a class) are those who have no social status (17:19). Denying Uriah burial in his family tomb further dishonoured him and was a mark of Jehoiakim's ruthless and total opposition to any who dared to challenge him or his policies.

6. The Intervention of Ahikam (26:24)

In yet another supplement to the trial narrative there is a brief note as to why Jeremiah did not meet the same fate as Uriah. Jeremiah enjoyed some support in Jerusalem, especially that of the influential figure of Ahikam who acted as his patron and protector. This does not refer just to the time of the trial and its immediate aftermath (as in NLT), but to the first part of Jehoiakim's reign. Here we sense some of the tension that existed in Jerusalem at that time. There were those who did not agree with Jehoiakim's pro-Egyptian policy, and they were sufficiently strong that the king and his supporters did not interfere with them if it could be avoided.

24. During these years Jeremiah did not meet with the same fate as Uriah because of the protection of Ahikam who acted as his patron. **Furthermore** ('ak, 'however', contrasts what happened to Jeremiah with what happened to Uriah), **Ahikam son of Shaphan supported**

---

12. A further 'to Egypt' is found in the Massoretic Text, but omitted by the NIV and NRSV, presumably on stylistic grounds. The Hebrew syntax is awkward but not impossible.

Jeremiah, and so he was not handed over to the people to be put to death. Ahikam was a very influential figure from one of the leading families in royal circles in Jerusalem, six members of which are known to have been active during the reigns of the last five kings of Judah.[13] His father Shaphan had been secretary/scribe to Josiah (2 Kgs. 22:12, 14; 2 Chron. 34:20), and both he and his father had been part of the high-ranking deputation that Josiah had sent to Huldah after the discovery of the scroll in the Temple. We know of three of Shaphan's sons: Ahikam, Elasah and Gemariah. Elasah served as one of Zedekiah's messengers to Nebuchadnezzar, and also carried Jeremiah's letter to the exiles (29:3). Though Ahikam himself does not appear to have been part of Jehoiakim's cabinet, his brother Gemariah was, and Ahikam's son, Gedaliah, seems to have been a chief minister in Zedekiah's cabinet and was afterwards governor of Judah under the Babylonians (39:14; 40:5). The family as a whole was well-disposed towards Jeremiah. Their attitude probably reflects the remains of the influence of Josiah on those around him as well as their political attitude towards Egypt. Gemariah put a room at Baruch's disposal (36:10, 25) and was one of the officials who tried to prevent Jehoiakim from cutting and burning Jeremiah's scroll, and later Gedaliah wished to protect Jeremiah. It was Micaiah, son of Gemariah, who first heard Baruch reading the scroll and reported this to the officials (36:11). Ahikam with his family connections had such standing in the community that he could act as a patron to Jeremiah, against whom even the king was not prepared to proceed. He was used by the LORD to give effect to his promise to protect Jeremiah.

The idiom 'supported'/'the hand of Ahikam ... was with Jeremiah' is not confined to this particular situation, but indicates Ahikam's attitude over a period of time. 'Hand' refers to his influence and power, which he exerted on behalf of Jeremiah. The phrase used contrasts with the earlier situation in which Jeremiah acknowledged he was in the hands of the court (v. 14) and also with the reference later in the verse to 'handing over to'/'given into the hand of' the people. This reflects the practice of stoning to death which was the sentence for blasphemy (Deut. 13:6-11; 21:18-21). It would seem that once the king's treatment of Uriah had made clear where he stood with

---

13. It is possible to read the evidence differently and suggest that there were two men with the name Shaphan, one who was Josiah's secretary and another the father of Ahikam. In 2 Kgs. 22:12 Ahikam son of Shaphan is listed before Shaphan the secretary among the members of the deputation sent to Huldah, and Shaphan's father is never explicitly identified as the secretary.

reference to prophetic criticism, anyone uttering similar warnings was under threat. The verdict given in Jeremiah's favour needed the protecting hand of Ahikam to ensure that it was not ignored. The general expression here, 'the people', is different from the technical use of 'all the people' earlier (vv. 11, 12, 16).

Although this chapter makes clear the difficulties and dangers facing Jeremiah, it is not without elements of hope. The religious situation in Judah and Jerusalem was dire, but there were still influential figures in the land who paid attention to the word of the LORD and were able to intervene effectively in events. The elders of the land are portrayed positively as men with a memory for the past, a willingness to speak up for justice in the present, and the ability to press unwelcome truths on their own generation. They saw that the lessons of history were being ignored and that those who were the opinion-formers of the nation and those who wielded political power in the land had subscribed to thinking that was inimical to the covenant of the LORD. We are also reminded of figures like Uriah who were faithful to the LORD in their day, but who have now become a footnote in history. The extent to which Jeremiah was assisted by one of the influential families of Jerusalem indicates that all hope for the land could not yet be given up.

But there were also gloomy signs: the character of the king, the hostile element among the officers and officials, and the popular desire to silence anyone who spoke out against the consensus view that the peace and prosperity of Jerusalem were unconditionally guaranteed by God. The word of warning had been sent repeatedly, but the people were not prepared to listen to it.

The trial of Jeremiah continues to attract attention because of the parallels and differences between it and various court scenes in the New Testament, notably the trial of Christ himself, but also those of Stephen (Acts 6:8–8:1ª) and of Paul (Acts 16:20-24; 21:27–25:26). In each case there was a struggle between truth and the views of a dominant religious ideology.

B. ZEDEKIAH'S CONSPIRACY (27:1-22)

Chapters 27–29
These chapters are frequently identified as having originally formed a separate collection because they share a number of distinctive features.

(1) Names which incorporate Yahweh are here generally spelled with -*yâ* rather than -*yāhû* as in the rest of the book. For instance, it is only in these chapters that Jeremiah's own name appears in the short

form, *yirməyâ*, rather than *yirməyāhû* as elsewhere.

(2) The name Nebuchadnezzar is spelled in that fashion in these
chapters (except for 29:21; indeed in 29:21-32 there are a number of
names with the longer spelling mentioned above), whereas elsewhere
in the book the form Nebuchadrezzar is found (for further details see
on v. 6).

(3) The text of chapters 27–29 is much shorter in the LXX where
27:1, 7, 13, 17, 20 are omitted. However, in the LXX but not found in
the Massoretic Text are isolated words and phrases in 27:15, 16. These
do not introduce new ideas, but draw out the significance of what is
already implied in the context, e.g. by referring to 'false prophets'. On
seven of the eleven occurrences of the name Jeremiah the Massoretic
Text includes the designation 'the prophet'. This is often identified as
an expansionistic feature as compared to the text used by the translators of the LXX. Though this addition is done more frequently in
these chapters than elsewhere, it is also meaningful in this context of
disputes with false prophets.

It is probable that these chapters were originally composed not long
after the events they describe as Jeremiah continued to grapple with the
problem of false prophecy that plagued Jerusalem. Perhaps the distinctive stylistic features indicate that he employed someone other than
Baruch as his amanuensis on this occasion. When the material was
later incorporated into what is now chapters 26–36, the stylistic
differences were retained (an instance of the care with which the text
was transmitted) and possibly the additional expressions of the
Massoretic Text were added.

Historical Setting
Chapters 27–29 share the same background. Within four years of the
conquest of Jerusalem in 597 BC, the government of Judah was
attempting to form a coalition with neighbouring states to throw off
Babylonian domination. The fact that the plot was never actually
activated explains why there is no extra-biblical reference to it. It does,
however, account for Zedekiah himself (or less probably, an embassy
sent by him) going to Nebuchadnezzar to reaffirm his loyalty as the
ruler of Judah and that of his subjects (51:59). Zedekiah was only
twenty-one years old when he was placed on the throne by Nebuchadnezzar, and as well as being seen as a Babylonian appointee—which
he undoubtedly was—he had to face the complicating factor that the
previous king, his nephew, Jehoiachin, was still alive in Babylon, and
considered by at least some of the people, and probably by the
Babylonians as well, to be the legitimate ruler. Zedekiah was often in

sympathy with the prophet, but powerless to act in the face of the opposition of a strong pro-Egyptian faction among the ruling elite in Jerusalem.

Carroll (1986:523-24) describes these chapters as a 'literary creation' drawn up in the fifth century BC to suggest that Babylon was the true centre of life for the LORD's people, but subsequently modified by a Judean redactor who placed after them chapters 30–31 which significantly refocused their perspective. However, there is no need to suppose such a substantial repositioning of the text. As it stands, it clearly tells the story of what happened to Jeremiah and the issues it raises were key ones for the community in Jerusalem and for the exiles in the years immediately before the fall of the city.

Chapter 27

In this chapter there are three similar messages from the LORD: to the nations (vv. 1-11), to Zedekiah (vv. 12-15), and to the priests and people (vv. 16-22). Note the mention of 'sword, famine and pestilence' in vv. 8 and 13, the command not to listen to the prophets in vv. 9, 14 and 16, the claim that they are prophesying falsehood to you in vv. 10, 14 and 16, and the injunction that safety could be found only by serving Babylon in vv. 11, 12 and 17. Jeremiah's message from the LORD was clear, but it was largely rejected in Jerusalem and by the detainees in Babylon, thus sealing the fate of the people. The reality of the events of 597 BC could not be gainsaid, but their significance was reinterpreted. The peace prophets said that what had happened was a minor, transient disturbance, and very soon the blip would be over and the blessing of the LORD would again be obviously enjoyed by the community. Normality, on their definition, would return.

1. The LORD's Message to the Nations (27:1-11)

1. Most Hebrew manuscripts read 'in the beginning of the reign of Jehoiakim' (NKJV), which is undoubtedly a textual corruption since it contradicts the mention of Zedekiah as king in vv. 3 and 12. It is also at variance with the introduction to the following chapter which is explicitly linked back to this one with the use of the phrase 'in the same year' (28:1), but that year is identified as the fourth year of Zedekiah. As there are good reasons for accepting the accuracy of the statement in 28:1, it must be concluded that there has been an error in the transmission of the text of 27:1, presumably the repetition of the phrase 'in the beginning of the reign of ...' leading to an erroneous assimilation to the statement of 26:1.[14] **Early in the reign of Zedekiah son of Josiah king of Judah** is in fact found in three Hebrew manuscripts and the Syriac (the verse is omitted in the LXX). It is also significant that this verse shows we can no longer associate the meaning 'accession year' (cf. 26:1) with the phrase 'early in the reign', as 28:1 definitely identifies it as the fourth year (594/3 BC), and indeed repeats the phrase. The expression seems rather to distinguish the early part of Zedekiah's reign when he was still loyal to Nebuchadnezzar from the later part when he was in open rebellion. **This word came to Jeremiah from the LORD.**

2. Although the first verse spoke of Jeremiah in the third person, it is clear (vv. 2, 12, 16) that he himself now takes up the narrative of how he was told to present his message by means of acted symbolism. **This is what the LORD said to me, 'Make a yoke[15] out of straps and crossbars and put it on your neck.'** A yoke was worn by oxen when ploughing, and consisted of a suitably shaped wooden bar which was placed across the necks of a pair of oxen and from which wooden pegs hung down around the animal's necks, being secured below the neck by leather thongs or straps. The end of the plough was attached to the middle of the yoke and passed back between the animals. Another style of wooden yoke had projections at either side and was intended for human use, for instance, in carrying two roughly similar loads on either side of the body. It is unclear precisely which type Jeremiah was here instructed to make. 'A yoke' in v. 2 is an NIV supplement (shared with the REB and NRSV).[16] 'Crossbars' (*mōṭōt*; 28:10, 12, 13) may refer either to an animal yoke, which Jeremiah would have had to carry in a lop-sided fashion, or to a yoke fashioned for human use, often for a captive or slave.

Though the shape of the yoke is unclear, there is no doubt about its significance. The animal that wore the yoke was one that had been

---

14. Calvin (1850, 3:348) argued for the authenticity of the Massoretic Text on the grounds that the prophecy was revealed by God in the reign of Jehoiakim but not promulgated until the time of Zedekiah. While the argument is ingenious, the special pleading involved is contrived and unsatisfactory.

15. The NIV does not translate *ləkā*, 'for yourself' (NJPS, NRSV). Unaccountably the NKJV has the plural 'yourselves' here. Since the LXX usually does not translate this phrase, its absence here does not necessarily indicate a difference in the text. This ethical/reflexive dative indicates the involvement of the subject in the outcome of the action (*IBHS* §11.2.10d).

16. The ordinary Hebrew word for an animal yoke (*'ōl*), which would include crossbar(s) and thongs, is used in 27:8, 11, 12 and 28:2, 4, 11, 14.

domesticated and was under the control of its owner. If it was a slave with a yoke on his shoulders, his status too was evident. Consequently, 'yoke' was used as a term for domination by another party (Deut. 28:48; 1 Kgs. 22:10-11; Ezek. 7:23). Jeremiah's message therefore was that the nations had to accept the political subjugation to Nebuchadnezzar. This would involve paying tribute to him and sending conscripts to serve in his army, but would have left their countries relatively intact.

How many yokes was Jeremiah to make? On the understanding that the yoke that was employed in Palestine had only one piece of wood, the plural 'crossbars' suggests that more than one is to be made. The Hebrew text reinforces that idea in that it says 'put them' (so NKJV and NASB) in v. 2, and also 'send them' in v. 3. This gives the impression that after he had worn a yoke round his own neck, Jeremiah took it off and presented it to the envoys of the surrounding nations, as well as delivering his message to them. There is no record of how they received this unusual gift.

3. Then send word to the kings of Edom, Moab, Ammon, Tyre and Sidon through the envoys who have come[17] to Jerusalem to Zedekiah king of Judah. 'Word' is a supplement where the Hebrew text reads, 'Send them' (NKJV, NJPS, REB margin, NRSV margin, most manuscripts of LXX[18]), referring to the yokes. To think in terms of permanent embassies in foreign capitals would be anachronistic at this period. The envoys had come to Jerusalem on a particular mission, presumably to discuss the current political situation. In Egypt around this time Psammetichus II (595–589 BC) had become Pharaoh. The Babylonian Chronicles show that the years 596–594 BC were troubled ones for Nebuchadnezzar, with major internal unrest in December 595/January 594 BC (Appendix §13). Word of this seems to have reached the small states on the western fringe of the empire, and their discussions were presumably to see if they could turn the developing situation to their own advantage. Nothing seems to have come out of it, however. But we do know that Zedekiah paid a visit to Babylon in his fourth year (51:59), perhaps after Nebuchadnezzar had got to hear of what had happened and possibly to reassure the emperor of his continuing loyalty. The nations are those mentioned in 25:21-22 and

---

17. In *malʿākîm habbāʿîm* one would have expected the participle to agree with its noun in definiteness (GKC §126aa; *IBHS* §37.5b), but perhaps the article is here to be understood as a virtual relative.

18. There is one LXX manuscript with a reading which suggests it did not have the final *mem* on *wəšillaḥtām*, so that it would read simply 'send'.

the oracles to the nations (46–51), with one notable exception, that of the Philistine cities which had been completely taken over by Babylon in 603 BC.

4. Give them a message for their masters and say. Literally, 'Command them to their masters'. Perhaps the force of the idiom is best brought out as in the NASB, 'Command them *to go* to their masters' and to relate the LORD's message that has been announced to them. **This is what the LORD Almighty, the God of Israel, says: 'Tell this to your masters'.** The universal sway of the LORD is asserted and also his identification with his people. Ambassadors would have been required to report in detail on what had taken place.

5. The verse begins with an emphatic 'I', calling attention to the LORD as Creator and requiring that all reality be interpreted in the light of that fundamental fact. **With my great power and outstretched arm I made the earth and its people and the animals that are on it.** 'Power and arm' are a variation of the phrase that is often found with the Exodus in mind ('mighty hand and an outstretched arm', 32:21), where it denotes the supreme might of the sovereign LORD. Here it refers to his power in creation (32:17). While the mention of the animals is a natural expansion of the thought of the totality of God's creation and his judgment on it, it also serves to lead into the thought of the next verse, the totality of Nebuchadnezzar's dominion. But before that there is also asserted the LORD's sovereign right to dispose of what he has created as he sees fit: **I give it to anyone I please.** While the Babylonians claimed the right to dispose of the lands they had conquered, there was a prior claim to determine their destiny from the LORD who had created them. Equally it was not the political and military strategy of the kings of these nations that would determine matters, but the good pleasure of God the creator who shapes the destiny of his creation.

6. Because of the LORD's control over events, opposing Nebuchadnezzar was equivalent to opposing the LORD. Using the same verb 'give' (v. 5) now rendered 'hand ... over' in the NIV, the LORD asserts that it is his pleasure to assign to Nebuchadnezzar control of the lands mentioned in v. 3. **Now I** (again *'ānōkî*, 'I', is separately expressed for emphasis) **will hand all your countries over to my servant Nebuchadnezzar king of Babylon.** The title 'servant' (cf. 25:9) does not necessarily signify that Nebuchadnezzar truly worshipped the LORD. Rather he was one whom the sovereign Lord of all had chosen to recognise as a vassal who will carry out his purposes at this time, principally by providing an army at the disposal of the Overlord to effect his purposes. In doing so Nebuchadnezzar was not aware of how his actions were divinely shaped. But the biblical presentation of the matter is more complex than that. Nebuchadnezzar is shown as acknowledging the superiority of Daniel's God (Dan. 2:46-47; 3:28-29), and also, after an experience of personal humiliation and suffering, as one who honoured and glorified the Most High in explicit terms (Dan. 4:34-35). There is no reason to suppose that the king ceased being polytheistic in his outlook, but he was vividly confronted with the truth.

'Wild animals'/'living one(s) of the field' may indicate all animals, particularly those that are not domesticated but live in their natural habitat (*HALOT* 310). **I will make even the wild animals subject to him** goes beyond an expression of his unlimited control over the lands (cf. 28:14). It seems to pick up the yoke imagery. If even the untamed animals will be subject to him, how much more the domestic animals who bear the yoke? It is therefore wisdom to accept the yoke of his dominion.

The spelling of the name Nebuchadnezzar/Nebuchadrezzar varies. Nebuchadnezzar spelled with an 'n' is probably derived from an Aramaic version of the name, which also gave rise to the Greek spelling, Nabochodonosor. The 'n' spelling is the one that has become standard in English, but spelling Nebuchadrezzar with an 'r', which always occurs in Ezekiel and generally in Jeremiah, is probably closer to the Babylonian original, Nabū-kudurri-uṣur, which was formerly interpreted as, 'May Nabu (the Babylonian god) guard the boundary ⌊stone⌋/succession rights', but is now reckoned to mean 'May Nabu guard my offspring' (Wiseman 1985:3). Nebuchadnezzar had taken over the throne in Babylon on the death of his father Nabopolassar in 605 BC, and he ruled until 562 BC. He was the major figure in the neo-Babylonian empire which went into rapid decline after his death (see Volume 1, Introduction §3.13).

7. All nations will serve him and his son and his grandson until the time for his land[19] comes.[20] There are two thoughts in this. Firstly,

---

19. The expression *'arṣô gam-hû'* places considerable emphasis on the suffix 'his' (GKC §135f; cf. REB 'his own') to make clear that the seemingly invincible empire will itself eventually fall.

20. This verse is omitted from the LXX. Keil (1873, 1:400-1) argues that it 'was rather omitted by the LXX simply because its contents, taken literally, were not in keeping with the historical facts'. On the other hand the lack of mention of an end to Babylonian domination fits in with the more gloomy picture of the later LXX reading of vv. 16-22.

Babylonian domination was not going to pass away quickly. Views differ as to whether mention of his son and grandson involves anything more than a standard expression for a long period of time. That would have been a necessary element of the message when the false prophets were indicating that Babylon's power would soon be eclipsed.

Nebuchadnezzar was indeed succeeded by his son Amel-Marduk (Evil-Merodach, 562–560 BC), but he ruled for only two years before being murdered and succeeded by Nergal-Sharezer (Neriglissar, 560–556 BC), his brother-in-law, who was an army general. After a reign of a few months in 556, Nergal-Sharezer's son, Labasi-Marduk, was murdered and the closing years of the neo-Babylonian empire were controlled by an Aramean line in the person of Nabonidus (555–539 BC), who ruled along with his son Belshazzar. Some have suggested that Belshazzar was in fact Nebuchadnezzar's grandson, because Nebuchadnezzar's daughter Nitocris married Nabonidus. That is not definitely established, but the thrust of this passage concerns the length of Babylonian rule rather than the precise line of succession.

However, a second fact is clearly stated. Babylonian rule will be brought to an end, because the duration of the empire is limited (cf. 24:10, and 9:15), and then the conqueror will be in his turn conquered. **Then many nations and great kings will subjugate him.**[21] The human empire is not the ultimate reality. When it has played the role that the LORD has assigned it, it too will be judged for its faults and found wanting. This is not simply a general observation on the inherent weakness and inevitable eventual decline of any political structure. Is not the history of the world the graveyard of grand and seemingly impregnable empires? What is specifically asserted is that the LORD controls the flow of earthly history, both as regards his own people and as regards the conduct of the nations (Isa. 47:6).

8. Warning is then issued to those who will not concede that acceptance of the power of Babylon is divinely ordained reality. **'If, however, any nation or kingdom will not serve Nebuchadnezzar king of Babylon or bow its neck under his yoke, I will punish that nation with the sword, famine and plague,' declares the LORD, 'until I destroy it by his hand.'**[22] If they did not submit to Babylonian

---

21. The REB rendering 'mighty nations and great kings will be subject to him' is possible. Indeed it is only ruled out on the basis of the flow of thought which requires a specification of what happens when his time comes.

22. 'Destroy it' renders the infinitive construct of *tāmam* (unusually used transitively) and the plural object marker 'them' rather than 'it' (for reasons of English style).

rule, it would inevitably trigger a process of destruction, imposed by
the LORD through Nebuchadnezzar. It is only here that Jeremiah
mentions 'sword, famine and plague' (14:12) in connection with
nations other than Judah. This seems to correspond to the policy
Nebuchadnezzar actually adopted with respect to conquered nations.
They were not treated too harshly at first—as Judah saw in the events
of 597—but in the face of continuing rebellion, punishment was swift
and severe.

9. Given the reality of Babylonian power, the fantasy of those who
urge opposite courses is to be disregarded. This is the first of three
warnings about the seductive allure of false prophecy (vv. 9, 14, 16).
'As for you' (masc. pl.) **so do not listen to your prophets, your
diviners, your interpreters of dreams**[23]**, your mediums or your
sorcerers who tell you, 'You will not serve the king of Babylon.'**
The warning is addressed to the foreign kings. Jeremiah accepts the
reality of the prevailing religious customs in pagan lands where there
were many who tried to tell the future by means which were forbidden
to Israel (Deut. 18:9-11): prophets who spoke a message revealed to
them by the gods were well-known figures; diviners tried to foretell the
future using omens (cf. Ezek. 12:16 of Babylonian practice); dreams
were frequently employed as the basis for generating messages thought
to be supernaturally granted (23:23-32; Deut. 13:3). The etymology of
'mediums' is obscure, with interpreters variously associating the term
with observation of clouds, bewitching with 'the evil eye', 'eyeing' or
being aware of the times, or humming as a means of conjuring up the
dead. Though the word 'sorcerers' (<√kāšap piel, 'to practise
magic/sorcery') is not found elsewhere in Scripture (but cf. 14:15),
associated terms point to the use of spells and charms. Jeremiah does
not here present an exhaustive list, nor necessarily one with exclusive
categories. There was a variety of ways in which the message of false
hope and rebellion might be generated, but all of them were to be
ignored even in foreign lands where they represented accepted
practice.

10. These foreign predictions agreed with those of the peace prophets
in Jerusalem that Nebuchadnezzar's power was going to be short-lived.
But their message was a delusion, 'for' (kî) **they prophesy lies** (šeqer,

---

23. The Massoretic Text presents the word ḥălōmōtêkem, 'dreams', as an
item in a list of in the middle of a list of persons. Many, dropping the *taw*,
translate as if the text read ḥōləmêkem, 'your dreamers'. The REB, however,
takes it as a participle, ḥōləmôtêkem, 'women dreamers', retaining the *taw*.

14:14) **to you that**[24] **will only serve to remove you far from your
lands.** Deportation (24:10) would be the first consequence of
Babylonian victory. The rulers of the surrounding peoples were only
too willing to listen to a message that told them what they wanted to
hear, but by being encouraged in this way their conduct will lead to
disaster. This consequence will come not merely because of Nebuchadnezzar's power, but because it is what the LORD has determined. **I will
banish you and you will perish.** Not accepting the warnings given
repeatedly and refusing to submit to Nebuchadnezzar would have horrendous consequences because such defiance ran contrary to what the
LORD had determined.

11. On the other hand, there is the alternative proposal: **'But if any
nation will bow its neck under the yoke of the king of Babylon and
serve him, I will let that nation remain in its own land to till it and
to live there,' declares the LORD.** The positive message is reinforced
by wordplay between two senses of the verb ʿābad, 'to serve' and 'to
till/cultivate'. Submission to Nebuchadnezzar will permit a nation to
continue to dwell in its own land and enjoy its produce. This part of the
message is set out briefly. It was the warning of the consequences of
rebellion that addressed the immediate situation directly; the prospect
of heeding that warning seemed remote.

Jeremiah's intervention in the diplomatic conference that was taking
place in Jerusalem would not have enamoured him to Zedekiah or his
courtiers. They thought they were on the point of pulling off a diplomatic coup—and here was this bizarre figure with a message that ran
counter to what they were trying to negotiate! We do not know how
the envoys reacted. Perhaps their superstitious inclinations led them to
be more susceptible to prophetic intervention. In any event, the
conspiracy does not seem to have gone any further. Calvin rightly
argues that the divine message to these foreign kings was primarily
intended to be a warning to Zedekiah. 'It was that the king might know
that it was wholly useless for these kings to promise their assistance;
for he had to do, not with the Chaldean king, but rather with the judgment of God, which is irresistible, and which men in vain struggle
with' (1850, 3:351).

2. The LORD's Message to King Zedekiah (27:12-15)

12. Jeremiah then records that he repeated the same message to

---

24. This seems to be a clear instance of ləmaʿan signifying consequence
rather than intention (cf. *IBHS* §38.3a, b).

Zedekiah. **I gave the same message to Zedekiah king of Judah. I
said, 'Bow your neck under the yoke of the king of Babylon; serve
him and his people, and you will live.'** Bowing under the yoke
(<√*bôʿ*, hiphil 'to make to enter', that is to lower the neck to come
under the yoke) links back to the symbolism of Jeremiah's prophetic
act. 'Your necks' is plural, as are the imperative verbs, because, as
v. 13 shows, the people as well as the king are in view. 'Serve him and
his people' is a variation that does not occur above, but balances the
reference in the following verse to 'you and your people' (both
singular). 'You will live' renders an imperative form (*wiḥyû*), which
expresses the consequence of the preceding command: serving
Nebuchadnezzar will result in life for Zedekiah and his people. The
gist of this message is the same as that in vv. 8-11 to the surrounding
nations. It was national suicide to pursue a policy of plotting against
Nebuchadnezzar, and Judah was in no way different from the other
nations in this regard.

13. **Why will you and your people die by the sword, famine and
plague with which the** LORD **has threatened any nation that will
not serve the king of Babylon?** This question presents the outcome of
disobedience to the exhortation being given by the LORD. It applies to
Judah the same logic as v. 8 did to the nations.

14. Again there is warning given not to listen to alluring voices
advocating a contrary, but seemingly more attractive, course. **Do not
listen to the words of the prophets who say to you, 'You will not
serve the king of Babylon,'** for (*kî*) **they are prophesying lies** (*šeqer*,
v. 10) **to you.** These words are addressed to the king and people in the
plural. While they reflect what is said in v. 9, there is no mention of the
diviners, interpreters of dreams, mediums or sorcerers, which were
much more prevalent in other nations. Not that they were absent from
Judah, but there the problem was the peace prophets who were
prophesying in the name of the LORD. Their lies were being eagerly
grasped by a nation that refused to hear the LORD's word through
Jeremiah.

15. The verse begins with 'for' (*kî*). The deception and falsehood of
the peace prophets arose from their lack of divine commission, and
consequent lack of an authentic divine word. **'I have not sent them,'
declares the** LORD**. 'They are prophesying lies in my name.'** This
relates specifically to the situation in Judah (14:14; 23:16, 21, 25, 26,
32). **Therefore** (*ləmaʿan*, 'with the result that', cf. v. 10), **I will banish
you and you will perish, both you and the prophets who prophesy
to you.** There is added the explicit warning that those who were

making false claims and leading the people astray would not be exempt from the judgment of the LORD. Specific illustrations of this are then given in 28:15-16 in respect of Hananiah and in 29:31-32 in respect of Shemaiah. These examples should have impressed on the people the validity of Jeremiah's message.

3. The LORD's Message to the Priests and People (27:16-22)

In the final section of the chapter Jeremiah delivers a similar message to the priests and the people, warning them about the delusive nature of the message of the false prophets, and urging them to avoid rebellion against Nebuchadnezzar since it would be suicidal. As with the warning given above to Zedekiah, what Jeremiah has to say to the religious establishment does not concern them alone. As leaders in the community their conduct influenced that of the nation as a whole.[25]

16. Then I said to the priests and all these people, 'This is what the LORD says: Do not listen to the prophets who say, "Very soon now the articles from the LORD's house will be brought back from Babylon." '[26] The NIV has two translations for the phrase *hāʿām hazzeh*: 'this people' when they are being thought of collectively, as a single unit, and 'these people' when the reference is more to the various individuals who are involved in the group. It is sometimes difficult to determine which nuance is present in the Hebrew. Nebuchadnezzar had taken gold items from the Temple when he had conquered the city

---

25. The LXX text of vv. 16-22 is much briefer, omitting especially the elements of hope to give a coherent, but gloomy, view of what was about to happen. Critical opinion differs as to whether or not this is due to the abbreviating tendency of the LXX or to the expansionist bias of the Massoretic Text. There are cogent arguments for retaining the MT. For instance, Holladay (1989, 2:116) argues for the authenticity of both vv. 13 and 17 on the grounds that there is then a chiastic structure. The text of the LXX (34:16-22) may be translated as follows (retaining the NIV as much as possible to facilitate comparison):

> 16 Then I said to you [pl.] and to all this people and the priests, 'This is what the Lord says: Do not listen to the words of the prophets who are prophesying to you saying, "Look! the articles from the Lord's house will be brought back from Babylon", for they are prophesying lies to you; I did not send them. 18 If they are prophets and if they have the word of the Lord, let them meet [intercede] with me. 19 For this is what the Lord says, Even the remaining articles, 20 which the king of Babylon did not take away when he carried Jehoiachin into exile from Jerusalem 22 will go to Babylon, says the Lord.'

26. With *-â* of direction, GKC §90e; *IBHS* §10.5b.

in 597 BC (2 Kgs. 24:13; see on 52:17-23). Indeed some articles had been taken in 605 BC also (2 Chron. 36:5-7). These were items that were of importance to the priests. The interest of the prophets arises not only because of their connection with the priests, but because of the significance of these items for the Temple, and the fact that on its sanctity their whole theology was based. They therefore, not being able to deny the fact that the articles had been removed, tried to minimise its significance, by proclaiming that 'very soon' (Hananiah in 28:3 makes it 'two years') the situation would be normalised. This of course involved the assumption that the power of Babylon would be significantly weakened, if not destroyed—and it was precisely this that Jeremiah was attacking, as leading the people into entertaining false hopes that would be their downfall. 'For' (*kî*) **they are prophesying lies to you.** Again the term *šeqer* is repeated.

17. It would seem that in vv. 17-18 Jeremiah himself speaks to the people as he urges them to ignore the false prophets. **Do not listen to them**, repeating the LORD's word of v. 16. Following what has already been said in v. 12, Jeremiah also points out the course of conduct that should be adopted: **Serve the king of Babylon, and you will live.**[27] This was of course easily misunderstood as defeatism and sedition. But Jeremiah was relaying the word of the LORD. If they did not pay attention, the prospect was grim. **Why should this city become a ruin** (*ḥorbâ*, 7:34)? This rhetorical question (echoing v. 13) was not asked to elicit information but to generate a response and make a point. Being taken in by the false prophets will remove the one remaining avenue whereby the city can retain a measure of independence. Instead only devastation will then await the city, the land (7:34), the palace (22:5) and the Temple (33:10).

18. Jeremiah next focuses more closely on the claims of the false prophets. The words continue to be his own. **If they are prophets and have the word of the LORD, let them plead with the LORD Almighty that the furnishings remaining in the house of the LORD and in the palace of the king of Judah and in Jerusalem be not taken[28] to Babylon.** Jeremiah argues by taking the claims of the

---

27. As in v. 12, the second imperative 'live' is being presented as the consequence of obedience to the first imperative (GKC §110f).

28. The Hebrew *ləbiltî bōʾû* (seemingly an imperative form) has long been recognised as a difficulty. It could be that after the preceding *yodh* another *yodh* has been omitted by haplography and we should read an imperfect, *yābôʾû* (cf. GKC §152x, 72o), or else transposing the *waw* and the *aleph*, read an infinitive *bôʾ*.

prophets at face value, and urges that as they are prophets they should act as such and really make a difference to what is going to happen in the land. Since they are making such a fuss about the articles from the Temple, Jeremiah challenges them to 'intercede' (<√*pāgaʿ*, 7:16) with the LORD on behalf of the articles that remain. Surely their prayers would be able to effect something against what they claim is a transient threat. Intercession played a very significant part in Jeremiah's estimate of what being a prophet involved (7:16). Of course, this challenge is ironic. It would have involved the peace prophets accepting Jeremiah's assessment of the situation because it was based on the word of the LORD as it had been given to him. However, the false prophets read the situation quite differently. For them there was a time of recovery coming, and it was not a matter of praying to avert further disaster, but one of waiting for the inevitable downfall of Babylon. Still, Jeremiah's exhortation was appropriate because the LORD's threatened catastrophe might be averted if the people responded suitably to his warnings. Submission to Babylon would let them remain in the land without further depredations.

19-20. He substantiates the need for such intercession by citing a prophecy of the LORD. **For (*kî*) this is what the LORD Almighty says about the pillars, the Sea, the movable stands and the other furnishings that are left in this city.** The pillars were Jachin (NIV Jakin) and Boaz which Solomon had made for the Temple (1 Kgs. 7:15-22; 2 Chron. 3:15-17). 'The Sea' was a large bronze basin that was used by the priests for washing (1 Kgs. 7:23-26; 2 Chron. 4:4-5). 'The movable stands' refers to the ten bronze stands on wheels that were used as supports for the basins in which sacrifices were rinsed (1 Kgs. 7:27-37; 2 Chron. 4:6). These and other bulkier or less valuable furnishings had been left in the Temple in 597 BC: **which Nebuchadnezzar king of Babylon did not take away when he carried Jehoiachin son of Jehoiakim king of Judah into exile from Jerusalem to Babylon, along with all the nobles of Judah and Jerusalem.** 'Nobles' renders *ḥōr*, 'free man, freeborn', a term that is used to refer to an upper class in whose hands the economic and political power in Judah had become concentrated.

21-22. The introduction to the divine saying is then resumed from v. 19: **Yes (*kî*), this is what the LORD Almighty, the God of Israel, says about the things that are left in the house of the LORD and in the palace of the king of Judah and in Jerusalem.** Jeremiah now actually cites the word of the LORD that he had received. **They will be taken to Babylon and there they will remain until the day I**

come for them. This flatly contradicts the expectation of the shalom prophets, but it was what did take place in 586 BC. When Jerusalem was captured, the city was totally ransacked with many of the people deported to Babylon and much plunder removed there also, among which were the Temple furnishings (52:17). But though they were transported to Babylon as part of the booty, they would not be forgotten by the LORD. He reveals that after the devastation and trauma of the Exile, there will be a time of restoration. The furnishings will not be permitted to lie in Babylon without limit of time, for the LORD says that he will act as the sovereign Lord and come to claim his own. 'Come for' is again *pāqad*, here used in a positive sense of scrutinising and responding favourably to their situation. **Then I will bring them back and restore them to this place.** 'Bring back' is literally 'bring up' (<√*‛ālâ*; NRSV, NKJV), not only of bringing up as reminiscent of the Exodus, but also of bringing up to the Temple in sacred procession. This was fulfilled by events under Cyrus in 536 BC (Ezra 1:7-11).

C. CONFRONTATION WITH HANANIAH (28:1-17)

This incident follows on from what is recorded in chapter 27, with Jeremiah still wearing the yoke that he had put on. The focus in chapter 28, however, is on the clash between two prophets, Jeremiah and Hananiah, who both claim to be presenting the truth as prophets of the LORD. They use similar language and both engage in symbolic action, but the difference between them is in the message that they bring. Jeremiah warns of the impending fall of the city as divine judgment on its sinful rebellion, and counsels that the only way to mitigate the looming disaster is to submit to Nebuchadnezzar because he has been divinely appointed to control Judah. Hananiah, on the other hand, seems to be a typical peace prophet. He asserts that the city has already suffered all that was going to befall it, and the people should be assured that Babylonian domination will soon be divinely overthrown, the booty taken from the Temple will be returned, and their rightful king Jehoiachin will once more sit on the throne in Jerusalem. It was, he argued, a time for having faith in the LORD's commitment and promises to Jerusalem, not for giving in to the hated Babylonian oppressor.

Who was really relaying the message of the LORD? How could the people tell? Indeed, a first glance at the two protagonists might well seem to favour Hananiah as the more creditable party. He was a respectable establishment figure with the support of the most influential circles in the land, whereas Jeremiah was an outsider, an eccentric, and dressed with a yoke round his neck so that it was difficult not to question his sanity as well as his orthodoxy. It was not easy for the people to determine where the truth of the matter lay in this classic confrontation of prophet against prophet. In the end the LORD intervened directly to provide conclusive verification of Jeremiah's status and to punish the impostor Hananiah; but even then the people were not prepared to listen.

1. Hananiah's Hopeful Message (28:1-4)

1. The introductory dating presents problems: **in the fifth month of that same year, the fourth year**[29]**, early in the reign of Zedekiah king of Judah.** There are three pieces of information: (1) 'in that year' undoubtedly refers to the same time as chapter 27, if for no other reason than the yoke Jeremiah wears, but there are other links as well.[30] These words are omitted in the LXX. (2) 'In the beginning of the reign of Zedekiah, king of Judah' has caused considerable problems, not as regards the reign of Zedekiah, but over the significance of the phrase which has been taken to be a technical formula for the accession year of a king (26:1), which brings it into conflict with the third piece of information. It is quite probable that the further omission of 'in the beginning of the reign' by the LXX, so that the Greek text is simply, 'in the fourth year of Zedekiah, king of Judah, in the fifth month', is an early attempt to iron out problems over what is written. (3) Because 'in the fourth year, in the fifth month' conflicts with the second phrase, the REB changes it to 'the fifth month of the first year', but the more reasonable approach is to recognise that the phrase in (2) refers not just to the initial months/accession year of Zedekiah's reign, but is a more general formula for the first part of his reign of eleven years, which would correspond to the period when Zedekiah was still acknowledging Babylonian authority. The fourth year 594/593 BC fits in well with what is known of events in Babylon, and the internal troubles there around that time. The emphasis on the first part of his reign is probably accounted for by the need to appreciate the background to the story. The precise month in which this happened is of significance as regards the speedy fulfilment of Jeremiah's prophecy

---

29. The kethibh *bišnat* (a construct form) is supported by 46:2; 51:29, so that the qere reading *baššānâ*, which is the expected form with the article (*IBHS* §15.3.1a), is unnecessary.

30. The NKJV rendering 'and it happened in the same year' points to the fact that v. 1 begins with the *waw*-consecutive construction *wayhî*, which fits in with the idea of temporal continuity.

regarding Hananiah's death in the seventh month (v. 17), and this
seems to favour a spring calendar being used.[31]

Jeremiah's opponent in this incident is an otherwise unknown
character, **the prophet Hananiah son of Azzur, who was from
Gibeon.** Hananiah was a common name in those days (two others with
the same name are mentioned in 36:12 and 37:13), but its meaning
'The LORD has shown favour' was eminently suitable for a shalom
prophet. Gibeon was located six miles (10 km) north-west of Jerusalem
in the territory of Benjamin, and was a priestly city (Josh. 21:17),
similar to Anathoth which lay only six miles away. Before the Temple
was built, Gibeon had been a major sanctuary with the sacred tent and
the bronze altar (1 Chron. 16:39; 2 Chron. 1:3). So Hananiah probably
had a similar background and upbringing to Jeremiah—indeed he may
have been a priest. In terms of outward credentials it was going to be
difficult to distinguish between these two men. Throughout the chapter
Hananiah is given the same title, 'prophet', as Jeremiah, but the LXX
with the benefit of hindsight rendered this *pseudoprophētēs*, 'false
prophet'. While true, this rendering obscures how difficult it was for
their contemporaries to discriminate between the two prophets.

Hananiah spoke to Jeremiah, where **said to me** is an indication of
how close this narrative is to Jeremiah, though it is subsequently
related in the third person. Hananiah accosted the prophet **in the house
of the LORD in the presence of the priests and all the people.** The
initiative at this juncture was Hananiah's. His attack on Jeremiah was
public, at a time when there were a good number of people present in
the Temple, probably a Sabbath, or a new moon.

2. This is what the LORD Almighty, the God of Israel, says shows
that both prophets used the same words to introduce their declarations,
and made the same claim to be relaying a message given to them by the
LORD. Indeed, the similarity extended even to the grammatical

---

31. On the basis of a spring calendar Zedekiah's fourth year was spring
594–spring 593 BC, and the fifth month would have been July/August of 594,
with Hananiah's death occurring in the seventh month, September/October
594 BC. On the basis of an autumn calendar, Zedekiah's fourth year was
autumn 594–autumn 593 BC. Because the months were counted from the
spring regardless of when the regnal year started, the fifth month of
Zedekiah's fourth year would have been July/August 593 BC. This causes
problems with the expression found in v. 17 where, if the seventh month is
taken as that of Zedekiah's fourth year, it would normally be interpreted as
September/October 594 BC—before the confrontation with Jeremiah! The text
does not, however, explicitly say that.

expressions they employed. Hananiah too used the prophetic perfect (see Volume 1, Introduction §7.2), when he says **I will break**[32] **the yoke of the king of Babylon.** This declaration was in direct conflict with the message of Jeremiah—a message he had not only proclaimed, but was also wearing, in the form of the yoke on his neck (v. 10).

Hananiah shared the convictions of those who were sure that the LORD's Temple in Jerusalem guaranteed that he would never desert that place, and so claimed the promises of the covenant in an absolute and unequivocal form. In that they could cite similar words from earlier prophets to substantiate their assertion that they were presenting the word of the LORD (for instance, Isa. 31:4-5; 33:17-22), they seem to have been genuinely convinced that they were applying revealed truth to the circumstances of their own day. As far as they could tell there were close parallels between the events of 701 BC and what was currently happening to them. Indeed had there not been news to the effect that Babylonian regime, or rather Nebuchadnezzar, was already beginning to crumble? That certainly seems to have stimulated the meeting of the envoys with Zedekiah. So sure is Hananiah of his position—and that of those who support him—that he confronts Jeremiah not only in front of his own supporters, the priests, but in public before the people to win their support also.

3. Hananiah then becomes more specific in a way which shows that he was not merely drawing on the general import of previous revelation. **Within two years**[33] **I will bring back to this place all the articles of the LORD's house that Nebuchadnezzar king of Babylon removed from here and took to Babylon.** This picks up the theme of 27:17-22, and reinterprets it in terms of a short, rather than a long, divine timetable. It is an emotional appeal for popular support in that the removal of the objects from the Temple as booty would have affronted the people. Holy objects are liable to arouse more passion than holy living. In making the specific claim that they will be returned within two years, Hananiah seems to have been projecting his own wishful interpretation onto reports of the current turmoil in the Babylonian empire.

---

32. That *šābartî*, 'I have broken', is a prophetic perfect is clear from the use of the imperfect *'ešbōr*, 'I will break', in v. 4 when the same phrase is repeated.

33. Literally, 'in continuance of two years (a dual form), days.' The expression is repeated in v. 11, and the use of 'days' in apposition is designed to be an emphatic and delimited statement (GKC §131d): 'within the space of two full years' (NKJV).

4. Perhaps we should envisage Hananiah looking about and gauging the reaction of his audience so far, because in v. 4 he makes a very bold statement not about material objects but about people.[34] '**I will also bring back to this place Jehoiachin son of Jehoiakim king of Judah and all the other exiles of Judah who went**[35] **to Babylon,'** **declares the** LORD. This contradicts Jeremiah's prophecy recorded in 22:24-27. The outcome described would seem to imply that the power of the Babylonians would be broken not just in Judah but also more generally. Such nationalistic sentiment would engender considerable support, and would in itself arouse no official ire from the king or his courtiers—after all what were they talking to the foreign envoys about? But to envisage the return of Jehoiachin inevitably meant the removal of Zedekiah, his uncle, as king. Though Zedekiah was a Babylonian appointee, he might conceivably have reckoned that success in rebelling against Babylon would have left him in control of an independent state; but if Jehoiachin were to return, Zedekiah's position would probably be untenable. Jehoiachin was still considered as king of Judah by the Babylonians (*ANET* 308); and, more significantly, that seems to have been the prevailing sentiment in Judah also. At various sites in Judah there have been uncovered clay seals with the impression, 'belonging to Eliakim steward of Yaukin'/Jehoiachin. These are unlikely to date from his brief reign, but may point to crown estates not having been made over to Zedekiah by the Babylonians but left to be administered on Jehoiachin's behalf—hardly a vote of confidence in their appointee. Zedekiah was no more than a regent, whose position was kept deliberately insecure by the Babylonians, and both he and those around him knew it.

After prophesying the return of the king and the other exiles, Hananiah elegantly completes his prophetic word by chiastically repeating the declaration of v. 2. What Hananiah has announced will come true 'for' (*kî*) the LORD has declared, **I will break the yoke of the king of Babylon.**

---

34. The LXX text of vv. 3-4 is considerably abbreviated: 'Within two years of days I will bring back to this place the articles of the Lord's house and Jehoiachin and the exiles of Judah because I will break the yoke of the king of Babylon.'
35. A *constructio ad sensum* in which a feminine singular collective noun, *gālût*, 'exiles', is followed by a masculine plural participle, *bā'îm*, 'going/ entering'.

2. Jeremiah's Rejection of Hananiah's Message (28:5-9)

5. Although Hananiah seems not to have named Jeremiah, he was undoubtedly the target of his words, and the prophet does not shirk the conflict. **Then the prophet Jeremiah replied to the prophet Hananiah.** His words and actions on this occasion have, however, caused problems for those who view Jeremiah as one who always denounced the people and who would therefore be expected to denounce Hananiah in no uncertain terms. But Jeremiah tried to use the occasion to argue for his position. What he had said and was doing had been assailed publicly, and so he spoke **before the priests and all the people who were standing in the house of the LORD.** But when he saw that nothing would be gained because of the closed mind of Hananiah and those who supported him, he left rather than see a riot occur. It does not seem that Hananiah's falsity was immediately apparent to Jeremiah, far less to those standing around in the Temple. He was not self-evidently an impostor, and Jeremiah seems to allow for the possibility of genuine new revelation from the LORD. But because Jeremiah was sure that the LORD had spoken to him, he had grave doubts about Hananiah. He was, however, content to wait until it was revealed where the truth lay.

6. He said, 'Amen! May the LORD do so![36] May the LORD fulfil the words you have prophesied by bringing the articles of the LORD's house and all the exiles back to this place from Babylon.' There is no phrase here to suggest that Jeremiah is relaying a divine word. At this juncture Jeremiah has no new prophetic revelation to announce. But he will not yield second place to Hananiah on the matter of patriotism. With 'Amen' (cf. 9:5; 11:5) he endorses the sentiment that the land would enjoy prosperity, and that what had been taken from it would be restored. We know of Jeremiah's heartfelt desires to see Judah prosper (8:18-9:1; 14:7-9; 17:16). These words are not ironic (*contra* Jones 1992:355). Jeremiah could endorse the sentiment of the utterance insofar as it was a wish, but he recognised it as a wish incapable of fulfilment. Furthermore Jeremiah says nothing about the yoke he is wearing round his neck. He has not gone back on the message he has delivered that submission to Nebuchadnezzar was the divinely mandated way forward for Judah.

7. Nevertheless (*'ak*) marks a sharp break of thought. He does not wish his statement in v. 6 to be misunderstood. What counted was not

---

36. Here we find the full imperfect form *ya'ăśeh* in a jussive sense (GKC §75t).

what appealed to one personally, but what was in accord with the
LORD's will. In dealing with the matter of which prophet should be
listened to, Jeremiah entreats Hananiah to pay close attention. **Listen
to what I have to say in your hearing and in the hearing of all the
people.** They too should know this, because the claims of the prophets
are being presented before them and their reaction to them will decide
their destiny.

8. Jeremiah's argument regarding determining the authenticity of a
prophetic message has two themes: (1) continuity with previous
acknowledged prophetic messages; (2) the test of fulfilment of the
prophetic word. It was by these tests that it might be established who
was a true prophet. **From early times**[37] **the prophets who preceded
you and me have prophesied**[38] **war, disaster**[39] **and plagues against
many countries and great kingdoms.** Now it must not be supposed
that Jeremiah is saying that previous prophets exclusively prophesied
about doom. That misunderstanding gave rise to the actions of the
earlier critics who deleted as not genuine passages in Isaiah, Hosea,
Amos, or the earlier prophets that spoke of future prosperity. Jeremiah
is talking about the main thrust of their message. As those sent by the
LORD to recall his people to the terms of the covenant, and to threaten
other nations—no matter how extensive their empires—with disaster in
view of their sin, their message was generally one of impending
judgment and disaster (e.g. Elijah in 1 Kgs. 17:1; 21:21-24; Micaiah,
1 Kgs. 22:17; Elisha 2 Kgs. 8:1; Hosea, Hos. 2:11-12; Amos, Amos 1–
4; Micah, Mic. 3:12; Isaiah, Isa. 2–6). Jeremiah is pointing to the fact
that his proclamation was in accordance with the general tenor of the
message of those who were indubitably recognised as prophets of the
LORD, and so there was an antecedent probability in favour of his message, which reflected theirs, also being true. 'Who preceded you and
me' is a statement of temporal priority; it says nothing about the
validity of either party's claim to be a prophet.

---

37. *min-hā'ôlām.* '*ôlām* is usually translated 'eternity', but here we can see
that the basic concept is of an indefinite time into the past (or future): 'from
ancient times' (NRSV); 'of old' (NKJV).

38. The *waw*-consecutive imperfect has here almost gained independent
force (GKC §111h).

39. The NRSV and the REB have 'famine', reading with many manuscripts
rā'āb for the Massoretic *rā'â*, 'disaster'. This change is found in many Hebrew
manuscripts, presumably under the influence of the frequent triplet 'sword,
famine and pestilence' (14:12), but that is not what is found here, and the
more general 'disaster' fits better with the preceding 'war'.

9. Jeremiah then contrasts the prophets who warned of impending judgment with one who brought a message of prosperity. The contrast between the many genuine messages of warning and the single prophet of prosperity is deliberate. **But** (there is no conjunction in the Hebrew; the alternatives are starkly juxtaposed) **the prophet who prophesies**[40] **peace** (*šālôm*, 6:14) **will be recognised as one truly sent by the LORD only if his prediction come true.** Because a prophet whose message is one of unconditional prosperity does not stand in the line of acknowledged prophets, Jeremiah emphasises the condition of Deuteronomy where fulfilment is given as a test of God-inspired prophecy: 'If what a prophet proclaims in the name of the LORD does not take place or come true, that is a message the LORD has not spoken. That prophet has spoken presumptuously. Do not be afraid of him' (Deut. 18:22). Consequently this test of the prediction of peace would require the passage of two full years to authenticate such a prophet as truly sent by the LORD.

The problem was that Hananiah was applying an old message inappropriately. Circumstances had changed, and the old message of prosperity for Zion because of the LORD's presence within her could no longer be applied unthinkingly. On their own the promises of the past could not take account of the people's subsequent failure to live up to the demands of their covenantal situation. Hananiah felt that the worst had already passed in 597 BC: they still had the Temple. Half the message did not in isolation have permanent validity and application. Discernment was needed to see which application matched current circumstances.

3. Jeremiah's Silence (28:10-11)

10. In contrast to Jeremiah's response which was reasonable and reasoning, Hananiah reacts with violence. **Then**[41] **the prophet Hananiah took the yoke off the neck of the prophet Jeremiah and broke it.**[42] The symbolic action of one prophet is designed to counteract the symbolic action of the other (compare the conduct of Zedekiah with respect to Micaiah in 1 Kgs. 22:24). At this time there were divided counsels in Jerusalem about the wisdom of resisting

---

40. An alternative interpretation would be to understand these imperfects as iterative, that is, referring to repeated actions in past time, rather than as futures.

41. Note the BHS marginal annotation 'half of the scroll by verses'.

42. The suffix on *wayyišbərēhû* is masculine, agreeing with *'ōl*, 'yoke', rather than with *môṭâ*, 'crossbar' (fem.), used in the previous clause.

Babylon. By wearing the yoke Jeremiah had made an impact on the people and had encouraged those who urged caution, so rather than engage in further debate, Hananiah adopts a dramatic gesture to impress his hearers that Jeremiah's word is ineffective. It is unclear precisely what Hananiah broke because a yoke was a strong piece of wood, designed to take stress. 'Yoke' (*môṭâ*) here may well refer just to the wooden pegs that kept the yoke itself in place (so Holladay 1989, 2:120). Either way the yoke could no longer be worn round Jeremiah's neck and fell to the ground.

11. Again Hananiah claims to speak in the name of the LORD, whereas Jeremiah in this encounter had not had any direct word from the LORD and had spoken on the basis of his own understanding of what had been previously said. **And he said before all the people, 'This is what the LORD says: "In the same way will I break the yoke of Nebuchadnezzar king of Babylon off the neck of all the nations within two years".'** This statement explains the symbolism of Hananiah's action. It reiterates the language of v. 3 with the additional detail that the deliverance from Nebuchadnezzar will extend more widely than Judah. Hananiah claims that what the nations are already experiencing is the yoke of Babylonian domination, and that this will shortly be removed. This addition directly contradicted Jeremiah's prophecy found in 27:6-11. By his action and by his message Hananiah is directly and personally rejecting the LORD's word and disobeying his command regarding subjection to Nebuchadnezzar.

At this the prophet Jeremiah went on his way. It would be wrong to suppose that Jeremiah was dumbfounded at this action, or that he had doubts as to whether the LORD had indeed changed his mind and relented. This is the action of a man who on meeting with implacable opposition realises the futility of speaking further. Having made his case, Jeremiah was content to let events prove who was in reality the prophet of the LORD.

4. Jeremiah's Return (28:12-17)

12. There are different perceptions about the time lapse between vv. 11 and 12. 'Shortly' (NIV) and 'sometime' (NRSV) are translators' supplements: the text does not indicate what length of time intervened. **Shortly after the prophet Hananiah had broken the yoke off the neck of the prophet Jeremiah, the word of the LORD came to Jeremiah.** But the narrator wishes to make clear that Jeremiah was not left without guidance as to how to respond to the challenge that had been made concerning his message. Furthermore, it is evident that

Jeremiah's experience was quite unlike Hananiah's; Jeremiah had the word of the LORD directly communicated to him in the way that was unique to those who were divinely accredited as prophets.

13. So Jeremiah is put in the position of taking the initiative. **Go and tell Hananiah.** He previously had had no direct revelation relating to Hananiah, and had had to wait until the LORD made clear how the dispute was to be resolved. Though Hananiah thought breaking the yoke would invalidate the message conveyed by its symbolism, it is now made clear that the symbolism is to be developed further to reinforce the message. **This is what the LORD says: You have broken a wooden yoke**[43]**, but in its place you will get a yoke of iron.** It would seem that unwittingly Hananiah had acted out the history of the people. By rebelling they would indeed break Nebuchadnezzar's domination of them, but only for a while. It would not be lasting freedom that they would achieve, but the imposition of an even severer regime from Nebuchadnezzar. 'A yoke of iron' had ever been a symbol of a hard and unrelenting oppression (Deut. 28:48), and the iron yoke would prove unbreakable (15:12), because ultimately it was the LORD's yoke, not Nebuchadnezzar's. By his action Hananiah had sought to signify that the domination of Babylon would be at most short lived, and in encouraging such an expectation he had not only rebelled against Babylon, but also against the LORD who had made it clear that in this matter Nebuchadnezzar was carrying out the divine decree.

14. The theme is elaborated in v. 14. 'For' (*kî*) **this is what the LORD Almighty says** points to his control of all the nations. He is also **the God of Israel**, and he has decreed that Nebuchadnezzar will dominate the nations. **I will put an iron yoke on the necks of all these nations to make them serve Nebuchadnezzar king of Babylon, and they will serve him** (cf. 27:6). It was not just Judah, the covenant people, who fell within the scope of the LORD's plans for the future; the surrounding nations would also be involved. The yoke they would then wear would require them to 'serve', presumably indicating more than an acknowledgment of political superiority. Like animals yoked to the plough, they would be compelled to carry out what Nebuchadnezzar required of them. To show how completely he will be in control of affairs in these lands, the LORD adds, **I will even give him control over the wild animals** (27:6).

---

43. The NKJV 'yokes of wood' and 'yokes of iron' preserves the plural of the Hebrew (*môtôt*). *'ōl* is found in v. 14, but in v. 12 it is the singular *môtâ*. *'ōl* refers to the whole yoke, whereas *môtâ* in the plural refers to the bars of the yoke, which would have been of wood or iron.

15. The narrative is compressed and there is a switch from Jeremiah being instructed about what he is to do to the middle of his implementation of those directions. **Then the prophet Jeremiah said to the prophet Hananiah**, indicates that Jeremiah had already carried out part of his commission on this occasion. He is thus in a position to announce: **Listen, Hananiah! The LORD has not sent you, yet you have persuaded this nation to trust in lies** (*šeqer*, 13:25). This is the indictment of a personal lawsuit against Hananiah on the grounds that he is an impostor. The fact that he had not been 'sent' (23:21) established that he was a false prophet. Jeremiah now knows this infallibly because the LORD has revealed it to him. Furthermore Hananiah's prophetic ministry had entirely arisen from misconception and had been based on delusion.

16. Consequently the divine sentence of condemnation follows: **Therefore** (*lākēn*), **this is what the LORD says: 'I am about to remove you from the face of the earth.'** In this statement there is a play on the fact that Hananiah was indicted as one who had not been sent (*šālaḥ*, qal perfect, v. 15); he is therefore sentenced to be removed/sent away (piel participle of *šālaḥ*). Jones (1992:358) suggests the play extends further to include the similar phrases 'off/from upon the neck of all the nations' (v. 11) and 'from upon the face of the earth'. **This very year[44] you are going to die, because** (*kî*) **you have preached rebellion against the LORD.** The sentence of death is pronounced on him because he had broken the law regarding false prophecy (Deut. 18:20). The words 'preached/spoken rebellion' (*dibber sārâ*) recall the requirement of Deut. 13:5 (cf. also 29:32) that those who urge the worship of other gods and turn the people away from serving and holding fast to the LORD must be put to death. By their messages, peace prophets such as Hananiah had sought to lead the people of God into conduct that was at variance with the requirements of the covenant. There is no attempt to gloss over what happens when human thinking is presented as divine truth: it is 'falsehood' (v. 14) and 'rebellion'. Comparison may also be made with the deaths of Pelatiah (Ezek. 11:13) and Ananias, whose name is in fact the Greek equivalent of Hananiah, though no significance should be attributed to this (Acts 5:1-11).

17. The sentence against Hananiah was carried into effect. **In the seventh month of that same year, Hananiah the prophet died.** That

---

44. In a temporal expression such as *haššānâ*, 'this year', the article has a demonstrative force (GKC §126b; *IBHS* §13.5.2b, also §10.2.2c).

is in September/October, within two months of the original incident.[45] One might wonder why it did not happen immediately. Would that not have given even greater authentication to Jeremiah and his message? Perhaps it is a sign of graciousness allowing Hananiah time to reflect and repent. Perhaps it allowed Hananiah's death to occur in a way that showed it was from the LORD and not humanly contrived whether by Jeremiah or anyone else.

This passage conveys a solemn reminder not to confuse our own desires, no matter how pious they may seem, with what God has revealed. Jeremiah is a model of carefulness in this respect, and Hananiah a warning of where presumption can lead. No matter how sincerely held his convictions were and no matter how laudable his vision of the future (even Jeremiah could add his Amen to it!), because it ran counter to what the LORD had revealed, it was a delusion. His hopes, and those he had encouraged the people to adopt, were doomed to be frustrated because they were not based on the foundation of the whole counsel of God.

D. CORRESPONDENCE WITH THE EXILES (29:1-32)

Jeremiah's confrontation with the false prophets was not confined to those in Jerusalem. Among the deportees in Babylon there were prophets promoting the view that their exile there would be short because Nebuchadnezzar's regime would soon collapse. Adopting such an outlook would hinder the divine purpose behind the Exile, which was that in Babylon the people would come to a renewed understanding of their relationship with the LORD, uncontaminated by the false ideas that had become prevalent in the existing regime in Jerusalem. If the events of chapters 26–28 show Jeremiah was indeed a true prophet, recognised as such by the officials of Judah and having his prophecy come true, then as the people considered their future, they ought to have been prepared to listen to what he has to say. His message did have an element of hope in that he foretold that the judgment, though long, would come to an end.

Most scholarly analyses of this chapter consider that there have been substantial additions made in the post-586 situation, but, while

---

45. See the footnote to v. 1. The expression does not definitely require that regnal years are calculated on a spring basis because here the expression might simply be understood in terms of an ordinary year. There is no mention of Zedekiah's reign, though it is evidently the seventh month following immediately after the fifth month of v. 1.

acknowledging that there are awkward transitions, particularly in the second part of the chapter, there is no need to depart from the *prima facie* interpretation that here we have the record of two communications Jeremiah sent to Babylon in the period shortly after 597 BC. Indeed, the roughness of the material suggests an early date for it rather than the work of subsequent redactor(s).

1. Jeremiah's Letter (29:1-23)

1. This is the text of the letter that the prophet Jeremiah sent from Jerusalem to the surviving elders among the exiles and to the priests, the prophets and all the other people whom Nebuchadnezzar[46] carried into exile from Jerusalem to Babylon. The translation 'letter' supposes that the present text is an abstract of a letter from which the conventional epistolary formulae have been omitted. However, *sēper*, 'scroll', can be used to refer to any written document, and it is possible that this chapter contains not so much letters sent to the exiles as a prophetic tract comprising several oracles, such as would constitute the first stage in the composition of the book of Jeremiah as we now have it. The scroll itself would probably have been made of papyrus, which would have been cut to an appropriate size, and rolled to make it easier to transport.

The phrase 'the surviving elders among the exiles'/'the remainder of the elders of the exile' constitutes a problem. If it refers to those who have survived the difficulties of the journey and the deportation (the noun *yeter* is used in reference to survivors in 39:9), why should special reference be made to the elders who survived, but not to the surviving priests, prophets, and others? Many have supposed that the reference is to some kind of trouble that had occurred in Babylon. At a time of internal difficulty, some prophets (vv. 21-23) were executed by Nebuchadnezzar, and it may be that there were elders who had become involved in that. This would then fit in with a dating of this letter around Zedekiah's fourth year, perhaps at the same time as chapter 28. However, the link between these chapters is thematic rather than chronological, and it is much more likely that this letter was written soon after the events of 597 BC.

In Babylon the deportees were permitted to retain much of their

---

46. In the Hebrew text Nebuchadnezzar is spelled with an *n* here (for the spelling of the name, see the discussion at 27:6). The phrase 'whom Nebuchadnezzar carried into exile from Jerusalem to Babylon' is simply 'to Babylon for the exile' in the LXX. It also omits 'the prophet' before Jeremiah and 'surviving'. As is its policy, it renders 'prophets' as 'false prophets'.

traditional customs and structures. Ezekiel was among those deported at this time, and in his prophecy the elders are portrayed as forming the core of the exiled community (Ezek. 8:1; 20:1).

2. The specification of the time at which the letter was sent also suggests that it was not long after the capture of Jerusalem in 597 BC, and so before the events of the preceding chapter. **This was after King Jehoiachin and the queen mother, the court officials and the leaders of Judah and Jerusalem, the[47] craftsmen and the artisans had gone into exile from Jerusalem** repeats the information of 24:1 with the addition of mention of the queen mother who was Nehushta (13:18), and of 'the court officials'. 'Court-officials' translates the plural of *sārîs*, which denoted a high-ranking palace administrator. Against a non-Israelite background, and particularly in exilic and post-exilic writings, the translation 'eunuchs' is appropriate, but that was not an Israelite practice (*TWOT* #1545). The officials may designate the domestic attendants of the king, as distinct from the 'leaders' (*śārîm*) who were the civil administrators of the country, with considerable political influence, and would have included the heads of the most important families in the land. Notice the inclusion in a similar list in 2 Kgs. 24:15 (qere) of 'the leading men of the land' (*'êlê hā'āreṣ*). The craftsmen and artisans would have been of particular interest to Nebuchadnezzar in view of the ambitious building programme he had initiated in Babylonia.

3. He entrusted the letter to Elasah son of Shaphan and to Gemariah son of Hilkiah, whom Zedekiah king of Judah sent to King Nebuchadnezzar in[48] Babylon. While certainty is impossible, it is highly probable that Elasah, who is not mentioned elsewhere, is a brother of Ahikam (26:24) and also of Gemariah (36:10). The Gemariah who is mentioned here is obviously a different figure, but his genealogy indicates that he may have been a son or grandson of Hilkiah (not Jeremiah's father, 1:1), the high priest who discovered the book of the law during the reign of Josiah (2 Kgs. 22:8-10). Shaphan, Elasah's father, had also been an influential member of Josiah's court, and the whole family remained favourably inclined towards Jeremiah (cf. 26:24). Here then we see the character of some of those who had

---

47. The NIV omits the conjunction 'and' which is found before 'craftsmen'. However, it adds 'and' before 'the leaders', which in the Massoretic Text may be epexegetic of 'court officials', or else may be the start of a second group of officials (Keil 1873, 1:410).

48. The Massoretic Text reads 'to Nebuchadnezzar king of Babylon to Babylon/Babylonwards'.

been left behind by Nebuchadnezzar, presumably because they were pro-Babylonian in their stance. Indeed Gedaliah son of Ahikam son of Shaphan was to be made governor by the Babylonians after the fall of Jerusalem (chap. 40). That Jeremiah had access to such figures and was able to send his letter by diplomatic mail indicates the extent to which he was in favour at this time—at least with some of the Jerusalem court—but it is unlikely that Zedekiah knew of the existence of the letter, let alone its contents. There was regular interchange of correspondence between the various parts of the empire, as this chapter bears witness, and these men would be carrying other mail as well.

But why were they going to Babylon? If this were in Zedekiah's fourth year, then it might have been part of his efforts to assure Nebuchadnezzar of his loyalty (51:59). There would, however, have been regular official contact between the provinces and the capital of the empire, and it is quite probable that these individuals functioned as royal messengers on a number of occasions and that this delegation took place soon after Zedekiah was left in charge in Jerusalem.

The letter that follows is given in substance rather than verbatim, as the absence of the opening address customary at this period indicates. It is in two parts: vv. 4-14 focus on the problem of the duration of the Exile, while vv. 15-20, after raising the question of false prophets, digress in vv. 16-19 into discussing the prevailing situation in Jerusalem, before resuming the principal theme in v. 20.

4. The main question facing the exiles was how they could maintain a real religious relationship with the LORD in a foreign land. They no longer had access to the Temple and its sacrifices. If they were to worship the LORD in an appropriate way and live true to the covenant, then this would seem to require a speedy return to the promised land. Indeed, there would have been doubts as to whether God would be interested in them at all in their residence in a foreign land. Such concerns are met by asserting the sovereignty of God in their exile. He continues to have plans for his people, even though for the immediate future they are not the sort of plans they would have anticipated or desired. **It said: This is what the LORD Almighty, the God of Israel, says to all those I carried**[49] **into exile from Jerusalem to Babylon.** There would presumably have been considerable confusion

---

49. 'I carried' exhibits one of those rapid switches in person (here from the third person to the first), which are a common feature of Hebrew poetry and prophecy (cf. GKC §144p). However, the REB rendering is not to be dismissed, where 'To all the exiles whom I deported from Jerusalem to Babylon' is taken as the heading of the letter, rather than immediately following 'says'.

as to what to think among the exiles, particularly as so many had identified belief in the LORD with the promises of the false prophets. This in itself would give rise to a crisis of faith—had the LORD let them down and deserted his people? Could they really rely on the covenant promises? The assertion that it was God who had controlled their destiny is made to assure them that they have not been forgotten, and that they play a particular part in the divine purpose. They were where they were by divine initiative and control (24:5); they had a future. Nebuchadnezzar was merely the agent whom the LORD had used to carry out his purposes. They should accept their circumstances, because the LORD was in control of them (note also v. 7).

5. The message that follows is revolutionary in its implications for their way of thinking, and is closely linked to the vision given to Jeremiah in chapter 24. There is a series of commands with the implication that if they are heeded the exiles will be granted security and prosperity by the LORD, but it is security in exile. They were to accept that their situation was from the LORD, who had decreed not immediate restoration but a long residence in Babylon. By acting on that basis they would be able to survive. **Build houses and settle down.** 'Build' and 'plant' recall Jeremiah's call. There may well have been reluctance to take up a settled abode in a heathen land, and particularly if the shalom prophets' revised estimate of only a two year stay there was in fact accurate. Jeremiah, however, presents the LORD's counsel to prepare for a long stay in Babylon. **Plant gardens and eat what they produce.** In Babylon the majority of the exiles were allowed considerable liberty. Those who had been leaders in the revolts against Babylon were led off in chains and imprisoned (2 Kgs. 24:15; 25:7, 27; for further details of their treatment, see on 52:31), but ordinary deportees were not imprisoned or treated as slaves in inhuman conditions in a concentration camp. While the speech of the Assyrian commander in 2 Kgs. 18:31-32 was undoubtedly an exercise in propaganda, there are substantial grounds for believing it generally true (though of course avoiding the negatives of deportation). Babylonian policies tended to mirror those previously practised by the Assyrians.

No doubt, the people were told where to settle. Both biblical (Ezek. 3:15) and other evidence points to the region of the city of Nippur sixty miles south-east of Babylon, where much work was needed to restore an area devastated by war. In that connection communities of exiles from several nations would be allotted certain tasks to perform for the regime through forced labour. They would have paid taxes and provided conscripts for the army (it was only in Roman times that the

Jews received a special dispensation in that respect). At the same time they were allowed freedom to have their own communal organisation (the existence of elders) and religious leaders (priests and prophets). There does not seem to have been any conscious policy of forced assimilation. They could continue to observe the ritual laws, the Sabbath and circumcision, all of which distinctives would have helped maintain their national identity and communal solidarity. They were free to communicate with their native land—though not of course to go back there. The mention of gardens rather than fields probably indicates that they were unable to acquire extensive land-holdings, but as tenants would have been allotted plots of ground in the vicinity of their houses.

6. Marry and have sons and daughters; find wives for your sons and give your daughters in marriage, so that they too may have sons and daughters. These marriages are of course within the exilic community as part of the process of settling down in Babylonia. The three generations in exile would correspond to the three generations of Nebuchadnezzar's descendants (27:7) and would span the seventy years that had been prophesied for the captivity (25:11). 'Find wives' contrasts with the circumstances of the first-generation exiles who are commanded to 'marry' since their parents would rarely be in exile with them and able to arrange marriages for them. **Increase in number there; do not decrease** (Gen. 1:28; Deut. 26:5). The promise of a numerous offspring, so much part of the Abrahamic covenant, is being transferred to a foreign land ('there' refers to Babylon). The same phenomenon of population growth had previously occurred when Israel was enslaved in Egypt (Exod. 1:7). The imposition of the covenant curse had broken the tie between the people and the land, but if in exile they were obedient to the LORD, they would enjoy renewed blessing.

7. The instructions go further, and again in a way that turns upside down the previous thinking of the deportees. **Also, seek the peace and prosperity of the city to which I have carried you into exile.** The NIV attempts to cover the whole range of ideas involved in šālôm ('welfare', 6:14) by employing the double rendering 'peace and prosperity'. The exiles are not to be ill-disposed towards the land they are in, even though they have been forcibly taken there. This was indeed the hardest part of the divine instructions. Psalm 137 reminds us of the bitterness that affected the later deportees. But while it was legitimate to criticise and oppose the evil perpetrated by Babylon, the exiles' attitude was not to be negative with respect to the pagan land they were in. Rather they were to promote its interests in every way open to them, because ultimately it was the LORD who had brought them there. 'The city' is probably used distributively, and not just referring to Babylon. The term can also apply to the region round a city, and the idea is 'in each city to which the LORD has brought you'. They are to exhibit the same concern for it as they once had displayed towards Jerusalem (Ps. 122:6-8).

The welfare of the land was not just to be sought by secular means. Pre-eminently it was to be by prayer. **Pray to the LORD for it,**[50] **because** (*kî*) **if it prospers, you too will prosper.** They had been separated from the worship of the Temple in Jerusalem, but that did not debar them from prayer, even on behalf of their captors. Their own fortunes were inextricably linked up with what happened to Babylon. 'Surely there is more in this than a prudential, pragmatic policy for survival. It rings true to the authentic mission of the priestly people of God, to exist in order to be the vehicle of God's blessing, God's *shalôm*, for those outside, even the oppressor himself' (Wright 1983:127). This is the same outlook on living in a heathen society that is promoted by Paul. 'I urge, then, first of all, that requests, prayers, intercession and thanksgiving be made for everyone—for kings and all those in authority, that we may live peaceful and quiet lives in all godliness and holiness. This is good, and pleases God our Saviour, who wants all men to be saved and to come to a knowledge of the truth' (1 Tim. 2:1-4).

Indeed, the advice conveyed to the exiles goes further than that: obedience to the commands of the LORD will lead to the reversal of the curse of the broken covenant. Deut. 28:30-32 lists the forcible break-up of marriage, loss of home, lack of enjoyment of vineyards and absence of children as aspects of the covenant curse on disobedience. Here these aspects of the curse are being divinely lifted from the exilic community, and that functioned as a precursor of further restoration at a later time. It is possible that the features of life mandated for the exilic community also functioned as a warning not to engage in armed insurrection against Babylon. In Deut. 20:5-7, building a new home, planting a vineyard and becoming engaged to get married were listed as valid grounds for being released from military service. The commands given to the deportees are such as would lead to a community legitimately exempted from warfare.

8. There then follow four verses, each of which begins with *kî*, 'for'.

---

50. The pronominal suffix on *ba'ădāh* is feminine singular, referring back to the feminine noun 'city' and not to *šālôm*, 'peace'.

They set out two main reasons (followed in each case by a subordinate reason) as to why the exiles should heed Jeremiah's advice. Verses 8-9 are one sentence that focuses on the false expectations of the prophets who were active among the exiles; vv. 10-11 are concerned with the plans the LORD has for their future.

Yes (*kî*), this is what the LORD Almighty, the God of Israel, says: 'Do not let the prophets and diviners among you deceive you'. The 'diviners' (14:14; 27:9) seem to have been an unauthorised intrusion into the lifestyle of Judah. They may have been among those transported to Babylon, or it may have been that on arrival some adopted practices prevalent there. **Do not listen to the dreams you encourage them to have.**[51] They seem to have gone looking for omens about the future. Is this an indication of their loss of confidence in the LORD, or the continuation of what they had been doing in Jerusalem anyhow? It is certainly a sign of a disoriented community trying to adjust to their changed circumstances.

9. The focus is on the false prophets who were saying the captivity would soon be over, and that the people should therefore not settle down. Such prophets were unauthorised and not to be listened to 'for' (*kî*) **'they are prophesying lies to you in my name. I have not sent them,' declares the LORD** (cf. 27:15). The people were being warned that the optimism promoted by the false prophets had no divine warrant.

10. Jeremiah then brings forward another saying of the LORD which presents a positive view of the future. In this way those who were in exile should be motivated and encouraged because there was a goal in view and what was happening to them was not pointless. 'For' (*kî*) shows that there is a divine logic behind the events that were to take place. **This is what the LORD says: 'When (*kî*) seventy years are completed[52] for Babylon.'** This refers back to the promise of 25:11-12. There will come a time when the LORD's righteous anger

---

51. 'The dreams' is 'your dreams'. The hiphil participle *maḥləmîm* (for its form cf. GKC §53o) does not occur elsewhere, but the sense of 'cause to have a dream' may be easily associated with it (cf. NRSV footnote). Alternatively the hiphil may be used simply in the same sense as the qal, 'to dream': 'your dreams which you dream', that is pointing to the interpretation of them given by the false prophets. 'Which they dream' (NASB, cf. NRSV) comes from the LXX which read *hēm ḥōləmîm* for *'attem maḥləmîm*. 'The women whom you set to dream dreams' (REB) reflects the change noted at 27:9.

52. *ləpî məlō't* 'according to the filling of ...', 'in keeping with ...', 'only after ...'.

against his people will have run its course and its purpose will be accomplished.

At that time they will be aware of their divine Overlord scrutinising their situation and acting to bring it into alignment with what he desires. **I will come** (<√*pāqad*, 'to visit', used in a good sense, cf. 15:15) **to you and fulfil my gracious promise to bring you back to this place,** referring to Jerusalem from where Jeremiah was sending the letter. Even though it seems like a long time, the outcome will be for good (27:22). 'Fulfil' (the hiphil of *qûm*) is used elsewhere to refer to making good the terms of the covenant (Gen. 6:18; 17:7, 19; Exod. 6:4). 'My gracious promise'/'my good word' (cf. 24:6, with which this passage is closely linked) refers to the pledge that the covenant king has committed himself to as regards the benefits he will bestow on his people. There is not, however, any promise for the period immediately ahead. The divine determination regarding Jerusalem has still to be executed fully, and the exiles already in Babylon will be joined by many more before the prophesied reversal of their fortunes will occur.

11. The way in which their circumstances will change, and the time scale on which such change will arise are divinely determined and reliable. **'For** (*kî*) **I know the plans I have for you,' declares the LORD, 'plans to prosper you and not to harm you, plans to give you hope and a future.'**[53] The LORD declares that he has certain ends in view and invites them to trust him. The 'I' in 'I know' is emphatic; 'I alone' (REB) or 'surely I' (NRSV) bring this out. 'Plans to prosper you'/ 'plans of *šālôm*' (6:14) points beyond the well-being described in v. 7 to the total blessing provided by the LORD. 'Hope and a future' reverses the order of the Hebrew, 'a future and hope', where 'future' (*'aḥărît*) refers to what is metaphorically behind one, and therefore unseen and unknown. Viewing the future in this way is the reverse of the English idiom. The two words probably convey one thought, a hopeful future (31:17), or the future you hope for. It is not something that will merely be a projection of human desires, but something divinely determined.

This is the essence of the divine message for those in exile. A shaft of light pierces the gloom of their present situation when the LORD says he has plans for their future. But realisation of these plans was contingent upon their attitude. They were called to exercise faith

---

53. The LXX text of vv. 11-14 is much briefer: 'I will plan for you a plan of peace, and not evil ⌐things⌐, to give these ⌐things⌐ to you. Pray to me, and I will answer you. Seek me and you will find me, because you will seek me with your whole heart, and I will reveal myself to you.'

without the accompaniments of Temple, sacrifice and sacred city, which the people had previously so identified with true religion that they had lost sight of the need to trust simply in God. He would deliver them, but on his time scale and not the one that they considered to be appropriate. The passing of the years would tend to encourage among them a right disposition towards the LORD, one of obediently waiting on his will, as opposed to the automatic claim they thought they had on his blessing.

12. Translations of v. 12 vary because it is uncertain how it is connected to v. 11. **Then you will call upon me** makes it seem like something that will occur after the hopeful future has arrived. **And come and pray to me, and I will listen to you.** What does 'come' imply—to the Temple, back to the land? Perhaps this is to be understood as a series of contingent futures: 'If you will call to me and come and pray to me, then I will listen to you'. This would indicate that in the Exile the people were to come in repentance before God and develop a faith relationship with him, which would be in accordance with the teaching of Moses as to what would happen after the disobedient Israelites had been scattered among the nations: 'When you are in distress and all these things have happened to you, then in later days you will return to the LORD your God and obey him. For the LORD your God is a merciful God; he will not abandon or destroy you or forget the covenant with your forefathers, which he confirmed to them by oath' (Deut. 4:30-31; cf. also Deut. 30:1-4). The future of the repentant nation sprang not only from the intrinsic compassion of God, but was also derived from his irrevocable covenant commitment. Though Israel had abandoned him, he had not abandoned them.

13. You will seek ($<\sqrt{b\bar{a}qa\check{s}}$, piel) **me and find me when** ($k\hat{\imath}$) **you seek** ($<\sqrt{d\bar{a}ra\check{s}}$) **me with all your heart.** *bāqaš* (piel) and *dāraš* (qal) are synonyms which are often used in combination to heighten the thought of attempting to communicate with God and to know his will. When this is done with genuine whole-hearted repentance (cf. 24:7), then the LORD will make himself known to those who approach him (2 Chron. 15:4, 15). The exiles are being informed that the restored status anticipated for them will be conditioned upon a genuine spiritual response from them, and it is this that they are expected to cultivate in their condition of captivity. The wording of the saying about seeking and finding the LORD follows closely that of Deut. 4:29: 'But if from there [their anticipated dispersion among the nations] you seek (*bāqaš* piel) the LORD your God, you will find him if you look for (*dāraš*) him with all your heart and with all your soul.' The people are being invited

to explore the divine provision already recorded as relevant to their
situation. As those who were experiencing the impact of the curse of
the broken covenant, they are assured that if they respond with a total
and exclusive commitment to the LORD, then he will be accessible to
them even in Babylon, and they will enjoy his favour.

**14. 'And I will be found[54] by you,' declares the LORD, 'and will
bring you back from captivity'.[55]** This makes clear the sequence
involved. Their seeking will precede their return. Those who come
back will already have approached the LORD in sincerity, and he can be
completely relied on to help them in time of crisis (Pss. 22:20; 27:9;
40:14; 63:8). The phrase 'bring back your captivity' (30:3) may also
mean 'restore your fortunes' (as in NIV footnote) without any
reference to an exile, and this seems to be its more basic meaning. Of
course, such a restoration of fortunes for those in exile is inevitably
connected with return to their native land.

**'I will gather you from all the nations and places where I have
banished you,' declares the LORD, 'and will bring you back to the
place from which I carried you into exile.'** Here there are two further
terms frequently used to describe the restoration the LORD will provide
for his people. It is a gathering ($<\sqrt{qābaṣ}$) from the many places to
which they had been dispersed; it is also a being brought back ($<\sqrt{šûb}$
hiphil). The LORD who acted in judgment against his people is the one
who will also effect their restoration. The thought reflects that of Deut.
30:4, 'Even if you have been banished to the most distant land under
the heavens, from there the LORD your God will gather you and bring
you back.' He is the one who matches his action to the spiritual
response of his people.

15. Many have argued that v. 15 is misplaced in this context, the
connection being between it and v. 21. But sense can be made of what
is said as it stands. The verse deals with the problem of the reaction of
the exiles to Jeremiah's message. It may be hypothetical as in NIV,
'You may say', or it may relate to what was known of their attitude,

---

54. Possibly *nimṣēʾtî* is a niphal tolerativum, 'I will let myself be found by
you' (*IBHS* §23.4f). Cf. also LXX, 'I will show myself'. The LXX omits the
rest of the verse.

55. The kethibh *šəbîtəkem* implies that the noun is derived from the root
šābâ, 'to take captive', but this is not now so generally favoured. The spelling
in the qere, *šəbûtəkem*, is associated with the root *šûb*, 'to come back'. In the
latter case the noun is a cognate accusative after the hiphil of the verb: 'I will
bring back your being brought back' and has the wider sense of restoring the
fortunes of someone as in Job 42:10 (*TWOT* #2311d; *NIDOTTE* 8740).

'You have said' (NRSV). 'For' (*kî*) **you may say, 'The LORD has raised up prophets for us in Babylon'** uses the language of Deut. 18:15, 18 ('raise up', the hiphil of *qûm* in connection with prophets) to show that the people were taking the prophets active among them as being truly accredited by God. There may be an element of surprise that the LORD's word should have extended, literally, 'to Babylon', but there is no doubt that the people were accepting their optimistic message, even in the face of the Exile of 597 BC, and were expecting a speedy return to Jerusalem. The converse of this is, of course, that they were rejecting what prophets like Jeremiah and Ezekiel had to say.

16. In opposition to them and their message,[56] Jeremiah insists that Jerusalem is not going to be spared. Judgment will come on the king and the remaining inhabitants of the city. The future does not lie with Jerusalem as it was then constituted, but with the exilic community. **But[57] this is what the LORD says about the king who sits on David's throne and all the people who remain in this city, your countrymen who did not go with you into exile.** Those left in Jerusalem assumed that they had been blessed by God and that the events of 597 BC were only a passing phase. Was there not a Davidic king (cf. 22:2) in Jerusalem? The reference in 'this city' is to Jerusalem, not Babylon; 'the king' is presumably Zedekiah and not the exiled Jehoiachin. Had not most of the population been left behind? Those who were in exile were only a small proportion of the people, and that did not annul the promise of inviolability for the city. What was more, they predicted that the situation of the exiles would be speedily reversed. Though articles from the Temple had been taken, it still stood, and services were continuing there. All that had happened was a temporary and minor reverse such as had happened before, e.g. in 605 BC. It would soon be over, and all would be well. Jeremiah's task was to counteract such facile optimism.

17. Yes (a translator's addition to indicate resumption of the main thought)**, this is what the LORD Almighty says: 'I will send the sword, famine and plague against them and I will make them like**

---

56. Verses 16-20 are not in the LXX. This is probably an instance of omission because the translators were unable to follow the train of thought, and the verses seemed to add little to what had been said elsewhere, though Archer (1991:146) suggests it is an instance of homoioarchton in which the eye of the copyist inadvertently slipped from the *kōh ʿāmar Yhwh* with which v. 16 begins to the similar opening of v. 21, especially since other verses began with *kî*.

57. 'But' renders *kî*, probably in an asseverative use (Keil 1873, 1:414).

poor figs that are so bad they cannot be eaten'. Though this saying
obviously reflects on the message of chapter 24, where threefold divine
judgment is also threatened (24:10), it can be understood without
knowledge of that particular prophecy. We have here the substance of
the message that Jeremiah had often repeated, though now there is one
difference. It is not being cited as a warning of what is in store for
Jerusalem, but as a means of undermining the false hopes engendered
in Babylon. The word[58] describing the figs is found only here, and
while it is of uncertain origin, there is no doubt that it describes them
as rotten. The LORD has already indicated that what is going to happen
in the immediate future is not release but further desolation.

18. So important is it for the exiles to realise that all that is to happen
to Judah has not yet occurred that v. 18 continues the theme by bringing together various elements of Jeremiah's preaching which would
have been well known to the exiles. **I will pursue them with the
sword, famine and plague and will make them abhorrent[59] to all
the kingdoms of the earth and an object of cursing and horror, of
scorn and reproach, among all the nations where I drive them.[60]**
The customary Jeremianic triad was not on its own sufficiently dire to
express all that would befall them. Additional terms have to be
employed. In the similar expressions in 24:9 and 25:18 'object of
cursing' renders qəlālâ (see also v. 22 below), but here it is the less
common word ʿālâ that is found, and it is more likely that it points to a
divinely imposed penalty for infringement of a solemn undertaking
than to the uttering of human words of disparagement (see 42:18 where
both words occur). For 'horror' see on 15:4; for 'desolation and
hissing', 18:16; 19:8; and for 'reproach', 6:10.

19. The reason for the judgment that would come upon them is their
disregard of the divine truth which had been revealed to them. Abuse

---

58. šōʿārîm may come from the root šāʿar, from which the word for 'gate'
comes, and hence the rendering 'split-open' (NASB), that is, like a gate split-
ting a wall. Alternatively, it may be from šāʿar III, 'to shudder' (cf. 5:30;
23:14), with the idea of horrid, disgusting, so rotten that you would shudder as
you tried to swallow it. Unusually, təʿēnîm, 'figs', is followed by a masculine
form here; usually it is feminine as in 24:2 (cf. GKC §132e).

59. The kethibh is lzwʿh (<√zāwaʿ, 'to tremble') for which the qere
transposes the ʿayin and waw to read ləzaʿăwâ, 'for an abhorrence'.

60. hiddaḥtîm (<√nādaḥ, 'to drive away') is not really 'I have driven them'
(NKJV, NRSV), perhaps suggesting a post-exilic origin for the passage. The
perfect is used in a future perfect sense, 'I shall have driven them', referring to
an action completed before the main verb in the verse.

of the privileges extended to them constituted the substance of the indictment against them. **'For** (*taḥat ᶜăšer*, 'in return for', 'as recompense for') **they have not listened to my words,' declares the LORD, 'words**[61] **that I sent to them again and again by my servants the prophets.'** This is a theme that recurs frequently in Jeremiah (cf. 7:25-26 and references there). The phrase 'my servants' is used to distinguish the true prophets of the LORD from those who were falsely presenting themselves as prophets. The conclusion of the verse is surprisingly, **'And you exiles have not listened either** (literally, but you did not listen),**' declares the LORD.** It is unnecessary to change this so that it refers to those in Judah 'but they would not listen' (NRSV; NJPS). It is rather turning and pointing the same charge at the recipients of the letter, that is, the exiles themselves.

20-21. Verse 20 constitutes another call for those whom the LORD had determined would be taken into exile to give heed, this time to judgment pronounced against the false prophets in their midst in Babylon. **Therefore** ('But ⌊as for⌋ you'), **hear the word of the LORD, all you exiles whom I have sent away from Jerusalem to Babylon.** The description of those addressed matches that of v. 4, and reminds them of who controlled the political and military forces that had shaped their destiny. They ought therefore to listen carefully to what further message he has sent as regards how they should behave. **This is what the LORD Almighty, the God of Israel, says about Ahab son of Kolaiah and Zedekiah son of Maaseiah, who are prophesying lies** (*šeqer*) **to you in my name.** These two prophets are not mentioned elsewhere, and we are not told exactly what their message was. However, there is no doubt that they were among the optimistic prophets who were putting it about that the Exile would be brief, and that the power of Babylon would soon be broken. Their future too was under the control of the LORD. **I will hand them over to Nebuchadnezzar king of Babylon, and he will put them to death before your very eyes.** They had already shared the fate of their fellow exiles, but now matters are going to move further. The LORD will act so that they will be arrested by Nebuchadnezzar and he will have them executed.

22. Because of them, all the exiles from Judah who are in Babylon will use this curse:[62] **'The LORD treat you like Zedekiah and**

---

61. The precise force of *ᶜăšer* here is problematic. The NIV and NASB understand it to follow from the preceding 'words'; the REB translates as 'when' as does the NRSV.

62. 'There shall be taken from them', i.e. a curse derived from their situation, a regular curse-formula.

Ahab,[63] **whom the king of Babylon burned in the fire'.** Burning by
fire had long been a form of execution in Babylon, and it was one to
which Nebuchadnezzar was prone to resort when there were any
threats to his authority (Dan. 3:6, 19-21). It was not employed by the
Persians to whom fire was sacred. There is a wordplay here between
'curse' (*qəlālâ*; 25:18; cf. also v. 18) and 'burned' (<*qālâ*, a relatively
rare word used also of roasted grain, Lev. 2:14), and probably also
with Kolaiah (*qôlāyâ*) in v. 21. The fate of these prophets would provide the exiles with a precursor of what the Babylonians would do to
Jerusalem (39:8) just as the LORD had threatened and forecast (17:27).

23.   For (*ya'an 'ăšer*, 'inasmuch as') **they have done outrageous
things in Israel; they have committed adultery with their neighbours' wives and in my name have spoken lies** (*šeqer*), **which I did
not tell them to do.** Translations vary as to whether they find two or
three reasons specified here. The NIV takes the first term 'outrageous
things in Israel'/'folly in Israel' as a general expression, which is then
made more specific in the following two respects. 'Outrage in Israel'
was a semi-technical phrase to denote serious disorderly actions that
were subversive of the covenant order among the people, usually of
gross uncleanness (Gen. 34:7, cf. also Deut. 22:21; Josh. 7:15; Judg.
20:6). Two such actions are specified: adultery (Judg. 19:23; 20:6, 10;
2 Sam. 13:12-13) and false prophecy (Job 42:8; Isa. 32:5-7).

    While these are the reasons for the divine action, it is unlikely that
Nebuchadnezzar or the Babylonians would have been greatly
concerned about the sexual morality of the exiles. There is evidence
that adultery was punishable by death in Babylon from the days of
Hammurabi,[64] but it is more probable that their prophetic activities
brought these men to the attention of the Babylonian authorities. If
they were going around prophesying the end of Nebuchadnezzar's
reign in Babylon and the restoration of subject peoples to their
homelands, there would have been no hesitation in acting against them
as fomenting rebellion within the empire. Those who assign this
correspondence to a later date suggest that they may have been implicated in the troubles in Babylon in Nebuchadnezzar's tenth year (595–
94 BC), but dissident activity would have been summarily dealt with at
any stage.

    What mattered, however, were not the intricacies of Babylonian

---

63. The spelling of the name as *'ehāb* rather than *'ah'āb* has arisen through
the omission of the second *aleph*.
64. The phrase 'with their neighbours' wives' makes it clear that committing
adultery (<√*nā'ap*, 3:8) is not here a metaphor for idolatrous behaviour.

politics, but the divine verdict on the conduct of Ahab and Zedekiah. **'I know[65] it and am a witness to it,'** declares the LORD. Their actions, even though conducted out of the sight of man, were not hidden from the LORD, and his knowledge would ensure that their action met with an appropriate penalty. 'Jeremiah here displays unlimited confidence in the power of the word of Yahweh to work through him across space and time' (Holladay 1989, 2:144).

2. Controversy with Shemaiah (29:24-32)

Jeremiah's letter to Babylon provoked at least one unfavourable response of which we are told here. Unfortunately, the structure of these verses is not altogether clear, and this has led to various reconstructions. The simplest understanding appears to be that vv. 24-25a are a divine command to Jeremiah to convey a message to Shemaiah, presumably by letter, since Shemaiah was in Babylon. The substance of the message is given in vv. 25-27, and incorporates in vv. 26-27 part of a letter Shemaiah had written to the priest Zephaniah urging him to rebuke Jeremiah. The sentence that is begun in v. 25 is not resumed after the citation of Shemaiah's letter. Instead it would seem that Shemaiah and the exiles are told how Zephaniah read the letter (v. 29) and how the LORD directed Jeremiah to respond to it by writing to the exiles denouncing Shemaiah and foretelling his fate. It is this that effectively concludes the thought of v. 25, though not the grammatical construction begun there.

It is probable that Shemaiah's letters to Jerusalem and Jeremiah's further letter to Babylon were written soon after the original letter to Babylon. It is unlikely that the fury of the false prophets permitted any lengthy period to elapse before they countered what Jeremiah had to say.

24. Tell Shemaiah the Nehelamite/'And to (or possibly 'concerning', NJPS) Shemaiah the Nehelamite you shall say' is less abrupt than the English translation might suggest. We know no more than what we have here about Shemaiah. He was a member of the community exiled

---

65. The kethibh *hwyd'* is a difficult form. The qere assumes (as in 2:25 and 8:6) that the *yodh* and *waw* should be transposed to read *hayyôdēa'*, 'the one who knows', but even so the presence of the article is unusual when it is omitted on the following *'ēd*, 'witness'. Is the kethibh to be read as *'ānōkî hû yōdēa'*, with the *aleph* of *hû'* not written, and the *hû'* used for emphasis (*IBHS* p. 298, note 30): 'I myself know'? A further option is to delete the word entirely (it is absent from the LXX) and read simply, 'I am witness, declares the LORD' (cf. NLT).

in 597 BC and was obviously a peace prophet who objected strongly to the message Jeremiah had sent to Babylon. Of 'Nehelamite' we cannot be certain whether it refers to his family or his place of origin.[66] The instruction given to Jeremiah on this occasion does not specify that a letter be sent.

25. The divine charge against Shemaiah is: **This is what the LORD Almighty, the God of Israel, says: You sent letters in your own name to all the people in Jerusalem, to Zephaniah son of Maaseiah[67] the priest, and to all the priests.** *səpārîm*, 'letters/scrolls', though plural, may be used to refer to just one communication,[68] but the mention of various groups suggests that Shemaiah made sure his message was widely publicised, and that several letters were involved. It is especially the one that was sent to Zephaniah the priest (21:1; 37:3) that is the focus of this divine response. The LORD's message begins with 'because' (*ya'an 'ăšer*, cf. v. 23): 'Because you have sent letters in your own name' (NASB). However, the citation of the text of the letter interrupts the construction, which is not resumed. But it is clear that the letter contained an accusation against Jeremiah. 'You' (masc. sing.) is emphatic, and 'in your own name' accuses Shemaiah of arrogating to himself authority and power he did not have. The charge does not focus on unwarrantably speaking in the name of the LORD, though that was undoubtedly involved. The pronouncement of judgment that logically completes this accusation is found in v. 32.

26. It is then the text of Shemaiah's letter to Zephaniah that is quoted. **You said to Zephaniah, 'The LORD has appointed you priest in place of Jehoiada to be in charge of[69] the house of the LORD'.** It is improbable that the Jehoiada mentioned here refers to the high priest

---

66. A connection between Nehelamite and *ḥālam*, 'to dream', to yield the meaning 'a dreamer' (*HALOT* 688), is implausible in view of the standard gentilic ending on *neḥĕlāmî*.

67. Maaseiah is the same name as that of the father of the peace prophet Zedekiah mentioned in v. 21. It is impossible to determine if they were in fact the same person.

68. This is favoured by the REB and NRSV. Compare 2 Kgs. 10:1-2; 19:14; 20:12; but note GKC §124b[1].

69. The Massoretic Text has a plural *pəqidîm* here, and it may be interpreted as a general statement 'so that there may be officers in the house of the LORD' (NRSV). Others following the LXX, Syriac, and Latin versions in reading a singular *pāqîd bebêt*, 'overseer ⌐in⌐ the house of ...' in place of *pəqidîm bêt*, 'overseers ⌐in⌐ the house of ...', supposing that there has been confusion of the *beth* for a *mem* and a consequent transposition of the *yodh* and the *daleth*.

from the reigns of Athaliah and Joash (2 Kgs. 11-12). Zephaniah was
not high priest, but as Temple overseer ranked next to him (52:24;
2 Kgs. 25:18). We know that Pashhur had held this office at an earlier
date (chap. 20), and he was probably succeeded by the otherwise
unknown Jehoiada. Shemaiah's message should not be interpreted as
an attempt from Babylon to displace Jehoiada and substitute Zephaniah
(though some have felt that such a move is needed to make sense of 'in
your own name' in v. 25). From the tone of Shemaiah's remark it may
be inferred that Zephaniah had only recently succeeded to that post,
and on that basis Shemaiah makes so bold as to instruct him in the
duties of his office. **You should put any madman who acts like a
prophet**[70] **into the stocks and neck-irons.** This punishment had
already been inflicted on Jeremiah by Pashhur (20:2), though this time
neck-irons[71] to keep the head immobile are added. 'Madman'/'mad'
was a derogatory term applied elsewhere to a prophet (2 Kgs. 9:11;
Hos. 9:7). By using this term Shemaiah was attempting to discredit
Jeremiah in the eyes of Zephaniah and the people of Jerusalem as a
whole. Ironically, the same term 'mad'/'deranged' (*məšuggāʿ*) was also
used in Deut. 28:34, 'The sights you see will drive you mad,' in
reference to the impact of the covenant curses on the disobedient
Israelites. This would be what Zephaniah and the people of Jerusalem
would experience when the city was captured.

This passage is of significance for the insight it yields into the way
prophets functioned in Jeremiah's time. The letter assumed that they
exercised their ministry at the Temple, and that they were under the
supervision of the priests there. Shemaiah's perception was no doubt
based on what he knew of the operations of the groups of prophets to
be found in Jerusalem, and it is less clear to what extent true prophets
conformed to that pattern of behaviour. But Shemaiah thought it
reasonable that Jeremiah would be under the high priest's jurisdiction.
'The jurisdiction of the priest was surely based mainly on the average
prophet's being active chiefly in and near the sanctuary. It could hardly
have been based solely on the nature of the prophet's activity. If
this is so, in Shemaiah's eyes Jeremiah must have conformed in large
measure to the normal pattern of prophetic procedure' (Ellison
1962:157).

---

70. The hithpael of *nābaʿ* is used here and in v. 27 with the implication of
'behaving like a prophet', where a person presents himself in a certain light
(an estimative-declarative reflexive, *IBHS* §26.2f).

71. *ṣînōq*, 'neck-irons', is a hapax which is possibly related to the more
common *zēq*, 'chain, fetter'.

27. So why have you not reprimanded Jeremiah from Anathoth, who poses as a prophet among you? Despite the events of 597 BC, Shemaiah refused to accept the truth of Jeremiah's prophecies, and wanted him treated as a sham. 'Rebuke' (<√*gāʿar*, 'to roar, bellow, rebuke') involves more than a verbal reprimand; it covers any action taken to bring a halt to an undesirable activity (Ruth 2:16; Mal. 3:11). 'Poses as a prophet' is probably the implication of the verb form used here,[72] rather than simply 'prophesies to you' (NASB, RSV), because Shemaiah is seeking to undermine Jeremiah's credibility.

28. Shemaiah then cited the substance of Jeremiah's letter to show how outrageous Jeremiah's conduct has been: he had not conformed to the prevailing opinion that the Exile was just a blip in the LORD's providential dealings with Jerusalem. 'For'(*kî ʿal-kēn* sets out the reason why Zephaniah should act)[73] **he has sent this message to us in Babylon: It will be a long time. Therefore** (a translator's supplement) **build houses and settle down; plant gardens and eat what they produce.** He gives the gist of v. 19 and cites v. 5.

29. That message is now broken off, and it would seem that vv. 29-30 are the narrator's comments to make clear the sequence of events. **Zephaniah the priest, however, read this letter to Jeremiah the prophet.** It is not clear what Zephaniah's attitude was towards Jeremiah. He seems to sit on the fence. He will read to him the letter that has been received, though if it came also for public reading, Jeremiah would have got to know about it anyhow. Zephaniah does not, however, act on the letter's contents. On two subsequent occasions he was involved in going to Jeremiah with a royal request that he obtain a message from the LORD (21:1; 37:8), which seems to indicate at least some recognition of Jeremiah's status. But he did not act on the basis of Jeremiah's warnings either, and his capture and death are recounted in 52:24-27.

30-31. After being made aware of the letter's contents, Jeremiah was divinely instructed as to how to respond: **Then the word of the LORD came to Jeremiah: 'Send this message to all the exiles.'** This is most probably the same occasion as v. 24. There is now presented a third oracle of judgment (in addition to those in vv. 16-19 and vv. 21-23) to which the exiles ought to pay attention. Like the second, it concerns

---

72. The verb is *mitnabbēʿ*, a hithpael participle. *HALOT* (659) takes as the meaning of this stem 'to exhibit the behaviour of a *nābîʿ*', 'to talk like one'.

73. *HALOT* (471) suggests that this phrase is used to introduce a reason which has existed for a long time but is only later discovered.

the existence of false prophecy in the community in Babylon. **This is what the LORD says about Shemaiah the Nehelamite: Because Shemaiah has prophesied to you, even though I did not send him, and has led you to believe a lie** (*šeqer*, 5:2). Shemaiah is clearly identified with the false prophets (28:15). It is not just a matter of his personal opposition to Jeremiah that is the crux, but of the damage he and the others were doing by creating confusion in Babylon regarding the course of conduct the exiles should adopt.

32. He will not escape the condemnation of the LORD, introduced by 'therefore' (*lākēn*). **This is what the LORD says: I will surely punish** (<√*pāqad*) **Shemaiah the Nehelamite and his descendants.** There are two aspects to the punishment. His line is going to die out: **he will have no one left among this people.** 'Left'/'living' or 'dwelling' (<√*yāšab*) uses the same root as that found in 'settle down' (v. 5). **Nor will he see the good things I will do for my people, declares the LORD.** As a consequence of his behaviour Shemaiah will have no part in the blessings the LORD has in store for his own, not just in terms of the eventual restoration from exile—he would be no different from the vast majority of his contemporaries in that respect—but even in terms of the preservation and encouragement extended to the community in exile. The reason for Shemaiah's punishment is clearly stated: **because** (*kî*) **he has preached rebellion against me** (28:16).

The community in exile was facing a crisis in their faith and in their personal circumstances. How should they react to the trauma of deportation? Were they to treat their present circumstances as temporary, or should they settle down for a long stay? Was it being true to the LORD to expect him to deliver them speedily (as promoted by Ahab, Zedekiah and Shemaiah), or should they accept that the LORD's word to them pointed to a lengthy, but not unlimited, period in Babylon (as presented by Jeremiah)? Often in crisis situations it is the optimistic word of a speedy resolution that seems to be called for, but optimism that is not based on divine revelation is pernicious and delusive. By engendering false hopes it leads to greater problems in the long run. Blind optimism is never the true answer to human cata-strophe; only a reaction based on the word of God will provide the genuine answers that are needed. In thinking through their dramatically changed circumstances of exile, the community was not to be beguiled by the alluring voices of a false resolution, but was rather to learn to hear and respond correctly to the message that comes from God.

It is a remarkable feature of Jeremiah's message that the community living in a pagan environment is not to dissociate itself from the concerns of those about them. Rather it is to seek their well-being. That did not mean that they were to condone their immorality, far less to participate in it. They are not, however, called on to rebel against the prevailing political authorities. Their aim is to witness to them and to draw them to the truth rather than to overthrow them by force. This still provides a model for witness to the 'unbelieving city'. There will again come a time when God's people will be urged, 'Come out of her, my people, so that you will not share in her sins, so that you will not receive any of her plagues; for her sins are piled up to heaven, and God has remembered her crimes' (Rev. 18:4-5; cf. 51:6, 9, 45). But for the present there is to be a ministry of intercession for both spiritual and material prosperity.

XI. THE RESTORATION OF ISRAEL

AND JUDAH

(30:1–33:26)

OUTLINE

A. Days are Coming (30:1-3)
B. Divine Intervention (30:4–31:1)
    1.   Do Not Be Dismayed (30:4-11)
    2.   Curing the Incurable (30:12-17)
    3.   The Restored People (30:18-22)
    4.   A Stern Warning (30:23–31:1)
C. The LORD's Favour (31:2-40)
    1.   To Israel (31:2-22)
    2.   To Judah (31:23-26)
    3.   To Israel and Judah Together (31:27-40)
D. Restoration to the Land (32:1-44)
    1.   The Prospect for the Besieged City (32:1-5)
    2.   A Field in Anathoth (32:6-15)
    3.   Jeremiah's Prayer (32:16-25)
    4.   The LORD's Response (32:26-44)
E. Promises of Peace and Prosperity (33:1-26)
    1.   Blessings for the Restored People (33:1-13)
    2.   Restoration of Royal and Priestly Lines (33:14-26)

The Book of Consolation.
Theme: Jeremiah was not just a prophet of gloom and collapse; he also had a mission 'to build and to plant' and nowhere is that more evident than in chapters 30–33, which are often termed 'The Book of Consolation'. Although messages of comfort and hope are found earlier (e.g. 3:14-18; 16:14-15; 23:3-8; 24:4-7; 29:10-14, 32), the main thrust of the prophet's ministry up to this point has been to present the LORD's warnings about impending judgment and catastrophe. While the note of punishment to come is by no means absent in chapters 30–33, the primary emphasis here is on the future that the LORD had determined for his people after judgment. The fact that in chapter 29 Jeremiah's messages to the exiles in Babylon looked forward to what would happen in the future made this a suitable juncture at which to add a collection of oracles of salvation.

The vision of restoration and renewed favour did not obviate the need for judgment; so it is not to be taken as originating in the hopeful thinking of the pious in the community. Nor is this to be read as a running commentary on events that unfolded in and after the Exile, which has then been retrojected into the ministry of Jeremiah. This is neither prayer nor history given the literary form of prophecy; rather it is prophetic declaration that is nothing less than God's pre-announcement of what he has sovereignly determined. Judgment and blessing are not here presented as alternatives, but as occurring in a sequence that was inherent in the covenant plan of God.

The LORD could not overlook the persistent rebellion of his people, and in the absence of repentance their repeated violations of their Overlord's commands drew down on them his righteous wrath. The honour and integrity of the LORD could not permit him to ignore rebellious conduct within his realm, but if the desolation of the land and the dispersal of the people had been God's final word on their destiny, then sin, not grace, would have had the ultimate say in determining the outcome of the divine plan of salvation. And that could not be. The rebellion even of the chosen people would not be allowed to frustrate the LORD's purpose; indeed, it would be used to further it. God provided for recovery on the far side of the abyss of judgment, and he had intended this from the beginning. This exercise of grace was no stopgap measure hurriedly thought up in the aftermath of the fall of the city, but had always been integral to the divine plan.

Composition: One viewpoint regarding the origin of the Book of Consolation assumes that it is necessary to wait until after the city has fallen, to the time of Gedaliah's governorship in Mizpah, to find a setting in which it would be appropriate to utter a word of hope (Clements 1981:351), and so these chapters are taken as composed in the early Exile. The inclusion of the material of chapters 32 and 33 makes this hypothesis difficult to sustain. Chapter 32 dates from late in the reign of Zedekiah, and interprets Jeremiah's purchase of the field in terms of chapters 30–31. It is therefore appropriate to view these four chapters as constituting a unit designed to present a message of hope. There can be no doubt that the Book of Consolation ministered powerfully to those who reappraised their position in the light of the fall of Jerusalem, and that was doubtless one factor behind the require-ment that these prophecies be written down (30:2). But they were also of immediate relevance to the situation of those in Jerusalem who were loyal to the LORD and were trying to discern the LORD's purpose for the nation. Though chapters 30 and 31 present the reality of future restoration, the background against which they speak is one of impend-ing judgment, not of executed judgment. Faith is instructed not to conjure up visions of the future based only on what earthly discern-ment pronounces possible. The promise of God breaks through the boundaries of human thinking because the power and wisdom of God are beyond being tied down by our perception. The focus for the future is not merely the re-establishment of the southern kingdom of Judah, but also, and more especially, the return of the exiles from the north and their reintegration with the south in one community dedicated to the service of the LORD.

The extent to which the former kingdom of Israel is mentioned has led to another approach to the Book of Consolation which suggests that chapters 30 and 31 present some of the earliest ministry of Jeremiah, perhaps reflecting a message of hope brought by the prophet to the remnants of the northern kingdom when Josiah was extending his influence there, possibly to be understood along with 3:14-18 (2 Kgs. 23:15-22; Thompson 1980:551-53). Jeremiah's use of Ephraim for Israel (31:6, 9, 18) might also indicate an early origin for these passages in that it would reflect the diction of Hosea, who is supposed to have influenced Jeremiah in his earlier ministry. The words, it is argued, were then reapplied with the addition of much briefer material relating to Judah either by the prophet himself or by later editors, and chapters 32 and 33 added to complete the message in a later setting. It has been suggested that this might have occurred during the reign of Jehoiakim or the early part of Zedekiah's, at a time when Nebuchad-nezzar's control of the region made it plausible to expect a return of the northern exiles (Holladay 1989, 2:160-61). Though there is insufficient evidence to rule out an early, northern provenance for some of the material, it does postulate the existence of an otherwise unattested northern ministry for the prophet, which is perhaps too speculative a scenario.

There is little room to doubt that these four chapters originated during Jeremiah's imprisonment in the closing years of Jerusalem's existence before its capture in 586 BC, and at a time when the city was already surrounded by the armies of Babylon. This would also fit in with the commandment to record the matter in writing: there was no other way in which Jeremiah in prison could communicate with the people for whom the message was immediately intended. Even those critics who see substantial post-Jeremianic editorial activity grant that there is nothing in this section that would indicate that the judgment of the Exile is in the past. It is still being worked out, and the idea of a late compilation is thereby ruled out.

Further, it does not seem improbable that while in confinement Jeremiah reviewed the LORD's dealings with his people from the time of Isaiah, and hence the Isaianic vocabulary and the inclusion of material regarding the northern kingdom. He certainly looked back to his own earlier sayings regarding the restoration of the nation (30:2), though this does not require that he had earlier engaged in a specific ministry to the north. Jeremiah drew personal comfort from the hopeful messages of earlier prophets, and he was also told that they contained matter of immediate relevance to the faithful within the beleaguered community. They could console themselves that the LORD was working through the catastrophe that was engulfing the nation. The written record of Jeremiah's vision would have increased impact for the shattered community when they considered it after the collapse of Jerusalem.

The lack of an introductory date to the Book of Consolation extends the scope of its divine promise of renewal in a way similar to the undated material in the concluding chapters of Isaiah. The future being mapped out here was in defiance of external political possibilities, being given by God alone. There is no attempt to trace out any political process by which this outcome would be achieved. What ultimately counted was that it was stated by divine warrant and its accomplishment was divinely guaranteed. This recovery would not originate in the debased institutions of Israel—Temple, priesthood, Davidic throne—but would involve a wonderful divine renewal of them. In the vulnerability of his people caused by their own sin, the LORD announces what the true basis of their hope must be: the LORD's commitment to his covenant and his determination not to let his people be destroyed and his purpose for them be frustrated.

A. DAYS ARE COMING (30:1-3)

1-2. This is the word that came to Jeremiah from the LORD is an introductory title also found elsewhere in the book (7:1; 11:1; 14:1; 18:1; 21:1). It tells of the LORD giving his message to his servant, and performs the literary function of marking a major division of the book. The substance of the particular command is given in v. 2: **This is what the LORD, the God of Israel, says.**

The command to **write** raises questions about the relationship between the prophet's ordinary ministry and the written record we have. Usually the prophet communicated with the people of his own day orally: they would expect to be addressed by him. The command to write seems to indicate a situation where the prophet is unable to carry out the normal pattern of his ministry. He is in confinement, but Baruch has access to him (32:13), and the message is committed to writing, presumably in a manner similar to that of the earlier occasion recorded in chapter 36. It may well be that the addition of the largely prose material in chapters 32 and 33 can be taken as dictated by the prophet to Baruch.

Modern scholars frequently have difficulty with the dating and concepts in these chapters because of the chronology they adopt for other texts such as Deuteronomy and Isaiah 40–66. There are undoubted links. But it becomes clear that, though Jeremiah's ministry is distinctive, he is brought to use language reminiscent of earlier prophets, and particularly the consolatory messages of Isaiah, to remind himself and others that there are two sides to the LORD's activity. All is not judgment. Furthermore the fact that judgment will not be permitted to have the final word in the destiny of Israel had been embedded in expositions of the covenant bond from earliest times (Deut. 30:1-5). Under the guidance of the Spirit the prophet is reflecting on previous revelation and is given greater insight into what was promised.

Jeremiah is told to record **in a book** (*sēper*, 'scroll') **all the words I have spoken to you.**[1] It would be going too far to assume that this involves making a written record of all his previous ministry. Verse 3 implies that the command is particularly concerned with messages of encouragement he had personally received from the LORD regarding

---

1. It is possible to understand *dibbartî* as an future perfect, 'which I shall have spoken to you' (*IBHS* §30.5.2b), but a similar construction occurs in 36:2 where the following temporal clause makes it clear that the words have already been spoken at the time the command to write was issued.

the recovery programme he would initiate for his people. It is evident that such words were not just a feature of the period when Jeremiah was confined to prison, but that some at any rate already existed, probably even in written form. Now Jeremiah is instructed to draw this material together into a connected whole. As he did so, recalling them to his mind would have had an uplifting effect on the spirit of the imprisoned prophet. Jeremiah then set out both old and new material in a form that was relevant to this particular period late in Zedekiah's reign.

3. The message of v. 3 is a summary of the theme of restoration, which is to be written down 'because'/'for' (*kî*) in this way the testimony regarding the grand prospect awaiting the people will be on permanent record so that there should be no doubt about what the LORD's intention had been throughout. The vision is presented in categoric terms, without any qualification such as the need for repentance on the part of the people. **'The days are coming,' declares the LORD** is a formula frequently used by Jeremiah (7:32), occurring in a positive sense five times in the Book of Consolation (also 31:27, 31, 38; 33:14). It is often taken as having an eschatological reference, but while it may refer to the distant future, it need not necessarily do so. It indicates a future of whose precise time reference the prophet is not informed. It is also the case that this formula avoids drawing attention to minor circumstances of the future presented by the prophet. There is the further inference that it is not a future that is going to arise out of nowhere, but is one that is already involved in the present. 'The use of the participle seems to suggest that something now existing has set up a chain of causation which must end in the event prophesied' (Ellison, 1964:10).

The phrase **when I will bring my people Israel and Judah back from captivity** (so also NKJV) or 'restore the fortunes of … ' (NRSV) occurs seven times in the Book of Consolation (v. 18; 31:23; 32:44; 33:7, 11, 26). The origins of the phrase are obscure, but it is now considered to mean, 'to turn a turning', that is, to effect a reversal of divine judgment and a restoration of the people to a state of well-being and prosperity. This is a more general concept than release from captivity and involves reinstatement in covenantal favour (29:14), often including divine action to correct what had led to the imposition of judgment (Bracke 1985:243). The broader thought is not redundant here in that the prophecy moves from the overall announcement of future blessings to give details about what would be bestowed. It is to proclaim this reinstitution of divine covenant favour that the Book of

Consolation was to be written. Mention is specifically made of Israel, which had been scattered by the Assyrians (2 Kgs. 17:6), to show that the reintegration of the fractured people of God would be effected in this time of future blessing.

'And restore (<√*šûb* hiphil) **them to the land I gave their forefathers to possess,' says the LORD.** For the land given to their forefathers, see on 7:7. 'Possess' (<√*yāraš*) is used not just of the conquest of the land after the Exodus, but also as part of the eschatological hope. Just as the curses of the broken covenant would involve the loss of the land (Deut. 28:63-64; 29:25-28), so after repentance there would be restoration to the land (Deut. 30:5). 'Possess the land' had developed in the vocabulary of the psalmists and Israel's piety as a picture of God's blessing (Pss. 25:12-13; 37:9, 11, 22, 29, 34; 69:32-36). 'To possess' is literally 'and they shall possess it', where the subject of the verb may be either the forefathers or the future generation. The salvation which the LORD promises the people centres on their return to the land, a theme taken up again in vv. 10 and 18. Undoubtedly there was material blessing involved in this promise, but it would be wrong to conclude that mere occupation of the physical territory of the promised land exhausted the provision that would be made for them. While the land provided the people with national identity and political integrity, its significance primarily derived from the fact that it was the arena of covenant blessing, the place where God's presence and spiritual bounty would be enjoyed. So it is only as they maintain a loyal relationship with the LORD in the land he has granted to them that Israel can realise the full potential of being the people of God. Furthermore, enjoyment of the land looked beyond present temporal and religious good to the full restoration of fellowship with God (Heb. 11:10-16). The possession or inheritance of the people of God in this life is but a foretaste of the eternal possession that is to be theirs. Though the full dimensions of final glory were grasped but dimly in Old Testament times, it is a mistake to consider them as completely unperceived.

B. DIVINE INTERVENTION (30:4–31:1)

1. Do Not Be Dismayed (30:4-11)

After the introduction in vv. 4-5a, the first block of material consists of three parts: vv. 5b-7, the time of trouble; vv. 8-9, freedom to serve God; vv. 10-11, 'Take Heart!'. This composite literary structure has threat (vv. 4-7) offset by promise (vv. 8-9) and assurance (vv. 10-11).

4. The superscriptions of vv. 4 and 5a seem somewhat repetitive after
the introduction of vv. 1-3. Presumably this reflects the way in which
the present section was gradually composed. The third person formula
marks off these words as the title of a document which deals with the
reunited people of God: **These are the words the LORD spoke
concerning Israel and Judah.** In its present position this refers back
to the introduction in v. 1, and far from Judah being a later addition to
this material, there is every reason to suppose that this joint future was
central to the original message.

5. This is what the LORD says is loosely linked to what preceded by
an initial *kî*, 'for', which functions to clarify what the words of the
LORD in v. 4 had in fact been. The message of vv. 5b-7 raises two main
questions: (a) who are the subjects of the verbs? and (b) what time is
being spoken of?

The NIV translation, **Cries of fear are heard**, tries to avoid the
awkwardness of the original, 'We have heard a voice of fear.' The
translators of the Septuagint achieved this by rendering, 'You have
heard', in agreement with the subjects of the imperatives 'Ask and see'
(v. 6). The NASB represents an emendation of the text to 'I have
heard', to conform to the subject of the second part of v. 6, 'Why do I
see?' It is possible to understand the text as similar to the divine speech
found in Isa. 6:8, 'Who will go for us?' (Holladay 1989, 2:171), but it
is more likely that we have here an unmarked quotation of how in a
vision the people describe their future experience. This sequence
would be similar to what is found in 31:17b-21 where a quotation of
what the people are saying precedes an announcement of salvation.
They are described as hearing voices before their source can be identified, but there is no doubt that the sounds are those of 'fear' (*ḥărādâ*), a
term which points to the shaking evoked by a sudden, overwhelming
and unusual event. The noun is used only here by Jeremiah, but the
corresponding verb occurs in the phrase 'make him afraid' at the end
of v. 10.

The further description, **Terror, not peace**, may be either what the
people are crying out in their fear, or it may be epexegetic of 'fear':
this is what has caused the cries. 'Terror' (*paḥad*) may refer either to
the emotion felt or to that which causes the reaction (48:43). 'Peace'
(*šālôm*, 6:14) is of course a reference to the total well-being that is to
be expected in the absence of war and in a right relationship with God.

6. The LORD then instructs those to whom Jeremiah brings the
message, (or it might be part of the future scene and addressed to the
'we' whose reaction is reported on in v. 5b), **Ask and see.** The verbs

are masculine plural, and call for consideration and reflection on the unnatural and incongruous behaviour that is occurring all around them. This is brought out by the ironic question: **Can a man** (*zākār*, a male) **bear children?** Though the same Hebrew verb can mean 'beget' as well as 'bear', the possibility of understanding the question in that way is immediately ruled out by what follows. **Then why do I see every strong man**[2] **with his hands on his stomach**[3] **like a woman in labour?** 'Stomach'/'loins' refers to the area between the ribs and the thighs. A woman in labour is an illustration Jeremiah frequently uses to depict abrupt, commanding pain (4:31; 6:24; 13:21; 49:24; 50:43). Here it refers to a reaction that is abnormal and unnatural: men, strong men, are suddenly experiencing disabling anguish. Rather than resisting what is facing them they are rendered helpless as they grope about trying to relieve their agony. What is more their experience will inevitably be incapable of a positive outcome: at least a woman can give birth to a child, but here these strong men are unable to do anything at all. **Every face turned deathly pale**[4] records the reaction as the blood drains away from their faces in their fright. This is a description of those who are panic-stricken and unable to cope with the pressure they are under.

7. How awful that day will be! renders a cry of despair, 'Woe! for (*kî*) that day is great'. Unusually there is no object expressed on whom the woe will come; it is simple a general statement that is made. This raises the second question mentioned above: what time period is specifically being looked at? Although the term 'the day of the LORD' is not directly employed, it undoubtedly provides the background for what is said here. The day of the LORD is the time when he intervenes in judgment against the wicked, whether they are the nations or his own people. It may refer to the day of God's final intervention in the affairs of earth, but it is equally applied to earlier times of judgment which are precursors of the final day. They too can be termed 'great' because of the awesome manifestation of divine wrath that is involved in that they presage the final day (Hos. 1:11[2:2]; Zeph. 1:14). **None**

---

2. The NIV 'strong man' tries to bring out what is often the force of *geber* (<√*gābar*, 'to be strong, superior', cf. 17:5).

3. A circumstantial noun clause (GKC §156c). This is the only occurrence of *ḥălāṣayim*, 'loins', in Jeremiah instead of *motnayim* (1:17; 13:1, 4, 11; 48:37).

4. *yērāqôn* is related to Hebrew words for 'green', and is used elsewhere of plant diseases. The Septuagint translates 'jaundiced', presumably indicating a sickly yellow-green colour.

will be like it. Though the absolute statement seems to refer to the day
of final judgment, the context renders it more probable that it refers to
the period anticipated in vv. 5b-6. But what specifically is in view?
While v. 8 might suggest that the reference is to the downfall of Babylon, historically we know of no exceptional circumstances affecting the
Jews at the time when Cyrus took control of Babylon. However, the
overthrow of Jerusalem and the end of the southern kingdom would be
a time of unprecedented physical and mental anguish for the people.
Indeed, it seems to be almost an understatement to say, **It will be a
time of trouble for Jacob**, but 'trouble' (*ṣārâ*, 'groan' 4:31) points to
the intense distress of the people as they experience the curse of the
broken covenant (Deut. 31:17). Jacob is used here to refer to the
people of God in their lowliness, and is not confined to the northern
kingdom; indeed, the immediate reference is to the south. The next two
oracles give greater content to this distress: as a time of foreign oppression (vv. 8-9) and of dispersal throughout the nations (vv. 10-11).

There is then a revolution in the message for which there has been
no immediate preparation. **But he will be saved out of it** has seemed
to introduce too great a contrast for some commentators who suggest
instead an ironic question is intended, along the lines of 'From it will
he be saved?' However, 'saved' (<√*yāšaʿ*) is repeated three times in
the passage, so that there is no mistaking the positive nature of what
the LORD is saying (vv. 10 and 11). Here we have the first glimpse of
the way in which divine power and grace will operate to transform the
situation of the people.

8. The theme of divine salvation is further explored in vv. 8-9, which
are treated as prose in the NASB, NRSV and NJPS. Although some
commentators regard these verses as a later insertion (Carroll
1986:575; Holladay 1989, 2:173), they perform an important role in
linking back to previous chapters where it was predicted that
Babylonian domination would come to an end and there would be a
restoration of the Davidic line. **'In that day,' declares the LORD
Almighty, 'I will break the yoke off their necks[5] and will tear off
their bonds; no longer will foreigners enslave them.'** 'That day' no
longer refers to the destruction of Jerusalem as in v. 7, but to the end of
the Exile. Anticipating the time of restoration (v. 3), the LORD
promises that there will be a dynamic irruption of divine power into a
situation of oppression and helplessness. 'I will break' and 'I will tear

5. Literally, 'his yoke from off your (masc. sing.) neck and will tear off your
(masc. pl.) bonds'. The LXX has 'their' instead of 'your' in both places.
'Them' at the end of the verse renders a singular, 'him', referring to Jacob.

off' show that it is divine intervention alone that can rid the people of
God of all the forces that dominate and exploit them. The language is
reminiscent of that used in Isa. 10:27 of the termination of Assyrian
oppression of Judah. It fits in well with release from Babylon, when
the imperial might of Babylon is no longer viewed as carrying out the
LORD's will (27:6), but seeking its own gain. 'His yoke' (see footnote)
points particularly to Nebuchadnezzar's domination of the land, though
he would have passed from the scene before the deliverance of the
people occurred. 'Bonds' refers to the leather straps which held the
yoke in place. Once the people had torn off the bonds of the LORD and
thought they had achieved real freedom (2:20), but now the change is
irreversible and for their good because it comes from the LORD
himself. He will provide them with true liberty from foreign servitude.
'Enslave' (<√‘ābad) is the first of three occurrences of the same root
(cf. 'serve', v. 9 and 'servant', v. 10). There are similarities to the
oracle of Hananiah (28:2), but now this liberation is presented in terms
of the divine timescale: not the wishful thinking of judgment averted,
but the outworking through exile and suffering of the LORD's purpose
to purify a people for himself.

9. After they have been freed from foreign domination, Israel and
Judah will be able to fulfil their destiny as the people of God. This is
not just a matter of individual obedience to the ethical imperatives of
the covenant; it extends to the religious and political organisation of
the nation restored to its rightful place in God's purpose. It was
certainly not a matter of Israel becoming a dominant political power,
but an opportunity for them to dedicate themselves to faithful service
of the LORD. 'They' refers to the whole people of God, brought back
into outward unity. There is a play on the use of 'serve' at the end of
the previous verse. **Instead, they will serve the LORD their God and
David their king, whom I will raise up for them.** To take this as
expressing some post-exilic hope of the restoration of a Davidic
monarchy among the Jews is to play down its obvious Messianic
reference. This 'David' is a reference to the righteous Branch of whom
Jeremiah had already spoken (23:5). David's reign set the standard for
a time of blessing for the people, both nationally and spiritually. In the
light of this, it is reasonable to find the realisation of the prophecy in
the coming of Jesus Christ, the true son of David. Notice how it is
brought out that there is no tension between serving the LORD and
serving the one who acts as his covenant king. These are two aspects
of the joint rule that is envisaged. Furthermore, this loyal king will be
one whom the LORD himself will appoint over them.

10-11. Because the LORD has decided to intervene on behalf of his people even though they will be in exile on account of their sin, it is possible to bring to them an immediate message of comfort which looks beyond the trauma they would experience and which encourages them to await the divine resolution of their affairs. The words are not initially addressed to the generation of the restoration who would personally experience the LORD's deliverance but to those of Jeremiah's day who had genuine faith in the LORD and were perplexed over what had happened to the promises of the covenant, and what was still to come upon the covenant people. Whether they were from the former kingdom of Israel and were already in exile, or whether they were from Judah, perhaps already in exile in Babylon, or perhaps shortly to be taken there, they could have renewed courage because what was happening was not fortuitous and pointless, but under divine control. The LORD's covenant commitment to them had not abated one whit.

In presenting this truth to the prophet the LORD made use of words that recalled those given through the prophet Isaiah in his later years when the loss of the northern kingdom of Israel was still a fresh and bitter memory in the south, and when there was an increasing breakdown in true religion in Judah. Assyria had indeed been turned back from the gates of Jerusalem in 701 BC in the days of the godly Hezekiah, but his son Manasseh did not walk in the ways of his father; rather he persecuted the faithful and introduced despicable pagan practices into the land. At that time too the LORD had given a message of encouragement, of restoration beyond the Exile already suffered by the north and inevitably awaiting the south if it persisted in its rebellious conduct. By using language which is reminiscent of that found in Isaiah's ministry at that time (Isa. 41:8-9, 13-14; 43:1, 5; 44:1-2), the LORD directed prophet and people alike to recall these prophecies of comfort to their minds. The LORD remained committed to what had been promised then. Indeed, events had moved on, and the fulfilment of these words was now even closer.

So do not fear, O Jacob my servant.[6] The verse begins, 'But as for you', and so focuses on those who match up to the description of 'my servant Jacob'. Jacob and Israel are both used here to describe the covenant people. Of course, such words of encouragement were not

---

6. Vv. 10-11 are virtually duplicated in 46:27-28. The fact that they are omitted in the corresponding passage in the LXX (chap. 37) probably arises from its practice of omitting duplicate passages that have already occurred (in this case in LXX 26:27-28).

addressed to the nation in general. Their national rebellion was going
to bring sweeping judgment on the people as a whole. But there were
also those who truly acknowledged the LORD as their covenant Overlord. They were not exempted from the catastrophe afflicting the
nation, but they were not left to cope on their own with what was
happening. The bond of the covenant is reciprocal, and so the LORD
not only recognises his servants' status before him, but implicitly
commits himself to act as their Overlord in defending and providing
for them. Those who could identify themselves in this description as
his servants would be able to draw strength from what the LORD was
doing in and through his act of judgment. **'Do not be dismayed**
(<√*ḥātat*, 1:17)**, O Israel,' declares the LORD.** The exhortation not to
be overwhelmed by their circumstances, particularly perhaps the length
of time during which divine judgment would be experienced by the
nation, is not presented as merely encouraging talk. It is grounded in
the fact of promised divine deliverance for those who are truly the
Israel of God.

I will surely (*kî*) **save**[7] **you out of a distant place, your descendants from the land of their exile.** The NIV treats the particle *kî* here
as an asseverative, 'surely', but it may just as readily be understood
causally, 'for' (NKJV, NRSV). The LORD's commitment to save them
is the reason why his people can take heart. 'Save' picks up the thread
of the promise from v. 7 and is repeated again in v. 11. 'A distant
place' shows that the land of exile reflects geographically what was
true of the nation as a whole spiritually. They were alienated and
distant from the LORD. However, when he acts in power to deliver
them, distance will not hinder him. Still, the mention of 'descendants'
at least hints that this deliverance will not be immediate. Nonetheless,
when the LORD acts, he will restore the full blessings of the covenant
to those who are truly his people. **Jacob will again have peace and
security, and no one will make him afraid.** The NIV treats the verb
šûb here as an auxiliary verb and renders it 'again'. More probable is
the rendering of the NKJV and NRSV, 'Jacob will return'. The LORD's
people would not be left as aliens and captives in a distant land, but
would be brought back to their proper place where they would enjoy
'peace' (<√*šāqaṭ*), the idea being one of tranquillity, absence of
disturbance and freedom from anxiety. 'Security' (<√*šā'an*) refers to
ease derived from an absence of unfavourable factors. It can denote
unwarranted ease manifesting itself in pride, but here the two terms

7. *hinnēh* plus a participle is used to announce an event as imminent, or at
least near at hand (and sure to happen) (GKC §116p).

combine to portray positively the 'quiet and ease' (NRSV) the LORD
will provide for his restored people. Similar encouragement is also
expressed in Hab. 2:4 and Heb. 12:5-11. 'No one will make ... afraid'
occurs 12 times in the Old Testament, and points to the absence of
outside interference that will prevail in the land. The phrase is used in
7:33 to describe conditions of desolation, but here it points forwards to
a future time when the people are living in harmony with their God.

11. Once more it is emphasised that the time of future blessing is not
mere wishful thinking, but grounded on the LORD's covenant commitment to his people. 'For (*kî*) **I am with you and will save you,'**
declares the LORD. This is a promise that is often uttered as a word of
assurance in Scripture (1:19; Exod. 3:12; Josh. 1:9; Matt. 28:19-20).
Again one ought to note that there is no verb expressed in the first
clause. The thought supports the idea 'I shall be with you', even in the
time of judgment and exile. **Though** (*kî*) **I completely destroy all the**
nations among which I scatter you, 'notwithstanding' (*ʿak*, 3:13) **I**
will not completely destroy you. The LORD speaks as the sovereign
ruler of the world. Although Babylon is not mentioned, it is in the
background. When the LORD intervenes, the political realities of the
day will be turned upside down. But whereas 29:7 had intertwined the
well-being of the people with that of their place of exile, at the time of
divine deliverance that connection will no longer hold. Their destinies
will be separated. Possibly there is a reflection on the way in which the
Israelites in Egypt were spared the impact of many of the plagues
(Exod. 8:22). So the people of God are assured that he is still
determined to work out his purpose through them, even if it is only a
small number who are left (4:27; 5:10, 18).

Further explanation is given of how the LORD will accomplish his
covenant purposes. **I will discipline you but only with justice; I will**
not let you go entirely unpunished. The LORD's punishment of his
people is never arbitrary. The curse of the broken covenant comes on
them because of their sin, and through it they receive what they
deserve. Divine justice required nothing less, but there is a limit to
what will be imposed. 'With justice' uses a different preposition from
10:24, perhaps giving the sense according to the standards of justice.
These words explain what is going to happen in the immediate future,
but placed as they are after the declarations of future prosperity, they
also act as a warning. Just as in the past, enjoyment of the land and the
blessings of the covenant are conditioned on loyalty and obedience.
The spiritual realities of the LORD's dealings with his people do not
change. Punishment is inevitable if the people violate the covenant.

The words used echo those of the declaration made to Moses, 'Yet he does not leave the guilty unpunished' (Exod. 34:7).[8] It is only by the wonder of divine grace that the standards of justice can be maintained and at the same time there is a remnant left through whom the LORD may bring his purposes to completion.

2. Curing the Incurable (30:12-17)

This section follows closely on the preceding. Indeed, it is really an extended commentary on v. 11, but now using the metaphor of ill-health and physical injury. These verses set out the present seemingly hopeless and incurable condition of Judah (vv. 12-14a) and what has brought it about (vv. 14b-15). There is no minimising of the trauma that Zion is experiencing, but astonishingly her enemies will be defeated (v. 16) and her health will be restored (v. 17). The impossible becomes possible with God, and this deliverance closely mirrors the two-sided nature of Jeremiah's ministry which involved both plucking up and planting (1:10). Again there are a number of themes that are also found in the later ministry of Isaiah.

12. The 'for' (*kî*) with which the verse begins indicates that this message is also presented as an explanation of the way in which the LORD is working to achieve his purposes (v. 3). Knowing why something is happening and what the outcome will be does not take away the pain of bitter experiences, but it does build up endurance. The introductory formula, **This is what the LORD says**, probably parallels that in v. 5, and sets this section as further exploring the LORD's programme for restoring the fortunes of his people. The message is addressed to Zion, as is indicated by the feminine singular 'you' and 'your' throughout,[9] and made clear by the explicit reference in v. 17. Zion is reminded that her redemption arises solely from God's gracious determination to save his people.

Zion is personified as a woman suffering from a seemingly fatal injury. **Your wound**[10] **is incurable** recalls the similar statement made by the prophet with respect to his own brokenness in 15:18; but the imagery is used of the impact on the people in 8:21-22; 10:19; 14:17.

---

8. The words of Exod. 34:7 are closer to this text in Hebrew than might appear from the NIV. In both verses the piel of *nāqâ* is preceded by the infinitive absolute.

9. The one exception to this is *tizʿaq* in v. 15, which must be second person masculine singular 'you cry out', and not third feminine singular.

10. *ləšibrēk* is probably an instance of emphatic *lamedh*, 'your particular hurt' (GKC §143e).

In the latter two references the language **your injury beyond healing**
occurs. Their 'injury', the blow they have sustained, is referred to
again in vv. 14 and 17. These were the national defeats, devastation
and loss of sovereignty occasioned by enemy invasion. The language
of incurable injury is used throughout Scripture to describe divine
chastisement for sin (Ps. 38:3-11; Isa. 1:5-6; Nah. 3:19). The essence
of the gospel message is that even in situations which are reckoned to
be beyond recovery, God declares that he is able to intervene and
restore (Isa. 53:4-5; 57:15-19; Hos. 6:1).

13. As translated in most English versions v. 13 seems to introduce
another element into the comparison, that of a lawsuit, **There is no one
to plead your cause** (the REB omits the words as a gloss). For the
phrase 'plead a cause' see 5:28; 22:16; it here suggests the people are
without an advocate in the courts of heaven, or perhaps without an ally
to seek favour for them with the Babylonians, anticipating the thought
of v. 14. Thompson (1980:558) eliminates this legal picture of the
people as out of place. However, mixed metaphors can occur in any
language. The picture then reverts to the patient who has sustained
irrecoverable injury: **no remedy for your sore, no healing for you.**
'Sore'/'hurt' refers to a injury or infection of the skin,[11] for which there
is no healing remedy. 'Healing'/'healing remedies' (*təʿālâ*) describes
the covering of a wound as new skin grows up over it (*HALOT* 1768).
However, rather than divide the verse into three lines (as is found in
the NIV and NRSV), the Massoretic interpunction of the text favours
taking 'for your sore' with the first part of the line, to read, 'There is
no one pleads the case for your healing; as for healing remedies, there
is none for you.'

14. Not only was there no known cure for her condition and no one
prepared to argue her case in court, but Zion had been deserted by
those nations which might have been expected to intervene on her
behalf. **All your allies have forgotten you** probably refers to Egypt
and Edom, to both of whom Judah had looked for support, but who
had deserted her in her hour of need. **They care nothing for you**/'do
not seek you' (<*dāraš*, cf. v. 17). Seeking is the action expected of a
shepherd in relation to his flock (Ezek. 34:6, 8). 'Among all her lovers
there is none to comfort her. All her friends have betrayed her; they
have become her enemies' (Lam. 1:2). But the people were not to take
it as a reason for self-commiseration as to their unfortunate situation.

---

11. *māzôr* probably refers to a suppurating ulcer or boil (only here and Hos.
5:13; *HALOT* 565).

The LORD had been active behind it all—and rightly so. 'For' (*kî*) **I have struck you as an enemy would**/'with the blow (*makkâ*, 'injury', v. 12) of an enemy' either presents the LORD as acting towards them as if he were their enemy or shows the LORD acting through the blows he had already permitted to come on them from the Babylonians. The same ambiguity is found in the following phrase. **And punished you as would the cruel**/'with the chastisement of a cruel one' (NKJV), **because your guilt is so great and your sins so many.**[12] These words are virtually re-echoed at the end of the following verse to emphasise the point. Zion found it difficult to concede that there was, or had been, anything wrong on her part. But she was no innocent sufferer unfortunately caught up in a drama that was no real concern of hers; nor had the LORD been unjust in permitting this calamity to come upon her. 'Punished'/'chastisement' uses language that normally refers to discipline intended to lead to reformed behaviour (2:30). Though the 'cruel one', the enemies of the people, seem to have the upper hand, there is a greater purpose in the LORD's covenant rebuke, and this will become evident in due course.

15. Why do you cry out over your wound (*šeber*, as in v. 12)**, your pain that has no cure?**[13] 'Why?' suggests that it was inappropriate to react in this way. 'Crying out' was normally an appeal to the LORD for help, but this infliction had come from the LORD and could not be averted. Judah was being urged to recognise that the blows of her enemies have been permitted by the LORD to chastise his erring people ('I will discipline you with justice', v. 11). This discipline, though painful, would ultimately open the way to restoration. What was more they had to acknowledge that there was no justifiable ground for complaining about their treatment. **Because of your great guilt and many sins I have done these things to you.** The words of the previous verse are repeated to emphasise that they were undergoing the penalties that were part of the curse they had been warned would come on covenant breakers. Crying out was unwarranted and it would be ineffective: they had no grounds for complaint against their Overlord.

16. Verse 16 begins rather surprisingly, 'therefore' (*lākēn*), which frequently heralds the imposition of judgment as a result of sin. But that is not what follows, and the word seems to be used here adversatively to indicate a contrast (16:14) rather than a consequence of their

---

12. The verb may convey the idea of strength as well as that of increased number; hence the RSV translation 'are flagrant'.

13. This verse is omitted from the LXX text, probably because of the substantial amount of repetition to be found in it.

sinfulness, or even their helplessness. The outcome for the people is
not left to human merit or demerit. Hope springs from the fact that it is
the LORD who is active in all these things (see also 15:19; 16:14), and
he will act to vindicate his name and those who are his. This derives
from the promise in the Abrahamic covenant, 'whoever curses you I
will curse' (Gen. 12:3). This pattern of correspondence between action
and judgment is explicitly traced out in three of the following clauses
to indicate the appropriateness of the punishment for the crimes that
have been committed. **But all who devour you will be devoured** (cf.
2:3; 5:17-18). Their oppressors will experience the fate that they have
meted out to others when they ransacked their territory and overwhelmed the inhabitants. **All your enemies will go into exile.** Here
too the correspondence principle is involved, because 'it is self-evident
that the judgment of exile upon Judah's enemies is also meant to correlate with the exile inflicted on her' (Miller 1982:69). **Those who
plunder you**[14] **will be plundered.** The identity of the nations involved
is not stated. But though it was divinely sanctioned, those involved are
still accountable. **All who make spoil of you I will despoil.** It is not an
impersonal process that will bring about their downfall, but the active
involvement of the LORD. Because the nations have overstepped the
boundary he has set they have made themselves liable to punishment
(49:32; 50:37; Ezek. 25:15; Nah. 3:11, 13). The repetition of 'all' in
three of the statements underscores the fact that there is no exemption
from divine scrutiny and accountability.

17. Here is the ultimate paradox: the provision of a cure for those
previously assessed as incurable. The relationship between v. 17 and
what precedes is expressed by $k\hat{\imath}$, which may be translated 'for'
(NKJV, NRSV), yielding the connection: 'The reversal of the fortunes
of your enemies will take place because I will act to restore you, which
inevitably has negative consequences for your oppressors.' Alternatively, the thought may be in terms of a contrast with vv. 12-13, which
leads to the NIV rendering, **But** ($k\hat{\imath}$) **I will restore you to health**/'I
will cause to come up lengthening'. The image is that of new skin
growing over a wound. This reversal of their spiritual and political
condition is by divine action: God will be their healer. **'And heal your
wounds,' declares the LORD.** But the reason for the reversal of their
enemies' fortunes is not just to be found at the level of divine action.

---

14. In many manuscripts there is a qere *šôsayik*, a participle from √*šāsâ*, 'to
plunder', rather than the kethibh *šō'ăsayik*, which may be an Aramaising form
šō'ăsayik (for *šōsəsayik*, from the related root *šāsas*, 'to plunder'; cf. GKC
§67s).

That action has been motivated at a deeper level by divine love for his
people as they are exposed to the taunts of their enemies. **Because** (*kî*)
you are called an outcast, Zion[15] **for whom no one cares.** An
'outcast' indicates one who has been put away by her husband (Isa.
62:4), and is a poignant picture of exiled Zion expelled from her
homeland. 'Cares for' echoes the neglect of her allies, which the LORD
had predicted would occur (v. 14). But the contempt of the nations for
Zion also slighted the LORD of the covenant and the adequacy of his
provision, being based on the misconception that judgment had
befallen the LORD's people because he was incapable of defending
them from the onslaughts of their adversaries. In fact he had been
acting in furtherance of his own purposes, and now he intervenes to
reverse his judgment and vindicate his name (Isa. 62:12).

3. The Restored People (30:18-22)

Again there is recorded a divine message in which salvation is promised. The LORD's resolution to save opens up before the people vistas
that had seemed too far-fetched to be capable of realisation. 'Jacob' is
still used to refer to the covenant people as a whole. It is out of keeping
with Old Testament prophecies of restoration to suppose that there is
foretold the reinstatement of a separate northern kingdom.

18. A more detailed picture is now built up of the restoration previously promised in general terms. **This is what the LORD says: 'I
will restore the fortunes of Jacob's tents.'** 'Restore the fortunes' is a
favourite expression in the Book of Consolation for the blessing to be
shown to the scattered people (cf. v. 3). While 'tents' may simply be a
poetic variant for 'house' or 'household' (Job 31:31), it is probable that
its use conveyed the notion of peace. Going to one's tent was a phrase
used for release from military service (Judg. 7:8; 20:8; 1 Sam. 13:2;
2 Sam. 20:1). The picture here is one of peacefulness and lack of
disturbance and disruption in the restored kingdom. The particular
reference to 'the tents of Jacob' reinforces this idea by recalling
Balaam's prophecy in Num. 24:5, 'How beautiful are your tents, O
Jacob, your dwelling-places, O Israel!' (see also Judg. 19:9; Mal.
2:12). This contrast to the scenes of devastation that had been
prevalent in the land is extended in **and have compassion** (<√*rāḥam*
piel; 13:14) **on his dwellings**, which focuses more on an urban than a
rural environment. There too conditions would be turned around

---

15. The LXX text does not refer to Zion. Instead it reads 'our prey' which
may suggest it read the Hebrew as *ṣêdēnû*.

because of the LORD's compassion, which is used here in a way that is in marked contrast to earlier passages where it was specifically said that the LORD would not have compassion (e.g. 21:7). This reversal of attitude is based on the fact that the LORD's punishment of his people would have run its course. In the light of the rebuilding programme mentioned in the second part of this verse, the LORD's pity would be physically evident in that their houses will be erected once more in their former sites.

In the second part of the verse, 'city' and 'palace' have no article in Hebrew, and the references could be taken in a general sense applying to all the cities of the land (so REB), but the mention of their leader and ruler in v. 21 certainly points to a specific focus on Jerusalem by that point. **The city will be rebuilt on her ruins, and the palace**[16] **will stand in its proper place.** 'On her ruins'/'mound' renders the word *tēl* (cf. also 49:2), a term still used for a site where ruins were levelled off to provide the foundations for new building. Rather than abandoning a location which had originally been chosen for strategic reasons, such as the existence of an adequate water supply, it was customary to redevelop it so that over time what might have once been a low hill suitable for defensive purposes could reach quite a height. The material preserved in the successive levels of these tels has proved to be a vital source of information for the archaeology of the Near East. 'In its proper place'/'upon its judgment' is a phrase of less certain significance. The word *mišpāṭ* basically indicates 'judgment, justice', and so can be used to indicate what is customary or usual (Gen. 40:13), that is, its accustomed site. Alternatively, the thought might be that it would be built in a way adjudged suitable or proper, perhaps even 'according to plan' (Exod. 26:30; 1 Kgs. 6:38).

19. From them will come[17] **songs of thanksgiving** refers to all the dwellings mentioned in the previous verse. The restored community will voice their joy in song (31:4; Isa. 51:11; Zeph. 3:14). **And the sound of rejoicing.** Their jubilation cannot be suppressed but will be evident throughout the land (cf. 31:3). This is in marked contrast to the absence of sounds of joy in the descriptions of catastrophe found in 7:34; 16:9; 25:10. Two further aspects of their future prosperity are envisaged. Both are divinely implemented, and in each the blessing is first stated positively and then negatively. **I will add to their**

16. *ʿarmôn* is not the usual word for 'palace'; it denotes a 'fortified place'.

17. There is a problem here in the Hebrew in that the verb 'will come out' is third *masculine* singular, and 'thanksgiving'/'songs of thanksgiving' (NIV) is *feminine* singular. Perhaps the masculine is used in a general sense.

numbers, and they will not be decreased refers not to the dwellings, but to the community, and contrasts with previous pictures of desolation (4:7, 29). Such an increase of numbers was part of the blessing of the covenant (Gen. 15:5; 22:17; Lev. 26:9), which would have been enjoyed in part by the community in exile (29:6), but obviously more fully after they returned to the land (23:3; Isa. 49:19-20; Zech. 10:8). **I will bring them honour, and they will not be disdained** (<√*ṣāʿar*, 'to be treated as insignificant'). Israel would become a country of such size and importance that it would be impossible to overlook and dismiss it in the affairs of the nations. Again this derives from the covenant blessing and action of the LORD who reverses their previous calamitous situation. 'The LORD will make you the head, not the tail' (Deut. 28:13).

20. In v. 20 the picture of blessing looks back to the restoration of what had been in the past. But it is God looking back. Just as the sin of mankind in Eden had not been permitted to usurp the divine purpose for the creation, so too here we can trace the same reality of God's sovereign determination and reclaiming love in the outworking of the history of the restored people. He had blessed the people in the past, and despite their sin that remained his intention. **Their[18] children will be as in days of old.** The reference seems in this context to be to their numbers, and may well be intended to recall the spectacular growth of the Israelite population during the years of oppression in Egypt (Exod. 1:7-10). **And their community** (*ʿēdâ*) **will be established before me** refers to the theocratic community, both in its political and religious aspects. As the people live together in loyal obedience to their covenant LORD, so they will enjoy his protection. **I will punish all who oppress them.** It is still envisaged that the restored people will experience hostility from foreign powers. To 'oppress' (<√*lāḥaṣ*) is to apply force so as to restrain or break. But this will not occur with impunity. 'Punish' (<√*pāqad*) refers to the visitation of a superior to inspect and reward. The divine king will protect those who are faithful to him from those who seek to harm them.

21. Attention is again given to the authority structure of the covenant community, and the theme of v. 9 is resumed, but now with no mention of David or a king. The avoidance of the word 'king' is probably a

---

18. In v. 20 and the first part of v. 21 the references in the Hebrew are in the singular, 'his children', 'his community', 'who oppress him', 'his leader', 'his own', 'his ruler', 'among him'. These continue the references to Jacob and 'his dwellings' found in v. 19. As Jacob here stands for the people of God, the plural rendering of many translations makes for clearer English.

politically and religiously motivated attempt to distance the coming leader from the inadequacies and disobedience of Judah's kings past and present. What is predicted will not in this respect be a rerun of the past. **Their leader** (*'addir*, 'distinguished'. 'mighty': 14:3; 25:34-36) **will be one of their own; their ruler** (<*māšal*, 'to govern', 'exercise authority': 22:30; 33:26; Mic. 5:2) **will arise from among them.** Their future ruler is not going to be a foreign oppressor, but rather someone who would fulfil the ancient requirement of Deut. 17:15, 'He must be from among your own brothers'. While both the terms 'leader' and 'ruler' are general ones which may in the first instance include others besides the Messianic king, there is no implication of denigration of the Davidic covenant. The terms point to a glorious, illustrious, effective leader, and can ultimately and fully apply only to the Messiah. The emphasis here, however, is on the fact that the restored people will be controlled by one who is himself an Israelite, a member of the community.

The words **I will bring him near and he will come close to me** do not in the first instance speak about familiarity or friendship between the ruler and the LORD, but are part of the vocabulary of the Israelite cult. It was presumption to seek access to God unbidden or in an unauthorised fashion (Exod. 19:21; 33:20). It was the privilege divinely accorded to the priests that they were brought near to the LORD as his court attendants, and even then they could approach him only under strictly regulated conditions (Lev. 10:1-3; Num. 16:5, 10). What then is the significance of this prerogative extended to the future ruler? It may point back to the exceptional role played by David or Solomon in cultic matters (2 Sam. 6:12-15; 7:18; 1 Kgs. 8:22). They did not act presumptuously as Uzziah later did (2 Chron. 26:16-20), and the anticipated ruler would show a Davidic concern for the worship of the LORD, and be permitted special access for consultation and intercession. However, if these words are taken as more directly Messianic, then it is probable that they arise out of the perception of Ps. 110, where the one who is expected is a priest–ruler. This was a combination that was common in the nations around Israel, but within the covenant community was a mark of the Messianic ruler (Ps. 110:4; Zech. 6:13). He would inaugurate a kingdom in which such access would be extended to the whole community (Ps. 65:4).

The extent of the privilege of the promised ruler is indicated by the question, **'For** (*kî*) **who is he who**[19] **will devote himself to be close to**

---

19. *mî hû'-zeh* is a very emphatic usage to show how incredible it would be for any to propose themselves for this role (GKC §136c).

me?' **declares the LORD.** To approach the LORD unbidden was to incur wrath more certainly than did any who entered the court of the king of Persia (Est. 4:11). Therefore no one would dare to take upon himself the task of ruling the covenant people in the restored community unless specially divinely commissioned. 'Devote himself'/ 'pledge his heart' denotes entering into a life-threatening undertaking. The risk is such that none would volunteer for the task of leading the new community and mediating between God and his people except one who is divinely appointed to the role and brought near by God himself.

22. The description of the restored community is completed by recalling the covenant promises.[20] The people are going to be established on the terms the LORD stipulates and so will be able to realise the ideal that had been set before them. **So you will be my people, and I will be your God.** It is not just a matter of national restoration to the outward blessings of the covenant, but recovery of the spiritual harmony of inner devotion to God and enjoyment of all he has committed himself to being for his people. This is the full meaning of the covenant relationship between Israel and her God, though without using the word 'covenant' itself. The conclusion here parallels the similar language of 31:1, with both verses marking the end of divine sayings.

4. A Stern Warning (30:23–31:1)

Both the extent and the theme of this short section are somewhat puzzling. For the arguments in favour of including 31:1 with the closing verses of this chapter, see the comments below on the verse. As regards the theme of vv. 23-24, it is significant that these verses are very similar to 23:19-20, which in the context of the exposure of false prophets expressed divine judgment coming upon Judah. Here the words are given a broader application, and 'the wicked' in v. 23 are all who oppose the true interests of God's chosen community, and principally foreign enemies who seek to oppress them. The promises of restoration will be fulfilled because of the LORD's action against those who are motivated by such hostility. There is probably, however, another aspect to the incorporation of these words here. There was a prevalent tendency to grasp the promises of the LORD and to forget his warnings. A stern warning (or is it a 'storm warning'?) is given that the future time of blessing, and its continuance, are not to be lightly

---

20. The verse is omitted in the LXX, again probably because it seemed repetitive and not adding to the description.

assumed as inevitable. Future generations must take care not to repeat the mistakes of the past.

23. See, the storm of the LORD will burst out in wrath.[21] This is identical to what is found in 23:19, but there are two changes from 23:19 in **a driving wind swirling down on the head of the wicked**. 'And' no longer introduces the clause, and the verb describing the action of the storm wind is also changed.[22] Previously it had been a swirling wind, indicating a turning, twisting circular motion; now it is 'driving', that is moving forwards and taking matter with it.[23] This wind too swirls down on the wicked as the LORD deals retributively with all who seek to oppose and thwart his ways.

24. There need be no uncertainty as to the outcome of the encounter of the wicked with the LORD's justice. **The fierce anger of the LORD will not turn back until he fully accomplishes the purposes of his heart** (cf. 23:20). The concluding words, **In days to come you will understand this**, look behind the future act of divine retribution to assure the people that they would eventually understand how the LORD had been working out his purposes in and through the events of history. For the moment much may have seemed obscure and perplexing, because there is always an element of hiddenness in divine disclosure. Not all can be told or understood at present, so the people are called on to walk by faith not by sight.

31:1 The first verse of chapter 31 occupies a transitional role in the Book of Consolation. This is reflected in Hebrew manuscripts, some of which put it as 30:25, and others as 31:1, which is what is found in English versions. The new start in 31:2, 'This is what the LORD says', also serves to reinforce the idea based on the similarity between 30:22 and 31:1 that the latter may suitably be taken with the previous chapter. Of course, chapter divisions would have been quite alien to Jeremiah, but he does ordinarily indicate the structure of his work.

31:1 echoes 30:22 in terms of the completeness and the harmony of

---

21. Usually the LXX omits verses that contain material that has occurred earlier, but that is not so here where vv. 23-24 are in the LXX text despite being substantially the same as 23:19-20.

22. The variation found in the NIV from 'whirlwind' in 23:19 to 'driving wind' here (both *saʿar*) is an adjustment due to the change of verb.

23. *mitgōrēr* is occasionally emended towards 23:19, *miṯḥôlēl*. It may well be the hithpolel participle of *gārar*, 'to drag, drag away' found in the qal in Prov. 21:7 and Hab. 1:15. Some take it as the hithpolel participle of *gûr*, a dubious occurrence of this root meaning 'to be a stranger' (cf. *NIDOTTE* 1:897).

the covenant relationship that will be experienced. **'At that time,'** **declares the LORD** refers back to the days to come (30:24), the time after the LORD's fierce anger has swept away his people's enemies and they have the leader whom the LORD brings near to himself, a time when they have understanding of his purposes. Then **I will be the God of all the clans of Israel**. The phrase 'all the clans/families' looks forward to a time when the ruptures that existed in the people will be reversed, both the rupture into the two kingdoms, and also the dispersion of the people, a process that had begun in 722 BC with the fall of Samaria. When the LORD restores his people it will be as a whole and into a unified body, no longer marred by the divisions in its religious and social life that should never have existed. Their restoration will go beyond territorial reinstatement and encompass all that is involved in a right relationship with their Overlord. This is part of the formula of the covenant bond, here cited in the reverse order from 30:22, probably to bring out the sovereign initiative of God that is required for this condition to prevail. **And they will be my people** shows how the LORD's sovereign action on behalf of his own will bring them to acknowledge what they have received from him and live lives of grateful obedience.

C. THE LORD'S FAVOUR (31:2-40)

The major theme of this section is the radical and lavish provision that the LORD will make for his people when he restores them to his favour. The theme is developed first in connection with the northern tribes of Israel/Ephraim in vv. 2-22; the focus then briefly switches to Judah in vv. 23-26; only to come to a grand conclusion embracing the reunited people in vv. 27-40.

1. To Israel (31:2-22)

OUTLINE

a. Everlasting Love (31:2-6)
b. Return of the Firstborn (31:7-9)
c. Journey's End (31:10-14)
d. Rachel's Grief (31:15-17)
e. Ephraim's Repentance (31:18-20)
f. A New Thing Created (31:21-22)

It is difficult to determine when the material in vv. 2-22 was originally

revealed to Jeremiah. Some find here a relic of a northern ministry of
the prophet during the time when Josiah was attempting to extend his
control in the area of the former kingdom of Israel. They argue that
these early oracles were subsequently updated by the addition of the
references to Judah to fit the changed circumstances that arose with
Babylonian hegemony. While this is possible, there is no positive
evidence to establish the existence of such a northern ministry.

Others such as Carroll note that the themes of restoration and joy
pursued in this section are such as to distance them from Jeremiah, and
contend that we have here a late insertion representing the hopes of
Judean society in the Persian period. 'The fictional Jeremiah created by
the tradition is temperamentally incapable of uttering such images of
love and merrymaking—the last representations of him in the tradition
are of his haranguing the communities in Egypt (44) and cursing the
Babylonians (51:59-64). Those are characteristic poses of the man
Jeremiah and it is against a backdrop of such images that the sudden
shift to love poetry and songs supportive of the people is so unlikely'
(Carroll 1986:588-9). However, the repeated use of Ephraim to refer to
the people of the northern kingdom militates against such a late date
for this material. Carroll's description also fails to recognise the
tension under which Jeremiah lived. He could not act so as to reinforce
the complacency of his own generation. His task was to awaken them
to the peril in which they lived. On the other hand, he had to be true to
the whole counsel of God, which did embrace a future of renewed
fellowship with the LORD and enjoyment of all that true peace would
bring to them. There was nothing that he wished for more than that his
people would again acknowledge the LORD and bask in the blessings
of covenant favour.

Dating of this passage is further complicated by the fact that it
draws on imagery found in Isaiah (particularly Isa. 60:1–62:12;
65:17-25; 66:7-14, 22-3). Those who subscribe to the view of late
authorship for Isaiah 40–66 are drawn to favour a late exilic or post-
exilic origin, but if the integrity of Isaiah is maintained, then there is no
difficulty in finding the phraseology of the earlier prophet being reused
as a similar message of comfort is extended to the people of God. The
thought of a time of future unity inevitably has to grapple with the
fragmented condition of the covenant people in Jeremiah's time. Looking back to how this unfortunate situation had arisen inevitably
involved considering the current circumstances of Israel/Ephraim.
What had happened to them pointed to the judgment to come on Judah
for its rebellion, and also to the possibility of future restoration. But the
point is clearly made that the restored people will be those who have

learned from their experience of divine chastisement (vv. 18-20).

The first three sub-sections (vv. 2-6, 7-9, 10-14) all develop with differing emphases the theme of return from exile in exuberant language which stretches beyond the historical experience of the return from Babylon to look forward to the eschatological harmony of the whole people of God as they gather in the New Jerusalem. These joyful scenes are then abruptly interrupted by a description of the grief caused by invasion and deportation (vv. 15-17), followed by the response of the suffering community as they recognise how wrong their conduct has been (vv. 18-20). The final sub-section (vv. 21-22) emphasises the astonishingly innovative course followed by the LORD in restoring the fortunes of his people.

a. Everlasting Love (31:2-6)

2. What follows the introductory words, **This is what the LORD says,** may be interpreted in two ways. On the one hand it may have a future reference and be a direct prophecy of the way God will bring back the exiles from Babylon. This is reflected in the NIV rendering: **The people who survive the sword will find favour in the desert; I will come to give rest to Israel.** On the other hand, it is possible to understand the words as looking back to what happened at the time of the Exodus. This is reflected in the NKJV: 'The people who survived the sword found grace in the wilderness—Israel, when I went to give him rest' (cf. NRSV; REB). The latter approach is supported by the fact that the perfect form of the verb *māṣāʿ* would ordinarily be translated by a past tense, 'found'; that the phrase 'find favour/grace' is associated with the Exodus, occurring five times in Exod. 33:12-17 in reference to the experience of the unmerited consideration and care of the LORD; that 'in the desert/wilderness' naturally suggests the time of the Exodus; and a similar structure of introductory speech formula followed by an historical resume before the start of direct speech may be detected in vv. 15-17 (Keown et al. 1995:107), though there the introductory words are repeated in v. 16. Such a flashback to the display of divine love at the time of the Exodus would be similar to that found in Hos.11:1-4, and the implicit argument would be that their past experience should lead to similar expectations for the future.

However, it is difficult to understand the phrase 'the people who survive the sword' as referring to the time of the Exodus, not even when the pursuing armies of Pharaoh (Exod. 14:9) or the activities of the Amalekites (Deut. 25:17-18) are taken into account, as was proposed by the medieval Jewish scholar Rashi. This phrase naturally suggests the circumstances of the people when Samaria fell in 722 BC or what would happen when Judah was overrun in 586 BC. This would indicate that the verb *māṣā'* should be identified as a prophetic perfect, 'will find' (see Volume 1, Introduction §7.2). 'In the desert/wilderness' would then be understood as an allusion to the experience at the Exodus, but the whole statement would be a direct prophecy of what the LORD intended to do for the exiles when they returned from Babylon. In this case the thought would be similar to 'I will lead her into the desert and speak tenderly to her' (Hos. 2:14). Coming up from Egypt and coming back from Babylon involved not just crossing similar physical terrain, but also learning similar spiritual lessons (Isa. 40:3-5).

The following words are variously understood because it is unclear whether Israel or the LORD is the subject of the verb 'come'.[24] Perhaps a continuation of the previous subject, 'the people', is the easiest assumption, and 'Israel' at the end of the verse is then a nominative absolute. This leads to a translation such as, 'Israel, when it went to find its rest' (NASB). However, when Jeremiah uses the relatively rare verb *rāga'* in 50:34, it has the sense 'to bring rest', and this fits in with the LORD being understood as the subject of the verb: **I will come to give rest to Israel**. Rest in the Old Testament is closely connected with Israel's occupation of the promised land (Exod. 33:14; Josh. 1:13; 23:1). The giving of rest then refers to their entry into the land, and the words can be understood both of the original settlement and of the return from exile. The word is used in the sense of 'to find rest/repose' in Deut. 28:65, 'Among those nations you will find no repose', and it is used here to indicate the LORD's fidelity towards the people he has taken to be his own. He promises that he will reverse for them the covenant curse of 'an anxious mind, eyes weary with longing, and a despairing heart' which afflicted them as exiles. Then they lived in a state of perpetual uncertainty as to what the regime would impose on them, but when the LORD restores them to the land he will provide them with settled conditions and security.

3. The LORD appeared to us[25] in the past, saying. As is indicated by

---

24. The matter is more complex than just determining the subject of the verb. *hālôk* is the infinitive absolute, which is used for the finite verb, but tense has to be inferred from the context, which is ambiguous. GKC §113dd suggests it may be the equivalent of a cohortative, 'Let me come to …'.

25. The Massoretic Text is 'to me' (*lî*), but translators have found this difficult. The LXX reads 'to him' (suggesting the text should be *lô*), a reading followed by the NASB and NRSV. It may, however, be that *lî* can function as a third person masculine form, especially in poetic contexts. 'Saying' is a supplement, and the Hebrew literally continues 'and everlasting love'.

the NIV footnote, the word rendered 'in the past' (Isa. 22:11) may also be translated in its more usual meaning 'from afar' (Isa. 5:29) or 'out of a distant place' (30:10). This fits in better with an exilic background for this declaration when their separation from the land of promise reinforced the people's feelings of separation from God. So taken as part of the divine speech begun in v. 2, this would then be a prophecy that in the Exile they would be aware (through prophets like Ezekiel) of the LORD's attitude towards them. However, the change to 'us'/'me' favours the view that the speaker is now Jeremiah himself expressing the ideal testimony of the people as a whole. 'In the past' then refers to the divine revelation at Sinai, where there was a declaration of God's love towards Israel (Exod. 20:6; Deut. 7:7-9; 10:15).

I have loved you[26] **with an everlasting love** looks back to the basis of Israel's relationship with the LORD as founded solely in the sovereign initiative and love of God, unmotivated by an obligation on his part towards those on whom he set his affection. This is the only use in Jeremiah of 'āhab, 'to love' with the LORD as the subject, though it is frequently used in Deuteronomy to present the basis of the covenant (Deut. 4:37; 7:8, 12, 13; 10:14, 15). Because divine love is 'everlasting', it opens the door to forgiveness even when the people have persistently rebelled and have forfeited all claim (if they ever had any) on the LORD. However, the LORD remains committed to them, and when repentance and a genuine response to the invitation of renewed fellowship are forthcoming, there need be no doubt about the LORD's response to his people. His everlasting love keeps the door constantly open for the returning prodigal.

The verb *māšak* used in **I have drawn you with loving-kindness** (*ḥesed*, 2:2) may be understood in two ways. It can mean 'to prolong' or 'to extend': 'I have continued my faithfulness to you' (NRSV). This use is reflected in the request, 'Continue your love to those who know you' (Ps. 36:10). Because of the unending nature of God's love, it is a committed, covenant love (*ḥesed*) so that he perpetually acts for the good of his people. This fits in with the sequence of thought between the two clauses, indicated by the 'therefore' (*'al-kēn*) with which the second clause begins (omitted in the NIV): eternal love and therefore acts of love that flow from it. A more specific expression of the same thought is, however, obtained if the verb is rendered 'to draw' or 'to drag', implying no help from the object being moved. It is used in this way when the Midianites 'pulled Joseph up out of the cistern'

---

26. The second person pronouns in the verse are feminine singular, referring to the people, as is made clear by the language of v. 4, 'Virgin Israel'.

(Gen. 37:28), and when something similar happened to Jeremiah (38:13). The prophet Hosea had used it in this way of the LORD's activity to 'draw' or 'lead' the people to himself: 'I led them with cords of human kindness, with ties of love' (Hos. 11:4). Possibly the picture is that of a farmer coaxing a recalcitrant animal to move to a place of safety or to better grazing. In a similar fashion the LORD had repeatedly sought to bring the people back to himself. As is frequently the case in the Old Testament, the object of God's love is the people as a group, not an individual, but there is no doubt that love is extended to individuals as well, those who are part of the group (Ps. 106:3) and who act in the way of which he approves (Ps. 146:8; Prov. 3:12; 15:9; 22:11).

4. Having shown what his past behaviour means for the future of the people, the LORD now presents a vision of what they will enjoy when restored to the land. Verses 4 and 5 are linked by the threefold emphatic repetition of 'again' (*'ôd*) at the beginning of successive lines (a feature preserved in the NRSV), marking three aspects of the decisive change back from exile. The first scene is that of rebuilding—a theme that was always part of Jeremiah's ministry. **I will build you up again and you will be rebuilt, O Virgin Israel.** The repetition of the verb serves to intensify the certainty of this restoration which encompasses more than the physical environment of the dwellings and towns of the land. The whole social, economic and religious fabric of the land will be regenerated. The address 'Virgin Israel' is found again in v. 21, and also in 18:13 (cf. 14:17; Amos 5:2). In the light of the geographic references in vv. 5 and 6 it is here a specific reference to the northern kingdom, but now with her squalid past forgiven and transformed by divine grace so that she is worthy of the epithet 'virgin' (Eph. 5:26-27).

The second scene pictures the joy which will be experienced by the people when they are restored to the land. **Again you will take up your tambourines and go out to dance with the joyful.** Tambourines were musical instruments with a circular frame across which was stretched a membrane of skin. They were held in one hand and beaten with the other. Archaeological evidence suggests that later tambourines had also pieces of metal hanging from them, which jangled when shaken. They were played by women in victory celebrations (Exod. 15:20; Judg. 11:34; 1 Sam. 18:6; Ps. 68:26), fitting in with the personification of Israel employed here. This contrasts with the melancholy picture of the people presented in 7:34 and 25:10.

5. The third scene presents the fruitfulness of the land, with 'plant' recalling the positive aspect of Jeremiah's message (1:10). **Again you**

will plant vineyards on the hills of Samaria. The vines were typically laid out on terraces on the hillsides, and their culture was impractical except in times of uninterrupted peace, because several years had to pass before a harvest was obtained. Samaria stood at the head of a fertile valley (Isa. 28:4) where vineyards would be found. There is here a reversal of the covenant curse under which those who tended the vines would not enjoy their produce (Deut. 28:30, 39, 51). **The farmers will plant them and enjoy their fruit.** 'Enjoy' is literally 'make common'. It refers to the legislation of Lev. 19:23-25 whereby the fruit of newly planted trees was not to be eaten for the first three years; in the fourth year it would be presented as a thank-offering to the LORD, though it could be redeemed; and in the fifth year it became available for ordinary use. The picture is thus one of a settled community in which the fruit is available for those who had planted it some years previously. So both town and country are re-established (cf. v. 24).

6. There is another vital dimension to the life of the restored community: there will be a return to the true worship of the LORD. The religious deviations of the past will no longer play a part in the life of the community. 'For' (*kî*) **there will be a day**; about that there should be no doubt. **When watchmen cry out on the hills of Ephraim** refers to those who looked for the first appearance of the new moon so that the time of the monthly festivals might be accurately determined. They are here stationed on prominent sites so that their vision would not be obscured and they might give accurate notice. They are not directly referred to in the Old Testament (but see Ps. 130), but are mentioned often in early Jewish literature. Having made the appropriate observations in the hill country of Ephraim (where Samaria itself was situated), they give the signal to proceed to Jerusalem: **Come, let us go up to Zion, to the LORD our God.** The noteworthy feature of the envisaged worship is that it is based on a reintegrated community (cf. 3:14). No longer would there be recourse to the divisive sanctuaries which had been a feature of the religious life of the northern kingdom (1 Kgs. 12:28-31). Bethel and Dan will be deserted; the days of tension and schism will be over; and the restored people will live in union and harmony. Here is the true outworking of the reforms Josiah had initiated.

b. Return of the Firstborn (31:7-9)
It is not immediately evident to whom the commands found in this section are addressed. The mention of the nations in v. 10 might

suggest that the LORD is calling for universal praise and rejoicing as his people return, but it is easier to see this sub-section as addressed to the people themselves, calling on them to celebrate their deliverance and acclaim their deliverer.

7. An initial 'for' (*kî*) suggests that what follows provides further motivation for the invitation of the watchmen in the previous verse. **This is what the LORD says** introduces another aspect to what the LORD will provide for his people. **Sing with joy[27] for Jacob; shout for the foremost/'head' of the nations.** 'Shout' (<√*sāhal* I) is here used positively of the joy of the remnant (8:16; 5:8; see possibly Isa. 12:6). The two phrases 'for Jacob' and 'for the foremost of the nations' are parallel, and given the explicit mention of Ephraim in v. 9, it is the northern kingdom that is being accorded this status (cf. Amos 6:1). This is grounded in the fact that God has chosen them (Deut. 26:19). It is not necessarily a term of political superiority (though it is used of David as the 'chief' or 'foremost ruler' in Ps. 18:44), but rather points to their key role in the divine unfolding of history. This had been obscured by the Exile, but now that God has restored them, shouts of elation are appropriate (Isa. 44:23; 48:20; 49:13; 51:11; 54:1; 55:12).

Make your praises heard,[28] and say: 'O LORD, save your people, the remnant of Israel.' There is a division of opinion as to whether it is 'The LORD has saved his people' (LXX[29]; REB), or 'Save, O LORD, your people' as in the Massoretic Text. The LXX reading fits in with the fact that the deliverance from exile is described as already underway, rather than something that is to be prayed for as still future. But the seeming awkwardness of the Massoretic Text argues for its originality. Prayer was an accompaniment of the return, as v. 9 shows, and the salvation in view is not merely deliverance from the Exile but from all that would oppose the people of God. The request to save (<√*yāša‘* hiphil; 4:16) is ultimately eschatological, for though its fulfilment is anticipated in various earthly acts of release, it is not exhausted by them. Here Jeremiah uses 'remnant' to refer to those who had survived the Exile and are now returning to the land (23:3). It is with them that hope for the future rests.

---

27. The noun is used as an accusative of respect, expressing the state or orientation of the subject (GKC §118q).

28. This is in fact two imperatives, 'Make heard! Praise!', bringing to five the number of imperatives in this exhortation.

29. The LXX reading, supported by the Targum, indicates the text should be read as *hôšia‘* ('he has saved') rather than the imperative *hôša‘* with a change in the pronominal suffix on *‘ammakā*, 'your people', to *‘ammô*, 'his people'.

8. The response to their prayer is divinely announced in what follows: **See, I will bring them from the land of the north and gather them from the ends of the earth.** Again, the language contains many echoes of Isaiah's prophetic descriptions of similar scenes (cf. Isa. 35:3-10; 40:3-5; 41:17-19; 42:16; 43:5-6; 44:3-4; 48:20; 49:9-13), in particular the presentation of the return from exile being a new Exodus. This is a motif found earlier in Jeremiah's prophecy (16:14-15; 23:7-8), with the realisation that what is now promised will so outstrip the old that it will pale in comparison and be almost forgotten. 'The land of the north', which had earlier constituted an ominous threat of enemy incursion (6:22-23), is now to be left behind as no longer determinative of the destiny of the people. They are divinely gathered (v. 10) from the distant lands into which they have been scattered (cf. Isa. 43:5; 54:7; 56:8). It is emphasised that **among them will be the blind and the lame, expectant mothers and women in labour.** There are two aspects to this picture. One is the universality of the return, which extends even to the most disadvantaged members of the community who would not normally be considered able or fit to travel. There is also an implicit contrast between the LORD's gentle care of the vulnerable and the brutality of the enemy forces that had descended upon the land and led the people captive. This return is not accomplished in human strength but in reliance on God. Along with the element of hope conveyed by the presence of women ready to give birth, this builds up into a picture of a people whom their divine Overlord carefully protects and reinstates as those who are significant to him.

A great throng will return. The NIV does not translate the final word 'to here' (cf. NRSV, NJPS).[30] This indicates the Palestinian perspective (cf. 3:18; 16:15) of Jeremiah as he speaks this word and militates against it originating in Egypt during his residence there after the destruction of Jerusalem. 'Throng' (NIV; NKJV) emphasises the large number of returnees, but the word *qāhāl* is frequently employed to describe the Israelites as a worshipping community, and it seems probable that this is the idea here. 'They shall return ⌐as⌐[31] a great assembly' (cf. NASB footnote).

---

30. BHS recommends revocalising *hēnnâ*, 'to here' (not 'to there' as in the NKJV) as *hinnēh*, 'behold', and transferring it to the beginning of v. 9. It is not clear whether the NIV has omitted it on these grounds, but the change is unnecessary.

31. An accusative of respect, expressing number (GKC §118q).

9. They will come with[32] **weeping; they will pray as I bring them back.** The combination of weeping and prayer is also found at 3:21, but here the weeping is a sign of joy rather than sadness. Instead of prayer the NRSV, relying on the LXX, has 'with consolations', whereas the Massoretic Text has 'with supplications'[33], which many have felt to be awkward (cf. v. 7), but again without adequate reason. As they are brought back (<√*yābal* hiphil, 'to conduct, guide along'; cf. 'led' 11:19), they express in prayer their awareness of the need for continuing divine assistance if they are to avoid the errors of the past.

In response to their heartfelt prayers God gives the assurance that he will guide them and provide for them. **I will lead** (<√*hālak* hiphil, 'to cause to walk') **them beside streams of water** is a picture of bountiful provision of resources, particularly water which is so important for survival in the heat of the east. However sad they may have been by the waters of Babylon (Ps. 137:1), leaving the abundance of water there and venturing into the desert was not to be lightly undertaken, but the LORD promises that he will make provision for them (Isa. 48:21) just as he had done at the Exodus from Egypt (Exod. 17:6; Deut. 8:15). After enduring conditions of God-abandonment as the punishment for their rebellion, they will enjoy a renewed experience of his love.

On a level path where they will not stumble. This continues the picture of the shepherd's care for his flock (cf. v. 10; Isa. 40:11). A 'level' or 'right' path was one from which unevennesses had been removed, and which was not strewn with obstacles (Ps. 107:7; Prov. 12:15; 14:12; 21:2). Paths were normally only straightened or levelled when a king was expected (Isa. 40:3). Here the people of God are being led on a road fit for a king.

The reason for this treatment is given as: **Because** (*kî*) **I am Israel's father.** The language of father in reference to God is infrequent in the Old Testament (3:19; Deut. 32:6; Isa. 63:16; 64:8), but it had been used at the time of the Exodus. The declaration of Israel's sonship preceded the Exodus and Sinai (Exod. 4:22), and designated their special status in comparison with the other nations. This bond contained within itself an element of permanence which injected hope into an otherwise hopeless situation: the father could not ultimately

32. The inseparable preposition *bə* is used to indicate accompanying circumstances (*IBHS* §11.2.5d).

33. The LXX points to reading the Hebrew as *tanḥûmîm*, 'comforts, consolations' (<√*nāḥam*), rather than the Massoretic *taḥănûnîm*, 'supplications for favour' (<√*ḥānan*).

disown his son (cf. Hos. 11:1). There does not seem to be here any reflection on Israel over against Judah, but rather on the people as entering into the fullness of the covenant promises already made.

The same thought is further expressed in, **and Ephraim is my firstborn son.** In royal dynasties of the ancient East primogeniture prevailed, and even in ordinary families the first-born was the heir and received a double portion of the inheritance (Deut. 21:15-17). As the first-born son, the people are the object of the care and protection of their heavenly Father. Ephraim was the second son of Joseph, who was elevated to a place of prominence in the family of Jacob by the patriarch's special blessing (Gen. 48:19-20). It had been the strongest tribe in northern Israel, with the capital Samaria lying in its territory. The term 'Ephraim' is used here in an extended sense as a poetic parallel for Israel. The emphasis in the passage is not that the north will enjoy special preference, but that they will not be excluded in the coming time of blessing. All Israel is God's first-born son and so the object of his special care and concern (Exod. 4:22; Deut. 32:6).

c. Journey's End (31:10-14)
The news of what happens to Israel is of such importance that it must be proclaimed throughout the world. It is not clear whether the prophet has had revealed to him a future scene which he now relates for the comfort of the people or whether the message is addressed immediately to the nations in confident expectation of the LORD's saving intervention (see comments on v. 11).

10. Hear the word of the LORD, O nations; proclaim it in distant coastlands. Again the language employed is reminiscent of that of Isaiah (Isa. 49:1). The nations are involved not only in receiving the message regarding what the LORD has done; they are also expected to relay that message to their furthest contacts. What they are to understand is that **he who scattered Israel will gather them.** It was not a sign of divine weakness or of lack of concern that the people had undergone such trials. Scattering among the nations (Lev. 26:33) was part of the curse of the broken covenant, and was frequently referred to by Ezekiel (e.g. Ezek. 5:10, 12; 12:14-15; 34:12). It was God punishing them for their sin, and so, when his intention to educate and reclaim them had been fully accomplished, he would act effectively to reverse this judgment on them. Scattering will be transformed into gathering: at the end of the dark tunnel is the light of God's recalling grace. He **will watch over his flock** (*ʿēder*, 13:17; Isa. 40:11; Zech. 10:3) **like a shepherd** indicates the care with which he will provide for his people and the tenderness of his action (23:3; Exod. 34:12; Pss. 95:6-7a; 100:3; Isa. 40:11).

11. The reason why the nations should pay attention is spelled out in terms of the deliverance the LORD will provide for his people. **For** (*kî*) **the LORD will ransom Jacob and redeem them from the hand of those stronger than they.** Other translations (such as the NRSV) take the verbs as referring to the past, that is, to action that has already occurred when the command to listen is issued to the nations. Either way this message was initially aimed at encouraging those who remained faithful in Judah that despite the immediate foreboding prospect there would be a later reversal of the condition of the people. To 'save' (v. 7) there are now added 'ransom' (<√*pādâ*, translated as 'redeem' in 15:21) which indicates transfer of ownership or release through purchase, and 'redeem' (<√*gāʾal*, a favourite word with Isaiah, Isa. 43:1; 52:9) which conveys much the same thought but with the additional aspect of it being the action of a close relative on behalf of a kinsman. 'Redeem' may be used in the broad sense of 'save from harm'; it had already been used of return from exile in Mic. 4:10. Though both words were employed of the LORD's action at the time of the Exodus ('ransom' in Deut. 7:8; 9:26, though rendered there as 'redeemed' in the NIV; 'redeem' in Exod. 6:5; 15:13), their use together is relatively rare (in addition at Ps. 69:19; Isa. 35:9-10; 51:10-11; Hos. 13:14). It is not the strength of the people that effects their release; they are in fact weaker than their enemies. Release from captivity is due solely to the LORD's intervention in power.

12. The people are no longer described as still on their travels (vv. 8-9). The trek is now over, and they are portrayed to the nations as having arrived at Jerusalem. **They will come and shout for joy** (the same word as in v. 7) **on the heights of Zion.** The description of the restored people is not focused on those from the former northern kingdom. In the unity of the restoration any thought of rival shrines as in the past is excluded and they all naturally move towards Jerusalem, the city of the LORD. The 'heights of Zion' (cf. 17:12) is a reference to the site of the Temple. It is not just political or territorial reinstatement that is in view, but religious restoration and covenant renewal which form the basis for enjoyment of their Overlord's provision. It is therefore the case that **they will rejoice**[34] **in the bounty/ 'goodness' of the LORD.**

---

34. 'Streaming to the goodness of the LORD' (NKJV) takes the verb as *nāhar* I, 'flow like a stream' (Isa. 2:2; Mic. 4:1), rather than *nāhar* II, 'be radiant' (Ps. 34:5; Isa. 60:5).

'Rejoice' points to the radiance of their expressions as they view and
enjoy what the LORD has given to them. His goodness in material
things is part of the total care their protector takes of them.

The grain, the new wine and the oil are often associated in
Deuteronomy as part of the blessings of the promised land (Deut. 7:13;
11:14). 'New wine' (*tîrôš*) is the fresh, unfermented juice of grapes,
associated with fruitfulness and enjoyment, and not a term used in
contexts of intoxication. It is a sign of divine blessing. The oil is that
obtained from olives. Since an olive tree took a long time to reach
maturity, enjoying its produce was a sign of long-term stability as well
as of a good harvest. Mention of **the young of the flocks and herds**
shows that animals as well as crops would flourish in the land. The
whole scene is one of great agriculture prosperity, as the LORD crowns
the year with his bounty (Ps. 65:11). This is a restoration of what
Canaan had been intended to be like for the people of God (Deut. 8:8).
As a consequence, **they will be like**[35] **a well-watered garden, and
they will sorrow** (<√*dāʿab*, 'to be weary', 31:25) **no more.** Continuity
of water supplies was also problematic in the east, and 'well-watered'
(Isa. 58:11) rules out any threat from this source. It all builds into a
scenario where the grief arising from weariness and sorrow which they
had experienced in the Exile will be a thing of the past, and Edenic
bounty will testify to renewed divine favour (Ezek. 34:25-31), a
resumption of paradise (Isa. 51:3). In this way the whole scene anticipates the final heavenly reconciliation between God and his people.

13. Such an overwhelming experience of the goodness of the LORD
leads to further exuberant expressions of joy. **Then maidens will
dance and be glad.** 'Then' points to this future time of blessing and
incorporates a solemn indication that the 'now' of estrangement and
rebellion involved a different scenario. Dancing was the recognised
opposite of mourning (Eccl. 3:4), and it was an accepted mode of
expressing emotion even in sacred contexts. **Young men and old as
well**[36] rather implies that they too will be dancing, whereas the main

---

35. *wəhāyətâ napšām* is literally 'their life (<*nepeš*, 2:34) will be'. 'Their
life shall become like a watered garden' (NRSV).

36. Instead of reading *yaḥdāw*, 'together', the REB translates 'will rejoice'
by revocalising the form to *yiḥdû* from the much rarer root *ḥādad* (or possibly
ḥādâ), 'to be merry', cf. Exod. 18:9 (so also the NRSV). Holladay (1989,
2:153, 186) and Carroll (1986:593-4) support this understanding in the light of
the parallel that would then exist with *śāmaḥ* and also of the LXX reading.
Bright (1965:274), however, suggests that the MT reading functions nicely to
describe the comprehensive extent of the rejoicing.

verb in Hebrew is 'be glad' and the focus is on all the people sharing as one in the joyful scene.[37] The contrast that had begun at the end of v. 12, 'they will sorrow no more', is then extended. **I will turn** (<√*hāpak*, 'to turn, overturn, transform'; not used here in a negative sense as in 2:21) **their mourning into gladness; I will give them comfort and joy instead of sorrow.** It is only by divine 'turning' that the present and impending bleak conditions will be transformed, but it can be done (Ps. 30:11).

14. The focus then reverts to the sacral implications of the scene, forming a closure with the initial mention of Zion in v. 12. The tribe of Levi had not been given territory in Canaan, and so the priests were largely dependent for their livelihood on their share of the offerings brought to the sanctuary. **I will satisfy**/'satiate/saturate the desire/life (<*nepeš*, cf. v. 12) of' **the priests with abundance**/'with fat'. 'Satisfy' refers to refreshing (v. 25) such as that obtained from a fall of rain. This may be a general reference to the prosperity and abundance of the land (Pss. 36:8; 63:5), which will be shared in by the priests, but it more probably paints a picture of the fat of the thank-offerings that would be generously offered. Neither priests nor people could eat the fat of the offerings (Lev. 7:23-24), but much fat from many offerings given in gratitude to the LORD also implied that more portions would become the priests' by right. **'And my people will be filled**/'satisfied, more than content' **with my bounty,' declares the LORD**, again referring to the 'goodness' which will be showered on the restored people.

d. Rachel's Grief (31:15-17)
There is then a sharp and sudden contrast in which scenes of future joy are replaced by a description of intense woe and desolation. This is a poetic description of great poignancy of the devastating impact deportation had had on the northern kingdom.

15. The time reference switches back from the future redemption the LORD will bring his people, especially Israel/Ephraim, to a scene of distress which may well have originally been intended as a history lesson for Judah. Confronted by a bold poetic presentation of the misery that had come on the northern kingdom, Jerusalem is challenged to assess her own prospects in the light of the past. **This is what the LORD says, 'A voice is heard**[38] **in Ramah, mourning and**

---

37. The main verb in the Hebrew is *tiśmaḥ*, 'she [i.e. a maiden] will rejoice', with the thought of dancing in the prepositional phrase *bəmāḥôl*.

38. *nišmāʿ* with long *ā* is the niphal participle; so this is viewed as an ongoing scene of grief.

great weeping.' There is an element of shock treatment here for there could hardly be a greater contrast from the joy that has just been described. 'Mourning'/'wailing' (*nəhî*, 9:20) describes the cries made over the dead. 'Great weeping' is 'weeping of bitterness' (*bəkî tamrûrîm*, cf. v. 21), a Hebrew idiom which expressed emotions of intense sorrow in terms of the sense of taste: what was unpalatably sour and bitter was used to represent experiences of misery and grief. Ramah was a town in Benjamin on the border between the two king-doms,[39] and so the scene is one of plaintive cries spreading north and south. **Rachel weeping for her children**. Although Rachel is not otherwise mentioned in the Old Testament as a figure from the past, she is here presented in a moving and graphic fashion. Rachel was the mother of Joseph and Benjamin, and so through Joseph was the grand-mother of Ephraim and Manasseh, the two most important northern tribes, which had been deported in 722 BC and which were undergoing brutal treatment as captives in foreign lands. The intense trauma of those events is portrayed by the personification of Rachel as a mother looking disconsolately for her children—and going on doing so.[40] **And refusing to be comforted** contrasts with the future reality of v. 13. At the time the message was given to Jeremiah there was only an intense sense of loss **because** (*kî*) **her children are no more.**[41] Looking north over their former territory, Rachel can no longer see her descendants because they have been removed. The poignancy of the scene is further intensified by the tragic life story of Rachel herself. She was the mother who had desperately wanted children (Gen. 30:1), but whose children had been a source of trouble to her. She had never herself enjoyed a settled home in the land of promise, dying on the way to Bethlehem after she had given birth to Benjamin with great difficulty (Gen. 35:16-19). 'In the stark simplicity of the phrase, "because they are not", the man himself unmarried and childless, has summed up the impassive wall which death presents before the reaching hands of love' (Welch 1928:213-4).

---

39. The Massoretic Text is *bərāmâ* without the article, which is unusual in that the place name generally has the article. To translate 'on a height' (NJPS footnote) or 'on high places' is not impossible.

40. 'Weeping' is a participle denoting continuing action. 'Refusing' is a per-fect form, possibly with a stative sense, 'she has refused to be comforted and continues to display such an attitude'.

41. Literally, 'because he is no more' (*kî 'ênennû*). The masculine singular is puzzling in view of the preceding plurals, perhaps the thought is 'each of them', possibly reflecting the use of *kullô*, 'all of him', in 6:13 and 15:10.

Interpretation of v. 15 has frequently been complicated by assuming that there must have been some connection between the mention of Ramah here and Rachel's tomb, so that the poetic figure is one of the mother of the people rising from her grave to weep over her lost children. But the location of Rachel's tomb is a matter of some uncertainty. The traditional site is just north of Bethlehem, based on understanding Gen. 35:16 to imply that she died and was buried close to Ephrath (the older name for Bethlehem). However, the rare term used in Gen. 35:16 for the distance involved is variously understood. The NKJV sees her death as occurring 'but a little distance to go to Ephrath', whereas the NIV suggests 'still some distance from Ephrath' as being more likely (though in Gen. 48:7 it has 'a little distance' for the same term). The mention in 1 Sam. 10:2 of her tomb being situated at the otherwise unidentified Zelzah does nothing more than locate it on the edge of Benjamite territory. Although Ramah, five miles (8 km) north of Jerusalem, lay on Jacob's route from Bethel to Bethlehem, it is by no means necessary to assume that Rachel's tomb was there. Ramah on the northern boundary of Judah was chosen as a place from which the former northern kingdom could be viewed and from which lamentation would be heard far and wide. That it was also the place where the inhabitants of Judah were assembled prior to their departure for Babylon (40:1) does not seem particularly relevant to the interpretation of this verse which focuses on the fate of the northern tribes over a century earlier.

There is another aspect to the situation arising from Matthew's citation of this verse which he found fulfilled in Herod's slaughter of the children in Bethlehem in the years after Jesus' birth (Matt. 2:16-18). It does not seem to be appropriate to follow Laetsch and take this as a direct prophecy of these events (1952:248-251). Keil is probably on sounder ground when he says, 'The destruction of the people of Israel by the Assyrians and Chaldeans is a type of the massacre of the infants at Bethlehem, in so far as the sin which brought the children of Israel into exile laid a foundation for the fact that Herod the Idumean became king over the Jews, and wished to destroy the true King and Saviour of Israel that he might strengthen his own dominion' (1873, 2:26). The references are undoubtedly in the first instance to the situation at the time of the Assyrian invasion of the northern kingdom, but by an analogical application Matthew sees Herod's action fulfilling Jeremiah's words in that it shared the same basic features and character: the LORD's people were suffering under the cruel and oppressive rule of a foreign king.

16. Since the desolation will be reversed, sorrow should give way to comfort (v. 13), and despair to hope. The divine words that follow are addressed to Rachel using the second-person feminine. **This is what the LORD says, 'Restrain your voice from weeping and your eyes from tears, for** (*kî*) **your work will be rewarded,' declares the LORD.** The end of tears frequently features in descriptions of the coming time of divine intervention (Isa. 25:8; Rev. 7:17; 21:4), bringing out that misery and its causes will both be transformed. The existence of the reward (*śākār*, 'wage') is strongly emphasised, in contrast to the negative aspect of the scene of the previous verse.[42] Scripture attaches significance to human actions (Ps. 28:4; Prov. 11:4), which are viewed as determinative of the course of history. The work of Rachel that is in view seems to be connected with her role as the mother of her people, probably not just that she gave birth to the children, but also to her being so concerned about their welfare. She is assured that the seemingly hopeless situation is in fact recoverable, and her reward is the fact that **they will return from the land of the enemy.** 'Return' is the first use of the root *šûb* in this passage, denoting physical return from enemy territory, the land of their captivity, to Palestine. It is found in this sense also in vv. 17 and 21, but see also vv. 18 and 19. The root occurs seven times in all in vv. 16-21.

17. The positive message is again strongly emphasised. **'So there is hope for your future,' declares the LORD.** 'You' still refers to Rachel as the mother of her people, and 'your future' ('the after of you'; cf. 29:11) looks to what is to become of her descendants. They will return from captivity, and so there will be a continuing presence in the land. **Your children will return to their own land**/'borders'. Again the root *šûb* is employed as in v. 16.

e. Ephraim's Repentance (31:18-20)
The way in which the return of the exiles will occur is spelled out in the following verses. The LORD has already spoken of the distress of Rachel as the mother of the northern tribes; he now turns to set out the attitude of the lost children.

18. The LORD recounts the confession of Ephraim. As with the language of 3:21-25, there is some doubt as to whether this has already occurred, or is yet future. **I have surely heard Ephraim's moaning.**

---

42. Note the contrast between the use of *'ayin* in 'they are no more' (v. 15) and the assertions using *yēš*, 'there is reward' (v. 16), and 'there is hope' (v. 17).

'Surely' (an infinitive absolute) suggests that Jeremiah's original
audience (the spiritually distressed in the pre-586 situation in Jerusalem) are being reassured that though there has not as yet been any
return of the northern tribes, their situation has not gone unmonitored
and the LORD is aware of any change in their outlook. The people who
had not responded to the LORD's goodness towards them and his
pleading with them through the prophets are expected to react to their
misfortunes in the Exile. They are said to be 'moaning' (<√*nûd*, 15:5),
a picture of someone rocking to and fro in grief (cf. REB: 'Ephraim
was rocking in his grief').[43] As they reflect on what has happened to
them, they confess to God, **You disciplined me like an unruly calf,
and I have been disciplined.** They had come to recognise that their
deportation was the LORD's chastisement of them, designed to effect
their restoration to a right relationship with him, and also restoration to
their land. 'I have been disciplined' is not just a statement of fact, but
also an acceptance of the purpose of the discipline.[44] The mention of
an 'unruly calf', that is one 'that needed to be trained for the yoke and
plough' (NLT; cf. 2:20), looks back to, and reverses, the imagery of
Hosea: 'the Israelites are stubborn, like a stubborn heifer' (Hos. 4:16)
and 'Ephraim is a trained heifer that loves to thresh; so I will put a
yoke on her fair neck. I will drive Ephraim, Judah must plough, and
Jacob must break up the ground' (Hos. 10:11). 'Unruly' is 'not
trained', where the picture is not so much one of formal, didactic
instruction, but of learning obedience to the farmer's commands by
repetition (*NIDOTTE* 2:802). The people now acknowledge that they
have been brought to accept what they had previously ignored, namely,
the place of the LORD in their lives.

They therefore plead, **Restore me, and I will return**, again the
root *šûb* is used twice, 'Bring me back and I will come back'[45] (echoing 3:7, 12, 14; cf. Lam. 5:21). Although the primary stress of the word

---

43. *mitnôdēd* is a hithpolel form, probably here (contrast 48:27) used in a
reflexive sense, 'bemoaning himself' (*HALOT* 678).
44. The first verb, 'you disciplined me', is piel (cf. 2:19), but the second is
niphal probably not just with a passive force, 'I was disciplined', but as
conveying a reflexive idea—'I accepted the discipline' for what it was (cf.
6:8), not just as some harsh fate that I must undergo. It would then be a niphal
tolerativum in which the subject allows something to happen to him or to have
an effect on him (GKC §51c; *IBHS* §23.4g).
45. Although most English versions render *we'āšûbâ* as 'and I shall come
back', it is an ordinary *waw* followed by the cohortative which after an
imperative is used to express purpose, 'so that I may come back' (cf. GKC
§108.d; *IBHS* §34.5.2b).

is on a physical return to the land, since this could not be accomplished without a prior turning to the LORD, there is undoubtedly spiritual renewal involved here. The people realise that they are powerless to help themselves, and so speak as those who put their hope in the LORD and in the covenant bond that unites them, **because** *(kî)* **you are the LORD my God.**

19. The confession of Ephraim continues by urging another reason why the LORD should intervene to help the people. 'For' *(kî)*[46] **after I strayed, I repented.** 'Strayed' also renders *šûb* in the sense of 'to go back, to turn away from' (cf. 8:4). They recognise their spiritual apostasy, but now plead with the LORD on the basis of their change of mind and heart (<√*nāḥam* niphal, 4:28). 'Like the NT parable of the prodigal son in the far country (Luke 15), the return in this case has a double dimension: it is a geographical return (from exile), and a return to a relationship that was spurned in the folly of youth' (Anderson 1978:472). **After I came to understand,**[47] **I beat my breast**/'I beat upon the thigh'. This was a recognised gesture of grief and consternation throughout the ancient world (Ezek. 21:12; 'And then he groaned and smote on both his thighs with headlong hands, and so in sorrow spoke' *Odyss.* 13:193). English versions tend to substitute a more readily understood action for the same spiritual experience (but note the NRSV, 'struck my thigh'). Ephraim did not merely gain a different intellectual perception of his situation, but was also overwhelmed by unfeigned anguish at what he had done. **I was ashamed and humiliated because** *(kî)* **I bore the disgrace of my youth.** 'Ashamed' (<√*bôš*, cf. 2:26) and 'humiliated' (<√*kālam*, 3:3) relate to what they had experienced as a nation when they were overrun and deported. They now speak on the basis of a more mature understanding of their history, and can see that what had been inflicted on them was the penalty of their wrongdoing. They describe their past conduct as a 'disgrace' (*ḥerpâ*; 'offensive' 6:10; 15:15), something from which they now disassociate themselves. For 'youth' as a reference to an earlier period in their collective history, compare 2:2; 3:24, 25; 22:21; 32:30. However, when Jeremiah first delivered this message, that was an

---

46. English versions are uncertain how to render *kî* here. The NRSV favours a causal connection, 'for', but the NKJV retains 'surely' from the AV. This emphatic understanding is supported by *IBHS* §39.3.4e, which suggests, 'indeed'.

47. The verb is *hiwwādə'î*, a niphal <√*yāda'*, 'to know'. The REB translates 'Now that I am submissive' relating the verb to an Arabic root meaning 'become quiet' (*TDOT* 5:450-51).

insight into their past that had not been accepted by Israel (or Judah). These words were spoken to lead them, particularly Judah, into greater self-understanding. It was only by consciously and wholeheartedly adopting such an outlook that the people would in the future be enabled to move towards restoration.

20. As they heard the LORD's response to this anticipated change of attitude on Ephraim's part, the people of Judah were encouraged to act appropriately themselves. Even though their history was a catalogue of failure, they would not be rejected because of the bond that existed between them and the LORD. The reflective question, **Is not Ephraim my dear son, the child in whom I delight?**[48] suggests a positive answer, but there is tension between expectation and reality. 'Dear' (*yāqār*) points to something that is highly valued and esteemed; 'delight' to the pleasure that is derived from it. **Though (*kî*) I often speak against him, I still remember him.**[49] The speaking against him (the phrase is ambiguous in that *dibber bэ* may also mean 'speak about', cf. 'mention' GNB) is in connection with his wrongdoing. The LORD did not overlook or condone Ephraim's transgression, but even so, the LORD 'will remember him' not simply as an act of wistful mental recall, but with a view to action, action that is here clearly intended to further his relationship with the LORD. **'Therefore (*ʿal-kēn*, 'on account of this') my heart yearns**[50] **for him; I have great compassion for him,' declares the LORD.** The LORD is not a detached, impersonal spectator in the downfall and suffering of his people, and it is that divine commitment which forms the basis for their restoration. The words differ but the sentiments parallel Hos. 11:1-4, 8-9. 'Yearns' (*<hāmâ*) has already been used to describe the intensity of Jeremiah's own emotion ('pounds', 4:19). God's compassion (*<√rāḥam*, 13:14; here intensified by the use of an infinitive absolute)

---

48. Literally 'a child of delight', possibly picturing him as a youngster dandled on one's knee (NJPS), although it may simply be an expression of intense pleasure ('delight', Isa. 5:7).

49. This translation does not bring out the force of the infinitive absolute *zākōr*. 'I earnestly remember him still' (NKJV), or perhaps 'I do really still remember him' (cf. RSV). With the further infinitive absolute in the next statement, this brings out the intensity of the divine response to Ephraim.

50. Literally 'my bowels make a noise'. The bowels (*mēʿayîm*, cf. 4:19) were viewed as the seat of the most intense emotions (cf. Isa. 16:11; 63:15), and hence the English versions use 'heart'. 'I thrill for him' (BDB 242); Bright (1966:275) and Carroll (1986:600) speak of the feminine aspect of God's love portrayed here in a mother's yearning for her child.

is aroused by personal attachment to Ephraim and emotional involvement with him. The verb is derived from the noun *reḥem*, 'womb', and
it is probably correct to find here, as many commentators do, an
anthropomorphic expression based on the love of a mother for her
child.

f. A New Thing Created (31:21-22)

The next section is clearly set apart from the preceding by a sudden
change of person. In vv. 18-20 the people had been collectively spoken
about as Ephraim, and hence the masculine references. But now the
theme changes from the 'dear son' to the 'unfaithful daughter' and the
verbs in v. 21 are feminine. But the message remains the same. It is a
word of encouragement to the people because of the astonishing
change in their circumstances that the LORD will bring about.

21. Although the commands are in the feminine singular, what
requires to be done are not actions commonly associated with women.
Set up road signs; put up guideposts. The road signs (*ṣiyyûn* is close
in sound to *ṣiyyôn*, Zion) are cairns of stones, such as would be left by
travellers across rough terrain to guide those who come after them.
'Guideposts' (*tamrûrîm*) is a homonym with 'bitterness' in v. 15,
suggesting the change that is to occur in their situation, from the depths
of despair to roadsigns towards freedom. There is also a strong
emphasis in the original that Israel is to act in this for herself.[51] The
people in exile are being commanded to get things ready for going
home. They are not to be passive and let others take action on their
behalf; they have to respond to the divine summons issued to them.
Take note ('put/set your heart/mind on') **of the highway, the road
that you take**.[52] 'Highway' does not necessarily refer to a busy road,
but to one that had been built up from the level of the surrounding
land. This was the way they had walked over in going into captivity.
Now they are to pay careful attention to the route that they had
travelled so that they would be ready to retrace their steps, or else the
idea is that of a first group of returnees marking out the way for
subsequent groups to follow. The picture of a highway leading to home
is one that is often found in Isaiah (Isa. 35; 40:3-5,11; 41:18-20; 42:16;
43:1-7; 44:3-4; 49:9-13). **Return, O Virgin Israel, return to your**

---

51. *lāk*, 'for yourself', is repeated with both commands.
52. The kethibh *hālāktî* is the archaic 2nd feminine singular perfect (GKC
§44h) for which the qere substitutes the usual form *hālākt* (pausal). There is
no change in meaning.

towns.[53] 'Return' is again the verb *šûb*. They are to be ready to go back to the cities that had been devastated. Virgin Israel (cf. v. 4) now refers to the exiles returning to their homeland.

22. How long will you wander,[54] **O unfaithful daughter?** The root *šûb* again appears in 'unfaithful', in the sense of one who goes away (3:14, 22). The term seems unusually negative in such close connection with the more positive term, 'Virgin Israel'. 'Wander' (<√*ḥāmaq* hithpael 'to turn this way and that') expresses emotional and spiritual instability, the restlessness of those who impatiently desire something else. This had been true of them as they had strayed from the LORD, but now he is going to transform them and their situation.

The second part of the verse is difficult to interpret. It presents the reason why they should now lay aside their hesitation: the LORD is going to intervene in an unprecedented fashion. 'For' (*kî*) **the LORD will create a new thing on earth**, or more probably 'in the land' because it is return there that is central to the concerns of the Book of Consolation. The occurrence here of the verb 'create' (*bārā'*, which is not found elsewhere in Jeremiah) points to an action of divine sovereignty and power. The word is used only with God as the subject, most often in reference to the original creation (Gen. 1:1, 21, 27; 2:3, 4), but also to a new heaven and a new earth (Isa. 65:16-18). So here we are led to expect that the LORD is going to undertake a major new initiative. Unfortunately the identification of what precisely is in view has proved vexatious. The NIV (probably correctly) takes the perfect verb 'has created' as an instance of a prophetic perfect, something in the future that is viewed as so certain that it is described as completed.

The difficulty that arises with the three Hebrew words, **A woman will surround a man,** does not lie in their separate meaning, but in what is to be inferred from their syntactic combination here. The word for 'woman' (*nəqēbâ*) is a colourless term for 'female' (Gen. 1:27). 'Man' (*geber*, 'strong man' 30:6) points to a male at the height of his power, a warrior capable of accomplishing much by his strength. 'Woman' and 'man' are without the article so that the statement is a general one. The verb (the polel of *sābab*, 'to go around', 'to surround') is used of various activities involving encirclement: of enemies hemming one in (Ps. 22:16, 19), of a liturgical movement around the altar (Ps. 26:6), of the LORD shielding his people

---

53. Note *'ēlleh*, 'these', without article (GKC §126y). 'These towns of yours' again suggests an origin in Palestine for this oracle.

54. For a second person feminine singular ending in *-în*, see GKC §47o. The paragogic nun is also discussed in *IBHS* §31.7.1a.

(Deut. 32:10) and protecting them in his covenant faithfulness (Ps. 32:7, 10). But what do the words mean in combination?

The early church interpretation that this was a prophecy of the Virgin birth is not exegetically tenable, but it did meet the requirement of being something distinctly new, which many subsequent interpretations have failed to achieve.

Calvin focused attention on the use of *geber*, 'strong man', and related the passage back to 30:6 where the Israelites were like women, without strength and without any effective assistance. The transforming power of God will mean 'that they will be superior in strength to their enemies, whose power filled the whole world with terror' (1850, 4:114). The new thing is therefore the radical change of the formerly weak people of God ('a woman') into a force that is able to overwhelm their enemies.

Another line of interpretation with a long history also identifies the woman as the people of God. This may receive some justification from the phonetic parallel between the verb *təsôbēb*, 'will surround', which has 'a woman' as its subject, and the earlier *šôbēbâ*, 'unfaithful'/ 'backsliding', referring to Israel. However, the *geber*, 'strong man', is now taken to be the LORD himself. The thought then is that whereas the LORD had previously surrounded his weak people with the care that flows from covenant fidelity, in the new situation which he will create, Israel will take the initiative and willingly embrace (the sense that 'surround' would then have in this passage) the LORD with covenant devotion. The thought is certainly one that fits the new covenant context of this passage, but the use of *geber* to refer to the LORD is not a common one, though the similar form *gibbôr*, 'powerful', is found in 32:18. A variation of this is reflected in the rendering, 'I have created something new and different, as different as a woman protecting a man' (GNB), where the startlingly unusual development which is referred to is probably the renewed devotion of Israel, which has been divinely brought into existence.

A fourth major style of approach to this passage emphasises that *nĕqēbâ*, 'woman', and *bārāʿ*, 'to create', are intentionally employed to indicate that Genesis 1 is the appropriate background for interpretation. Whereas in the past Rachel had been deprived of her offspring, she was now going to have a future because the LORD will empower her to 'enfold a man (a son) as a sign of Yahweh's gracious gift of new life in the land. ... It is Yahweh who opens the womb and gives a future. So the Jeremianic text, when viewed in its poetic context, announces that the way into the future is opened by Yahweh who, in a miracle of creation, gives the people new life by restoring them to their land and giving them a posterity, a future. The old age, symbolised by Rachel weeping for her lost sons, will be superseded by a new age when Virgin Israel will be fruitful' (Anderson 1978:476-77).

It cannot be said that the obscurity of the saying has been totally resolved, but explanations along the lines of the third option above seem most probable. The context has emphasised that the LORD will take action to bring the people back to the land; now it is shown that he will work transformingly to create within them the right spirit that will enable them to continue to live in the land enjoying his favour.

> The new thing that God creates consists in this, that the woman, the weaker nature that needs help, will lovingly and solicitously sur-round the man, the stronger. Herein is expressed a new relation of Israel to the Lord, a reference to a new covenant which the Lord, ver. 31 ff., will conclude with his people, and in which he deals so condescendingly towards them that they can lovingly embrace him. This is the substance of the Messianic meaning in the words. (Keil 1873, 2:30)

2. To Judah (31:23-26)

There then follows a short section which mirrors the preceding vision of future good for the people of the north with one which foretells a similar destiny for the people of Judah. It was not the case that Judah had been totally omitted from what went before in that the promises of vv. 6 and 12 regarding the future worship at Zion strongly implied that there would be a time of blessing there, but this is now made clear.

23. This is what the LORD Almighty, the God of Israel, says raises the question of the significance of Israel here: is it the northern king-dom, or the united, ancient covenant people? It is extremely probable that it is the latter which is meant in this formal title of the God who was worshipped in the Temple (7:3). The blessing he has in store for his people does not exclude those in the south, though the oracle implies that there will be a time of national disaster before the blessing is enjoyed. **When I bring them back from captivity, the people**[55] **in the land of Judah and in its towns will once again** ('ôd, v. 4) **use these words** looks forward to the coming time of divine blessing. 'Bring them back from captivity' is a somewhat ambiguous phrase which the NIV footnote renders 'restore their fortunes' (30:3). Both meanings coincide when the people have in fact been exiled, though the broader meaning is the more likely. They are now depicted as

---

55. 'The people ... will once again use' is literally 'they ... will again say', an indefinite use of the plural (GKC §144g).

returning to the land, enjoying renewed prosperity and settling in once more throughout the length and breadth of Judah.

At this time of renewed favour the people will recognise the source of their improved circumstances. They employ traditional language: **The LORD bless you, O righteous dwelling, O sacred mountain.** Though it is possible that 'righteous' conveys the idea of 'legitimate' (23:5), the proper place for the people to dwell, it is more probable that 'righteous dwelling' is used to indicate the place where right standards of behaviour prevailed. This would contrast with the situation that had previously existed in Jerusalem and had occasioned her downfall, when her conduct defied the covenant norms. 'Dwelling' (*nāweh*) is an old word used to describe the land of promise as the place where the divine shepherd cares for his flock (10:25; 50:7; Exod. 15:13), and this is now recognised as the place where the LORD and his people will enjoy true fellowship. The mountain referred to is Zion or Moriah where the Temple was built. It may by extension refer to the whole city (Ps. 2:6; Isa. 66:20). It is 'sacred'/'holy' (cf. 1:5), set apart because the LORD had chosen it for the Temple where he presenced himself in the midst of his people. This saying does not of itself assume a previous destruction of the Temple and the city, though it would well fit in with that scenario, but can refer to a time of spiritual renewal characterised by the LORD again dwelling in the midst of his people.

24. The renewed occupation of the land will involve contentedness and social harmony. **People will live together in Judah and all its towns**[56]**—farmers and those who move about with their flocks.** The emphasis is on 'together' (*yaḥdāw*, as a united community). It involves both city-dwellers and those living in the countryside.[57] Those who were 'farmers'/'farm-workers' were hired help rather than smallholders, and 'those who move about' in the land were perhaps the shepherd boys. The point is that they are not the wealthy or the upper classes, but those of the lowest levels of society. They too are part of this scene of social cohesion and security.

---

56. The NIV has simplified the construction of the first part of this verse. 'They will live in it (*f.*), Judah and all his towns together.' The feminine 'it' probably refers back to 'the land of Judah' in the previous verse.

57. There is a puzzling *waw*-consecutive perfect: 'farmers and they will move on with the flock'. 'Those who move on with the flock' is probably based on reading, with some versional support, a construct participle *nōsə'ê* rather than a third person plural qal perfect, *nāsə'û*. A construct participle before a noun with a preposition is a possible construction (GKC §130a). It is generally agreed that three classes of people are referred to here: townspeople, farm-workers, and shepherds.

25. This will come about because the LORD will revive the land. 'For' (*kî*) **I will refresh the weary and satisfy the faint.**[58] The description is primarily one of the physical condition of the people. 'Refresh' (<√*rāwâ*, hiphil) is a metaphor based on saturation with water (cf. 'give abundant drink' NJPS), a picture of the relief and reinvigoration it gives to a weary individual (<*nepeš*, 2:34), that is one who is physically drained. The note of the totality of the blessing is lost in the NIV translation. *kôl*, 'every', qualifies 'the faint'/'every faint life'[59] (<*nepeš*, 2:34). All who are faint who will be satisfied/filled with the bounty of the LORD's provision. But there are spiritual implications as well, because the LORD is acting out of concern for their total welfare. As they go about their legitimate callings, they will know God's blessing. The language of 'satisfy'/'fill' is used in the gospels of the blessings of the kingdom (Matt. 5:6).

26. The brief section concludes with a comment which has no real parallel in Jeremiah. **At this I awoke and looked around. My sleep had been pleasant to me.** Keown et al. (1995:124, 128-29) suggest that this is a speech of the restored (and refreshed) exiles echoing that which is formally introduced in v. 23. But Zechariah records his personal experience regarding the visions he received (e.g. Zech. 4:1), and this verse seems to fulfil a similar function. Clearly it was while asleep that Jeremiah had received the message of vv. 23-25 from God. It is contrary to all that we know about Jeremiah to suppose that this sleep is a reference to some ecstatic experience during which Jeremiah's personal consciousness was suppressed. Despite his earlier strictures on dreams (23:25), they were not categorised as totally improper, but only those that had not been divinely given. It may be that like Zechariah's visions this revelation, though given while the prophet slept, involved more than the passive reception of a dream.

The revelation of future blessing afforded Jeremiah considerable personal satisfaction. (This had not been the case with all the revelation he received, 20:7-10.) It may be that he was all the more ready to add this personal detail because of accusations that he delighted in

---

58. The NLT rendering, 'For I have given rest to the weary and joy to the sorrowing', is a bold paraphrase which takes the perfect verbs as referring to completed actions rather than relating them to the time of the preceding verb in v. 24. The perfects in v. 25 refer to actions which will be completed before v. 24 will occur, and are therefore better translated as futures (future perfects).

59. *dā'ăbâ* may be a perfect before which a relative has to be supplied, 'every individual ⌊who⌋ has become and so is weary', or it may be an adjective based on an Aramaic participle *dā'ēb*.

uttering gloomy and condemnatory words about the people. Jeremiah intensely desired the good of the land, and took pleasure in its coming prosperity and the opportunity to announce it. But what then is the significance of 'I looked around'/'I saw'? It may just be part of the picture of someone roused from restful sleep and adjusting to wakefulness. But the idea may go beyond that. The verb 'to see' is used to indicate mental perception, and so the thought may be that as Jeremiah mused upon what he had been permitted to see in his dream he came to realise the wonder of what was yet to be. On the other hand, 'looked around' may also convey a grimmer thought: as he considered the circumstances of his own day, Jeremiah was aware of the contrast between what he saw about him and the future reality God promised.

3. To Israel and Judah Together (31:27-40)

OUTLINE

a.   From One Generation to the Next (31:27-30)
b.   The New Covenant (31:31-34)
c.   The Reliable Bond (31:35-37)
d.   Jerusalem Rebuilt (31:38-40)

Although it is convenient to consider the remainder of chapter 31 as four sections, it is in fact set out in a tripartite structure (vv. 27-30, vv. 31-37, vv. 38-40) as the repetition of the introductory formula indicates. However, vv. 35-37 constitute a separate expansion of the thought of vv. 31-34 rather than being integral to it, and it is more satisfactory to treat them as a separate sub-unit. Here Jeremiah presents the united blessing that will come to the people from the LORD.

a. From One Generation to the Next (31:27-30)
27.   This is the first of three sections which begin with the same formula, **'The days are coming,' declares the LORD** (vv. 27, 31, 38).[60] The clause begins with 'Behold!' (not translated in the NIV), probably to emphasise the reality and imminence of what is being talked about. The significance of the time reference in this phrase is much debated, but it seems to point to a future scene, the precise time

---

60.   *hinnēh yāmîm bāʾîm*, 'Behold! days ⌊are⌋ coming'. The NIV unnecessarily varies the translation of this phrase at the beginning of v. 31.

of which is not revealed, but which is certain because the coming events are already rising out of present circumstances (30:3). What will happen will be a development of factors that are already at work. Therefore those who by faith accept the divine analysis of the situation can be confident that what is foretold will come to pass.

Here the LORD gives his promise regarding a time **when/'and' I will plant the house of Israel and the house of Judah with the off-spring of men and of animals.** The future era of blessing affects equally both parts of the people, who will then be reunited. They are likened to fields which by divine action will be resown. God will scatter 'seed', here rendered 'offspring', so that the devastated land will once more be occupied by people and domestic animals. The metaphor found here presupposes that drawn in Hosea 2:23, where the same verb *zāra'* (here used with its cognate noun), 'to sow, scatter' (NIV uses 'plant' because of the changed metaphor), describes the people as divinely re-established in the land. A similar picture of the revitalisation of the land is found in Ezek. 36:10-11. This is the reversal of the covenant curse that had been described in 4:23-29, and points to a renewal of the covenant promise of offspring/seed (Gen. 12:7; 22:17).

28. What will happen is the realisation of the commission given to Jeremiah when he was called (1:10). The six verbs used then are here repeated, along with 'watched' (1:12) and the additional term of judgment 'bring disaster' (from the same root as 'disaster' in 1:14). **'Just as I watched over them to uproot and tear down, and to overthrow, destroy and bring disaster, so I will watch over them to build and to plant,' declares the LORD.** The divine activity which had not let his people sin with impunity and so had brought the curse of the broken covenant on them is now viewed as completed. But the same thoroughness will be exercised as regards their good. In this way they would learn even from the bleakness and rigour of the divine imposition of judgment to anticipate the comprehensiveness with which the promised blessing would come upon them.

29. There is then presented another aspect of the reversal of the people's situation in the time of blessing. In v. 23 it was foretold what the people would once again say when they began to seek divine blessing on their land; so now **in those days** (that is, the time of restoration, 3:16) **people will no longer say** presages an abandonment of sentiments which call into question divine righteousness.[61] The proverbial

---

61. In v. 23 'they will again say' is *'ôd yō'mərû*; in v. 28 'they will no longer say' is *lō'-yō'mərû 'ôd*.

saying, **The fathers have eaten sour grapes, and the children's teeth are set on edge**, is also found in Ezek. 18:2 and represents a common view of the exilic period that the people were suffering unjustly and unnaturally for what their forefathers had done. Rather than acknowledge their own sinfulness, in an attitude of self-exculpation they blamed their upbringing and society for what had gone wrong. 'Set on edge' (<√$qāhâ$) is 'to be blunt' as in, 'If the axe is dull (<√$qāhâ$) and its edge unsharpened' (Eccl. 10:10). It is here used to describe the effect of eating unripe or sour fruit (I always substitute rhubarb for sour grapes in trying to envisage the sensation), but the significant feature is the alleged anomalous intergenerational transfer of the consequences. 'Our fathers sinned and are no more, and we bear their punishment' (Lam. 5:7). Such an attitude led those in exile to allege, 'The way of the LORD is not just' (Ezek. 18:25, 29). This was spoken in a spirit of self-righteousness which was blind to their own deficiencies, not least their refusal to respond to the entreaties of the prophets. There was no doubt about the sin of their forefathers and the fact that it had consequences, but it was also emphatically the case that the present generation were as guilty as their ancestors, if not more so (16:10-13). However, in days to come this will no longer be a matter of contention because the people will recognise the error of their ways and no longer seek to justify themselves over against God.

30. There then is set out the view which would become generally acknowledged among the restored people. **Instead** (*kî 'im*, 'but rather'), **everyone will die for his own sin; whoever eats sour grapes— his own teeth will be set on edge.** This was not the introduction of some new doctrine of individual responsibility, but rather the restatement of basic teaching. 'Fathers shall not be put to death for their children, nor children put to death for their fathers; each is to die for his own sin' (Deut. 24:16). However, individual responsibility was always presented as existing alongside the corporate, communal aspect of living—a feature of life that is often suppressed or denied in the individualistic culture of the west. It is, however, the accumulated decisions for good or bad of past generations and of others of our own generation that set the scene for our living. We are judged not only for the contribution we personally make to our culture and the legacy we leave to subsequent generations, but also for how we react to the parameters that condition our living. Both individual and communal responsibility ('No man is an Island, entire of itself; every man is a piece of the Continent, a part of the main', John Donne, *Devotions* 17) have to be acknowledged as both having a role in determining our destiny. As a consequence of divine intervention the restored people will be able communally and individually to begin a new history without a catalogue of past misdemeanours to account for (cf. v. 34).

b. The New Covenant (31:31-34)

Covenant was the basic religious metaphor of the Old Testament. Its use drew on the knowledge people had of the way the great kings of ancient empires exercised sovereignty over other peoples. They frequently regulated the affairs of their vassals by stipulating in a treaty the behaviour they expected from them, and by threatening dire consequences on disobedience and promising blessing on loyalty and obedience. In the same way the LORD as Israel's 'great king' (Pss. 47:2; 48:2; 95:3; Mal. 1:14; Matt. 5:35) entered into a covenant relationship with his people in which he set out the blessings he would provide for them, and also the conduct that he expected from them.

But if the LORD as Israel's covenant king has brought the curse of the broken covenant upon his errant subjects for their disobedience and unfaithfulness, is there any way forward after that? Can rebels be reinstated in divine favour? Can chronic apostasy be forgiven? Can it be cured? Here such questions are answered in terms of the divine institution of 'a new covenant'. This is the only Old Testament passage where that precise phrase occurs, though similar terms are found elsewhere. The New Testament both in its title and in its content takes up and develops this theme extensively.

31. The introductory phrase **'The time is coming,' declares the LORD**, is the same as that which began v. 27 ('Behold! days ⌐are⌐ coming'), and points forward to the period when the LORD will act to restore the fortunes of his people. The precise timescale is not stated, but there is the idea that what is to come is already determined and has in fact begun to emerge. Such a background sets the scene for understanding the clause, **when I will make a new covenant.** The concept of newness may be taken in two ways: either what is brand new (Exod. 1:8; Deut. 32:17; 1 Sam. 6:7), or what is new in the sense of renewed (Lam. 3:22-23). The idea of brand newness is favoured here by the previous use of 'new' in v. 22 accompanied by the verb 'create', which usually implies the bringing into existence of what had not been previously present. On the other hand, the Septuagint used the Greek word which indicated not the brand new, but the new edition of something already existing.[62] There is much in the passage itself to indicate

---

62. The LXX usage of *kainos* ('new' edition) rather than *neos* (brand 'new') is continued in the New Testament.

this element of continuity. Apart from the continued use of the word covenant itself, there is the identity of the parties to the covenant and the basic dimensions of the relationship established, 'I will be their God and they will be my people' (v. 33).

When the covenant is stated to be **with the house of Israel and with the house of Judah**, this resumes the theme found in v. 27, and common throughout the prophets, that when the LORD restores his people it will not be as two divided, and often hostile, kingdoms, but as one united people of God.

32. The situation that will prevail when the new covenant is established is first described negatively. **It will not be like the covenant I made with their forefathers when I took them by the hand to lead them out of Egypt.** This obviously looks back to the time of the Exodus, and so the comparison that is being instituted is not between the new covenant and the Abrahamic covenant, but between the new covenant and the Sinai or Mosaic covenant. 'When' renders a Hebrew phrase that is 'on the day' (NASB; cf. 7:22), but this is not to be restricted to a specific day, such as the night of the Exodus. It is to be taken of the whole experience of the people, perhaps stretching as far as the Settlement. It is instructive to note that the LORD's covenant dealings with the people are not characterised by a reference to Sinai—to the giving of the law as such, but by what constituted his proper claim of overlordship over them, namely, his deliverance of them from the bondage of Egypt. Taking them by the hand is not found elsewhere in the Old Testament to describe this event, but denotes the care and tenderness he displayed towards them in his dealings. Subsequently at various junctures in their history the people had renewed their covenant commitment to the LORD and had pledged their continued loyalty to the covenant instituted at Sinai (Exod. 34:1; Josh. 24:19; 2 Chron. 29:10). But when the LORD here speaks of a new covenant, he makes it clear that what he has in mind is not another covenant renewal ceremony such as that under Josiah where the terms of Sinai were reaffirmed. That had not led to a long-term solution in the past and something more was needed.

There are two ways of understanding the second part of the verse. **Because they broke my covenant** takes it as expressing the reason for the new covenant. Alternatively, it may be a second description of the covenant, a relative clause, 'my covenant which they broke' (NKJV).[63] Despite their oath of loyalty and protestations of sincerity and commitment, they had broken the Sinai covenant almost as soon as it was

---

63. *'ăšer* is probably parallel with the first occurrence, and there is a two part description of the covenant, '—which covenant of mine ...'

established (Exod. 32; Num. 14; 16; Jer. 7:25-28; Ps. 95:8-11; Acts
7:51-53). The word rendered 'broke' (<√*pārar*, 11:10) may well go
beyond the idea of violating the terms of the covenant by breaking the
stipulations in it, to encompass the idea of rendering the covenant null
and void. God would then be saying, 'They annulled my covenant by
their repeated breaking of it and the persistent refusal to amend their
ways in spite of my pleadings with them through the prophets.' In that
case the existing covenant arrangements provided no basis for any
further relationship between God and the people. As had been the case
in the first place, the subsequent history of the LORD and his people
would be rooted in his sovereign and unconditioned determination to
begin anew with them. When he had said he loved them (v. 3), they
had not been empty words but divine reality, which he would again
express in a covenant. It was not the covenant form that had been at
fault for the breakdown of the relationship, but their rebellion.

'**Though I was a husband to them,' declares the LORD** brings
out the strong contrast between the behaviour of the people and of
God.[64] As indicated in the NIV footnote the verb 'to be a husband'
(*bāʿal*) may also be used to denote 'to be lord or master', and in view
of the fact that this is a covenant context and of Jeremiah's previous
use of the word (cf. 3:14), there are grounds for adopting the latter
rendering. But it is not merely the fact of the LORD's suzerainty that is
being emphasised. It is also his loving care that has been spurned. He
was not a stern ruler over them, and so their disobedience and ingratitude was all the more culpable. There is no note of harshness in the
language whichever translation is adopted.

The New Testament citation of this verse in Heb. 8:9 follows the
Septuagint text which had 'I turned away from them' expressing the
LORD's revulsion at their behaviour. Though this reading could easily
be explained in terms of a slightly different Hebrew text, the construction does not fit so well into the Hebrew text.[65]

33. The positive description of the new covenant is found in vv. 33
and 34. The introductory *kî* is probably used adversatively here after 'it

64. Note the use of *hēmmâ*, 'they' and *ʾānōkî*, 'I'. There is no Hebrew word
corresponding to 'though', but the balanced contrast of the original is well
brought out in this way.
65. The LXX *ka'gō ēmelēsa autōn*, 'and I disregarded them', probably arose
from reading *gāʿaltî*, 'I abhorred them' (the Greek verb is weaker than the
Hebrew would have been in that case), but it does not seem to do justice to the
contrast in the Hebrew. This meaning would have been more naturally
conveyed in a consecutive construction.

will not be like' at the beginning of v. 32; hence 'but' (NKJV, NRSV) **'this is the covenant that I will make with the house of Israel after that time,' declares the LORD.** 'The house of Israel' here refers to the united people of God. The aberration of the divided monarchy has been passed over not only because of the double reference in v. 31 but also because of the focus on the one people at the time of the Exodus in the preceding verse. 'After that time'/'those days' constitutes a problem in that it seems to refer back to the days which are said to be coming when the new covenant is made in v. 31. However, it is more probable that the reference is not back to v. 31, but merely denotes after the time when the people's fortunes will be restored and they will be brought back to the land. This would fit in with the basic structure of Exodus, when the formal enactment of the covenant at Sinai follows the effective divine act of redemption in the Exodus. Similarly the new covenant is not presented as a result of human action or merit. It too is a suzerainty covenant whose terms are divinely dictated and which comes into existence solely at the sovereign initiative of God. The verbs throughout this section emphasise what 'I', the LORD, will do.

But the LORD not only formally inaugurates the covenant and determines its terms; he also acts to transform the character of his vassals. This is how loyalty and obedience will be secured. **I will put my law in their minds and write it on their hearts.** The mention of law (*tōrâ*) refers to the LORD's instruction for his people, which constitutes an essential element in the continuity between the Mosaic and the new covenants. The difference between the two covenantal administrations lies in the mode of presentation and bestowal of the instruction. Many aspects of the Mosaic covenant were external. The law was written on tables of stone (Exod. 31:18; cf. 32:15f; 34:8; Deut. 4:13; 9:11; 10:4) which remained for Israel as an external standard for their conduct. This outward presentation of the law to the people made it easy for them to be satisfied with an external fulfilment of its terms. They could delude themselves that they were loyal to the LORD while their hearts were far from him. The need for heart engagement had always been present, however, even in the Mosaic covenant (cf. heart circumcision in Deut. 30:5-6; 'it is in your mouth and in your heart so you may obey it', Deut. 30:14). In the new covenant the law is to be put in their minds and written on their hearts. Both the terms *qereb*, 'inner being' (used in an extended sense of the psychic centre of human life; here translated 'mind' but equally used of the emotions and will) and *lēb* ('heart', but including the intellectual aspects of an individual's inner life as well as the emotional) are according to Hebrew idiom in the singular. It is not valid to draw from this any inferences as to the collective nature of the experience. What is emphasised is the contrast with the largely external presentation of the law to the people through the covenant mediator. Now rather than being put before them,[66] God undertakes to make an inner copy of it. What is referred to here seems to be the greater measure of the Spirit which is to be present to engender spiritual life in the new age. The old covenant had been given a new lease of life in Jeremiah's day by Josiah's reformation, but the people's allegiance to it had been only superficial, and so in this new arrangement genuine spiritual change is envisaged.

I will be their God, and they will be my people. This had always been the essence of the covenant relationship. It transcended any merely external political arrangement by instituting a personal bond between the parties to the covenant (Exod. 29:45; Lev. 26:12). That bond had always been real, meaningful and effective as regards God's commitment to the covenant; now it will really be present in the response of the people because of the inward activity of God's Spirit.

34. No longer will a man teach his neighbour, or a man his brother, saying, 'Know the LORD.' This is not to be understood as doing away with a teaching ministry, nor yet as rendering obsolete any exhortation one to the other. The repetition 'neighbour' and 'brother' brings out clearly the reciprocal covenant obligations that existed within the nation, but in the situation envisaged the need for teaching the facts of the faith or for exhorting to greater personal loyalty would be obsolete. The knowledge talked of here goes beyond a mere knowledge of the facts of revelation to include an inner commitment to a party who is known. Lack of knowledge ($<\sqrt{yāda^c}$, 2:8) had been perceived by Hosea as the root sin of the northern kingdom (Hos. 4:1; 6:6), and it was the same problem that persisted in the south. It did not mean that there was widespread ignorance of the details of the law. The flaw arose from a personal lack of acquaintance with the character and will of the God they professed they served. Under the arrangements of the new covenant this deficiency is rectified. There is a call to a living faith (9:24; John 17:3; Gal. 4:8-9), which will not need to be addressed to any because all will equally acknowledge the supremacy of the LORD in truth and will have intimate personal knowledge of the LORD to whom they will be totally committed. **'Because ($k\hat{\imath}$) they will all know me, from the least of them to the greatest,'[67] declares the**

---

66. *nātan lipnêhem*, 'to put before them' is used of law in 9:12; Deut. 4:8; 11:32; 1 Kgs. 9:6. That contrasts with its being 'put' (also *nātan*) within them.

67. Twice in this expression the adjective is used with the article to express a superlative (GKC §133g).

LORD. This phrase may be mean 'from the youngest to the oldest', or
'right across the social spectrum'. The emphasis is on the universality
of the knowledge which is the product not just of outward teaching but
of the action of the Spirit of God (Isa. 54:13; Joel 3:1; Isa. 11:9).

The heart commitment involved in truly knowing God will come
about because of the prior divine actions of forgiveness and not
remembering. **For** (*kî*) **I will forgive their wickedness** (*ᶜāwôn*, 2:22)
and will remember their sins (*ḥaṭṭāt*) **no more**. This is the basis of
newness of the covenant. In the Mosaic covenant forgiveness of sin
was presented through many intermediaries and sacrificial offerings,
but in the new covenant forgiveness will be known about in such a way
that all will genuinely recognise the LORD as their sovereign and
provider because of the method by which he forgives and blots out
iniquity. The details of how this is possible are not spelled out here. In
particular this revelation of the new covenant is silent about who in the
new covenant will assume a mediatorial role corresponding to that of
covenant figures like Abraham and Moses. At one level there is no
need for a Moses to come down the mountain with tablets of stone and
set the law before the people. But that was not all that mediating
figures provided under the Sinaitic administration of the covenant.
There is no hint here of the coming one whose prerogative it is to
forgive sin (Luke 7:47). What is emphasised is the liberating experience of knowing that the root cause of their estrangement from their
God has been dealt with, and will not be brought up again to haunt
them. 'Remembering' is here not a case of divine forgetfulness, but
rather of not calling to mind with a view to action.

In considering these verses in their total scriptural context we must
strive to do justice to two aspects of the message. In the first instance
the new covenant spoke to the people of Jeremiah's day, on the verge
of the Exile, of a time of renewal beyond that Exile. But equally,
though the historical reality of the return from Babylon constituted an
astounding fulfilment of God's promise to restore, it did not exhaust
what is here promised and foretold (Heb. 8:8-13; 9:15-22; 10:16-17).
There is no doubt that the ultimate realisation of this prophecy is found
not in the earthly reality of the New Testament church but in its
glorified heavenly consummation. At present, however, there has been
divinely brought into existence in the Christian church a greater fulfilment of this promise. Just as those believing Jews who entered into the
covenant newly set before them by God were enabled to experience in
measure the wonder of his gracious provision here clearly detailed, so
to an even greater extent those who are covered by the blood of the

new covenant inaugurated by Jesus Christ enter into that same provision, which will be completely consummated at the Lord's return. This is not to impose on the Old Testament text an alien message, but to see in the successive fulfilments of the prophecy that which Scripture assures us is there. In Jeremiah's day the future prospects of the people of God were presented in terms of the national destiny of the people who were then the embodiment of the church of God. With the realisation of the universal aspect of the covenant promise (Gen. 12:3; Acts 3:25) the way Jeremiah and his contemporaries understood these promises is not negated or reversed, but broadened and internationalised. The new covenant does not exclude Israel after the flesh, but includes it on the same basis as it does those from all nations who receive the mercy of God and have faith in Jesus Christ.

c. The Reliable Bond (31:35-37)
These verses add a pledge of permanence to the arrangements of the new covenant by showing that God is the one whose power and disposition prevails in the natural realm, and so also in the spiritual realm. The language is called hymnic in that it is similar to that found in many psalms where the divine attributes, which are the basis for praising God, are listed in a number of relative clauses. The continuity of the created order is an expression of divine trustworthiness, which prevails also in spiritual matters.

35. This is what the LORD says, he who appoints the sun to shine by day, who decrees the moon and stars to shine by night[68] looks back to the creation ordinances of Gen. 1:16, although here the sun and moon are clearly named as such. 'Decrees' (<*ḥōq*, 'task, obligation, boundary, limit, law') relates to the fixed order God has imposed on his creation (Job 26:10; 38:10; Prov. 8:29; cf. 5:24; 33:25), and which he pledged himself to perpetuate in the Noachic covenant (Gen. 8:22). The permanence of the divine arrangements in nature indicates the permanence that may be expected of the new covenant. All is under his providential care. **Who stirs up**[69] **the sea so that its waves roar—the LORD Almighty is his name** points to the power and control of the

---

68. 'Who gives the sun for a light by day, the ordinances of the moon and the stars for a light by night' (NKJV) reflects the structure of the Hebrew where there is one relative clause, and *ḥuqqōt*, 'ordinances, decrees', is a noun. The NIV translates using an additional relative clause, perhaps following a suggestion to read a participle *ḥōqēq*, 'appointing' instead of *ḥuqqōt*, 'ordinances'.

69. Note the form is *rōga'* and not *rōgēa'* (GKC §65d).

God who has decreed these arrangements of the natural world. No
natural phenomenon can occur contrary to his wishes. It is certainly in
terms of divine omnipotence that similar words are found in Isa. 51:15,
and mention of the Lord of hosts who has power over the natural
realm reinforces the idea of omnipotence (cf. also Isa. 17:12; Ps. 46:3).
For 'roar' see 5:22; 6:23.

36. The Lord then links his disposition and control of the natural
world with his arrangements for his people: the latter will exist at least
as permanently as the former. **'Only if these decrees vanish from my
sight,' declares the Lord, 'will the descendants of Israel ever cease
to be a nation before me.'** The use of the political term 'nation' (*gôy*)
and not the kinship term *'am*, 'people', raises the question as to the
extent to which this statement relates to the perpetuity of a Jewish
state. However, the term 'nation' had always been given a significant
role in the covenant promises, being found for instance in Gen. 12:2
and Exod. 19:6. It did indeed point in the first instance to the Old
Testament reality of the nation state of Israel as an embodiment of
divine rule upon earth. But the scope of the theocracy was not intended
to be restricted to the geopolitical realities of Palestine. That was only
a temporary feature of the age before the advent of Christ. Just as
membership of 'the descendants/seed of Israel' is no longer to be reckoned as a matter of physical descent but has been extended to include
all those who exhibit the same faith as the patriarchs, so too the
outward form of their collective organisation has been internationalised. Abraham is now truly 'a father of many nations' (Gen. 17:5;
Rom. 4:17) and so is 'heir of the world' (Rom. 4:13). Wherever those
who are of the faith of Abraham are now found living in the covenant
community which is Christ's church upon earth, there the nation of the
faithful is to be found, for they truly are those who are 'before me'.

37. There is then added a further assurance[70] conveyed by means of
assertion of an impossible condition. This answers Jeremiah's question
in 14:19. **This is what the Lord says: 'Only if the heavens above
can be measured and the foundations of the earth below be
searched out.'** These were tasks beyond mankind—and still are.
Human inability to perform such a calculation stands in dramatic
contrast to God's ability to control the universe (Ps. 95:4). But only if
these impossible requirements were fulfilled, **'will I reject all the
descendants of Israel because of all they have done,' declares the
Lord.** The previous promise assured continuance of Israel as an entity.

---

70. The LXX places v. 37 before v. 35.

The focus now is on the possibility of rejection. God will only totally reject Israel on moral grounds in the unlikely event that the heavens can be measured. The emphasis is on the reality of divine non-rejection, but it is phrased in such a way that it does not automatically include all the seed of Israel. 'All the descendants' leaves open the possibility that some will be rejected because of their sin. It does, however, give the assurance of 'a remnant chosen by grace' (Rom. 11:5).

d. Jerusalem Rebuilt (31:38-40)

These three verses open another vista on the future in which a rebuilt Jerusalem is seen. It may seem an anticlimax to have to consider obscure topological references regarding an ancient city, and indeed difficulties arise as to the details of the vision. In some respects it was fulfilled at the time of the return from the Exile and the rebuilding of the Temple in the days of Haggai and Zechariah, and perhaps even more so in the time of Nehemiah. But the geographical particularity of this vision should not be permitted to obscure the underlying reality of spiritual well-being for the city where God has been pleased to dwell, and that truth is ultimately fulfilled in ways that go far beyond the geography of Palestine.

38. Though the phrase, **The days are coming** (v. 27), is not fully represented in the Hebrew text, there is little doubt that that is what is intended.[71] It will be a time **when this city will be rebuilt for me**[72]. 'This city' points to a Jerusalem origin for the saying. 'Rebuild' is one meaning of the ordinary word for 'build', and does not necessarily imply that the city is already razed to the ground (though that is made likely by v. 40). Jeremiah is looking forwards to the time when the restoration will occur, not merely the physical repair of the site, but the rededication of it to the LORD who will then be able to presence himself in the midst of his people. The thought is more fully developed in v. 40.

But first to emphasise the completeness of the restoration, there is given a description of the bounds of the city. **From the Tower of**

---

71. The qere supplies $b\bar{a}^c\hat{i}m$, 'coming', for a word that has been wholly omitted from the Massoretic Text, but is found in several manuscripts and in the early versions. Perhaps b^cm was omitted by haplography because of the following n^cm.

72. The NIV substitutes 'for me' for 'for the LORD'. It is also possible that $lyhwh$ indicates 'by the LORD' as well as 'in the LORD's honour' (REB) or as his possession ('as my city' GNB).

Hananel to the Corner Gate. The tower of Hananel is also mentioned in Neh. 3:1; 12:39; and Zech. 14:10. It was on the north-east corner of the city wall, north of the Temple. The Corner Gate (2 Kgs. 14:13 and 2 Chron. 25:23; 26:9; Zech. 14:10) was on the north-west corner of the city. This description therefore covers the north side of the city moving west.

39. The use of a measuring line to determine the extent of the restored city is found also in Ezek. 40–48 and Zech. 2. Possibly it evoked memories of the original allotment of the land (Ps. 16:6). **The measuring line**[73] **will stretch from there straight**[74] **to the hill of Gareb and then turn to Goah.** The wall seems not to have been built, and only its future course is marked out. Neither of these places have been identified, but given that the description here proceeds in an anticlockwise direction it has been presumed on the basis of this passage that they have been given as the north-west and south-west limits of the city. At least part of the hill is included within the bounds of the rebuilt city.

40. The description in v. 40 continues the boundaries of the city along its south-western flank. **The whole valley**[75] **where dead bodies and ashes are thrown** refers to the valley of Ben-Hinnom, which had been desecrated by Josiah (2 Kgs. 23:10; cf. 7:32-33; 19:11-13). The ashes may be the fatty remains of wood burned in sacrifices (Lev. 6:3). But these would hardly have been deposited in the Valley of Ben-Hinnom which was an unclean place. Ashes seem to have been deposited to the north of the Temple area. The reference is possibly to illicit worship. The Hinnom Valley on the south-western and southern sides of the city was where the people of Jerusalem had burned their children as sacrifices and where the LORD had said that there would be so many dead bodies when he punished them that they would be unable to bury all of them (7:31-32). Because this site is here taken within the holy city, its character is to be transformed.

---

73. The qere *qāw* substitutes a later contracted form for the earlier *qəwēh*, construct singular of *qāweh*, found in the kethibh.

74. *negdô*, 'before it', i.e. the measuring rod, and so straight out over the hill Gareb.

75. GKC §127g argues that the article being usual after *kol* has been mechanically added here in error to the construct. *IBHS* §12.3c analyses the situation differently arguing that it is a case of nouns in apposition indicating the material of the leadword, 'all the valley, the corpses and the ashes', and so the NIV translation, 'The whole valley where dead bodies and ashes are thrown'.

All the terraces[76] has caused some problems, but the NIV rendering is the most probable, referring to the ledges on the hillside where cultivation took place. **Out to the Kidron Valley on the east as far as the corner of the Horse Gate,** which lay on the south-east corner of the Temple courts (Neh. 3:28). Omitted from this description is the eastern periphery round the Temple where the Kidron Valley itself formed the boundary. Although the land indicated contains a greater area than was occupied either before or after the Exile, the stress is not on the size of the city or the population it can hold, but rather on the fact that it all **will be holy to the LORD.** There is no mention of the Temple, because the whole city will be ready and fit for the divine presence (cf. Zech. 14:10-11). **The city will never again be uprooted or demolished.** Two verbs from Jeremiah's commission (1:10) are used here, and the message is spelled out that what was impending as a result of their sin would not be allowed to happen again under the new arrangements. The vision obviously extends well beyond the post-exilic period because Jerusalem was later destroyed again. It combines into one view the deliverance from the Exile and the redemption by the Messiah. 'Never again' (*lō'* ... *'ōd lə'ōlām*), 'not ... any more for ever' (RSV) introduces an eschatological perspective into this promise which is eventually fulfilled in the New Jerusalem.

Again these sections present the message of divine deliverance in Old Testament categories, which have to be interpreted in the light of the total revelation of the New Testament. What was once described in terms of the physical entity of a city in Palestine is not set aside but is rather taken up into the grander reality of the Jerusalem which is above (Gal. 4:26), 'the heavenly Jerusalem, the city of the living God' (Heb. 12:22), 'the city that is to come' (Heb. 13:14), 'the Holy City, the new Jerusalem' (Rev. 21:2). In the same way the promises made to Israel as Abraham's descendants are not negated but extended. There is no national or racial boundary to those who may inherit the covenant. 'If

---

76. The kethibh has *haššərēmôt*, while the qere has *haśśədēmôt*, which some take as 'fields of death', perhaps from Mot, the Canaanite god of death, and a reference either to sites where he was worshipped, or as a term for cemeteries. Despite the fact that many manuscripts have the qere reading, the LXX has a transliteration of the kethibh, which points to its early existence. The translation 'terraces' draws on the existence of an Ugaritic term *šdmt*, which is often mentioned in connection with vines. Its root also fits in with the idea of terraces. But notice the double change involved with *d* substituted for *r*, for which it could easily be confused, and also the interchange of *ś* and *š*. For further information, see *NIDOTTE* 4:50.

you belong to Christ, then you are Abraham's seed, and heirs according to the promise' (Gal. 3:29). 'The Israel of God' (Gal. 6:16) in
whom the covenant is realised are those characterised by dependence
on, and loyalty to, Jesus Christ. This does not supersede the Old Testament promises, but extends it graciously. 'For there is no difference
between Jew and Gentile—the same Lord is Lord of all and richly
blesses all who call on him, for, "Everyone who calls on the name of
the Lord will be saved" ' (Rom. 10:12-13).

D. RESTORATION TO THE LAND (32:1-44)

In the second part of the Book of Consolation (chapters 32 and 33),
prose narrative replaces the poetry of the previous two chapters as the
focus switches to events in Jeremiah's life. Both chapters, however,
continue to deal with the promised reversal of the fortunes of the
besieged, and soon to be exiled, people. Their future is in the hands of
the LORD, the all-powerful Creator. Although he is the one who has
brought judgment on his people, he is also shown as the one who will
bring them deliverance (32:42-44; 33:6-7), and who may be
approached in times of distress to shed light on events that would
otherwise be incomprehensible (32:25).

In chapter 32, when it was evident that deportation from Jerusalem
by the Babylonians was imminent, the general encouragement of previous chapters that there would be a return to the land was given more
specific illustration in terms of Jeremiah's purchase of a field and the
measures taken to preserve the accompanying legal documentation.
After the historical background to the incident is set out (vv. 1-5), the
actual purchase and associated legal formalities are described in detail
in vv. 6-15. Though Jeremiah carried out the LORD's instructions, he
was puzzled by their implications and so brought the matter before the
LORD, seeking clarification (vv. 16-25). The divine response is
recorded in vv. 26-44: the doom of the city is certain, but beyond that
the LORD is committed to bringing his people back and revitalising
their attitude towards him. The theme of the new covenant from 31:31
is developed in terms of an 'everlasting covenant' (v. 40) which will
entail renewed devotion and fidelity on the part of the restored people.

1. The Prospects for the Besieged City (32:1-5)

1. Though this chapter is linked thematically to what has preceded, the
formal, dated introduction indicates that this revelation was originally
separate from the message about the new covenant. What is related

here has to be understood against the dark background of Jerusalem under siege by the Babylonians. **This is the word that came to Jeremiah from the LORD in the tenth year**[77] **of Zedekiah king of Judah, which was the eighteenth year of Nebuchadnezzar.**[78] The divine message is not related until v. 6 because further information is needed to set the scene. As in 25:1 the dual dating involving the years of Nebuchadnezzar's reign serves to point out who was really the political master of the land. The siege of Jerusalem had begun in the tenth month of Zedekiah's ninth year (2 Kgs. 25:1), that is, on 15th January 588 BC, whether one reckons Zedekiah's regnal years from spring or autumn 597 BC (Appendix §11). His tenth year (588/587 BC) was therefore some time into the siege.

2. Background information is provided both about what was taking place outside the city, affecting all its inhabitants, **the army of the king of Babylon was then besieging Jerusalem**, and about the situation within the city, particularly as it affected one person, **and Jeremiah the prophet was confined in the courtyard of the guard in the royal palace of Judah.** The date and duration of the siege of Jerusalem have not yet been finally resolved, but it is known that at one point the Babylonians temporarily lifted the siege due to Egyptian invasion from the south (37:5-11). Malamat (1968:152-153) reckons that this occurred a year after the start of the siege, during the spring of 587 BC (Appendix §12). Jeremiah took advantage of the lull to try to make his way out to Anathoth, but was arrested and remained incarcerated till the city fell (37:11-16). Accordingly it is to the second phase of the siege that this verse refers. However, Jeremiah's imprisonment itself involved a number of stages. At first he was placed in confinement in Jonathan's house for many days (37:16), but later at Zedekiah's instructions removed to the courtyard of the guard (37:21). At a still later stage he was again temporarily confined in the cistern of Malchiah (38:6), only to be released once more and kept in the courtyard of the guard (38:13). It is not clear whether it was during his first or second imprisonment that this incident occurred, though the

---

77. The kethibh is *baššānāt* a construct form, while the qere is the absolute *baššānâ*, cf. 28:1. Either may be read, with the construct in the kethibh understood to be in a merely formal apposition to the following 'the tenth' (GKC §134p).

78. For once it is the Massoretic Text that is parsimonious in its use of titles here as compared with the LXX, 'king Nebuchadnezzar, king of Babylon'. The LXX, however, makes up for this by omitting 'of Judah' both in this verse and the following, where it also does not have 'the prophet'.

evidence of vv. 24 and 36 favours a time when the siege was well advanced. For the location of the 'courtyard of the guard' and conditions there, see on 37:21.

3-4. Verses 3-5 add further background detail to the episode. **Now Zedekiah king of Judah had imprisoned him there, saying, 'Why do you prophesy** (a participle, indicating the ongoing character of Jeremiah's ministry) **as you do?'** Although it was initially because of the hostility of the court officials that Jeremiah was placed in custody, it was by the king's command on both occasions that he was put in the court of the guard (37:21; 38:10). For 'shut up' (<√*kālā*', 'to detain, imprison'), see on 37:15, 18. Possibly Zedekiah is referring to the same period of Jeremiah's activity as the officials do in 38:1, that is, during his first imprisonment in the courtyard of the guard. The king's question is not really an attempt to obtain information, but is an indignant remonstrance that Jeremiah should behave in such a treasonable fashion by claiming the city would fall (cf. 34:2). **You say, 'This is what the LORD says: I am about to hand this city over to the king of Babylon, and he will capture it.'** Zedekiah as a politician expecting the support of all the people in a time of national crisis was unable to comprehend how the prophet was not doing all he could to implore divine blessing on the nation and destruction on its enemies. To declare instead its powerlessness to remedy the situation was treachery. What was more, it was an act of ingratitude to Zedekiah who had intervened to ameliorate the prophet's personal circumstances (37:21).

4. But it was not only the fate of the city that Jeremiah spoke about; he also foretold the destiny of the king. **Zedekiah king of Judah will not escape** (<√*mālaṭ* piel, 'to deliver oneself' especially by physical departure from a perilous situation) **out of the hands of the Babylonians but** (*kî*) **will certainly be handed over to the king of Babylon, and will speak with him face to face**/'mouth with mouth' **and see him with his own eyes.**[79] Literally, 'his eyes will see his eyes'. Flight from the Babylonians would not be a viable option. Instead there would be personal confrontation with their king, but the meeting would certainly not be one of agreement and harmony as our idiom of seeing eye to eye would suggest. Indeed, when the meeting did take place, Nebuchadnezzar slew Zedekiah's sons in his presence and then had his eyes gouged out (39:7). The last person Zedekiah would have seen was

---

79. The kethibh '*ynw* is supplied in the qere with an additional *yodh* to give the regular pronominal suffix form '*ênāyw*. This is merely a difference in spelling.

Nebuchadnezzar himself. This is reflected also in the prediction that he would be brought to Babylon but would not see it (Ezek. 12:13). The summary Zedekiah gives here of Jeremiah's message reflects that found in 34:2-3, which had been delivered earlier, probably before the Babylonians encircled the city.

5. 'He will take Zedekiah ⌊to⌋ Babylon,[80] **where he will remain until I deal with him,' declares the LORD.** The nature of what is intended by 'deal' ($<\sqrt{p\bar{a}qad}$) is not immediately evident; it could be used favourably (27:22; 29:10) or unfavourably (6:15; 49:8). It might conceivably be the case that the LORD would intervene in favour of Zedekiah, but such an outcome is militated against by the king's continuing disobedience. There is no direct record of how Zedekiah died, but see the prophecy in 34:4-5. **'If ($k\hat{\imath}$) you fight against the Babylonians, you will not succeed.'**[81] This is in accordance with the message that Jeremiah had given when the Babylonian forces were advancing against the city (21:4-7). The verbs in the second sentence are plurals, addressed to the king and his counsellors, or to the community at large. Jeremiah as the LORD's prophet had consistently announced that the king would not be blessed in his military endeavours if his strategy ran counter to that proposed by the LORD.

2. A Field in Anathoth (32:6-15)

Despite the immediate certainty of the desolation and misery that would ensue with the capture and looting of the city, Jeremiah was instructed to give a practical demonstration to show that the LORD's purpose of ultimate restoration still stood. He was directed to buy a plot of land which was already in enemy hands and to take steps that he, or his heirs, could prove ownership at a future time of liberation. Roman history records a later similar act of patriotic faith in the purchase by auction in Rome at full market value of the very plot of land on which Hannibal had set up the camp of the approaching Carthaginian forces (Livy *History of Rome,* 26.11).

---

80. The noun as an accusative is used for motion towards a place (GKC §118f).

81. At the end of v. 5 the LXX does not have, 'if you fight against the Babylonians, you will not succeed', and begins v. 6 with the fuller, formal introduction, 'And the word of the LORD came to Jeremiah.' In this way it indicates that the remainder of chapter 32 functions as a response to Zedekiah's inquiry. However, there is no further mention of Zedekiah and the prospect of restoration in vv. 36-44 is too distant to hold out hope to Zedekiah. It is better therefore not to adopt the sequence the LXX suggests.

6-7. Jeremiah said, 'The word of the LORD came to me' resumes
from v. 1 after the extended background information. The narrative
also changes to being autobiographical, but it is unclear who
constituted the prophet's audience as he related the message he had
received. In it he had been told that **Hanamel son of Shallum your
uncle is going to come to you and say, 'Buy my field at Anathoth,
because** (*kî*) **as nearest relative it is your right and duty to buy it.'**
When we last heard of Jeremiah's relatives, his relationship with them
had been more than a little strained as they were plotting to kill him
(12:6). The prophet's absence from family weddings and funerals
(required by the LORD to warn of the suffering about to come on the
nation) would hardly have improved matters (16:5-9). Perhaps this
meeting is a sign of rapprochement, but more probably it is an indication of desperation. The name Hanamel (meaning 'God is gracious')
occurs only here in the Old Testament.

What Jeremiah would be asked to do related to the old custom of
kinship redemption required in Israel (Lev. 25:25). Land was the gift of
God to the family, and if it was likely to pass out of their control, a
near relative was expected to purchase it. It would of course revert to
the original owner at the time of the jubilee (Lev. 25, 27; Num. 35;
Deut. 19). However, the nearest relative was not always in a position to
purchase the land, or willing to do so. That is illustrated in the story of
Ruth (Ruth 4:3-4). So here Jeremiah may not have been the first to be
approached, but if others had a prior right, they have refused, and the
prophet is now approached. There is nothing to suggest that Hanamel
was acting with any duplicity in the matter, except of course for the
fact that at that time the land in question would have been in the area
of Babylonian control. We are left to guess at Hanamel's motivation.
He may well have come into Jerusalem for safety during the invasion,
and now be in financial straits. Moreover, in v. 6 it is not stated how
Jeremiah should react when this would happen; he is simply informed
in advance. His 'right' (*mišpāṭ*, for this use of the term compare Deut.
21:17) was to perform the duties expected of a near relative ('duty'
renders *gəʾullâ* <*gāʾal*, 'to redeem'), having first refusal as regards
buying the property and probably also being obligated to buy it if at all
possible.

8. The sequence in the narrative implies there was no great lapse of
time. **Then, just as the LORD has said, my cousin**[82] **Hanamel came**

---

82. Literally, it is 'son of my uncle', which helps clear up the potentially
ambiguous 'Hanamel son of Shallum your uncle' in v. 7, where in the Hebrew
either Hanamel or Shallum could be being referred to as Jeremiah's uncle.

to in the courtyard of the guard and said, 'Buy my field at Anathoth in the territory of Benjamin. Since (*kî*) it is your right to redeem it and possess it, buy it for yourself.' The courtyard of the guard was a place not so much of imprisonment as of protective custody where friends could visit. Hanamel's speech is couched in formal terms because it is part of a public transaction regarding property transference. 'Redeem' and 'possess' are reversed from the order of the Hebrew text (cf. NKJV, NRSV). With the right of possession/ inheritance Jeremiah was accepting part of what the LORD had allotted to his people. 'Possess' is an additional term from v. 7 and perhaps indicates that the circumstances were such that Jeremiah was not merely redeeming the land (that is, buying the right to use it until the next jubilee when it would revert to its original owner) but inheriting it (perhaps Hanamel was childless and his family line dying out; but in that case, was Jeremiah's situation any different?). The message that was conveyed by this transaction was that what happened to Jeremiah's land-inheritance set the pattern for what would happen with the land as a whole.

There is also the question of what sort of land Jeremiah and his relatives from priestly families could have owned. Numbers 18:20, 23-24 had forbidden Aaron and his descendants from having any share in the inheritance of the land. But there were Levitical cities throughout the land, of which Anathoth was one (Josh. 21:18), and such cities had pastureland attached to them where cattle and sheep might graze (Lev. 25:34; Num. 35:5). Property might also have come into a priestly family through marriage.

I knew that this was the word of the LORD. This is unusual in that Jeremiah did not ordinarily have any doubts about what was and what was not a divine message. Perhaps on this occasion, the speedy fulfilment of the prophecy regarding his cousin's arrival was what made clear to the prophet how he should act in these circumstances. (Compare the arrival of Cornelius' messenger in Acts 10:19-21 as confirmatory of the divine message.) Though no direct order is recorded, yet in v. 25 Jeremiah presents matters as divinely commanded, so that this is probably another instance of compressed narrative.

9. So I bought the field at Anathoth from my cousin Hanamel and weighed out for him seventeen shekels[83] of silver. A shekel was approximately equivalent to 0.4 ounces (11.4 grams); so Jeremiah

---

83. The Hebrew is unusual 'seven shekels and ten', but the reason for this is not evident.

would have paid about 7 ounces (194 grams) of silver. It is difficult to
know whether or not this was a high or low price for the field, because
we do not know its size. But Menahem had imposed a fifty-shekel tax
on wealthy Israelites (2 Kgs. 15:20), so seventeen shekels might
indicate it was a fairly small plot of land. Since coinage only became
common in Palestine during the Persian era, the silver used in the
transaction had to be weighed on scales (v. 11).

10-11. There then follow details of the way in which the transaction
was effected. The various actions Jeremiah performs present a picture
of exactness and deliberation. This was not done unthinkingly or in a
hurry; his actions were of significance for the distant future of Judah. **I
signed and sealed the deed,**[84] **had it witnessed, and weighed out the
silver on the scales.** In the light of v. 12 'signed the deed'/'wrote on
the scroll' indicates some form of signature rather than writing out the
text of the deed. Seals were used from earliest times as a means of
identification and authentication. They were impressed on lumps of
clay or pottery vessels and hundreds survive from 8th and 7th century
Israel and Judah. Further details of what the witnesses did are given
later in the verse. The weighing of the money was done on 'scales',
two plates or pans (note the dual form *mōʾznayim*) suspended from a
bar or beam held in the hand or on a support. What was to be measured
was placed in one pan, and weights of known magnitude were placed
in the other until the cross-beam was steady and horizontal. **I took the
deed of purchase—the sealed copy containing the terms and conditions**[85]**, as well as the unsealed copy.** The form of such a legal deed
has become clearer in the light of archaeological material from
Elephantine in Egypt at a slightly later period (King 1993:90). One
piece of papyrus was used, on which the deed was written twice with a
space between them. The papyrus was torn in the middle sufficiently to
let one copy be rolled up, tied tight with cord and sealed with clay
seals, while there remained attached the second open copy of the deed.
The sealed copy could not be tampered with, and the open copy was
available for consultation. The witnesses would place their seals also

---

84. The article is used generically to indicate a typical item of a class (*IBHS*
§13.5.1g), or for a person or thing as yet unknown, but expected to occur in a
context (GKC §126s).

85. It is not clear what difference is intended between 'terms' (*hammiṣwâ*,
'the commandment') and 'conditions' (*haḥuqqîm*, 'the testimonies'). Perhaps
the former stated that there had been a sale, identifying the object and the
price paid, with the latter indicating more detailed conditions of sale, possibly
for instance that the transfer lasted until the next jubilee.

on the document, or possibly add their signatures to the outside of the
sealed copy. If questions arose about the document, the sealed copy
could be opened in court.

12. Jeremiah proceeds to take steps to ensure that the deed is properly
deposited for future reference. **And I gave this deed[86] to Baruch son
of Neriah, the son of Mahseiah, in the presence of my cousin
Hanamel[87] and of the witnesses who had signed the deed and of all
the Jews sitting in the courtyard of the guard.** This is the first
mention of Baruch in the narrative of the prophecy, although he has in
fact been assisting Jeremiah from much earlier (around 605 BC). For
further details regarding Baruch, see chapter 45. A bulla is a small
lump of clay with an impression from a seal (such as those used in
v. 11), and one has been found from this period with the inscription
'belonging to Berechiah son of Neriah the scribe'. Almost certainly
this belonged to Baruch (Avigad 1978), as did another naming
'Berekhyahu son of Neriyahu son of Mahseiah', using the alternative
long forms of the first two names. The witnesses added their names to
the scroll in the form of signatures, as Jeremiah himself had already
done (v. 10).

As the courtyard of the guard was part of the palace precincts, there
was easy access to persons who could act as witnesses, since many
would be going to and from the palace on business. This is an early
occurrence of the term Jews. 'Jew' (*yǝhûdî*) signifies not a member of
the tribe of Judah, but an inhabitant of the territory of Judah, the
southern hill country of Palestine (cf. 2 Chron. 30:1-18). In the neo-
Babylonian era the word came to be used of Israelites in general,
whether in Judah or in the Diaspora. Here their presence indicates that
the matter was done 'in open court'. It adds another dimension to the
proceedings. What was witnessed was not just the purchase of a field;
it was also prophetic proclamation, and in days to come these men
could confirm what had been said and done by divine authority.

13-14. In their presence I gave Baruch these instructions relates to
the further instructions given to Baruch which represent the standard
storage practice of the times and are here vital to making clear the

86. Literally, 'the scroll, the purchase' which GKC explains as possibly in
apposition rather than an incorrect use of the article (§127h).
87. *dōdî*, which would normally be translated, 'my uncle', that is, 'my
father's brother', is here probably used in an extended sense of any male relative. Alternatively, one may with a number of manuscripts, the LXX and
Syriac add the words 'son of', because there is no doubt that Hanamel was
Jeremiah's cousin (v. 8).

symbolism of what was going on. As v. 14 presents the instructions as a word of the LORD, it seems that either Jeremiah has had another vision, or else the report in v. 6 is only an extract of what he had been told on the first occasion. **This is what the LORD Almighty, the God of Israel, says: Take these documents, both the sealed and unsealed copies of the deed of purchase, and put them in a clay jar so that they will last a long time.** This method of preservation has been witnessed in a number of places. The jar would be sealed with pitch, and documents could be kept inside indefinitely, as happened at Elephantine and Qumran. This is an additional precaution, quite apart from the sealed copy. It implies that it is anticipated that the deeds will need to be preserved for some time. It is not known if there was an early public records office in which such jars were stored or if they were kept by the individuals concerned.

15. There is then added the perspective against which the rationale of the act could be gauged. **For** (*kî*) **this is what the LORD Almighty, the God of Israel, says: Houses, fields and vineyards will again be bought in this land.** Far from being pointless, Jeremiah's purchase anticipates the restored conditions which the LORD predicts when normal buying and selling will occur once more. What Jeremiah has done has to be assessed against that background. At present he has bought a field to which he has no access and which has zero market value because it is occupied by the enemy. But the LORD promises to bring an end to the current social and economic dislocation of the land. Consequently what Jeremiah paid out has not been squandered. There will come a time when normal commercial activity will be resumed, and Jeremiah's field will again have value. 'Fields and vineyards' are used to describe all agriculturally significant land (as distinct from unproductive wilderness and scrub), which will be restored to its rightful owners. But still there is the ominous shadow of 'again': there must intervene an interval when this state of affairs will not prevail.

3. Jeremiah's Prayer (32:16-25)

The prayer may be divided into four sections: (a) general descriptive praise of the Sovereign LORD (vv. 16-19); (b) thanksgiving for God's particular goodness (vv. 20-23a); (c) confession of sin and a cry of distress (vv. 23b-24); (d) assurance of God's purpose and submission to him (v. 25). Similar lengthy prose prayers are found in Neh. 9:6-37 and Dan. 9:4-19, which are also structured along comparable lines. Daniel too was praying in circumstances where there was tension between God's revealed word (in fact the very word revealed to Jeremiah as

Dan. 9:2 makes clear) and the events of his day. The LORD also answered him with a word of reassurance and promise. When humanly
speaking everything seems hopeless, the will and purpose of God can
create possibilities undreamed of by mankind ('immeasurably more
than all we ask or imagine', Eph. 3:20).

**16. After I had given the deed of purchase to Baruch son of
Neriah, I prayed to the LORD** relates to the public action Jeremiah
had taken in vv. 13-15. Now he shows that although he obediently
carried out what was required of him, without giving others any hint of
problems, yet on reflection he was quite as baffled as any by what had
occurred. It was not a matter of the significance of the transaction. He
had delivered the clear message of v. 15 that this purchase was a token
of good in that there would be a future for the land beyond the impending catastrophe. Jeremiah's problem seems rather to have been to
reconcile the certainty of both the judgment and the grace of God. That
at any rate is where v. 25 focuses.

Jeremiah had been commanded at various times not to intercede on
behalf of the people (7:16; 11:14; 14:11). Here the same verb (*pālal*
hithpael) is used in a broader sense of bringing a matter before the
LORD. It is frequently recorded of the prophet that he came before the
LORD in prayer at times of distress and danger, though this verb is used
to describe his action only here and in 42:2-4. At this point Jeremiah is
in custody, but the focus of his prayer is not on his critical personal circumstances, but on the perplexing theological problem of how the
LORD's promise of future blessing could be reconciled with the
imminent prospect of national overthrow.

17. It is often argued that this prayer (certainly up to v. 24) is a later
interpolation at this point because its language is more that of public,
congregational utterance, and its themes are inappropriate to Jeremiah's immediate circumstances. On the contrary, this is a sublime and
apposite prayer, indicating Jeremiah's profound grasp of how to
wrestle with divine matters that go beyond him. He tries to take a
broad perspective, and begins with what he is sure of, the character and
saving work of God. The language does reflect many parts of Scripture, but it is no mechanical reiteration. Rather the divine attributes that
are remembered are such as to intensify the situation Jeremiah found
himself to be in.

Ah (*'āhāh*), **Sovereign LORD,** uses an ejaculatory phrase that only
occurs elsewhere at 1:6; 4:10; 14:13, and points to the spirit of restlessness and turmoil the prophet was experiencing. The prayer would thus
seem to be one of complaint or distress. The address 'Sovereign LORD'

(*'ădōnāy Yhwh*, 1:6) is frequently found in Isaiah and Ezekiel, and acknowledges the LORD's supremacy and his capacity to enforce his will. **You have made the heavens and the earth by your great power and outstretched arm.** The latter phrase is frequently used for God's work in salvation (v. 21), but here it is applied to creation in a statement that parallels 27:5. It is the fact that **nothing is too hard for you**[88] that perhaps makes possible the resolution of the combination of devastation and restoration. The thought, which echoes 'Is anything too hard for the LORD?' (Gen. 18:14a), is taken up in the LORD's answer in v. 27. 'Hard' (<*pālāʿ* niphal) points to an action that causes someone wonderment or bewilderment because it is beyond their capacity to carry it out. But for God there is nothing that is extraordinary or amazing, and he is the omnipotent one whose resources can be called on through prayer.

18. Jeremiah expresses the justice of God's judgment using language drawn from Exod. 20:5-6; 34:6-7. **You show love to thousands.**[89] 'Show love' is in Hebrew idiom 'do love' (*ḥesed*, 2:2); it describes an emotional commitment that flows through into practical action. **But bring the punishment for the fathers' sins into the laps of their children after them.** 'Bring the punishment for sin'/'requite the guilt' (<*šālēm* piel, 'to repay, impose a penalty' and *ʿāwōn*, 'guilt', 2:22) shows that the LORD's covenant commitment is not undiscriminating, and his retribution on those who despise his covenant exactly matches the extent of their infringement. The curse on disobedience is an ineluctable reality (Exod. 34:7). 'Into the laps of their children' pictures the fold of a long eastern garment being used to carry away what is allotted to them (used literally in Ruth 3:15; Prov. 17:23; and metaphorically in Isa. 65:6; Ps. 79:12). This statement brings once more to the fore the problem of intergenerational relationships and the justice of God (cf. 31:29-30). The fathers' conduct both sets a precedent for behaviour that the following generation will imitate and also distorts their social and religious environment so that further acts of rebellion are more likely.

Jeremiah then expands in vv. 18b-19 on these themes, looking first at the power of God, and then at the fact that his ways are just. The title, **O great and powerful God**, is language that is found both early (Deut. 10:17) and late (Neh. 9:32; cf. Dan. 9:4; Neh. 1:5). In Jeremiah it is only here and in a similar context of retribution in 52:56 that God is described as *ʿēl*, a generic term for deity, which is qualified by

---

88. For the construction, *IBHS* §14.4f; GKC §133c, 152b, cf. v. 27.
89. It may be that 'generations' is to be added, cf. Deut. 7:9.

'great' (10:6) to indicate that he alone is truly worthy of being called God. 'Powerful' (*gibbôr*, 'valiant warrior') is used of the LORD in many places such as Ps. 24:8; Isa. 10:21; Deut. 10:17. He is compared to a military champion, and as such he uses his incomparable power and might to triumph over his foes (Isa. 42:13). He is the one who can be relied upon to bring victory or salvation (Zeph. 3:17). Whatever claims may be made on behalf of others, Jeremiah, in terms of the common faith of Israel, confesses that this God is the one **whose name is the LORD Almighty**. This hymnic language (10:16; 31:35) reflects the acclamation in worship of the LORD who rules over and has at his disposal the armies of heaven.

19. Great are your purposes[90] **and mighty are your deeds**[91] are phrases with no exact parallels elsewhere, but the thought reflects the sentiments of many passages (Pss. 66:5; 147:5; Isa. 28:29). 'Purposes'/'counsel' refers to divine policy, planning which is comprehensive in scope and which achieves results, as may be seen in creation (10:12). The LORD can therefore effectively intervene in history, here the history of the world and not only of his chosen people. **Your eyes are open to all the ways of men**. Again the phrase lacks exact parallels, but the sentiment is a basic perception of Israel's faith (16:17; Prov. 5:21). Because the LORD keeps events on earth under his ongoing scrutiny, his actions are not arbitrary but based on the evidence which is fully known to him. **You reward everyone according to his conduct and as his deeds deserve.** Compare 17:10.

20. Jeremiah then considers the way in which the LORD had already intervened in the flow of earth's history. **You performed miraculous signs and wonders in Egypt and have continued them to this day, both in Israel and among all mankind, and have gained the renown that is still yours.** 'Miraculous signs and wonders' refer to deeds that could only be effected by divine power and which therefore attest God's supremacy. The LORD had displayed his power on various occasions throughout the history of the people. 'And have continued them' is an NIV supplement which rightly brings out the force of the terse phrase 'to this day'. Despite the NJPS rendering, 'won renown in Israel and among mankind to this very day', there seems no good reason to depart from the Massoretic accentuation which takes 'both in Israel and among all mankind' with the first part of the verse, extending the LORD's sphere of action temporally down to the present and geographically from Egypt throughout the world.

---

90. Epexegetic genitive, GKC §128x.
91. *ʿălîlîyâ* occurs only here, but cf. *pəlîlîyâ*, Isa. 28:7.

In the ancient Near East it was accepted that the fate or fortune of a nation and the productivity of its land played a determinative role in the reputation of its national deity (Block 2000:108). The events of the Exodus were a clear manifestation to the nations of the power of the LORD (Exod. 15:14-16), and Israel's occupation of the land was intended to be so also (cf. 33:9).

21-22. Jeremiah then focuses on the LORD's dealings with Israel from the time of the Exodus until his own day. **You brought your people Israel out of Egypt with signs and wonders, by a mighty hand and an outstretched arm**[92] **and with great terror. You gave them this land you had sworn to give to their forefathers, a land flowing with milk and honey.** These verses reflect Deut. 26:8-9, the material being recast from Moses' original address to suit its use in prayer, and with some internal reordering. The clause 'you had sworn to give to their forefathers' is also incorporated, possibly from Deut. 26:3, but the designation is one that is frequent in the Pentateuch. It was by divine action that the people had been brought out of Egypt, and it was as a consequence of divine fidelity to the covenant promises made to the patriarchs that they were given right of possession in Palestine, a land renowned for its agricultural and pastoral abundance (11:5; Exod. 3:8).

23. What was more, the right of occupation given to the people was one that they exercised. **They came in and took possession of it.** 'Took possession'/'inherited' makes it clear that their status as regards the land was dependent on the LORD's bestowal of it; it was not theirs by right of conquest or purchase. They were the LORD's tenants in his land, and so Jeremiah moves on to give a résumé of their tenancy. They did not respect the rights of their divine landlord and covenant suzerain. **But they did not obey you or follow your law;**[93] **they did not do what you commanded them to do.**[94] Jeremiah uses three expressions of similar meaning to intensify the way in which their

---

92. The prosthetic *aleph* before *zərûaʿ* is found only here and Job 31:22 (GKC §85b), and possibly reflects Aramaic influence.

93. The kethibh *wbtrwtk* might be read as *ûbətōrôtekā*, 'and in your laws' (so LXX), but usually the plural is *tôrōt* written with two *waw*s, and it is unusual for a plural pronominal suffix to have the *yodh* omitted. The qere transposes the *waw* and the *resh* to yield *ûbətôrātəkā*, 'and in your law', which is the form found in many manuscripts, the Vulgate, Syriac and Targum.

94. The clause is asyndetic and epexegetic: 'all that you commanded them to do, they did not do.' The expression is more forceful than the NIV rendering might suggest. 'They have done nothing of all that you commanded them to do' (NKJV, NRSV).

misconduct is specified: disobedience (3:25), not following the law (44:10, 23), not doing what was commanded (11:8). At this point Jeremiah's prayer is unusual. He has confessed the sin of his people, but he does not go on to plead for mercy and forgiveness. Presumably he considered that this was forbidden by divine injunction (cf. v. 16). Rather he acknowledges the justice of what is befalling the city and its inhabitants. **So you have brought[95] all this disaster upon them.** It was the inevitable consequence of their conduct.

24. Jeremiah then gives a graphic description of a specific aspect of how the judgment of the LORD was tightening its grasp on the city. **See** (*hinnēh*, 'behold') **how the siege ramps are built up[96] to take the city.** The siege ramps were mounds of stones and soil built up to the height of the city walls to permit access (6:6). The higher they got and the closer in they came, the more surely was the city's doom sealed. Jeremiah is setting out the circumstances in which he is approaching God in prayer. The siege has almost been concluded: why now be told to buy a field? How is God working in this situation? Jeremiah is looking for understanding of what is happening, even though there is no explicit plea to this effect. In some respects this resembles the petition of Moses in Num. 11:21 where Moses in perplexity approached the LORD, setting out the circumstances he was in and the instructions the LORD had already given, but making no direct entreaty in the matter. Jeremiah, like Moses, felt it was sufficient to set the situation before the LORD. **Because of the sword, famine and plague** (cf. 14:16; 25:16) **the city will be handed over[97] to the Babylonians who are attacking it. What you said has happened, as you now see.** How is it possible for there to be deliverance after all this?

25. Over against the current reality of the siege, Jeremiah sets the command of God. He begins with a contrasting, 'But ⌐as for⌐ you, you have said'. The title with which he addresses God (*'ădōnāy Yhwh*, v. 17) shows there is no insubordination involved; rather it is a subordinate trying to grasp the rationale of the superior's orders. **And though[98] the city will be handed over to the Babylonians, you, O**

---

95. *taqrēʿ* for *taqrēh*, cf. 13:22; Deut. 31:29. This is the only hiphil occurrence of *qārāʿ* II (qal 'to meet'), and it emphasises divine causation.

96. Literally, 'the siege ramps come to the city', an unusual personification.

97. *nittənâ*, perfect niphal of *nātan*, a prophetic perfect, expressing the certainty with which the event is viewed (cf v. 25).

98. *wəhāʿîr* is a *waw*-disjunctive (inter-clausal *waw* plus non-verb), setting up contrasting circumstances and hence translated 'though' in the NIV; 'yet' (NKJV).

Sovereign LORD, say to me, 'Buy the field with silver and have the transaction witnessed.' The command to buy the field is not explicitly related in the first section of the narrative, but Jeremiah had no doubt that this was what he should do. It is unlikely that he was expressing confident faith when he said, 'You say to me.' It was an incongruous, seemingly absurd command given the imminent sack of the city. Jeremiah is prepared to acknowledge great truths about the LORD in the abstract, but when it comes to working in the ordinary situations of life, he hesitates. He does not say, 'It is impossible', but brings matters before the LORD and in effect asks, 'Can this really come about?'

4. The LORD's Response (32:26-44)

OUTLINE

    a.   Certain Doom (32:26-35)
    b.   Covenanted Prosperity (32:36-44)

The LORD's response to Jeremiah's perplexity is set out in two parts (vv. 28-35 and vv. 36-44) with similar introductions, both of which follow on from the introductory argument of v. 27.

a. Certain Doom (32:26-35)
26-27. Then the word of the LORD came to Jeremiah introduces the LORD's response as he takes up the matters raised by Jeremiah. The prophet is challenged through his own confession in v. 17 being turned back against him as a question probing his faith. 'Behold!' (*hinnēh*) sets out the premise on which an argument will be based. Here it is the fact that, **I am the LORD, the God of all mankind.** 'Mankind' (*bāśār*, 'flesh') points to the weakness and transience of humanity. The fuller expression 'God of the spirits of all mankind/flesh' occurs at Num. 16:22; 27:16. This is a categorical assertion of the all-embracing rule of the one true God. The conclusion to be drawn from this is expressed in a rhetorical question, expecting a negative answer. **Is anything too hard for me?** If he is the God for whom 'nothing is too hard' (v. 17), then surely Jeremiah should be able to trust him to reverse even such a situation of catastrophic judgment. The God who rules over all mankind is able to carry out his will in the face of seemingly invincible and irreversible displays of earthly power. Jeremiah may not be able to anticipate how it will be done, but let him be in no doubt that God can

do it. He is called on to exercise faith in the LORD whose control over events is such that even after handing the city over to Nebuchadnezzar (vv. 28-29a), he can ensure that it will eventually be restored and repopulated (vv. 37-41).

28. The formula, **Therefore** (*lākēn*), **this is what the LORD says,** introduces the first consequence of the LORD's sovereign power and control (cf. v. 36). Because he is so powerful, there can be no doubt that he will execute the judgment he has decreed against Jerusalem. **I am about to hand this city over to the Babylonians and to Nebuchadnezzar king of Babylon, who will capture it.** The prophetic messenger will witness that the message he had delivered was no idle threat.

29. **The Babylonians who are attacking this city will come in and set it on fire** presents information that had been already given in 21:10, 14; 37:8. **They will burn it down, along with the houses where the people provoked me to anger by burning incense on the roofs to Baal** (19:13, though here Baal replaces 'the host of heaven'; cf. 7:9, 18) **and by pouring out drink offerings to other gods.** The provocative acts of the citizens of Jerusalem have not lessened and have brought on them this judgment. Although 'burn it down' (*śārap*) and 'burning incense' (*qāṭar*, piel) are unrelated words in Hebrew, the thought is related, and serves to bring out the justice of the LORD's retribution.

30. The reason for the impending judgment is broadened out from their current idolatry to include the history of the past. 'For' (*kî*) **the people of Israel and Judah have done[99] nothing but evil in my sight from their youth.** 'Youth' is an indeterminate period in early life. In 2:2 their youth had been the time when they had just become a nation and when there had been a seeming loyal response to the LORD—but it had not lasted (3:24-25). The mention of both the northern and the southern kingdoms brings with it the thought that the south, Judah, will not escape what has already befallen the north. **'Indeed** (*kî*, either emphatic or, more probably, restating the reason for the judgment)**, the people of Israel have done nothing but provoke me with what their hands have made,' declares the LORD.** The reference to Israel takes in the whole of the covenant people. What their hands have made certainly includes the idols they worshiped (1:16; 7:18-19), but it may be a more general reference to all their actions (Deut. 31:29).

---

99. The perfect of *hāyâ*, 'to be' followed by a participle expresses durative action, 'they have been doing' (cf. NASB).

31. A third reason for the judgment the LORD has brought on them focuses on what took place in Jerusalem. 'For' (*kî*) **from the day it was built until now, this city has so aroused my anger and wrath**[100] probably does not refer back to the Jebusite days of the city. 'Built' indicates the major period of expansion of the city under David (2 Sam. 5:6-10) and Solomon (1 Kgs. 9:15, 19). Throughout its occupation by the covenant people, this city had so angered the LORD that he declared **that I must remove it from my sight.** The fact that this provocation occurred over a prolonged period indicates that now that God has decided to act there is no possibility of last minute reprieve.

32. The indictment (cf. 7:12; 11:17) continues, especially emphasising the totality of the involvement of the people by listing various groups. **The people of Israel and Judah have provoked me by all the evil they have done—they, their kings and officials, their priests and prophets, the men of Judah and the people of Jerusalem.** The initial mention of Israel and Judah continues their association in wrongdoing. The various groups of public figures (cf. 2:26; 8:1; 17:25) implicates the leadership of the land in initiating and promoting this defiant misconduct. But Judahite society as a whole is mentioned because rebellion was rife and not just a phenomenon associated with the powerful and influential.

33. The nation had perpetrated such heinous wrongdoing in spite of repeated warnings (7:24). **They turned their backs to me and not their faces** (2:27); **though I taught**[101] **them again and again** ('beginning early': 2:13, 25; 25:3, 4), **they would not listen or respond to discipline.** The unresponsiveness of the people to the LORD's discipline is also remarked on in 2:30; 7:28; 17:23. Judah had become so inured to such behaviour that it was impervious to pleas to reconsider and change.

34. The height of their provocation against the LORD was that **they set up their abominable idols in the house that bears my Name and defiled it.** The accusation of this verse is similar to the second part of 7:30. Repeatedly over the centuries the people had been drawn into idolatry, culminating in the reign of Manasseh (2 Kgs. 21:2-7). Though Josiah had purged the Temple (2 Kgs. 23:4, 6-7, 11-12), it was not long before Judah had reverted to its former ways. The reformation had

---

100. The construction is unusual: 'on my anger and on my wrath this city has been with respect to me' (cf. 52:3). Hence the supplement 'provocation' (NASB, NKJV).

101. An infinitive absolute used in place of a finite verb form, GKC §113ff.

only touched the surface of the problem; there had been no deep and
widespread inner change. The clearest evidence for the religious decay
in Jerusalem at this time is the evidence of Ezekiel 8 which the prophet
dated as occurring on the fifth day of the sixth month of the sixth year
of their captivity (17th September 592 BC).

**35. They built high places for Baal in the Valley of Ben-Hinnom to
sacrifice their sons and daughters to Molech.** This verse is similar to
7:31 and 19:5, though in the former place the high places are said to be
'for Topheth'. Molech (2 Kgs. 23:10) was a deformation of the word
for king (*mlk*) by vocalising it with the vowels of *bōšet*, 'shame'. Since
'king' was often used in the ancient Near East as a title for a god, it
expressed utter contempt for the deity involved. There is the possibility
that the god involved was a deity of the underworld, which may indicate how, in its Greek form Gehenna, the 'Valley of Ben-Hinnom'
later became a term for the definitive hell of the last judgment which
the fires and human sacrifices of the valley foreshadowed. 'To sacrifice' here (<*ābar*, hiphil, 'to cause to pass through') has sometimes
been understood as passing through a fire in some sort of dedication
ceremony, but the parallel expressions in 7:31 and 19:5 are quite clear
that children were slain. **Though I never commanded, nor did it
enter my mind, that they should do such a detestable thing and so
make Judah sin.**[102] There should be no doubt that the LORD had never
authorised or contemplated such action. For 'detestable thing'
(<√*tā'ab*), see on 2:7.

b. Covenanted Prosperity (32:36-44)
The second part of the LORD's answer to Jeremiah's prayer is
altogether different in its tone. The LORD for whom nothing is too hard
will restore the fortunes of his people.

36. By rearranging the order of the clauses in v. 36 the NIV obscures
the structural parallel with v. 28. The verse here begins, 'But now',
introducing a contrast to what had been previously said, followed by
'therefore (*lākēn*), this is what the LORD says' (as in v. 28). **You are
saying about this city, 'By the sword, famine and plague it will be
handed over to the king of Babylon'; but this is what the LORD,
the God of Israel, says.** 'You' is plural, but it is unclear who they
might be. The LXX reads a singular 'you', but that avoids rather than
solves the problem of the plural reference. It is unlikely that it is a

---

102. The form *haḥăṭî* in the kethibh has the final *aleph* omitted; it is
provided in the qere (cf. 19:15).

reference to Jeremiah and those associated with him in view of the loneliness of Jeremiah in the city, let alone in prison. It is possible that there was a group in Jerusalem who, recognising the inevitability of the city's fall, had adopted the words of the prophet's message, but not the reasoning behind it or all that he had predicted, and who were saying with deep pessimism and utter despair, 'It will be given (prophetic perfect) into the hand of the king of Babylon, by the sword and by the famine and by the pestilence'. What had been threatened had arrived, and they did not see any future for the city whose end had surely come. But there is a contrast between the view expressed by this group, and what the LORD had to say on the matter.

37. I will surely gather them from all the lands where I banish[103] **them in my furious anger and great wrath**/'in my fury and in my anger and in great wrath' (21:5; Deut. 29:27). The future scene is vividly presented as the prophet is urged to consider what the LORD proposes doing. **I will bring them back** (*hăšibōtîm* <√*šûb* hiphil) **to this place and let them live** (*hōšabtîm* <√*yāšab* hiphil) **in safety** reinforces its message by the assonance between the two verbs used: the change in the people's circumstances will be brought about by divine intervention in grace, restating the themes of 31:8-10. 'This place' refers to Judah, cf. Ezek. 36:11, 33; Hos. 11:11. For 'live in safety', see on 23:6.

38. Their future condition is viewed as the supreme realisation of the covenant. The essential bond of the covenant relationship will be truly realised when the LORD intervenes to restore his people. **They will be my people, and I will be their God,** restating the formula found at 24:7 and 31:33, though there in reverse order (see also 7:23; 11:4; 31:1).

39. Along with the restoration of the covenant relationship, the people will become the subjects of divine renewal. **I will give them single-ness of heart and action**[104]/'one heart and one way'. 'Heart' refers to all the inner being of mankind: the capacity to think, to feel emotions,

---

103. Although *hiddahtîm*, 'I banished them', is a perfect, it is not neces-sarily to be taken as a prophetic perfect, or even as a reference to those who had already been exiled in 605 or 597 BC. The perfect in the subordinate clause is here functioning with its basic significance as an action already complete from the point of view of the main verb. 'I will gather them from where I shall have banished them'; for which the NIV's present tense is a suitable English equivalent.

104. The LXX reflects *'ahēr*, 'another', rather than *'ehād*, 'one'.

to make decisions and to control one's behaviour. It is possible to find
here a prophecy of the harmony that will exist among all who are the
people of God. 'The gift of "one heart and one way," singular, to
"them," plural, signifies unity and solidarity among God's people'
(Keown et al. 1995:160). Such unity does indeed play a significant role
in prophetic accounts of the restoration. But it is improbable that such
a societal effect is primarily what is in view. Hebrew idiom generally
uses 'heart' in the singular even when referring to a group of people,
and what is principally in view here is inner moral integrity whereby
there will no longer experience vacillation between rival loyalties but
each will individually display single-minded devotion to God, and so
the people as a whole will be transformed. This is the answer to the
psalmist's prayer, 'Give me an undivided heart, that I may fear your
name' (Ps. 86:11). The absence of inner tension with renewed personal
commitment is expressed in a variety of ways in the Old Testament.
Totality of commitment to their covenant Overlord was enjoined in
Deut. 6:5, 'Love the LORD your God with all your heart and with all
your soul and with all your strength.' This required heart circumcision
(Deut. 10:16), which ultimately could be provided only by the LORD.
'The LORD your God will circumcise your hearts and the hearts of your
descendants, so that you may love him with all your heart and with all
your soul, and live' (Deut. 30:6). The prophet Ezekiel also spoke of the
divine provision of an 'undivided/one heart' and 'a new spirit in them'
through removal of their heart of stone and the gift of a heart of flesh
(Ezek. 11:19-20; 36:26-27). Jeremiah had earlier spoken of the
remnant being given a heart to know the LORD (24:7) and of God
directly writing his law on their hearts (31:33). It would be by divine
intervention that the people would be inwardly transformed so that
they were unequivocally committed to the LORD. This singleness of
heart is only partially accomplished on earth and so remains a goal that
is constantly to be striven for (John 17:21-23; Eph. 4:13).

Their inner loyalty would then find natural expression in action.
'Action' translates the word 'way' (*derek*), which denotes the outward
course of conduct as distinct from the inner orientation. The restored
people will no longer try to combine conflicting lifestyles. **So that
they will always/'all the days' fear me for their own good and the
good of their children after them.** This fear ($<\sqrt{yar\bar{e}^c}$) is the total
reverence towards the LORD that characterises those in a right relationship to him, a reverential awe that respects the LORD's commands
as well as his person. Not only does it bring good (covenant blessing)
on them, it also redounds to the good of subsequent generations, which
is a notable feature of the LORD's covenant dealings with his people.

40. I will make an everlasting covenant with them. The term
'everlasting covenant' is found elsewhere (50:5; Isa. 55:3; 61:8; Ezek.
16:60; 37:26) and contrasts with the outcome of the original covenant
relationship. It was in the nature of all covenants that their terms and
conditions were intended to be perpetually binding, but the problem
being addressed here is that the violation of the Mosaic covenant by
the people had brought on them the covenant curse. When the LORD
restores his people, he will take action so that his covenant people will
not draw down on them such a curse as will deprive them of the blessings of the covenant.

The terms of the everlasting covenant are then set out.[105] These are
not only divinely stipulated, but principally consist of what the LORD
commits himself to do. There will be an unceasing outpouring of
divine blessing: **I will never stop doing good to them.** 'Stop' uses the
root šûb, 'to turn away from', which so often related to the people's
apostasy, but which is negated here as a pledge of the constancy of the
LORD's provision. There is, however, another word in the text: 'I will
not turn away from them' (NJPS), or even more literally 'from after
them' (mēʿaḥărêhem), repeating almost exactly the phrase 'after them'
in the previous verse and indicating the intergenerational nature of this
provision. Also, the covenant bounty of the LORD will include an
important gift: **and I will inspire** (<√nātan, 'to give, set') **them to
fear me.** This fear (<√yārēʿ, cf. v. 39) is the attitude of awe and respect
that leads to enduring commitment, **so that they will never turn away
from me.** 'Turn away' (<√sûr, 'to change course or direction', 5:23;
17:5) is frequently used of moral or spiritual abandonment of what is
right. The new heart the LORD gives will lead to perpetual attachment
to him.

41. Not only will the people be joyful when the LORD intervenes to
restore them (31:12-13); the LORD will derive pleasure from the new
arrangements. **I will rejoice in doing them good** (Deut. 30:9; Isa.
62:5; 65:19). The LORD's pleasure is not just in bestowing good on
them: he rejoices 'over them' (NKJV), or on account of them. His
reverent and obedient people are a source of pleasure to him, and so he
delights in bestowing on them further tokens of his favour. This especially is seen in the security they enjoy in the land. **And will assuredly
plant them in this land with all my heart and soul.** 'Assuredly'/'in
truth' refers to what is done 'faithfully' (beʾĕmet), with complete

---

105. A colon is used in the NIV text after 'with them' to perform the same
function as ʾăšer, 'that', 'namely that', introducing a specification of what
constituted the covenant.

reliability in what he has committed himself to do. 'With all my heart and soul' (*nepeš*, 'being', 'inner self'; 6:8), which frequently occurs in Deuteronomy to denote the response required of the LORD's people, is here uniquely turned to denote his commitment. With v. 39 (and in contrast to v. 35 where 'mind'/'heart' is also used) this shows that on both sides it is total commitment and unswervingly loyalty that brings about the fullness of covenant blessing and enjoyment.

42. The introductory words 'for' (*kî*) **this is what the LORD says** indicate a new section of thought, which expresses the ground for the previous assurance. Confidence in the fulfilment of these promises can be derived from the fact of the LORD's action in imposing the covenant curse on the people. **As I have brought all this great calamity on this people, so I will give/**'bring' (repeating the root *bôʿ* hiphil) **them all the prosperity I have promised them.** These words summarise the previous argument, bringing together the certainty of both the judgment and the future blessing (31:38) because both are the fulfilment of the word of the reliable God. Frequently in Jeremiah we have the phrase 'bring calamity/evil upon' (4:6; 6:19), but only here 'bring prosperity/good'.

43. But then the picture moves on to deal with the more specific matter Jeremiah had raised, namely the buying and selling of land. **Once more fields[106] will be bought in this land of which you say.** This again raises the perplexing problem of who 'you' plural refers to. It seems that it is the population in general who say of the country around Jerusalem, **It is a desolate waste** (*šəmāmâ*, 4:27), **without men or animals, for[107] it has been handed over to the Babylonians.** The description is repeated in 33:10, 12. Accepting that this describes the attitude of the people before the fall of the city, there is much to commend the translation, 'This land will be like a desert where neither people nor animals live, and that it will be given over to the Babylonians' (GNB). The first clause has no expressed verb in Hebrew, and the perfect verb in the second may be treated as a prophetic perfect, describing the future as certain (this is how the NIV translates exactly the same expression in vv. 24, 25). However, 'handed over'/'given into the hand of' may indicate the control the Babylonians had already been divinely permitted to exercise over the countryside of Judah before the fall of the city. But the LORD reiterates his promise that the countryside will be reinhabited, once the Babylonians have completed their

---

106. It is probable that the Hebrew *haśśādeh*, 'the field', is a collective singular (GKC §126m).

107. 'For' is a translator's supplement; the clause is asyndetic.

divinely assigned task of punishing his people for their misdeeds.

44. By recalling the procedure by which Jeremiah had bought the field at Anathoth (vv. 11-12), **fields will be bought for silver, and deeds will be signed**[108]**, sealed and witnessed** forms an inclusion which brings the section to an end. This portrayal of the restored land corresponds to that of the restored city found in 31:38-40. Once again farms and property will be freely traded in the restored community (v. 15). To bring out the completeness of what is envisaged there is a listing of all the places that will be involved, beginning with Benjamin, probably because of the reference to Anathoth: **in the territory of Benjamin, in the villages around Jerusalem, in the towns of Judah and in the towns of the hill country, of the western foothills and of the Negev.** Similar lists occur at 17:26 and 33:13. The reason for all this will not be some blind turn in the events of history, but because of the LORD's sovereign action. **'Because I will restore their fortunes,' declares the LORD.** 'Restore their fortunes' (30:3) denotes the reversal of the LORD's judgment against them and the reinstitution of the covenant blessings graciously made for them.

When the siege ramps are in process of construction round the city, it takes great faith to believe that there is a prosperous future beyond the imminent collapse. Already there had been substantial hardship and loss of life, and the dislocation that would be involved in their impending deportation to an enemy land did not hold out any immediate amelioration of their conditions. But the very God who unequivocally announced that the disaster would come on his people also provided a lifeline for them if they would put their trust in him. By his command to Jeremiah he vividly set before the people that his dealings with them and their land were not going to end with catastrophic judgment. Their sin would be punished, but that would not terminate his commitment to them, and beyond all that they would have to endure in the immediate future as the judicial consequences of their sin, he would act to ensure that there would be a new start.

E. PROMISES OF PEACE AND PROSPERITY (33:1-26)

Chapter 33 develops motifs that have already occurred in the Book of Consolation, but it is not merely an appendix to what has gone before.

---

108. The second, third and fourth verbs are infinitives absolute, substituting for a finite form of the verb as occurs a number of times in Jeremiah (GKC §113z).

While it undoubtedly continues the theme of chapter 32 regarding the bright times to come when the LORD restores the fortunes of his people, it brings into clearer focus the international implications of the LORD's work among his people (v. 9), and also the Davidic, Messianic figure by whom the restoration will be advanced. This is the theme of the second part of the chapter (vv. 14-26), whereas in the first part the emphasis is more on the restored conditions in the land.

1. Blessings for the Restored People (33:1-13)

OUTLINE

a. Rebuilding Judah and Jerusalem (33:1-9)
b. Joy in the City (33:10-11)
c. Flocks in Abundance (33:12-13)

The first section of the chapter is further divided by the introductory formulae in vv. 1, 10 and 12 into three sub-sections. Although the city would experience devastation in the immediate future (vv. 2-5), beyond that the LORD would provide abundant peace and prosperity for his people (vv. 6-9), restoring their joy (vv. 10-11) and reversing the desolation of their defeat (vv. 12-13).

a. Rebuilding Judah and Jerusalem (33:1-9)
1. While Jeremiah was still confined in the courtyard of the guard indicates that the circumstances which are described in 32:1-2 still prevail, with the Babylonians besieging the city. Perhaps v. 4 suggests there has been some deterioration in the circumstances of the city. **The word of the LORD came to him a second time** recalls 1:13, but here the second message is linked thematically with the first in chapter 32, though it is impossible to say how closely they followed one another in time.[109] The word of the LORD brought a message of hope to the prophet in prison, just as much as it spoke vibrantly of their future

---

109. Translating 'while he was still confined' as 'while he was again confined' (*'ôdennû* can have this meaning), Holladay (1989, 2:226) suggests the sequence: confinement in the court of the guard (32:2), release (37:4, 12), subsequent imprisonment in a dungeon (37:15-16), transference by the king to the court of the guard (37:21). It is then on this second occasion that this revelation was given.

destiny to a people imprisoned in a besieged city.

**2. This what the LORD says, he who made the earth, the LORD
who formed it and established it—the LORD is his name.** 'The
earth' is a translator's supplement; the text reads simply a feminine
form 'it' three times (cf. NKJV). This may be understood as a general
reference to the plans of God. 'The reference of the suffixes ... is
evident from the contents of the propositions: the Lord does what he
says, and forms what he wants to make, in order to accomplish it, *i.e.*
he completes what he has spoken and determined on' (Keil 1873,
2:61), with 'formed' (<√*yāṣar*) being understood in the sense
'planned' (as in Isa. 22:11; 37:26).[110] But many modern translations
follow the example of the LXX in understanding the feminine suffixes
to refer to the earth. If that is so, such creation language (*'āśâ*, 'to
make' and *yāṣar*, 'to form' occur in Gen. 1–2) may reflect the thought
of 32:17. In either rendering, this divine description is introduced here
to undergird the completeness with which Jeremiah may put his trust in
the LORD who wields such power and control. The use of participial
phrases to describe God as Creator and the emphatic conclusion, 'the
LORD is his name', identify the description as coming from, or
modelled on, those employed in the worship of God. The phrase 'the
LORD is his name' is a similar to 31:35. It is only with a confident
grasp of the true identity of the one who speaks that there will be genuine reliance on the announcements he makes.

3. The invitation in **Call to me** is singular and may be addressed to
Jeremiah himself, but the singular could also be used of the people
thought of as a whole. They are invited to call on God, that is to set
before him their situation and seek his assistance. The experience of
calling on God and being answered by him is recounted by the psalmists (Pss. 50:15; 91:15), who generally expected an answer not in the
form of some verbal communication, but as divinely provided deliverance from distress and danger. In this passage, however, the terms
seem to be used in a somewhat different way. It is an invitation to
prayer which the LORD will answer by providing Jeremiah with
specific further information. **And I will answer you and tell you**

---

110. In both these passages in Isaiah *yāṣar* in the sense 'to plan' is found
with a feminine pronominal suffix used to refer to an indefinite reality, the
nature of which has to be surmised from the context. Keown et al. (1995:170)
suggest that the most likely object of the participles is the phrase in v. 3, 'great
and unsearchable things' (NIV).

great and unsearchable[111] **things you do not know.** The LORD, who
alone is able to provide it, will reveal to the prophet what till then had
lain beyond the scope of human investigation. Such grand vistas of the
future will sustain the prophet and the people in the traumatic days that
lie ahead.

4. But before taking up the theme of hope in v. 6, the LORD reiterates
his warning about impending judgment. There is not going to be an
easy transition to the good days to come. Even so those who are
identified as falling under God's judgment are also identified as those
for whom he provides hope. **For** (*kî*) **this is what the LORD, the God
of Israel, says.** In speaking as 'the God of Israel', the LORD acknowledges the bond that unites him with his people. Though he cannot
disregard their transgression, they remain his people.

The second part of v. 4 and the first part of v. 5 are obscure, and
many have supposed that some words have slipped out. The LXX is of
little help in reconstructing what the original might have been, in that
apart from reading 'ramparts' for 'sword' and omitting 'coming' in
v. 5 it reflects the same text. **About the houses in this city and the
royal palaces of Judah that have been torn down** is relatively clear.
Presumably the reference to 'the royal palaces'/'houses of the kings'
reflects additional structures such as that built by Jehoiakim
(22:13-14). But were these houses and palaces inside or outside the
city walls? The choice influences who should be identified as tearing
them down, and for what purpose. **To be used against the siege
ramps and the sword** (NIV) implies that the buildings are inside the
city and are being commandeered by the inhabitants of the city as they
patch the walls to strengthen the city defence (as illustrated on an
earlier occasion by Isa. 22:10) or repair any damage done by the
enemy. The royal properties would have been constructed of the best
stone, and so would have been an excellent source of material for
reinforcing the walls. However, since 'to be used against' is an expansion of the Hebrew 'to' (*'el*), others have suggested that the properties
that were torn down were on the slopes outside the city wall and were

111. The Massoretic Text has *baṣurôt*, 'inaccessible', but six Hebrew manuscripts, the oriental kethibh and the Targum have *naṣurôt*, 'hidden', probably
reflecting Isa. 48:6. But *baṣurôt* literally means 'fortified' (cf. 34:7). In
combination with 'great' it is elsewhere used of the strong cities of the
Canaanites (Deut. 1:28; 9:1; Josh. 14:12). It occurs in 15:20 in reference to the
impregnability of a wall. Its use here, though not otherwise attested, fits in
with Jeremiah's preoccupation with the siege. What was otherwise
inaccessible to man, God would tell.

razed by the besieging troops to construct the siege mounds. The REB goes one stage further and takes ʿel, 'to', as equivalent to the preceding ʿal, 'about', and renders, 'about the houses in this city and the royal palaces of Judah which are razed to the ground, about siege-ramp and sword', eliminating any reference to repairs of the battered walls. For 'siege ramps', see on 6:6 and 32:24. 'Sword' here refers to the military might of the Babylonian forces.

5. In the fight with the Babylonians is the NIV rendering of a difficult phrase which is literally 'ₗtheyₗ are coming in to fight the Babylonians' (cf. NRSV margin). The participle 'coming' is masculine and it is improbable that it is used to refer to the feminine nouns, 'siege ramp' or 'sword'. The unspecified subject of 'coming' can then only be the inhabitants of the city, but it is unclear how they can be said to 'come in'. Hence the NRSV recasts the thought to 'The Chaldeans are coming in to fight and to fill them with the dead bodies of those whom I shall strike down', but this requires emendation of the text. **They will be filled**[112] **with the dead bodies of men I will slay in my anger and wrath.** With 'I will slay' (a prophetic perfect $<\sqrt{nākâ}$ hiphil, 'to strike') there is a transition to direct speech, which is awkward in English. The NIV tries to smooth this by indicating the direct speech beginning somewhat earlier, and by making what precedes 'they will be filled' an extended specification of the theme of the LORD's speech. The citizens' activities will only result in filling with corpses the houses and the palaces. Either this reflects the fact that these buildings have indeed been destroyed and their rubble moved to the scene of fighting, which is where the corpses of the city's defenders are to be found, or else the reference is to the sites of the former houses and palaces which are used to receive the slain because the traditional burial grounds were outside the city and inaccessible during the siege. The presence of these corpses would have brought ritual uncleanness to the city (Num. 19:11-20) as well as constituting a health hazard.

This would all occur because of the LORD's anger against his people. **I will hide** (another prophetic perfect) **my face from this city because of all its wickedness.** The gesture is an indication of anger and withdrawal of the LORD's favour and support resulting in vulnerability to enemy onslaught and subsequent loss and destruction (Deut. 31:17; Isa. 8:17; 54:8; 64:6). This is the cumulative consequence of the people's wrongdoing.

---

112. Formally this phrase is 'and to fill them' in parallel with the preceding 'to fight the Chaldeans'.

6. A quite different situation is then unexpectedly envisaged in which the judgment already pressing upon the city will be reversed, and there will be a time of renewal and blessing. These are the 'great and unsearchable things you do not know' (v. 3). **Nevertheless,**[113] **I will bring health and healing to it.** The 'it' (feminine singular) to whom recovery is granted is 'this city' of the previous verse. The LORD will 'bring health'/'cause to come up lengthening', a metaphor drawn from skin growing over a wound (8:22). 'Healing' is a more general term used in several promises earlier in the book (6:14; 8:11, 15, 22; 14:19; 15:18; 30:13). **I will heal my people** (lit. 'them') **and will let them enjoy abundant peace and security.** The NIV rightly interprets the 'them' who are healed as the LORD's people. Such healing reverses the situation of the previous verse where the LORD 'smites' the people. Here what is in view is the physical devastation brought on the land by the enemy forces. The situation will be divinely turned around. Instead the LORD will 'let enjoy'/'reveal' ($<\sqrt{g\bar{a}l\hat{a}}$, piel; in other stems this verb means 'to exile'). 'Abundant' (*'ǎteret*) occurs only here. It is generally translated 'abundance', though translators note the word as of uncertain meaning (NRSV, NJPS). Holladay proposed changing the vowel pointing so as to read *'āteret*, with which he associated the meaning 'fragrance' (1989, 2:223). 'Peace' (*šālôm*, 6:14) and 'security' (*'ĕmet*, 4:2) constitute the essence of this renewed state.

7. I will bring back Judah and Israel from captivity. This is the phrase which recurs throughout the Book of Consolation (30:3). Here the NIV puts 'fortunes' in the margin and 'captivity' in the text as better suiting the context. Both parts of the divided people will share in this restoration (30:18; 31:4, 31). When the LORD promises that he **will rebuild them as they were before**, 'them' presumably refers to the lands and not to the people. This is the positive aspect of Jeremiah's message (using $\sqrt{b\bar{a}n\hat{a}}$, 'to build'), and contrasts with 'torn down' in v. 4 ($<\sqrt{n\bar{a}ta\d{s}}$, 'to tear down', 1:10). 'As they were before'/'as at the beginning' refers to the time when the people were united under David and Solomon (3:18; 30:3; 31:27).

8. But it is not just restored economic and social well-being that is promised. The fundamental aspect of the restored land is that it is the location where there will be experienced spiritual renewal from the LORD. **I will cleanse them from all the sin they have committed**

---

113. 'Nevertheless' is a translator's supplement. The Hebrew brings out the contrast by quickly switching the focus from the LORD's anger to his healing with *hinnî ma'ǎleh-lāh*, 'Behold me bringing up to her!', not woe but healing.

against me and will forgive all[114] **their sins of rebellion against me.**
In this promise sin in all its aspects is effectively dealt with, as is indicated by the repetition of 'all' and the variety of terms that are employed. 'Cleanse' (<√ṭāhēr, piel) views sin as pollution and defilement. Sin (ʿāwōn, 2:22) points to both the offence and the guilt that is its consequence. 'Commit' (<√ḥāṭāʿ) points to sin as missing the mark or falling short of the required standard of conduct, while 'rebellion' (<√pāšaʿ, 2:8) refers to action taken in defiance of a lawful superior. Over against this misbehaviour which should have ensured perpetual banishment from the land there is set the power of divine cleansing and forgiveness (<√sālaḥ, 31:34). This statement gives greater detail regarding the way in which restoration will be accomplished. Unlike 32:36-41 where judgment is followed by restoration but without any exploration of the mechanism by which this transition is effected, here it is revealed how the LORD will effectively deal with the situation so that his people may enjoy untroubled possession of the land. The comprehensiveness of the divine provision for the sin of the people is reminiscent of that of the Day of Atonement when 'atonement will be made for you, to cleanse you. Then, before the LORD, you will be clean from all your sins' (Lev. 16:30), where the root ṭāhēr, 'to cleanse', is used twice.

9. The forgiven and restored people will dedicate their lives to the LORD's service, and this will redound to his glory. **Then this city will bring me renown, joy, praise and honour before all nations on earth that hear of all the good things**/'goodness' **I do for it.** 'Renown, joy' is literally 'a name of joy', presumably a reputation that causes God to rejoice. 'Renown, praise and honour' (cf. 13:11) are clearly here the LORD's and not the city's. The restoration of Jerusalem will witness to the nations and lead them to acknowledge all that the LORD has done for his people and to acclaim his great salvation. He is the one who can give life to what is dead. **And they will be in awe and will tremble because at the abundant prosperity**/'all the goodness' (the same phrase as earlier in the verse) **and peace I provide for it.** The nations will react in wonder and amazement at what the LORD has provided for his people ('totality of goodness and totality of well-being', šālôm, 6:14). Their reaction is not yet portrayed in terms of submission to the LORD, but it is the first step along the path of Gentile reverence towards him. 'Fear' (<√pāḥad) can be used to describe both

---

114. The kethibh *lkwl* seems to be a simple spelling variation, reading *kôl* plene and without the maqqeph. The qere represents the same text more conventionally spelled *ləkōl*.

the quaking of terror (36:16; Isa. 51:13) or of joy (Ps. 119:161).
'Tremble' (<√rāgaz, 'to quiver, shake') indicates physical trembling of
the lips and legs caused by extreme fear (Hab. 3:16). The peace the
LORD provides for his people comes after chastisement for their sin. It
is not the peace that the false prophets had predicted, which would
have occurred instead of disaster and quite apart from the moral and
spiritual state of the people.

b. Joy in the City (33:10-11)

The next two brief sections look beyond the circumstances of Jerusalem's fall to present aspects of the subsequent restoration the LORD
will bring about. Because they incorporate descriptions of the city as
captured and sacked, they are generally dated after 586 BC. While it is
not impossible that the prophet was given advance information about
the conditions that would later prevail, it is more likely that this section
of the Book of Consolation contains the latest prophecies that Jeremiah
incorporated into his book (cf. discussion of vv. 14-26), and that the
sayings of vv. 10-13 were first revealed to him in the immediate
aftermath of the sack of the city.

10. This what the LORD says: 'You (plural) **say about this place,
"It is a desolate waste, without men or animals".'** 'This place' is a
reference to Jerusalem (7:3). The NIV hides the nature of the divine
speech by leaving to the end of the verse 'once more' ('ôd, cf. 32:15)
which is emphatically placed first, 'Once more there will be heard in
this place of which you are saying ...', to make clear that this is an
oracle about transformation. The people are presented as looking
around and saying of the city that it was a 'desolate waste' (hārēb,
'dry' and so 'waste'; then applied to cities that had been devastated),
'without men or animals' (32:43). This could hardly be said to apply to
the crowded conditions that occur in a siege. It suits rather what
prevailed after the collapse of Jerusalem, and might be presented in
advance or come from Jeremiah's ministry in the months after the fall
of the city. To the dejected people, the LORD declares he is not going
to permit the current state of affairs to continue indefinitely. **Yet in the
towns of Judah and the streets of Jerusalem that are deserted,
inhabited by neither men nor animals, there will be heard once
more** points forward to the divine reversal of the present emptiness
and eerie stillness of the ruined sites. The thought of 'absence of' ('ên)
is repeated twice in the saying of the people and three times in the
LORD's description ('absence of man, absence of inhabitant, absence
of animal'). It is a ghost town, no longer able to function, condemned

to hopelessness, until the LORD intervenes.

11. The way in which the silence will be broken is described first of all in general terms, **the sounds of joy and gladness**, before being made more specific in terms of two scenes. Firstly there will be **the voices of bride and bridegroom** (where the NIV switches the Hebrew order of 'bridegroom and bride' to conform to our idiom). Family life will be restored, weddings will take place with all their associated celebrations and rejoicing, and the curse set out in 7:34; 16:9; 25:10 will be annulled. This is a sign not only of the return of normality but also of the survival of the people, with the promise of generations to be born. Also the restored city will resound to **the voices of those who bring thank-offerings to the house of the LORD, saying, 'Give thanks to the LORD Almighty, for** (*kî*) **the LORD is good; his love endures for ever.'** It is envisaged that the Temple will be again be in use[115] and will be filled with the joyful worship of those who bring thank-offerings in acknowledgment of the special blessings bestowed on them by the LORD. The ancient songs of praise will once more resound through the streets of Jerusalem. The chorus that is here cited is one that is found in a wide range of texts (1 Chron. 16:34, 41; 2 Chron. 5:13; 7:3, 6; 20:21; Ezra 3:11; Pss. 100:5; 106:1; 107:1; 118; 136). It expresses the essence of Israel's covenant perception of the LORD as providing for his people all that a great king should, and doing so with that 'love'/'covenant commitment' (*ḥesed*, 2:2) that is uniquely his.

This scene of rejoicing will occur solely because of the LORD's gracious intervention. **For** (*kî*) **I will restore the fortunes of the land as they were before,' says the LORD.** 'Restore the fortunes' repeats the phrase 'bring back from captivity' in v. 7, and 'as they were before' (*kəbāriʾšōnâ*, 'as at the beginning') also reflects that verse.

c. Flocks in Abundance (33:12-13)

The imagery of the second future scene seems initially to be that of prosperity in the countryside matching the scenes of joy in the restored cities. It is, however, possible that the location of pastures within the towns of Judah is meant to suggest more than shepherds and flocks of sheep. This was a common metaphor for rulers and their subjects, and

---

115. One feature of this saying that militates against it being set in the aftermath of the fall of the city is how little it makes of the loss of the Temple. This was a major part of the trauma involved in the loss of the city, but here there is no mention made of its restoration. It is just assumed to be there, and that is surprising if these words are first spoken after 586 BC.

it may be that we have here an alternative description of the security and prosperity of the people. If so, the introduction of those who rule in the land provides a suitable link to the following section.

12. The introductory formula is somewhat expanded from that of v. 10: **This is what the LORD Almighty says**, and picks up the divine epithet used in the praise of v. 11. The divine speech begins with 'again'/'once more' (*'ôd*) as in v. 10, which is also echoed in the initially bleak description: **in this place, desolate and without men or animals—in all its towns there will again be pastures for shepherds to rest their flocks**. 'Pasture' is *nāweh* (10:25). 'Rest' (<√*rābaṣ*, hiphil, 'to cause to lie down') presents a picture of security and contentment. The language is also used of the LORD as the divine shepherd (Ps. 23:2; Ezek. 34:14-15).

13. The rural geography of the land is set out in reverse order from 17:26 and 32:44. Though it envisages a more restricted scene of restoration than that found later in Ezekiel 47 (probably because it arises out of the fact that Jeremiah was in the first instance addressing people in Jerusalem before the city fell), the list is inserted to show there is no area exempt from the LORD's restoring power. **'In the towns of the hill country, of the western foothills and of the Negev, in the territory of Benjamin, in the villages around Jerusalem and in the towns of Judah, flocks will again pass under the hand of one who counts them,' says the LORD.** The picture is that of a shepherd counting his flock as they pass under his hand into the fold (Lev. 27:52; Ezek. 20:37). This reflects the individual care bestowed by the shepherd on his flock, a theme taken up in the New Testament (Luke 15:3-7; John 10:1-18). The restoration to the land reverses the woe pronounced on the shepherds of the people (23:1-2) and leads to the fulfilment of the promise of 23:4, 'I will place shepherds over them who will tend them.' Instead of the chaos and disorientation of the Exile there will be structure and care.

2. Restoration of Royal and Priestly Lines (33:14-26)

OUTLINE

a. The Righteous Branch (33:14-16)
b. Perpetuity of King and Priest (33:17-22)
c. Covenant Succession (33:23-26)

From v. 14 to the end of chapter 33 is not found in the Septuagint (LXX), and this combined with what are felt to be significant divergences from the thought of Jeremiah has led many to view the passage as a later insertion. Various proposals have been advanced as to its possible origin, reflecting in themselves the diversity of critical opinion as to how the book of Jeremiah received its present form. But absence from the LXX does prove a late origin for these words. It is now generally acknowledged that the LXX translators used Hebrew manuscripts that differed significantly from those preserved in the Massoretic Text (MT). However, this alternative manuscript tradition is only attested in fragmentary Hebrew texts and by the evidence of the LXX itself, where readings at variance with the MT may also occur because of the translation style employed, because of deliberate omissions and additions made by the translators, or because of the vicissitudes of the subsequent transmission of the LXX manuscripts. It is, however, improbable that the text should have suffered such a large omission due to a mistake on the part of scribes, and there is also no obvious reason why it should have been suppressed by the LXX translators. It seems probable therefore that there were Hebrew manuscripts of Jeremiah which did not contain these verses.

Such a conclusion is consonant with the hypothesis that Jeremiah was largely his own editor and that the final form of the text as represented by the MT was extant in the early years of the Exile. The Book of Jeremiah was composed and doubtless copies made at various stages over the years of Jeremiah's ministry. At the end of chapter 33 we are probably dealing with some of the latest material revealed to Jeremiah, and it would seem that these verses were not in earlier copies of his work. There is no good reason to doubt the explicit statements of vv. 19 and 23 that we have here the record of revelation given to the prophet himself.

Although it has also been argued that the 'Hebrew style, the anthological nature of the passage, and the themes it sets forth' raise grave suspicions about its authenticity (Holladay 1989, 2:228), these doubts are not sufficiently significant to resolve the issue, particularly if the words come from the very end of Jeremiah's ministry and deliberately recall what had been said earlier with a view to reinforcing the consolatory aspect of his ministry. It was of considerable importance to emphasise that the message of encouragement was not a stop-gap measure introduced after the collapse of Judah, but had been divinely intended and earlier revealed (30:2). Holladay also argues that the most substantial datum for establishing a setting for the passage is the intimate link it sets out between the Levitical priests and the

Davidic king, which seems to him to indicate a post-exilic setting in which civil and religious authorities cooperated in ruling the land. However, interest in those who will officiate in the sanctuary arises naturally out of the descriptions of the restored land, and need not reflect post-exilic conditions.

a. The Righteous Branch (33:14-18)

This section follows on well from the previous verses where the curse on the shepherds of the people has been reversed and new, caring shepherds have been provided for the flock. Then, as in 23:5-6, the thought moves from rulers in general to the supreme Messianic ruler.

14. 'The days are coming,' declares the LORD, 'when I will fulfil the gracious promise I made to the house of Israel and to[116] the house of Judah.' 'Days are coming' is the formula that has already been found on a number of occasions (30:3; 31:27, 31). Its employment here seems to locate the fulfilment of this section at a time subsequent to the provision of the shepherd/rulers described in vv. 12-13. There will then be realised the promise of 23:5-6 in terms of the united people of God (30:3; 31:31). The promise is described as 'gracious'/'good' (cf. 29:10) not only because it conveys good to the people, but also because it comes from their covenant king's determination to do them good. It is a promise that bestows covenant benefits guaranteed by the LORD himself. In this it shares the same characteristics as the blessings divinely bestowed on covenant obedience (Deut. 28:1-14). Not one word fails of all the good promises that he makes (1 Kgs. 8:56).

15. It is promised that in the future time of blessing the Davidic dynasty will also be restored. **In those days** (that is, the time of restoration, 3:16) **and at that time I will make[117] a righteous Branch sprout from David's line; he will do what is just and right in the land.** The passage is based on 23:5. Indeed many Hebrew manuscripts add 'and a king will reign wisely/act prudently' as in 23:5, though it is

---

116. The preposition rendered as 'to' is first *'el* and then *'al*. There is no need to discriminate between these words as they are often interchanged (e.g. 18:11; 23:35). This reduces the cogency of Holladay's argument that it is a sign of a particularly careless and inelegant style in these verses (1989, 2:228).

117. The verb differs between the two passages: in 23:5 it is *wahăqimōtî*, a *waw*-consecutive perfect with a future sense from the hiphil of *qûm*; in this verse it is *'aṣmîaḥ*, the imperfect hiphil of *ṣāmaḥ*. Though the thought is more graphically expressed here, it is substantially the same in both passages because of the presence of the cognate noun, *ṣemaḥ*, 'branch'.

unlikely to be original here. The metaphor of a shoot sprouting from the Davidic tree/dynasty is used to refer to the Davidic king as in 23:5, and his conduct is set out in the same terms as there.

Commentators are divided over whether or not vv. 15-16 are prose or poetry. The NIV and NKJV treat them as poetry in the same way as 23:5-6, but the REB and NRSV prefer prose here, and the NJPS takes both passages as prose. The difference is of little importance unless we assume that poetry is in some way more authentically Jeremianic than prose.

16. In those days (repeating the phrase from the previous verse) **Judah will be saved and Jerusalem will live in safety.** 'In safety' echoes the character of the provision made under the new covenant (32:37). The sentence as a whole repeats the promise of 23:6, but with 'Jerusalem' replacing 'Israel'. This is done to permit a subsequent change of reference in the following sentence. **This is the name**[118] **by which it will be called: The LORD Our Righteousness.** The title is transferred from the Messiah to the city of Jerusalem. The significance of this is variously assessed. But if the title referred to the fact that the Messianic king would be the very embodiment of the truth that the LORD is the one who provides and constitutes all that is involved in righteousness for his people, then the restored and renewed city of Jerusalem embodies that truth as well. The city is renamed because the character of the ruler who is provided for her by the LORD conveys a new status to the city as his capital. Such a variation in what Jerusalem will be called is a device that is frequently employed to bring out the change that will occur when the LORD looks on her with favour once more (3:17; Isa. 62:2-4; Ezek. 48:35; Zech. 8:3).

17. The reason why this outcome may be confidently expected derives from the LORD's covenant commitment. **For** (*kî*) **this is what the LORD says: 'David will never fail to have a man**[119] **to sit on the throne of the house of Israel.'** 'Sitting on the throne' is the language of effective royal government (Exod. 11:5; 2 Sam. 7:13, 16; 1 Kgs. 1:13). This confirms the promise of the Davidic covenant: 'Your house and your kingdom will endure for ever before me; your throne will be established for ever' (2 Sam. 7:16). It especially reflects the form in

118. 'Name' does not occur here (unlike 23:6); it is simply, 'This ⌞is⌟ that which one will call to her.'

119. Literally, 'a man will not be cut off to David', where the verb is the niphal of *kārat*, used to refer to divine punishment of an individual by separating him (presumably through death) from the community of God's people (Gen. 17:14; Exod. 12:15; Num. 15:30-31).

which David cited the promise, 'If your descendants watch how they live, and if they walk faithfully before me with all their heart and soul, you will never fail to have a man on the throne of Israel' (1 Kgs. 2:4; cf. also 1 Kgs. 8:25 = 2 Chron. 6:16; 1 Kgs. 9:5 = 2 Chron. 7:18). However, 'a temporary loss of the throne is not thereby excluded, but only such a permanent loss as would be caused by the family of David becoming extinct, or by the kingdom in Israel either passing over to some other family, or in some way or other coming to an end' (Keil 1873, 2:72-73).

18. But the promise of permanence and continuity is not confined to the house of David. It is stated in similar terms for the Levitical priests. Mention of the priests in this way is not, as some have supposed, at variance with the rest of Jeremiah's prophecy. Undoubtedly in passages such as 6:13, 20:1-6 and 26:11 he conveyed many criticisms of the behaviour of the priests of his day—but he did so equally regarding the kings of Judah (and those who claimed to be prophets as well, but the office of the prophet is not brought in here because of its extraordinary nature, not being part of the ordinary constitution of the theocracy). Neither with king nor with priest was Jeremiah denying that they had a legitimate place in God's arrangements for his people, but those who held these offices had to live up to their responsibilities. As true and faithful shepherds would be provided for the people, so too would there be a legitimate priesthood. Jeremiah, himself of priestly stock, no doubt had wondered by whom the worship of those who went up to Zion (31:6) would be conducted, and by whom the thank-offerings would be made (v. 11). He now has revealed to him (and through him to the people) that the LORD issues a similar guarantee regarding the priesthood as he does regarding the Davidic king.

Nor will the priests, who are Levites,[120] **ever fail to have a man to stand before me.** The language of the Davidic covenant promise is employed also of the Levitical priests in connection with their sacred duties, described in the phrase 'before me' ('to stand' is a translator's supplement). This is the language of service, especially Temple worship (1 Kgs. 21:29; Ezek. 30:9). Three aspects of the priests' duties are specified. The first is **to offer burnt offerings,** the basic Old Testament sacrifice in which the animal was totally consumed with fire. The last item, **to present sacrifices,** is a general expression covering all the sacrificial ritual. However, the middle term, **to burn**/'cause to smoke'

---

120. The phrase *hakkōhănîm halwîyim*, where the two nouns 'the priests' and 'the Levites' are placed in apposition, is characteristic terminology in Deuteronomy (e.g. Deut. 18:1).

($<\sqrt{q\bar{a}tar}$ hiphil) **the grain offering**, is an unusual expression. What grain offering is being referred to? Is it that of the priest (Lev. 6:23)? It is more likely to be the regular burning of a handful of the normal grain offering (cf. Lev. 2:2) or it may refer to the stated daily offering which was accompanied by a grain offering (Exod. 29:38-46; Num. 28:1-8). Snaith (1971), however, proposed that it referred to the priest's offering which was part of the installation ceremony for priests (Lev. 6:23; 9:15-17). The implication is then of a steady succession of new entrants into the priesthood rather than of the perpetuation of the daily sacrifices. In any event, the emphasis is on the fact that this will take place **continually**/'all the days'.

The fulfilment of these promises indicates that they cannot be understood in a literal fashion. For millennia no earthly Davidic king has ruled over Israel and the Levitical worship of the Temple has ceased. Premillennial interpreters frequently find the fulfilment of the Levitical promise in restored Temple worship in a future dispensation, but even that does not satisfy the literal requirement of there being no break in the line of such priests. This does not square with events during the period after the destruction of the Jerusalem Temple in AD 70, and if the reference is taken to be in some still-future millennium, the reinstitution of animal sacrifice is quite contrary to the teaching of Scripture that there can be any place for further sacrifice after the final offering by Jesus Christ (Gal. 3:1-3; Heb. 10:1-16). If instead it is supposed that some modified form of commemorative offerings will then be used in place of the sacrifices named here, it is equally permissible to assume that the priests who offer them are also to be understood in a similarly modified sense.

Indeed there can be little doubt that both the Davidic and the Levitical aspects of the promise are to be understood in the same way. Using language drawn from past and present theocratic institutions, the LORD assured the people of Jeremiah's day of his continued provision for them of suitable rulers and of legitimate priests. With the greater light given by New Testament revelation it can be seen that just as it was indicated that the provision of rulers would culminate in the 'righteous Branch' (v. 15) who is the consummation of the Davidic promise and 'king of kings' (Rev. 19:16), so too it has become clear that the consummation of the priestly promise is also to be found in the Messiah. Furthermore, because of the union between Christ and his people, they are granted the same status he himself has. 'You have made them to be a kingdom and priests to serve our God, and they will reign on the earth' (Rev. 5:10).

b. Perpetuity of King and Priest (33:19-22)
The need to reassure the people at such turbulent times was such that
the same promises as are found in vv. 17-18 are now presented in a
different fashion in this brief saying.

19-20. The introductory formula, **The word of the LORD came to
Jeremiah**, suggests that this was originally a separate saying that has
been incorporated by Jeremiah in this place because of its thematic
associations. The certainty of the LORD's purpose is brought out by the
use of a contrary-to-fact condition (cf. 31:36-37). **This is what the
LORD says: 'If you can break my covenant with the day**[121] **and my
covenant with the night, so that**[122] **day and night no longer come at
their appointed time.'** 'You' is a plural of general reference.' The
covenant referred to is that of Noah where the LORD guaranteed the
regular succession of day and night which he had instituted at creation
(Gen. 8:22). It is impossible for these ordinances to be set aside by
human ingenuity, as had already been emphasised (31:35-36).

21. Because it is inconceivable that the expressed condition can be
fulfilled, the contingent outcome is emphatically denied. **Then my
covenant with David my servant—and my covenant with the
Levites who are priests**[123] **ministering before me—can be broken
and David will no longer have a descendant to reign on his throne.**
The Hebrew text deals firstly with the Davidic promise and then with
that relating to the priests (as in vv. 17-18). David is called 'my
servant' twenty-one times in the Old Testament, particularly in Samuel,
Kings and Psalms. It is used in Jeremiah only in this chapter (vv. 21,
22, 26). The phrase 'my servant' was used of Abraham (Gen. 26:24)
and Moses (Num. 12:7), where it denoted their privileged relationship
with the LORD, and the place they occupied in his purposes (see also
25:9). The LORD's promises to David that his throne would endure are
said to be 'for ever' (2 Sam. 7:13, 16), 'an everlasting covenant,

---

121. *bərîtî hayyôm* and *bərîtî hallāylâ* are unusual expressions in that they
would seem to be construct chains where the construct has a pronominal suffix (but cf. also v. 25). There are a number of similar examples elsewhere (e.g.
Lev. 26:42; cf. GKC §§128d, 131r).

122. This clause is literally, 'even so that there be not daily and ⌊by⌋ night in
their time.' The *wə* before *ləbiltî* is probably epexegetic, 'even'. *yômām-
wālaylâ* seem to be adverbs, 'daily and nightly', used to convey the regular
alternation of day and night. However, *yômām* recurs in v. 25 in the same
combination (cf. also Neh. 9:19) so that it might have been possible to use it
as an alternative for *yôm*.

123. Notice that this reverses the order of the words from v. 18.

arranged and secured in every part' (2 Sam. 23:5). In Num. 25:10-13 the promise given to Phinehas that he and his descendants should have the priesthood as their rightful possession is termed 'my covenant of peace' and 'a covenant of a lasting (*ôlām*, 'in perpetuity', 'for ever') priesthood'. This seems to be the basis for the later reference to a covenant with Levi (Neh. 13:29; Mal. 2:4, 8). 'Ministering' (<√*šārat* piel) is the term used for the activities of the priests in the sanctuary.

22. To the promise of perpetuity for the Davidic and priestly lines, there is now added a promise of increase in their numbers. **I will make the descendants of David my servant and the Levites who minister before me**[124] **as countless as the stars of the sky and as measureless as the sand on the seashore.** The comparisons with the stars/'host of heaven' and with the sand on the shore are reminiscent of the promises to Abraham (Gen. 15:5; 22:17). The sand of the sea which cannot be measured (<√*mādad* niphal) uses a rare term that links back to 31:37. The patriarchal promise still holds, but will be worked out through those who are the descendants of David and the Levites.

Again, this promise is couched in language that reflects the stage of revelation that had been reached in Jeremiah's day. While there would be a partial fulfilment in the provision of rulers and priests in the post-exilic community, the consummation of the promise is found in its realisation in the New Testament church. No longer is it confined to certain groups within the people of God to be rulers and priests, but it is true of all those who by faith are Abraham's seed (Gal. 3:26-29) that they are a 'royal priesthood' (1 Pet. 2:9), already made a kingdom and priests to serve God (Rev. 1:6), but also still awaiting the complete fulfilment of that promise (Rev. 5:10). This grand reality could only be dimly perceived by Jeremiah, but its unfolding in the fullness of time was the ultimate intention of the LORD who revealed to his prophet the lines along which his work of restoration would proceed, both in the immediate and in the more distant future.

c. Covenant Succession (33:23-26)
23. To set out even more clearly and categorically the divine assurances that have been given regarding the restoration of the people, Jeremiah adds one further message from the LORD to bring the Book of Consolation to a conclusion. The formula, **The word of the LORD**

---

124. Holladay (1989, 2:227) exaggerates in calling the text here 'bizarre' because a plural construct is followed by an object pronoun. But Jeremiah does have phrases such as *'ĕlōhê miqqārōb* and *'ĕlōhê mērāḥôq* in 23:23, which wider use of the construct is not uncommon (GKC §130a).

came to Jeremiah, again indicates revelation given on a separate occasion (v. 19).

24. The LORD calls Jeremiah to consider the situation around him. **Have you not noticed/'seen' that these people are saying?** In some respects this introduction resembles Jeremiah's initial visions (1:11, 13) as well as what happened on a later occasion (24:3), but rather than looking at a physical object, Jeremiah is invited to assess what is being said. It is not clear who 'these people'/'this people' are. Normally one would assume it to be a reference to the nation of Judah, so that the thought is that as they consider their circumstances, they despairingly conclude that the LORD has abandoned them and will have no more to do with them (31:27, 31; 32:20). However, the language of the later part of the verse suggests that 'this people' refers to the heathen as they look in mockery on the downfall of LORD's people (cf. Ezek. 35:10; 36:20). **The LORD has rejected the two kingdoms he chose.**[125] 'Kingdoms' is literally 'families' (NIV margin), and the reference might be to (a) in the light of v. 22, the descendants of Levi and the descendants of David, (b) in the light of v. 26, the families of Jacob and David, or (c) the two kingdoms of Israel and Judah. If the words are understood to be the speech of heathen nations, the last seems most probable.

The following words, **So they despise** (<√*nā'aṣ*, 14:21; 23:17) **my people and no longer regard them as a nation**, can hardly relate to the people's self-perception, but constitute their enemies' assessment of their fate. When they looked at the condition of Israel and Judah, it provided clear proof that they had been written off by their God, and so they treated them with contempt as dispersed captives and refugees, no longer a nation.

25-26. Over against this disparaging attitude, which no doubt reinforced the doubts of the people themselves, there is set the assurance of God, again expressed by means of a contrary-to-fact condition. **This is what the LORD says: 'If I have not established my covenant with day and night and the fixed laws of heaven and earth, then I will reject the descendants of Jacob and David my servant and will not choose one of his sons to rule over the**

---

125. This clause, 'the two kingdoms/families he chose' is fronted for emphasis and picked up again in 'them', the pronominal suffix on *wayyim'āsēm*, 'he has rejected them'. The first construction is not completed, and the *waw*-consecutive is only loosely connected with what precedes and functions as a sort of *waw* of apodosis (GKC §111h; 143d).

descendants of Abraham, Isaac[126] **and Jacob.'** The divine commitment to the regular succession of day and night is again referred to (v.
20), along with the more general 'fixed laws (<*ḥoq*, 31:35) of heaven
and earth' which is probably the 'natural' law divinely imposed on
creation. There can be no doubt that the LORD as Creator has structured the created realm in this way and has continued to preserve this
order. Consequently there should be no doubt regarding the
inviolability of his covenant purpose regarding the structure and
preservation of his chosen people. The LORD had committed himself to
be Abraham's God and the God of his descendants after him (Gen.
17:7), and will not go back on the promises made to the patriarchs. He
will also maintain his commitment to David that his house and throne
would be established. The use of the phrase 'the descendants of
Abraham, Isaac and Jacob' reminds the people of their true status in
God's sight and of the series of promises the LORD had made to them,
and counters the way they have been written off by others and by
themselves. There should be no confusion on the matter: he will not
reverse his sovereign choice of those who are to be his people.

The fact that the LORD has not rejected them will be clearly seen in
the action he will take. **For** (*kî*) **I will restore**[127] **their fortunes and
have compassion on them.** 'Have compassion' picks up the theme of
30:18 and 31:20. 'Restore the fortunes'/'bring back from captivity'
ends the Book of Consolation by picking up the phrase first used in
30:3. The LORD will act to reverse the judgment he is rightfully imposing on his people. His grace and commitment will ensure that they will
be kept as the people of God. His power is capable of reversing the
most hopeless of situations, and the commitment he has given ensures
that this will occur.

---

126. This is one of the four occasions in the Old Testament where the spelling is *yiśḥāq* rather than *yiṣḥāq*.

127. The qere and many manuscripts read *'āšîb*, a hiphil imperfect, and the
kethibh reads *'āšûb*, a qal imperfect. The same situation prevails in 49:39, and
evidently both the qal and the hiphil are acceptable with this idiom so that the
meaning remains the same.

XII. THE NEED FOR FAITHFULNESS

(34:1–36:32)

OUTLINE

A. The First Phase of the Siege (34:1-22)
    1. The Doom of the King (34:1-7)
    2. A Broken Covenant (34:8-11)
    3. Freedom to Fall (34:12-22)
B. The Rechabites (35:1-19)
    1. The Prophet's Challenge (35:1-5)
    2. The Faithful Response (35:6-11)
    3. Learning the Lesson (35:12-17)
    4. Faithfulness Rewarded (35:18-19)
C. The Enduring Witness of the Scroll (36:1-32)
    1. The Writing of the Scroll (36:1-4)
    2. The Scroll Read to the People (36:5-10)
    3. The Scroll Read to the Officials (36:11-19)
    4. The Scroll Read to the King (36:20-26)
    5. The Scroll Rewritten (36:27-32)

The Book of Consolation has ended, and the narrative of the following three chapters depicts scenes not of restored blessing but of the moral and spiritual malaise which had corrupted the nation and swept it to its doom. The three chapters are in reverse chronological order. Their focus is not on the historical or military aspects of the situation, but on the moral disintegration of the king and the people alike, who could not be trusted to keep their word. Chapter 34 considers the behaviour of the people of the city in respect of a solemn commitment they had given to obey the law regarding the release of bondservants. They reneged on their pledge and exposed their word to one another as worthless. Chapter 35 uses the conduct of the Rechabites as an object lesson in what faithfulness to a solemn commitment ought to entail, but the people of Judah did not display such fidelity to the covenant bond they had entered into with the LORD. This is traced back in chapter 36 to an incident in the reign of Jehoiakim when the king revealed his utter disrespect for the LORD. If the head of the nation was prepared to destroy the word of God, then it was all too evident what spirit was prevalent in Jerusalem. When the people rejected the LORD, their behaviour not only set in train internal social mistrust and disintegration but also drew down upon themselves the wrath of God.

A. THE FIRST PHASE OF THE SIEGE (34:1-22)

Chapter 34 records two incidents in the closing years of Zedekiah's reign: a message delivered to him by Jeremiah (vv. 1-7), and a blatant example of opportunism and half-heartedness in a solemn commitment (vv. 8-22). Zedekiah had rebelled against his overlord, Nebuchadnezzar, who began to take counteraction late in 589 BC, advancing into Judah, and first seizing the outlying defensive fortress cities before tightening his grip on the capital. 52:4 implies the siege of Jerusalem began early in 588 BC, possibly in January. In that there is no mention of the investment of the city in vv. 1-7, the first incident may have occurred shortly after Nebuchadnezzar and his armies made their incursion into the land late in 589 BC. The second incident spans a period beginning towards the end of the first phase of the siege, when conditions were worsening and the anticipated assistance from Egypt had not yet materialised, and extending into the subsequent lull in the siege.

1. The Doom of the King (34:1-7)

This message brought to Zedekiah at the start of the final siege of

Jerusalem differs from those recorded elsewhere (21:1-7; 37:3-10, 17-21; 38:14-28) in which Zedekiah inquires of the LORD regarding what is going to happen to the city. In this encounter it is the LORD who takes the initiative and approaches Zedekiah through the prophet. This suggests that this is the earliest of these incidents.

1. While Nebuchadnezzar king of Babylon and all his army and all the kingdoms and peoples in the empire he ruled were fighting against Jerusalem and against all its surrounding towns presents a formidable picture of the forces Nebuchadnezzar brought with him against Jerusalem. There is a three-part specification of the composition of those ranged against the city: 'all his army', 'all the kingdoms of the land of the rule of his hand' and 'all the peoples'. We do not have precise details about all who were involved, though 35:11 mentions Aramean armies, and Psalm 137:7 and the prophecy of Obadiah indicate Edomite involvement. However, it was accepted procedure that the emperors of the ancient world were provided with military manpower by vassal peoples, and so the Babylonian army would have been a multi-national force. The impressive list of the armies ranged against Judah (a similar build up of words is found in Ezek. 26:7) shows how hopeless their situation was when faced with 'all' the military and political might of the empire. It is probable that Nebuchadnezzar was employing as large a force as he could, not because he felt that Judah on her own was going to prove a particularly intractable opponent, but because of the threat of Egyptian intervention. In the winter of 601/600 BC the Egyptians had already fought the Babylonians to a stalemate (if not worse), and Nebuchadnezzar was determined to avoid that happening again. The description of the army reinforces earlier predictions regarding Nebuchadnezzar's power (27:6-7).

In these circumstances of impending doom, **this word came to Jeremiah from the LORD.** This introductory formula occurs first in the Hebrew verse, and is found also at 7:1; 11:1; 18:1; 21:1; 30:1; 32:1. It points to the divine initiative in the matter.

2. The LORD commanded Jeremiah to approach the king. **This is what the LORD, the God of Israel, says: Go to Zedekiah king of Judah and tell him.** Jeremiah had a number of encounters with Zedekiah during the period of the siege, but this is the only one recorded where he was commanded to approach the king. The message he had to bring was not one of comfort. **This is what the LORD says: I am about to hand this city over to the king of Babylon, and he will burn it down.** 'Hand over'/'give into the hand of' (vv. 20, 21; 32:28, 36) is to place something or someone under the authority and control of another. Zedekiah's bid for independence is doomed to failure. What is more the ensuing disaster will leave his capital a charred ruin—a fate that was foretold for Jerusalem time and again. In 597 BC the city had been captured and booty taken, but the next time the Babylonians forces came they would not leave until the city was burned to the ground (vv. 21-22; 21:10; 37:10; 38:18). 'He shall burn it with fire' (NKJV) represents the invariable Hebrew idiom for this form of destruction. It was a destiny that befitted a nation whose king had burned the scroll of the LORD's word (36:32) and a city that had offered its children to Baal by fire (7:31; 19:5).

3. The introductory 'But as for you' (wəʿattâ) with which v. 3 begins shifts the focus from the doom of the city to what awaits the king. He will have to face the full consequences of his rebellion. **You will not escape from his grasp but** (kî) **will surely**[1] **be captured and handed over to him.** It is this saying that forms the basis for Zedekiah's later summary of Jeremiah's message in 32:3-5. **You will see the king of Babylon with your own eyes, and he will speak with you face to face.** That was no word of encouragement. Nebuchadnezzar was the overlord against whom he had rebelled. Such conferences between suzerain and errant subject kings were a feature of eastern diplomacy, and there could be little in the prospect to comfort Zedekiah. Their encounter is briefly recorded in 39:5-7; 52:9-11; and 2 Kgs. 25:6-7. For the same idiom regarding 'mouth' and 'eye', though in the opposite order, see on 32:4, which summarises this address. Zedekiah is also told, **And you will go to Babylon.** Being taken captive to the overlord's capital was in one respect a relief for a rebellious vassal: he had been spared summary execution. Zedekiah is forewarned of the outcome of the siege so that he would not trust in relief coming from Egypt, but would act on the basis of the warnings given and so submit to Nebuchadnezzar before the full consequences of his folly came on him and his land. This is conditional prophecy designed to stir up its recipient to appropriate action to avoid the inevitable outcome of his present conduct.

4. There is then a modification of the preceding statement. **Yet** (ʿak) suggests some mitigation of the expected outcome. However, there is a command given, **hear the promise/'word' of the LORD, O Zedekiah king of Judah. This is what the LORD says concerning you: You will not die by the sword.** Some (e.g. Nicholson 1975, 2:91) have

---

1. Infinitive absolute qal before a niphal form of the verb (*IBHS* §35.2.1d).

suggested that the initial words should be translated as a conditional clause, 'if you hear (i.e. obey) the word of the LORD'. In that case Zedekiah would capitulate to Nebuchadnezzar and so spare his people much suffering, and it is promised that then his own fate would be mitigated. Holladay (1989, 2:234) refers to the choice that is offered to Zedekiah in 38:17-18, and suggests that a similar choice is implied here as well. This would then continue the conditional prophecy and its outcome would be contingent on Zedekiah falling in with what the LORD directed him to do. On the other hand, the prophecy may be understood as an absolute promise. In that case the king is presented with a less harsh future than might have been anticipated for one who had rebelled against Babylon. It would seem that the LORD was trying to induce him to respond to the counsel given to him, or it may reflect the fact that irresolute Zedekiah was an unfortunate and somewhat pathetic character caught up in a situation that overwhelmed him, rather than being as notoriously wicked as the incorrigible Jehoiakim.

5. You will die peacefully (*bəšālôm*). The exact significance of this phrase is uncertain. It is wrong to suppose that it is a prophecy that proved false because Zedekiah's death in Babylon was hardly characterised by *šālôm*, peace. Nor is it necessary to understand it as an unfulfilled outcome because Zedekiah did not comply with the condition in v. 4. In fact Huldah had prophesied in identical terms regarding Josiah (2 Kgs. 22:20), and he had died in battle. A variety of suggestions have been proposed for the significance of 'peacefully' in such contexts: in Jerusalem, in free conditions, or through natural causes. The last option seems to fit this context as Zedekiah did not die in battle or from Babylonian reprisals. We know that he had his eyes put out and was led off in fetters to Babylon where he died in prison (52:10-11), though the circumstances of his death are unrecorded. It is also prophesied that he will be afforded an honourable burial. **As people made a funeral fire in honour of your fathers, the former kings who preceded you, so they will make a fire in your honour and lament, 'Alas, O master!'** 'Lament' (<√*sāpad*), wailing that did not aspire to the more formal *qînâ*, was traditional on the death of a king (22:18). The funeral fires do not refer to the practice of cremation which was not followed in Israel or Judah.[2] It may refer to burning of incense, but is more probably a special fire lit in honour of the dead.

---

2. What happened to Saul was an exception probably to prevent further indignity being done to his remains. Amos 6:10 may imply burning in circumstances of epidemic. Burning might be added to the death penalty (Josh. 7:15, 25; 1 Kgs. 13:2; 2 Kgs. 23:20).

Note that in 2 Chron. 16:14 in connection with Asa's funeral the spices and perfumes are on the bier, while the fire is a separate item (cf. also 2 Chron. 21:19). There is no mention of the location where this fire in honour of Zedekiah would be lit; presumably this came true when at a later date the Jews were permitted to mourn the passing of their former king. There is then added a very emphatic conclusion to stir Zedekiah up to take advantage of the message given. 'For' (*kî*) '**I myself make this promise,' declares the LORD.**[3]

6. Jeremiah's diligence in carrying out the commission given him is recorded, though it would hardly be a popular message to bring to a king. **Then Jeremiah the prophet told all this to Zedekiah king of Judah, in Jerusalem.** It is not, however, the case that the delivery of this message resulted in Jeremiah's imprisonment. That only occurred in the interval between the two stages of the final siege of Jerusalem, and the circumstances of v. 7 are such as to indicate that this incident took place earlier than that. It is frequently suggested that 'in Jerusalem' at the end of v. 6 makes no sense here. Where else could Jeremiah speak to him? But rather than supposing that it is a mistaken reduplication of 'in peace' from the beginning of v. 5, it may reflect that Zedekiah had been away from the city during the initial stages of the Babylonian incursion, perhaps inspecting the troops in the outlying fortresses, and it was on his (enforced) return that Jeremiah spoke to him.

7. There is then added further detail about the prevailing military situation. Jeremiah delivered the message **while**[4] **the army of the king of Babylon was fighting against Jerusalem and the other cities of Judah that were still holding out—Lachish and Azekah.** 'For' (*kî*) **these were the only fortified cities left in Judah.** Nebuchadnezzar's campaign involved capturing the surrounding cities, isolating the capital, and then bringing the full force of his army against it. Lachish and Azekah were the only two fortified cities outside Jerusalem remaining uncaptured. Lachish, which in area was much larger than Jerusalem itself, was about twenty-three miles (43 km) south-west of the capital (and so halfway to Gaza), and Azekah was eleven miles (20 km) north of it, and some eighteen miles (33 km) from Jerusalem. They were built to defend the capital from assaults from the west and south-west, that is, by the Egyptians or Philistines. At this stage they

3. Literally, 'Word I myself speak', with *dābār*, 'word', brought forward, and *'ănî*, 'I', expressed to form a strong asseveration.
4. *Waw*-disjunctive (*waw* followed by a non-verb) introducing a clause of attendant circumstances.

were obviously functioning as vital links in communicating with Egypt. It does not seem that the Babylonians advanced further south than this at this juncture.

The background to the verse has been considerably illumined by the finding of twenty-one pottery sherds/ostraca at Lachish, preserved in the ruins of this period (King 1993:80-83). On these sherds were notes from officers of outlying garrisons to their commander at Lachish, informing him of their situation. Ostracon IV describes a time when a local outpost could no longer see the signal fires at Azekah. Presumably it had been captured, and the military dispatch comes from shortly after the events related here.

2. A Broken Covenant (34:8-11)

The underlying problem in the community is then explored in terms of an incident where the people went back on an agreement they had voluntarily entered into. This showed their lack of trustworthiness in their dealings with one another. However, as the agreement was also a covenant which they had entered into under solemn religious sanctions, it also uncovered their lack of a sense of true responsibility before God. They thought he was one who could effectively be forgotten about; their pledges in his presence and using his name could be rewritten to suit their own purposes and nothing would come of it.

This episode begins towards the end of the first stage of the siege of Jerusalem by the Babylonians. This had begun in January 588 BC (39:1), and was to last until July 586 BC (39:2). At one stage the Egyptian forces moved north to aid Judah, and Nebuchadnezzar raised the siege for a time to allow this threat to be dealt with (v. 21). Precisely when this occurred is not certain, but late winter of 588 BC and the spring of 587 BC seem probable (see Appendix §12). Before the Egyptian army had made an appearance on the scene, the people entered into this agreement, and then when the siege had been lifted, they reneged on their commitment.

8. The word came to Jeremiah from the LORD is not immediately followed by that word (cf. v. 12) but by an extended description of the circumstances in which it was given (cf. 32:1, 6). **After King Zedekiah had made a covenant with all the people in Jerusalem to proclaim freedom for the slaves.** The Hebrew for 'make a covenant' is literally 'cut a covenant' (*kārat bərît*), and the phrase occurs here and in vv. 13, 15, and 18; see the last for the background to the idiom. The making of the covenant seems to have originated with Zedekiah. He was a weak man, who frequently permitted his good intentions to be overruled by the pressure of political circumstances. It is probable that he introduced this measure as a means of obtaining divine favour during the siege, and that it was part of a larger package of religious reforms (cf. v. 18). The slaves who are spoken of are Hebrew slaves, who had become such during the economic oppression of the previous century. Covenant legislation (Exod. 21:1-4; Deut. 15:12) had always envisaged such slavery as being temporary, and now, to show loyalty to the LORD, Zedekiah proposes falling in with what should have prevailed, but most probably did not. One may wonder what motivated the king's advisers and those in the city who owned such slaves. It may have been a matter of convenience. If the slaves became freemen, they could be expected to help defend the capital, but this does not explain why the women were released, and there does not seem to be any adequate reason why slaves could not have been used in various aspects of defending the city. Alternatively, it may have been the case that slaves who were usually employed on the land had been brought into the capital as the Babylonians drew close, but then in the hardships of the siege they became just so many extra mouths to feed. At any rate the king made the proposal, and the others agreed, and it was solemnly entered into.

'Proclaim freedom'/'release' (dərôr; also vv. 15 and 17, twice) echoes the regulations regarding the jubilee (Lev. 25:10; cf. also Ezek. 46:17) rather than regulations regarding the release of slaves in the sabbatical year (Exod. 21:2-10; Deut. 15:12-18) where a different word is used. The phrase is also found in Isa. 61:1 in a sabbatical context. Perhaps here Zedekiah is taking advantage of the prevailing situation to bring into operation a number of long-neglected requirements. The closest parallel to his action regarding the slaves is that of Nehemiah in Neh. 5:1-13.

9. The conditions of the agreement are set out. **Everyone was to free[5] his Hebrew slaves, both male and female; no one was to hold a fellow Jew in bondage.** 'To hold in bondage' (cf. Lev. 25:39) indicates using them either as bondservants or as slaves of even lower status to carry out tasks. The use of the word 'Hebrew' is significant. It was not usually employed as a self-designation, and seems to occur principally in contexts where the people are themselves subject to oppression. Here it may be employed to refer back to Deuteronomic

---

5. Literally, 'to send away/dismiss ⌊as⌋ ḥopšî', a term used mainly to describe the economic and social status of emancipated Hebrew slaves (e.g. Exod. 21:2, 5, 26f.; Deut. 15:12f, 18), and so their return to ordinary life. The masculine adjective is used to refer to both males and females (GKC §132d).

legislation. 'A fellow Jew' (literally 'a Jew his brother') brings out the
bond of covenant community that was intended to characterise the
covenant people's relationships with one another. 'Jew' (*yəhûdî*) is a
relatively late term, not used before the fall of Samaria. Its first occurrence is in 2 Kgs. 16:6, and referred to one who lived in the tribal area
of Judah. The term became more common in the exilic period to
designate one of Israelite descent regardless of his place of residence
(32:12).

10. A solemn undertaking was made. **So all the officials and people
who entered into this covenant agreed that they would free their
male and female slaves and no longer hold them in bondage. They
agreed, and set them free.** 'Agreed' (twice <√*šāmaʿ*, 'to hear', 'to
obey') indicates their willingness to comply with Zedekiah's initiative.
'To enter into the covenant' is to assume its obligations (2 Chron.
15:12; Ezek. 16:8). Subsequently they carried out what they had
committed themselves to. All the slaves were set free, including those
who had not served for six years.

11. However, that was not the end of the matter. **But afterwards they
changed their minds and took back[6] the slaves they had freed and
enslaved them again.[7]** 'Bring into subjection' (<√*kābaš*) is a strong
verb, indicating subjugation of what resists or is unwilling. Nothing is
said of how they found their slaves, or how they established their rights
over them. It is the fact of their going back on their word that is
emphasised in the text, not what occasioned it. However, if the release
of the slaves took place just before the end of the first period of siege,
it is improbable that the slaves would have been able to leave the city.
It has been reasonably conjectured that the change in attitude of the
former slaveowners is connected with the lifting of the siege by the
Babylonians. When the city was under siege, their slaves were a
liability, but with the unexpected change of circumstances—did they
begin to think in terms of a Babylonian defeat?—the slaves were
forced back into bondage.

3. Freedom to Fall (34:12-22)

12. It is against this background of covenant violation that the text

---

6. Notice the wordplay between qal of *šûb* in *wayyāšûbû*, 'they changed
their minds', and the hiphil of *šûb* in *wayyāšîbû*, 'they took back'.

7. The kethibh, *wykbyšwm*, indicates a hiphil, *wayyakbîšûm*. This form does
not occur elsewhere, though it might be justified here as conveying an
intensive force. The qere substitutes a more usual qal form *wayyikbəšûm*.

resumes from v. 8 with **then the word of the LORD came to Jeremiah.**[8] But first there is a recapitulation of the history of Israel, with special emphasis on their own former circumstances as slaves, to underline the significance of the divine requirement regarding the treatment which should have been shown to slaves.

13. This is what the LORD, the God of Israel, says: I made/'cut' (cf. v. 8) **a covenant with your forefathers when I brought them out of Egypt, out of the land of slavery.** 'Your' is masculine plural and refers to the people of Judah and Jerusalem. 'The house of bondage' is literally 'the house of slaves' and points to the treatment that they had experienced while they were in bondage in Egypt (Exod. 13:3, 14; 20:2; Deut. 6:12), which should have conditioned their attitude towards other slaves. 'Remember that you were slaves in Egypt and the LORD your God redeemed you. That is why I give you this command today' (Deut. 15:15). They were therefore required to pay particular regard to how they treated their fellow covenant members who fell on hard times and became bondslaves.

14. I said, 'Every seventh year[9] **each of you must free any fellow Hebrew who has sold himself to you.**[10] **After he has served you for six years, you must let him go free.'** These words are not found in precisely this form in either Exod. 21:2-6 or Deut. 15:12-17, but resemble most closely Deut. 15:12: 'If a fellow Hebrew, a man or a woman, sells himself to you and serves you six years, in the seventh year you must let him go free.' The phrase 'has sold himself to you' (or 'has been sold to you'[11]) shows that the type of slavery envisaged is that of one who in economic straits voluntarily sold himself to pay of his debts. This bondservice was not allowed to continue for longer than six years, but that need not imply Zedekiah took this action in a

---

8. The NIV does not translate 'from the LORD' (cf. NKJV, NRSV), which, though redundant, is more likely to be a feature of Hebrew style than a scribal insertion which ought to be omitted.

9. The Hebrew here is perplexing: *miqqēṣ šebaʿ šānîm*, 'at the end of seven years'. The legislation clearly envisages freedom being granted at the end of six years (Exod. 21:2; Deut. 15:12). Hence the RSV (following the LXX) reads 'at the end of six years', but there is no need for emendation of the text as the same phrase is found in Deut. 15:1. It would seem best explained by the habit of counting both the first and final year in such time expressions.

10. The change here to a second person singular is suggested by Holladay (1989, 2:241) as an indicator that this material is being quoted.

11. The niphal verb *yimmākēr* might be rendered either reflexively, 'sold himself', or passively, 'been sold'. It is the same verb in Deut. 15:12.

sabbatical year. Over an extended period there had been a general disregard of the precepts of the covenant, and it is quite probable that many slaves had not been released at the appropriate time. As part of his programme of religious reform, Zedekiah had all who were Hebrew slaves freed. In the divine speech, the point being made is that this legislation had been established shortly after the Exodus, **your fathers, however, did not listen to me** (<√*šamaʿ*, v. 10) **or pay attention** (cf. 7:24). What the LORD had required had not been put into effect because of Israel's disobedience.

15. Lately, however, things had taken a different turn. **Recently**[12] **you**[13] **repented** (<√*šûb*) points to a change of attitude and conduct. It was an action that God approved of in that they **did what is right in my sight.** No longer treating them as slaves, **each of you proclaimed freedom to his countrymen**/'neighbour'. What was more, they went so far as giving solemn religious sanction to the arrangements they made. **You even made a covenant before me in the house that bears my Name.** They had solemnly ratified the new arrangements by a religious ceremony in the Temple itself. This would have involved calling on the LORD to act as a witness to the arrangements made, and also to act as the one who would enforce the curses of the covenant on any who violated its terms. But see also 'my covenant' in v. 18.

16. But now you have turned round and profaned my name. 'Turned round' (<√*šûb*) is exactly the same word as 'repented' in v. 15. They had first of all turned in repentance, dissociating themselves from their forefathers' disobedience, but now the same term is used ironically (cf. 11:10) to describe how they have turned again in disobedience. Furthermore, because they had pledged themselves before the LORD, it was not just a matter of wilfully disregarding the agreement they had entered into; they had also 'profaned'/'defiled' (<√*ḥālal*, 16:18) God's name by repudiating what they had solemnly undertaken before him. **Each of you has taken back the male and female slaves you had set free to go where they wished.** The last phrase renders the Hebrew phrase which might be literally rendered 'according to their souls/desires' (<*nepeš*, 2:34). They had been freed to do what they wished, and go where they wanted. Obviously in the

---

12. *hayyôm*, 'recently', is literally 'today'. Perhaps the use here is in contrast with the period mentioned in v. 13, where 'when' (NIV) renders *bəyôm*, 'in day of'.

13. 'You', *ʿattem*, is expressed to effect a contrast with the behaviour of their fathers, and so, though the pronoun is the second, and not the first, word in the sentence, it warrants the translation, 'But recently you for your part ...'

siege conditions that prevailed their options in that regard had been
quite limited. But their wishes were not taken into account when **you
have forced them to become your slaves again.**

17. Verses 17-22 spell out the consequences of this perfidy.
Therefore (*lākēn*)**, this is what the LORD says** indicates the beginning of the verdict of the LORD based on the evidence just cited. **You
have not obeyed** (<√*šāmaʿ*, v. 10) **me; you have not proclaimed
freedom for your fellow countrymen.** The nature of the personal
bond between them is here pointed out by the phrase 'for your fellow
countrymen'/'every one to his brother and every one to his neighbour'
(NKJV), where the addition of 'brother' to the 'neighbour' mentioned
alone in v. 15 clarifies the bond of kinship that existed. This is the
indictment they have to face.

In one of the many wordplays found in this section, the LORD's
judgment gives an ironic twist to the situation. They had treated
matters as merely playing with words; so the LORD shows what playing
with words can lead to. **So I now proclaim 'freedom' for you,
declares the LORD.** The freedom the LORD proclaims is freedom from
being his servants and so from being under his protection (Lev. 25:55).
This does not leave them free to do whatever they want because,
released from divine guardianship, they will inevitably experience
'freedom' to fall by the sword, plague and famine. This is the recur-
ring Jeremianic triad of catastrophes (cf. 14:12), though only here with
'plague' coming before 'famine'. **I will make you abhorrent**[14] **to all
the kingdoms of the earth** (cf. 15:4; 24:9; 29:18).

18. This verse shows that the broken covenant had been ratified using
the most solemn of procedures. This is described elsewhere in Scripture only in Gen. 15:7-21, but similar procedures were common in the
ancient East. The parties to the agreement cut an animal in two and
walked between the pieces of the slain animal in a ceremony of
enacted self-malediction. They were saying, 'May the gods in whose
names I enter into this undertaking ensure that this fate befalls me if I
do not keep the terms of this agreement'. **The men who have violated**
(<√*ʿābar*, 'to transgress', cf. v. 19) **my covenant** raises the problem of
which covenant is being referred to. The covenant made by Zedekiah
and the people seems to have been a one-sided agreement. They agreed
and walked through the pieces. The slaves were not called on to do
anything. Nor was Yahweh a party to that covenant (as distinct from
being a witness). However, the release of the slaves may have been

---

14. For the kethibh/qere here, see on 15:4.

part of a general ceremony of covenant renewal. It is quite probable that Zedekiah is trying to imitate the behaviour of his father Josiah in renewing the nation's commitment to the Mosaic covenant. The most obvious way in which this renewal impacted on life in Jerusalem was in connection with the treatment of slaves. There is then a second charge, **and have not fulfilled the terms of the covenant they made**/'cut' **before me.** This refers particularly to the breach of the solemn agreement to free the slaves. **I will treat like the calf**[15] **they cut in two and then walked between its pieces.** The LORD will ensure that using his name in the covenant ceremony was no empty form, for he will bring down on their heads the very malediction with which they had cursed themselves. 'Cut' ($<\sqrt{k\bar{a}rat}$, v. 8) is the same word as just used for to make/cut a covenant. 'Pieces' ($<\sqrt{b\bar{a}tar}$, 'to cut in pieces') was used in Gen. 15:10 with respect to Abraham cutting up the animals used in the covenant ritual. Since they have gone back on their word, those who went between the cut pieces will themselves be cut to pieces.

19. The participants in the covenant ceremony included all who were sufficiently wealthy to have owned bondslaves. **The leaders of Judah and Jerusalem, the court officials, the priests and all the people of the land who walked between the pieces of the calf.** 'Walked' ($<\sqrt{\bar{a}bar}$, 'to pass through'; Gen. 15:17) involves an untranslatable play on the Hebrew root which is also used in the sense of 'pass beyond', 'transgress' and so has been translated 'violated' in v. 18. This wordplay draws attention to the heinous nature of their conduct: those who had committed themselves by walking through the pieces walked away from their commitment. 'The leaders of Judah and the leaders of Jerusalem' are specified as two groups (cf. NKJV). Perhaps these royal advisers and officials were distinguished by their place of service. 'Officials' ($<s\bar{a}r\hat{i}s$, cf. 29:2) probably refers to Zedekiah's personal attendants. 'The people of the land' refers not to all no matter what their circumstances, but to the upper classes (1:18). No mention is made of the royal family or the prophets.

20. The LORD before whom the covenant was solemnised gives the assurance that their actions will not pass unrequited. **I will hand them**

---

15. The Hebrew construction has been perplexing principally because of the distance in the Hebrew of 'the calf' $h\bar{a}$'$\bar{e}gel$ from the verb 'I will treat' $wan\bar{a}tatt\hat{i}$. But it seems to be a case of $n\bar{a}tan$ followed by two accusatives to indicate to 'treat A like B', and there is no need to emend to $k\bar{a}$'$\bar{e}gel$, 'like the calf'. The absence of the preposition makes the statement even more stark.

over[16] **to their enemies who seek their lives** (cf. 21:7). **Their dead bodies will become food for the birds of the air and the beasts of the earth.** Having one's unburied body become carrion for scavenging animals was a curse frequently found in treaty documents. It is also threatened in 7:33; 16:4; 19:7; Deut. 28:26. But such a fate was what those who had acted so perfidiously in connection with the covenant had brought upon themselves. Note that this applies to those listed in v. 19, which does not include the king.

21. But the role of the king is not be passed by in silence. **I will hand Zedekiah king of Judah and his officials over to their enemies who seek their lives, to the army of the king of Babylon, which has withdrawn from you.** 'Hand over'/'give in the hand of' repeats the warning of v. 2, and the description of their enemies matches that of the previous verse. 'Officials' (<śar) refers to the groups mentioned as 'leaders' in v. 19, that is, the political and military advisers of the king. No distinction is made between his fate and theirs, presumably because Zedekiah had given in to their representations on the matter and had not maintained his policy. 'Which has withdrawn from you' shows that at this point the advancing Egyptian forces had caused the Babylonians to lift the siege of the city—temporarily (37:5-8). It was then that the ruling classes in Jerusalem thought that they had done enough to secure deliverance from Babylon and reneged on the commitment they had given to their former slaves—and to the LORD.

22. I am going to give the order, declares the LORD, and I will bring them back to this city. 'Bring back' is yet another variation on the theme of the verb šûb (here a hiphil). The departure of the Babylonian armies was only a temporary feature (37:8). There should be no doubt that they will return as the instruments of the LORD's judgment upon such treacherous people who have violated their covenant undertakings. He is in control of the movements of the Babylonian army. **They will fight against it, take it and burn it down. And I will lay waste the towns of Judah so that no one can live there.** What their enemies do is effectively that which the LORD himself has carried out. Archaeological evidence indicates that there was widespread destruction of settlements and fortresses during this period (9:11).

---

16. The Hebrew object marker 'ôtām serves to resume the list from the previous verse.

B. THE RECHABITES (35:1-19)

This chapter relates an incident that occurred over ten years before that of chapter 34. The events have been brought together here because of their thematic connection. In chapter 34 we have the culminating instance of the inconstancy and lack of commitment displayed by the people of Judah and Jerusalem, even with regard to pledges they had themselves undertaken before the LORD. By way of contrast, this chapter relates an instance of constancy and obedience on the part of a group known as the Rechabites, which Jeremiah uses to expose more starkly the covenant infidelity of the people in an attempt to shame them into reconsidering their attitude towards God. Perhaps there is also a link in that the slaves and the Rechabites would be considered second class members of the community.

1. The Prophet's Challenge (35:1-5)

Jeremiah is instructed to bring the Rechabites to a room at the Temple and offer them wine to drink. Because their ancestor had instructed them not to consume wine, they refuse the offer.

1. This is the word that came to Jeremiah from the LORD during the reign of Jehoiakim son of Josiah king of Judah does not of itself indicate when in Jehoiakim's reign from 609–598 BC the incident occurred. The information given in v. 11 regarding the invasion of Nebuchadnezzar does, however, narrow the options to around 605 BC, or 600–598 BC. Furthermore the mention in v. 11 of Aramean involvement makes the latter period more probable in the light of 2 Kgs. 24:2. This was towards the close of Jehoiakim's reign when he had revolted from Nebuchadnezzar, who was unable to bring his army immediately against Judah. Instead he sent marauding parties from the north to harass the land. Such forays would have been particularly effective against a nomadic people such as the Rechabites.

2. Go to the Rechabite[17] family/'house of the Rechabites'. Although some commentators (e.g. Holladay 1989, 2:247; Carroll 1986:651) contend that this is a reference to a building in Jerusalem in which they were then living, the testimony of v. 9 seems to rule this out. 'House of

---

17. The NIV idiosyncratically spells the word in the unfamiliar form of 'Recabite' (and similarly the name 'Recab'), presumably to avoid the *ch* combination being pronounced as in *ch*urch rather than lo*ch*. This is a quite unnecessary change from a familiar form, and it is not adopted by most English versions.

the Rechabites' is rather a fixed expression to refer to the clan or family.[18] Though enemy harassment had forced them to give up living in the countryside, they might have found a spot to pitch their tents outside the walls of Jerusalem. There would be no space to do so in the inner city, and the siege of 597 BC had not yet begun. Perhaps, like the many others who would have fled to the capital, they had been forced to sleep wherever they could in the streets. Their numbers are not known, but do not seem to have been a large group.

Apart from this chapter, our information about the Rechabites is sparse. They were related to the Kenites, the Midianite tribe from whom Moses' father-in-law, Jethro, came (1 Chron. 2:55), and who associated themselves with the Israelites and accompanied them when they entered into the land. There appear to have been two groups, one settling in the north in the territory of Naphtali (Judg. 4:11, 17; 5:24), and the other on the southern borders of Judah (1 Sam. 15:6; 27:10; 30:29). If their nomadic lifestyle pre-dates Jonadab, then they could have been located in different regions at different times. Certainly groups in the north might have migrated south at the dissolution of the northern kingdom. Attempts to identify them as craftsmen, and in particular, as chariot makers derive from the fact that the same three Hebrew consonants that are the basis of the name 'Rechab' also form the word *rēkāb*, 'chariot', but there is nothing in the text to warrant this association. It is favoured by those who want to see the Rechabites not as a religiously motivated group who eschewed certain practices because of their potential for spiritual corruption (there are parallels with, but no direct connection to, the Nazirites; Num. 6), but as a craft guild that avoided settled society and also alcohol lest any inadvertently disclose the secrets of their trade.

However, the evidence points to their behaviour as springing from cultural and religious rejection of the perceived dangers of the settled lifestyle in the cities of Palestine. Their particular traditions derive from Jonadab son of Rechab (vv. 6, 8, 10, 14, 16, 19) who is mentioned in 2 Kgs. 10:15-27 as associating with Jehu when he set out to eliminate the worship of Baal in the northern kingdom, 842 BC. Jonadab (a shorter form of the name Jehonadab[19]) took an active part in the slaughter of the Baal worshippers in their temple. He was

---

18. Notice also that in v. 5 the phrase *bêt hārēkābîm*, 'the house of the Rechabites' (vv. 2, 3, 18), is replaced by *bǝnê bêt hārēkābîm*, 'the sons of the house of the Rechabites', which makes clear that 'house' is used in the sense of 'family'.

19. The longer form is found in this chapter in vv. 8, 14, 16, 18, 19.

passionately committed to the worship of the LORD and this seems to have been the basis of his instructions to his descendants—instructions which they carried out for the succeeding two and a half centuries.

Jeremiah is further divinely directed, **And invite them to come to one of the side rooms of the house of the LORD and give them wine to drink.** The side rooms were chambers attached to the outside of the Temple, or possibly, erected in one of its courtyards. They were used as storerooms or for accommodation of Temple officials. However, the significant feature of the divine command is that the Rechabites were to be invited to consume alcohol—something which they had been specifically prohibited from doing (v. 6).

3. Jeremiah then relates how he complied with the instructions given to him. **So I went to get Jaazaniah son of Jeremiah, the son of Habazziniah, and his brothers and all his sons—the whole family of the Rechabites.** Jaazaniah seems to have been the patriarch of the clan at the time. The 'Jeremiah' mentioned here is of course someone other than the prophet, the name being fairly common at the time (1:1). 'Sons' might refer to followers rather than children, but it is more likely that the description is of an extended family group of no great numbers.

4. I brought them into the house of the LORD indicates into the Temple precincts, not into the Temple building itself. We know that for a while Jeremiah was denied access to the Temple (36:5). This incident might come from 605 BC, just before his exclusion, but given the facts set out in v. 1, it is more probable that there was a relaxation in the official attitude towards Jeremiah during the confused closing months of Jehoiakim's reign, at which juncture the prophet resumed his public ministry.

Jeremiah mentions particularly where he brought them, but unfortunately the details are obscure to us in that we have no precise information about the location of the additional rooms at the Temple. **Into the room of the sons of Hanan son of Igdaliah[20] the man of God.** It is Hanan who is called 'the man of God', a title that is only found here in Jeremiah, but is used elsewhere in the Old Testament to indicate a prophet of great stature or indisputable piety (used of Moses in Deut. 33:1 and Samuel in 1 Sam. 9:6, but notice also of unnamed prophets in 1 Sam. 2:27 and 1 Kgs. 13:1). It is possible that Hanan, who is not otherwise mentioned in Scripture, was indeed a genuine

---

20. This is a longer form of Gedaliah, a fairly common name (cf. 38:1; 40:5).

prophet. The mention of a room in the Temple precincts may indicate that he was also a priest, but the specific reference is to his sons (possibly his followers rather than his family), which means that he himself was probably not a contemporary of Jeremiah. The fact that Jeremiah is permitted access to this room suggests that at least there was a measure of sympathy between the prophet and this group, but we cannot really say more than that. **It was next to the room of the officials** (<*śar*). The reference is to court officials (rather than Temple officials), for whose use a room had been specially set aside since the Temple was adjacent to the palace. The description, **which was over that of Maaseiah son of Shallum the door-keeper,** suggests that the first two rooms were on an upper floor. Maaseiah may have been the father of the priest Zephaniah (21:1). The 'door-keeper'/'keeper of the threshold' held an eminent office in the hierarchy, coming third in rank after the high priest himself. There seem to have been three such officials (52:24 = 2 Kgs. 25:18), corresponding to the three principal entrances to the Temple. They had guards under their command to help them carry out their duties, which included monitoring those coming into the sacred precincts because there were specific rules regarding ritual purity that stipulated who might enter the Temple and what sacrifices they might bring with them. They also supervised the collection of gifts to the Temple (2 Kgs. 12:9) and possibly also its physical upkeep. So the Rechabites, a marginal group of vagrants/refugees, were being brought into the chambers of the highest circles of Judahite society. What Jeremiah was doing with them was not being done in a corner. It was meant to serve as an object lesson, though what lesson was intended is not yet stated.

5. The third part of the instructions given by the LORD in v. 2 is now carried out. **Then I set bowls full of wine and some cups before the men of the Rechabite family and said to them, 'Drink some wine.'** The test is not conducted by merely asking questions. The choice is put before them as compellingly as possible. The bowls were large containers from which the individual drinking cups would be filled. Jeremiah in his own name invites them to drink so that it is not just a matter of refusing wine set before them, but of spurning the hospitality extended to them by the prophet in such a fine setting. The Rechabites were being put on the spot as regards where their loyalties lay.

2. The Faithful Response (35:6-11)

6. But they replied, 'We do not drink wine, because (*kî*) **our forefather Jonadab son of Rechab gave us this command: "Neither**

you nor your descendants must[21] **ever drink wine".'** It was a
standing ordinance, and not just something one-off, applicable in a
particular situation. The question that is thus raised is Jonadab's
motivation in issuing this command. It seems plausible to associate it
with his anti-Baal stance. Drunkenness was frequent in the ancient
Near East, and had become a feature of Canaanite worship. Jonadab
was seeking to dissociate his descendants from Baal worship and all its
impurities. He therefore imposed on them a lifestyle that would not
involve them in situations where he judged the influences of Baalism
would be more keenly felt. Abstinence from wine indicated complete
attention given to the LORD and had been a feature of Israel's life
before God in the wilderness (Deut. 29:6; cf. also Dan. 1:8). Wine, on
the other hand, was a symbol of confusion (51:7).

7. They proceed to set their obedience to this specific requirement in
the context of a basic commitment to a whole series of commands
which they are determined to keep. **And you must not build houses,
sow seed or plant vineyards; you must never have any of these
things, but** (*kî*) **must always/**'all your days' **live in tents.** The cultivation of vines involved a sedentary life, and Baal worship seems to have
been more prevalent in the settled communities of the land. By
maintaining a nomadic lifestyle, they would be protected to some
extent from accommodating and apostatising pressures, and in this way
Jonadab felt the religious purity of the group would be maintained.
Then (*ləmaʿan*, 'in order that' or 'so that', of purpose or consequence)
you will live a long time in the land where you are nomads. Their
attitude to the land was to be that of nomads/resident aliens (<*gēr*),
people who were only passing through, without citizen rights and
dependent on the hospitality and goodwill of the residents of the land.
But free from the corruptions of Canaanite religion they would be able
to enjoy God's blessing.

There is nothing in this incident which reflects on the correctness of
Jonadab's position. It would be wrong to take the chapter as endorsing,
or mandating, an ascetic lifestyle, or an absolute prohibition on the
consumption of alcohol. Undoubtedly what these people were doing
was not wrong. If it had been, they would not have been commended
as they were, but it is not suggested that this is the only, or even the
desired, response to the problem of maintaining a godly lifestyle when
the surrounding culture is permeated by paganism. The matter would
be discussed extensively by Paul in 1 Corinthians.

---

21. 'Must' is intended to bring out the force of the strong, apodictic prohibition using *lōʾ*, rather than *ʿal*, with the imperfect.

8-11. The focus of the chapter is on obedience. Verses 8-10 provide us with the testimony that the Rechabites are able to give of their lifestyle in obedience to the commands given by their forefather. **We have obeyed everything our forefather Jonadab son of Rechab commanded us. Neither we nor our wives nor our sons and daughters have ever drunk wine or built houses to live in or had vineyards, fields or crops. We have lived in tents and have fully obeyed everything our forefather Jonadab commanded us.** 'Obey' ($<\sqrt{š\bar{a}ma}$', which basically means 'to hear', and so 'to pay attention to', 'to heed', and also 'to obey'; vv. 10, 13, 14, 15, 16, 17, 18) is a keyword in the chapter: really listening impels to obedience. The particular details of their obedience are spelled out in a series of negated infinitive constructs. They have followed him completely, and would have continued to live in the open country had not external circumstances compelled them to come to stay in Jerusalem. Presumably they anticipated resuming their former lifestyle once that became practicable. **But when Nebuchadnezzar king of Babylon invaded this land, we said, 'Come, we must go to Jerusalem to escape the Babylonian and Aramean armies.'** This would seem to indicate that they recognised that their commitment was not absolutely binding, but that they would carry it out as far as they were humanly able. 'Babylonian' here, as throughout Jeremiah (21:4), is in Hebrew 'Chaldean' and this may be of significance for our understanding of 'Aramean'. In the Old Testament the term usually refers to the tribes found north of Israel in the area around Damascus, but there were also eastern Aramean peoples many of whom lived a semi-nomadic existence throughout Mesopotamia. It may be that they are referred to here, but 2 Kgs. 24:2 suggests that the troops Nebuchadnezzar at first used were mainly levies drawn from vassal states in the region. **So we have remained in Jerusalem.** This is a plea based on the special circumstances that prevailed. The rest of the narrative accepts that their presence in Jerusalem had not compromised their loyalty.

3. Learning the Lesson (35:12-17)

Jeremiah's conduct in trying to get teetotallers to consume wine would no doubt have stirred up considerable interest and amusement. But the sign is not left uninterpreted. Its significance for the people of Jerusalem lay in the contrast between the principled and resolute behaviour of the Rechabites and their own conduct. This use of the other people as an object lesson for Judah is similar to that found in 2:9-13 in terms of the allegiance of the nations to their own gods. Here the Rechabites' display of constancy and fidelity had condemned Judah in the circumstances of Jehoiakim's reign, and it continued to expose Judah's unfaithfulness.

12-13. The testimony of the Rechabites as to their past practice and their refusal to surrender their principles even though invited to by a prophet of God in circumstances which the hospitality of the East would have led them to accept his offer of wine is now used to bring home to the people of Judah the difference with their own position. **Then the word of the LORD came to Jeremiah, saying: 'This is what the LORD Almighty, the God of Israel, says: Go and tell the men of Judah and the people of Jerusalem, "Will you not learn a lesson and obey[22] my words?" declares the LORD.'** The full title of the LORD is used to emphasise his claim to Judah's obedience. That Jeremiah is told to 'Go' shows that he is to present this message not in the room in which the test of the Rechabites' allegiance to their principles took place, but perhaps in one of the outer courts of the Temple where many more people would be found. Having gone outside, the prophet is to challenge them in the LORD's name that they should note well what the example of the Rechabites was saying about their own conduct. There was still the possibility of repentance which would have averted the coming cataclysm, if only they would 'learn a lesson'/'receive instruction' (*mûsār* <√*yāsar*, 2:30). The LORD as the divine instructor urges them to let their conduct be corrected by the example given by the Rechabites. If they do that, then they will truly hear and obey (<√*šāmaʿ*) the LORD's words.

14. Jonadab son of Rechab ordered his sons not to drink wine[23] and this command has been kept. To this day they do not drink wine, because (*kî*) **they obey their forefather's command.** 'Forefather'/'father' may be used here to refer to the founder of the group, rather than implying that all were directly descended from him. But though the command given to them came from one man, two hundred and fifty years before in the reign of Jehu, they still obeyed it. However, the people of Judah had ignored the repeated message of

---

22. The NIV like the NRSV presents learning the lesson and obeying the LORD's words as if these two actions were synonymous. The Hebrew suggests, however, that the lesson is that of the overriding need for fidelity to instructions given. 'And obey', literally 'to obey' (*lišmōaʿ*; cf. NKJV), is then the consequence of accepting correction.

23. *hûqam* is a singular hophal perfect followed by ʿ*et* before the subject as can occur with a passive verb, 'There has been performed the words of Jonadab ...' (GKC §121b; *IBHS* §10.3.2b).

their God. **But I** (*wə'ănōkî*, 'and I', marks a sharp contrast) **have spoken to you again and again.** This is part of the divine speech, indicating the effort made by the LORD ('rising early and speaking', 7:13) to gain his people's attention and their hearts. But his attempts, though unremitting, have proved fruitless. **Yet you have not obeyed me.** Now the keyword 'obey' (<√*šāma'*) is negated. The people were listening to their own inclinations, not the directions of the LORD.

15. Again and again I sent/'rising early and sending' (cf. 7:25) **all my servants the prophets to you.** Judah could not complain about lack of warnings, or about the clarity of the message that was delivered to them. **They said, 'Each of you must turn** (<√*šûb*) **from your wicked ways and reform your actions** (cf. 7:3); **do not follow other gods to serve them'** (cf. 7:6; 11:10). Repentance and reformation should be accompanied by absolute dissociation from the cult of heathen gods, and then their renewed loyalty to the LORD will not go unrewarded. **Then you shall live[24] in the land I have given to you and your fathers.'** Jeremiah had not been the first to approach them in this way (cf. 25:4-5). Repeatedly the message had been proclaimed by a long line of prophets of the LORD, but to no avail. **But you have not paid attention or listened to me** (cf. 7:26). 'Listen' (<√*šāma'*, 'to hear') is one of the repeated keywords in this narrative. The endeavours of the prophets did not bring about any change in their attitude.

16. The verse begins with 'for' (*kî*), not to suggest a reason for Judah's disobedience, but to justify making the immediately foregoing statement.[25] The people of Judah can be rightly charged with not paying attention because comparison with the behaviour of the Rechabites clearly brings out the negligent nature of Judah's response to the LORD. **The descendants of Jonadab son of Rechab have carried out the command their forefather gave them, but these people have not obeyed me.** 'These people' is used to refer to them, even although they are being directly addressed, to indicate the degree of alienation that has entered into the relationship because of their conduct.

---

24. *ûšəbû*, 'and dwell!', is an imperative after an imperative and a jussive, expressing a consequence expected with certainty (GKC §110i). There is also a play on the words 'turn' (<√*šûb*) and 'live' (<√*yāšab*, 'to dwell, inhabit'): repentance leads to residence in the land of promise.

25. This use of *kî* is described in BDB, 473, 3.c: 'sometimes it [i.e. *kî*] is explicative, justifying a statement by unfolding the particulars which establish or exemplify it.'

17. Inevitably they will experience the judgment of the LORD on their disobedience. **Therefore** (*lākēn*), **this is what the LORD God Almighty, the God of Israel, says: 'Listen! I am going to bring on Judah and on everyone living in Jerusalem every disaster I pronounced against them.'** The reason for this action is then given. 'Because' (*yaʿan*) **I spoke to them, but they did not listen; I called to them, but they did not answer'** (cf. 11:11). Disaster is the inevitable consequence of continued disobedience in the face of direct divine instructions as to how they should live, and also in the face of repeated divine remonstrance and entreaty that they had got things wrong and should repent before it became too late.

4. Faithfulness Rewarded (35:18-19)

The testing of the Rechabites was used not only to present Judah with an object lesson in obedience—a lesson that obviously condemned them. It also was the occasion of divine blessing being pronounced on the Rechabites, which was no doubt intended to act as a further stimulus to reformation on the part of Judah.

18. It may be that Jeremiah addressed these words to the Rechabites before leaving the room (that is, after v. 11) and that the narrative of the blessing has been delayed to highlight the contrast with what awaits Judah.[26] Otherwise, we are to understand that the Rechabites followed Jeremiah out into the Temple courtyard. **Then Jeremiah said to the family of the Rechabites, 'This is what the LORD Almighty, the God of Israel, says: "You have obeyed the command of your forefather Jonadab and have followed all his instructions and have done everything he ordered".'** Their complete obedience (*kol*, 'all', is used twice) to their ancestor's injunctions was the basis for the blessing that was to be extended to them.

19. **Therefore** (*lākēn*) introduces the divine verdict, but here it is one of promise, not condemnation. **This is what the LORD Almighty, the God of Israel, says: 'Jonadab son of Rechab shall never fail to have a man to serve me.'** 'To serve me' is literally 'to stand before me'. It is used of a servant waiting to attend his master, but pre-eminently of priestly service of the LORD (15:1). 'Never' is literally 'not ... all the days', reflecting v. 7. The idiom is that of covenant

---

26. The NRSV brings out well the *waw*-adversative construction with which v. 18 begins: 'But to the house of the Rechabites Jeremiah said'. There is no indication of temporal sequence as 'then' (NIV) might suggest; it is rather a juxtaposition for rhetorical effect.

blessing, such as has been set out in connection with the seed of David and the Levites (33:17-18). Its use here associates the Rechabites with the covenant community and not only asserts the continuance of the Rechabite line, but also more specifically their continuance as those who will be engaged in divine service.

But how did this promise come true? There are possible indications in Scripture of Rechabites in succeeding centuries. For instance, Machijah son of Rechab who is said to be the ruler of the district of Beth-hakerem (literally the 'house of the vineyard', though it would be too much to read from a place name of this sort anything about the life-style of this individual). He is mentioned as repairing the Dung Gate (Neh. 3:14), which seems at variance with the previous lifestyle of the Rechabites. There are also Jewish traditions that by marrying into priestly families the Rechabites later were given the function of bringing wood for the altar. Some early travellers in the East reported that they had found people claiming to be descendants of the Rechabites, but these reports have not been substantiated (Keil 1873, 2:92).

C. THE ENDURING WITNESS OF THE SCROLL (36:1-32)

For a second time the narrative moves backwards to consider another key incident in the decline of faithfulness in Judah. For twenty-three years Jeremiah had borne witness to the need for heart reformation in Judah, because otherwise the LORD would send disaster upon the nation. Many times during those years Jeremiah's 'foe from the north', announced as the LORD's chosen instrument to punish his people, must have seemed like a bogeyman, thought up to frighten little children. Were not the real facts of the matter that the northern power of Assyria was collapsing rapidly? How could disaster come from the north, from Mesopotamia, when the powers there were so busy fighting one another?

The events of 605 BC showed how quickly the international scene could turn around. Nebuchadnezzar led Babylonian forces to take over where the Assyrians had left off. Babylonian records show that at this time Nebuchadnezzar took general control of Syria–Palestine from the Egyptians. Jerusalem was encircled and hostages taken (see Appendix §7). Then in October 605 BC–March 604 BC Nebuchadnezzar waged a six-month campaign in Syria–Palestine during which all the kings of the area brought tribute to him. There is no reason to suppose that an exception was made of Jehoiakim. Ashkelon refused to submit, and Nebuchadnezzar marched against it, took it and devastated it in

December 604 BC. Would not this partial realisation of Jeremiah's warnings serve to make the people more attentive to his message? The account of this chapter shows that even in the light of these ominous events the nation would not acknowledge its guilt before the LORD.

This chapter also gives insight into the dynamics of government in Judah at this time. We see the role and influence of the leading ministers of the government, and possibly also of another group, the king's personal attendants. In trying to understand what is going on in the book of Jeremiah it is important to notice the difference between the regimes of Jehoiakim and Zedekiah. Jehoiakim is presented as a resolute but unscrupulous king, someone who exploited his position for his own ends. He was, however, served by officials who had been trained under Josiah and who retained respect for the word of God and for his prophet. As we can see in this chapter, while these men recognised the king's ultimate authority, they did try to sway him into taking a more prudent course of action (v. 25). The situation was to change, however, with the exile of 597 BC. Zedekiah, Nebuchadnezzar's appointee as ruler of Judah, did not have the full support of the people, many of whom considered the exiled Jehoiachin to remain their true king. Furthermore, Zedekiah was irresolute and hesitant. Perhaps Nebuchadnezzar had installed him for the very reason that he was no threat to anyone. However, the previous royal advisers were now in exile, and their successors were largely second-rate men who incited the king to adopt most ill-judged measures and who were out of sympathy with Jeremiah and the message he brought.

In the ominous period when the Babylonians were tightening their grip of the region, Jeremiah was instructed to prepare a scroll containing the warnings he had been uttering throughout his prophetic ministry. After a delay, the scroll was publicly read by Baruch, and it was then drawn to the king's attention by his senior advisers. Despite their protests King Jehoiakim took it upon himself to burn the scroll containing the word the LORD had revealed through Jeremiah. This act of extreme bravado and folly on the part of the king marked a turning-point in relationship between the LORD and his people. The political regime had now openly repudiated its allegiance to the LORD.

Though Jehoiakim wanted his own way, that was not to be. The rewritten scroll served as a sign that the word of the LORD cannot be set aside by human endeavour, however forceful and radical. The burned scroll testified that the king and the people he led had no time for the word of the LORD, but they would not on that account escape its dire predictions. The word of the LORD would not pass away, and their obstinacy would bring on them the predicted calamity.

The king's reaction to the scroll that was brought to him deviated starkly from that of Josiah, his father, in similar circumstances a generation earlier. In 2 Kgs. 22 we find recorded what happened during restoration work in the Temple, when the scroll of the law was found. The contrast between the penitence shown on the one occasion and the impenitence on the other could not be more striking. Both kings had to face a demand that the ways of the nation be reformed—but how differently they reacted! Josiah's reverent response gained a reprieve for the nation, whereas his son's intransigence sealed its doom.

The detail recorded in this chapter indicates that the information it contains derives from an eyewitness to the incidents recorded. That eyewitness was most probably Baruch himself, and it is likely that he was personally involved in the composition of this part of the book. The chapter also attracts attention through the detail that it provides about how this prophecy was preserved (and probably other ancient prophecies too). There is nothing to suggest that this was the first time Jeremiah had written down his message. At any point in time dissemination of information in the ancient Near East was effected by word of mouth—and it was in that way the prophets too conducted their ministry—but it was also the case that all important matters were preserved in writing. Opinions will doubtless continue to vary as to whether what was done on this occasion was typical prophetic procedure. Scholarly investigation has also failed to achieve a consensus as to what the two scrolls of this chapter have in common with one another, and with the completed book of Jeremiah. But that should not induce us to adopt views such as those of Carroll (1986:662-8), that the scrolls are in fact a fiction based on 2 Kgs. 22:8-13 designed to boost the authority of Baruch (and his successors, the Deuteronomistic scribes of the Exile and later), and that this narrative was conceived to function as a literary parallel to chapter 26. Scholarly flights of fancy should not divert us from the information provided here. Undoubtedly we cannot give precise answers to every question because the chapter was not written to satisfy our curiosity about the composition of prophetic books. Its focus is on the wickedness of the king, and the reasons for the disaster that overtook Jerusalem in 597 BC and again in 586 BC.

1. The Writing of the Scroll (36:1-4)

1. Once more the time period alters. **In the fourth year of Jehoiakim son of Josiah king of Judah, this word came to Jeremiah from the LORD** takes us back to the year of autumn 605–autumn 604 BC

(Appendix §9). In the early summer of 605 BC Babylonian forces under
the crown prince Nebuchadnezzar had defeated the Egyptians at
Carchemish on the Euphrates, which spelled the end of Egyptian
domination of Syria–Palestine. Nebuchadnezzar chased the Egyptians
south, and defeated them again at Haran. No doubt he would have
gone further, but his father died in August of that year and he had to
return home to assume the throne. The regime in Judah had to decide
which side to ally itself with in the uncertainties of the reshaped
political landscape. Jehoiakim favoured alliance with Egypt, but the
dominant power was now undoubtedly Babylon, especially when the
following year Nebuchadnezzar returned and sacked Ashkelon on the
Philistine plain (December 604 BC). For those who had eyes to see it,
the foe from the north that Jeremiah had spoken about throughout his
ministry had finally arrived.

2. Jeremiah was commanded to deliver his message in a way that
differed from what had prevailed earlier. **Take a scroll and write**[27] **on
it.**[28] The scroll is described using a rare double description, literally,
'scroll of a document' (*məgillat-sēper*), a combination found here in
vv. 2 and 4, and elsewhere only in Ps. 40:7 and Ezek. 2:9. *məgillâ*,
'scroll', denotes something that has been rolled up, and is used on its
own eleven times in the chapter. *sēper*, 'document', which is elsewhere
rendered 'scroll', refers to something that is written, or written upon,
occurring six times on its own in the chapter. The significance of the
composite expression is uncertain. Probably it indicated a scroll of
sufficient length to contain a fair amount of writing, such as would be
used for an important document, and points to its status. The form of
Jeremiah's scroll was as impressive as the message it contained.
Scrolls often consisted of pieces of leather or parchment sewn together,
but here the ease with which it was burned (v. 23) may indicate it was
made from papyrus. The papyrus was fairly narrow, about 10 inches
(25 cm) high, and would be rolled lengthwise on two pieces of wood.
Scrolls could be up to 30 feet (9 m) long. The writing would be in
columns of a standard width and would run from top to bottom and
right to left. The scroll would be read as the papyrus was rolled off the
left stick onto the right one. We further notice that while the command
to write is given to Jeremiah, it is not in fact executed directly, but

27. The *waw*-consecutive perfect construction is used here to express the
second imperative. Usually this implies that the second action follows on after
the first, but in v. 28 the same two actions are expressed using imperatives
(Joüon, §119l).
28. *'ēleyâ* for *'āleyâ*, as often.

through the use of Baruch as an amanuensis.

The theme of this scroll is **all the words I have spoken to you concerning Israel, Judah and all the other nations from the time I began speaking to you in the reign of Josiah till now.** While the preposition *'al*, 'concerning', may also be translated 'against' and that hostile note may seem warranted by the fact that the subject is impending 'disaster' (v. 3), the message in fact constitutes one last appeal for repentance, and so a more neutral rendering is preferable. Contrary to some critics (e.g. Driver 1906:5, 'None of Jeremiah's prophecies were committed to writing till the fourth year of Jehoiakim'), it is overwhelmingly probable that over the years Jeremiah had kept records of what had been revealed to him. For generations prophets had kept written records (Isa. 8:1). Given the importance to Jeremiah of his call and his total acceptance that the revelation he received was of divine origin, it is intrinsically and culturally unlikely that he had taken no steps to keep a permanent record of it. But previous to 605 BC Jeremiah had not gathered this together for public proclamation.

The extent of the material in Jeremiah's First Scroll is unclear. There are those who see Jeremiah as being supernaturally empowered on the occasion to recall from memory all his previous ministry so that Baruch could write it down. More probably Jeremiah was reading from various scattered sets of notes, possibly on parchment or even on pottery sherds, so as to bring his material into a connected order. Though 'all' might be taken to comprise the totality of the revelation he had previously received, later in the chapter this scroll is read comfortably three times in one day (and also substantially recounted), so that if virtually all the material up to say chapter 19 is to be included on this scroll then there might have been difficulties. Also if v. 32 refers to earlier messages, then what is intended here could not be absolutely all. What was required was a presentation that summarised the whole scope of the LORD's message through the prophet. The mention of 'all the other nations' indicates that the First Scroll contained at least some of what is now found in chapters 25 and 46–51. While its precise contents are a matter of speculation, chapters 1–7 were almost certainly present. There is no doubt that this concentrated form of Jeremiah's message, bringing together what had delivered on many occasions over the years, should have made a powerful impression on its hearers by its total impact—and with some it did.

3. The purpose of the exercise is outlined in the words: **Perhaps when the people/'house' of Judah hear about every disaster I plan to inflict on them**. 'Perhaps' introduces a note of doubt. It does not rule out the possibility of repentance, but assesses its probability realistically in view of the previous intransigence of the people in the face of repeated warnings. It is not revealed in advance how the people will react when they are once more confronted with the word of God. There may not have been much hope of success, but God was not going to cast off his people lightly. Time and again there will be spelled out to them the dire consequences of their attitude and actions. Here the written word is used to make it more solemn. It is not an ephemeral message that is being presented to them, but one on the same level as that which was regularly read from the Pentateuch by the priests at Temple services. The hearing that is looked for is not merely outward, but with inward acceptance (cf. 26:3). The thought that is expressed is, 'Perhaps the house of Judah will hear ... in order that/so that[29] each of them will turn' (cf. NASB, NKJV). The LORD is acting in this way with a view to achieving the result that **each of them will turn from his wicked way**, because hearing the divine warning read from the scroll was intended to evoke the response of repentance ('turn' <√šûb).

Then I will forgive their wickedness (ʿawon, 2:22) **and their sin** (ḥaṭṭāʾt, 2:35). Divine forgiveness is not offered to a people who show no awareness of the culpability of their own actions.

4. Jeremiah carries out the LORD's instructions by summoning his friend, Baruch, who appears for the first time chronologically in the narrative (the references in chapter 32 are to events a dozen years later). It was not as if Jeremiah himself could not write (32:10; 51:60), but that the length and the complexity of assembling the material required that he be assisted by someone skilled in writing. We can see what it cost Baruch to be associated with Jeremiah at this time in chapter 45 (further information about Baruch is given in the introduction to that chapter). **So Jeremiah called Baruch son of Neriah, and while Jeremiah dictated all the words the LORD had spoken to him,[30] Baruch wrote them on the scroll**. Throughout the chapter the term 'dictate' is used to render Hebrew phrases conveying the idea of 'from

29. Hebrew shares with many languages a blurring of the difference between purpose (final or telic) clauses and consecutive (consequence) clauses. Though ləmaʿan is generally a telic particle, it may also function as a consequence indicator. It is primarily the context that has to be used to determine the matter (Joüon §§168d, 169g, i; *IBHS* §38.3).

30. The Hebrew is somewhat ambiguous: 'all the words of the LORD that he spoke to him' where the 'he' may be the LORD or Jeremiah, and the 'him' correspondingly either Jeremiah or Baruch. The NIV understanding is probably correct, that is 'all the words the LORD had spoken to' Jeremiah.

the mouth of'. It was as Jeremiah spoke that Baruch wrote down what he heard.

2. The Scroll Read to the People (36:5-10)

5. It is not clear if the arrangements regarding the reading of the scroll were made immediately it was complete, or whether they were given closer to the time it was read. **Then Jeremiah told Baruch, 'I am restricted; I cannot go to the LORD's temple.'** We do not know what lies behind this. The word translated 'restricted' ($<\sqrt{}$'āṣar) does later refer to imprisonment (33:1; 39:15), but that cannot apply here, because subsequently there is no impediment to Jeremiah going into hiding (v. 19). It is unlikely that the matter is one of ceremonial impurity, because that could be rectified through the appropriate ritual. It is more probable that he had been prohibited (cf. Neh. 6:10) by the Temple authorities from coming into the Temple and speaking there, presumably as a result of what he had said on a previous occasion, either the address of chapters 7 and 26, but most likely as a consequence of Passhur's action (20:2).

Others, however, have suggested that the reason for the restriction lay at a deeper level. Calvin (1850, 4:350) suggested that the prophet was prohibited by a secret revelation. Certainly when the word 'restricted' is used in Gen. 16:2, where Sarai says, 'The LORD has kept me', the sense is that of 'prevented me.' Indeed, it may be possible to see why the LORD acted in this way. 'But the real reason for Jeremiah's exclusion has to do with the prophetic sign to be enacted. It is the LORD himself who restrains Jeremiah from entering the Temple, even if he uses intermediate means. It is essential that Jeremiah himself does not read his own oracles and distances himself from them because they are now to take an independent life as God's word to his people' (Jones 1992:441-2). While one would reject the implicit suggestion that the prophet's oracles were initially his own words rather than the LORD's word, the idea that the witness of the scroll will be independent of the prophet does seem to have merit. The written word of the prophetic scroll is to become as much a covenant document as the scroll of the Law.

6. The message of the LORD is going to be heard because the written word will allow Baruch to proclaim it in place of the prophet. Rather than having the scroll read elsewhere in the city where an equally representative company might have gathered, Jeremiah directed Baruch to read the scroll at the Temple, the normal site for prophetic proclamation (cf. 11:6), where crowds would gather. **So you**[31] **go to the house of the LORD on a day of fasting and read to the people from the scroll the words of the LORD that you wrote as I dictated.** It is uncertain what 'a day of fasting' refers to. In the Mosaic law only on the Day of Atonement were the people to 'afflict their souls' (Lev. 16:29), a phrase that increasingly came to be interpreted in terms of fasting. But the Day of Atonement occurred in the seventh month (September/October), and the scroll remained unread until November/ December 604 BC (v. 9). The fast day was probably an additional one, called in a time of national emergency (1 Sam. 31:13; 2 Sam. 1:12; 2 Chron. 20:3; Joel 1:14; 2:15). Jeremiah instructed Baruch to act on this occasion and to set out the message to the people as a whole (not just the king and his advisers) because the crisis was one that affected the whole nation. Perhaps the Temple congregation would be in a more receptive mood than usual if this fast had been called because of the presence of the Babylonian army in the region. The Babylonians who had just destroyed the city of Ashkelon on the coastal plain were the instruments of the LORD's judgment, and the only way of avoiding total disaster was to recognise that fact and comply with the LORD's advice.

The need to communicate with everyone is emphasised by the addition of **Read them to all the people of Judah who come in from their towns,** literally, 'also in the ears of all Judah'. This idiom 'in the ears of' (found earlier in the verse and also in vv. 10, 13, 14, 15 twice, 20, 21 twice) does not denote giving a message privately or secretly, as English idiom might suggest, but a public proclamation (2:2). The whole people and not just the king and his courtiers were to be challenged with the message, because nothing less was at stake than the continuing existence of the nation. So it is addressed not just to the townspeople of Jerusalem, but to those from the surrounding districts who have gathered for this special act of worship in the Temple.

7. Jeremiah echoes the **perhaps** that was present in the LORD's assessment of the matter (v. 3). The reception that will be given to the LORD's word has not been announced beforehand. **They will bring their petition before the LORD** is literally 'their petition will fall before the LORD' with the attitude of the petitioner humbly prostrate on the ground before his superior being transferred to that which he presents (37:20; 38:26; 42:9; Dan. 9:18, 20). This is a more graphic alternative to the expression 'come before' (Pss. 79:11; 88:3; 119:170;

---

31. The 'you' (*'attâ*) is expressed to constitute an emphatic contrast with the *'anî*, 'I', of v. 5.

Job 34:28). 'Petition' (<√ḥānan, 'to be gracious) incorporates a request for mercy, here for deliverance from the threatened execution of judgment. But to be acceptable in the courts of heaven this plea has to be accompanied by true repentance. **And each will turn from his wicked ways.** The dire warnings of what will happen might stir up an appropriate response. **For** (kî) **the anger** (ʿap, 4:8) **and wrath** (ḥēmâ, 4:4) **pronounced against this people by the LORD are great.**

8-9. Baruch complied completely with the instructions given him. **Baruch son of Neriah did everything Jeremiah the prophet told him to do; at the LORD's temple he read the words of the LORD from the scroll.** The repetition of LORD (which occurs even more closely in the Hebrew[32]) emphasises the propriety of the LORD's word being read in the LORD's Temple. The details of how this took place are then spelled out more clearly in v. 9. **In the ninth month of the fifth year of Jehoiakim son of Josiah king of Judah,** that is, November/December 604 BC. No matter which month was taken as starting the year, the months were always numbered from the spring. Using a Tishri (autumn) start for the regnal years implies a lapse of at least two months between the completion of the scroll and its being read.[33] **A time of fasting before the LORD was proclaimed for all the people in Jerusalem and those who had come from the towns of Judah.** The phrase 'proclaim a fast' (qārāʿ ṣôm) is also found in 1 Kgs. 21:9, 12; 2 Chron. 20:3. Here it is a plural verb 'they proclaimed' which the NIV treats as equivalent to an anonymous passive, but which probably implies the people called it (a practice found also in Jonah 3:5; Joel 1:14; 2:15). It need not indicate that this was done in defiance of the Temple authorities, or against the king's will. It would certainly have required royal permission, but it was not a matter of royal initiative. As events were to show Jehoiakim was not in a penitent mood, but the emergency was on such a scale that the desire to implore divine assistance was widely felt. Earlier suggestions that the fast was called because of a crop failure or as a time of remembrance of the capture of Jerusalem the previous year (Keil) now seem less probable in the light

---

32. Literally, 'everything which Jeremiah the prophet had commanded him with respect to reading from the scroll the words of the LORD ⌊in⌋ the house of the LORD.'

33. A spring regnal calendar would imply an even greater lapse of time, of at least eight months, possibly longer. The LXX extends the period when the scroll lay unread by substituting the 'eighth' for 'fifth' year of Jehoiakim. This is supported by Holladay (1989, 2:255-6), but it is difficult to establish any reason for the scroll being written so far in advance of its proclamation.

of the information we have about Nebuchadnezzar's capture of
Ashkelon.

**10. From the room of Gemariah son of Shaphan the secretary,
which was in the upper courtyard at the entrance of the New Gate
of the temple, Baruch read to all the people at the LORD's temple
the words of Jeremiah from the scroll.** 'Secretary' (*sōpēr*, 'scribe')
refers to one of the statesmen of Judah, and may indicate Gemariah's
own status.[34] We also know that his father Shaphan had held a similar
rank under Josiah (2 Kgs. 22:3), and during the course of his official
duties the book of the law had been discovered and he had read it and
reported its contents to Josiah, who then instituted sweeping reforms in
response to its contents. (See 2 Kgs. 22 and note especially vv. 3, 8,
10.) His sons continued to be prominent in the court, and to have much
sympathy with the message of Jeremiah. Gemariah was a common
name at this time, and this Gemariah is not the same as the one
mentioned in 29:3, but was a brother of Ahikam, who has already been
shown to be well disposed to Jeremiah (26:24). Another son of
Shaphan, Elasah, took Jeremiah's letter to Babylon (29:3). Micaiah
(v. 11) and Gedaliah the governor after 586 (40:5) were grandsons of
Shaphan. A bulla or stamp seal impression inscribed 'belonging to
Gemariah son of Shaphan the scribe' was found in Jerusalem in 1983,
and though the identification has been disputed, it is fairly certain that
it belonged to him. Baruch being a trained scribe was acquainted with
these men, having been educated with them. He therefore had no
difficulty in obtaining use of the room which was one of several
around the Temple and in its courts for storage and meetings.

The room was in the upper courtyard, which is generally taken to
be the same as the inner courtyard mentioned in 1 Kgs. 6:36; 7:12. It is
called 'upper' here because it stood above (cf. 1 Kgs. 7:12) the outer
courtyard where all the people were standing. The New Gate of the
Temple (26:10) was probably the same as the Benjamin Gate (20:2),
and we are to envisage Baruch either at a window or in the doorway of
this room. From there he had a vantage point over the Courtyard of the
People and could read out the message 'in the ears of all the people'

---

34. If it is argued that 'the secretary' (*sōpēr*, the same word as 'scribe', used
also of ministerial office) was the designation of only one high-ranking official at any time, then the term in v. 10 applies to Shaphan, because v. 12
clearly shows that Elishama held the rank of secretary at this juncture. But
there were probably a number of men with various responsibilities who held
this title. There are two men mentioned as 'secretaries' in the list of
Solomon's officials in 1 Kgs. 4:3.

who were in the courtyard below him. We are not told what their reaction was, but as he does not seem to have been interrupted, there must at least have been a willingness to hear out what the prophet had to say through Baruch. Possibly it was not uncommon for prophetic announcements to be made on such occasions, although the length of the message and its delivery by an intermediary were certainly unusual— quite apart from its contents. This call to repentance was not the sort of message that the peace prophets proclaimed.

3. The Scroll Read to the Officials (36:11-19)

11. When Micaiah son of Gemariah, the son of Shaphan, heard all the words of the LORD from the scroll shows that he had been waiting to find out what was taking place in his father's room and had listened carefully as Baruch read the scroll. No doubt he had been asked to keep a watchful eye on proceedings. He then took the news regarding Baruch to his father and the other members of the royal cabinet. Given that the officials were in general well-disposed towards Jeremiah, we need not suppose that there was any malice in this, but rather a measure of their interest and awareness of how public morale might be affected at such a critical juncture. Perhaps they would have to intervene again (cf. 26:10).

12. He went down to the secretary's room in the royal palace, where all the officials were sitting. The movement 'down' fits in with the relative height of the Temple and the palace (cf. 22:1; 26:10). Again the term 'secretary', which could refer to an ordinary scribe, is here the title of a royal minister. In his room the council of advisers to the king are found during the course of a meeting (rather than being gathered specifically to wait for word as to what Baruch was about). Five officials are listed: **Elishama the secretary, Delaiah son of Shemaiah, Elnathan son of Achbor, Gemariah son of Shaphan, Zedekiah son of Hananiah, and all the other officials.** Although we know no more of Delaiah and Zedekiah[35] than their presence at this incident, we have some information about the others. Elishama may have been the grandfather of the assassin of Gedaliah (41:1), and, if so, was connected to the royal family (cf. also 2 Kgs. 25:25). A seal impression has survived from this period with the inscription, 'Elishama, servant of the king'. In that Gemariah had a room in the Temple area, it might have been that his responsibilities as a secretary

---

35. There is nothing to suggest that his father Hananiah is to be identified as Jeremiah's adversary in chap. 28.

were more of an ecclesiastical nature, whereas Elishama had a political role. In Solomon's court there had been two Secretaries of State: one for civil and one for military affairs (1 Kgs. 4:3; cf. 52:25).

Elnathan (26:22) had been involved in the extradition of Uriah the prophet from Egypt, but his attitude towards the scroll (v. 25) suggests that he was by no means outrightly hostile to the prophets. His daughter had married Jehoiakim (2 Kgs. 24:8) and he was no doubt experiencing an intense conflict of loyalties. Elnathan's father had also been involved in the aftermath of the discovery of the scroll in Josiah's reign (2 Kgs. 22:12), a factor underlying v. 24.

13. After Micaiah told them everything he had heard Baruch read to the people from the scroll. While he related to them the entire substance of what he had heard, it need not be supposed that was able to repeat the contents of the scroll verbatim. It was when Baruch read it that the officials heard all that had been written.

14-15. All the officials sent Jehudi son of Nethaniah, the son of Shelemiah, the son of Cushi, to say to Baruch, 'Bring the scroll[36] from which you have read to the people and come'. The name Jehudi is the same word as the gentilic 'Jew' (34:9). He is also given an impressive genealogy, which some have felt to be unwarranted for an otherwise unknown individual. But there seems no reason to assail it on textual grounds. Cushi is not a true proper name but another gentilic, and may indicate one of Cushite, or Ethiopian background, who had become naturalised. If the rule of Deut. 23:8 to exclude the descendants of certain converts until the third generation was applied in such circumstances, that may be the reason for the extended genealogy. He acted as an executive officer for the council of officials who were unwilling to proceed without assuring themselves of the evidence. There is nothing stated at this point about their reaction to the news they have received, and this keeps up the tension in the story. **So Baruch son of Neriah went to them with the scroll in his hand.** He complied with their request (order?), and was received in a friendly fashion. **They said to him, 'Sit down, please, and read it to us.'** Again, Baruch complied. **So Baruch read it to them.** This is the second time that day the scroll was read in full.

16. The reaction of the officials is one of obvious alarm. **When they heard all these words, they looked at each other in fear.** The

---

36. 'The scroll' is brought to the start of the clause for emphasis. It is the scroll that is the focus of attention, not Baruch.

expression[37] is very terse. 'Fear' ($<\sqrt{pāhad}$) often denotes religious fear, and could indicate that they were treating God's word with profound respect. But it goes beyond that. It is a picture of significant looks and gestures being exchanged as the words are read out. What they heard confirmed their worst suspicions. Their fears were probably not focused on the content of Jeremiah's message—after all he had been presenting such a word for over twenty years, although having the gist of all his messages related continuously may well have stirred up forebodings on their part. First and foremost they were politicians, and their fear focused on the king's reaction to these words being repeated publicly at this sensitive time. This also indicates that the scroll as well as condemning the religious aberrations of the people spelled out the political consequences of their transgression. Criticism of a lack of religious devotion would not have troubled Jehoiakim, but predictions of military disaster and the overthrow of his regime would. Because the officials knew this, it led to their extreme unease.

However, they did not let that deflect them from their duty. **And said to Baruch, 'We must[38] report all these words to the king.'** This was not with the desire to cause trouble for Baruch and Jeremiah. Their office obliged them to report to the king the public delivery of such a message, which warned of the destruction of the city and urged a pro-Babylonian view—counter to the king's policy. This document was an important factor in vital political discussions of the day.

17. Before making their report, however, they question Baruch about the way in which the document was obtained. **Then they asked Baruch, 'Tell us, how did you come to write all this? Did Jeremiah dictate it?'[39]** It was obvious from the message itself that it originated with Jeremiah, but it may be that this was a collection of old oracles. Was it something that Baruch had drawn up on his own initiative, or had Jeremiah in a prophetic capacity intended that they be read in this way at this time? Were they hoping that the force of the condemnatory word had been exhausted by whatever had happened in 605 BC? Or was their concern to ensure that it was exactly what Jeremiah wished to

---

37. *pāhădû 'îš 'el-rēʿēhû*, 'a man feared towards his neighbour'.

38. The force of the infinitive absolute here seems to be that of obligation or necessity (Joüon §23h).

39. 'Did Jeremiah dictate it?' renders one word *mippîw*, 'from his mouth', which is taken as having the force of a separate question. There is no explicit mention of Jeremiah. 'Neither the troubled officials nor the secretary needed to ask or explain who "he" was. There was only one man in Jerusalem who was capable of issuing such a message' (Welch 1928:154).

have made known at that particular juncture?

18. 'Yes,' Baruch replied. Baruch assured them that it had been 'from his mouth'. He spelled out the details of the process. **He dictated**[40] **all these words to me, and I wrote them in ink on the scroll.** The verb used for 'dictating' is the same as that for 'reading' in vv. 6, 8, 10 and 14. It is not, however, decisive as regards whether or not Jeremiah was reading from previously written material, as it may simply mean 'call out'. The ink used would have been carbon (soot) in a solution of gum or olive oil.

19. The officials, many of whom were the sons of those who had been advisers to Josiah, show their sympathy towards Jeremiah. They tell Baruch to hide (the imperatives are singular) and take Jeremiah with him. **Then the officials said to Baruch, 'You and Jeremiah, go and hide. Don't let anyone know where you are.'** 'Hide' ($<\sqrt{s\bar{a}tar}$) is used to refer to a response of concealing oneself or others for the sake of protection from a life-threatening situation. The officials were aware of how the king was liable to react when public opposition to official policy was voiced (26:22-23). That they acted in this way indicates the respect they had for Jeremiah; indeed, many of them may well have accepted the cogency of his message. Since it was sure to provoke the king, the officials were anxious to shield the prophet from royal fury. Their need-to-know policy also indicates their political adroitness. It will leave them able to say truthfully that they do not know where the prophet and his assistant are. So by their recommendation the officials are able to resolve for the moment their conflicting loyalties between God and the king.

4. The Scroll Read to the King (36:20-26)

20-21. After[41] **they put** (yet another occurrence of the versatile *pāqad*) **the scroll in the room of Elishama the scribe**, which was most probably the same as the scribe's room mentioned in v. 12, their action shows that they well anticipated the violent reaction that the king would display. It is uncertain whether leaving the scroll behind

---

40. The imperfect *yiqrāʿ* implies that the process took place over a period of time (GKC §107b; Joüon §113f). It is consistent with a number of sessions being involved. The document was evidently of some length.

41. The NIV reverses the order of the Hebrew clauses (contrast NKJV), but the avoidance of the *waw*-consecutive construction at the beginning of the second clause indicates that the second action took place before that reported first (Joüon §166j).

was due to fears about its safety if brought to the king, or to enable the courtiers to engage in a measure of crisis management by presenting a suitably toned-down version of the message. **They went to the king in the courtyard and reported everything to him.** They moved 'courtyardwards'; it is not implied that the king was outside in the cold weather. The courtyard was in the inner part of the palace, and round it would be grouped the royal apartments. 'To him' is the Hebrew idiom 'in the ears of' (cf. v. 6). But when Jehoiakim heard his officials' digest of the scroll's contents, he was not satisfied their oral report and directed Jehudi to bring the scroll to him. **The king sent Jehudi to get the scroll, and Jehudi brought it from the room of Elishama the secretary and read it to the king and all the officials standing beside**[42] **him.** The scroll is now read in separation from both the prophet and his amanuensis.

22. Further details are then given of the scene to prepare the reader for what follows. **It was the ninth month**, that is Kislev (November/December), when it would be cold in Jerusalem. **And the king was sitting in the winter apartment, with a fire**[43] **burning in the brazier in front of him.** The 'winter apartment'/'house' might have been a separate residence, but it was more probably a room in the palace, probably with a southern exposure, and suitable for keeping warm. Often in two-storey buildings the upper apartments were favoured for summer conditions, being more exposed to any breeze, and the lower rooms were warmer for winter. There would also be a hollow in the floor where a brazier, a metal tray for holding coals, could be placed (or a ceramic firepot filled in a similar fashion). Indeed, in royal apartments there might even have been a proper 'hearth' (NKJV). The word rendered 'brazier'/'firepot' could be understood in this way also.

23. But Jehoiakim was intent on more than having the scroll read to him in comfortable surroundings. **Whenever**[44] **Jehudi had read three or four columns of the scroll.** In his youth Jehoiakim would have

---

42. Literally, 'over him', as he was seated, and they were standing.

43. 'Fire ... in the brazier' renders *wə'et-hā'āḥ* in the MT, that is, the object marker preceding 'brazier', *'aḥ*, apparently an Egyptian loanword. The LXX rendering *eschara puros*, 'brazier of fire' (43:22), shows that it read *'ēš*, 'fire', rather than the object marker. BHS records that 'fire' also occurs in the Syriac and Targum. Various suggestions have been put forward to account for the presence of the object marker, for instance that it occurs with the subject before a passive verb (*IBHS* p419, note 4; see also GKC §117l).

44. For the use of *kə*, 'when', with a repeated action, see Joüon §123x.

received an education befitting a royal prince, and would no doubt
have been able to read for himself, but it was more dignified for an
attendant to read the scroll to him. The 'columns', literally 'doors',[45]
were written down the papyrus page. While it was possible to write on
both sides of a sheet of papyrus, the reverse side was rough and would
have been avoided in preparing such an important document as this. A
long scroll was composed of sheets of papyrus that were glued
together. Probably it was after hearing the message that had been written in several columns covering one of the constituent sheets, **the king
cut them off**[46] **with a scribe's knife**[47] **and threw**[48] **them into the
brazier.** The scribe's knife was a penknife to trim the stalks used as
pens and also the edges of the papyrus roll. What was ordinarily used
to make preparation for writing is here used as an instrument to destroy
what has been written. The form of the verb 'cut off' implies that this
went on a number of times, **until the entire scroll was burned in the
fire.**[49]

What did the king hope to achieve by burning the scroll? Was it an
act of cynicism and contempt, or the reaction of a thoroughly frightened man trying to control what was beyond him? 'It may not be
extravagant to say that Jehoiakim believed that only by burning the
scroll and destroying the prophetic *dābār* [word] could he prevent the

---

45. *delet* is cognate with the Akkadian *daltu* which can also refer to a leaf of
a writing board covered with wax, but the references to burning and to ink rule
out it being a hinged writing board that was used on this occasion. Hicks
(1983) argued that the reference is to a piece of parchment of a similar size
and that what the king cut were the sutures that bound the various pieces of
parchment into a scroll.

46. *yiqrāʿehā*, 'he would cut it (fem.)', is imperfect expressing repeated
action in the past (GKC §107e). 'The king' is not expressed in Hebrew
sentence and this suggests that the subject of 'cut' is Jehudi, no doubt acting
on the king's instructions. But it is possible to take the king himself as the
subject of the verb. The feminine singular pronominal suffix refers to a
plurality of things (GKC §135p; *IBHS* §16.4c).

47. *taʿar* is used elsewhere to refer to a razor for shaving hair from the head
or body (Num. 6:5; 8:7; Ezek. 5:1). The scribe's knife was apparently of
similar size and shape.

48. The infinitive absolute continuing a finite verb, as in 14:5, 32:44.

49. There is probably no significance to be attached to the variation here
'into (ʿel) the fire which ⌊was⌋ in (ʿel) the brazier' and 'on (ʿal) the fire which
⌊was⌋ on (ʿal) the brazier.' In each case the NIV suppresses one element in the
Hebrew expression to give 'into the brazier' on the first occasion and 'in the
fire' on the second.

prediction from working itself out' (McKane 1965:121). Jehoiakim's treatment of the scroll was influenced by semi-magical ideas of its inherent power. By ostentatiously destroying it he sought to counter the power of God's word, just as Hananiah would later do by breaking Jeremiah's yoke (28:10-11). But his gesture of brazen defiance was ineffective in the face of the power of God.

24. There is then added a significant commentary on this scene. **The king and all his attendants who heard all these words showed no fear, nor did they tear their clothes.** A different word is used here for 'attendants'/'servants' (*<ebed*) from that for 'officials' (*<śar*). Given the reaction described in v. 16 (where the word for 'fear' is the same) and v. 25, it may well be that we are to understand 'attendants' here as a group of personal servants of the king, such as those named in v. 26, rather than the officers of state, whose attitude, as v. 25 reveals, continues to be a mixture of respect for the scroll and desire to preserve their own standing with the king. But the main point being made is that the king did not react as his father Josiah had done when he had been presented with a scroll containing the word of the LORD. 'When the king heard the words of the Book of the Law, he tore his robes' (2 Kgs. 22:11)—a display of grief and sorrow. Jehoiakim was not going to let anything interfere with his plans. He tore the scroll and not his clothes.[50] His action of frustrated fury reflected a desire to destroy the power of the prophet's words and to live in defiance of the divine word. He was king, and he would decide what was going to happen next.

25. Some, at any rate, of the officials had tried to dissuade him. **Even though[51] Elnathan, Delaiah and Gemariah urged the king not to burn the scroll, he would not listen to them**. They were not at all happy at the king's course of conduct, and were prepared to risk his disfavour and wrath by expostulating with him. Did Elnathan take the lead because of his closer relationship with the king? But their entreaties were of no avail. The king refused to 'listen'/'hear' (*<√šāmaʿ*). At one level he had heard the word, but he did not display the response of obedient submission that should have characterised his

50. There may be a play between *qāraʿ*, 'to tear, rend', and *qārāʾ*, 'to read' (v. 23), to emphasise the action that should have occurred.

51. *gam* may be used to introduce a concessive clause (GKC §160b), and that may well be appropriate here: 'Though Elnathan and Delaiah and Gemariah had entreated ..., he did not listen to them.' The *waw*-consecutive sequence has been interrupted, and this verse presents explanatory information about what had happened prior to this juncture.

reaction to the word of the LORD. It was not just the particular message delivered at that time that was set aside. By refusing to heed the demands of God's word he had turned his back on his own status as the LORD's covenant king. He had not yielded with respect to his Overlord and his stipulations. He was determined to be autonomous and have his own way.

26. The king, not content with destroying the scroll, set out to destroy those who had produced it. **Instead, the king commanded Jerahmeel, a son of the king, Seraiah son of Azriel and Shelemiah son of Abdeel to arrest Baruch the scribe and Jeremiah the prophet**. 'A son of the king' may not refer to one of Jehoiakim's own sons for, if that had been the case, 'his son' would have been the expected expression. Since Jehoiakim himself was only about thirty years old at this time, would he have had a son sufficiently old to act in this way? The answer to that is not clear cut; a king's son was often married in his early teens. A clay bulla has been found that reads, 'belonging to Jerahmeel, son of the king' (Avigad 1978). While this might indicate he was a member of the wider royal family ('a royal prince' REB), it is more probable that the term describes a court official who enforced royal orders. There is some evidence from Egypt of the existence of such an official, and those who in Scripture are given such a title seem to have acted in the same way (38:6; 1 Kgs. 22:26). Seraiah (there are three others with the same name mentioned in Jeremiah: 40:8; 51:59; 52:24) and Shelemiah are otherwise unknown.

However, the king's intention was divinely frustrated. **But the LORD had hidden them**.[52] The well-intentioned counsel of the officials (v. 19) had left it a matter for Jeremiah and Baruch to see to themselves, but there was a higher hand superintending events and their efforts at concealment were made effective by the LORD's gracious action. His prophet and his assistant were not left to their own resources. It is not known how long they stayed hidden. But Jehoiakim must eventually have passed from the matter, because the incident with the Rechabites (chap. 35) shows Jeremiah active in Jerusalem and able to enter the Temple area most probably in the closing months of Jehoiakim's reign.

5. The Scroll Rewritten (36:27-32)

27. Though the king thought he had resolved matters in his own favour by destroying the scroll, that was not to be the end of the story.

---

52. The LXX has 'they hid themselves', probably by assimilation to v. 19.

The word of God cannot be suppressed by human opposition. The scroll was rewritten, and it now contained even more scathing words of condemnation. **After the king burned the scroll containing the words that Baruch had written at Jeremiah's dictation, the word of the LORD came to Jeremiah.** We are not told what period of time elapsed, but it may well have been fairly immediately, and we are to take it that Jeremiah and Baruch spent the time of their concealment in producing this second edition of Jeremiah's collected prophecies.

28. The LORD's message was not allowed to pass into obscurity. **Take[53] another scroll and write on it all the words that were on the first scroll, which Jehoiakim king of Judah burned up.** This need for a second scroll resembles the way in which the Decalogue had to be rewritten after the first set of stone tablets had been smashed by Moses (Exod. 32:19; 34:1).

29. But there was more than just a reissue of the scroll. Jeremiah is further commanded, **Also tell Jehoiakim king of Judah.** It is not certain if Jeremiah was being instructed to encounter the king face-to-face at this time. The Hebrew preposition (ʿal) before Jehoiakim may also be translated 'concerning' (NASB, NRSV) or even 'against'. Taking it as equivalent to 'to' (ʾel) is justified by other passages in Jeremiah and by the personal address in the following divine word, but even so, a personal confrontation with the king in the years following this incident seems unlikely. It may be that some other way of delivering this indictment was used. **This is what the LORD says: You[54] burned that scroll and said, 'Why did you write on it that the king of Babylon would certainly come and destroy (<√šāḥat, 5:10) this land and cut off both men and animals from it?'** The question seems addressed to Jeremiah, but that is improbable. It is probably a rhetorical presentation of Jehoiakim's concerns. He focused on what the scroll implied about the inroads of the foe from the north, and in the prevailing circumstances there could be no doubt as to the identity of that foe. The king questioned Jeremiah's right to say such things to the subversion of royal policy and public morale. Quite apart from his spiritual lack of perception, at a political level the king had not learned the lessons of the years of Assyrian domination: that Judah was unable to withstand the might of the Mesopotamian powers and that attempts

53. Literally, 'Return, take for yourself', where the verb šûb, 'return', is used as an auxiliary verb with the sense 'repeat, do again', and ləkā is an ethic dative denoting Jeremiah's personal involvement in what is done.

54. The expressed ʿattâ is emphatic, 'You are the one who …', or 'You personally …'

at resistance merely brought on savage reprisals. For the fate of man
and beast, see on 9:10-11; 32:43.

30. Jehoiakim's irreverent attitude will not be permitted to go
unpunished. **Therefore** (*lākēn*), **this is what the LORD says about
Jehoiakim king of Judah: He will have no one to sit on the throne
of David; his body will be thrown out[55] and exposed to the heat by
day and the frost by night'.** The sentence of judgment is as usual
introduced by 'therefore' to show that it is based on the evidence of the
situation. The phrase 'one sitting on the throne of David' indicates a
true successor, and that was not to be. Jehoiachin, his son, ruled for
three months before being taken into captivity in Babylon, from which
he never returned, and his uncle, Zedekiah, succeeded him in Jerusalem. A similar prediction regarding the casting out of the corpse of
Jehoiakim is found in 22:18-19. We have no historical account of
Jehoiakim's death, but it occurred in suspicious circumstances. Many
have supposed he was murdered by a pro-Babylonian party so that the
city might be spared the full rigours of Babylonian wrath in 597 BC.
2 Kgs. 24:6 says nothing about the circumstances of his burial, but
mention of frost would fit in with the time of his death in December
598. It is not impossible that after Jerusalem was captured in 597 BC
the corpse of Jehoiakim was exhumed and exposed as part of the
Babylonian reprisals for his rebellion (Josephus, *Ant.* 10.6.3 adds
significantly and implausibly to the biblical account of Jehoiakim's
death). Some have indeed supposed that the prophecy was written
retrospectively in the light of such action.

31. Verse 31 perhaps shows us that the people were generally in
sympathy with the line taken by the king. **I will punish** (<√*pāqad*, the
action of the sovereign Overlord) **him and his children and his
attendants for their wickedness; I will bring on them and those
living in Jerusalem and the people of Judah every disaster I
pronounced against[56] them, because they have not listened** (cf.
35:17; 19:15). 'Attendants'/'servants' (<*ebed*) may well refer to the
group mentioned in v. 24. The punishment also extended to the
inhabitants of Jerusalem and the people of Judah because they had
fallen in with the lead given to them by the king. Those in positions of
authority are accountable to God for their actions, but that does not
leave their subjects without responsibility. They too have to consider if

55. *hāyâ* with the passive participle brings out the durative aspect of this
future exposure (Joüon §121e).
56. *'ălêhem*, 'to them', may again be understood as equivalent to *'al*,
'against', so the NIV, NKJV, and probably the NRSV.

the conduct of public affairs in the land is in terms of God's law—and then act appropriately.

32. We are next told that Jeremiah carried out the task of preparing a second scroll. Nothing is said about him taking the message to Jehoiakim! **So Jeremiah took another scroll and gave it to the scribe Baruch son of Neriah,**[57] **and as Jeremiah dictated, Baruch wrote on it all the words of the scroll that Jehoiakim king of Judah had burned in the fire.** 'Scribe' is used here of Baruch in its ordinary sense of 'writer', one who had received the highest educational training available in the land. No doubt it was a profession that gave entry to the privileged class of the day and opened doors into government employment, but Baruch was not a Secretary of State. There is also added the information, **And many similar words were added to them.**[58] Given that the composition of this Second Scroll followed shortly after the destruction of the first, it need not have been the case that these words resulted from new divine revelation, but rather that much had been omitted in the summary given in the First Scroll. After all, it had been looking back on twenty-three years of prophetic ministry. If, as is probable, we have here an account of the beginning of the present book of Jeremiah, then this mode of composition might well indicate how material was added to it (see Volume 1, Introduction §2.2). It is improbable that here we have a redactorial note describing the start of a process by which subsequent groups expanded on the original Jeremianic material. The plain implication of the text is that Jeremiah was responsible for an expanded version of his original scroll. The oblique mode of expression may have been used to account for the fact that the additions were not all written by Baruch. It is only claimed that he was responsible for the rewritten original material.

The word of God may be dismissed and destroyed, but it will not go away. The LORD is the one who cannot be defeated, and he takes steps to ensure that his message is rewritten and repromulgated. The furious actions of Jehoiakim are exposed in all their folly. His faithlessness in resisting God's demands has resulted in a more comprehensive scroll and in sentence being passed against the king. Only by truly listening and submitting to the word of the LORD can the blessing and security

---

57. The LXX reads, 'And Baruch took another scroll and wrote …', giving greater prominence to Baruch's role in the matter as he acts on his own initiative.

58. The position of *kāhēmâ*, 'like them', makes it possible to translate it also as 'as many words as them', indicating a possible doubling of the size of the scroll (Naegelsbach 1871:316).

of the covenant be known and enjoyed.

We also see that those serving the LORD are kept by him according to his promise: 'They will fight against you but will not overcome you, for I am with you and will rescue you' (1:19). The fortitude of his servants in the face of hostility does not go unrewarded. That is a truth which is illustrated in the even darker days that are described in following section of the book.

XIII. THE SIEGE AND FALL OF JERUSALEM

(37:1–39:18)

OUTLINE

A. During a Lull in the Siege (37:1-21)
    1. A Royal Delegation (37:1-5)
    2. The Enemy Will Return (37:6-10)
    3. A Defecting Prophet? (37:11-16)
    4. The Prophet in Prison (37:17-21)
B. Rescued from a Cistern (38:1-13)
    1. Official Hostility (38:1-6)
    2. Unexpected Intervention (38:7-13)
C. The Final Interview (38:14-28a)
    1. The Royal Oath (38:14-16)
    2. Surrender or Else (38:17-23)
    3. Palace Intrigue (38:24-28a)
D. The Fall of the City (38:28b–39:18)
    1. Military Administration (38:28b–39:3)
    2. Zedekiah's Fate (39:4-7)
    3. The Devastation of the Land (39:8-10)
    4. The Prophet Well Treated (39:11-14)
    5. Ebed-Melech's Reward (39:15-18)

A period of eighteen years elapses from chapter 36, but the placing of the material here is not haphazard. Chapters 37–44 deal with the final years of Jerusalem, its destruction and the aftermath of its fall. They are presented against the background of the unresponsiveness of king and people alike to the message that had been delivered to them time and again by Jeremiah. What ensues are the events that constitute the vindication of Jeremiah's prophetic ministry. Neither earlier under Jehoiakim nor later under Zedekiah had there been a proper response to Jeremiah, which might have averted the catastrophe, or mitigated its effect.

The material in this block is arranged mainly chronologically. There are sections (39:1-10; 40:7–41:15) where Jeremiah is not mentioned at all, and the appendix in chapter 45 focuses on the role and suffering of Baruch. This raises questions as to whether these chapters can be classified as simply biographical in their concern. Though they present a coherent sequence of events, with much basic historical information, suggesting again that Baruch, or a figure like him, helped prepare these sections, Jeremiah is not merely recording events for the historical enlightenment of posterity, or even to show that he had been in the right in his earlier claims to be a true prophet of the LORD. Jeremiah is speaking to the survivors of the collapse of Jerusalem and is pleading with the generation that had experienced the trauma of the devastation of their former way of life to learn the lessons of the past and avoid its pitfalls. Many were no nearer to repentance than they had been before the fall of the city, and so the prophet was urging them to consider their position in relation to the LORD. Even in the grim circumstances of Babylonian domination, there was the possibility of a brighter future because of the LORD's control of events. A change for the better is here anticipated in terms of the LORD's reward and protection to those who act faithfully even in dark circumstances (the prophet himself and Ebed-Melech, chaps. 37–39; Baruch, chap. 45), and in chapters 40–44 the same message is presented negatively: divisions and rebellious behaviour will retard or divert blessing.

At one level this narrative continues the message of the need for faithfulness. During the years of the siege when the pressure on Jeremiah was greatest, he did not flinch in his determination to present the message the LORD had entrusted to him. His witness to the divine revelation that capture was certain and mitigation of the situation could only be effected by surrender was reckoned treasonable by the Jerusalem establishment. But his steadfast commitment to what the LORD had revealed to him and his faithful submission to all that brought on him in terms of suffering and imprisonment was eventually rewarded after the city was captured. But there is also in the narrative a warning for the suffering community that there was no easy way out for the prophet during his years of suffering. 'No raven feeds the prophet in his hunger; no angel stops the lion's mouth' (Von Rad 1965:207). Apart from the intervention of Ebed-Melech in the closing days of the siege, there was no external relief for the prophet, yet he remained faithful through to the end. So those whom Jeremiah addressed among the displaced people of Judah could find in the prophet one whose own life and circumstances were a living illustration of the conduct they were now called on to display. Survival and deliverance were possible even in the most unpromising of circumstances if only they would commit their ways wholeheartedly to the LORD and wait for his promised intervention in their situation.

The first section of material takes in chapters 37–39 and is concerned with events leading up to the fall of Jerusalem. The capture of Jerusalem is described in chapter 39, but before that conditions in the besieged city are set out, particularly as they affected Jeremiah himself. He is twice imprisoned, and though he is repeatedly approached by King Zedekiah for guidance, the king cannot bring himself to act as the prophet advises him.

A. DURING A LULL IN THE SIEGE (37:1-21)

1. A Royal Delegation (37:1-5)

In this section we are introduced to the individuals who will be the focus of the narrative in the following chapters. The principal characters are the king and the prophet, with various state officials whose presence in the background casts a menacing shadow over the scene.

1. Zedekiah son of Josiah was made king of Judah by Nebuchadnezzar king of Babylon. Zedekiah was originally known as Mattaniah. He was a son of Josiah by the same mother, Hamutal daughter of Jeremiah of Libnah, as Jehoahaz, who had been deposed by the Egyptians in 609 BC (52:1; 2 Kgs. 23:31; 24:18). After the surrender of the city in 597 BC, Nebuchadnezzar had appointed the twenty-one year old Zedekiah as king, but many of the people, both at home and among the exiles in Babylon, still regarded Jehoiachin as their legitimate ruler, and were waiting for his early restoration (28:4). Zedekiah had been placed in an unenviable situation where to patriots in Judah his position was compromised: he was simply a Babylonian puppet. The difficulties of his situation were compounded by flaws in his character. He was not strong-minded and decisive, but weak and vacillating. He did not possess the strength of character to deal with the stressful situation in his own court caused by the pro-Egyptian policy favoured by the majority of his advisers.

Nebuchadnezzar had imposed a vassal treaty on Zedekiah in which he pledged his allegiance to his Babylonian overlord by means of an oath taken in the name of his own God (2 Chron. 36:13), seemingly continuing a practice of the Assyrians in the western part of their empire where vassals swore fealty not in the name of their suzerain's gods, but in the name of their own. It was to the breach of this oath that Ezekiel pointed when explaining Zedekiah's fate at the hands of Babylon (Ezek. 12:11-16; 17:11-21). Jeremiah emphasises rather the breach of the LORD's standards involved in Zedekiah's conduct. Certainly the king was fully aware of what would happen to him personally if he went back on his solemn oath. But he was unable to resist the domestic pressure to renounce his commitment to Babylon, and this precipitated the rebellion that led to Judah's downfall.

Zedekiah was not hostile towards Jeremiah. He was not unscrupulous like Jehoiakim, but is portrayed as a rather pathetic figure who is swept along by currents that were too strong for him to withstand. He had no real influence on policy in Jerusalem, which was in any event overshadowed by the struggle between the superpowers of Egypt and Babylon. Certainly there is no suggestion that it was Zedekiah's conduct that was responsible for the overthrow of Jerusalem. That had already been decreed. He is, however, shown to be responsible for the lack of amelioration of the city's fate, and for his own sad end. Here is a man who is a mixture, who might have moved either way, but who through his own weakness is drawn to his doom. Faced with the demands of the divine word, an irresolute, half-hearted response is not a viable option. Only complete submission will suffice.

He reigned in place of Jehoiachin son of Jehoiakim may look back to the prophecy of 36:30 that Jehoiakim would have no son after him on the throne. Zedekiah was Jehoiachin's uncle,[1] and it is probable that he was thought of as merely ruling as regent for the exiled king. The phrase 'reigned ⌐as⌐ king' (*wayyimlok-melek*) is an unusual one, and may reflect this subordinate status of Zedekiah (but compare its use in 23:5). Coniah (NIV margin, NKJV, NRSV) is an abbreviated form of the name Jeconiah (see 22:24), itself a variant form of Jehoiachin.

---

1. In 2 Chron. 36:10 he is referred to as Jehoiachin's brother (NRSV), but the term '*āḥ* is used there in its wider sense of kinsman (NASB, NJPS).

2. Verse 2 sets out the scene for the following dark events. Though Zedekiah did on occasions look favourably on Jeremiah, that was not the general tenor of his reign, which was instead characterised by continuing refusal to accept the word of the LORD. **Neither he nor his attendants nor the people of the land paid any attention to the words the LORD had spoken through[2] Jeremiah the prophet.** 'His attendants' ($<\sqrt{}$ _ebed_) seems here to refer to his court officials, but see on 36:24. Though 'the people of the land' may be used as a technical term for the upper classes in Judah (1:18; 34:19), here it probably refers to populace in general (36:10, 24, 31). The picture is one focusing on the king, but involving Judah as a whole, in that they all refused to 'pay attention' ($<\sqrt{}$ _šāma‘_, 'to hear', 'to listen') to the warnings given by Jeremiah on the LORD's behalf. Their attitude was an assertion of their own competency to direct their affairs and a rejection of the LORD's superintendence. This culpable reliance on their own ingenuity precipitated their downfall. These words were written to those who already knew the outcome of events, and constituted a warning to them not to display the same misguided reaction.

3. Zedekiah himself is somewhat of an enigma. For all that he failed to respond to Jeremiah's message, still he could not leave the prophet alone. He behaved as a man who was inwardly convinced of Jeremiah's status as a prophet, but who was not prepared to act consistently on that basis. **King Zedekiah, however, sent Jehucal son of Shelemiah with[3] the priest Zephaniah son of Maaseiah to Jeremiah the prophet with this message: 'Please pray to the LORD our God for us.'** This is the second delegation that Zedekiah sent to Jeremiah to ask him to pray for a miraculous deliverance. The deputation consists of two of Zedekiah's chief officials. Jehucal is met with elsewhere (38:1). Later his attitude towards Jeremiah was certainly one of hostility in that he called for his death (38:4). Zephaniah seems to have been more favourably inclined towards the prophet. He had been a member of the earlier delegation sent by Zedekiah to the prophet (21:1), and when he had been written to from Babylon with complaints against Jeremiah, he took no real action (29:25). In asking Jeremiah to

---

2. _bəyad_, 'by the hand of, by the agency of' is used to show the role of the prophet as an intermediary in communicating the divine word (Hag. 1:1, 3; 2:1; Mal. 1:1).

3. The NIV 'with the priest Zephaniah' suggests that Jehucal was the senior party in this mission, but the Hebrew _wə'et_ is the object marker and not the preposition, and the two are set down side by side with no indication of subordination.

pray (<√*pālal*, 'to intercede') the king is acknowledging his status as a prophet of the LORD. However, in the light of the information given in v. 5 it would seem that the request that was presented was that the lifting of the siege should become permanent and that the Babylonian army that had gone should stay away. No doubt the court was hoping for a reversal of fortune such as that which had been experienced in the days of Hezekiah (701 BC, 2 Kgs. 19:37) when the Assyrian armies abandoned their siege after the king had sent a deputation to the prophet Isaiah requesting prayer. But the point to note is that what Zedekiah and his courtiers were looking for was divine endorsement of *their* policy. They expect a prophet to engage in efficacious intercession for divine blessing to accrue to them on their own terms. It does not reveal a willingness to listen to the word of the LORD to them and to act in obedience to it. They have the political and military insight to recognise that the circumstances of the city are desperate, but still they lack the spiritual perception to see how inadequate and demeaning their attitude is towards the LORD.

4. Two pieces of information provide the background that is required to assess what is said in v. 3. First, we are told **Now[4] Jeremiah was free to come and go among the people, for he had not yet been put in prison.**[5] 'Put' renders the verb *nātan*, 'to give', used here and in vv. 15, 18; 52:11 as a technical term for 'to imprison'. Later we read of Zedekiah sending for Jeremiah when he is in confinement (v. 17; 38:14). Prison was not used then as a penalty for law-breaking, but was rather custody while a matter was under investigation. That fate awaited Jeremiah (v. 15), but here it is emphasised that he was still at liberty.

5. Secondly, we are told **Pharaoh's army had marched out of Egypt, and when the Babylonians who were besieging Jerusalem heard the report about them, they withdrew[6] from Jerusalem.** The Pharaoh referred to is Hophra (589–570 BC), who had recently ascended the throne (cf. 44:30). No doubt the pro-Egyptian party had been promised help by him. There is evidence in Lachish Ostracon II

---

4. *Waw*-disjunctive (*waw* plus a non-verb as a clause connector) here introduces background information. The sequence is continued with another *waw*-disjunctive at the beginning of the next verse.

5. The kethibh seems to have the form *hakkəlî'*, 'the prison', an unusual form for *kele'*, 'prison' (vv. 15, 18). The qere offers *hakkəlû'*. The same variation is found in 52:31.

6. For *'ālâ mē'al*, compare 21:2. The verb here is niphal, perhaps with a reflexive sense, 'took themselves up from upon'.

338

that army officers had been sent to Egypt seeking assistance. The presence of the Egyptian army in southern Palestine led the Babylonians to lift their siege—temporarily as it turned out (34:21-22), because the Egyptians declined to engage them.

2. The Enemy Will Return (37:6-10)

6. After this deputation from the king had arrived, **then the word of the LORD came to Jeremiah the prophet.** But there was conveyed an uncompromisingly negative message—not at all what the king wanted to hear. Morale in the city had been boosted by the lifting of the siege, as no doubt it had several years earlier when the Egyptians had held their own against Babylon. If that previous occasion had been understood as discrediting Jeremiah's oracles, it is possible that the recent events led to a similar reaction. Though the Babylonian forces had not gone far, many people would be of the view that they would never come back. But the LORD refused to fall in with the political analyses of the court and set before them what he required to be done.

7. The LORD who rules over the nations of earth shows how completely he knows and can predict what the superpowers of the day will do. Their actions fall not only within his cognisance but also within his control. **This is what the LORD, the God of Israel, says: Tell** (plural; addressed to the members of the delegation) **the king of Judah, who has sent you to inquire of me, 'Pharaoh's army, which has marched out to support you** (plural: the king and people)**, will go back to its own land, to Egypt.'** 'Inquire' (a more neutral term than 'pray for', v. 3) might indicate seeking information from the LORD as to how events would turn out, but in the light of the request for intercession in v. 3 it is more probable that what Zedekiah wanted was miraculous intervention. But he should be in no doubt that the Egyptian army had brought only brief respite; there would be no lasting deliverance from that quarter. The hopes that Judah and the other states in the region placed in Egypt would prove delusive.

8. Then the Babylonians will return and attack this city; they will capture it and burn it down/'with fire'. It is not Egypt that is going to be influential in the affairs of Syria–Palestine, but Babylon. Jerusalem is doomed because it has rebelled against its Overlord in heaven as well as its political overlord on earth, and nothing will deflect the catastrophe about to overwhelm it.

9-10. Verses 9 and 10 add a footnote to that message, reinforcing the inevitability of Judah's imminent downfall by engaging in rhetorical exaggeration. **This is what the LORD says: Do not deceive**

yourselves, thinking,[7] 'The Babylonians will surely[8] leave us.' 'For'
(*kî*) **They will not!** As they saw the Babylonian army departing, the
people in Jerusalem were naturally relieved, but any tendency to
euphoria had to be checked. They should not persuade themselves that
this was a permanent turn-around. Over the years they had consistently
underestimated the threat posed by Babylon. Ultimately this was
because it was not a matter of assessment of military intelligence
reports. Behind the political challenge to their nation was the divine
sentence of judgment. It was the LORD who was their enemy, and it
was their spiritual blindness that was clouding their judgment at other
levels as well. There was no possibility that the LORD was going to lift
what he had determined to impose on the city. **Even if** (*kî ʿim*) **you
were to defeat the entire Babylonian army that is attacking you
and only wounded[9] men were left in their tents, they would come
out and burn this city down**/'with fire' (34:2; 38:3). Even if the
Judah's troops (or, more realistically, with the help of their Egyptian
allies) were to effect a defeat on Babylon, the casualties resting from
their grievous wounds in their tents would be sufficiently strong to
overcome the city, given the LORD's determined purpose against it. No
matter how hopeful circumstances might appear, they were to take no
consolation or encouragement from that. The LORD had determined
what would happen, and he was not going to be deflected.

3. A Defecting Prophet? (37:11-16)

11. The rest of the chapter is concerned with two later incidents. The
first also occurs during the lull in the siege. **After**[10] **the Babylonian
army had withdrawn from Jerusalem because of Pharaoh's army.**
There was probably a three-month period (around January–March 587
BC) when the troops were withdrawn. This period allowed some
supplies to get into the city (though the surrounding countryside would

---

7. Literally, 'Do not cause to rise your desires, saying, …', where *nepeš*,
'desire' (2:34), is used in the plural to express the idea of inner hopes or of
'self' (GKC §139f).

8. *hālôk yēləkû* strengthens the idea in the verb; here = 'to depart'.

9. *meduqqār*, 'pierced through' with a lance or sword and so usually
mortally wounded, but in this instance the stabbing has not been fatal.

10. The verse begins oddly in the Hebrew *wəhāyâ*, perhaps to indicate a
disjunctive clause of circumstances, 'Now it was when …' Keil (1873, 2:106)
suggests it is a later usage for *wayhî*, referring to 3:9 (cf. also 38:28; 40:3).
GKC §112uu can only suggest reading *wayhî* for *wəhāyâ*, but the idiom
occurs too often to make that a satisfying expedient.

already have been devastated by the Babylonians) and also permitted
many to desert from the city. Both these factors probably led to the
prolongation of the siege when it was resumed. Also the numbers
trying to leave the city laid the background of suspicion against which
Jeremiah's actions were assessed.

**12. Jeremiah started to leave the city to go to the territory of Ben-
jamin.** Jeremiah was from Anathoth in the territory of Benjamin, and
so this journey, which was made possible by the lifting of the siege,
was back to his home town. It is not entirely clear why he was going
there, but the NIV rendering, **to get his share**[11] **of the property
among the people there,** is quite probable. The verb ḥālaq, 'to
divide', 'to share', can refer to the apportioning of land (Josh. 19:51;
Mic. 2:4; Joel 3:2; Dan. 11:39). Perhaps the background is to be
sought in the upheaval caused by the Babylonian invasion, accompanied by the death of a relative there, in which case 'people' (ʿam)
refers to his kinsfolk. It is not clear what connection, if any, exists with
his subsequent purchase of Hanamel's field (32:7), which occurred
while Jeremiah was in detention, whereas here he is obviously still at
liberty. It is unlikely that the properties involved are the same, though
the background circumstances might be related. Certainly whatever
naivety Jeremiah displayed in thinking that his departure would be
unhindered, escape was not in his mind. He stayed with his people to
the end, and his protestation in v. 14 was entirely justified.

13. But when he reached the Benjamin Gate, which was on the
north side of the city and so called because the road to the territory of
Benjamin went through it (20:2; 38:7; Zech. 14:10),[12] **the captain of
the guard**[13]**, whose**[14] **name was Irijah son of Shelemiah, the son of**

---

11. laḥăliq seems to be for ləhahălîq, cf. GKC §53q which takes the form as
hiphil with elided he, but suggests reading a qal infinitive. It is only here that
the hiphil of ḥālaq occurs. The NIV renders the hiphil as 'to get his share of
the property'; compare 'receive a portion' (BDB 324) and 'take part in
dividing' (HALOT 323). The translation of the AV, 'to separate himself', was
based on a medieval Jewish understanding of the verb as 'to divide oneself',
and so 'to separate', but that does not fit the circumstances, or Jeremiah's
protestation.

12. Keil (1873, 2:106) notes that it was for the same reason also called the
Gate of Ephraim (2 Kgs. 14:13; Neh. 8:16).

13. The title occurs only here. For baʿal cf. IBHS §9.5.3b. In place of 'the
captain of the guard, whose name was Irijah' the LXX has 'and there a man
with whom he lodged, Serouia'.

14. Disjunctive waw introducing circumstantial clause.

Hananiah, arrested him and said, 'You are deserting to (<√*nāpal*,
'to fall' away to; 21:9) the Babylonians!' The suspicions of the officer
on sentry duty were not without foundation when all that Jeremiah
himself had so publicly said is considered, including the fact that he
had urged the people to submit to Babylon (21:8-10; 38:2), and
evidently considerable numbers had done so (38:19; 52:15). However,
it was a most improbable time to try to defect, in that the Babylonians
had raised the siege and were now miles away.

**14. 'That's not true!' Jeremiah said. 'I am not deserting to the
Babylonians.'** 'That's not true!'/'A lie' (*šeqer*, 5:2): Jeremiah's
protest was categorical, but it was not believed. **But Irijah would not
listen** (<√*šāmaʿ*, 'to hear'; v. 2) **to him.** The same deafness that
afflicted the policy makers of Jerusalem prevails also with the soldiers
on sentry duty. Their discernment and willingness to consider what the
prophet is saying has been subverted by official propaganda. They too
can assess the prophet only as a traitor. Their officer entertained no
protests: **instead, he arrested Jeremiah and brought him to the
officials.** These were not the same body of men who had shown
considerable sympathy towards Jeremiah years earlier (chap. 36). If
those men had survived the events of 597 BC, they were at this time
among the deportees in Babylon. The officials left with Zedekiah were
an altogether inferior group, who were possibly in a more defiant mood
given the turn of events which had seen the siege lifted.

15. They were angry with Jeremiah. This account is evidently not
given from the point of view of the officials. To them 'it was
intolerable that he should use his prophetic immunity in order to
destroy the morale and resistance of the soldiers and civilian population of Jerusalem, and what appeared to be an attempt to desert and
join those Jews who were already with the Babylonians proved to the
satisfaction of the *śārîm* that the intention of his previous speeches had
been seditious and that he had had clandestine relations with this
treacherous political faction' (McKane 1965:125). Therefore they **had
him beaten**[15] **and imprisoned**[16] **in the house of Jonathan the**

---

15. The verbs here *wəhikkû*, 'and they beat', and *wənatənû*, 'and they
imprisoned/put', are *waw* plus perfect. The sebirin, Massoretic corrections for
unusual forms, read instead imperfects (*wayyakkû* and *wayyittənû* respectively). GKC §§112f, tt suggests that the first verb is perfect because of the
continuance of the action, but the second is probably an error in the text.

16. 'Imprison' is literally 'put (<√*nātan*, v. 4) ֽin֯ the house of binding (*bêt
hāʾēsûr*)'. 'Prison' at the end of the verse renders *bêt hākeleʿ*, 'house of
restraint/confinement'.

secretary, which (*kî*, 'for') **they had made into a prison.** It is likely
that the number of would-be deserters at this time had required additional accommodation for them, and the secretary's house was taken
over for this purpose. Here Jonathan is the holder of the same office as
Elishama in a previous administration.

16. It is unclear whether v. 16 is to be read along with v. 15 as in most
English translations or whether it starts a new paragraph as in the
NIV.[17] The verse begins with 'for' (*kî*), which seems to introduce a
further clarification of the prophet's confinement, and is one of a series
of summary statements found in this history contributed by Baruch (cf.
37:21; 38:13, 28; 39:14) that marks off the various stages in the narrative. **Jeremiah was put into a vaulted cell in a dungeon, where he
remained a long time.** It would seem as if Jonathan's house had
attached to it a separate building, a 'dungeon'/'the house of the cistern-
pit' (*bêt bôr*, used as a technical term for 'prison' in Exod. 12:29). A
bôr, 'pit', could be dug, but it was more frequently hewn out of the
rock, and filled by rainwater, which in the city would be run-off from
the roofs of the houses. The sides of such a pit would be plastered to
retain the water for use during the dry season (cf. 'cistern', 2:13). This
pit, however, seems to have been used for storage of commodities such
as grain, in that there were cells/cellars there. It was in such an
underground prison that Jeremiah was confined in airless, gloomy, and
probably damp conditions. It certainly seems to have constituted on its
own a threat to his health (v. 20). Jeremiah in prison is in some senses
a paradigm for what had happened to the word of the LORD as well as
to the messenger who brought that word. The word was having no
freedom to impact on the life of the nation; it too was in confinement.
The leaders of the nation closed the prophet's mouth and ministry by
imprisoning him in part of the domain of the ruling party in Jerusalem.

4. The Prophet in Prison (37:17-21)

These verses present an unexpected sequel to Jeremiah's detention. It
had seemed that the political regime had silenced a troublesome
agitator opposed to the prevailing policy. He had been beaten and
incarcerated. Meanwhile the Egyptian army retreated, the Babylonians
returned in force, and the siege of Jerusalem resumed and dragged on,
while conditions within the city deteriorated. The king, the ostensible
head of the regime, was troubled about his own situation, about the

17. In that case one might adopt Keil's approach and take *kî* = 'when', introducing a subordinate clause connected to what follows (1873, 2:107).

wisdom of official policy, and about what awaited the city. So he became irresistibly drawn to hear what the silenced voice of the prophet had to say about affairs. So though the establishment thought that the word of the prophet, which is the word of God, had been stifled, the personal doubts of the king led him to speak with the prophet. The king, however, is Zedekiah, and so rather than conducting an open interview, he approaches the prophet clandestinely, for Zedekiah was as much trapped by his own advisers as by the Babylonians.

17. Jeremiah was confined in these circumstances for 'many days', during which time we are to understand that the Babylonian army resumed the siege of the city (v. 21 implies as much). The influential men of the city thought they had dealt with the word of God by imprisoning Jeremiah, but the need for the light from God was acutely felt in the deteriorating situation, and especially by the king, who had Jeremiah brought to him, not out of compassion for the prophet but because he was looking for something more certain than the prevailing conjectures of his politicians. **Then King Zedekiah sent for him and had him brought to the palace, where he asked him privately, 'Is there any word from the LORD?'** Zedekiah is here torn two ways. He has respect for Jeremiah, indeed he privately seems to recognise that he is a true prophet of the LORD, and hence his request if there has been further revelation for the city in its distress. But at the same time he does so 'privately'/'secretly' (38:16), so that his court officials, and perhaps also the people, do not get to hear about it. They were antagonistic to Jeremiah, and Zedekiah does not want to do anything that will rub them up the wrong way. He is a king who is ruled by those around him.

Jeremiah recognises that the king's primary concern is for his own position, and he answers on that basis. **'Yes,' Jeremiah replied,**[18] **'you** (sing.) **will be handed over to the king of Babylon.'** To the king's terse question, Jeremiah gives an equally terse response, which exhibits his unquavering resolution to be true to what the LORD had revealed to him, no matter what difficulties it might bring to him personally. Since there has been no change in Zedekiah's position (cf. 32:4; 34:3), there can be no change in Jeremiah's message. Otherwise the prophet would have been seeking favour with men at the expense of being true to the word of the LORD.

---

18. An affirmative answer was given by repeating the emphatic word in the question, in this case *yēš*, 'there is' (GKC §150n).

18. Then Jeremiah said to King Zedekiah, 'What crime have I committed (<√*ḥāṭat*, 'to sin') **against you or your officials or this people, that** (*kî*) **you** (plural) **have put me in prison?'** Jeremiah took advantage of the audience with the king to seek to remedy his own position in relation to the judicial proceedings that had been taken against him. His question was an assertion of his innocence and he asked that proper charges be brought so that he might be able to defend himself. Though the royal officials had been the ones to beat and imprison him (note plural 'you'), it was the king who was ultimately responsible for what went on within his realm. He knew where Jeremiah was being held but had taken no action to secure his release. If he returned him there, he would be more directly implicated in his death (v. 20).

19. What is more, not only is Jeremiah innocent as regards the more recent allegations made against him; events have also proved him to have been in the right over many years with the warnings he brought. **Where[19] are your prophets who prophesied to you, 'The king of Babylon will not attack you or this land'?** The prophecy that Jeremiah had made had been fulfilled. It was therefore incongruous that he was the one who was imprisoned, whereas those whose message had been shown by events to be false were not punished. It may have been the case that the peace prophets had taken comfort in the raising of the siege and had suggested that their prophecies were coming true. Such hopes had been frustrated, and Jeremiah was pointing out to the king the injustice of the situation where the prophet who had spoken truly was the one who was in prison.

20. On the basis of his innocence and the fulfilment of what he had foretold, Jeremiah addressed a specific plea to the king. **But now** (*'attâ*, probably used inferentially, 'in these circumstances', rather than temporally; cf. 2:18; 7:13), **my lord the king, please listen.** This is an honorific form of address, acknowledging the king's status. **Let me bring my petition before you: Do not send me back to the house of Jonathan the secretary, or[20] I will die there.** The request is literally, 'Let my petition fall before you' (36:7). To send him back to where he had been incarcerated would be a virtual death sentence.

21. Zedekiah says nothing, but he does act. Perhaps he did not want to have on his own hands the death of a man whom he considered to be a

---

19. The kethibh is *'ayyô* presumably *'ayyēh* with a third masculine singular suffix. The qere reads simply *'ayyēh*.

20. A negative final clause introduced by *wə-'al* (GKC §109g).

prophet of the LORD, but Zedekiah having the character that he had came up with a compromise. Rather than freeing him, **King Zedekiah then gave orders for Jeremiah to be placed** (here we have *pāqad* again, in the sense of to deposit something or someone under the control of another) **in the courtyard of the guard.** This was attached to the palace, and those who were in custody there enjoyed much better conditions, being able to receive visitors and to conduct business (32:2; cf. also Neh. 3:25). We no longer have precise details about the layout of the royal complex in Jerusalem, but it seems likely that the official buildings were grouped round and looked out to a large central enclosed courtyard. As this courtyard was constantly under the scrutiny of the royal guards, it was known as the courtyard of the guard. There is no reason to suppose that Jeremiah was then living in the open air. No doubt he had shelter of some sort while still being under the scrutiny of the guards. However, those confined in this way would have enjoyed air and sunlight in a manner that was impossible in an underground cell such as the prophet had previously occupied.

The king also made provision for Jeremiah's needs, **and given**[21] **bread from the street of the bakers each day until all the bread in the city was gone.** A loaf (*kikkār*) described something round, which was the shape of the bread. We have here a glimpse into the structure of ancient Jerusalem with all the bakers gathered into the one street (and presumably those plying other trades grouped themselves in a similar fashion). The conditions were already those of siege, but as long as there was food Jeremiah was to receive some. The round flat loaf he was to be given seems to have been standard siege rations. The bread supply was to run out on the day that the city wall was breached (52:6).

There then follows one of the summary statements (cf. v. 16) that Baruch used to punctuate the story of Jeremiah's suffering. **So Jeremiah remained in the courtyard of the guard.** It is clear where power really lay in Jerusalem—and it was not in the hands of the king (cf. 38:5).

---

21. An infinitive absolute continuing a finite verb (GKC §113z). There are two possible ways of understanding this. On the one hand 'placed' and 'given' may relate parts of Zedekiah's commands (NIV, NKJV, NJPS); on the other hand, these verbs may record the consequences of those commands (NASB, NRSV; so also LXX). The REB adopts a mixed approach by taking the first verb as relating the content of the command regarding Jeremiah's imprisonment and the second as historical narrative regarding his rations.

B. RESCUED FROM A CISTERN (38:1-13)

Chapter 38 contains two incidents, first that of Jeremiah's imprisonment and release (vv. 1-13), and then that of a further interview with
the king (vv. 14-28). There are certain features that resemble what has
already been narrated in chapter 37: the hostility of the officials,
imprisonment in a cistern or a place connected with a cistern, release
from there into the court of the guard through favour obtained from
Zedekiah, an interview with Zedekiah. This has suggested to some that
chapter 38 is a doublet of chapter 37 (e.g. Skinner 1922:258-59; Bright
1965:233; Nicholson 1975, 2:118; Thompson 1980:637). If that was
so, then it would seem that the final editing process of the book took
place at some remove from Jeremiah and his closest associates, who
would have been able to recognise the double nature of the accounts. It
is not sufficient to say that there are double accounts elsewhere in
Jeremiah. This is far from proved. Repetitions of similar material in
different addresses is of a different nature from consecutive repetition
of the same sequence of events in what is a closely written historical
account.

But there is no need to conclude that chapter 38 is a doublet of
chapter 37. There are significant differences: in chapter 37 there is an
account of his arrest, which is lacking in chapter 38; in chapter 38
there are many details given of how Jeremiah is removed from the pit,
there are no such details in the account of his coming from the house
of the pit in chapter 37; further his original place of imprisonment is
connected to the house of Jonathan the secretary, whereas later it is the
property of Malkijah, the king's son, that is involved. Also, the one
account mentions Ebed-Melech while the other does not. In chapter 37
it is Jeremiah himself who procures his better conditions from the king;
in chapter 38 there are two interviews with the king, and it is the first
by Ebed-Melech that procures Jeremiah's release. This in itself is sufficient to demonstrate that two separate incidents are described (cf.
Holladay 1989, 2:282). It is further significant that the omissions from
the second narrative, such as there being no account of Jeremiah's
arrest, are precisely those which are logically required if it does follow
the first historically. The only contrary evidence occurs in 38:26
(which see) where mention is made of the house of Jonathan the secretary. For arguments that this is a double account, see Jones 1992:454-6.

1. Official Hostility (38:1-6)

1. This chapter then takes up the story with Jeremiah confined in the

courtyard of the guard (37:21). Here Jeremiah was able to conduct
business, and also to speak to any who came to the palace and to the
soldiers stationed there. It was here that four of the officials,
**Shephatiah son of Mattan, Gedaliah son of Pashhur, Jehucal son
of Shelemiah, and Pashhur son of Malkijah heard what Jeremiah
was telling all the people.** Jucal (NIV margin) is an abbreviated form
of Jehucal (37:3); Pashhur son of Malkijah is mentioned in connection
with the first royal delegation to Jeremiah (21:1); but the other two
individuals do not occur elsewhere. Gedaliah might have been a son of
Pashhur son of Immer who once had Jeremiah put in the stocks (20:1-
2). These men were evidently of the pro-Egyptian party which was
dominant in Zedekiah's court at this time. They therefore were horrified that the king's action had enabled Jeremiah to continue to
proclaim the same message he had been relaying all along—that the
only way forward was to surrender to Babylon.

There are, however, commentators who consider that Jeremiah
speaking to 'all the people' either directly or through intermediaries is
an improbable scenario when he is held in prison. They therefore argue
that 'heard' should be translated as a pluperfect 'had heard'[22] and they
take these words as prophecies that Jeremiah uttered before his arrest
(e.g. Bright 1965:226, 230). But this is to overestimate the severity of
confinement in the courtyard of the guard. Unlike the dungeon cells,
Jeremiah has by royal command been removed to a place where his
freedom to move about is inhibited, but not the access others have to
him. Note the mention of 'all the Jews sitting in the courtyard of the
guard' (32:12) in the description of conditions at this period. So while
the verse does not describe a public sermon such as those once
delivered by Jeremiah in the Temple, it is making clear that what he
was saying was a matter of public knowledge. 'Sitting in public prison
Jeremiah continues his loud spoken sermons to the people of Jerusalem, not caring for the hushes of the guards' (Holt 1999:165). This is a
testimony to his personal boldness and his conviction that a response
was urgently required to mitigate the consequences of the imminent
fall of the city. It is also a further indictment of the officials. They had
heard (<√šāmaʿ) and knew full well the warning that Jeremiah had
brought.

2. It was not a new message that Jeremiah uttered. Since so much of

---

22. There are occasions when the context indicates that a *waw*-consecutive
imperfect is to be understood as a pluperfect (Gen. 12:1; Exod. 4:19; *IBHS*
§33.2.3a). English translations generally avoid such a rendering here because
it presupposes a particular theory of the composition of Jeremiah.

what he had warned about had already come to pass, the people ought to have been in no doubt that they would not escape the full measure of divine justice, and therefore they should act as they had been advised. **This is what the LORD says: 'Whoever stays in this city will die by the sword, famine or plague, but whoever goes over to the Babylonians will live.[23] He will escape with his life; he will live.'** This message is substantially the same as the one Jeremiah gave when the siege began, including the graphic phrase 'escape with his life'/'have his life (*nepeš*, 2:34) as booty' (21:9). The LORD's message has been consistent throughout. Of course, by saying that continued resistance was futile and by urging the people to align themselves with the enemy forces, Jeremiah was uttering what the officials could interpret only as high treason. But Jeremiah's message was not born out of a lack of patriotism, or out of fear for his personal safety, or for some personal advantage. He was the loyal spokesman of the LORD, and he had a deep concern for the well-being of his people. They could not escape the impending catastrophe, but they could rescue their own lives by prompt surrender to the Babylonians. Whatever would then happen to them would not be glorious or grand, but it would be better than the horrors of life in a city under prolonged siege or the massacre that would ensue when the city fell.

What Jeremiah was saying had been known for some time, and therefore it at first seems puzzling that the officials had not acted against the prophet at a much earlier stage. But the tensions of the siege no doubt led to divided counsel even among the higher echelons of Zedekiah's advisers. Their first attempt to silence Jeremiah had failed because of the king's intervention. Although they had a considerable hold over the king, they continue to observe the constitutional niceties and direct their request to him. If anything happened to the prophet, these politicians wanted the blame spread round as much as possible. They therefore use Jeremiah's continuing declaration of the LORD's word as grounds for moving against him a second time.

3. Jeremiah's message to the people who listened to him in the courtyard of the guard had another strand to it. **And[24] this is what the LORD says: 'This city will certainly be handed over to the army of the king of Babylon, who will capture it.'** While this is indubitably the message the LORD required to be delivered and which Jeremiah

---

23. The kethibh is *yiḥyeh* and the qere is *wəḥāyâ*. Both forms are grammatically possible, but there is no good reason to depart from the kethibh, cf. 21:9.

24. Here the NIV introductory 'and' is an addition; surprisingly the Hebrew text is without a conjunction.

had already announced (21:7; 32:28; 34:2), there can be little difficulty in seeing how the officials would have analysed it as sapping morale, and engendering a spirit of defeatism by reminding the populace that the LORD had decreed that the city would fall.

4. So once more Jeremiah's life is in danger. **Then the officials said to the king, 'This man should be put to death.'** The officials demand the death penalty, and they state their reason for it. The NIV does not translate the emphatic connective *kî-ʿal-kēn*, 'for inasmuch as', which might point to what is presented as a previously unrecognised factor (see 29:28 and the comment there). **He is discouraging**[25] **the soldiers who are left in this city, as well as all the people, by the things he is saying to them.'** 'Discouraging'/'weakening/causing to relax the hands' is an idiom that denotes dejection and loss of nerve/morale (for the opposite idiom, see on 23:14). The same phrase is found in Lachish Ostracon VI written probably two years earlier (*ANET*, 322), but there it is used regarding the behaviour of some of the officials from the Jerusalem nobility who were perceived as undermining the morale of the population. Obviously at that time there was considerable debate in the city as to the advisability of surrendering to the Babylonians. 'For' (*kî*) expands on the reason already given. **This man is not seeking the good of these people but** (*kî ʿim*) **their ruin** (*rāʿâ*). This indicates the difference between the prophet and the politician. The people's good (*šālôm*, 'peace', 'total well-being') can be sought either by worldly stratagem, or by conformity to the message of God. Those who rely on the former cannot get to grips with the motives of the latter, and the reality of what it is that they point to. To continue in the face of the divine message is not heroism but blind obstinacy. When the two courses of action move forwards to the culminating crisis, an irreconcilable gulf of hostility opens out between them.

5. He is in your hands,' King Zedekiah answered. 'For' (*kî*) introduces the reason that the king gives for his response. **'The king can do nothing**[26] **to oppose you.'**[27] These are the words of a man who acknowledges his own powerlessness. What a change from the situation that had prevailed in Jehoiakim's day (cf. chap. 36)! But Zedekiah

---

25. As if the verb *rāpeh* was final *aleph* rather than final *he*, the form *mərappeʿ* is found instead of *mərappeh* (GKC §75rr).

26. The Massoretic Text has the imperfect *yûkal*, whereas a participle would be the expected construction (and seems to be reflected in the LXX). However, the participle of this verb is not attested elsewhere.

27. The object marker *ʿetəkem* is probably used instead of the preposition *ʿittəkem*, 'with you'.

did not have a popular support base because he was seen as a
Babylonian appointee—even though he is now opposing them. Many
people still viewed Jehoiachin as their rightful king, and indeed the
Babylonians may have encouraged this. The officials constituted a
powerful pressure group who were able to ensure that they had their
own way. It is not likely that Zedekiah personally wished to see
Jeremiah killed. His attitude both before and after shows that the king
stood somewhat in awe of the man who was as fearless and
uncompromising as he himself was vacillating and intimidated. Given
that on other occasions Zedekiah did succeed in modifying the actions
of the officials (37:11-21; 38:7-13), it seems probable that the powerlessness to which he refers here is the impossibility of anyone, even a
king, defending Jeremiah's speech from charges of treason. What precisely was it that was implied by 'he is in your hands'? Given that the
officials had demanded the death penalty it does not seem possible to
read these words in any other way than Zedekiah acquiescing in their
demand.

6. But we do not read of Jeremiah's execution. The course followed
shows that the officials themselves were acting under constraint. They
seem to be trying as hard as possible to clear themselves of being
directly responsible for the prophet's death. It is one thing to have him
executed by the direct command of the king's officials; it is quite
another should he die while in custody, particularly of starvation or
natural causes—just another casualty of the siege. **So they took
Jeremiah and put[28] him into the cistern of Malkijah, the king's
son, which was in the courtyard of the guard.** For the term 'the
king's son' see on 36:26 where it is used of a member of Jehoiakim's
entourage. Malkijah lived in the vicinity of the courtyard.[29] Unlike
Jonathan's cistern which had been dry, this cistern (*bôr*, 37:16) was
evidently used to store rainwater, and though empty, remained damp
and unhealthy. It was also fairly deep because it is recorded of the officials, who had certainly no concern for Jeremiah's well-being, that

28. Translations vary on how to render *šālak* (hiphil) here. 'Cast' (NKJV) or
'threw' (NRSV) convey the primary meaning of the word, but 'put' (NIV,
REB) and 'put down' (NJPS) are also found so as to bring the rendering into
harmony with the description given in the second part of the verse. Perhaps
the sense is 'abandon' (cf. Ezek. 16:5; Gen. 21:15; Exod. 1:22) (*NIDOTTE*
4:127).

29. The REB omits 'Malkijah, the king's son'. This facilitates identifying
the cistern as the same one mentioned in 37:15-16 and also the reference in
v. 26, but lacks manuscript support.

they lowered Jeremiah by ropes into the cistern. This is a more particular description of their action which had first been described in general terms. Their care is consonant with their intention that he should not die by their direct action. Food could have been thrown down to him in the cistern, but he would have been unable to escape unaided through the narrow aperture in the neck of the bulbous cavity. **It had no water in it, only** (*ki ʿim*) **mud, and Jeremiah sank down into the mud.** The absence of water may have been due to the season of the year, or possibly, if it was fed from an external supply, through the siege. The lack of water meant that he did not die immediately of drowning, but he was being virtually condemned to a slow death in the wet mud. Jeremiah's circumstances were literally those that were often employed by the psalmists metaphorically as epitomising a life-threatening situation (Pss. 28:1; 30:4; 40:3; 88:5, 7; 143:7).

2. Unexpected Intervention (38:7-13)

The detail with which Ebed-Melech's intervention is related indicates that it has a significance beyond being the means used to effect Jeremiah's release from what would have inevitably proved his place of death. Tribute is paid to the courageous conduct of someone who was a nonentity in terms of the political structures of Jerusalem. However, he was prepared to speak out on behalf of justice and fair play for one who was being oppressed. His concern about the treatment of others led him to act with compassion and consideration on their behalf. Because he trusted in the LORD and because that trust was given practical expression in acting for the LORD and for his prophet, he was given a divine guarantee of deliverance whereas the so-called people of God, trusting in the delusion of 'the Lie', were being swept to their doom.

7. Given the extreme danger that the prophet's life was in, it is unlikely that there was any great delay before he was rescued. Help came to him from an unexpected source—a foreign slave. **But Ebed-Melech, a Cushite, an official in the royal palace.**[30] Ebed-Melech, literally 'king's servant', seems to have been a name given to him on his being brought as a slave into the royal palace/king's household. 'Cushite' indicates he was from Nubia, that is northern Sudan, or else, in accordance with the traditional understanding of the term, from Ethiopia further to the south. It is quite probable that he was in charge of the king's domestic arrangements (cf. Obadiah's role as overseer of

---

30. *Waw*-disjunctive introducing an explanatory clause.

Ahab's household in 1 Kgs. 18:3), and if this extended to the king's harem (Zedekiah seems to have had many wives, vv. 22-23), then it is probable that Ebed-Melech was in fact a 'eunuch', though the word may also signify simply a court official.[31] While the degenerate circumstances in Judah might have led them to follow eastern practice in the matter despite contrary legislation, it is equally probable that he was a eunuch before coming into the king's possession. Certainly he was someone who was in frequent contact with the king and well-known to him; but still he was an outsider, debarred from the cultic community. Yet the conduct of this alien and slave brings light into the dark events engulfing the dying city, and is instrumental in preserving Jeremiah's life.

Zedekiah does not seem to have wanted to know what Jeremiah's fate in the hands of the officials had been, but Ebed-Melech **heard that ($k\hat{\imath}$) they had put Jeremiah into the cistern.** Presumably he knew the nature of that cistern, as it was in the palace environs, and appreciated the danger that the prophet was in. There is added the information, **while[32] the king was sitting in the Benjamin gate.** It seems that the king, sitting on a throne, was going about his duty of administering justice and hearing complaints. Consequently Ebed-Melech would then have easy access to him probably at the Benjamin gate that led into the Temple rather than the one in the north of the city wall (37:13). Though the latter would have been a key location in the defences of the city, and the king might very well have gone there to inspect them and encourage his troops (Malamat 1968:155), he would hardly have been sitting at such an exposed site. It seems rather that we have the ironic picture of the king being petitioned to correct a miscarriage of justice which he himself was largely responsible for.

8-9. Knowing where the king was, **Ebed-Melech went out of the palace and said to him, 'My lord the king, these men have acted wickedly in all that they have done to Jeremiah the prophet.'[33]** He

---

31. In this verse the expression *'îš sārîs*, 'a eunuch man', seems to point in the direction of *sārîs* being understood as 'eunuch', rather than in its more extended sense of 'official', which would not have required the addition of 'man' (cf. NIV margin).

32. *Waw*-disjunctive introducing an explanatory clause.

33. Ebed-Melech's speech is given quite differently in the LXX: 'You (sing.) have acted wickedly ⌊in⌋ what you have done to kill this man through hunger for there is no longer bread in the city.' This is a direct attack on the king. The Massoretic Text seems a much more probable approach to an eastern monarch, even one as weak as Zedekiah.

has no hesitation in bringing the matter to Zedekiah's notice, and in condemning the officials. **They have thrown** (the same word as 'put' in v. 6) **him into a cistern, where he will starve to death**[34] **when** (*kî*) **there is no longer any bread in the city.** Jeremiah's problem was much more immediate than that, but Ebed-Melech is speaking in the stress of the moment and is pressing home the gravity of Jeremiah's situation. He would not of course know when the bread would run out, and what would happen then (in point of fact at the same time the city walls were breached), but he was sure that Jeremiah would receive no supplies in his underground prison.

10. Zedekiah evidently had a conscience in the matter, probably intensified by his respect for Jeremiah. He was easily swayed: what he did seems often to have been a matter of who had spoken to him last. **Then the king commanded Ebed-Melech the Cushite, 'Take thirty men from here with you**[35] **and lift Jeremiah the prophet out of the cistern before he dies.'** 'Commanded' is probably not used to indicate a decisive intervention on Zedekiah's part, so much as noting that Ebed-Melech can now act on the king's authority. Many are suspicious of the number 'thirty' as being too high for the task required, and read instead 'three' (so REB; NRSV). Although one Hebrew manuscript has this reading, there is no real need to make the change.[36] Quite possibly the show of force reflects the possibility that there would be opposition to the move from the officials, who had just had Jeremiah put in the cistern. Not all the men were needed to pull him out of the cistern.

11. The detail given in vv. 11-13 of Ebed-Melech's rescue indicates that this report goes back to an eye-witness. Indeed, the emphasis on the consideration shown the prophet may well point to Jeremiah himself as the source of the information. **So Ebed-Melech took the**

34. Literally, 'and he has died in his place because of the famine.' The *waw*-consecutive imperfect (*wayyāmot*) would naturally suggest a past rendering, but here it probably expresses the certain consequence, 'and he is sure to die', viewing it as a logical or necessary consequence of what precedes (GKC §111l). *IBHS* takes it as an exceptional, epexegetic use (§33.3.1f). Another possibility is to repoint the consonants to read *wəyāmut*, 'and he will die' (BHS).
35. Literally, 'in your hand', that is under your direction and control, rather than just 'with you' (NIV, NRSV).
36. The emendation is from *šəlōšîm*, 'thirty', to *šəlōšâ*, 'three'. It is urged that with 'thirty' one would expect the singular *'îš*, but both constructions are possible.

men with him and went to a room under the treasury in the
palace. He took some old rags[37] and worn-out clothes from there
and let them down with ropes to Jeremiah in the cistern. Ebed-
Melech made good use of his inside knowledge regarding the domestic
arrangements of the royal household. There is some dispute as to
where the rags were found. By a slight emendation the NRSV has 'to a
wardrobe of the storehouse'.[38] While rags would presumably be readily
found there, our knowledge of what was the case in the confused
conditions of the siege would suggest that the text be left as it is.

**12-13. Ebed-Melech the Cushite said to Jeremiah, 'Put these old
rags and worn-out clothes under your arm to pad the ropes.'** He
was showing consideration for the strain that Jeremiah would be under,
with the ropes cutting into his flesh, particularly if the mud was deep
and viscous. No doubt it was with real gratitude that **Jeremiah did so,
and they pulled him up with the ropes and lifted him out of the
cistern.** The suggestion is that the prophet was considerably weakened
by his ordeal. Of course, the lift was vertical; Jeremiah could not have
scrambled out unaided. This episode in Jeremiah's story is then
concluded with one of the summary statements characteristic of
Baruch's style (cf. 37:16): **and Jeremiah remained in the courtyard
of the guard.** He is returned to his previous place of detainment, but at
least the immediate threat to his life has been lifted. Of Ebed-Melech,
more will be recounted in 39:15-18.

C. THE FINAL INTERVIEW (38:14-28a)

There is then described the final interview between Jeremiah and
Zedekiah. There are no certain indications as to when it took place in
relation to the preceding incident, but it probably occurred only weeks
before the fall of Jerusalem. It is part of the world of intrigue and pressure as the crumbling regime faced up to the stresses and strains of the
ever intensifying siege of the city. The king and his officials were
intensely suspicious of one another, and though neither party will

---

37. *bəlôyē* for *bəlôʾyê* (GKC §8k) from √*bālâ*, 'to be worn away'. There is a
softening of the *yodh* to *aleph* in v. 12, *bəlôʾê*. The kethibh has *haśśəḥābôt*,
whereas the article is omitted in the qere, *səḥābôt*, because it is not present
with the following *məlāḥîm*, 'torn'.
38. The change is from *ʾel taḥat haʾôṣār*, 'to under the treasury', to *ʾel
meltaḥat haʾôṣār*, 'to the wardrobe of the storehouse', cf 2 Kgs. 10:12, which
would of course be a more likely place for clothing, but there is no manuscript
evidence for such a reading.

admit it, it was only a matter of time till the inevitable happened.

1. The Royal Oath (38:14-16)

14. **Then King Zedekiah sent for Jeremiah the prophet and had him brought to the third entrance**[39] **to the temple of the LORD.** We do not know where precisely this entrance lay, but presumably it was from the palace into the Temple and may have been the same as 'the royal entryway outside the temple of the LORD' (2 Kgs. 16:18). If this was a covered walkway restricted to royal use possibly only on state occasions, then its shadows would have afforded Zedekiah a suitable place for a secret interview. Certainly Zedekiah hoped he would be unobserved there—and he was partially correct in that assumption (v. 27). This reinforces the picture of a man who lacked confidence in anything he did and who lived in fear of those around him.

'I am going to ask you something,' the king said to Jeremiah. The king was no doubt regally dressed while Jeremiah's condition showed how he had been living recently, but still it is Zedekiah who is the suppliant as the interview begins. Though in the event the king does not actually get round to posing his question, it is clear that he wants information from Jeremiah about the LORD's attitude to what is going on, and how the siege will end. Zedekiah does not want to change his own course of action. It is rather that he is hoping against hope that the LORD will relent and not carry out his threat—even at the last moment. **Do not hide anything from me** suggests that the king was well aware that Jeremiah's recent treatment might make him fearful of speaking. He might not be prepared to tell all he knew for fear of the consequences.

15. The response Jeremiah makes does reveal his anxiety about how the king will act. Had it not been with the king's approval that he had been consigned to the cistern (v. 5)? As there had been no change in the message the LORD had given the prophet to deliver, it was not improbable that the king might react negatively to the bearer of the message. **Jeremiah said to Zedekiah, 'If ($k\hat{\imath}$) I give you an answer, will you not kill me?**[40] **Even if ($k\hat{\imath}$) I did give you counsel, you would not listen to me.'** Jeremiah reasons that an answer true to his divine commission would only lead to the resurrection of the charge of

---

39. The adjective is definite, though the noun is not (*IBHS* §14.3.1d).

40. The negative question is rhetorical, expecting a positive response. This is reinforced by the use of the infinitive absolute *hāmēt* before the finite verb. Perhaps the force of what Jeremiah says is brought out by, 'You will certainly kill me, won't you?'

treason and undermining morale. He also recognises that Zedekiah is
not going to listen (<√*šāmaʿ*), no matter what advice is given him. He
had previously received repeated warnings, and the possibility was
remote of a different response this time.

16. Zedekiah, however, is a man consumed with anxieties and doubts.
He is at his wits' end, and will do anything to hear a favourable
response. **But King Zedekiah swore this oath secretly to Jeremiah:
'As surely as the LORD lives, who**[41] **has given us breath/**'made us
for this life' (*nepeš*, 2:34)**, I will neither kill you nor hand you over
to those who are seeking your life.'** 'Secretly' emphasises the
unusual nature of the oath, which would normally involve a public
commitment to a course of action, but Zedekiah's weak personal position was such that he was trying to keep everything as quiet as
possible. The reference to the LORD as the giver of breath (*nepeš*, the
breath and life that constitutes an animate being) involves the implied
malediction that if he does not keep his word, then the LORD, who has
the power of life and death in his hands, should take Zedekiah's life
away. No doubt Zedekiah acted sincerely in giving this commitment,
but one might well wonder what degree of reliance could be given to
the word of this weak and temporising monarch, even when it was
bolstered by an oath.

2. Surrender or Else (38:17-23)

17. Though Zedekiah's ability to carry out the commitment he has
given might be questioned, nonetheless Jeremiah replies to him. **Then
Jeremiah said to Zedekiah, 'This is what the LORD God Almighty,
the God of Israel, says: "If you surrender**[42] **to the officers of the
king of Babylon, your life** (*nepeš*, cf. v. 16) **will be spared and this
city will not be burned down/**'with fire'**; you and your family will
live".'** Jeremiah emphasises that the message he is giving comes from
the LORD himself (for the full designation, see on 7:3). Zedekiah is
being confronted with the absolute authority of God. But the message
is not what Zedekiah wants to hear because it is identical to what

41. In the Massoretic Text the *ʿăšer* is preceded by an unpointed object
marker *ʾt*, with no accompanying qere, which would presumably have recom-
mended its omission. If *ʾet* is read, it would function in a way similar to 27:8,
'with regard to him who created us' (cf. GKC §17b).

42. *yāṣāʿ*, 'to go out', rendered 'surrender' in many translations. It is
accompanied by the infinite absolute *yāṣōʿ*, untranslated in the NIV, but the
NRSV has, 'if you will only surrender'. Perhaps the thought is 'if and only if
you surrender'.

Jeremiah has announced many times before (cf. 21:4-10; 32:4; 34:2-5). The need to surrender is urgently pressed upon the king. He would have to submit to the officers of Nebuchadnezzar because the emperor was not encamped at Jerusalem but at Riblah 200 miles (370 km) to the north (39:5; 2 Kgs. 25:6). The mention of the Babylonian 'officers' introduces an ironic contrast with Jeremiah's own situation where the 'officials' (also *śārîm* in Hebrew) were causing him so much trouble.

Of course, Zedekiah's surrender would not be the same as that of a private individual. If the king capitulated, the whole city would be surrendering. But if he complies with the divine word, he is given three divine guarantees: his own life would be spared, his family would be spared, and the city would escape conflagration. None of these were automatic consequences of his surrender. On the contrary those who rebelled against an overlord such as Nebuchadnezzar would normally be subject to harsh and humiliating treatment, especially when they had held out against him for a long time. Subject kings were frequently mutilated and then killed to discourage others from rebelling. The LORD promises to intervene to modify the Babylonian treatment of Zedekiah and Jerusalem, but it would take faith in the word Jeremiah has brought for the king to venture on that promise.

18. There is, however, the stark alternative. **But if you will not surrender to the officers of the king of Babylon, this city will be handed over to the Babylonians and they will burn it down**/'with fire'; **you yourself** (*'attâ* expressed for emphasis) **will not escape from their hands.** Continued resistance will meet with destruction, and it is implied the king will be captured and at the mercy of Babylon. His worst fears will be realised.

19. Momentous issues were at stake for Zedekiah and his people. In his response we see the measure of the man. **King Zedekiah said to Jeremiah, 'I am afraid of the Jews who have gone over to the Babylonians, for the Babylonians may hand me over to them and they will ill-treat me.'** Zedekiah for the moment considers the possible consequences of obedience, and one scenario in particular causes him particular consternation. He draws Jeremiah into the circle of his political confidants (were any others left?) and candidly sets before him his inmost thinking. 'Am afraid' (<√*dā'ag*, 'to be anxious, concerned') expresses an emotional response to a threat, real or potential. Zedekiah is concerned for his own well-being if, as he imagines might be the case, the Babylonians hand him over to those Jews who had already defected to them (39:9; 52:15). There is no doubt that the

verb 'ill-treat' is a strong one.[43] It is not just a matter of verbal abuse.
He may have his life, but he is supposing that he will be subjected to
considerable physical harassment (cf. Num. 22:29; Judg. 19:25; 1 Sam.
31:4; 1 Chron. 10:4.), though we know of nothing to suggest that
Nebuchadnezzar would adopt this course of action. It does not seem
that these defectors were acting in response to Jeremiah's prophecy,
but had gone over to the Babylonians for their own reasons. It may
well be that their hostility to Zedekiah is the fallout from earlier
disputes within the ruling circles in Jerusalem, as hinted at in the
Lachish Ostraca (see on v. 4). It is not the ordinary people the king is
afraid of, but leading citizens, perhaps even courtiers, who had fled
after their advice had been rejected. Zedekiah focuses on the
indignities and sufferings he would personally have to endure and
ignores the plight of his people, especially if the siege continues until
the city is overwhelmed by the Babylonians.

20. Jeremiah speaks to sway the king towards a more sensible policy.
'They will not hand you over,' Jeremiah replied. If the king is
rejecting the right course of action by thinking of possible reprisals
against himself, the prophet acts to stem that loophole by ruling out
categorically the outcome Zedekiah envisages. He again urges Zedekiah to hear what the LORD is saying to him. **Obey the LORD by doing
what I tell you. Then it will go well with you, and your life will be
spared** (cf. v. 17). The king could have surrendered to the LORD (by
surrendering to the Babylonians as directed) and by so doing would
have been permitted to live. But under pressure from those around him
and being unwilling to venture in faith upon the promise of God, the
king rejected the prophet's counsel and drew down upon himself his
sad end.

21. If the prospect of the good outcome promised to obedience does
not induce Zedekiah to comply, then Jeremiah seeks to impel him to
respond by spelling out the dire consequences of disobedience. **But if
you refuse to surrender, this is what the LORD has revealed to me.**

22. The NRSV begins the verse with 'a vision', which seeks to bring
out the force of *wəhinnēh*, 'and/but behold'. What follows is a description of the scene the LORD has revealed to the prophet and which he
vividly portrays for the king. **All the women left in the palace of the
king of Judah will be brought out to the officials of the king of
Babylon.** The women referred are not the king's own wives, who are

---

43. *hittʿallēl bə* <√ʿālal I, 'to drink again and again' (?), hithpael 'to deal
mischievously with someone'.

mentioned in v. 23. Nor is their being left a reference to some disaster, as if to point to those who have survived the famine in the siege. It seems rather to reflect the practice that when a king died or was removed, the concubines in his harem and other household attendants were left in the palace for his successor (2 Sam. 16:21-22). This group of women will be handed over to the Babylonian officials, an act indicative of their now being the ones in control. The women reckon that their interests have not been adequately looked after, and as they are led out it is envisaged they turn and reproach Zedekiah, taunting him with his weakness and irresolution. **Those women will say to you: 'They misled you and overcame you—those trusted friends of yours.'** The first sentence of this sneering song is drawn from Obadiah 7.[44] Its metrical pattern in Hebrew suggests that it might have been sung in tones of mocking condolence. (The song is in the 3:2 metre known as *qinah*, often associated with a lament, but here addressed to the king it obviously serves another function.) Jeremiah is predicting that this man who will not surrender because he feared the abuse of the deserters will have to endure the abuse even of the women of the palace as a consequence of his conduct. He had allowed himself to be deceived by his 'trusted friends'/'men of his peace' (*šālôm*), those who had promised him that they would act to promote his welfare, but who in the end deserted him (Jeremiah's own experience in 20:10; cf. also Ps. 41:10). The reference may be to other nations who had said they would be allies in the uprising against Babylon, or it may be a more specific reference to the false prophets and to the court officials who had forced him into certain lines of action, but who are no longer at his side.

Your feet are sunk[45] in the mud; your friends have deserted you. The women will express themselves as certain that the king is in mortal danger. His feet are stuck in the mud[46]—a situation of danger and loss (cf. Ps. 69:14). Jeremiah warns him that he will then be in the life-threatening situation that he himself has just experienced, but he will not have an Ebed-Melech to come to his side. 'Deserted'/'turned back' is a standard phrase for withdrawal under military or psychological pressure. Zedekiah will be on his own.

---

44. The only difference is the substitution of *hissîtûkā* for *hiššî'kā*.

45. The Massoretic Text has a hophal *hotba'û*; the REB reads as a hiphil *hitbî'û*: 'they stuck your feet in the mud'.

46. The word for 'mud' here is a hapax *bōṣ*, and not the same word as in v. 6. As the situation is life-threatening, the translation might also be 'mire', what is found on the soft floor of a swamp.

23. All your wives and your sons will be brought out[47] **to the Babylonians.** Perhaps the king may be induced to think of others for a while, or perhaps he will see this as even more indignity heaped upon himself and what little dignity or honour he has left. **You yourself will not escape from their hands but** (*kî*) **will be captured by the king of Babylon**/'but in the hand of the king of Babylon you will be caught'; **and this city will be burned down**/'with fire'.[48] There will be no escaping the outcome. With this stark presentation of the alternatives Jeremiah has set clearly before the king the choice he has to make. The king makes no response to what has been said to him. It would seem that at one level he accepted that Jeremiah was speaking the truth, but at another he cannot bring himself to act on the basis of what the prophet has said. All he can do is to try to limit the impact of the interview on his immediate personal predicament. The king fears his advisers more than Babylon—and more than the LORD.

3. Palace Intrigue (38:24-28a)

When the king sent for Jeremiah in 37:11-21, it was Jeremiah who presented his request to him and the king granted it. On this occasion, it is the king who makes a request of Jeremiah.

24. Zedekiah has not received the answer he wanted. He focuses instead on his own situation in the palace politics of those desperate days. **Then Zedekiah said to Jeremiah, 'Do not let anyone know about this conversation, or**[49] **you may die.'** This is probably not Zedekiah going back on his word (v. 16) so much as him expressing his helplessness if the officials find out that Jeremiah has been

---

47. The Hebrew is a hiphil participle *môṣî'îm*, continuing what the prophet has seen in vision. However, there is no expressed subject (cf. 'They will also bring out all your wives and your sons', NASB). While the participle may be revocalised as a passive hophal, *mûṣā'îm* (with the Vulgate and the Targum), that leaves the object markers to be explained. It seems better to supply some undefined subject with the hiphil participle (GKC §144i; *IBHS* §4.4.2).

48. The MT has *tiśrōp*, reflected in the NIV margin, 'you will burn this city' or 'you will cause this city to be burned'. The same consonants may, however, also be pointed as a niphal *tiśśārēp* (the form found in v. 17), 'the city will be burned.' This is supported by the LXX and Targum, Syriac and a few manuscripts. In that case *'et* will be used not to mark the object but to mark a new subject. The *waw*-disjunctive will be setting the two outcomes side by side as part of the same overthrow of the city.

49. *wəlō'* + an imperfect may be used to express a negative final clause, 'so that you may not die' (GKC §109g).

speaking to the king. The pro-Egyptian party at court would not be slow to seek the prophet's life if they could bring further charges against him.

25-26. Zedekiah knew that the officials were keeping a close eye on all that was going on, and so he provided a cover story for their conversation. **If** (*kî*) **the officials hear that** (*kî*) **I have talked with you, and they come to you and say, 'Tell us what you said to the king and what the king said to you; do not hide it from us or**[50] **we will kill you,' then tell them, 'I was pleading with the king not to send me back to Jonathan's house to die there.'** In the event Zedekiah's suspicions in this matter proved well founded. He equally had no illusions about the unscrupulous nature of the officials. The most puzzling feature is the reference to Jonathan's house, in that this relates to the first period of imprisonment (37:15), and Jeremiah's request at that time. Many would then see this as a displaced fragment from that story, or as evidence that chapters 37 and 38 are relating two differing versions of the one event. But there are many other possible ways of explaining the words. They may reflect the distraught state of Zedekiah's mind. He is saying, 'Tell them what we were talking about last time,' in the knowledge that they will be convinced that Jeremiah was talking about his own safety. Another option is that Zedekiah is suggesting that in the interview he proposed treating Jeremiah harshly and that the prophet had urged him not to return him where he had been before.[51] Even so, it has to be acknowledged that this remains a puzzling feature of the narrative.

27. The king was correct in his assumption that the interview would not pass unnoticed. Indeed the behaviour of the officials seems to display suspicions about the king's motives as much as a desire to ensnare the prophet. **All the officials did come to Jeremiah and question him, and he told them everything the king had ordered him to say.** Was the prophet right in this? It may be that a plea for his

---

50. 'Or' represents the same construction as in v. 24.

51. Nicholson (1975, 2:118) argues that 'although the underground prison in which Jeremiah was confined is described in 38:6 ... as the pit or cistern of Malchiah the king's son and to have been located in the court of the guardhouse, 38:26 clearly implies that it was the same as in 37:11-16, that is, the house of Jonathan.' Nicholson does so in process of concluding that the accounts are divergent accounts of one and the same course of events. He also speculates (1975, 2:120) that 'it may be that the cistern referred to was located in the house of Jonathan, but was popularly known, for some reason or other, as the cistern of Malchiah'.

safety was involved in the earlier conversation, and the king's cover story was to limit Jeremiah's reply to only part of what they had been talking about. Certainly the officials had no right to demand an account of what had passed between the king and the prophet, and so Jeremiah would not have been culpable in telling them part, but not all, of the truth (cf. 1 Sam. 16:2-3). **So they said no more to him, for** (*kî*) **no one had heard his conversation with the king.** 'Said no more to him' is literally 'and they were silent from him', a condensed form of speech involving both the idea of stopping speaking and also moving away from him. They had no evidence to proceed since the 'conversation' (literally, 'word') had not been overheard. To that extent at any rate Zedekiah had been successful.

28a. Again Baruch concludes an episode in his life of Jeremiah with a summary statement (cf. 37:16). **And Jeremiah remained in the courtyard of the guard until the day Jerusalem was captured.** The prophet was not sent back to the dungeons, but was left in the less restrictive conditions of the courtyard of the guard.

D. THE FALL OF THE CITY (38:28b–39:18)

Chapter 39 is not concerned to provide military information about how Jerusalem was captured. The fact of the fall of the city is briefly related in vv. 1-3, focusing more than anything else on the military administration that the Babylonians installed. The main concern of the narrative is to show how the fall of the city affected the destiny of various people: King Zedekiah (vv. 4-7), the city and the population of the land (vv. 8-10), Jeremiah himself (vv. 11-14), and Ebed-Melech (vv. 15-18). The people and their rulers had faced the choice set before them by the LORD: surrender to Nebuchadnezzar and live, or fight against Babylon and perish. They had repeatedly chosen the latter option, and now the consequences had come upon them. But within this general judgment there was divine discrimination because there were those who displayed personal loyalty to the LORD.

It is frequently alleged that the chapter has been subject to considerable textual corruption (see the discussion at vv. 1 and 4). Related to this is the question of the relationship between chapter 39 and other parallel passages, particularly 52:4-16 and 2 Kgs. 25:1-12. It may well be that the textual corruption is considerably less than many suppose. Judgments reflecting what is or is not a natural transition, or way of presenting incidental information, vary from culture to culture, and care must be taken that we do not impose our ideas on the ancient text.

The assessment of Thompson is well worth endorsing: 'Part of the problem for modern commentators is that they do not always understand the methods of the ancient compilers, who had their own ways of handling parentheses, of adding explanatory sentences, and of interrupting the flow of an argument. Some of our own attempts to unravel an ancient editor's work would seem quite unnecessary to him' (1980:645).

1. Military Administration (38:28b–39:3)

38:28b This is[52] **how Jerusalem was taken** renders the last clause of 38:28 in the Hebrew. Different translations have different techniques for dealing with it: it is omitted by the REB (cf. also Holladay 1989, 2:268); taken at the beginning of v. 3 by the NRSV (cf. also Bright 1965:245); rendered 'and he was ⌐there⌐ when Jerusalem was taken' and left at the end of chapter 38 by the NKJV. While omission may be argued for on the basis that the phrase is not found in the LXX and Syriac versions and also a few Hebrew manuscripts, it is probable that the difficulty of understanding the phrase led to its being deliberately omitted. The NKJV approach has the merit of doing justice to the conjunction *ka'ăšer*, 'when', but it is unlikely that Jeremiah is the subject of the introductory verb, which seems rather to be part of a regular transitional formula, 'Now it came to pass that when Jerusalem was taken …' It is probable that the construction was originally closed by the words of v. 3, and that vv. 1-2 were subsequently added as an extended parenthesis to indicate more precisely when the city fell. When was 'subsequently'? The inclusion of vv. 1-2 in the LXX argues for this insertion being early rather than late, and there is no evidence that requires the insertion to be later than the final editing by Jeremiah and Baruch. It is difficult to know how best to present the matter in an English translation as the use of a long parenthesis at such a point in a sentence is not good English style. Equally rearranging the text by moving the phrase two verses later seems overly drastic as a remedy. The NIV approach is as suitable a compromise as any, namely, leaving the phrase where it occurs in the Hebrew text and rendering it as a title, though perhaps 'This is what happened when Jerusalem was taken' might reflect the original more closely.

1. In the ninth year of Zedekiah king of Judah, in the tenth month, Nebuchadnezzar king of Babylon marched against Jerusalem with his whole army and laid siege to it. The dates for the

---

52. For the translation of *wəhāyâ* cf. 37:11.

siege substantially agree with those in 52:4-7a and 2 Kgs. 25:1-4a,
though here no day of the month is given for its start. The date would
be 15th January 588 BC (see Appendix §11). The prophet is not
mentioned in this section which sets out the political and military background against which his ministry is placed. In a very real sense,
however, this is the turning-point in Jeremiah's life because now his
warnings of doom have been realised and his ministry vindicated.

**2. And on the ninth day of the fourth month of Zedekiah's
eleventh year, the city wall was broken through.** The precise length
and terminal date of the siege are a matter of controversy (Appendix
§11), but it would seem that after a siege lasting in total some thirty
months, the city fell on 18th July 586 BC. This information emphasises
that Jeremiah's predictions did come true, and it also forms a bridge to
the next part of Jeremiah's story, in the period after the fall of the city.
Both the narrative concerning the prophet and that concerning the
people to whom he brought the message of the LORD move forwards
together as the events of history unfold, a history that had their interests and circumstances inextricably interlinked. 'Broken through'
($<\sqrt{b\bar{a}qa^c}$ hophal,[53] 'to split, break open') refers to a breach being made
in the city's defences permitting entry into the besieged town. Fighting
might continue for some time thereafter, depending on any secondary
defence works and the layout of the town, but a breach of the city walls
meant that the situation was irrecoverable.

3. Jeremiah had forecast that the Babylonian forces would be successful, and now what had seemed inconceivable to the establishment party
in Jerusalem had occurred: the enemy was in control of the sacred city
and was setting up a military administration to control the situation.
**Then all the officials of the king of Babylon came and took seats in
the Middle Gate: Nergal-Sharezer of Samgar, Nebo-Sarsekim a
chief officer, Nergal-Sharezer a high official and all the other officials of the king of Babylon.** Many feel that this verse is intruded
here, being a mangled version of v. 13. Verse 13 is not, however, a
duplicate of this verse. It refers to the circumstances some weeks later.
It would seem that this information is presented here not only to bring
out that Jeremiah's prophecy was fulfilled in general terms, but also in
specific details, this being the fulfilment of 1:15. We are uncertain
where the Middle Gate was. One possibility is that it was in a wall
separating the upper part of the city, where the palace and temple were,
and the lower part of the city. Alternatively it might be in the middle of

---

53. For a discussion of the use of the hophal here see *IBHS* §28.1c.

the northern wall of Jerusalem where a gate structure from this period
has been identified (*ABD* 2:853). Here the leading officers of the army
are administering the affairs of the city which is under their control. At
this point, Nebuchadnezzar was further north at Riblah.

The names and ranks of the officials have caused considerable
perplexity. In the LXX and so also in the NKJV there are identified six
personal names: 'Nergal-Sharezer, Samgar-Nebo, Sarsechim, Rabsaris,
Nergal-Sarezer,[54] Rabmag'. In the NRSV (cf. NIV margin) there are
four names and two titles: 'Nergal-sharezer, Samgar-nebo, Sarsechim
the Rabsaris, Nergal-sharezer the Rabmag'. The repetition of the name
Nergal-Sharezer is not of itself a problem, in that it seems to have been
fairly common (*contra* Bright 1965:243). But information from
Babylon about the names and positions of Nebuchadnezzar's officials
suggests reading the words of the Hebrew text in different combina-
tions to yield the NIV text has some merit. Nergal-Sharezer would
represent the Akkadian Nergal-šar-uṣur, which means 'May Nergal
protect the king'. At this time he was ruler over a province of Samgar,
corresponding to the Akkadian Sin-magir, a district of Babylonia. He
seems to have been Nebuchadnezzar's son-in-law, and is to be identified with Neriglissar, who became ruler in Babylon in 560 BC after
removing Nebuchadnezzar's son, Amel-Marduk.

The second official would be Nebo-Sarsekim. He is described as
rab-saris, a diplomatic or military rank, which reflects the title *rab ša
rēši*, 'chief who is at the head', a Babylonian political/military official,
often a provincial governor of a newly captured province. To render it
'the chief eunuch' (REB) fails to convey its significance in current
Babylonian practice. The third name, Nergal-Sharezer, is described as
rab-mag, a title whose precise significance is still unknown, but *rab*
designates a royal official or military commander (synonymous with
śar, but used only of non-Israelites). It may designate someone of highest rank under the king. These are the men who were responsible for
capturing Jerusalem and setting up the new administration.

2. Zedekiah's Fate (39:4-7)

The LXX lacks vv. 4-13, probably caused by confusion between the
similar lists of names in vv. 3 and 13. What is said here fits into the
flow of the book as part of the fulfilment of what has already been
foretold. The king who had twice had Jeremiah imprisoned is now

---

54. The NKJV spelling reflects variations in the Hebrew manuscripts
between *sin* and *šin* in both occurrences of this name. The Massoretic Text has
śar-ʿeṣer on both occurrences.

taken captive, and his former prisoner will enjoy freedom (v. 14). This
is the difference that accepting the word of the LORD makes.

**4.   When Zedekiah king of Judah and all the soldiers saw them,
they fled** (<√*bārah*, 4:29). For the incident see 52:7-11 and
2 Kgs. 25:4-7. This raises questions about the sequence of events. If
only part of the city was captured at the time of v. 3, then this means
that they recognised it was impossible to continue defending the upper
city, and decided to flee. Ezekiel had symbolically predicted their
escape (Ezek. 12:12-13). The king who could not make up his mind
now makes a decision too late, and abandoning his people to their fate,
ignominiously sneaks out of the city. **They left the city at night by
way of the king's garden, through the gate between the two walls,
and headed[55] towards the Arabah.** The king's garden (gardens were
often a feature of palaces in the east) may have been on the south-
eastern slope of the city, near the junction of the Hinnom and Kidron
valleys. It is described as being near the pool of Siloam (Neh. 3:15).
Which gate they used is a matter of conjecture, as is the significance of
the phrase 'between the two walls'. Some have supposed that there
was a double wall at some point round Jerusalem, but that would seem
to require more than one gate. The REB favours the phrase being taken
as the name of the gate: 'through the gate called Between the Two
Walls'. This would also fit in with a location at the meeting of two
walls, that round the upper city and that round the lower city. The
precise location is unknown, but in that they were escaping towards the
Arabah, the valley of the river Jordan and the rift valley stretching
south through the Dead Sea to the Gulf of Aqaba (cf. 2:6). Presumably
the gate was on the east side of the city. Keil identifies it with the
Horse Gate (Neh. 3:28), others with the Fountain Gate, or even the
Fish Gate in the north wall. Holladay (1989, 2:292) proposes that they
were seeking refuge in Ammon as others did at this time (40:14;
41:15).

5.   Though they were able to make their exit, they were not totally
undetected. **But the Babylonian army pursued them and overtook
Zedekiah in the plains of Jericho. They captured him and took him
to Nebuchadnezzar king of Babylon at Riblah in the land of
Hamath, where he pronounced sentence on him.** Riblah was an
Aramean city situated about halfway along the course of the river

---

55.   *wayyēṣēʾ*, 'and he went out'. Some manuscripts, Theodotion, Syriac and
Vulgate have 'they left', but it is probable that the focus is particularly on the
king as escaping. 2 Kgs. 25:5 and Jer. 52:8 mention that the soldiers all
scattered from him. That is why the text focuses on Zedekiah here.

Orontes, commanding a great length of the river valley in the ancient kingdom of Hamath. It had been a tributary state to David and Solomon (2 Sam. 8:10; 1 Kgs. 4:21-24), and it was a strategic area for the control of Syria–Palestine, at the centre of communications to north and south. Riblah had served as the Egyptian headquarters for military operations in the area when they tried to aid the collapsing Assyrian Empire (2 Kgs. 23:33), and when Nebuchadnezzar defeated the Egyptians, he retained Riblah as his headquarters for operations in Syria–Palestine. Although Nebuchadnezzar was in the field with his armies, he was not personally present at Jerusalem at this juncture. For the phrase 'pronounced sentence on him', see on 1:16.

6. The sentence was not one that was out of the ordinary for those days, no matter how horrific and brutal it seems now. **There at Riblah the king of Babylon slaughtered the sons of Zedekiah before his eyes and also killed all the nobles of Judah.** 'Slaughtered' (<*šāḥat*) is a word usually employed for the killing of animals, and so probably conveying the brutality with which Nebuchadnezzar acted. 'Nobles' (<*ḥōr*; 27:30) is a wider term than the 'officials' of preceding chapters, but they would certainly have been included among them.

7. Then he put out Zedekiah's eyes and bound him with bronze shackles to take[56] **him to Babylon.** 'Bound' here refers to being manacled with 'bronze shackles'/'a pair of bronzes'. The last thing Zedekiah would remember seeing was the death of his own sons. This was a common punishment for captives (Judg. 16:21), and would have been considered appropriate in view of the treachery Zedekiah had perpetrated against Nebuchadnezzar, 'the king who put him on the throne, whose oath he despised and whose treaty he broke' (Ezek. 17:16). This combination of actions fulfilled the apparently conflicting prophecies of 32:5 and 34:3 that he would see the king of Babylon and be taken to Babylon, but that he would not see Babylonia (Ezek. 12:13). Unlike Jehoiachin who had voluntarily surrendered and who was eventually treated in kindly fashion by the Babylonians (52:31-34), Zedekiah who resisted to the end is treated brutally after his capture.

3. The Devastation of the Land (39:8-10)

8. The focus of this summary account then switches back to the fate of the city of Jerusalem. From elsewhere (52:12 and 2 Kgs. 25:8) we know that these events occurred one month after the breach of the city

---

56. *lābî*ʿ for *ləhābî*ʿ, GKC §§3q, 72z.

walls and were carried out under the direction of Nebuzaradan, mentioned in the next verse. **The Babylonians set fire to the royal palace and the houses of the people.** The unusual expression 'the houses of the people'[57] has led to the surmise that some words have been omitted from the text. Thus the REB translates 'the house of the LORD and the houses of the people'. (Compare 52:13 where the list includes the house of the LORD and all the houses of Jerusalem). It is certainly strange that there is no mention of the Temple here, because the phrase 'house of the people' could not refer to it.

The Babylonians also **broke down the walls of Jerusalem**, but it is not necessary to suppose that all the walls were completely levelled, only that sufficient of the fortifications were demolished as to prevent the city from becoming a military threat again. As a city open to its enemies, Jerusalem could not function as a centre for Egyptian intrigue against Babylon, or have a garrison stationed there by Egypt to further her own purposes.

9. Nebuzaradan commander of the imperial guard[58] carried into exile to Babylon the people who remained in the city, along with those who had gone over to him/'the falling ones who had fallen/ deserted to him' (cf. 21:9), **and the rest of the people.**[59] We know that Nebuzaradan had been sent to Jerusalem with a specific commission after the city fell (52:12). He was therefore omitted from the list of officials in v. 3, but included in that of v. 13, as having arrived in the interval. His name represents the Akkadian '⌐The god⌐ Nabu has given offspring', and he is given the title *rab ṭabbaḥîm*, literally 'chief of the slaughterers'. This is unlikely to mean chief executioner, but is a title originally related to butchers. In the same Babylonian document that tells of Nergal-Sharezer as ruling over Samgar, we find Nebuzaradan called chief cook. The one who controlled the king's food became a very powerful man, and the title itself became frozen as a military term for the leader of an influential body of troops. It should be noted that both those who had deserted to the Babylonians and those who had been captured were taken into exile. Of course, many in the city would have succumbed to famine and plague during the siege, and others would have been killed in the conflict (21:8-9; 38:2). 'To him'

---

57. To translate it in this way assumes an otherwise unknown collective use of *bayit*, 'house'.

58. The title is treated as unique and definite (*IBHS* §13.4b).

59. Omitted by the NLT presumably on the grounds of dittography with the similar expression earlier in the verse. The REB translates as 'and any remaining artisans'.

probably refers to the king of Babylon, rather than to Nebuzaradan personally.

10. But Nebuzaradan the commander of the guard left behind in the land of Judah some of the poor people, who owned nothing; and at that time he gave them vineyards and fields.[60] The Babylonians did not want an empty area, but a controlled border state between themselves and Egypt. Those who were taken away constituted the influential classes in the community, though some leaders were left (v. 14; 40:7–41:18). The poor were presumably expected to be sufficiently grateful to their conquerors for the land grant made them that they would not be inclined to engage intrigues or revolt. Generally the poor (<*dal*) are viewed as not totally destitute, but as suffering economic hardship. They can sacrifice and be taxed (Lev. 14:21; Amos 5:11). Here, however, they have nothing. This was to be expected after the prolonged siege. Possibly they represent those from the countryside who had fled into Jerusalem for refuge, and after the capture of the city were left totally destitute. Overall, the picture is no longer one of a land flowing with milk and honey, but of a devastated and ruined community.

4. The Prophet Well Treated (39:11-14)

This is still part of the section not found in the LXX. This omission means that the LXX text does not have Jeremiah released twice.

11. There now follow two sections which are concerned with individuals involved in the calamity that had come upon Jerusalem. In vv. 11-14 the focus is on Jeremiah. **Now Nebuchadnezzar king of Babylon had given these orders**[61] **about Jeremiah through Nebuzaradan commander of the imperial guard.** One may well wonder about the nature of Nebuchadnezzar's interest in the prophet. It was more than just involving him in a general edict to treat with consideration those who had been following a line favourable to Babylon. It is quite possible that the interrogation of deserters had made clear that Jeremiah was proclaiming that the Babylonians would take the city and advocating submission to Nebuchadnezzar. Given the superstitious nature of the Babylonians, it is easy to see how the king would have issued a command that such a prophet be kept alive. There

---

60. The word *yāgēb*, 'field', is a hapax whose meaning has been determined principally by its association with vineyards.

61. The *waw*-consecutive imperfect has to be translated as a pluperfect to maintain the proper time sequence.

is also the possibility of influence from the not insignificant Jewish presence in the Babylonian court.

12. The orders were: **Take him and look after him; don't harm**[62] **him but**[63] **do for him whatever he asks.** For Jeremiah submission to Babylon was not a matter of being pro-Babylonian, but of acting on the basis of divine revelation. But 'set your eyes on him' indicates careful consideration for his well-being, and this was the Babylonian response to what they knew about his conduct. It is Jeremiah's own choice that is to prevail.

13-14. **So Nebuzaradan the commander of the guard, Nebushaz-ban a chief officer, Nergal-Sharezer a high official and all the other officers of the king of Babylon sent**[64] **and had Jeremiah taken out of the courtyard of the guard.** Nebushazban (from the Akkadian name Nabū-šuzibanni, 'May ⌐the god⌐ Nabu save me') is mentioned only here. He may have arrived with Nebuzaradan during the month after the city wall was breached. He is given the title *rab-saris* (cf. v. 2). We are not certain that he was a replacement for the similarly entitled Nebo-Sarsekim in v. 3, but this seems likely as what is presented here is the group of high officials who are involved in setting up an administration in the newly captured city.

That they are said to take him 'out of the courtyard of the guard' is often felt to constitute a difficulty in comparison with 40:1 where Jeremiah is found by Nebuzaradan in chains among the captives at Ramah, five miles (8 km) north of the captured city. Three main types of explanation have been advanced for this. (1) The editor of this portion of Jeremiah's history had two conflicting accounts of what happened to the prophet after the capture of the city, and included them both. We cannot be sure which is right. This involves distancing the narratives from Jeremiah, and assuming the editor was not unduly worried by the conflicting statements. (2) It is proposed that the account in v. 14 is highly condensed. Jeremiah was released by Nebuzaradan only once, and that took place at Ramah. There was after all a month's delay between the breach of the city wall and the arrival of Nebuzaradan, and it is quite reasonable to suppose that during this

---

62. A monosyllable beginning with *resh* which unusually has a *dagesh euphoristicum* after the preceding stress (GKC §22s).

63. The kethibh has *kî ʿim*, 'but rather'; the qere has simply *kî*, the *ʿm* being unpointed (GKC §17b).

64. The repetition 'they sent' is resumptive in Hebrew because the list of names intervenes between the singular verb which is at the beginning of v. 13 and what follows here.

time the Babylonians had taken all the males from the city to a transit camp at Ramah, and that Jeremiah was taken along with them. The Babylonians took Jeremiah from the courtyard of the guard, but their action to release him was sometime later after his identity had been ascertained. (3) It is argued that Jeremiah was released twice. The phraseology of this verse, it is claimed, need only imply that on the first occasion his release from the courtyard of the guard was arranged at the highest levels of the Babylonian command. After this he was taken back into detention by some zealous Babylonians in the confused aftermath of the city's capture, and moved with other prisoners to Ramah. This scenario gains plausibility from the fact that Jeremiah decided to remain among his own people with a view to encouraging them (v. 14 end). When his detention came to the notice of the authorities, he was again released by Nebuzaradan. In favour of this view is the mention in 40:5 of Jeremiah going back to Gedaliah, as if he had already been with him.

As for the Babylonian officials, on his first release **they handed him over to Gedaliah son of Ahikam, the son of Shaphan, to take him back to his home.** Gedaliah (the name means 'the LORD is great') is not the same person as the Gedaliah mentioned in 38:1; rather this is the first mention of the individual whom the Babylonians made the native governor of the devastated province of Judah. He came from the third generation of an illustrious family whose history we can trace back to the time of Josiah. In Jehoiakim's reign his father had given protection to Jeremiah (26:24). We may presume that he was pro-Babylonian as a result of Jeremiah's influence, for his family had always been well-disposed towards the prophet. A seal impression from this period has been found at Lachish, inscribed, 'Belonging to Gedaliah, over the house', a term that was used for the chief administrative official of the king. If this did indeed belong to Gedaliah son of Ahikam, then he had occupied a high position in Zedekiah's government.

'Take ... back' renders the hiphil of $yāṣā^c$, which has the sense 'to take away', 'to lead off'. Having been placed under Gedaliah's custody, Jeremiah was led off by him 'to his home'/'to the house'. Since Gedaliah already appears to have official status in the Babylonian regime, it is unlikely that we are dealing with a building in Jerusalem. It is more probable this is the governor's residence which would have been situated at Mizpah. **So he remained among his own people** (another summary statement marking a distinct phase in Jeremiah's history; cf. 37:16) is unlikely to refer to Jerusalem, which at this stage was being emptied of its surviving inhabitants. The same

phrase is found in 40:6 where it clearly refers to residence at Mizpah.
The point is that Jeremiah identified with the ordinary people of the
land and did not accept any special favours from the Babylonians so
that there should be no doubt as to where his loyalty lay. For Jeremiah
to be released twice, it must be assumed that after staying in Mizpah,
the prophet's regard for the well-being of the people led him to move
about among them so that he subsequently became detained along with
some of them. However, the emphasis in the passage is on the freedom
that the Babylonians bestowed on him and their concern for his
welfare.

5. Ebed-Melech's Reward (39:15-18)

There then follows a section which is concerned with Ebed-Melech. It
is generally considered to be misplaced here in that in terms of
temporal sequence it follows 38:13. As a matter of chronology that is
correct in that the LORD's oracle to Ebed-Melech undoubtedly
followed soon after his rescue of Jeremiah, and certainly before the
city wall was breached. However, the placement of this oracle here is
not a matter of dislocation, but to effect a contrast with the fate of
Zedekiah. It is presented as another aspect of the way in which the
LORD worked even in the confusion of the captured city to ensure the
well-being of those who trusted in him. We are not told that Ebed-
Melech escaped, but that is the clear implication.

15. While[65] **Jeremiah had been confined in the courtyard of the
guard, the word of the LORD came to him** refers back to the time of
38:13. **Go and tell Ebed-Melech the Cushite, 'This is what the
LORD Almighty, the God of Israel, says: I am about to fulfil**[66]
(<√*bôʿ* hiphil, 'cause to come, bring to pass') **my words against this
city through disaster, not prosperity. At that time they will be
fulfilled before your eyes.'** There is sometimes felt to be difficulty
about 'Go and tell'. Could Jeremiah do this while in confinement? It
may just be a conventional prophetic formula (13:1; 19:1; 35:1), or else
since Ebed-Melech was a royal servant who would have access to the
area of the courtyard, when he came there, Jeremiah was to take the
initiative and approach him. The message Jeremiah brings begins with

---

65. The *waw*-disjunctive indicates here that the following section does not
follow chronologically on what has been described. It is included here for
thematic reasons to form a contrast with the experience of Zedekiah, and also
as a parallel to the experience of Jeremiah.

66. The kethibh is *mēbî*, with the *aleph* dropped as in 19:15, whereas the
aleph is supplied in the qere *mēbîʿ* (GKC §74k).

a summary of what he had been saying all along. The LORD had determined to bring on the city 'disaster' (*rāʿâ*, 'evil') and not 'prosperity' (*tôbâ*, 'good'), and Ebed-Melech will personally witness the catastrophe.

17. However, Jeremiah is to assure Ebed-Melech that he will be safe in the impending disaster. **But I will rescue** (<√*nāṣal* hiphil, 'to snatch away', 1:8) **you on that day, declares the LORD; you will not be handed over to those you fear.** Those of whom he is afraid are not the officials in Jerusalem. The time of capture of the city would not particularly expose him to their wrath; they would have quite enough on their hands. It rather refers to the Babylonians. It is probable that as a member of the king's household Ebed-Melech feared ('dread' <√*yāgar*, 22:25) for his life. What the LORD had promised to Jeremiah in 1:8 is here extended to Ebed-Melech.

18. However, Ebed-Melech can stop worrying 'for' (*kî*) the LORD assures him that he will protect him. **I will save you**/'I will surely deliver you' (NKJV) is an emphatic statement of the LORD's intention to save (<√*mālaṭ* piel, 'to bring into safety').[67] **You will not fall by the sword but will escape with your life, because you trust in me, declares the LORD.** It is not what he has done for Jeremiah that is made the basis of his deliverance, but rather this faith in the LORD. From this we can tell that throughout Ebed-Melech was motivated not just by humanitarian concerns for Jeremiah, but by his commitment to the LORD, foreigner though he was. For 'escape with your life' see on 21:9; 38:2. Ebed-Melech's readiness to risk his life for what he thought was right before God is rewarded by his deliverance (Mark 8:35). Jerusalem, Zedekiah and his officials had a misplaced confidence in their own ingenuity and political dexterity, and as a result they had been overwhelmed.

---

67. 'Save' is *mallēṭ* the piel infinitive absolute followed by the finite verb form *ʿămalleṭkā*, 'I will bring into safety'. The piel has a factitive sense (*NIDOTTE* #4880).

XIV. JEREMIAH AFTER THE FALL OF

JERUSALEM

(40:1–45:5)

OUTLINE

A. Gedaliah's Governorship (40:1–41:18)
    1. Jeremiah's Release (40:1-6)
    2. The Community at Mizpah (40:7-12)
    3. Unheeded Warnings (40:13-16)
    4. Gedaliah's Assassination (41:1-3)
    5. Ishmael's Treachery (41:4-10)
    6. Recovery and Flight (41:11-18)
B. Rejecting Prophetic Guidance (42:1–43:7)
    1. Request for Guidance (42:1-6)
    2. Guidance Given (42:7-18)
    3. Prophetic Exhortation (42:19-22)
    4. Guidance Spurned (43:1-7)
C. Ministry in Egypt (43:8–44:30)
    1. Preparations for Nebuchadnezzar (43:8-13)
    2. Dialogue with the Jews in Egypt (44:1-30)
D. A Word for Baruch (45:1-5)

What can possibly come after the end? Well, the fall of Jerusalem did not lead to Judah being totally evacuated. There were still people there—though not many—and the Babylonians set up an administration in the land, appointing Gedaliah as governor. Unfortunately these arrangements did not last, because Gedaliah was assassinated by his fellow countrymen (chaps. 40 and 41). The group which had gathered round Gedaliah then disregarded Jeremiah's advice and moved to Egypt, taking the prophet and Baruch along with them (42:1–43:7). The last record that we have of Jeremiah's life is of his ministry among the expatriate Jewish community in Egypt where despite all that had happened there was still no real willingness to listen to the prophet's word. This block of narrative concludes with a brief oracle addressed to Baruch promising that his life will be preserved (chap. 45).

A. GEDALIAH'S GOVERNORSHIP (40:1–41:18)

The timescale of Gedaliah's governorship is not made clear. It was probably a very brief affair which ended with his death in September/October 586 BC, just a few months after the fall of the city (cf. Holladay 1989, 2:287). However, it may be that he was in power for a longer period. The third deportation from the land listed in 52:30 occurred around 582 BC. If it is understood to be the result of Babylonian reprisals for the assassination of their appointed governor, then Gedaliah may have ruled for two or three years (Bright 1965:253-54; Thompson 1980:657). This provides additional time for the population movements mentioned in v. 11.

1. Jeremiah's Release (40:1-6)

1. The introductory sentence, **The word came to Jeremiah from the LORD after Nebuzaradan commander of the imperial guard had released him at Ramah,** lacks any corresponding divine oracle to Jeremiah. Indeed, there is no explicit divine word until 42:9. Some (e.g. Bright 1965:244 and Carroll 1986:698) have sought to reconstruct such an oracle from the seemingly Jeremianic words of Nebuzaradan in vv. 2-3, but that involves too great a rearrangement of the text to be acceptable. Others consider that Jeremiah finds a word from the LORD in what Nebuzaradan says to him in offering him his freedom (Keown et al. 1995:235; cf. 32:6-8). The most satisfactory understanding is that this heading corresponds to that in 1:1-3, which related to the period up to the capture of the city. This is then a title for the following section of the book, up to chapter 45, which is deliberately presented as a supplement to the main part of Jeremiah's ministry. 'Word' then does not indicate simply message, but history as well.

The remainder of the verse then sets out the historical setting of what is to follow. The details given amplify what has already been said about the favourable treatment the Babylonians extended to Jeremiah. For the problem of whether there were one or two releases of Jeremiah, see on 39:14. **He had found Jeremiah bound in chains**[1] **among all the captives from Jerusalem and Judah who were being carried into exile to Babylon.** The word rendered by the NIV 'found' (<√*lāqaḥ*) here and in v. 2 is generally understood as 'taken' (so NASB, NRSV, NKJV), on the understanding that Nebuzaradan was unaware of his identity at that stage when the population was being moved out of the captured city to a transit camp at Ramah where their future would be decided.

2-3. When the commander of the guard found Jeremiah,[2] **he said to him** fits in with a particular search being made for Jeremiah. The speech that follows is often felt incongruous to be on the lips of a heathen Babylonian. **The Lord your God decreed this disaster for this place. And now the Lord has brought it about; he has done just as he said he would.** The reason for the preceding statement is then given. **All this**[3] **happened**[4] **because (***kî***) you (plural) people**[5] **sinned against the Lord and did not obey** (<√*šāmaʿ*) **him.** It seems rather that the words are those of Jeremiah. Two factors may account for this. One is that heathen speakers are often presented with their words cast in the form that a Jewish speaker would have used. The thought is the foreigner's, but the expression is not. Here then there is no need to suppose that Nebuzaradan had become a worshipper of the Lord. The speech does not imply more than a polytheist's belief that

---

1. The kethibh is *baʿăziqqîm*, whereas in the qere *bāʿziqqîm* the same word is spelled with syncopation of the first syllable, though *aleph* is orthographically retained (GKC §35d; cf. v. 4). *ʿăziqqîm* occurs only in 40:1, 4 for chains used as handcuffs.

2. The use of *lǝ* before the object may be interpreted as evidence of Aramaic influence in the language (GKC §117n).

3. The kethibh has simply *dābār*, 'word', but the qere in view of the following demonstrative puts the article before the noun, *haddābār*, 'the word'.

4. It is difficult to account for *wǝhāyâ*, 'and it will happen', the perfect with *waw*-consecutive (GKC §112pp, qq).

5. 'People' is a NIV supplement to indicate that in the Hebrew this and the following verb are plural, referring to the nation as a whole, whereas 'your' in v. 2 and 'you' in the following verse are singular, referring to Jeremiah.

each nation had its patron deity.

On the other hand, there is ample evidence that the intelligence gathering and propaganda machines of foreign kings were very familiar with the thinking and outlook of the people they were attacking (2 Kgs. 17:24-28; 2 Kgs. 18:25; Ezra 1:3-4). It is not at all impossible, indeed it is highly likely, that Nebuzaradan had a very good knowledge of what Jeremiah had been saying, and could have presented a summary of it to him. But why should he have wanted to do so? One way of taking the words is to understand them as an apology for what had happened to Jeremiah, if indeed he had been rearrested after being initially freed. In terms of the presentation of the narrative, here is another instance of a foreigner (compare Ebed-Melech) having greater insight into the ways of the LORD than those who were ostensibly his people.

4. But (*wə'attâ hinnēh*, 'but now behold') moves the focus of the narrative from the general situation to Jeremiah's particular predicament. **Today I am freeing[6] you** (singular) **from the chains on your wrists.** Nebuzaradan acts in terms of the commission given him by Nebuchadnezzar. He frees Jeremiah and sets before him various courses of action from which he may make his choice. **Come with me to Babylon, if you like, and I will look after you.** For 'look after'/'set one's eye on', compare 39:12. It may well have enhanced Nebuzaradan's position at home to have been seen to act as patron to an influential pro-Babylonian prophet, whose words had come terribly true. **But if you do not want to, then don't come.[7] Look, the whole country lies before you; go wherever you please.** There was no compulsion on Jeremiah, and he was invited to settle in any part of the land he felt inclined to.

5. The beginning of v. 5 has been variously translated.[8] The phrase

---

6. GKC §106m consider that the perfect is used here to represent the action as accomplished, while *IBHS* §30.5.1e suggest a perfect of resolve, in which the speaker announces his intention to do something, but it might equally be a performative perfect, 'I ⌊hereby⌋ free you'.

7. <√ḥādal, 'to end, stop', but used here in the sense 'leave off', that is, do not even start the journey.

8. The Massoretic Text is obscure. *wə'ôdennû lō'-yāšûb wəšûbâ* seems to mean, 'and he was still not turning. And turn!'. The early versions seem to have had the same Hebrew text and attempted to make sense of it as best they could. Another alternative to the approaches mentioned is to translate 'before Jeremiah could answer' (REB, NIV margin), reading a hiphil *yāšîb*, 'he could make to return ⌊an answer⌋'.

seems to indicate the circumstances under which Nebuzaradan spoke, and might be translated either 'And while he had not yet gone back', or **However, before Jeremiah turned to go**. It would seem as if Nebuzaradan gave him an opportunity to consider the proposals put before him, and then **Nebuzaradan added, 'Go back** ($<\sqrt{šûb}$, 'to return') **to Gedaliah son of Ahikam, the son of Shaphan, whom the king of Babylon has appointed over the towns of Judah, and live with him among the people, or go anywhere else you please.'** Nebuzaradan does not so much put forward a third proposal in mentioning Gedaliah, as give a specific instance of what might be involved in staying in the land. Presumably there was some measure of security in being with Gedaliah, and it would serve Babylonian interests to have there one who had been so well disposed towards them in the past. The towns of Judah had been devastated, but the phrase is still used to indicate the extent of Gedaliah's rule. **Then the commander gave him provisions and a present and let him go.** It is not clear what constituted the 'provisions and a present'. It may just have been an hospitable gesture for the journey,[9] but the same word is used later for the allowance given to Jehoiachin (52:34), and it may indicate that ongoing provision was made for Jeremiah's upkeep at the governor's house. It was certainly a display of favour towards the prophet.

6. So Jeremiah went to Gedaliah son of Ahikam at Mizpah and stayed with him among the people who were left behind in the land. Again (cf. 39:14) the note is struck of Jeremiah among the people. Mizpah, with the article, means 'the watchtower', and was the name of six or seven sites. In this instance it has usually been located at Nebi Ṣamwil, five miles (8 km) north-west of Jerusalem (cf. Holladay 1989, 2:294-95), though more recently scholars have argued for Tell en-Naṣbeh, a site in Benjamite territory eight miles (13 km) north of Jerusalem, in a strategic position on the road north from Jerusalem. Here, unlike most sites of this period, no evidence of devastation has been found. The town became the centre for the community which remained in the land as they sought to build a future for themselves.

Jeremiah's decision to stay enables us to put into perspective his earlier advice to yield to the Babylonians. He was not simply arguing acquiescence in the political realities of the day because Babylon's power was invincible and any other policy was doomed to frustration. His desire

---

9. Earlier derivations suggested *'ăruḥâ* $<\sqrt{'ārah}$, 'to be on the road', and so a 'travelling allowance', but it is now argued that the word refers to one's daily meal (*NIDOTTE* 1:513; cf. 52:33-34).

was to see the good of his people advanced by their acknowledging the LORD's interest in them and provision for them. Even though in chapter 24 he had predicted that the future of the people lay with those who were deported to Babylon and not those who were left in the land, because the need of the community left behind was greater, he recognised that he still had a ministry towards them and opted to stay with them. Jeremiah was not motivated by personal ease or ambition but by a desire to see the LORD's cause advanced among his people.

2. The Community at Mizpah (40:7-12)

There is no further mention of Jeremiah until chapter 42. Instead there is a section which focuses on the community who were left in Judah by the Babylonians as they tried to adjust to the trauma of their changed circumstances. At first there seemed to be an emerging unity round the figure of Gedaliah, who attempted to bring the various groups together. The prospect facing them was dire. Their land would have been looted by their conquerors and everything of value removed. The economic and social fabric of the land was utterly disrupted. Many cities, like Jerusalem, were reduced to rubble, and others survived at subsistence level. Indeed the massive death toll caused by fighting, disease and famine meant that there were fewer demands being made on their diminished resources. There was a measure of prosperity (v. 12) but from a much depleted agricultural base. The scene portrayed is clearly one where survival of the people depended on coming together under an acceptance of the Babylonian regime and recognising that life would be a struggle.

7. The narrative of vv. 7-9 gives more detail than the account in 2 Kgs. 25:22-24, with which it shares a number of expressions. **When all the army officers and their men who were still in the open country** refers to the groups of soldiers who had not been in Jerusalem during the final siege and who had hidden in remote areas of Judah, presumably harassing the Babylonians as much as possible. For 'open country' (*śadeh*) see on 17:3. When they **heard that** (*kî*) **the king of Babylon had appointed Gedaliah son of Ahikam as governor over the land and had put him in charge of the men, women and children who were the poorest in the land and who had not been carried into exile to Babylon**, they responded favourably to this turn of events. Gedaliah was someone whom they knew personally, and it was part of the wisdom of the Babylonians at this juncture that they had installed a native governor rather than one of their own number. Gedaliah's precise title is not given: 'had appointed … as governor'

renders the hiphil of *pāqad*, which does specify his precise role. Miller
and Hayes (1986:423) speculate that he was made king, replacing
Zedekiah on the throne (cf. 41:1, 10), but that this title is not used here
or in Kings because it was not acknowledged by the Jews on the
grounds that Gedaliah was not of Davidic descent.

The land was very unsettled after the recent turmoil of invasion and
occupation, and the Babylonians tried to provide a measure of stability
for the area. They did not want to have an unoccupied zone which it
would have been easy for Egypt to move into, nor did they want any
further insurgency—a fact which might have led them to appoint
someone not related to previous rulers of Judah who had proved
troublesome. By giving land to people of the poorer classes (39:10) the
Babylonians were trying to keep some population in the area, and
furthermore resumption of farming would have assisted logistic
problems if ever their troops had to move south against Egypt. So the
situation was not the same as that which had prevailed in the northern
kingdom after its defeat, when the Assyrians introduced colonists into
the area. Local people were left in charge with a measure of self-
reliance.

8. The soldiers who had been in the field were willing to talk, and
they came to Gedaliah at Mizpah—Ishmael son of Nethaniah.
According to 41:1, Ishmael was a grandson of Elishama, and so of
royal descent. **Johanan and Jonathan the sons of Kareah**. Johanan
plays a significant role in the following narrative as one who is suspicious of Ishmael, and who later leads the group into Egypt. **Seraiah
son of Tanhumeth** is otherwise unknown, while **the sons of Ephai**[10]
the Netophathite would have come from Netophah, which may have
been 3½ miles (5½ km) south-east of Bethlehem. **Jaazaniah**[11] **the son
of the Maacathite** (Maachah was a district in Syria, south-east of
Hermon, what is now known as the Golan Heights), **and their men.**
An agate seal found in a tomb at Mizpah bore the inscription, 'belonging to Jaazaniah the servant of the king', and may refer to this
individual. The guerrilla forces gather with Gedaliah to see what their
future might hold.

**9. Gedaliah son of Ahikam, the son of Shaphan, took an oath to
reassure them and their men. 'Do not be afraid to serve the
Babylonians,' he said.** It would seem that their main worry was over

10. The kethibh is *'ôpay*, Ophai; the qere is *'êpay*, Ephai. Versions differ in
which spelling they prefer.

11. What is found here is Jezaniah, a contracted form of the name Jaazaniah,
used in full in 2 Kgs. 25:23.

Babylonian reprisals against them for their activities. If they were to come into the open, would it not be inviting arrest and deportation for themselves? Gedaliah urges them to copy what he himself had done in recognising the new state of affairs, and trying to make the best of it. It is probable that over the previous years Gedaliah had been a member of the (minority) group at court who had been arguing in favour of reaching a settlement with the Babylonians. The terms of Gedaliah's oath are not stated; presumably he gave a solemn commitment to act as their guardian and to ensure that they came to no harm. In this way Gedaliah sought to ease tensions within the residual community in the land. **Settle down in the land and serve the king of Babylon, and it will go well with you**. This commitment was designed as the basis for all parties to live together in the land. The NLT rendering, 'Stay here', is misleading. As the next verse makes clear, Gedaliah was not proposing that they remain with him at Mizpah, but that they occupy part of Judah.

10. The pronouns which begin the two parts of the verse (*waʿănî* ... *wəʿattem*, 'and I ⌊for my part⌋ ... and you ⌊for your part⌋') set out the two sides to the bargain that Gedaliah is proposing. He is presented as a responsible figure, trying to balance the need to keep the Babylonians from taking any further action and the need to have the respect and authority among his own people that would enable him to function effectively as governor. **I myself will stay at Mizpah to represent you before the Babylonians who come to us.** 'Represent you before' is literally 'stand before' ('you' is a translator's supplement), an expression that is related to being in a superior's presence (15:1) and that may also signify presentation of a request (Gen. 18:22). Gedaliah obviously envisaged a time when the Babylonian army had left the land, and officials came from Nebuchadnezzar to check up on what was happening. He undertook to neutralise any future trouble with officialdom over these groups who had come out of hiding by acting as an intermediary on their behalf. Although appointed by the Babylonians, he will not simply act as they direct.

In the meantime the people were to be active. The economy of the country needed to be revived. **But you are to harvest the wine, summer fruit and oil, and put them in your storage jars, and live in the towns you have taken over.** These crops ('summer fruit' would include items such as dates and figs) are those that would have grown with little attention during the time that the army was encamped in the land. In the aftermath of the city's fall, the groups who have returned are to gather as much as they can so as to tide them over the winter.

Jerusalem fell in the fifth month, and was burned in the sixth month. It was at the same time that these fruits would have been ripening (July/August). The towns had been devastated by the Babylonians, but now the enemy forces had left, there would be no difficulty in groups of men finding places to stay in the ruins and making them the centre of their operations. Though *tāpaś*, 'to take hold of, seize', can be used of violent seizure, that is unlikely here. There was no one left to resist in the towns devastated by the Babylonians. With a bit of work the remaining population could provide sufficient food for themselves. What is more, these products were items of trade with any surplus being available for barter for other commodities.

11-12. There were also groups of refugees returning from further afield. **When all the Jews in Moab, Ammon, Edom and all the other countries heard that (*kî*) the king of Babylon had left a remnant in Judah and had appointed Gedaliah son of Ahikam, the son of Shaphan, as governor over them, they all came back to the land of Judah from all the countries where they had been scattered.** This would have occurred over a number of months as groups who had fled before the Babylonian army accepted the regime under Gedaliah and returned to Judah. They too were able to make provision for themselves by gathering in what had grown untended in the land. **And they harvested an abundance of wine and summer fruit.** It is being made clear that the group gathered round Gedaliah was not going to suffer hardship in the following period. Along with the number of those who returned, the scene that is pictured is one of potential for building up a significant community centred round Mizpah, though under Babylonian hegemony. But that possibility was soon to be tragically disrupted.

3. Unheeded Warnings (40:13-16)

It is difficult to know when the following warnings came to Gedaliah. The time hint in 41:1 does not mention a year. Some suggest that this was all played out in the immediate aftermath of the fall of Jerusalem. Others think that several years have passed, and the assassination of the Babylonian Governor of Judah is what precipitated the further deportation to Babylon mentioned in 52:30 as occurring in 582 BC.

In terms of the narrative the significant point is that the new ruler of the people who at first displayed prudence and sagacity is shown to have character defects as well: he did not give due weight to well-intentioned (and accurate) warnings. Like Zedekiah who did not listen to the warnings of the prophet Jeremiah, Gedaliah does not listen to the warnings of his own officers.

13. Johanan son of Kareah and all the army officers still in the open country came to Gedaliah at Mizpah. Johanan was loyal to Gedaliah, and eventually succeeded him. The description of these forces as being 'in the open field' may be either to distinguish them as a group from the returned refugees mentioned in v. 11-12, or it may be that they were 'still' (an NIV interpretative addition) in the open country, not having yet taken the opportunity to settle down as Gedaliah had suggested in v. 10.

14. They tell Gedaliah of the threat to his life. Indeed they are surprised that he has not already heard about it. **And said to him, 'Don't you know**[12] **that** (*kî*) **Baalis king of the Ammonites has sent Ishmael son of Nethaniah to take your life?'** (<*nepeš*, 2:34). The name and status of Baalis are now attested by a clay seal that has been found. He may have been perpetuating Ammonite hostility against Babylon, and so against Gedaliah who had accepted governorship under them. Ammon had participated in the war conference earlier (27:3), and it seems to have revolted against Babylon at the same time as Judah, although Nebuchadnezzar had turned his attention to Judah. It may be that when Zedekiah escaped from Jerusalem, it was Ammon he was making for. Ishmael was of the royal blood (41:1), and possibly viewed Gedaliah as a quisling whom he wished to kill because of his collaboration with the enemy forces. There may, however, be a more personal note also, in that he, one of the royal family, had been passed over in favour of Gedaliah whom he viewed as an upstart. That may explain his action when he took Zedekiah's daughters away with him (41:10).

Though he had been warned, Gedaliah was not prepared to accept the truth of the report that was brought to him. Perhaps he had rejected such reports already, and his attitude does not change on hearing it again. **But Gedaliah son of Ahikam did not believe them.** He himself was a man of unquestioned sincerity, and he was not prepared to entertain doubts about the position of others. He accepted Ishmael's commitment to work towards bettering conditions in the land under Babylon, and wished to rise above the factionalism that had so marred the situation in Jerusalem in previous years.

15. There then followed a secret approach from Johanan to try to get

---

12. In *hăyādōʿ tēdaʿ*, the interrogative particle with the infinitive absolute comes before the finite verb and so conveys a note of surprise at his seeming ignorance.

Gedaliah to grasp the seriousness of the situation that had to be faced. **Then Johanan son of Kareah said privately to Gedaliah in Mizpah, 'Let me go and kill[13] Ishmael son of Nethaniah, and no one will know it. Why should he take your life** (cf. v. 14) **and cause all the Jews who are gathered around you to be scattered and the remnant of Judah to perish?'** Johanan had obviously a very clear understanding of what would be likely to follow the assassination of the Babylonian appointed governor: reprisals from Nebuchadnezzar on a massive scale. In the face of this the community would be dispersed and what they had been trying to build up would be lost. Survival required that the remaining community stayed together. The rhetorical question introduces a reason why action should be taken, and Johanan is in no doubt that a pre-emptive strike is the best way to dispose of the very real threat that has been posed.

16. But Gedaliah son of Ahikam said to Johanan son of Kareah, 'Don't do[14] such a thing!' He gave as his reason, 'for' (*kî*) **what you are saying about Ishmael is not true.** It may well be that Gedaliah's response of horror to Johanan's proposal of anticipatory counter-assassination was the correct one, but he refused to countenance Johanan's information, saying bluntly of it 'a lie!' (*šeqer*, 5:2). No doubt many rumours were circulating in those unsettled times, but it would have been prudent to take some action.

4. Gedaliah's Assassination (41:1-3)

1. The narrative here and also in 2 Kgs. 25:25 does not specify which year is referred to by **in the seventh month** (Tishri, September/October), but there is no indication of any gap so that these incidents may well have occurred within two months after the destruction of the city in early August 586 BC, and are part of the upheaval in the land at that time. Indeed Jewish tradition dates Gedaliah's assassination to this period and claims that the fasts of the seventh month mentioned in Zech. 7:5 and 8:19 (they were held on the third of Tishri, after the two-day celebration of the religious new year) were in commemoration of this event (cf. 52:4). An alternative date one year later would allow for the return of the various groups that are mentioned, while a date up to

---

13. Where a clause is introduced by ordinary *waw* and the prefix conjugation after a volitional form in the preceding clause, the second clause expresses purpose or a result, 'Let me go to slay'. This construction is often difficult to distinguish from two successive volitional forms (*IBHS* §39.2.2a).

14. The qere unnecessarily changes the kethibh *ʿal-taʿaś* into *ʿal-taʿăśēh*, probably to avoid hiatus before the following *aleph* (GKC §75hh) (cf. 39:12).

five years later would provide a plausible scenario for the additional deportation that is mentioned in 52:30. But the evidence that exists seems very much to support the idea of the same year. Gedaliah's governorship is thus a brief interlude that is brought to a sudden end by the treachery of Ishmael. This outcome provided a definitive answer to the question whether the community in Judah that had submitted to Nebuchadnezzar constituted the way forward for the people.

Ishmael son of Nethaniah, the son of Elishama, who was of royal blood and had been one of the king's officers[15] is a puzzling figure whose motivation is obscure. In many ways he seems to be the prototype of the amoral modern terrorist for whom the cause for which he is fighting has largely receded into the background and who derives his satisfaction from increasingly violent and attention-grabbing atrocities. Ishmael was quite prepared to act as an agent of the Ammonites, but his conduct at times seems both cunning and irrational. It appears he still entertained the notion that the power of Babylon might be thwarted, and perhaps also that he could head the re-establishment of the Davidic line in Jerusalem. Mention of his being of the royal household may also suggest that because of the cruelty shown to Zedekiah and his household, who would have been Ishmael's distant relatives, he might have been intent on revenge against Babylon and all who were siding with it, and it perhaps indicates in addition an element of jealousy against Gedaliah whom he would have viewed as an upstart. It is unclear who Elishama was. He is either the figure mentioned in 36:12, or the son of David (2 Sam. 5:6; 1 Chron. 3:8; 14:7), so that Ishmael was of a collateral line. It seems more likely to be the former, and Ishmael is one of the offspring of the numerous polygamous marriages of the kings.

He came with ten men to Gedaliah son of Ahikam at Mizpah. Gedaliah had been warned about his intentions (40:13-16), but he was not prepared to act on the basis of rumour, and assumed that all were as well-intentioned as he himself was in their attempts to salvage something out of the ruins of Judah. Gedaliah would, of course, have been personally acquainted with Ishmael from earlier times when they would both have been active in court circles in Jerusalem. Equally, in

---

15. The Hebrew is 'and the chief officers of the king', but it is reasonable to take *min* as understood before the phrase. The word *rab* is used elsewhere only of Babylonian officers. The phrase is omitted in the corresponding passage in 2 Kgs. 25:25 and the LXX. Hayes and Miller (1986:423) speculate that Ishmael was an officer under Gedaliah as king and under whose authority he had placed himself.

Gedaliah's attempts to bring coherence to what was happening in the country, it was essential for him to be on good relations with the guerrilla chiefs who had begun to resettle in the land. As a preliminary to the delicate negotiations that were to take place between them, Gedaliah entertains Ishmael hospitably: **while they were eating together there.** The oriental view of the bonds of friendship created by participation in a common meal was such that Ishmael's treachery is intensified by the form it took.

2. Ishmael son of Nethaniah and the ten men who were with him got up and struck down Gedaliah son of Ahikam, the son of Shaphan, with the sword. 'Got up' and also the following 'struck' and 'killed' are all singular verbs, emphasising the initiative and leadership of Ishmael in the matter. The others were simply his henchmen in this act of perfidy against their unsuspecting host. But its repercussions went further than murder and a breach of hospitality. **Killing the one whom the king of Babylon had appointed as governor over the land** points to the political implications of the assassination as a setback to Nebuchadnezzar's hopes that Judah would return to some level of normality. Babylonian reprisals could now be anticipated. Ishmael had achieved his objective of destabilising the country, and that was very much what the Ammonites also wanted, as they had eyes on Judah's territory.

3. Ishmael also killed all the Jews who were with Gedaliah at Mizpah. His actions went beyond the assassination of Gedaliah to include others. At first sight those referred to seem to include all the population of Mizpah that had gathered round the governor, but since v. 10 mentions 'the rest of the people who were in Mizpah', the reference here is probably to the establishment that Gedaliah kept with him in his official residence, or to his guests at that particular meal. It would not have been an impossible feat for eleven men to have killed the Jewish officials who constituted Gedaliah's presumably quite modest entourage. Though these men might have been more suspicious than Gedaliah himself, it is unlikely that they would have anticipated the outrage that occurred and were probably unable to do much to rally round Gedaliah. Ishmael killed them **as well as the Babylonian soldiers who were there,** presumably a small contingent allocated to Gedaliah to act as his personal bodyguard. Ishmael and his men had obviously given some forethought to the way in which they could overcome them. We do not know where Jeremiah was while this was going on (he next appears in 42:2). Certainly he was not at the official residence because his well-known attitude towards Babylon would have made him a prime target for Ishmael who was motivated by anti-Babylonian sentiment.

5. Ishmael's Treachery (41:4-10)

4. The day after Gedaliah's assassination, before anyone knew about it, a puzzling incident occurs. Obviously word of what had happened had not got out of Mizpah; indeed it may be that even in the town itself the treachery at the governor's residence was not yet known about.

5. But Mizpah, 'the Watchtower', was well situated to let Ishmael know in advance that a body of men was approaching. **Eighty men who had shaved off[16] their beards, torn their clothes and cut themselves came from Shechem, Shiloh and Samaria, bringing grain offerings and incense with them to the house of the LORD.** Shechem was forty-five miles (72 km) north of Jerusalem and was a major city in a key mountain pass in the centre of the former northern kingdom. Shiloh was nineteen miles (31 km) north-east of Jerusalem, midway between Bethel and Shechem. The site had never recovered from its devastation centuries earlier, and is perhaps mentioned here because of its previous status as a religious centre (7:12).[17] Samaria, seven miles (11 km) north-west of Shechem and forty-two miles (67½ km) from Jerusalem, had been the strategically located capital of the northern kingdom. Though the term may be used of the area surrounding the city, that is less likely here in combination with the names of two settlements. This substantial group of pilgrims represents those who had remained loyal to the LORD in the north, particularly after Josiah's reformation when shrines there were destroyed and worshippers were directed to the Jerusalem Temple. Even though that had now been razed, this group did not revert to the earlier practices of the north.

The seventh month (v. 1) was the beginning of the religious year, and during it fell both the Day of Atonement and the Feast of Tabernacles, so that pilgrims going to the Temple would be not unexpected. Things had of course changed from the old days. The dress of the pilgrims suggests that they had taken a special vow, or that they were mourners. Indeed, it may be that their vow was connected with the fall of the city. Hair was normally considered a sign of strength and

---

16. 'Shaved' and 'torn' are passive participles in the construct, 'shaved ones ⌐with respect to⌐ beard and torn ones ⌐with respect to⌐ clothes' (GKC §116k).

17. The LXX reads Salem instead of Shiloh, and this fits in better with the order in which the names are listed. Salem was possibly a site near Shechem (Gen. 33:18, NIV margin).

dignity, but when shorn, it became an emblem of shame and devastation (48:37; Isa. 7:20; 15:2). Cutting oneself as a sign of mourning was a heathen practice that was forbidden in the law (cf. 16:6), but even so seems to have been practised to some considerable extent. While the word that the NIV renders 'grain offerings' can also be used to signify sacrificial gifts in general, it seems probable that what is indicated here is that they were going with non-bloody sacrifices to the site of the now ruined Temple, to maintain some semblance of the worship that had been previously found there. It is not necessary to assume that another (temporary) temple with a burnt offering altar (and possibly an incense altar) had been erected, or that the house of the LORD refers to a sanctuary at Mizpah itself (*ABD*, 4:880).

6. Ishmael son of Nethaniah went out from Mizpah to meet them, weeping as he went.[18] The fact that Ishmael too adopts a posture of weeping shows that he knew something about the party before he approached them. It was not the case that he was dealing with, say, a Babylonian detachment that constituted a threat to him, but with a group whom he can put at ease by subterfuge. By getting them off their guard, he perhaps hoped to lead them into a situation where they would be more vulnerable to attack by his own much smaller group of men. **When he met them, he said, 'Come to Gedaliah son of Ahikam.'** Ishmael assumes that the pilgrims know about Gedaliah's appointment as governor, and goes further in his deception of these men by issuing them an invitation they could not refuse, though paying their respects to the governor may have been their intention anyhow. Some sort of ambush would no doubt have been necessary to overcome the group, but the motive behind their murder is unclear. Had he wished to, he might easily have concocted a cover story to explain Gedaliah's absence. It may be that he wanted to commit an atrocity of such a magnitude that the Babylonians had to take some action, so that the land would experience even more upheaval. The slaughter of the pilgrims would certainly seem to indicate that Ishmael was not acting out of any misplaced respect for the true traditions of Judah, but more like one consumed by bloodlust.

7. When they went into the city, Ishmael son of Nethaniah and the men who were with him slaughtered[19] **them and threw**

---

18. Note Hebrew idiom 'going and weeping', here the infinitive absolute of *hālak* followed by a participle rather than a second infinitive (GKC §113n).

19. Again the Hebrew verb is singular, to denote the initiative and responsibility belonged to Ishmael.

them[20] **into a cistern.** The cistern (*bôr*, 2:13; 37:16) was a large underground reservoir for water. Its history is further outlined in v. 9. It was a suitable place for dumping corpses that one did not wish easily found. The pollution of the water supply would also render Mizpah more difficult for others to inhabit.

8. There is then a digression which tells of how some of the pilgrims escaped the fate of the majority. **But ten of them said**[21] **to Ishmael, 'Don't kill us!** 'For' (*kî*) **we have wheat and barley, oil and honey, hidden in a field.'** These men bargained with Ishmael when they saw what was about to happen to them. They owned a variety of produce. Wheat and barley were the two main grain crops in Palestine, and they would have been in short supply in the south after the Babylonian army had occupied the land for three harvests. Oil (olive oil) and honey (a basic source of sweetening) were both much appreciated commodities. But where were these provisions stored? It was common in Palestine to preserve grain and foodstuffs in underground storage chambers, which often had concealed entrances to prevent theft. But pilgrims would not have such sites at their disposal as they travelled, and so the reference must be either to stores they had at home or to a temporary cache they had made as they travelled south. The latter seems more probable and may provide an indication of the unsettled state of the land after the withdrawal of the Babylonian forces. At any rate, whatever the location of these stores, by appealing to Ishmael's self-interest, these men succeeded in negotiating their survival. **So he let them alone and did not kill them with the others.**

9. Additional information is provided to bring out the horrific barbarity of the action perpetrated by Ishmael. **Now the cistern where he threw all the bodies of the men he had killed along with**[22] **Gedaliah was the one King Asa had made as part of his defence**

---

20. 'And threw them' is a supplement, which may be implied by the terse Hebrew 'into the inside of the cistern', a pregnant construction (GKC §119gg). The slaughtering could hardly have taken place in the cistern.

21. 'But ten men were found among them and they said ...' (cf. NASB, NKJV). 'Were found' might imply in English that a search was made. The Hebrew idiom merely implies that they happened to be present.

22. The use here of *bəyad*, 'at hand of'/'by the hand of', is obscure. It seems to mean 'at the side of', or perhaps with reference to the subterfuge used in v. 6, 'by means of Gedaliah' (cf. Job 15:23). The NRSV and REB follow the LXX to read 'the great cistern', from a supposed original *bôr gādôl hûʿ*, instead of *bəyad gədalyāhû hûʿ*.

against[23] **Baasha king of Israel.** The phrase 'along with (*bəyad*)
Gedaliah' is a puzzling one. It may indicate 'at the side of' Gedaliah,
that is, next to where his corpse lay, or it could also be translated
'because of Gedaliah' (NASB), and would then indicate that all these
actions were because of his collaboration and their countenancing of
it.[24] There is no other biblical information about the construction of
this cistern, but we do know that Asa had undertaken considerable
defensive building at the site (1 Kgs. 15:22; 2 Chron. 16:6), and ensuring a water supply in the event of siege would have been a standard
part of such military works. This information would then indicate the
size of the cistern, by way of its being able to hold perhaps over a
hundred corpses. The particular cistern referred to in the text has not
been identified, though numerous cisterns have been found at the more
northerly site argued for as the location of Mizpah (Tell en-Naṣbeh, cf.
40:6). The traditional more southerly site has not yet been excavated.
Ishmael son of Nethaniah filled it with the dead. This is probably
intended to bring out a contrast with the defensive nature of Asa's
work, and the fraternal blood letting associated with Ishmael.

**10. Ishmael made captives of all the rest of the people who were in
Mizpah.** This assumes that the slaughter of v. 3 was limited to those in
the governor's palace. There were others who had take up residence in
the town itself or on farms close by. Presumably these people would
have been without arms and so were not in a position to resist
Ishmael's relatively small band of determined men. There were some
notable persons who had been entrusted to Gedaliah, whom Ishmael
might be able to use as hostages. **The king's daughters** may well not
refer to Zedekiah's own daughters. It is unlikely that they would have
been left behind by the Babylonians, especially when it had been
predicted that the king's wives and children/sons would be captured
(38:23). It may therefore here be a general description of women born
to the royal family as a whole (cf. 36:26). That the Babylonians
entrusted these women to Gedaliah indicates the status they accorded
him as continuing the royal line of Judah (and their capture by Ishmael
would indicate his pretensions in the matter). Alternatively, Hayes and
Miller suppose that the king referred to is Gedaliah who had been
appointed by Nebuchadnezzar to succeed Zedekiah, but whose regal
status was never recognised by the Jews because he was not of Davidic

---

23. 'As part of his defence against' renders the Hebrew *mippənê*, 'from the
face of, because of'.
24. Many modern versions follow the LXX in reading *bôr gādôl hûʿ*, 'it was
a large well', in place of *bəyad-gədalyāhû hûʿ* (cf. BHS).

descent (1986:423). **Along with all the others who were left there, over whom Nebuzaradan commander of the imperial guard had appointed** (<√*pāqad*) **Gedaliah son of Ahikam**, these people were now kidnapped and forced to leave the city. We note the absence of any mention of Jeremiah or Baruch, but this may not be significant as there were other figures obviously not in Mizpah at that time either, such as Johanan. But those who were there were led off by Ishmael back to his sponsor. **Ishmael son of Nethaniah took them captive and set out to cross over to the Ammonites.** 'Cross over' (*'ābar 'el*) is also used of rejecting one regime and aligning oneself with an opposing party (1 Sam. 27:2).

6. Recovery and Flight (41:11-18)

11-12. Ishmael's success was short lived. Someone may have escaped, or events may have been observed from a distance. At any rate we are told that **when Johanan son of Kareah and all the army officers who**[25] **were with him heard about all the crimes** (*rā'â*, 'evil') **Ishmael son of Nethaniah had committed**, they took appropriate countermeasures. It is interesting to speculate why Johanan had not been present, but presumably Ishmael had been waiting a favourable opportunity for putting his plan into action, and that would have been provided by Johanan's absence. He and the group of officers with him **took all their men and went to fight Ishmael son of Nethaniah. They caught up with him near**[26] **the great pool** (literally, 'many waters') **in Gibeon.** This great pool is presumably the same one mentioned in 2 Sam. 2:13 as the scene of a skirmish between David's men and Ishbosheth's supporters. At that site (el-Jib) there has been excavated a cistern hewn to a depth of over 80 feet (24 m) into the rock with steps to provide access to the stored water. Gibeon's situation, six miles (9½ km) north-west of Jerusalem, makes it much more likely that the site of Mizpah is the southerly one, otherwise Ishmael in trying to go to Ammon (v. 10) had actually travelled south-west rather than east (cf. Holladay 1989, 2:294). However, his direction of travel may not have been dictated by the available routes to Ammon so much as by prevailing circumstances, and especially his knowledge of where Johanan and his men were. That Ishmael did not manage to go far indicates that Johanan and his detachment had been close to Mizpah.

---

25. It is not clear whether 'who were with him' refers to the officers or to the forces (so NKJV). 'That were with him' (NASB) and 'with him' (NRSV) avoid making a choice. The difference is not significant.

26. *'el* in a locative sense, 'at, by, near' (*IBHS* §11.2.2a; GKC §119g).

13-15. When all the people Ishmael had with him saw Johanan son of Kareah and all the army officers who were with him, they were glad. This reaction of joy indicates that the lack of support for Ishmael's policy, quite apart from relief at escape from further atrocities. The people with Ishmael presumably excludes his own men. Those whom he had taken captive do not appear to have experienced any effective constraint on their movement. They had been hustled unwillingly away from Mizpah and now that the arrival of a large party of rescuers led Ishmael to think of his own safety, he was unable to detain them any longer. **All the people Ishmael had taken captive at Mizpah turned and went over to Johanan son of Kareah.** There may have been some fighting, for we then note that as Ishmael makes his escape he has two fewer men than before. **But Ishmael son of Nethaniah and eight men of his men escaped from Johanan and fled to the Ammonites.** It is not implied that Ishmael was in Johanan's power, but that he escaped being captured by him. We know no more about Ishmael's career. His mission had not been a total success, but it had achieved its primary objective in wrecking the possibility of there being set up in Judah an administration under Babylonian oversight which would have been able to restore a semblance of normality to the land.

16. Gedaliah's death left Johanan in charge of the group of survivors so that he had to face the challenge of what to do next. **Then Johanan son of Kareah and all the army officers who were with him led away all the survivors from Mizpah whom he had recovered from Ishmael son of Nethaniah after he had assassinated Gedaliah son of Ahikam.** Presumably the first move was from Gibeon back to Mizpah. Then having gathered possessions and provisions they moved south. The list of those involved is given as **the soldiers,**[27] **women, children and court officials he had brought from Gibeon.** It is difficult to see how soldiers were involved in those rescued. Presumably the men in that group were unable to offer resistance. The women would have include the king's daughters. Children refers to very young children: toddlers (*tap*). 'Court officials' (*sāris*, 38:7) were presumably not those of Zedekiah's court in Jerusalem, but those who

---

27. Most translations are similar to the NIV and assume there is only one group referred to, e.g. 'the mighty men of war' (NKJV), 'the men who were soldiers' (NASB), though the REB has two groups, 'men, both armed and unarmed'. The Hebrew is 'men, the men of war'. Perhaps the last phrase is a gloss that has crept into the text from a misunderstood *gəbārîm* ('men', MT) taken as *gibbôrîm*, 'warriors'.

had acted as officials in Mizpah. It may even be that the word retains its root significance here of eunuchs, and these were men the keepers of the harem, there to protect the 'king's daughters' (v. 10).

17-18. The small band moved south to territory outside Babylonian influence. **And they went on, stopping at Geruth Kimham**[28] **near Bethlehem on their way to Egypt.** A temporary resting place is found outside Bethlehem, six miles (9½ km) south-west of Jerusalem. Geruth Kimham, or Chimham, may mean the lodging place[29] of Chimham (its site is unknown), who may be the same person as the son of Barzillai who received land near Bethlehem from David (2 Sam. 19:37). They had left the immediate area of the slaughter, but were still uncertain as to what they should do in future. Their dominant emotion was that of fear, and their objective was clear, **to escape the Babylonians.** 'For' (*kî*) **they were afraid of them because** (*kî*) **Ishmael son of Nethaniah had killed Gedaliah son of Ahikam, whom the king of Babylon had appointed as governor over the land.** They entertained no doubts as to what Babylonian policy would be towards a conquered people that had assassinated the local ruler Babylon had installed.

B. REJECTING PROPHETIC GUIDANCE (42:1–43:7)

The survivors of the massacre at Mizpah were bewildered by the turn of events and were uncertain as to what their future held, but they began to move south towards Egypt, that is, away from the Babylonians. As they travelled, they approached Jeremiah to request divine guidance as regards what they should do (vv. 1-6). After ten days the LORD revealed how he would act compassionately towards them if they remained in the land (vv. 7-18). This was a test of their faith, because staying there risked Babylonian reprisals and represented a willingness to venture their lives on the effectiveness of divine protection. If they refused to accede to the LORD's directions, calamity would follow them. Despite Jeremiah's exhortation to trust the LORD (vv. 19-22), the leaders of the group suspected the prophet's motives and continued to lead the people to Egypt (43:1-7). These survivors thus failed the testing of their faith, and so the community in Egypt did not represent the way forwards towards restoration.

---

28. Many manuscripts read with the qere *kimhām*. The kethibh, *kmwhm*, is impenetrable because of the long vowel represented by the *waw*.

29. *gērût* occurs only here, but may be related to *gēr*, 'a temporary resident', and so a place where temporary residents stay, an 'inn' or 'khan' (cf. NASB margin).

1. Request for Guidance (42:1-6)

The greatest difficulty in understanding this passage is to read correctly
the underlying nuances of those who speak. In particular, are the
people who seek Jeremiah's assistance genuine in their approach, or
are they merely seeking divine endorsement of what they have decided
already? Increasingly it becomes evident that it is the latter that is the
case.

**1. Then all the army officers, including Johanan son of Kareah
and Jezaniah son of Hoshaiah, and all the people from the least to
the greatest approached.** At first sight it seems encouraging that there
is such a unanimous approach to the prophet. The phrase 'from the
least to the greatest' is a merism, which by indicating polar opposites
provides an inclusive designation of everything in between as well. It
could indicate from the poorest to the richest, from the least to the most
influential, or from the youngest to the oldest. The fact that on any
understanding the whole community was involved indicates the
uncertainty that had enveloped the survivors. They had undergone
traumatic experiences when Jerusalem fell, and what little order they
had subsequently recovered in their lives had been shattered by
Gedaliah's assassination and their own kidnapping. Now driven by
fear of Babylonian reprisals they were seeking safety in Egypt.

There is no indication in the text of any dissension within the
community regarding what they should do. It is rather that they were
confused as to what the future held. Two of the army officers are
named as being involved in this approach. Johanan has already figured
prominently in warning Gedaliah and rescuing those he kidnapped.
Jezaniah is less easily identified. Even though he is also an army
officer, he is probably not the same person as the Jezaniah (Jaazaniah)
of 40:8, because that man is denominated 'the son of the Maachathite'.
On the other hand, it is possible that he is the same person as Azariah
son of Hoshaiah mentioned in 43:2, or perhaps his brother. The
Septuagint in both places[30] has the name Azariah, but with a different
patronymic, son of Maaseiah.

2. Jeremiah the prophet reappears in the narrative without any
indication of where he had been. The easiest assumption is that he had
been staying with Gedaliah at Mizpah, been kidnapped by Ishmael, and
subsequently rescued by Johanan. It does, however, have the problem
of how he had escaped being killed at Mizpah. Jeremiah was old by

---

30. Because of the different chapter numbers these references are 49:1 and
50:2 in the LXX.

this time, and the rigours he had undergone in the siege, and especially in his imprisonment at that time, may have taken their toll on his frame. It may be that his silence and non-participation in the intervening events can best be explained by weakness. However, a good case can also be made that Jeremiah had been absent from Mizpah at the time of Ishmael's massacre and that he had been contacted by the fleeing survivors as they moved south and taken along with them.

The people approached Jeremiah, recognising his status as a prophet and asking him to intercede on their behalf. They seemed sincere when they **said to him, 'Please hear our petition'**/'let our petition fall before you'. This phrase describes Jeremiah's action in 37:20, and more significantly in 36:7 it is used of the action the people should take to respond appropriately to Jeremiah's warnings. It may here indicate the urgency with which they brought their situation to the prophet's attention. However, the content of what they ask Jeremiah to do, **and pray** (<√pālal hithpael, 'to intercede' [7:16] followed by 'on our behalf') **to the LORD your God for this entire remnant,** contains a note of the distance they perceive between themselves and God. In this and the following verse 'the LORD your God'[31] presents them as unable or unprepared to acknowledge any direct link between themselves and God, and as leaving the matter of dealing with the LORD to another.

They perceive themselves as a 'remnant' (šəʾērît, 23:3), those of God's people who have been left after judgment. They urge Jeremiah to act on their behalf because of the circumstances they find themselves in. **For (kî) as you now see, though we were once many, now only a few are left.** They urge him to act for them because their numbers have already been significantly depleted by Ishmael's slaughter at Mizpah. There may also have been some who had not joined them in their flight and who may have gone to stay with other groups scattered throughout Judah. But this particular set of refugees are traumatised by all that has happened to them, and are feeling particularly insecure because of the drop in their numbers.

3. Pray that the LORD your God will tell us where/'the way in which' **we should go and what**/'the thing which' **we should do.** They are asking that God extend favour to them in view of their being almost annihilated, but the nature of their request is puzzling: is it a request for general guidance or for specific directions? 'Way' (derek) may be used to describe obedience to the requirements of the covenant

---

31. A few manuscripts and the Syriac have 'our God' (cf. 37:3), but the Massoretic Text is to be preferred as the more difficult and better attested text.

(21:8; Deut. 5:33; 8:6; 19:9), but they are not looking for instruction in
the demands of the law. Equally, it is improbable that they were asking
for a divine road map to give them knowledge about the route to
Egypt. Probably they were reassessing their whole situation and were
asking in uncertainty whether they should go to Egypt at all. But there
is an ominous note in the text. Although uncertain about what they
should do, the people had already concluded that there was no
possibility of staying in the land because of the inevitable hostility of
the Babylonians. They were genuine in wishing divine light on their
path, but they had already foreclosed on some possible responses,
ruling them out, perhaps not consciously, as incredible. They were
seeking divine endorsement on their reading of the situation, and were
not open to the LORD's interpretation of their circumstances. 'Pray to
the LORD on our behalf' (v. 2) echoes the words of Zedekiah in 37:3,
and neither he nor the people here were prepared for an answer that
turned their preconceptions upside down. Similarly here, the LORD
does not ignore the people's approach as if all they were wanting was a
divine seal of approval on what they had already decided to do, but he
challenges the mixed-up nature of their petition for light on their path.
True faith will not dictate the parameters within which the LORD must
respond.

4. 'I have heard you,' replied Jeremiah the prophet. This answer
indicates that he agreed to do what they had requested. Jeremiah no
longer sees himself as being under a ban on interceding for the people
(7:16). That had come to an end with the judgment that fell upon the
city. In the changed situation it is appropriate that he resume his
prophetic task of approaching God on behalf of the people. **I will
certainly pray to the LORD your God as you have requested**/'in
accordance with your words'. But his approach to God on their behalf
imposed certain obligations upon them. It would not be a profitable
exercise unless they recognised that he is the LORD their God and not
(as in v. 2 and 3) simply Jeremiah's God. Moreover, it is probable that
when he says, **I will tell you everything the LORD says**/'answers you'
and will keep nothing back from you, Jeremiah was anticipating that
matters might well not be dealt with in terms of the frame of reference
the people themselves had suggested.

5. The people solemnly commit themselves to obey whatever directions Jeremiah will bring them from the LORD. **Then they said to
Jeremiah, 'May the LORD be a true and faithful witness against us
if we do not act in accordance with everything the LORD your God
sends you to tell us.'** 'True' (*ʾĕmet*, 10:10) relates to the reliability of

the LORD, as 'faithful' (<√'āman, cf. Deut. 7:9; Isa. 8:2) does also. They acknowledge that he will be an accurate and dependable witness who will bear testimony to their pledge. He will also fulfil the role of judge if they fall short in their obedience. The strength of the people's commitment given here makes their subsequent lack of compliance an even more heinous transgression.

6. One wonders if the addition of v. 6 with its twofold commitment does not indicate too much of a desire to protest their obedience. **Whether it is favourable or unfavourable, we will obey** (<√šamaʿ) **the LORD our God, to whom we**[32] **are sending you, so that it will go well with us, for**[33] (*kî*) **we will obey** (<√šamaʿ) **the LORD our God.** Rather than confirming their sincerity the repetition of 'we will obey' raises the possibility of self-doubt, that the people were trying to talk themselves into the appropriate attitude. The phrase 'whether it is favourable or unfavourable'/'good or evil' is an abbreviated form of the idiomatic expressions 'to be good in the eyes of' = 'to be pleasing to' (BDB 374) and 'to be bad in the eyes of' = 'to be displeasing to' (BDB 948). They were consumed with anxiety and uncertainty, and all unreservedly committed themselves to responding appropriately to whatever message was brought to them. 'Are sending' is one of a number of occurrences in this chapter of the verb 'to send' (also in vv. 5, 6, 9, 20, 21) which relate to the prophet delegated by the people to act on their behalf before God and also commissioned by the LORD to relay his message to the people.

2. Guidance Given (42:7-18)

7. Ten days later the word of the LORD came to Jeremiah. It was no immediate response that the people received from the prophet (cf. 28:11-12, and the seven days of Ezek. 3:16). The message Jeremiah relayed was not one that he thought up. The ten days were not a time of introspective meditation, as though the prophet sought within himself for some answer, though they may well have been a time of prayer. Certainly it was a revelation from the LORD that the prophet received. Why did God leave the people in suspense so long? We can only

---

32. The kethibh has *'ănû*, 'we', as the first person plural pronoun. This is the only time it occurs in the MT, and the qere substitutes the normal written form *'ănaḥnû*. However, *'ănû* became common in post-biblical Hebrew, and may well have occurred in colloquial speech of Jeremiah's day.

33. *kî* here may be used as an emphatic: 'Yes indeed, we will obey the LORD our God'. That would tend to reinforce the idea that they are talking themselves into what they perceive as the correct response.

speculate; but if their inquiry comes after a hurried journey from
Mizpah, then the time for reflection might have made them more
responsive to the word that comes to them. It was a time of crucial
decision, and it would determine their fate. Therefore they were not to
be hasty or to be allowed to bounce themselves into a hurried decision
because of their anxiety. It is difficult to say if their fears of
Babylonian reprisals would have increased or decreased with the passage of time.

8. When he has been given the message of the LORD, the prophet
reacts. **So he called together Johanan son of Kareah and all the
army officers who were with him and all the people from the least
to the greatest.** No doubt all concerned had kept asking the prophet
over this period if there had been any response from the LORD, and so
he summoned all who had asked him to hear the reply. The numbers
involved would not have been very great. For the phrase, 'from least to
greatest', see v. 2 (6:13; 8:10; 16:6; 31:34).

9. **He said to them, 'This is what the LORD, the God of Israel, to
whom you sent me to present your petition, says.'** He reminds them
that it was on their initiative that guidance was sought so that they
might be the more ready to receive the word that has come. The divine
response is structured by the two 'ifs' with which vv. 10 and 13 begin
in a way reminiscent to the possibilities that were set before Zedekiah
prior to the fall of the city (38:17-18). First the divinely commended
course of action is set before them, and the blessing that would follow
it (vv. 10-12). Then the course of action they already seem committed
to is condemned, and its fearful consequences set forth (vv. 13-18).

10. **If you stay**[34] **in this land** is the option which they had implicitly
ruled out as being untenable, but it is to that the LORD directs them,
challenging them to have faith in him and not in human calculations of
probabilities. Implicit in this option is the continuation of Gedaliah's
policy of acceptance of Babylonian overlordship as part of the divine
chastisement of his people. If they acquiesce in this, their obedience
would be richly rewarded. **I will build you up** (cf. 24:6; 31:4; 33:7)
and not tear you down; I will plant you and not uproot you. The

---

34. The infinitive absolute is given in the MT as *šôb*, the infinitive absolute
from *šûb*, 'to return', but since the following verb is *tēšəbû*, from *yāšab*, 'to
dwell', and the infinitive absolute generally serves to emphasise the cognate
verb, there seems to have been a scribal error here in the MT omitting the
yodh. GKC §19i suggests that there may have been aphaeresis of the weak
initial consonant, but it is more probable that the form is an early scribal error.

four verbs used here are all found in Jeremiah's inaugural vision (1:10), but now they are set in a context of hope and deliverance. (Compare also 18:7-9 where the verbs are set in a similar context.) If the people are obedient to the LORD, then there is the prospect of blessing for them. They are in fact being offered the same terms as the community in Babylon who have been designated as the ones with whom the future of the people lies (cf. 31:28). **For** (*kî*) **I am grieved**[35] **over the disaster I have inflicted on you.** 'Grieve' (<√*nāḥam*, 18:8, 10; Joel 2:14) does not convey the idea of a change of divine purpose as if God had been wrong in bringing judgment on Jerusalem ('repent', RSV; 'relent', NASB, NKJV), far less the idea of conveying an apology for what has occurred ('am sorry', NRSV). It is a reaction of pity and of compassionate sorrow over the catastrophe and suffering that had been divinely inflicted on Jerusalem. There is no suggestion that it was an unmerited imposition, but still the LORD in his love would rather rescue and build up the people. But there is no possibility of evading the divine demand: the people must follow the path of obedience. The sentence has been executed, and there is the prospect of recovery—but it remains conditioned on the 'if'.

11. The people had ruled out remaining in the land because of their fear of Babylonian reprisals. This was no far-fetched scenario, but a response that could reasonably be anticipated. Therefore the LORD addresses himself directly to their need. **Do not be afraid of the king of Babylon, whom you now fear.**[36] The injunction to put away their fear (the content of which is spelled out in v. 18) is repeated for emphasis and reinforced by specific divine pledges in the matter. **Do not be afraid of him, declares the LORD, for** (*kî*) **I am with you and will save** (<√*nāṣal* hiphil, 'to rescue', 1:8) **you and deliver** (<√*yāšaʿ*) **you from his hands.** For God's presence to deliver, see on 1:8, 19b. It is not that their fears were groundless humanly speaking, but rather that they are given a divine pledge of deliverance so that they may overcome their fears. The challenge is to respond in faith to the LORD.

12. I will show you compassion[37] **so that he will have compassion**

35. The tense of this perfect verb is variously rendered. The perfect may be a future perfect, 'I shall have grieved/relented', and hence a future rendering; or it may be a present perfect of an attitude or emotion already adopted, 'I have and still do grieve/relent'.
36. Notice the use of the participle to express the ongoing reaction.
37. Literally 'I will give you compassion', perhaps meaning 'I will obtain it for you' (Gen. 43:14; 1 Kgs. 8:50).

on you and restore you[38] **to your land.** There is a sequence involved
that begins with God. The people were focusing too much on the man,
the king of Babylon, and had forgotten about the one who is king of
all. It is because of his divine determination to show them compassion
(*raḥămîm*, 16:5) when they obey him that the attitude of the Babylonian king will surely be changed by God himself. It may be that he
would spare them (after all they had been Ishmael's victims not the
perpetrators of the calamity) so that after being in exile they would join
in the eventual restoration to Palestine. More probably, however, the
restoration to the land envisaged here is not that which had been
prophesied as taking place after the eclipse of Babylonian power. The
promise is specifically addressed to this small group who were then
near Bethlehem. They would be immediately restored by Nebuchadnezzar either to their original landholdings—remember many of them
had only recently returned either from foreign lands or had given up
guerrilla activities against him—or to temporary arrangements such as
those that had prevailed under Gedaliah at Mizpah. This would have
presaged the eventual return of all the deportees.

13. The message does not, however, stop there. A second, darker
option has also to be spelled out. **However, if you say, 'We will not
stay in this land,' and so disobey the LORD your God.** This does not
describe a future response, so much as the continuation of their already
existing attitude, 'if you continue to say' (NRSV).[39] They had already
adopted this attitude, and if they persisted in it now that the LORD had
explicitly rejected it, there would be no doubt ('and so'[40]) that their
conduct was wilful disobedience.

14. And if you say, 'No, 'but' (*kî* after a negative) **we will go and
live in Egypt, where we will not see war or hear the trumpet** (cf.
4:19) **or be hungry for bread'** (cf. Amos 8:11) does not introduce a
second condition, but rather expands on the attitude expressed in v. 13.
Egypt must have seemed a haven of tranquillity to the Judahites whose
land had been torn by war and invasion over the years from 609 BC
when Josiah had fallen at Megiddo. There had been invasion, foreign
domination, disaster and destruction. Although Egypt had been
involved, indeed had been defeated at Carchemish in 605, the

38. The REB 'will let you stay' involves reading the hiphil *wəhēšîb* as
wəhôšîb, from *yāšab*, 'to dwell', rather than *šûb*, 'to return'.
39. The Hebrew has a participle *'ōmərîm*, probably indicating ongoing
activity both at present and into the future, rather than simply in the future, as
in the NASB 'if you are going to say'.
40. The Hebrew is *ləbiltî šəmōaʿ*, the negative with the infinitive construct.

Babylonians had not invaded Egypt itself, and so the people view it as a land untouched by war, not startled by the alarm of the war trumpet, or feeling the ravages of famine. That is where they want to live. But both Jeremiah (2:36; 37:7) and Ezekiel (Ezek. 17:11-18; 29–32) were insistent that going to Egypt was not the right policy. In bringing forwards 'and live' the NIV rearranges the order of the clauses from the Hebrew which ends with a defiant 'and there we will stay' (NRSV).

15-16. However, if they persist in that attitude, **then** (*'attâ*) **hear the word of the LORD, O remnant of Judah.** The remnant are those left from the professing covenant community here represented by the small group with whom the prophet is dealing (v. 19; 43:5; 44:12, 14). 'Then' followed by 'therefore' (*lākēn*) forcefully presents the bleak future under divine condemnation that awaits them. **This is what the LORD Almighty, the God of Israel, says.** The full title given to the LORD indicates the solemnity of the address and how crucial their response to it would be (7:3). **If you are determined to go to Egypt and you go to settle there, then**[41] **the sword you fear will overtake you** (39:5) **there, and the famine you dread** (<√*dā'ag*, cf. 17:8) **will follow** (<√*dābaq*, 'to cling to, stick to, stay close') **you into Egypt, and there you will die.** The 'there' used in the final clause of v. 14 to refer to Egypt is repeated in v. 15 and occurs three times in v. 16, emphasising the degree of estrangement from the LORD that they will experience if they persist in going to Egypt. What is more, there will be a decided difference between the outcome they hoped for—life in Egypt, as described at the end of v. 14—and the grim reality that is set out at the end of v. 16. 'Determined'/'set your faces' is a Hebrew idiom for being of a decided attitude, tenaciously clinging to a certain course of action—a picture of those who had turned in that direction and would allow nothing, not even the word of divine warning, to deflect them. Egypt may have remained untouched by the series of disasters up until then, but there was no guarantee that would continue. They were deluding themselves by their predictions of what the future might hold, and the LORD was warning them that the very things they hoped to escape would come upon them in Egypt.

17. Indeed,[42] **all who are determined to go to Egypt to settle there**

---

41. Very rarely does the transitional verb 'and it will be ⌊that⌋' agree in gender and number with the following subject, but it does so at the beginning of vv. 16 and 17 (GKC §112y). See also the following footnote.

42. Rather unusually the verse is introduced by the personal idiom *wəyihyû*, 'and they will be' (*waw*-conjunctive) rather than the normal impersonal usage *wəhāyâ*, 'and it will be' (cf. v. 16).

**will die by the sword, famine and plague; not one of them will
survive or escape the disaster I will bring on them.** The Jeremianic
triad of disasters is again pronounced upon the disobedient (7:20;
14:12; 21:7, 9). It is the height of perversity and folly to pursue a
course of action knowing that it will lead to disaster.

18. A solemn warning is then given that their situation in Egypt will
become like that which had prevailed with respect to Jerusalem. There
had been a reversal of judgment in v. 10 on condition of obedience, but
ignoring the LORD's warnings will result in the catastrophe of Jerusalem being repeated. 'For' (*kî*) introduces the reason for the disaster that
will come. **This is what the LORD Almighty, the God of Israel, says:
'As my anger and wrath have been poured out on those who lived
in Jerusalem, so will my wrath be poured out on you** (7:20; 44:6;
cf. 32:31; 33:5; 36:7) **when you go to Egypt. You will become an
object of cursing** (cf. 24:9; 25:18; 29:18) **and horror, of condemnation and reproach; you will never see this place again'** (cf. 42:18;
44:12; and also 29:18; 24:9; 25:18). 'Curse' (*ʾālâ*) is a metonymy for a
person put under a curse (19:18). Going to Egypt does not remove
them from the reach of the LORD. Their disobedience will ensure that
the curse of Jerusalem follows them.

3. Prophetic Exhortation (42:19-22)

There then follows a prophetic reinforcement of the divine message.
Because it presupposes that the people have decided to go to Egypt,
some scholars have argued that it is misplaced and should follow
43:1-3 (Bright 1965:252, 256, 258; Holladay 1989, 2:285). This is
unnecessary. Jeremiah has correctly assessed the mood of the people
and their intention is clear before the episode at the beginning of chapter 43. Indeed the group's goal has already been stated in 41:17.

These verses also challenge the perception of Carroll that in chapters 1–25 Jeremiah becomes increasingly passive until in chapters 37–
45 he is 'almost inert' (1986:669). The prophet does not hesitate to
announce the divine word—when he has received it. But he will not
presume. He is the messenger, not the originator of the message.

19-20. Having relayed the message that God had given him, the
prophet reinforces its warnings as he speaks to the people. Their negative reaction was evident both from the way in which the LORD's
message had been expressed, and also no doubt from their faces as
they stood around listening to him. **O remnant of Judah, the LORD
has told you, 'Do not go to Egypt.'** (For the negative *ʾal* used here,
see on 43:2.) The address, 'remnant of Judah', has an element of hope

in it, in that much good had been predicted about the remnant who survived the LORD's judgment (23:3; 31:7; Isa. 37:32; 46:3). But they are to be in no doubt about what the LORD had said to them. It is only death that will face them in Egypt. **Be sure of this:**[43] **I warn you today** (cf. 11:7) **that** (*kî*) **you have made a fatal mistake**[44] **when** (*kî*) **you** 'yourselves' (an emphatic use) **sent me to the LORD your God and said, 'Pray to the LORD our God, for us; tell us everything he says and we will do it.'** 'A fatal mistake' renders 'you erred at the price of yourselves' (<*nepeš*, 2:34), because what was at stake was their own lives (17:21). It was not wrong that they had asked the prophet to intercede with God, but they had not been inwardly prepared to obey no matter what he said and had pledged themselves to an obedience that they were not really committed to.

21-22. I have told you today, but you still have not obeyed the LORD your God in all he sent me to tell you. Jeremiah is able to sense from their previous actions and the expressions of those he is addressing that the clarity of the message had not made any difference in their reaction to what was said to them. They must then be absolutely in no doubt about what is going to happen. **So now, be sure of this: You will die by the sword, famine and plague in the place where you want to go to settle.** cf. 29:18.

4. Guidance Spurned (43:1-7)

Although the people and their leaders had requested that Jeremiah seek divine guidance for them in their uncertain circumstances, it is now made explicit that they were in no mood to listen to anything that ran counter to what they had already virtually decided to do. They rejected Jeremiah's proclamation and claimed that he was prophesying falsely. Then they moved south into Egypt, and surprisingly they took Jeremiah and Baruch with them. In this move there came to an end any hope for the restoration to divine favour of the community left in the

---

43. Both here and in v. 22 'be sure of this' is followed by *kî*, 'that', introducing the content of what they are to be aware of. In both verses the infinitive absolute precedes the finite verb *yādaʿ*, 'to know', to reinforce the idea of the verb: 'know this absolutely'.

44. The kethibh *htʿtym* seems to involve a scribal error in transposing the second *taw* and the *yodh*. The qere corrects this to *htʿytm*, to be read as *hitʿêtem* (<√*tāʿâ*, 'to wander off, roam'), 'you have caused yourselves to wander'. *bənapšôtêkem*, 'in your souls', may be taken as, 'You erred in your hearts' (so NIV margin, NASB, cf. REB), or else as in the NIV text and the NRSV as an example of *beth pretii*, stating the price or cost of their action.

land, and as the rest of chapters 43 and 44 show, the community already in Egypt had also departed far from the LORD. There were left only those deported to Babylon, whom Jeremiah had already identified as 'the good figs' (24:5).

1. The response to Jeremiah's prophecy yields insight into the mind of those who constituted the group of refugees. **When Jeremiah finished telling the people all the words of the LORD their God—everything the LORD had sent him to tell them**, the response was immediate, and it was for rejection. It is emphasised that this was their reaction even though the LORD had a special claim on their loyalty in that he was 'their God', and even though Jeremiah had conveyed to them the totality of the divine response—warnings and all. What they do cannot be minimised as occurring through panic and ignorance; it was deliberately done in the face of solemn and explicit advice to the contrary as they rejected the blessing that had been promised if in faith they stayed in the land.

2. Azariah son of Hoshaiah and Johanan son of Kareah and all the arrogant men said to Jeremiah. Azariah's identity has already been discussed, see on Jezaniah (42:1). The fact that he is mentioned here before Johanan suggests that on this occasion he took the initiative and became the spokesman for those who opposed Jeremiah's advice. They are called 'arrogant' ($<\sqrt{z\hat{\imath}d}$, 'to boil' and hence metaphorically 'to act presumptuously, insolently'; *TWOT* #547), not just because they had a high opinion of themselves, but because they wilfully assume authority or rights not legitimately theirs. Such people consider that God's laws do not apply to them (Ps. 119:21, 51, 69, 78, 85, 122), and invalidly reject God's counsel for the nation (Neh. 9:29) by not paying regard to important principles such as respect for the needs and rights of others.

The tactics they adopt are to accuse Jeremiah of being a false prophet. **You are lying!**/'speaking falsehood (*šeqer*, 5:2)'. **The LORD our God has not sent you to say, 'You must not go[45] to Egypt to settle there.'** The accusation Jeremiah had frequently made against others (8:8; 14:14) is turned against him: he is the one whose message is false because he has not been divinely sent (23:21). Gedaliah had similarly discounted Johanan's advice as false (40:16). The leaders of

---

45. Jeremiah's words are not quoted quite accurately. In 42:19 the negative particle is *'al* which is used to express a one-off specific prohibition; here the particle *lōʾ* is substituted. This normally expresses a permanent prohibition (GKC §107o), and raises the possibility that there was an attempt to exaggerate what Jeremiah had said to make it appear quite unreasonable.

the remanent community were no better than those of Judah before the Exile at discerning truth. It was of course difficult to substantiate or to disprove a charge of false prophecy, though the accuracy of what Jeremiah had said regarding Jerusalem should have constituted an adequate corroboration of his status. However, the people and their leaders had committed themselves to obey whatever word he brought to them from the LORD. They were not prepared simply to say that they were going back on their pledge because the message has not been to their liking. They were genuinely surprised by what had happened and unable to comprehend how 'the LORD our God' could say anything which ran so contrary to the obvious realities of their situation. They therefore rationalise their rejection of the prophetic word by arguing that Jeremiah must have been 'got at' by some pressure group or other. Were they used to such ways of influencing prophets from the old days in Jerusalem? On this occasion, the only person they could find to focus their story on was Baruch, who elsewhere appears surprisingly little in the history of Jeremiah.

3. But (*kî*) Baruch son of Neriah is inciting (<√*sût*, 'to entice, draw away') **you against us to hand us over to the Babylonians, so that they may kill us or carry us into exile to Babylon.** Baruch seems to have survived the fall of Jerusalem as Jeremiah's attendant, and he is present here still performing that role. As Jeremiah was now old, it may have seemed reasonable to suggest his attendant could exercise undue influence over him. Baruch had had access to the highest circles in Jerusalem before it fell. His support of Jeremiah identified him as one of the pro-Babylonian party, and the story that is put out about him here makes it probable that he was seen as a strong character who still possessed influence. So it was possible to hint that he wanted the group to fall into the hands of the Babylonians. Then given Jeremiah's good standing with Babylon and his obvious non-involvement in Gedaliah's death, perhaps Baruch could advance his own position. On the other hand coming under Babylonian rule would have meant death for army officers who had failed to protect the Babylonian-appointed governor.

The spin they put on the situation was improbable. The man who at great personal cost had refused to tailor his message to suit the desires of the kings of Judah was hardly likely to do so under pressure from an attendant, no matter how great a friend or how needed a helper. But if his opponents were prepared to go to such lengths in setting up a cover for their actions, then what more can be said? In face of the charge of falsehood the only course open was to wait to see whose word God would honour through fulfilment.

**4-5. So Johanan son of Kareah and all the army officers and all
the people disobeyed the LORD's command to stay in the land of
Judah.** Whatever plausibility the cover story for their response
possessed, the verdict recorded on them is simply one of disobedience:
'they disobeyed/did not listen' (<√*šāma'*). The options had been set
before them and they had made their choice, even though it was
obviously contrary to God's will and their own previous commitment
(42:5-6). **Instead, Johanan son of Kareah and all the army officers
led away** (<√*lāqaḥ*, 'to take') **all the remnant of Judah who had
come back to live in the land of Judah from all the nations where
they had been scattered.** The army officers were obviously in a position to impose their will on the small group gathered around them. 'All
the remnant of Judah' seems to refer to this group and not to all the
Jews in the land, because there were still many others left. The group
that moved south comprised a number of parties including refugees
who had gone abroad at various stages during the Babylonian
campaign against Judah (40:11-12) but who had returned when
Gedaliah was set up as governor. They need not all have been resident
in Mizpah, but they had acknowledged Gedaliah as their leader. The
unsettled status they possessed on their return is marked by the word
translated 'to live' (<√*gûr*, 'to sojourn') which generally refers to those
who reside in a land as resident aliens. Surely an unusual phrase to
employ here!

6. They also led away all the men (<√*gābar*, 17:5)**, women and
children and the king's daughters** 'and/even every person' (*nepeš*,
used collectively for individuals comprising a group) **whom Nebuzaradan commander of the imperial guard had left with Gedaliah
son of Ahikam, the son of Shaphan.** This verse may be a further
explanation of the 'remnant' mentioned previously, but it seems more
likely (as the NIV takes it) to indicate a different party, namely those
who had been captured by the Babylonians when the city fell and who
had been placed under Gedaliah's control (40:7; 41:10, 16). For the
identity of the 'king's daughters' see 41:10.

Tagged on at the end, there is a third party consisting of **Jeremiah
the prophet and Baruch son of Neriah.** They are also 'taken',
presumably against their will. It is difficult to see why the group took
along with them a prophet whose word they rejected as being false and
who they claimed was seeking to undermine their community. It may
well reflect the inconsistency of those who are not fully persuaded of
the truth of the story they themselves have invented. It is also the case

that there may well have been some among them who continued to acknowledge Jeremiah as a prophet, and who did not wish to see him badly treated. It may be that here we have a recurrence of their earlier attitude towards the ark and the Temple. They recognised Jeremiah as a divinely authenticated prophet, and so he is taken 'as a lucky charm by Jews who have decided that the only future lies in refuge in Egypt' (Goldingay 1984:17).

7. So they entered Egypt in disobedience to/'for (*kî*) they did not obey (*šāmaʿ*)' the LORD and went far as Tahpanhes. Again the disobedience they were displaying is underlined. Tahpanhes (cf. 2:16) was an important border community on the northern frontier of Egypt in the north-eastern Nile delta, known to the Greeks as Daphne. Here they seem to have stopped to work out what would happen next. Presumably there was already a Jewish community there—this group would not have been the first to flee to Egypt, quite apart from the Jewish propensity to move for purposes of trade. Among their fellow countrymen they would find assistance, and in Egypt they considered they were beyond Babylonian reprisals.

C. MINISTRY IN EGYPT (43:8–44:30)

There are records of two episodes in Jeremiah's ministry in Egypt. The first (43:8-13) is addressed to the group he has travelled south with, as well as other Jews residing in Tahpanhes. The second set of material in chapter 44 describes an interchange with the wider Jewish community in Egypt in which Jeremiah warns them of the consequences of their continuing idolatry.

1. Preparations for Nebuchadnezzar (43:8-13)

We do not know how much time elapsed before Jeremiah was instructed to perform actions that formed the basis for a prophetic message regarding what awaited Egypt, and more particularly the Jewish community there. Taking refuge in Egypt in defiance of the LORD's warning did not exempt them from the attentions of Nebuchadnezzar.

8. Though moving to Egypt brought an end to the separate history of the community that had gathered round Gedaliah and to the prospects it had of maintaining a presence in Judah, the LORD did not leave them to their own devices. **In Tahpanhes the word of the LORD came to Jeremiah.** The LORD's last word to this group, even though it was disobedient, had not yet been spoken. They were not to think that acting in defiance of his will would ensure them safety in Egypt. Their perception of security in Egypt was an illusion because of the universal sovereignty of the LORD.

9. Jeremiah's message to the Jewish community was to be preceded by symbolic action. **While the Jews are watching, take some large stones with you and bury** (<√*ṭāman*, 'to hide by burying'; cf. 13:4-7) **them in clay in the brick pavement at the entrance to Pharaoh's palace in Tahpanhes.** Both 'clay' and 'brick pavement' are words of uncertain meaning. *meleṭ* occurs only here and may refer to clay used as mortar in the construction of the pavement. *malbēn*, 'brick pavement', is found in 2 Sam. 12:31 and Nah. 3:14 and in both passages is connected with bricks. Pharaoh's palace was probably the administrative centre in the town, where the local governor may have stayed, and Pharaoh too when he visited the area. A similarly named building is known to have existed during this period in a border town, Elephantine, in the south of Egypt (Bright 1965:263). Jeremiah's public action is designed to make an impression on the Jewish community. At the site of Tahpanhes a paved area has been identified in front of a major building, which may be what is referred to here. The problem which arises is that it is difficult to envisage the Egyptian authorities standing by and letting a group of refugees dig up the approach to a major government building. Even if we suppose that the action took place at some distance from the palace, it is still unlikely that lifting a brick pavement would have been permitted, and especially if the authorities got any hint of the subversive nature of what was being symbolised. There may thus be some scope for the explanation advanced that this action was only to be mimed. The prophetic action and word served to emphasise that Egypt did not provide a haven where they could shelter from the LORD's judgment.

10. As was usual, the symbolic action was accompanied by a verbal explanation. **Then say to them, 'This is what the LORD Almighty, the God of Israel, says: I will send for my servant Nebuchadnezzar king of Babylon, and I will set his throne over these stones I have buried here; he will spread his royal canopy[46] above them.'** The word rendered 'canopy' occurs only here, and its meaning is uncertain. 'Spread' is often used of erecting a tent, and fits in with the idea of a

---

46. The kethibh is *šaprûrô* or *šarôrô*, the qere *šaprîrô*, a word which only occurs here, but is associated with *šiprâ*, 'beauty, splendour'. *HALOT* (1636) does not favour a derivation from an Akkadian root meaning 'sceptre' and indicates that either a sumptuous tent over his throne or a carpet under it would fit the use of *nāṭâ*, 'to spread'.

royal pavilion, but it would also suit the proposal that the reference is to the carpet on which the throne would be set. It is explained that the stones Jeremiah buried would provide the foundation on which Nebuchadnezzar's throne would be set because the Babylonian monarch is going to come to Egypt in accordance with the LORD's summons. Indeed, Nebuchadnezzar is given the title 'my servant' to underline the fact that the action will be in accordance with the LORD's will, even though he himself may not recognise that (25:9; 27:6). There are three points being made: (1) that Nebuchadnezzar's dominion will extend to Tahpanhes, to Egypt; (2) his rule will have a stable and effective basis on top of the divinely placed stones; and (3) all this is to be done by divine warrant, and so will further God's purposes.

11. By divine decree Nebuchadnezzar's presence in Egypt will spell disaster. **He will come**[47] **and attack Egypt, bringing death to those destined for death, captivity to those destined for captivity, and the sword to those destined for the sword.** Though these words remind one of judgments pronounced against the community earlier by Jeremiah (15:2), they are not specifically directed at the Jews, but include the Egyptians also. The point is that Egypt which the refugees thought so safe a place to be in will undergo what Judah had already experienced. There is then the subsidiary thought that the Jewish community will not be exempt, and for them the action of God's servant will bring the just punishment of their disobedience.

12. He will set fire to the temples of the gods of Egypt; he will burn their temples and take their gods captive. Burnt temples and looted images carried in triumphal parade to the temple of the victor's gods were customary features in conquests of the day. But the first verb in the Hebrew is 'I will set fire' (NIV margin)[48]. Although this seems awkward as an English mode of expression, it brings out the parallel with expressions such as 'I will set his throne' in v. 10. What the one who has been designated God's servant does is effectively what is done by God himself, because it is the outworking of his will. The LORD kindles the fire and Nebuchadnezzar is the instrument he

---

47. The kethibh is *ûbāʾâ*, the qere *ûbāʿ*. The kethibh may be retained with a mappiq in the final *he* to give a third feminine singular suffix referring to the land ⌐of Egypt⌐.

48. *hiṣṣattî* in the consonantal text would be *hṣty*. The LXX, Syriac and Vulgate all have a third person rendering, 'he will set fire', presumably reading *hiṣṣît*. This might have arisen by metathesis of the *taw* and *yodh* to give a consonantal text *hṣyt*, and probably does not reflect a different text but rather the perceived awkwardness of the first person.

uses to carry through his threat.

As a shepherd wraps his garment round him, so will he wrap Egypt round himself involves a comparison that has been variously understood. At first sight the simile would seem to focus on the ease with which Nebuchadnezzar will gain control of Egypt. He will wrap himself with Egypt as easily as a shepherd picks up his cloak and puts it round him. The simile would be suggested by the frequent use of 'shepherd' as a metaphor for a ruler. However, there is a second far less elegant meaning based on a homonym ʿāṭâ II, 'to delouse' (cf. LXX and Arabic; *HALOT* 814). Nebuchadnezzar will delouse Egypt 'as a shepherd scours his clothes to rid them of lice' (REB), that is, he will absolutely pillage it, taking from the land all that he can find. It is also said **and depart from there unscathed** (bəšālôm, 'in peace' in the sense 'complete, unharmed, having suffered no loss'). This would be quite a different departure from that which he experienced in 600 BC when he was suffered heavy losses at the hands of the Egyptians as he tried to overwhelm them.

13. There in the temple of the sun in Egypt he will demolish (<√šābar I, 'to break', piel 'to smash') **the sacred pillars** may refer to a temple dedicated to the sun god Re (at Tahpanhes, or anywhere in the land), or it may be a more specific reference to Heliopolis (situated about six miles [9½ km] north-east of modern Cairo) and its famous temple to Re, which was approached through two rows of obelisks, carved pillars. Heliopolis, 'city of the sun', may correspond to the Beth-Shemesh, 'temple/house of the sun', which is here explicitly designated as 'in Egypt' to distinguish it from the place of the same name in Judah. This was not the normal Hebrew designation of the city, which was usually called On. It too would be ravaged by Nebuchadnezzar. **And will burn down the temples of the gods of Egypt.** The last clause resumes the thought of v. 12a, and marks the verses as being a unit.

Commentators are divided on the extent to which the prophecy came true. There is a fragmentary description from Babylon of a campaign Nebuchadnezzar made to Egypt in his thirty-seventh year (568/7 BC), but it appears to have been a foraging raid rather than an attempt to subjugate the country. Pharaoh Amasis submitted to Babylonian control, retained his throne and remained on good terms with Babylon thereafter. Nebuchadnezzar was certainly the victor and as there was virtually no resistance, this fits the description of him as 'unscathed' (v. 12). While there is no evidence of widespread destruction of Egyptian temples at this time, the Babylonian records are fragmentary (*ANET*, 308). Indeed it is possible that there was an earlier invasion around 582 BC (see on 46:13), and the lack of extant records leaves it open that there were other hostilities in the following decade.

2. Dialogue with the Jews in Egypt (44:1-30)

OUTLINE

    a. Lessons not Learned (44:1-14)
    b. The Queen of Heaven (44:15-19)
    c. The Prophet's Warning (44:20-23)
    d. Divine Judgment (44:24-30)

Chapter 44 contains a sermon and the response to it from the time of Jeremiah's ministry in Egypt. It does not follow directly on from chapter 43, as those addressed are now from the larger community of all the Jews resident in Egypt. It is not clear how this message was delivered. Certainly the interaction in vv. 15-29 suggests that there was some occasion when representatives of quite a number of immigrant groups were gathered, both men and women, probably for some religious festival. Another suggestion is that Jeremiah moved round the land and visited many of these groups, and what is recorded here is a typical sample of the reaction he got in various places. The text does not allow us to determine which, but the conversations read more naturally if viewed as taking place on some specific occasion. The words seem to be the last of Jeremiah's recorded ministry, and were uttered before the events predicted in v. 30. We do not know when Jeremiah died, but if he arrived in Egypt in late 586 BC he was already in his mid-fifties, and quite possibly over sixty years of age. The period up to 580 BC then seems to be a feasible date for the events of this chapter, with Jeremiah adding them very soon thereafter to his almost completed prophetic works.

The Jews in Egypt presented Jeremiah with as big a challenge as any he had faced in his earlier ministry. In spite of the cataclysm that had swept Judah and Jerusalem away, the Jewish enclaves in Egypt remained thirled to the worship of pagan gods, particularly the Queen of Heaven. The lead in the matter was taken by the women of the community, but not without their husbands' knowledge and connivance. When the prophet confronted them with their conduct, they openly defended it (vv. 15-19). Jeremiah therefore warned them that they inevitably faced the same doom as had overtaken their homeland.

Modern scholarship often finds here the work of a Deuteronomic editor, probably in Babylon, or possibly among the community that returned from there to Jerusalem after 539 BC. He is seen as engaging in a polemic against the Jewish communities in Egypt which had been substantially affected by syncretism and were viewed as apostate by those who returned from Babylon. The chapter has therefore, it is argued, been crafted to expose the disobedience of the Jews in Egypt, and implicitly to bolster the claims of the Jerusalem community to be the true remnant who upheld the orthodox standards of the religion of the LORD. But this is to read into the text much that is not there, and there seems little reason for not finding here a genuine account of the closing ministry of Jeremiah. Many of the thoughts and phrases reflect what had been said earlier because the same problems had existed earlier. For instance, the worship of the Queen of Heaven occurs in this chapter and also in 7:18. Unfortunately those in Egypt displayed the same stubbornness as their forefathers and they too rejected the call for repentance.

a. Lessons Not Learned (44:1-14)

The message Jeremiah is given for the Jews residing in Egypt has three clear parts: (1) vv. 2-6 are a résumé of past history; (2) vv. 7-10 set out the present consequences of similar actions; and (3) vv. 11-14 are God's word of judgment upon his people.

1. This word came to Jeremiah concerning all the Jews living in Lower Egypt—in Migdol, Tahpanhes and Memphis—and in Upper Egypt. 'In Lower Egypt'/'in the land of Egypt' here signifies the area of the delta, where three important Jewish communities were to be found. Migdol ('watchtower', 'fortress'; also occurs as a placename in Exod. 14:2; Num. 33:7; Ezek. 29:10; 30:6) was a Semitic loanword used by the Egyptians, and here it refers to a site about twenty-five miles (42 km) north-east of Tahpanhes. For the location of Tahpanhes, see on 43:7. Both Migdol and Tahpanhes were border towns to the east of the Nile delta. However, Memphis (Hebrew, Noph) was situated at the head of the delta, fourteen miles (22 km) south of the modern Cairo, and was the capital of Lower Egypt. 'Upper Egypt'/'the land of Pathros' (from an Egyptian word meaning 'the southern land') stretched from just south of Memphis down the Nile Valley to Aswan. It is known that there were several Jewish groups in this area. Many probably went to Egypt as economic migrants, but others would have been refugees, starting at the time of the Assyrian invasions in the late eighth century BC. Their numbers would have been considerably augmented by those fleeing from the more recent Babylonian incursions (24:8).

Apart from these chapters in Jeremiah, our sources regarding early Jewish colonies in Egypt consist of legal documents and letters in the Elephantine papyri of the later Persian period. Elephantine was near the southern border of Egypt, at the First Cataract of the Nile. We find there Jewish settlers who were aware of many of the practices of the Mosaic law, such as the Sabbath legislation, and feasts like Passover and Unleavened Bread. But they had a temple which displayed certain structural similarities to that in Jerusalem, and in it they worshipped Yahu (Yahweh), including offering sacrifice. Furthermore there is strong evidence that their beliefs were tainted with syncretistic ideas probably of Canaanite origin (v. 17).

2. This is what the LORD Almighty, the God of Israel, says: You saw the great disaster (*rā'â*) I brought on Jerusalem and on all the towns of Judah. For the divine titles, see on 7:3. It need not be supposed that this experience was true only for the recent arrivals from Mizpah. 'You saw' need not imply that they were eyewitnesses, but that they were acquainted with the facts of the matter and prepared to acknowledge them. By making this reference to what had actually recently happened and not merely to what had been threatened, the following warning was made more impressive. The disaster that had come on the land was incontrovertible; there was destruction wherever you turned. **Today they lie deserted and in ruins**/'a ruin (*ḥorbâ*, 7:34) and there is no one dwelling in them'. It need not be contended that there was no population at all in any of the towns of Judah. Their numbers were, however, very small. The cities had been ransacked, and it was an impoverished remnant that was left living in very straitened circumstances. The ruins contrasted with their former prosperity.

3. There should have been no doubt as to the reason for this calamity: **because of the evil they have done.** Again there is a play on the two meanings of *rā'â*: 'disaster' from God (v. 2) which was the condign punishment of their 'evil' and was imposed by God on the people of Judah and Jerusalem to match their wrongdoing. Specifically their sin is identified as the worship of other gods, which denied the uniqueness of the LORD and marred the unswerving and exclusive loyalty to the LORD demanded in his covenant with the people. **They provoked me to anger by burning incense and by worshipping other gods that**

neither they nor you nor your fathers ever knew (cf. 11:17; 19:4;
32:32). 'Burn incense' (<√*qāṭar* piel, 1:16) occurs only outside the
Pentateuch and is used almost exclusively in the context of illegitimate
idol worship. Reflecting the fact that there were a substantial number
of Jews already in Egypt before 586 BC, 'you' here is specifically the
Jewish community in Egypt, distinguished from the 'they' who are the
Jewish people in Judah before the fall of Jerusalem. Obviously those
who engaged in false worship were aware of the identity of the gods
they claimed to be worshipping. The knowledge spoken of is that of
the true devotion and commitment that was required from those who
genuinely acknowledged the overlordship of the LORD (7:9; 19:4;
Deut. 13:6; 29:26; 32:17). What is being said in this phrase is that this
worship violated their covenant relationship with the LORD and their
unique acknowledgment of his rights over them. When the people
turned away from the LORD, they aroused his anger.

4. But it was not the case that judgment came on them immediately.
Over the years the LORD made every effort to reclaim his erring
people. **Again and again I sent my servants the prophets, who said,
'Do not do this detestable thing that I hate!'** (7:25; 25:4). The
prophetic ministry was not designed as a threat to the people, but as
means whereby the LORD graciously pled with them to abandon their
wilful ways and avert the disaster that would otherwise come on them.
For 'detestable thing', see 7:10; 32:35; 44:22. The practices involved
in the worship of other gods were acts of disloyalty which spurned the
LORD's expressed will and intruded into the people's relationship with
him.

5-6. Despite the warnings they received, their forefathers had
continued with their disobedient conduct. **But they did not listen or
pay attention; they did not turn from their wickedness or stop
burning incense to other gods.** For 'not listening' cf. 7:13b, 26; 11:8;
25:4, 7; 29:19; 34:14; 35:14-15. In such circumstances it was
inevitable that the divine execution of wrath would not be postponed
indefinitely. **Therefore** (simply 'and'), **my fierce anger was poured
out;**[49] **it raged against the towns of Judah and the streets of Jerusalem and made them the desolate ruins they are today** (cf. 42:18;
7:20). The matter was clear and obvious. The fires of destruction were
the outward reality coming from the fire of God's wrath. What had
been threatened (7:16-20) had now arrived.

---

49. The durative stative perfective is found with quasi-fientive verbs,
indicating an ongoing emotional response (*IBHS* §30.5.3c).

7. But the facts of history are one thing; learning their lessons for present behaviour is quite another. The obvious need not be so obvious after all if people are looking somewhere else, or have deficient vision. In vv. 7-10 there is an obvious intensification of the emotional tension from a sorrowful but calm recital of the facts of history to a challenging and indignant questioning of those addressed. **Now** (wəʿattâ, introducing a conclusion of present relevance, cf. 7:13) **this is what the LORD God Almighty, the God of Israel, says: Why bring such great disaster on yourselves** (<nepeš, 2:34) **by cutting off from Judah the men and women, the children and infants, and so leave yourselves without a remnant?/**'so as not to leave a remnant to you?' Judah here no longer refers to the people in the land, but to those of Jewish extraction, linked together by common religious bonds and background, wherever they were situated. In particular, those in Egypt were behaving in such a way that they were in danger of bringing on themselves the same fate as had come upon the land of Judah. A catastrophe involving all age groups in the community was going to have such a devastating effect that they would be left with no descendants at all. They would be 'cut off' (<√kārat), that is, declared to be no longer members of the community of the people of God and judicially separated from it.

8. Specific allegations are then made against the Jews in Egypt. **Why provoke me to anger with what your hands have made** (cf. 1:16),[50] **burning incense to other gods in Egypt, where you have come to live?** This makes clear that worship of pagan gods lies behind their condemnation. Though it was common for those from other nations if they moved from one land to another to change the gods to which they pledged allegiance (or at any rate to add to the ones they venerated), such modifications were forbidden to those who were the people of the LORD. No matter where they lived, they should have nothing to do with false worship. The consequence (ləmaʿan) of such idolatry is clear: **you will destroy yourselves/**'be cut off with respect to yourselves' (repeating the verb kārat from v. 7) **and make yourselves an object of cursing and reproach** (for both terms see 24:8) **among all the nations on earth.** For the final phrase, see 26:6.

9. The rhetorical question of v. 9 (for the use of rhetorical questions, see 3:6; 7:17) seeks to bring home the lesson to be learned from

---

50. Many Hebrew manuscripts read a singular form bəmaʿăśēh yədêkem, 'by the work of your hands', rather than the plural bəmaʿăśê, 'by the works of', found in the Massoretic Text. The difference would not affect the NIV translation.

history. **Have you forgotten the wickedness committed by your fathers and by the kings and queens**[51] **of Judah and the wickedness**[52] **committed by you and your wives in the land of Judah and the streets of Jerusalem?** The 'you' referred to here continues to be the Jewish communities in Egypt viewed in solidarity with those who had lived in Judah. There is a fivefold repetition of 'wickednesses' (*rāʿôt*) in Hebrew which intensifies the effect of the question by emphasising how frequently they had acted in this way. It is also noticeable how there is mention made here of the womenfolk, in that it leads on into the subsequent discussions where the women play a prominent role because they were so highly involved in the pagan cults to be found throughout the community (vv. 15, 19).

10. To this day begins to turn towards the present application of this history lesson. **They have not humbled themselves or shown reverence**/'feared' (<√*yārēʿ*, 32:39-40), **nor have they followed my law**/'walked in my law' (9:12; 26:4) **and the decrees I set before you and your fathers.** The switch to 'they' at the beginning of the verse probably indicates that v. 9 principally had those who had resided in Judah in mind, though those addressed and their wives were also implicated. 'You and your fathers' points back to the common origins and obligations of both groups. Their response was woefully inadequate: they were not 'humbled', (pual <√*dākāʿ*, 'to crush'), that is, they have not been overwhelmed by awareness of their wrongdoing (Ps. 51:17; Isa. 19:10; 57:15), nor did they display an attitude of reverence towards God (<√*yārēʿ*, 'to fear', 5:22). For 'decrees' see 9:12; 26:4. Israel's violation of the law and the statutes of the covenant is a central theme in Jeremiah (7; 11; 17:19-27; 34:8-22).

11. The solemn **therefore** (*lākēn*) begins the pronouncement of judgment on them. **This is what the LORD Almighty, the God of Israel, says: I am determined to bring disaster on you.** 'I am determined'/'I have set my face against' is a Hebrew idiom for being resolute and unyielding (21:10). Here there is a clash of wills, because in the next verse we are told of the similar determination of the people. But the LORD has decided that judgment must fall on them. Again 'disaster' re-echoes the 'wickedness' of v. 9 (cf. also v. 3). It is then made clear what this disaster will entail: **and to destroy all Judah.** They are to be

---

51. Literally, 'and the wickednesses of his wives', a distributive singular use of the suffix, which is generally taken to indicate each king's wives (GKC §145.l), though Keil (1873, 2:159) favoured understanding it of the nation as a whole, that is, the wives of both the fathers and the kings.

52. The plural is written without *yodh* in the plural suffix (GKC §91k).

destroyed/cut off (<√*kārat*, vv. 7, 8), that is, they will be subject to judgment because they have offended God (Exod. 12:15), no longer being recognised by him as his people. In this context 'all Judah' must refer to all the Jews living in Egypt whom Jeremiah is now addressing.

12. I will take away the remnant of Judah who were determined/ 'set their faces' (v. 11) **to go to Egypt to settle** (<√*gûr*, 43:5) **there.** Where there is a clash of wills between God and man, the outcome is inevitable. It is built up in a succession of phrases, many of which have occurred earlier in Jeremiah's preaching, but to dismiss what is found here as merely a redactional collocation of clichéd phrases is to undermine the solemn message that is being delivered and driven home by the force of sheer repetition. **They will all perish** (<√*tāmam*, 'to be complete/at an end') **in Egypt** is followed by a specification of how this will occur: **they will fall by the sword or die from famine. From the least to the greatest, they will die** (<√*tāmam*) **by sword or famine.** For sword and famine, see on 14:12. **They will become an object of cursing and horror, of condemnation and reproach.** As in 42:18, the accumulation of penalties brings out the ominous burden imposed on the people as they are brought to their end. 'From the least to the greatest' (literally 'from small and as far as great', cf. 42:1) is another example of merism, a figure of speech which points to two extremes of a class as a way of including all in the statement being made (e.g. Gen. 44:12; Deut. 1:17).

13. I will punish (<√*pāqad*) **those who live in Egypt with the sword, famine and plague, as I punished Jerusalem.** The question arises as to whether this involves the Egyptians or not. Although the focus is on the Jewish community, it would seem that all Egypt will be engulfed in calamity from which the refugees will not be exempt. So they will come to share in Jerusalem's fate just as they have participated in Jerusalem's rebellion.

14. None of the remnant of Judah who have gone to live in Egypt will escape or survive to return to the land of Judah, to which they long/'have lifted up their desires' (<*nepeš*; cf. 22:27) **to return and live;** 'for' (*kî*) **none will return except** (*kî 'im*) **a few fugitives.** 'Escape' and 'fugitives' come from the root *pālaṭ*, 'to bring to safety', whereas 'survive' (<√*śārad*) points to one who escapes from the battlefield. The final clause has often been dismissed as a redactional insertion which conflicts with the previous picture of total annihilation (v. 7). It should rather be seen as a glimpse of divine grace in the midst of condemnation of the people. It is not a lame ending but makes even more stark the severity of the impending calamity in that it is just fugitives that are seen returning. Previously Jeremiah had been able to hold out the hope of eventual restoration (cf. 29:18-19; 32:29-35), but this is not possible for a community so set on perpetuating the errors of the past by failing to recognise the obedience they owed to the LORD. The future prospects for those living in this way in Egypt were bleak.

Despite all that has happened in Jerusalem this chapter brings us back to the problems of chapter 2, worship of pagan gods. Nothing has been learned even though idolatry had brought disaster on the nation (2:8, 23). Note the parallels with chapter 7: 'ruin' (7:34), 'offend me' (7:18); 'sent prophets' (7:25); 'commit abomination' (7:10); 'listen/ incline ear' (7:24); 'pour out' (7:20); 'so now' (7:13). Jeremiah's message remained the same because its lessons had not been learned.

b. The Queen of Heaven (44:15-19)

Jeremiah's ministry was met with total rejection and brazen obstinacy. We are here given a very clear insight into the mindset of those who spurned the message of the LORD in that age and in ours. Their opposition involves a blatant reinterpretation of history which completely omits the fact of sin and plays down the claims of the LORD upon them. It was probably not just among the Jews living in Egypt that there were those who thought the decline in their national fortunes had begun with Josiah's reforms which were aimed at ensuring the exclusive worship of the LORD.

15. There are three groups indicated as joining in a common defiant response to Jeremiah. **Then all the men who knew that (kî) their wives were burning incense to other gods.** The first group of men seem to have been involved in the idol worship through their wives. The women had taken the initiative in the matter, but they were not acting clandestinely. The men knew and acquiesced. The second group consists of **along with all the women who were present.** This indicates that in the first instance there is a specific occasion in mind, possibly a religious festival which women could attend. That in itself may have indicated the presence of an element of syncretism. These two groups together are described as **a large assembly** (qāhāl), a term often used of a cultic gathering (cf. 26:17).

There is then added a third group: **all the people living in Lower and Upper Egypt.** It is not certain that the phrase should be translated 'in Lower and Upper Egypt'. The NIV footnoted alternative 'in Egypt and Pathros' (cf. v. 1) is misleading in that it does not show that 'and' is a supplement.[53] Literally, it is 'in land of Egypt, in Pathros', and the

---

53. The only textual evidence for the addition of 'and' is in the Syriac.

second phrase could be interpreted as epexegetic of the first.[54] That would mean that the third group consisted of others (presumably Jews) who came from the area of Pathros and who were not so involved in the pagan worship. More probably the phrase is added here not to indicate their presence on the particular occasion being described, but to set out the general response that was given to Jeremiah's message from Jewish groups throughout Egypt. The repetition of 'all' serves to underline how widespread the reaction was.

16. They **said to Jeremiah.** Their response is united and decided. **We will not listen** (<√*šamaʿ*) **to the message you have spoken to us in the name of the LORD.** Their refusal is not, of course, simply a matter of hearing the message; it is principally a rejection of the content of the message, which they will not accept or obey (cf. 43:1-2). This is to perpetuate the attitudes which had prevailed in Jerusalem and which had ensured its downfall.

17. 'For' (*kî*) introduces the reason why this would be their response. Their actions will be determined by what they thought was right. **We will certainly** (an infinitive absolute) **do everything we said we would.** 'Everything we said we would' renders a Hebrew idiom 'everything that came out from our mouth' which generally seems to be used in the context of making a vow (Num. 30:3, 13; Deut. 23:24). They had undertaken to perform certain actions, be it burning incense or offering libations, and they are not to be deflected from that. **We will burn incense to the Queen[55] of Heaven and will pour out[56] drink offerings to her just as we and our fathers, our kings and our officials did in the towns of Judah and in the streets of Jerusalem.** This is indirect corroboration of the extent to which the whole community had become involved in the corrupt worship in Judah prior to its overthrow. For the mode of worship, see on 7:16-19. The reference is to the widespread worship of a fertility goddess who was known in Akkadian as Ishtar, at Ugarit as ʿAthtart, and in Egypt as Isis.

---

54. Keil (1873, 2:162) proposed that 'in Pathros' is not epexegetic of the preceding phrase but should be taken as qualifying the verb *wayyaʿănû*, 'and they answered', indicating where the large assembly was gathered. While this is grammatically tenable, it does not take account of the fact that in the Hebrew text twenty words separate the phrase from the verb.

55. The Massoretic Text has *limleket*, which seems best explained as indicating a euphemistic substitution of *limleʿket*, 'to the service of heaven'. *lmlkt* was probably originally read as *ləmalkat*, 'to the queen of ...'

56. This is an instance of the infinitive absolute used without the preposition *lə* repeated to continue the previous infinitive construct (GKC §113e).

The Hebrew form of the name is Ashtoreth, and the Greek form Astarte. The Elephantine papyri of the late fifth century provide very clear evidence of the syncretism of Jewish worship in Egypt at that time (cf. v. 1). In an unashamed mixture of Israelite and Canaanite beliefs, they provided the LORD, Yahweh, with a consort, Anat-Yahweh. This group had existed for a considerable time prior to 400 BC, and it is not implausible to suppose its origins dated back to the time of Jeremiah.

Jeremiah's hearers presented a counter-theology of history to justify their actions by looking back to the time when idolatry had been rampant. **At that time we had plenty** ($<\sqrt{s\bar{a}ba^{\,c}}$, 'to be satisfied/ satiated', 31:14) **of food and were well off** ($<\underset{.}{t}\hat{o}b$, cf. 22:16) **and suffered no harm** ($r\bar{a}^{\,c}\hat{a}$). Though these terms were associated with the LORD's blessing of the land and its people, here they are used presumably in reference to the reign of Manasseh when idolatrous practices were openly fostered in Judah and enjoyed state sponsorship. That period was also a time of relative peace because Manasseh was a vassal of Assyria, the dominant superpower, and Egypt was not sufficiently powerful to challenge Assyrian domination of Syria–Palestine. The people attest their commitment to the worship of the Queen of Heaven because it works: history had shown that was the way to experience prosperity.

18. Those responding to Jeremiah contrast the state of affairs that had prevailed under Manasseh with what happened when Josiah introduced his reformation of the idolatrous practices of the land. **But ever since we stopped burning incense to the Queen of Heaven and pouring out drink offerings to her, we have had nothing and have been perishing**[57] **by sword and famine.** This bears testimony to the effectiveness (at least outwardly) of Josiah's reformation, but the earlier reference to the cult of the Queen of Heaven in 7:17-18 shows that Josiah's zeal was unable to wipe out entirely what had become a long-standing practice, and after his death it enjoyed a resurgence. In the popular thinking of the ancient world a lack of the necessities of life was the result of offending a deity. The people argued that it was because of the prohibition of the worship they formerly engaged in that shortages and disaster came upon them. Perhaps they were reflecting even on the period before Josiah's death at Megiddo in 609 BC, but certainly the evidence points to a profusion of troubles thereafter: droughts are mentioned in 3:3; 12:4; 14:1-6; 23:10, and there were also the repeated Babylonian incursions. The argument that is presented is

---

57. The form $t\bar{a}mn\hat{u}$ seems an Aramaising form for $tamm\hat{o}n\hat{u}$ (GKC §67dd).

based on the fallacy that because first A occurred and then B, A was the cause of B (*post hoc, ergo propter hoc*). They evidence no perception of the covenant demands of the LORD upon his people, and of their persistent failure to live up to the requirements that he imposed. There is therefore selectivity in the evidence they use to bolster their argument. They had no awareness of the LORD, no sense of having offended him, and an explicit focus on the enjoyment of material peace and prosperity.

19. The women added/'said' is a supplement to the Hebrew text required by the sense of the passage. **When** (*kî*) **we burned**[58] **incense to the Queen of Heaven and poured out**[59] **drink offerings to her, did not our husbands know**[60] **that we were making cakes like her image**[61] **and pouring out drink offerings to her?** Here is a strange mixture of pagan practice and an appeal to the law of the LORD. The argument seems to be that what Jeremiah was urging was a course of action that would involve them in renouncing their vows already taken (cf. v. 17). There was provision for a husband to disallow a vow his wife had taken without his knowledge, so that it became null (Num. 30:7-15). The women were saying to Jeremiah you have no right to ask us to make void our vow to worship the Queen of Heaven because our husbands knew about it all along. We cannot be accused of acting on

58. 'Burned' renders the participle *məqaṭṭərîm*, which indicates the ongoing nature of their action: 'used to burn' as a regular practice. It is also masculine. This is a possible use of the masculine instead of the feminine (GKC §145u), and its presence here may well account for the mistaken omission from the Hebrew text of some phrase such as, 'And the women said' (Lucian's recension of LXX), or 'And the women answered and said' (Syriac). But quotes are not always introduced, and it may be that these phrases are translators' supplements rather than any indication of what was in the Hebrew text before them.

59. *ûləhassēk*, 'and to pour out', is an instance of the infinitive construct used instead of the infinitive absolute as a continuation of the finite verb (an idiom found in later usage, *IBHS* §36.3.2). The infinitive construct hiphil usually has *î* (*IBHS* §36.1.1b; GKC §53k).

60. Literally, 'Were we making cakes … without our husbands?' The force of *balʿădê*, 'without', has to be gauged from the context. It might simply be without their knowledge, but also possible are without their approval (RSV), without their knowing and helping (NLT), or without their being involved (NRSV).

61. *ləhaʿăṣbâ* (the preposition *lə* with the hiphil of *ʿāṣab* I, 'to make an idol'; 'to copy', *HALOT*, 864) is unusually without mappiq in the *he* to indicate a third person feminine singular suffix (GKC §§58g, 91e), 'to form an idol of her'.

our own. Our actions were legal and binding and so our vow must
stand.

c. The Prophet's Warning (44:20-23)

There are two parts to Jeremiah's response. The first is found in
vv. 20-23 where Jeremiah himself disputes with the people regarding
their defiance. Then in vv. 24-30 he repeats the substance of the
message he had already conveyed to them.

**20. Then Jeremiah said to all the people, both men and women,
who were answering him.** It may be that the NIV translation here is
too terse. Taking the switch from the first ʿel to the subsequent three
occurrences of ʿal as being significant for the meaning of the passage
(though these prepositions are often used interchangeably in Jeremiah),
it may be translated, 'Then Jeremiah said to all the people, against the
men and against the women, even against all the people who were
answering him'. This would make clear that he was stoutly opposing
the response given him and the thinking that lay behind it.

Jeremiah agreed that the worship and non-worship of the Queen of
Heaven was the key to interpreting what had happened in the recent
past, but not in the way the people understood it. By insisting on bringing in the LORD into the picture, the prophet shows that such worship
led not to prosperity but to disaster which came as the LORD's (merci-
fully) delayed response to their conduct. **Did not the LORD remember
and think about the incense burned in the towns of Judah and the
streets of Jerusalem by you and your fathers, your kings and your
officials and the people of the land?** Remembering is of course with
a view to action (2:2). 'Think about' renders the phrase 'it (a feminine
used in a neuter sense) entered/came up on his mind' (cf. 7:31; 19:5;
32:35), that is, he was aware of and noticed what was going on. The
question is phrased argumentatively. 'Is it not the case with respect to
the incense ... that the LORD remembered them?'[62] He is urging the
people to recognise what was clear and patent—at least to the prophet.
They were, however, determined to interpret things in another way.
There is a clash of ideologies in their differing interpretations of their
recent experience. The historical facts of their economic and political
history are not in dispute, but rather the basic religious presuppositions
employed to structure the perception of those facts and give coherence
and meaning to them. For 'the people of the land', see on 1:18.

---

62. The ʿōtām, 'them' is resumptive. It might refer to all the groups listed
(NKJV) or to the incense, in which case it is unusual in that it is plural,
perhaps because of the repeated acts of idolatrous worship that are in view.

22. When the LORD could[63] **no longer endure your wicked actions and the detestable things you did** indicates that the time sequence involved was determined by the LORD's forbearance of their wrongdoing. For 'because of the evil', compare 21:12; 4:4. Their conduct had become so obnoxious to the LORD that he had to act to vindicate his name and to assert his right as the God of the covenant to the loyal obedience of those who were his people. By bringing on them the judgment he had threatened, **your land became an object of cursing and a desolate** (4:7) **waste without inhabitants, as it is today** (cf. vv. 6, 12).

23. Jeremiah repeats his argument. The people were unwilling to accept the explanation of their situation that the prophet was advocating, and so he felt compelled to restate it in an effort to make them understand. They were not going to be left in any doubt as to what had gone wrong. There are two aspects to the charge against them. Firstly, the rituals that were involved in pagan worship constituted a deviation from the standards the LORD had set: **Because you have burned incense and have sinned against the LORD.** Then the matter is rephrased in such a way as to bring out the broader covenant violations that they had perpetrated. Because you **have not obeyed him or followed his law or his decrees** (<*ḥuqqâ*, 5:24) **or his stipulations**, 'consequently' (*'al-kēn*) **this disaster has come upon**[64] **you as you now see.** 'Stipulations' (<*'ēdût*) occurs only here in Jeremiah and refers to the laws that have been divinely imposed on the covenant community. They disregarded what the LORD had set out as his covenant requirements, and he had eventually brought on them the destruction of their land and their expulsion from it.

d. Divine Judgment (44:24-30)
24. The second part of Jeremiah's rejoinder is found in vv. 24-30. Much of what he says had already been uttered in vv. 11-14, though perhaps the expression of it is now even stronger. There is a greater element of irony in his response, which seems to have dealt more with the situation of the women, though not exclusively so. **Then Jeremiah said to all the people, including the women, 'Hear the word of the LORD, all you people of Judah in Egypt.'**
25. This is what the LORD Almighty, the God of Israel, says: You

---

63. *yôkal* is an imperfect probably indicting the continuance of the LORD's forbearance.
64. *qārā't* on analogy of final *he* forms rather than *qārə'â* (GKC §74g).

and your wives have shown[65] by your (masc.) **actions what you
promised when you said,**[66] **'We will certainly carry out the vows
we made to burn incense and pour out drink offerings to the
Queen of Heaven.'** It is not clear what the respective roles of the
husbands and wives were. Had the husbands themselves taken this
oath, or was it a matter of being complicit in the actions of their wives?
For 'Queen of Heaven'/'service of heaven', see on v. 17.

Go ahead then, do[67] **what you promised! Keep** (fem.) **your**
(masc.) **vows!** is an ironic dismissal as the community is left to the
deadly consequences of the course of action it has committed itself to.
It is the only place in the Old Testament where Israelite vows are said
to be directed at a god other than Yahweh. They have been speciously
arguing that they must go on with what they have started since they
have entered into a vow and thus committed themselves to that course
of action. The impact of these words would have been more graphic if
we suppose them uttered at an assembly convened for the purpose of
syncretistic, or even pagan, worship with the cakes and incense already
prepared for the festivities.

26. However, their determined resistance to the LORD's way will not
be engaged in with impunity. Verse 26 begins with the **But**/'therefore'
(*lākēn*) that often precedes the announcement of judgment. **Hear the
word of the LORD, all Jews living in Egypt: 'I swear**[68] **by my great
name,'** says the LORD, **'that no one from Judah living anywhere in**

---

65. The second person references in this verse are of mixed genders: listing
them in the order they occur in the Hebrew, 'promised'/'spoken' is feminine,
'your mouth' and 'your actions'/'your hands' are masculine, 'shown' is
masculine, 'do'/'fulfil' and 'keep'/'do' are feminine, but then 'your vows' is
masculine. Keil (1873, 2:165) explained the feminines as arising from the
extent to which the women initiated this form of worship. Indeed 'you
women' (REB following LXX) reads *'attēnâ hannāššîm* in place of *'attem
ûnəšêkem*, 'you and your wives' (MT). It may, however, simply be a linguistic
development that second masculine plural forms were substituted for feminine
ones to which there was an increasing aversion (GKC §§144a; 145t).
66. Literally, 'you both spoke by your mouth and fulfilled by your hands
with respect to saying'.
67. Literally, 'certainly fulfil your vows and certainly do your vows' where
both verbs 'do'/'fulfil' (<√*qûm*) and 'keep'/'do' (<√*'āśâ*) are strengthened by
the addition of infinitives absolute, which the NIV brings out by 'Go ahead
then'. The use of the infinitives absolute echoes the similar construction in the
people's declaration, 'We will certainly carry out/do' (<√*'āśâ*).
68. Possibly a performative perfect, 'I hereby swear' rather than a past
action, 'I have sworn' (NKJV).

Egypt will ever again invoke my name or swear, "As surely as the Sovereign LORD lives".' The LORD swears by himself because there is none greater he can invoke (22:5; 32:22; 49:13; 51:14). His 'name' is a designation for all that he has revealed himself to be in his works of power. For 'great name', see on 10:6. In the face of such defiance the LORD asserts his sovereignty and vindicates his integrity. Because their actions have ruptured the covenant tie that bound them together, the LORD renounces their right to be his people and to invoke his blessings or sanctions in commitments they undertake. But it goes beyond that. Given the connection with what follows in v. 27, the reason why they will not invoke his name any more is that they will not be alive to do so.

27. The divine repudiation of the people is not a mere technicality, because the LORD continues to exercise active sovereignty over them. **For** (literally, 'Behold!') **I am watching** (<√šāqad, 1:12) **over them for harm, not for good.** This divine watchfulness emphasises that there is nothing hidden from the scrutiny of God, and that though he may not seem to act immediately, yet he is letting nothing go unobserved (1:12; 21:10). There is, however, a division between the outcome for the community in Egypt and the exiles in Babylon, over whom the LORD has committed himself to watch for their good (31:28). Here those who act in defiance of his will are warned that they do so at their own peril. **The Jews in Egypt will perish by sword and famine until they are all destroyed.** This prophecy is not to be understood absolutely, as if none at all were to survive. As the next verse shows, what is being presented is a picture of very widespread disaster. Nor does it seem likely that the words are to be understood only in some restricted sense, as for instance, referring only to those Jews who came down after the destruction of Jerusalem. What is being condemned is the pagan worship that was found largely throughout the Jewish communities living in Egypt, and the devastation to come upon them will extend over the same group.

28. But the community will not be totally eradicated. As at the end of v. 14 where a similar sweeping prediction is made only to be modified, here too there is a subsequent qualification of the absolute disaster foretold in v. 27. **Those who escape the sword/**'fugitives of the sword' (<√pālaṭ, v. 14) **and return to the land of Judah from Egypt will be very few.**[69] The general 'all' of 'until they are all destroyed' in

---

69. *mətê mispār*, 'men of counting', whose number can be counted and who therefore were few (*TWOT* #1263; cf. Deut. 4:27; 33:6; Ps. 105:12).

v. 27 is thus susceptible of modification. It is not clear if the subsequent phrase **then the whole remnant of Judah who came to live in Egypt** refers to some who continue living there after the disaster or to a remnant which moves back into Judah. However, the main emphasis is on the fact that they **will know whose word will stand—mine or theirs.**[70] This is the crux of the matter. It is a case of conflicting ideologies. The proof of which is right will be seen in what eventually occurs. When the LORD's judgment comes upon them, the truth will be made clear, and so the remnant that survive will be able to look back and understand all that has happened.

29. The people are then given a specific sign, an external reality that points beyond itself and that will act as a warrant for believing in the message that has been given them. **'This will be the sign to you that (kî) I will punish you in this place,' declares the LORD.** The punishment was to take place in Egypt; there was no exemption there from the LORD's judgment. The sign is given specifically **so that you will know that (kî) my threats of harm against you will surely stand.**[71] This brings out the conflict. In v. 25 they were ironically urged to 'do'/'fulfil' their vows. Now the same vocabulary and construction is used[72] to show that the LORD's threats will be certainly carried out.

30. Rather unusually the sign that the prophecy of judgment on the Jews will be fulfilled is itself a prophecy, one of judgment that will come on the Pharaoh who then ruled Egypt. **This is what the LORD says: 'I am going to give Pharaoh Hophra king of Egypt over to his enemies who seek his life** (cf. 21:7)**, just as I handed Zedekiah king of Judah over to Nebuchadnezzar king of Babylon, the enemy who was seeking his life.'** It should be noticed that the verse does not predict, what at first glance it might seem to say, that Pharaoh Hophra would be handed over to Nebuchadnezzar. Hophra, otherwise known as Apries, ruled from February 589 BC. It is fitting that his fate is compared to that of Zedekiah, in that he had been his ally, sending troops during the siege of Jerusalem (37:5). Those who sought Hophra's life were Egyptians. After trouble in Libya in 570 BC, Hophra sent a courtier to take charge of the Egyptian forces and

---

70. Literally, 'from me and from them', where *min*, 'from', marks the author or authority from whom a standard or truth originated (*IBHS* §11.2.11d).

71. The LXX omits the words 'in this place so that you will know that my threats of harm against you will surely stand', probably by scribal error skipping from one occurrence of *'ālêhem*, 'against you' to the following.

72. 'Will surely stand' renders the emphatic construction *qôm yāqûmû*, an infinite absolute followed by the finite verb.

suppress the revolt. But the army made the courtier, Ahmose (also known as Amasis), king. For a few years he seems to have shared control of the land with Hophra, but eventually defeated him, and procured his death in 568 BC (cf. 46:17). It was at this time of internal confusion and weakness that Nebuchadnezzar invaded Egypt (43:13). This prophecy could have been uttered by Jeremiah at any time after his arrival in Egypt. It does not imply that he survived there until 570 BC, when he would have been in his seventies. He may have done so, but we do not know. The focus of Scripture is not ultimately on those who are the messengers, but on the message and the one who sent it. It is only when God comes as the Word with his own message that the significance of the messenger and the message merge.

Here we have as acute an analysis as may be found anywhere in Scripture of what happens when the same agreed historical facts are interpreted by two rival ideologies/theologies. The interpretative matrix employed by each side seems able to accommodate the acknowledged facts and employ them to reinforce its own prior faith commitment. However, the total witness of Scripture points to two features that break through the short-term impasse. One dimension of the scriptural message is the historical grounding of faith in the LORD. Scripture does not call on us to base our perception of what is occurring around us merely on the experience of the immediate past; it also enjoins that we recall and obey the LORD's law, decrees and stipulations (v. 23), that is, it points to the covenantal structures of the past grounded in divine intervention to save and to establish his people. Without the beacon provided by the overall historical claims of the LORD, a foreshortened perspective may well assert that ideologies are equally compatible with events. But where is the Queen of Heaven now? Where had she been in Israel's past?

Equally, the acceptance of rival ideologies as displaying equal plausibility is shattered by the eschatological dimension. Present actions have future consequences which are assigned by the God of justice and holiness. Though in Jeremiah's day the fall of Jerusalem was diversely interpreted as the consequence of desertion of the Queen of Heaven, the *predicted* fall did in fact constitute a solemn divine warning regarding the inevitability of judgment. That is repeated here in v. 30. To act as if that is not so is to suppress basic instincts implanted in human nature regarding right conduct and accountability.

D. A WORD FOR BARUCH (45:1-5)

In chapter 45 there is a switch back from Jeremiah's ministry in Egypt around 580 BC to the period before the fall of Jerusalem, and to the critical year 605/4 BC. The inclusion of this passage here seems to function at a number of levels in the structure of the book.

Looking back to the last passage which is out of chronological sequence, namely the word of encouragement and promise of future hope to Ebed-Melech (39:15-18), we see similarities not only in their general theme but also in their particular vocabulary, for instance, 'I will let you escape with your life' (v. 5 and 39:18). Both these passages mitigate what appears to be a scene of total destruction and a dead end to the cause of the LORD. With Ebed-Melech it had been the destruction of Jerusalem; here what is said of Baruch serves to offset the disaster prophesied for the Jews in Egypt. There is, of course, a greater temporal dislocation in this instance, but the connection is still present in that Baruch is mentioned in 43:3. He is one of those who have faith in the LORD, and whose survival through the judgment that engulfed his generation is a token of the LORD's mercy.

It is also obvious that the mention of Jehoiakim's fourth year looks back to the incident recorded in chapter 36, so that that chapter and this form an inclusion round the historical narrative about the siege and fall of Jerusalem and its aftermath. In the Septuagintal ordering of the text chapter 45 (found there as 51:31-35) brings the prophecy to a conclusion, before the addition of the obviously later appendix of chapter 52. In this way the material about Baruch comes in the same position to the whole prophecy as a colophon, which would in ancient writings be found at the end of a work giving its name and possibly information about the scribe who copied it (see Volume 1, Introduction §2.6). Baruch then follows a recognised ancient pattern of writing by including a brief postscript about himself at the end of what he had produced as scribe and editor on Jeremiah's behalf. Lundbom argues that this chapter functions as an 'expanded colophon' that originally brought Jeremiah's scroll of chapter 36 to an end (1986:99-100). He considers that this provides evidence of Baruch's role as a scribe in the production of Jeremiah's scrolls and also of Baruch's involvement in the writing of the subsequent histories. Possibly in the promise of survival in v. 5, it anticipates the time when the younger Baruch will be left as a witness to the career and teaching of his mentor.

The additional information of this chapter also forms an apposite conclusion in that there is a significant verbal association between v. 4 and 1:10. This makes it probable that this passage was also located here to form an inclusion with the words at the beginning of the prophecy.

1. This is what Jeremiah the prophet told Baruch son of Neriah in the fourth year of Jehoiakim son of Josiah king of Judah, after Baruch had written on a scroll the words Jeremiah was then[73] dictating. The time reference is back to the events of chapter 36, the fourth year of Jehoiakim being 605/4 BC, using the same formula as 36:1. It may well be that structurally the position of chapters 36 and 45 is explained by the way they bracket the material of chapters 37–44. Baruch had been employed by Jeremiah as his amanuensis in preparing the scroll of messages that the LORD had given to him over the years regarding the situation in Judah. Though the NIV 'after' suggests that the scroll was completed and then this message was given, 'when he was writing' (NJPS) seems a more probable translation.[74] So Baruch's lament (v. 3) was uttered as he was writing the first scroll (the second scroll was not written until after the events of the following year), and it was the serious nature of the contents of the scroll that had such a traumatic impact on him. Baruch must have told Jeremiah of his feelings, and the prophet brought the matter before the LORD, from whom he then received this message to relay back to Baruch. Here we see Jeremiah who was so often involved in ministering to the needs of the nation bringing spiritual solace to an individual. More than that, we see God himself dealing not only with the nation as a whole, but also individually with those who were his and engulfed in the movements and catastrophes of their day and generation.

In 32:12 Baruch's name is given in full as Baruch son of Neriah the son of Mahseiah. Nothing is known about his father or grandfather,[75] but the fact that they are both named suggests that he belonged to one of the upper-class families in Jerusalem. His brother Seraiah (51:59) held a high position in the court of Zedekiah. Josephus describes Baruch as of 'a very illustrious house' and 'highly educated' (*Ant.* 10.9.1). Indeed, the attribution of later apocryphal works to Baruch

---

73. The 'then' of the NIV translation brings out the reference in the Hebrew phrase *haddəbārîm hāʾēlleh*, 'these words', where 'these' is made specific by the time phrase that follows in the Hebrew text 'in the fourth year …'

74. *bəkotbô* could indicate either 'while he was writing' or 'when he had written'. The latter would indicate a reaction after all that had been said came home to him.

75. There is a Maaseiah (*maʿăśēyāhû*) mentioned in 2 Chron. 34:8 as ruler of the city in Josiah's reign, but that name differs in two consonants from Mahseiah (*maḥsēyâ*).

shows the significance attributed to him in the ancient world. He has
fared less well in more recent times with authors such as Carroll treating him as a fictional character whereby the 'tradition created and
developed a subsidiary figure to accompany Jeremiah' (1986:723).
Carroll's interest in developing this thesis is derived from the
significance he attaches to the late deuteronomic school which he
holds responsible for the character and book of Jeremiah also.

2.   This is what the LORD, the God of Israel, says to you, Baruch.
What the LORD has to say is by way of response to Baruch's own
statement (v. 3) in which the LORD is referred to in the third person. It
is thus more probable that Baruch addressed Jeremiah than the LORD
in prayer, and that the LORD is now responding to Jeremiah's intercession on his behalf.

3.   You said, 'Woe to me!' gives expression to Baruch's feelings of
sorrow and anguish at the cumulative impact of the words he has been
writing out, which certainly included the oracles of chapters 2–6. The
scribe has been affected by the message in much the same way as the
prophet had been (4:19). 'For' (*kî*) **the LORD had added sorrow to
my pain**. This may simply be an expression to indicate that the LORD
had allotted him an experience of intense spiritual anguish. Alternatively, it is possible to think of the 'pain' (30:12-15) as the feeling that
Baruch already had regarding the situation in the land in his own day,
and that that has now been given a dimension of greater sorrow (8:18)
by the task of setting down Jeremiah's message in writing. The pain he
felt at the people's corruption would thus reflect the pain that Jeremiah
too had experienced (15:10, 18; 20:18). Living in a generation when
the word of God is despised is never an easy experience for those who
have a heart commitment to the LORD. **I am worn out with groaning
and find no rest.** This sentiment comes from Ps. 6:7, and expresses
how Baruch felt as he wrote down the message and grieved over what
was being said about the impending calamity on the land, and the
refusal of the people to heed the warnings that had been repeatedly
given to them. Anxiety over the future well-being of the nation of
which they are part deprives even those who have faith in the LORD of
a sense of rest (*mənûḥâ*) in such troubled times.

4.   The LORD then instructs Jeremiah to give this particular message to
Baruch. ⌞**The LORD said,**⌟ **'Say this to him: "This is what the LORD
says, I will overthrow what I have built and uproot what[76] I have**

---

76.   *ʾēt ʾăšer* with *ʾēt* introducing the subject is a somewhat unusual
construction.

planted, throughout the land".' The supplement, 'The LORD said', serves to make clear that what follows is no longer Baruch's speech. The two clauses introduced by 'what' could equally well cover people as well as places or things. The final clause may be understood as either particular, 'that is, the whole land' (so NASB, NRSV) or else as universal, 'so it will be with the whole earth' (REB). In favour of the universal rendering is the fact that the following verse mentions 'all people' which seems to include more than just those dwelling in Judah. There is also mention of the whole earth in 25:15. But the particular theme of the impending catastrophe on the disobedient covenant people makes the translation 'land' more natural here. It is the whole land of promise that the LORD has built and planted.

However the verbs, which are also used in 1:10 and similar passages throughout the book (31:28), are here used in an arrestingly different pattern. No mention is made of the positive sequel of building and planting after the LORD's judgment has come upon the land. 'Build' and 'plant' no longer set the agenda for the future, but refer to what has been done in the past. Poignantly that work is seen as about to be destroyed. The thrust of the passage is not simply to reiterate the certainty of the coming judgment, but to emphasise what it involves for the LORD himself. It is his own work that he is having to destroy. Before Baruch becomes overwhelmed with grief at the situation that he finds himself in, let him remember what is involved in it for the LORD, and that will act as a corrective to excessive indulgence in self-commiseration. The LORD's own concern will surpass that of any individual.

5. Verse 5 begins with a strong contrast 'But as for you'. If that was how matters stood with the LORD, then Baruch should be able to see his own circumstances in a different perspective. **Should you then seek great things for yourself?**[77] The implication is that Baruch's grief was not only for the calamities about to fall on his nation, but also for what that would mean in terms of his own personal ambitions. He was of a well-placed family and had been trained as a scribe who could have expected a distinguished career in public service in front of him. Accepting the truthfulness of Jeremiah's message, and recognising the intransigence and spiritual blindness of his generation, he realised that these options were going to be swept away from him in the coming disaster. He is urged, **Seek them not.** He will find his true portion and destiny in something other than the advancement the world seeks (cf.

---

77. There is no explicit interrogative; the interrogative sense is derived from the context (GKC §150a).

Ps. 131:1). Living in a generation that is under the curse of God's judgment, his priorities are to be governed by the divine message rather
than human hopes. His faith is not to be viewed as a step on the ladder
of self-advancement; it is sufficient reward in itself. The challenging
note in the LORD's word to Baruch reflects the way in which the
prophet himself was answered on several occasions (12:5-6; 15:19-21).

Ambitions based on worldly promotion ('for yourself') will be frustrated, **'For** (*kî*) **I will bring disaster on all people,' declares the
LORD.** 'All people/flesh' generally has in view mankind in their
weakness and transience (12:12; 25:31; 32:27). It therefore seems to
have in view a disaster that goes beyond the bounds of Judah. More
probably, the thought is that what is to come upon Judah when the
LORD of the covenant punishes his covenant people for their
disobedience is an event that would have universal significance and
implications.

In the troubled and disastrous times in which he lived, however,
Baruch was given a personal message of hope. Although the LORD
would pour out his wrath on his disobedient people, he would still be
discriminating towards those who had not rejected him. Baruch shared
the promise given Ebed-Melech (39:18). **But wherever you go I will
let you escape with your life.** The plural 'wherever'/'in all the places
that' invites the application not only to Baruch being safe when Jerusalem falls, but as being safe whatever happens after the rebellious
Jewish community in Egypt meets a similar end. Baruch's safety will,
however, only be at the expense of flight, and the phrase 'I will give
your life (<*nepeš*, 2:34) to you as booty' (38:2) indicates that he is just
going to escape with his life and no more. It would not be a comfortable experience, though it promised deliverance. In the face of the
overwhelming judgment of God there is still scope for divine
discrimination and rescue.

XV.   THE LORD'S WORDS

AGAINST THE NATIONS

(46:1–51:64)

OUTLINE

A. Oracles Against the Nations (46:1)
B. Against Egypt (46:2-28)
    1. Egyptian Ambitions Frustrated (46:2-12)
    2. The Conquest of Egypt (46:13-24)
    3. Egypt's Future (46:25-26)
    4. Reassurance for Jacob (46:27-28)
C. Against the Philistines (47:1-7)
D. Against Moab (48:1-47)
    1. Impending Overthrow (48:1-10)
    2. Unsettling the Complacent (48:11-13)
    3. Warriors No More (48:14-17)
    4. Judgment on Moab's Cities (48:18-25)
    5. The Doom of the Defiant (48:26-33)
    6. A Jar No One Wants (48:34-39)
    7. Destruction and Restoration (48:40-47)
E. Against Ammon (49:1-6)
F. Against Edom (49:7-22)
    1. Inevitable Doom (49:7-13)
    2. Sudden Invasion (49:14-19)
    3. Complete Destruction (49:20-22)
G. Against Damascus (49:23-27)
H. Against Kedar and Hazor (49:28-33)
I. Against Elam (49:34-39)
J. Against Babylon (50:1–51:64)
    1. Superscription and Introduction (50:1-3)
    2. Babylon's Fall and Israel's Return (50:4-20)
    3. The LORD's Work in Babylon (50:21-32)
    4. The Invincible Purpose of the LORD (50:33-46)
    5. Proud Babylon Shattered (51:1-33)
    6. Israel's Plea Answered (51:34-44)
    7. Destruction Inevitable (51:45-53)
    8. The God of Retribution (51:54-58)
    9. Seraiah's Mission (51:59-64)

The theme of the next part of the book of Jeremiah clearly distinguishes it as a separate section in the prophecy. The Septuagint, the Greek translation made in the third and second centuries BC, not only places these oracles after 25:13a, but also has them in a different order, and with several textual differences. Many commentators feel that the earlier position is the original one. In the Massoretic Text (MT) there is a logical progression both in terms of geography—from south-west to north-east—and probably also in terms of time of delivery. Beginning with Egypt the second superpower of the day may have been viewed as a suitable link to chapter 44, and also as providing a balance with the concluding section of the Oracles which deals extensively with Babylon, the dominant power of the era. However, the theme of the section is not primarily the destiny of these nations, great and small, but the LORD's determination and power which structures all that occurs on earth. The balance in the Massoretic ordering probably indicates that it is a later arrangement of the material than the more haphazard Septuagintal collection.

Were the Oracles composed by Jeremiah? Skinner represents a major strand of early criticism which held that they did not originate with Jeremiah. It was argued that the prophet could hardly have urged Judah to submit to Babylon and at the same time announced judgment upon Babylon. But this now seems a theologically superficial contention. While Babylon was the instrument of divine judgment on Judah, Babylon was still held responsible for her actions and would be required to account for them before the Judge of all the earth. Bright and Holladay hold that some of these oracles originated with Jeremiah. However, since Jeremiah was installed as a prophet to the nations and since such oracles are a feature of the records of all prophetic ministries except that of Hosea, there is no real reason to suppose that Jeremiah did not utter such oracles.

Were the Oracles against the Nations part of the first or second scrolls of chapter 36? How was the book subsequently expanded? The material of chapters 37–45 is consecutive and obviously to be taken together, but the variations that occur between it in the MT and in the LXX would indicate two editions. Because of the LXX connections with Egypt it is tempting to take the Hebrew original underlying the LXX as originating there during the closing years of the prophet's life. Certainly the position of chapter 45 (LXX 51:31-35) in the LXX material as a colophon dealing with Baruch supports the view of his involvement in the original production of this text. The MT text seems to have been produced after that. There is no need to posit a long line of editorial revision and expansion. The editing could have taken place

Order of the Oracles against the Nations.

	MT	LXX (Rahlfs edition)
Elam	49:34-39	25:14-20
Egypt	46:2-28	26:2-28
Babylon	50:1–28:64	27:1–28:64
Philistia	47:1-7	29:1-7
Edom	49:7-22	30:1-16
Ammonites	49:1-6	30:17-21
Kedar	49:28-33	30:23-28
Damascus	49:23-27	30:29-33
Moab	48:1-47	31:1-44

during Jeremiah's lifetime. If it is appropriate to see greater Babylonian connections with the MT text, it might have been prepared by Jeremiah and Baruch in Egypt for transmission to Babylon. The major reshaping of the order of its material may have been deliberately carried out to give it greater relevance to those in Babylon as they grappled with the problems of that empire's sovereignty and destiny.

A. ORACLES AGAINST THE NATIONS (46:1)

1. This is the word of the LORD that came to Jeremiah the prophet concerning the nations[1] constitutes a title that covers all the material in chapters 46–51. If it is accepted that these chapters have been moved from after 25:13, where the preceding verses in the chapter acted as an introduction, then this title (which does not occur in the LXX) was added at the time of their relocation probably by, or under the supervision of, Jeremiah himself.

The question has to be considered: how did these oracles function in Jeremiah's ministry? From the beginning Jeremiah had been called to be a prophet not only to Judah and Jerusalem but also to the nations (1:5, 10), and so it is not surprising to find material dealing specifically with them. The oracles are consistent with the note of judgment sounded against all nations (including some not mentioned in 46–51) in chapter 25.

There is considerable critical discussion of these oracles, and their

1. The formula is unusual with the absolute use of *ʾăšer* (GKC §138e[2]); compare 14:1; 47:1; 49:34; and contrast 1:2.

connection with Jeremiah. Most of the arguments against his authorship are highly impressionistic and subjective, for instance, the wide
variety of styles that are employed here, as if Jeremiah were limited to
one particular mode of composition. There is also pointed out an
historical incongruity between the prophet advocating surrender to
Babylon and at the same time predicting its eventual doom. These are
often advocated on the basis of the oracle being the product of human
wisdom. If they are of divine origin, then there is no incompatibility
between the prophet asserting an immediate course of action on the
one hand, and at the same time presenting Babylon as liable to God's
judgment for her behaviour.

There are oracles against the nations in all the prophetic books
except Hosea (e.g. Isa. 13–23; Ezek. 25–32; Amos 1–2). Indeed three
prophecies, Obadiah, Jonah, Nahum, focus on the nations rather than
Israel. It has been suggested that there are in total forty such
prophecies which are characterised by being about the destiny of one
distinctly named foreign nation, proclaiming a catastrophe that will
occur in its history (Hoffman 1982:78). Frequently the cause of the
impending calamity is traced back to the nation's sin. This reflects the
belief that the sovereignty and power of the LORD were not limited to
the one nation, but that he was the ruler of the earth. The universalistic
overtones of the nations being subject to his control, and so liable to
his judgment for their misdeeds, are nowhere asserted more clearly
than in these oracles. If anything, the oracles in Jeremiah are
distinguished by the fact that they do not single out the sins which the
nations committed for special mention, but rather focus on the impending execution of the LORD's judgment against them. They are very
vividly expressed in a variety of moods, and frequently here, as elsewhere, Jeremiah draws on language that was already well known from
previous prophets. Equally we have to observe that the earthly power
which God will use to overwhelm these nations is permitted to remain
in relative obscurity. The disaster that was impending for each nation
was that of war, but the enemy is not brought to the forefront (49:2
which mentions Nebuchadnezzar is exceptional), though the oracles
against Babylon make much more of the identity of the foe that will
come from the north. This also serves to keep the focus on the control
and sovereignty of the LORD. He is the one who has set himself against
the godless self-confidence of the nations.

It is possible that the Oracles against the Nations reflected a development of an earlier style of oracle in which the LORD as the divine
warrior pronounced disaster on his enemies. Those nations who
attacked the covenant people drew down upon themselves the wrath of

their covenant Overlord who had committed himself to protect and defend his own people. The oracles then were an expression of impending doom on the enemies of Israel, and therefore a means of providing reassurance to God's people that he would act on their behalf. However, because of the people's inclination to seek security in foreign alliances, divine denunciation of those nations also served notice on Israel to avoid such entanglements. In Jeremiah it is only Babylon that is specifically identified as having mistreated Judah. However, the LORD's sovereignty extended over the nations and he judged them for their mistreatment of others with whom they were in alliance (48:1-2, 45; 49:1-2). It is unlikely that the oracles were intended to be heard by the nations, but they constituted an affirmation of the LORD's international sovereignty. Nations which do not honour divine standards of conduct will be judged for their behaviour. The pretensions of every nation come under the scrutiny of the Lord of all the earth.

It is also the case that Oracles against the Nations would have gained the prophet a domestic audience. There would be a readiness to hear their enemies being condemned, and from the prophet's point of view, some of his audience might begin to perceive that the faults of others were not really so different from their own. If they did not make the connection, then the prophet might very well make it for them (Amos 1–2). But there was also the theological point regarding the equity of divine judgment. God's people were not being singled out unfairly when they were punished for their sins; the same standards operated for all nations. The LORD did not condone sin wherever it was to be found. Particularly in Jeremiah the LORD's evenhanded treatment of all nations means that there is also a message of hope for four of them: Egypt (46:26), Moab (48:47), Ammon (49:6), and Elam (49:39).

It is unlikely that the prophet travelled to those nations against whom he spoke, or that he took steps to have his message conveyed to them. The only prophet of whom it is explicitly recorded that he engaged in ministry to a foreign people in their own land is Jonah. The ministries of the southerner Amos in Israel and of Jeremiah in Egypt were interacting with the covenant people.

B. AGAINST EGYPT (46:2-28)

In the Oracles against the Nations as ordered in the Massoretic Text, the first oracle focuses on Egypt, the second superpower of the day which presented the alternative to Babylon that seemed so attractive to Judah's leaders but which was exposed as a delusive option by

Jeremiah. The LORD had revealed to him that he had decreed the dominance of Babylon as the instrument he would use to accomplish his purposes among the nations. Ever since the time of Moses Egypt had been regarded as hostile to the LORD and his people, and though their political involvement in Palestine had been minimal for several centuries, as Assyrian power declined during Josiah's reign, there was renewed and increasing Egyptian influence to her north. There is therefore an initial assertion of the LORD's sovereignty over Egypt.

There are two main sections to the prophecies given against Egypt. Verses 2-12 relates to the situation in 605 BC, whereas vv. 13-28 come from a less well-defined period and end with two appendices (vv. 25-26 and vv. 27-28) to the main material, in the first of which there is a positive note sounded regarding Egypt's future, and in the second a prediction regarding the survival of the people of God, which contains at least an element of hope. The oracle can therefore be viewed at various levels. When originally given, it was a word of hope for Judah that Egypt would not triumph, and therefore also a word of warning against trusting in Egyptian power. In later years when Jeremiah formed this collection it continued to speak of the LORD's power and his ordering of the affairs of the nations to further his purposes. This is especially true with the final sections which point to the salvation he would give.

1. Egyptian Ambitions Frustrated (46:2-12)

This oracle functions at two levels. On the one hand, it is a word of exultation over Egypt as receiving her due on the day of the LORD's vengeance (v. 10). On the other hand, when uttered by Jeremiah in the confused conditions after Carchemish, it constituted a powerful argument against the policies of the pro-Egyptian party in Jerusalem. It would be folly to trust in a power that had been so thoroughly defeated. This would have reinforced the message Jeremiah had been given that Judah should submit to Babylon.

2. The prophecies of this chapter (vv. 2-12 and 13-28) are given the heading, **Concerning Egypt.** No power lies outwith the ambit of the LORD's discernment and decree. The first oracle is then located in quite definite historical circumstances (cf. v. 13 for the second). **This is the message against the army of Pharaoh Neco king of Egypt, which was defeated at Carchemish on the Euphrates River by Nebuchadnezzar king of Babylon in the fourth year[2] of Jehoiakim**

---

2. For the construction see GKC §134p.

son of Josiah king of Judah. With the collapse and impending demise
of Assyria, Egypt, which had been fairly passive in her foreign policy
for centuries, began to take greater interest in the affairs of Syria–
Palestine during the later reign of Psammetichus I (664–610 BC).
Pharaoh Neco II (610–595 BC) continued to deploy the army and
resources that his father Psammetichus had built up, and it was as Neco
brought reinforcements north to help the Assyrians in 609 BC that
Josiah was killed at Megiddo. For the next four years the Egyptians
were based at Carchemish and exercised control over Syria and
Palestine, including Judah. But then in 605 BC Nebuchadnezzar moved
against the Egyptians. He is called 'king of Babylon' here proleptically
because at the time of the battle he was still crown prince under his
father Nabopolassar. Nebuchadnezzar completely routed the Egyptians
at Carchemish and chased them south, gaining control of Syria–
Palestine. He would no doubt have followed them into Egypt had not
the death of his father necessitated his return home to assume the
throne. The Battle of Carchemish was thus a turning-point in the
history of the area, as it disposed of the Egyptian challenge and
ensured Babylonian hegemony over those lands previously dominated
by Assyria.

The date given in this verse constitutes one of the main challenges
for those constructing a chronology of this period. The difficulties are
set out in Appendix §6. There is no doubt that the battle took place in
the second quarter of 605 BC, probably around the middle of May.

3. The first stanza of the poem (vv. 3-6) without identifying who is
addressed contains a vivid description of a call to arms, which is astonishingly followed by a rout. Though Egypt itself is introduced in the
second stanza of the poem (vv. 7-12), the enemy the Egyptians have to
face is never clearly identified. Here only the reference to the
Euphrates (v. 6) explicitly ties in with historical events. This presentation effectively emphasises that it is the LORD himself who works
through the power that defeats Egypt, whatever that power may be;
Egypt is having to face the LORD's campaign against her.
**Prepare your shields, both large and small, and march out for
battle!** The poem begins abruptly with the brisk plural commands that
set an army on its way. 'Prepare' (NIV, NRSV) does not really convey
the idea behind ʿārak, which always involves the idea of setting things
neatly in order, and so here 'line up' in formation (cf. NKJV margin)
with their shields in place, ready to move forward in disciplined array.
But whose army is being described: that of the Egyptians or of their
enemy? The picture of a state of high alert could apply to either side,

but if there is a deliberate de-emphasis of the identity of those opposing Egypt, then this may be taken as addressed to the Egyptian forces
by their officers. There may be a sarcastic twist to the words because
their preparations are going to prove ineffective (Nah. 2:1; 3:4)
because they have not appreciated who their real enemy is (v. 10).

The small shield, which is mentioned first, hence the order 'buckler
and shield' (NKJV), would have been held in the left hand, and carv-
ings suggest it was round and used principally to protect the head. It
probably consisted of leather stretched across a wooden frame, and
was oiled to help parry blows (2 Sam. 1:21; Isa. 21:5). The larger
shield would have been either oval or rectangular in shape and used to
protect the whole body. When advancing into battle such shields would
have been used to form a moving barrier capable of deflecting enemy
missiles from the soldiers, most of whom did not wear body armour.

4. As the foot-soldiers get into battle-array, further commands are
issued to the cavalry and chariot-forces. Such evidence as exists
suggests it is improbable that the Egyptians used cavalry as distinct
from chariotry to any great extent at this period, though the
Babylonians had made good use of the more versatile and mobile
cavalry for centuries. If then these words refer to cavalry rather than
chariotry, they are heavily ironic because this was a deficiency in
Egyptian resources. **Harness the horses, mount the steeds!**[3] **Take
your positions with helmets ᴌonᴊ! Polish your spears, put on your
armour!** 'Mount' is the first use of the verb ʿālâ, 'to go up', which
recurs in vv. 7, 8, 9, and 11 (twice) as an integrating theme in the
poem. 'Take your positions' conveys the idea of military preparedness,
'poised to strike' (*NIDOTTE* 2:500). The helmets were probably made
of leather, though later metal became common. Helmets were only put
on at the time of battle because they were quite uncomfortable to wear
in the heat. 'Whet your lances!' (NRSV) does not seem to render the
verb accurately. The idea of polishing a spear seems to have been to
make it glisten in the sun and so seem more horrendous to the enemy.
On the other hand, the translation 'lance' indicates what sort of
weapon it was, not one for throwing but rather for thrusting at the
enemy. Because armour was costly and sophisticated, it was not widely
available to armies of this period. For those who could afford it, it consisted of a sort of chain-mail in which between four hundred and six
hundred metal plates were attached with difficulty to a leather
undercoat.

---

3. The NIV, NRSV and NASB take *happārāšîm* as an object, 'Mount the
horses', but it may be a vocative, 'Mount, O horsemen!' (RSV, NJPS).

5. The description of the battle preparations is then suddenly interrupted by, **What⁴ do I see?** The question does not ask for information but is a rhetorical device employed to introduce a note of surprise, as is the use of 'I'. The LORD is the speaker as the conclusion to the verse makes clear, but what attention is being drawn to is the fact that after all these preparations, a battle, if not victory, would have been expected. Instead six brief clauses follow quickly one after the other, conveying the abrupt and panic-stricken confusion of a routed army. **They are terrified, they are retreating, their warriors are defeated.⁵ They flee in haste⁶ without looking back**/'they do not look back'. Where there had been advance (v. 3), there is now retreat; previously they had stationed themselves in battle formation, but now they flee in haste. Confidence is replaced by terror. For 'terrified' (<√ḥātat), see on 1:17. 'Warriors' is also another motif word in this poem, occurring again in vv. 6, 9 and 12 (twice). Here its use is ironic: this is what these strong men have come to. The delay until the third verb in identifying the subject as warriors also increases the note of astonishment. Yes, notwithstanding appearances to the contrary, these are warriors. **'And there is terror on every side,' declares the LORD.** The sixth element of the description is the phrase that is found elsewhere in Jeremiah's message (6:25; 20:3, 4, 10; 49:29). It was probably a traditional proverbial expression for devastating panic where no matter in which direction one turned the threat to life was such as to cause hope to be abandoned.

6. The impossible situation the army has found itself in is then conveyed by two terse statements. **The swift cannot flee nor the strong escape.** The Hebrew idiom expresses the conviction that neither of these outcomes can occur⁷ no matter how swift or strong (the same word as used for 'warriors' in v. 5) the individuals are. 'Escape' (<√mālaṭ piel, 'to deliver' from danger, generally with a human subject) will be impossible. There is then introduced for the first time in the poem a specific piece of information. **In the north by the River**

---

4. *maddua* is literally 'Why?' (as in most English versions). The thought is, 'Why do I see ⌐what I do⌐?', followed by a description of the scene.

5. *IBHS* (page 375 note 32) suggests that a qal passive form has here been pointed as a hophal. 'Beaten down' <√kātat, 'to beat fine, pound down'.

6. Literally, 'they flee a flight', *ûmāôs nāsû*, an internal accusative before the verb (cf. 16:19; GKC §117q).

7. The use of *ʿal* with the jussive rather than expressing a prohibition ('Do not let the swift flee away, nor the mighty man escape'; NKJV) conveys the view that flight is an impossibility (GKC §107p).

Euphrates they stumble and fall.[8] 'In the north' here is a geographical description and does not seem to be related to Jeremiah's earlier words about the foe from the north (cf. v. 20). 'Stumble' (<√*kāšal*, 'to totter') is often the prelude to falling (cf. v. 16), but here 'fall' is used in the sense of meeting their death in battle. The question that is raised is whether this is a description after the event, or a prophecy of it. In themselves the words could be taken either way. Certainly the time frame of v. 2, which is editorial and intended to locate the poem in its historical setting, does not determine it as being composed after the defeat at Carchemish. Understood as uttered after the event, there is a strong ironic, taunting note in the words. Taken as uttered before it, they warn that all human preparations are capable of being overturned in a moment.

7-8. In the second stanza of the poem (vv. 7-12), the taunting note is even more clearly expressed. It begins back before the battle, and points to the pride with which the Egyptians had undertaken their campaign. All the strength of Egypt had been poured out in anticipation of victory just as the great river Nile poured out its waters. **Who is this that rises like the Nile, like rivers of surging waters?** NKJV translates 'like a flood' rather than 'like the Nile'. Though *yəʾōr* may be used to refer to other rivers, it is the standard term for the Nile, which in an Egyptian context is undoubtedly the correct translation. Throughout this section there is a play on the word 'go up'. It has already occurred in v. 4 of mounting the steeds, but it recurs here in v. 7, v. 8 (rise: twice), v. 9 (charge!), v. 11 (twice: go up!, healing). 'Rises'/'goes up' refers to the annual inundation of the Nile, when it bursts its banks. This was known about throughout the east as a regular and reliable phenomenon. The 'rivers' are probably a reference to the various distributaries that are to be found in the delta region (cf. Exod. 7:19; 8:1). The same theme is repeated in v. 8, which gives an answer to the question of v. 7. It brings out the steady surging of the waters, and provides a contrast with the staccato and impulsive commands before battle. **Egypt rises like the Nile, like rivers of surging** (<√*gāʿaś* hithpael, 'to rise and fall perpetually'; 5:22; 25:16) **waters.** The spread of her influence and military power over the surrounding lands was as irresistible as the inundation of the Nile.

Then the poem turns to consider the motives behind her aggression.

---

8. Translations vary in their rendering of the tenses: the NKJV takes them as prophetic perfects, i.e. futures; the NRSV and NASB as pasts; the REB like the NIV uses present tenses, which leaves the matter undecided.

She says,[9] **'I will rise**[10] **and cover the earth/'land'; I will destroy**[11] **cities and their people.'**[12] The expansionist dreams of the Egyptian regime were spurring on their endeavours. However, while the Nile's flooding was of benefit to all, Egypt's policies are to cause havoc. 'Surging' also conveys the fact that the Nile also sinks; was it implied that this would happen to Egyptian ambitions too?

9. There is then a switch back to the instructions of the army officers (or to the ironic commands of the LORD as he prepares the Egyptian army for its come-uppance). **Charge, O horses! Drive furiously,**[13] **O charioteers! March on, O warriors!** We are back at the time of vv. 3-4, with the three commands perhaps reflecting the three main types of Egyptian force, though, as has been mentioned, cavalry was not an Egyptian strong point. Battle is about to begin, and Egypt puts all her allies and mercenary forces into the conflict. Those who constitute the army are listed as **men of Cush and Put who carry**[14] **shields, men of Lydia who draw the bow.** Cush refers to the region south of Egypt on the Nile, traditionally Ethiopia, but more accurately Sudan (13:23). Put has not been positively identified, but was probably Libya (though Bright 1965:306 argued for the east coast of Africa). The 'men of Lydia'/'Ludim' were from Lydia, though the term may be used of mercenaries from Asia Minor generally. Herodotus tells of

---

9. Translations vary in their renderings of *wayyōmer*, 'and he said'. 'He' is found in the NKJV; 'it' is in the NRSV; the REB supplements 'says Egypt'. The NASB gives another identity to the unidentified speaker, by rendering, 'And He has said, "I will rise and cover ⌞that⌟ land",' making the speaker God. That seems an unlikely turn in the thought of the passage. The NIV 'she' is an accommodation to the personification of the country as a woman.

10. The form *'a'ăleh*, 'let me bring up' (an army?), is a hiphil, whereas the English translations treat it as if it were a qal, *'e'ĕleh*, 'let me go up'. Perhaps the confusion is from the preceding occurrences of *ya'ăleh*, which could be either qal or hiphil in form.

11. *'ōbîdâ* is an unusual form for *'a'ăbîdâ* (GKC §68i). That it is a cohortative form would seem to imply that the two preceding forms should be taken as cohortative also.

12. Literally, 'a city and those dwelling in her'. *'îr*, 'city', is being used indefinitely, cf. 8:16.

13. *hālal* III 'to be confused, deluded' (25:16; 50:38; 51:7), is here used in the hithpoel 'behave like mad' to describe chariots driven in an unusual manner or speed, ('storm through', Nah. 2:4).

14. 'Carry' <√*tāpaś*, 'to take hold of', generally by gripping or handling an object, occurs twice, but the NIV treats its second occurrence as a scribal error unlike the NJPS which renders, 'the Ludim who grasp and draw the bow!'

Ionian and Carian settlers in the Delta forty years earlier (*Hist.* 2:153), and Greek and other mercenaries had been numbered among the Egyptian forces during the reign of Psammetichus I, so that there is no need to take this as another reference of some sort to Libyan force. They 'draw'/'tread' the bow, that is, use their feet or knees to bend it while strings are fitted.

10. Though the Egyptian army commanders urge on all the men under them, it will be to no avail. Neither the preparations of vv. 3-4 nor the reinforcements that are brought forward in v. 9 will deflect disaster. **But** (*waw*-disjunctive) **that day belongs to the Lord, the LORD Almighty—a day of vengeance, for vengeance on his foes.** 'Lord' is Adonai, reflecting the universal control of God, while 'LORD Almighty/of hosts' indicates the powers that he has at his command. It is his day, in that he so exercises his power and control that the outcome is one that accords with his will. He is going to bring vengeance (<√*nāqam*, 5:9; 11:20) 'on his foes' (*miṣṣārāyw* is deliberately used because of its similarity to *miṣrayim*, 'Egypt'), that is, he is going to vindicate his name and purpose against those who defy him. It may be that their opposition has been seen in their attitude to his people, and these words are often associated with the way in which the Egyptians had defeated Judah at Megiddo and killed Josiah. That has not gone unnoticed by the ruler of all.

The sword will devour till it is satisfied, till it has quenched its thirst with blood. This imagery develops a common Hebrew expression, 'the mouth of the sword', and uses it to express the carnage that will develop on that day (cf. 2:30; 31:14). What is done is not just a matter of an international clash. It is the LORD claiming his due. **For** (*kî*) **the Lord, the LORD Almighty, will offer sacrifice in the land of the north by the River Euphrates.** 'Sacrifice' is a metaphor for slaughtering rebellious nations in judgment (cf. Isa. 34:6) which will occur through the slaughter of their armies.

11. The defeated Egyptians are taunted because there is nothing they can do to remedy their situation. They had been the ones who were going to go up and overwhelm the earth (v. 8); well, let them now go up. There is a twofold edge to the mention of Gilead. It was in the area of Syria–Palestine that came under Egyptian control in the years between Megiddo and Carchemish (609–605 BC). Since it was now firmly in Babylonian hands, there is the taunt that the Egyptians cannot now do what they had once done. Also there is the thought that Gilead was famed as a source of medicinal remedies. **Go up to Gilead and**

get[15] **balm, O Virgin Daughter of Egypt.** For Gilead and balm, see
on 8:22. The description of Egypt as 'Virgin Daughter' probably
derives from the fact that since the withdrawal of the Assyrians around
660 BC her relative isolation had protected her domestically from the
impact of calamitous defeats such as are now to come upon her. **But
you multiply[16] remedies in vain** (*laššāwʿ*, 44:30); **there is no healing
for you.** 'Healing' (<√ʿālâ, 'to go up', as in 30:13) denotes the coming
up of new skin to cover the wound. Despite all their going up to seek
remedies, their attempts to remedy their military defeats will be to no
effect. They have defied the LORD and there is no human stratagem
that can extricate them from the consequences of their folly.

**12. The nations will hear[17] of your shame[18]; your cries will fill the
earth** (cf. 14:2) intensifies Egypt's agony as others get to know of her
defeat. *qālôn*, 'shame', points to the disgrace and dishonour that result
from being vanquished. Others will treat them with contempt, and they
will no longer be able to intervene decisively in the affairs of Palestine,
as Judah found to her cost in the years before the fall of Jerusalem.
There would be no possibility of covering up the matter and producing
a public record with a spin in their own favour—something the
Pharaohs were not averse to. They were divine, and how could a god
be defeated? But this defeat will be known about by all. The picture of
the confused rout of her army takes up the two ideas of 'stumble' and
'fall' from the last verse of the first stanza, and so brings the poem as a
whole to a conclusion. 'For' (*kî*) **one warrior will stumble over
another; both will fall down together**. Egypt's power has not
brought her the victory she expected because she did not really identify
who her foe was: not Babylon, but the LORD who is directing the
affairs of the nations to suit his own purposes.

---

15. The verbs 'go up' and 'take' are feminine singular imperatives in view
of the personification employed.

16. The kethibh is *hirbîtî*, representing the old feminine ending, cf 2:33; 3:4.
The qere substitutes *hirbêt*.

17. The verbs 'will hear', 'will fill', 'will stumble' and 'will fall' are all
perfects. Unlike most other English versions which translate these with past
tenses, the NIV treats them as prophetic perfects, referring to a future situation
which is conceived of as certain to occur. The choice between the two styles
of translation depends on whether this prophecy as a whole is viewed as a
prior announcement of impending defeat or as a taunting description of what
has already occurred.

18. The REB 'cry' represents a reading *qôlēk*, 'your voice' (LXX), rather
than *qəlônēk*, 'your shame', which is the more unusual word (13:26).

2. The Conquest of Egypt (46:13-24)

Jeremiah's second poem about Egypt (vv. 13-24) has more difficulties connected with it than the first. These are both linguistic and in terms of its setting. The poem is again in three stanzas with the first and last (vv. 14-17 and vv. 20-24) describing the disaster the Egyptians experience and the middle stanza (vv. 18-19) exploring the reasons for it. If the poem was uttered prior to the fall of Jerusalem it would have reinforced Jeremiah's advocacy of a change in official policy away from favouring Egypt. The prophet showed that Egypt should have been written off as a realistic source of assistance and that Judah should do as the LORD urged and submit to Babylon.

13. This is the message the LORD spoke to Jeremiah the prophet[19] about the coming of Nebuchadnezzar king of Babylon to attack Egypt is unspecific as to the date of this attack. Three options are mooted: (1) around 604 BC, (2) around 582/81 BC, and (3) around 568 BC. After the Egyptians had been routed at Carchemish and chased south, Nebuchadnezzar had to give up his pursuit in 605 BC to take the throne of Babylon. He did, however, return to the area in 604 BC, capturing Ashkelon, the Philistine city. It could have been at this time that he pressed hard on Egypt, but the new introduction here favours a different scenario from v. 4. There was also the major battle in late 601 BC where the two sides fought to a standstill. But that was not a Babylonian victory and to take it as the reference here would imply that Jeremiah had wrongly anticipated the outcome. Though there was also the move against the Egyptian forces during the siege of Jerusalem (37:5), a more sustained campaign against Egypt does not seem to have occurred until 582/81 BC. The evidence for this rests on the statement of Josephus (*Ant.* 10.9.7) that in the twenty-third year of his reign, after subjugating the Ammonites and Moabites, Nebuchadnezzar attacked Egypt. The Babylonian Chronicle for this period has not yet been discovered so that Josephus cannot be corroborated. In that he also records that Nebuchadnezzar slew the currently reigning king and set up another, whereas Hophra is known to have reigned from 589 BC until at least 570 BC, there is a tendency to discount his evidence. The final option is a date around 568 BC, but again we have little evidence concerning this (see on 43:13).

It is uncertain whether the poem anticipates events or describes the

---

19. This formula is also found in 50:1. Keil (1873, 2:183) suggests that the use of *dibber* and not *hāyâ* might indicate it was not uttered in public by Jeremiah, but only written down.

outcome of hostilities. If the events are those of 604 or 601 BC, it must have anticipated them as fuller details would have been expected in a description. If it is dated to 588 BC, it might refer to the poor showing of Hophra who returned home without engaging the Babylonians. Most probably it anticipates what occurred around 568 BC, and may have been uttered at any time in the preceding years.

14. Announce this in Egypt, and proclaim it in Migdol; proclaim it also in Memphis and Tahpanhes. For 'announce' and 'proclaim', see on 4:5. These words are addressed to a number of people, probably messengers or heralds who are viewed as going to these cities throughout Egypt with their news and with a summons to get ready for action. Their general destination is given first, followed by the names of three representative Egyptian cities in Lower Egypt. For Migdol, see on 44:1; for Memphis (Noph) and Tahpanhes, see on 2:16. Situated in the delta area, these cities would have been among the first to feel the impact of Babylonian aggression launched from the north. **Take your positions and get ready, for** (*kî*) **the sword devours those around you.** The call to action is in the singular: perhaps the people are being viewed as a group in the response that is expected of them. 'Those around you', neighbouring states, have already experienced the impact of Babylonian military might in Palestine.

15. But as in the previous poem the sounds of preparations are followed by an abrupt and puzzled change: **Why will your warriors be laid low?**[20] As the text stands (followed also by the NASB, NKJV and NJPS), the description is one of an army being devastated. The verb 'be laid low' (<√*sāḥap*, niphal) occurs elsewhere only in Prov. 28:3 (qal) to describe how a driving rain 'washes away' or 'beats down' the crop. That gives a vivid picture of the defeated and bedraggled forces. 'Your warriors' (<*'abbîr*, 'mighty one, strong one') uses a noun which may refer to stallions (8:16; 47:3; 50:11) or bulls (Ps. 50:13) as well as being an epithet of God ('the mighty one of Israel, or the mighty one of Jacob' Gen. 49:24; Isa. 1:24; 49:26). It is used of soldiers and men of importance in Judg. 5:22; 1 Sam. 21:8; Job 24:22; 34:20; Lam. 1:15. However, the following verb 'be laid low' is singular, as is also 'stand', and the 'them' of 'push them down'. While the plural noun could be taken as a distributive usage implying each and every one of them and hence the following singulars (GKC §145l), this discrepancy has led to other readings of the text being favoured.

---

20. The verbs in this and the following verse are prophetic perfects, portraying the future defeat as certain to occur.

Following the LXX,[21] the NRSV and the REB take the reference in 'warriors' to be to the bull-god, possibly using a plural of majesty. 'Why has Apis fled? Why did your bull not stand?' Apis was the bull-god worshipped at Memphis, and revered as the son of, or an aspect of, the god Ptah. Since images of deity were carried into battle, and the flight or capture of such an image would be interpreted as the defeat of those worshipping that particular god, it is possible that Nebuchadnezzar's success is being portrayed as the vanquishing of a prominent Egyptian god. The bull has fled.

They cannot stand, for (*kî*) **the LORD will push them down.**[22] Their inability to maintain their position again points to the fact that the ultimate enemy against whom they are contending is not the as yet unnamed Babylonians, but God himself. When he pushes, none is able to keep his place.

16. As their subsequent speech makes clear, this verse refers to the foreign troops who formed a significant contingent of the Egyptian forces. **They will stumble**[23] **repeatedly; they will fall over each other.** In their confused panic the soldiers get in each other's way as they attempt to escape (cf. use of 'stumble' and 'fall' in vv. 6 and 12). **They will say, 'Get up, let us go back to our people and our native lands, away from the sword of the oppressor.'** The mercenaries brought from Asia Minor (cf. v. 21) had mainly settled in the eastern delta, but now the attack has been so devastating in its impact that they do not think of retreating to their base in the delta, but of quitting Egypt altogether. For 'the sword of the oppressor', see on 25:38.[24]

---

21. The LXX reads, 'Why has Apis fled? Your chosen calf has not remained.' This was obtained by dividing the consonants of the uncommon verb *nišḥap* into *nās* (from the more frequent root *nûs*, 'to flee') and *ḥap*, referring to Apis, the Egyptian god: 'Haf has fled'. This also fits in with the following singulars. 'Your calf', singular, is also favoured by the reading *'abbîrēk* found in many Hebrew manuscripts.

22. *hādap* is used for the movement of an object or person from one point to another, often with physical force; used for overthrow of idols in 1 Sam. 5:1-12; and of cattle shoving one another in Ezek. 34:11.

23. The Hebrew is obscure. Literally, 'he increased one stumbling'. The LXX renders 'your multitude has failed', reading *rubbəkā* for *hirbâ* (hence the NRSV). The REB reads *'erbəkā*, 'your mixed multitude'.

24. *ḥereb hayyônâ* is anomalous if taken as a participle following a noun in that the noun in anarthrous. It is more likely to be a construct chain, with the feminine being of neuter significance, 'oppression', but cf. GKC §126w, 'the sword which oppresses (?)'.

17. There they will exclaim[25] continues the reaction of these mercenary forces. 'There' probably does not mean back in the safety of their
native lands, but 'there' in the situation caused by the oppressor's
sword. Like soldiers everywhere involved in a debacle caused by the
incompetence of their leaders, they have scathing comments to make
about Pharaoh. **Pharaoh king of Egypt is only a loud noise.** Another
way of understanding this is that this is a title, 'Loud noise', they give
to Pharaoh. 'Noise' ($<\sqrt{šā^c ôn}$ II, 'roar, uproar, confusion, 25:31) was
no doubt chosen because of the overtones of the homonym $šā^c ôn$ I,
'desolation, destruction, ruin' (24:31; Ps. 40:3). He makes a noise that
only leads to ruin. Furthermore, **he has missed his opportunity.** He
has shown himself incapable of making vital decisions at the right
time. Because the Hebrew verb 'missed' ($he^c ĕbîr$) resembles to a
certain extent the name Hophra ($hopra^c$, 44:30; Egyptian $W^c ḥ$-yb-r^c,
HALOT 341) it has been suggested that there is a play on his name
here (Bright 1965:306; Holladay 1989, 2:330). This is not proven, but
plausible in that other evidence suggests Hophra was an impetuous
ruler who often displayed a woeful lack of sound judgment (*ABD*
3:286-87).

**18. 'As surely as I live,' declares the King, whose name is the
LORD Almighty.** This is one of three passages in Jeremiah (also 48:15
and 51:57) where 'declares' ($n^c um$) is followed not by the LORD (that
is, Yahweh), but by 'the King' (cf. also 5:22; 23:24; *TDOT* 9:113),
who is then further described as the sovereign ruler in contrast to the
derisory title accorded to Pharaoh. The true source of direction and
authority does not lie with any Pharaoh—god though he claimed to
be—but with the LORD of hosts, in whose control lie the forces of
heaven and earth. He declares what is going to happen, that is, what he
is going to bring about, and guarantees the accuracy and truthfulness of
what he says with a solemn oath.

The divine statement is introduced by $kî$, which here functions to
introduce what is asserted by the oath. **One will come who is like
Tabor among the mountains, like Carmel by the sea.** The precise
point of this comparison is not clearly stated. 'Surely as Tabor is
among the mountains, and as Carmel by the sea, so shall he come'
(NKJV) makes the point of the remark the obvious certainty of the
coming of the unidentified party. 'Surely one shall come *who looms up*
like Tabor among the mountains, or like Carmel by the sea' (NASB)
seems a more probable understanding. Tabor, at the east of the Valley

25. 'Give Pharaoh ... the name' (NRSV) follows the LXX which seems to
have read $qir^c û šēm$ for $qār^c û šām$.

of Jezreel, is a relatively isolated peak. It is not particularly high (1843 feet, 562 m), but its isolation makes it dominate the surrounding countryside. Similarly, at the western end of the Valley of Jezreel, Carmel (470 feet, 143 m at the coast, but the Carmel range rises to over 1700 feet inland) on the Mediterranean coast dominates the coastline. The focus of the poem thus turns from the situation among the Egypt forces to the individual who will cause such panic. Perhaps with a reference to Egyptian art where Pharaoh was portrayed as taller than other men, the predicted conqueror is described as a dominating figure who will tower over Pharaoh and control Egypt.[26] That Nebuchadnezzar is not named makes the prediction all the more ominous. But there can be no doubt that the ultimate power is not Nebuchadnezzar, but the LORD who announces and decrees his coming.

19. Therefore the advice is issued, almost in tones of sorrow. **Pack your belongings for exile, you who live in Egypt**/'daughter dwelling in Egypt' (NASB). The term 'daughter' explains the subsequent feminine references and the choice of 'heifer' as a figure for Egypt. Perhaps the term also conveys overtones of helplessness. They may as well get ready now, **for** ($k\hat{\imath}$) **Memphis will be laid waste** ($\check{s}amm\hat{a}$, 2:15) **and lie in ruins** ($<\sqrt{n\bar{a}\d{s}\hat{a}}$, cf. 2:15 footnote) **without inhabitant.** The references to exile and ruins may be a way of saying that a fate similar to that which befell Jerusalem awaits the city of Memphis which had regained much of its former political and religious significance in Egypt under Psammetichus I and his successors. There is no evidence that Nebuchadnezzar ever captured Memphis though it was taken by the Persian emperor Cambyses in 525 BC.

20. The second stanza of the poem (vv. 20-24) covers the same ground again. **Egypt is a beautiful[27] heifer** presents a picture of a prosperous agricultural economy. The choice of 'heifer' seems to be out of place given that it was bull worship that was practised in Egypt (v. 15). One wonders if it is just a matter of grammatical congruence with 'daughter' (v. 19) or if there are negative overtones. Certainly what awaits her is not pleasant. **But a gadfly is coming against her from**

26. Holladay (1989, 2:325-6) argues that Tabor is an isolated peak and may here refer to Egypt or the Pharaoh who will be isolated and thrown into the sea. Another suggestion is that the mention of Tabor and Carmel designates the line of the Egyptian retreat after Carchemish, but that seems to be too early to fit the setting of this poem.

27. The Massoretic $y\partial p\bar{e}h$-$piyya$ is most probably to be reconstructed as $y\partial p\hat{e}piyya$, 'most beautiful'. See also GKC §84[b]n.

the north.[28] A 'gadfly'/'a nipping/biting one' (*qereṣ* only occurs here, but the corresponding verb *qāraṣ* means 'to narrow' or 'to pinch') has not been precisely identified. However, it is not to be thought of as a minor irritant, but as some sort of insect whose bite would drive cattle to distraction, possibly causing them to stampede in their wretchedness. A similar illustration using flies and bees is found in Isa. 7:18. By this time Jeremiah's mysterious description of the foe from 'the north' meant only one power—Babylon. It would cause havoc in Egypt, but its impact would not be fatal to the land.

21. **The mercenaries** (*śākîr*, 'one who is hired') **in her ranks are like fattened calves.** The mercenaries (cf. v. 16) were well treated by Pharaoh because his power depended upon them. They are compared to 'calves of the stall' (Amos 6:4; 1 Sam. 28:24; Mal. 4:2), those the farmer has penned up and carefully fed so that they will be ready for eating on some special occasion. These pampered troops will be unfit for fighting and only slaughter awaits them, but they will not stay for that. 'For' (*kî*), as in v. 16, **they too will turn and flee together, they will not stand their ground, for** (*kî*) **the day of disaster is coming upon them, the time for them to be punished.** 'Flee' and 'not stand' reflect v. 15. For 'day of disaster' see on 18:17; and for 'time for them to be punished' see on 9:23; 23:12.

22. A third animal comparison is then employed. **Egypt**[29] **will hiss**[30] **like a fleeing serpent as** (*kî*) **the enemy advances in force; they will come against her with axes, like men who cut down trees.** The picture seems to be one of a serpent that has been disturbed in its lair in the undergrowth as foresters come to fell trees. It then slithers away in helpless retreat. The imagery would have been suggested by the extensive use of the coiled serpent as a symbol of divine power in Egypt, probably to represent Pharaoh's ability to strike in deadly fashion against all that dared to oppose him. But now he is just a disturbed and frightened snake slithering away. The reference to the felling of trees may reflect the practice of ancient armies as they prepared siege

---

28. The MT *bāʿ bāʿ*, rendered by the NASB 'A horsefly is coming from the north — it is coming!' (cf. also NJPS), may be a case of repetition for emphasis. However, many Hebrew manuscripts and ancient versions such as the LXX and the Syriac read *bāh*, with mappiq in the *he*, 'against her', and this is followed by the NIV, REB and NRSV.

29. *qôlāh*, with mappiq, 'her voice' or 'her sound', has a feminine pronominal suffix referring back to 'daughter of Egypt' in v. 19.

30. 'Hiss' (NIV) is not in the MT and reflects the LXX. MT is literally, 'her sound like the serpent ⌊as⌋ it goes.'

works against a city. In Israel such felling was strictly controlled by covenant law (Deut. 20:19-20), but other nations would have acknowledged no such limitations.

23. Forests were not a feature of Egyptian topography. The figure is employed to refer to her resources in general. **'They will cut down her forest,' declares the LORD, 'dense though (*kî*) it be.'** Felling of a complete forest will be easily accomplished because of the size of the enemy forces. Their numbers are described using yet another animal comparison. 'For'(*kî*) **they are more numerous than locusts, they cannot be counted.** There is in the original a wordplay between numerous and locusts.[31] This is a common hyperbole in the Old Testament for a vast number (cf. Judg. 6:5; 7:12). All these images combine to present Egypt as helpless and passive before the foe who advances against her. It is an uneven contest with numbers and aggression being stacked on the other side.

24. The section is brought to a close with a further statement of Egypt's doom. **The Daughter of Egypt will be put to shame, handed over to the people of the north.** This resumes the description of v. 19. Female captives were roughly treated in ancient warfare, and the inhabitants of the land are here given into the power of their enemies to use and abuse as they like. 'The people of the north' forms an inclusion with 'the north' (v. 20) to conclude this stanza.

3. Egypt's Future (46:25-26)

This section is the first of two supplements to the main oracles about Egypt. It is a prose summary of what has already been said (the REB is exceptional in recognising poetry here), but concludes with a surprising statement regarding subsequent Egyptian restoration (v. 26b). This seems to come from revelation given to Jeremiah towards the close of his ministry.

25. The LORD Almighty, the God of Israel, says: 'I am about to bring punishment on Amon god of Thebes, on Pharaoh,[32] on Egypt and her gods and her kings, and on those who rely on

---

31. *rabbû*, 'they are many'; *'arbeh*, 'locust ⌐swarm⌐'.

32. The MT has a double mention of Pharaoh (cf. NKJV, NRSV). This may be a scribal error, and, if so, it is probably the first occurrence that is intrusive in that the second is linked into the phrase 'Pharaoh and those who are trusting in him'. English translations that retain both references to Pharaoh make the final 'on Pharoah and on those who rely on him' epexegetic of what precedes, but it is hard to see any justification for this in the Hebrew text.

Pharaoh.' The LORD says he is about to exercise his oversight of the king of Egypt by bringing punishment (<√*pāqad*) on all connected with Egypt. The Hebrew repeats the preposition 'on' six times,[33] which gives the statement a solemn, inescapable overtone. Amon god of Thebes (the Greek name for the city; the Hebrew name of the city was 'No') was the deity worshipped there, who, combined with the sun god Re, became the state deity of Egypt. Thebes was the chief city of Upper Egypt, being 325 miles (600 km) south of Memphis. It is now best known for the remains at Luxor and Karnak. The city was plundered by Cambyses in 525 BC (cf. v. 19). Pharaoh himself will not be exempt from the LORD's retribution—the whole political and religious apparatus of Egypt will suffer. The identity of 'those who rely on/put their trust in Pharaoh' depends on the setting of this saying. It most naturally reads as a reference to the Egyptians themselves, but if it was originally uttered before the fall of Jerusalem, then it would also have had very clear implications for the pro-Egyptian party in Judah. If uttered after 586 BC, then it might well reflect on the Jews who had moved south to find shelter in Egypt. In either case the message emphasised that the initiative and sovereignty are the LORD's.

26. The theme of the LORD's irresistible power is continued in the next verse. **I will hand them over to those who seeking their lives** (cf. 21:7), **to[34] Nebuchadnezzar king of Babylon and his officers.** This is a clear statement of who is involved in what the LORD will accomplish (cf. 21:7; 44:30). But then there is a surprising declaration that all will not be lost. **'Later, however, Egypt will be inhabited as in times past,' declares the LORD.** This glimpse of hope is one that is found in other prophecies against the nations (cf. 48:47; 49:6, 39), but this verse is not in the LXX, perhaps reflecting that Jeremiah added it to his final revision of his prophecy. Carroll (1986:772) considers the sentiment to be at odds with all that is said elsewhere in Jeremiah about Egypt and consequently takes it to be a late post-exilic addition to the text. However, this is not negation of what Jeremiah has prophesied earlier, but a temporal limitation, and that is true of many things that Jeremiah had to say. Furthermore such a view of Egypt's future was not exceptional in the wider prophetic context (Isa. 19:18-25; Ezek. 29:13-16). What is prophesied here concerning Egypt is not its total destruction, but a period when it will be punished followed by

33. The first 'on' in the NIV is in fact *'el* while the remaining six are *'al*. There is no difference in meaning.

34. In *ûbəyad*, 'and in hand/control of', the conjunction is probably a *waw* explicativum.

a period of settlement and prosperity as formerly. The victory of Nebuchadnezzar and his plans for Egypt will not be the ultimate determinant of its destiny, but what the LORD wills for it.

4. Reassurance for Jacob (46:27-28)

A glimpse of Egypt restored leads into the message of the final two verses. They have already occurred in substantially this form at 30:10-11, though there are verbal and spelling differences.[35] Jeremiah adds them here to give hope to the people of God regarding their destiny. If there can be a future for Egypt, then how much more must that be the case for those whom the LORD had claimed as his own. In the LXX these verses come between the oracles against Egypt and those against Babylon to which they serve as a sort of introduction. Here the salvation oracle (similar to Isa. 41:8-13) points to the LORD's care for his people and connects what happens to Egypt to the destiny of the people of Judah. They have not been directly mentioned in what has been said so far in this chapter, but the downfall of Egypt and the hegemony of Babylon were realities that impinged directly on their lives in the shadows of the great powers. They are again reminded that the overwhelming political realities of the day are under divine control and will not be permitted to frustrate what the LORD has in view for his people.

27. Do not fear, O Jacob my servant; do not be dismayed, O Israel. 'For' (kî) I will surely save you out of a distant place, your descendants from the land of their exile. Jacob will again have peace and security, and no one will make him afraid. See on 30:10.

28. 'Do not fear, O Jacob my servant, for (kî) I am with you,' declares the LORD. 'Though (kî) I completely destroy all the nations among which I scatter you, I will not completely destroy you. I will discipline you but only with justice; I will not let you go entirely unpunished.' See on 30:11. In both statements Jacob is given reason for hope. It is not a contentless feeling of well-being about the future, but a positive expectation grounded in what the LORD has revealed about his purposes, even when his rule involves difficult times for his people. There is a future for the people of God even in the upheavals that are occurring around them.

---

35. The second occurrence of 'Do not fear, O Jacob my servant' (v. 28) is not found in 30:11. The phrase 'to save you' (30:11) is not present in 46:28.

C. AGAINST THE PHILISTINES (47:1-7)

The second in the collection of Oracles against the Nations moves
northwards from Egypt to the southern coastal plain of Palestine where
the Philistine pentapolis of Ashkelon, Gaza, Ashdod, Gath and Ekron
had been located (see map 1). Many details of Philistine history remain
obscure (we have no records of their own), though they were
undoubtedly a non-Semitic people associated with the Greek islands
but probably not originating there. They were professional warriors
who, having been repulsed by the Egyptians during the reign of
Rameses III around 1190 BC, settled in the eastern Mediterranean,
particularly in south-west Canaan, where they had maintained outposts
from an early date. While they were militarily dominant in the area,
culturally they assimilated to Canaan. Their power was broken by
David, but they continued their separate existence during the period of
the monarchy, occasionally proving troublesome neighbours. At some
stage Gath was destroyed. In the later centuries they became more
involved with agriculture (olive oil) than with military or trading enter-
prises. Because their territory was strategically situated on the coastal
route north from Egypt, they were often subject to invasion from north
or south. After a brief period of independence when the Assyrians
withdrew from the area around 620 BC, the Philistines came under
Egyptian control. This too did not last long, for after Carchemish in
605 BC the Babylonians took over control of Syria–Palestine, and the
Philistines suffered extensively at their hands in 604 BC (v. 7). However, after an abortive Babylonian move against Egypt in 601 BC,
Pharaoh Neco again extended his zone of influence into Philistine
territory, capturing Gaza. This re-establishment of Egyptian control
only lasted for two years before the area became a Babylonian
province and hence had no representation at the Jerusalem conference
in 594 BC (27:3; Volume 1, Introduction §3.10). But the Philistines
continued to exist in some form until the time of the Maccabees. Other
prophecies concerning the Philistines are found at Amos 1:6-8; Isa.
14:29-32; Ezek. 25:15-17; Zeph. 2:4-7; and Zech. 9:5-7.

   The oracle describes an imminent disaster that will affect all
Philistia. The threat to them comes 'from the north' (v. 2) but the real
power at work is the LORD himself (vv. 6-7), who controls and directs
the political and military powers of the day.

**1. This is the word of the LORD that came to Jeremiah the prophet
concerning the Philistines, before Pharaoh attacked Gaza.** For the
introductory formula, cf. 14:1; 46:1; 49:34. Determining when Pharaoh

attacked Gaza has caused perplexity, particularly because, as so often
in the Old Testament, the particular Pharaoh involved is not identified.
There are two main possibilities. The reference might be to Psammetichus I who sought to extend Egyptian influence into Philistia in
the years before his death in 610 BC. Alternatively, the reference may
be to the brief seizure of Gaza by the Egyptians under Neco in the
period 601–600 BC. What has to be appreciated is that this heading
does not indicate that the following poem describes an Egyptian attack
on Gaza. It is therefore irrelevant to note that the oracle that follows
talks of a movement from the north (v. 2), whereas an Egyptian attack
would normally be expected from the south. This makes improbable
and unnecessary suggestions such as an Egyptian attack from the north
after Pharaoh Neco had defeated Josiah at Megiddo,[36] or an attack four
years later by the defeated Egyptian forces after Carchemish, taking
Gaza as they moved south in rout.

It seems best to understand the title as indicating that this oracle
was given while Philistia enjoyed a period free from foreign domination after the withdrawal of the Assyrians and before the Egyptians
made their presence felt. The heading to the oracle was placed there at
a time when a more recent attack on Gaza was known about (as is
prophesied in v. 5), but the prophecy itself pre-dates the renewal of
Egyptian influence in the area. Further, since the destroyers of the
Philistines are not identified in the poem as the Babylonians, this fits in
with Jeremiah's ministry before Carchemish in 605 BC when the foe
from the north remained unnamed.

As for the prophecy itself, it was fulfilled both in the events of
December 604 BC when the Babylonians sacked Ashkelon and
deported its people to Babylon, and also in their later recapture of the
area. Although the Philistines were traditional enemies of Israel, there
is no hint in the oracle as to why this doom was currently being
pronounced against them. However, it did make clear that their enjoyment of independence was going to be brief.

2. The poem is in two parts. The first and longer section is from v. 2 to
v. 5, and describes the catastrophe about to come on the Philistines.
**This is what the LORD says, 'See how the waters are rising in the
north; they will become an overflowing torrent.'** The invading
forces are described in terms of a river in flood, similar to those in

---

36. This suggestion was based on an account by Herodotus (*Hist.* 2.159),
where after Megiddo Neco is said to have captured Kadytis, which is taken to
be Gaza. While the identification is not implausible, a move back south at that
juncture is unlikely.

46:7-8 with reference to the Egyptian forces and the Nile, and in Isa.
8:7 to the Assyrian army and the floods of the Euphrates. The river
here is one whose water level is rising 'from the north' (cf. 46:20;
1:13-14), that is, in the north and flowing south from there. The picture
is very much a Palestinian (rather than Egyptian or Mesopotamian)
one. It will be like a winter torrent, which floods the land on either side
of it. The picture is of a threat which cannot be stemmed and which
will bring destruction to all it approaches. **They will overflow the
land and everything in it, the towns and those who live in them** (cf.
8:16b). The depredations of the invading troops will sweep them away
as effectively as the river in spate, and they will cause terror and
distress to the local population. **The people will cry out; all who
dwell in the land will wail** (<√*yālal*, an onomatopoeic term for
wailing or lamenting, 25:34). The invasions of old caused just as much
disruption and hardship as those of modern times.

3. While the previous description of the invasion had used the metaphorical language of a flood, now there is a change to the harsh reality
of military might. **At the sound of the hoofs of galloping steeds**
(*'abbîrîm* cf. 8:16), **at the noise of enemy chariots and the rumble of
their wheels.**[37] The technique of describing the sounds made by the
approaching enemy forces was also employed in 46:3-4, 9. The well-
disciplined ranks of the Babylonian forces would strike terror into the
hearts of their opponents. The war horses of the cavalry presented a
dire threat to the lightly armed infantry of the day and the impact of
their thundering advance was reinforced by the clatter of the chariots.
Their wheels were massive, often as high as a man, and any not able to
get out of their way fast enough would be crushed under them. Even
without any fighting, the impact of the invasion would be devastating.
So demoralised and panicked will the population be that **fathers will
not turn** (<√*pānâ* hiphil, cf. 'look back' 46:5) **to help their children;
their hands will hang limp.** They are unable to help their families
because terror has frozen them into immobility. The NKJV takes the
slackness of their hands as an indication of 'lacking courage' but
'sheer helplessness' (NJPS) conveys a more accurate impression of
their inability to react.

4. Verse 4 gives the ultimate reason for the invasion and the panic.
For (*'al*, 'because of') **the day has come to destroy** (<√*šādad*; 4:13

---

37. The root *šā'aṭ*, 'galloping'/'stamping', occurs only here. 'Noise' (*raša'*)
may refer to an earthquake or to physical shaking caused by fear. Here it
describes the vibration and clatter made by the chariots as they rattle over
rough ground. For the combination of *qōl* and *hāmôn* see 10:13.

and used 13 times in chaps. 48, 49, 51) **all the Philistines.** 'The day' indicates the time that the LORD has determined (cf. 46:10, 21), as is made clear in the second part of the verse. The LORD is coming in power to overthrow the Philistines by means of the invading army. It is not clear how the second part of the reason relates to the first, though it is probably a second aspect of the day, as the NIV indicates by adding the supplement 'and': **and to cut off all survivors who could help Tyre and Sidon.** But why are these two towns mentioned? They were Phoenician cities further to the north. While there is no record of any treaty between Phoenicia and the Philistines at this time, it is not improbable that some understanding existed because of their common economic and maritime interests. Still, given the focus on the Philistines in the oracle, it is surprising that there is any mention of others.

Not unlike the presentation in 46:10, the reason for the impending devastation is that it has been divinely decreed. 'For' (*kî*) **the LORD is about to destroy the Philistines, the remnant from the coasts of Caphtor.** Caphtor is now fairly certainly identified as Crete, though perhaps also including other islands in the Aegean. It was from there that the Philistines moved when they came to Palestine (Amos 9:7; Deut. 2:23), and 'remnant' points to the extent to which their numbers had been subsequently depleted. But the LORD is going to act against them and they will be subject to further diminution.

5. Gaza was a major city in the fertile coastal plain in south-west Palestine. It was separated by sand dunes from the sea some 2½ miles (4½ km) distant, and lay on the vital north–south land route along the Mediterranean coast. 'Baldness has come upon Gaza' (NKJV, NRSV) pictures the city as a victim of devastation caused by the aggressor. This somewhat more passive rendering is more suitable than **Gaza will shave her head in mourning.** While cutting off one's hair was a gesture employed in grief, the depiction is rather of the city as a victim, incapable of any response.

Ashkelon will be silenced[38] points to the numbness of her grief. The city was situated ten miles (16 km) north of Gaza. **O remnant on the plain** refers to the cities mentioned, and points to the survivors who remained in the open area around them. 'Plain' (*'ēmeq*, 'valley') describes a low-lying area that could be broad enough for the cultivation of crops. Others have suggested a connection with an Ugaritic root that means 'strength'; hence 'the remnant of the Philistine power'

---

38. The rendering 'cut off' (NKJV) or 'is destroying' (NRSV) treats the root as *dāmâ* III, niphal, 'to be destroyed' rather than *dāmâ* II, niphal, 'to be silent'. Traditionally these two roots were not distinguished.

(REB; cf. NRSV[39]). **How long will you cut yourselves?**[40] Another mourning gesture, which though forbidden in Israel (Deut. 14:1), was practised among the surrounding nations (5:7; 16:6; 41:5).

6. The second part of the oracle against the Philistines consists of an address regarding the sword of the LORD (51:35-37; 12:12), which introduces a theme not found in the Oracle against Egypt. Verse 7 seems to be a response to v. 6, and so the NIV and REB indicate two speakers here. The first could possibly be those who are suffering, as indicated by the NIV supplement of 'you cry'. **'Ah, sword of the LORD,'** ⌊**you cry,**⌋ **'how long till you rest?'** The sword of the LORD was a symbol of divine judgment. The cry of the people would seem to involve them in recognising that the LORD was in some way behind their disaster. They in no way acknowledge the propriety of his action, but speak out against it and wish to be rid of it, questioning how long it will continue. So they urge the sword, **Return**[41] **to**[42] **your scabbard; cease** (<√*rāgaʿ*, 'come to rest, cease activity') **and be still.** The terror-stricken populace long for a cessation of hostilities and for the removal of the menace that is overwhelming them. 'Be still' (<√*dāmam* I, 'to stand still, keep quiet') echoes the 'be silenced' of v. 5.

7. The reply is then given by means of a wondering question, asked according to the NIV punctuation by the LORD himself, though it might also be taken as a question of the prophet regarding the sword of the LORD. **But how can it rest**[43] **when the LORD has commanded it, when he has ordered it to attack Ashkelon and the coast?**/'when he has appointed it against Ashkelon and against the coast there?' Ashkelon was the only town of the Philistine pentapolis that was on the sea-coast of the Mediterranean. It was attacked and captured by Nebuchadnezzar in December 604 BC, when he claimed 'he turned the city into a mound and a heap of ruins' (Wiseman 1956:68), an outcome

---

39. This represents a change from the RSV, which followed the LXX in emending the word to 'Anakim', the race of giants, some of whom were to be found in Joshua's time in this area (Josh. 11:22), but it is improbable that they had survived till this stage.
40. The verb is singular agreeing with the collective remnant.
41. The niphal of *ʾāsap* is also found in Isa. 60:20 meaning 'withdraw'.
42. *ʿal* is evidently used here for *ʾel*.
43. The MT has *tišqōṭî*, 'you will be quiet'. In the light of the following *lāh*, 'to her', most translations treat this as an erroneous copying of the word from the previous verse where it fits, and read instead the third feminine singular *tišqōṭ*, 'it [the sword] will rest' (cf. LXX). However, sudden switches of person are not impossible in Hebrew style, and the MT may well be correct.

amply attested to by modern archaeology. What was happening was under the control and supervision of the LORD, and it would not cease until all he had appointed had been accomplished.

It may well be asked, What end did this revelation serve? There is no suggestion that it was delivered to the Philistines; so its purpose could not have been to induce them to repent. There is no hint that judgment was overtaking the Philistines because of certain specific offences; so it is unlikely that it was addressed to Judah to remind them of the justice of the LORD. It is rather a bleak description of an unidentified northern invader overwhelming Philistia, and as such served to remind Judah of what had been prophesied concerning the foe from the north that would come upon her. It was all very well to be prepared to listen to such words against one's traditional enemies, but they were not the only ones threatened by the LORD's directive.

D. AGAINST MOAB (48:1-47)

Having recorded the position regarding the LORD's verdict on Philistia, Jeremiah now moves east across the hill country of Judah and the Dead Sea to set out what he has been told regarding Moab, the enemy who took advantage of Israel and mocked her in her distress. Moab's ruin had been previously predicted in Amos 2:1-3 and Isa. 15–16 (cf. also Zeph. 2:8-11; Ezek. 25:8-11). Indeed the intermittent hostility between the nations goes back to the period of the settlement in Canaan when the Israelites occupied territory the Moabites considered to be theirs. It was at this early period that Moab's eventual downfall was foreseen by Balaam in connection with the rising of a Star from Israel who 'will crush the foreheads of Moab' (Num. 24:17).

The Oracle against Moab is lengthy and contains a number of textual difficulties (e.g. in vv. 9, 15, 32). There are also divergent views regarding the extent to which it should be treated as poetry.[44] As

---

44. The NRSV prints as prose vv. 1a, 10, 12-13, 21-27, 34-39. The NKJV has verse from v. 1b , apart from vv. 40a and 47b, as does the NIV. Apart from the title 'Concerning Moab' the NASB reads vv. 12-13, 21-28a, 34-39 as prose. The REB treats vv. 12-13, 15b, 21-24, 34-40a, and 47b as prose. The possible variations between poetry and prose may be of significance for attempts to discern the literary history of the chapter, particularly if differing genres are assigned to different sources. If one understands the chapter as coming from Jeremiah, who would use either style as seemed appropriate, then determining in which category particular verses are to be placed plays a relatively minor role in the interpretative task.

regards the interpretation of the passage, however, there are two main
difficulties: uncertainty as to the particular historical events reflected in
the prophecy, and grasping how and why so much of what Jeremiah
says derives from earlier oracles against Moab, particularly those
found in Num. 22 and 24, and Isa. 15–16. The fact that these and a
number of other quotations and allusions are found in this passage
clearly shows that it is Jeremiah who is drawing on earlier Scripture
rather than the other passages all being dependent on Jeremiah.
However, far from reading as a composite of other passages, the
material shades gradually from one topic to another, and is not easily
divided into sections.

The oracle seems disproportionately long in relation to the political
significance of Moab. It is difficult to account for its length unless
some particular crisis occurred during Jeremiah's ministry. Certainly
the disappearance of Moab in the years after the fall of Jerusalem
makes it improbable that this section is a later invention that has been
attributed to Jeremiah, though it has been frequently argued by critics
that over the years this Oracle attracted to itself pieces of material from
various sources. But again one must ask, Why?

1. Impending Overthrow (48:1-10)

1. Concerning Moab is a brief title for these sayings about Moab, a
nation which lived on the plateau bounded by the Dead Sea on the
west, the desert to the east, and the rivers Arnon in the north and Zered
in the south (see Map 1). Originally its territory had stretched further
north up the whole of the eastern shore of the Dead Sea, but the northernmost section had been occupied by the Ammonites, from whom
Israel took it and allocated it to Reuben (principally) and also to Gad.
The Moabite Stone records that this northern territory was retaken by
Mesha, king of Moab, around 850 BC. However, Moab's independence
did not last long, and it fell under Assyrian domination. Assyrian texts
contain records of four Moabite kings paying tribute during the reign
of Ashurbanipal (668–627 BC). The subsequent decline of Assyrian
influence led to another brief interlude of independence, but it is generally assumed that Moab was one of the nations which submitted to
Nebuchadnezzar in the aftermath of Carchemish (605 BC). Moabite
contingents were employed by the Babylonians to bring pressure on
Judah after Jehoiakim's rebellion (2 Kgs. 24:2; 599/98 BC). However,
the Moabites' loyalty was not to be totally relied on. They sent envoys
to the conference that took place in Jerusalem in 594 BC, presumably to
discuss opposition to Babylon (27:3). Josephus records that in 582 BC

Moab was devastated by Babylon, which would have occurred at the
same time as there was a further deportation from Judah (52:30). Not
long after this Arabs moved in from the east and occupied the country.
This is what the LORD Almighty, the God of Israel, says indicates the divine origin of this oracle, but that does not mean that
Jeremiah will not at times reflect on what the LORD had said earlier.
The LORD who is in control of the hosts of heaven is also in control of
the destiny of Moab, and that fact does not bode well for her, because
the oracle begins with a message of dire trouble to come. **Woe to
Nebo, for** (*kî*) **it will be ruined** (<√*šādad*, extensive and complete
ruin). 'Woe!' (*hôy* plus a third person reference) announces disaster.
Nebo was not the mountain of that name from which Moses viewed
Canaan before his death (Deut. 32:49; 34:1), but a city located nearby,
lying in the territory north of the Arnon. It, along with Kiriathaim, was
assigned to the tribe of Reuben (Num. 32:37-38; Josh. 13:19), and both
are mentioned on the Moabite Stone. The cities of Moab were
extensively ruined in Nebuchadnezzar's campaign of 582 BC.
Kiriathaim will be disgraced and captured. Kiriathaim is probably
to be identified as El Quraiyāt about five miles (8 km) north-west of
Dibon. It is not certain if the next line mentions a further site. **The
stronghold will be disgraced** (<√*bôš*, 2:26) **and shattered** (<√*ḥātat*,
1:17). The NIV treats the description as being of Kiriathaim itself, but
a footnote indicates that the word *miśgāb*, 'stronghold'/'fortress' may
be a proper name, Misgab (as in the REB).[45] The location of such a site
is unknown, and it is perhaps better to follow the NIV and most
English translations.

What happens to Nebo and Kiriathaim spells out disaster for the
rest of the country. They had formed Moab's front line to the north and
once they had fallen territory further south lay exposed to invading
forces. Again a major translation problem is to know how to translate
the Hebrew perfects. They may be prophetic perfects because Moab's
future doom is presented as so certain that it is conceived of as already
complete (NIV, NLT). Alternatively, the perfects may be true past
tenses, and the whole passage may be rendered as commenting on the
doom that has already overtaken Moab (NASB, NKJV, NRSV).

---

45. The presence of the article with *hammiśgāb* probably favours the
reference being to Kiriathaim, and the accompanying verbs 'will be disgraced
and shattered' are both feminine forms, which are more likely to refer to the
name of a town, since the noun for 'fortress' is masculine. However, the
gender of the verbs may have been assimilated to the feminines used earlier in
the verse.

However, it is generally accepted that v. 8, for instance, speaks of events that are still future, and it is on balance preferable to have the same stance throughout (see also vv. 12 and 16).

2. Moab will be praised no more (cf. 49:25; 51:41). Perhaps there is a hint that Moab was known for self-praise (v. 29; Isa. 16:6; cf. also the language of the Moabite Stone, *ANET* 320-21), but it is predicted that the country as a whole is no longer going to be able to boast about itself, or be lauded by others. **In Heshbon men will plot her downfall.** Heshbon, at the southern end of the Transjordanian plateau and eighteen miles (29 km) east of the northern end of the Dead Sea, was a well-known city in the northern territory which Moab only controlled in times of expansion. It was the former Amorite capital of Sihon (Num. 21:26; Deut. 2:24), and had been originally allocated to Reuben (Num. 32:37; Josh. 13:17). At this juncture it was in the control of the Ammonites (49:3), and so represents a border town in which men were plotting the downfall of the land. There is in Hebrew a wordplay between Heshbon (*ḥešbôn*) and 'they will plot' (*ḥāšəbû*) to bring out how appropriate it was that this action against Moab should take place in that town. **Come, let us put an end to**/'cut off' (<√*kārat*) **that nation.** The identity of Moab's adversaries is not stated.

Another wordplay is found in the line, **You too, O Madmen, will be silenced**, between the name of the town (*madmēn*) and 'be silenced' (*todōmmî*)[46] referring to the silence of those who lie killed by the sword. The location of Madmen (rendered as Madhmen in the REB to avoid confusion with the unrelated English word) is unknown. Presumably it lay within Moabite control when this oracle was first uttered. **The sword will pursue you** (cf. 9:15). 'Will be silenced' and 'will pursue' render Hebrew imperfects. If the previous perfects are treated as past references (cf. v. 1), then this oracle was uttered when the destruction of Moab was half completed. However, the NIV rendering of all the verbs as futures is preferable.

3. Listen to the cries from Horonaim treats the word 'voice' ('a voice of crying' NKJV) as equivalent to a command to listen. Horonaim (also found in Isa. 15:5) is mentioned on the Moabite Stone. The dual form of the name suggests a meaning such as 'two caverns', or else a lower and upper city, but its location is a matter of dispute. Perhaps it lay on the other side of hills from Luhith. **Cries of great**

---

46. For a discussion of the possible roots involved, see on 6:2 and 8:14. Here the verb seems to be the qal of *dāmam* I, 'to keep quiet/rigid', though *dāmam* III, 'to perish', is also possible.

havoc and destruction involves a supplement of 'cries of'. Other
versions (NASB, REB, NKJV, NRSV) take 'Devastation (*šōd*, 20:8)
and great destruction (*šeber*, 4:6)' as what was cried out. Each time
one of the great cities of Moab is mentioned it is accompanied by a
prediction of impending catastrophe to drive home the theme that there
is inescapable judgment about to engulf the country from which its
centres of economic and military might will not be exempted.

4. Moab will be broken (<√*šābar*); **her little ones**[47] **will cry**[48] **out.**
The term 'little ones' (<*ṣāʿîr*, 'insignificant/helpless ones') may refer to
her children, or to all her citizens in their misery, and is employed
because of assonance with 'cry out' (<√*zāʿaq*). 'Their cries are heard
as far as Zoar' (REB) follows the LXX. Zoar is associated with
Horonaim in v. 34 and Isa. 15:5.

5. In the first clause of v. 5 the subject is not identified, and so the
rendering as an indefinite plural in English is appropriate. 'For' (*kî*)
they go up the way to Luhith,[49] **weeping bitterly as they go;** 'for'
(*kî*, picking up and extending the initial clause of the verse) **on the
road down to Horonaim anguished cries**[50] **over the destruction**
(*šeber*, cf. v. 3) **are heard.** The picture of the escapees as they leave
their ruined cities with great weeping consists of two balanced halves:
the route up to Luhith and the route down to Horonaim (cf. Isa. 15:5,
though there the figure is applied differently). These two places have
not been definitely located, though the link in Isa. 15:5 with Zoar, near
the south of the Dead Sea, suggests that they were in the southern part
of Moabite territory.

6. The impending destruction has been described, and now those to be
caught up in it are addressed. The only way of escape will be to go into

---

47. The kethibh has the form *ṣəʿôreyhā* for which the qere reads *ṣəʿîreyhā* as
in 14:3 where the term is used for 'servants', but see following note.

48. 'Cry' in v. 4 is *zəʿāqâ*, whereas in v. 3 'crying' is *ṣəʿāqâ*. The spellings
seem to be interchangeable. However, the clause is literally, 'they caused to be
heard the cry of her little ones'. The 'little ones' are understood as the logical
subject of the verb by the NIV (and also NRSV, NKJV, NJPS). But the LXX
read, 'Their cry is heard as far as Zoar', reading *ṣôʿărâ* by transposing two
consonants in the kethibh *ṣʿwryh* (RSV, REB).

49. The kethibh reads *hlḥwt*, presumably *halluḥôt*, 'tablets', which is
unintelligible. The qere is *halluḥît*, 'the Luhith', a hill referred to in Isa. 15:5.

50. The Hebrew is unusual 'anguished ones of cries of destruction'. In the
first part of the verse the verb 'go up' is masculine singular, which contrasts
with 'they hear', an indefinite plural, equivalent to a passive. The NIV has
taken the first as a collective reference to the 'little ones'.

a desolate spot far from any habitation that would attract the attention
of invading forces. **Flee! Run for your lives**/'save (<√*mālaṭ* piel,
32:4) your lives' (<*nepeš*, 2:34); **become**[51] **like a bush in the desert.**
The NIV marginal reading, 'like Aroer', a town in Moab on the north
bank of the Arnon river, reflects the Hebrew text, but the resulting
comparison between refugees and a city is obscure, and Aroer was not
in the wilderness. Changing the word slightly (from *kəʿărôʿēr* to
kəʿarʿār, cf. 17:6 and the Vulgate) gives the understanding of a low-
growing bush, possibly a 'juniper' (NASB, REB margin), indicating
that the fugitives will have only minimal resources with which to
survive in difficult conditions. The LXX translates 'wild ass' (probably
reading *kəʿārôd*) and that is followed by the NRSV so that the fugitives
are likened to a wild donkey free to roam in the wilderness—possibly a
more optimistic picture. A third type of translation draws on the use of
the word in Ps. 107:17 where it is generally rendered 'destitute' (and
so REB here). This is again a more negative picture of the suffering
that awaits the refugees. While the majority of English translations
favour the first option (which should probably be adopted), the other
possibilities cannot be completely discounted.

7. The doom that is about to come on them and the consequent need to
flee are not accidents, but consequences. They are the divine verdict on
their behaviour. 'For' (*kî*) introduces the reason why they are urged to
flee. **Since you**[52] **trust in your deeds and riches** indicates a
materialism that relied on their achievements and national wealth—
'riches' here is more than silver and gold; it embraces all the natural
resources of the fertile plateau area of Moab. 'Deeds' refers to what
they have accomplished as a nation. But 'trust' (<√*bāṭaḥ*, 'to rely on,
find refuge in') is virtually a description of a religious attitude towards
material possessions, and it will ultimately be seen to be misplaced.
You too will be taken captive. 'Too' probably being explained, as
along with Judah, which may reflect a situation after 597 or 586 BC.
      And Chemosh[53] **will go into exile, together**[54] **with his priests**

---

51. The feminine plural form *wətihyệnâ* may be explained as a masculine
with an energic *nun* (Bright 1965:314), or it may reflect a text where the
preceding *napšəkem* was in fact plural *napšêkem* (Holladay 1989, 2:341).
      52. This 'you' and the 'your' of 'your deeds' and the 'you' with 'be taken
captive' are all feminine singular, presumably referring to the land of Moab.
      53. *kəmîš* seems to be a copyist's error for *kəmôš*, but *IBHS* page 28 note 79
cite evidence from Ebla showing the same form of the name as here. One
piece of evidence for the widespread worship of this god is in the name Carchemish (*karkəmîš*, 'fortress/quay of Chimish').

and officials. Chemosh was the principal god of the Moabites (Num. 21:29; and was also revered by the Ammonites, Judg. 11:24), and it is known that the deity had been widely worshipped in northern Syria and Mesopotamia many centuries earlier (some have supposed that was the area where the Moabites had originated, though Gen. 19:37 indicates an early connection with Lot). It is uncertain whether Chemosh was a deity of the underworld, or an astral deity. The Moabite Stone refers to him as Ashtar-Chemosh, and Ashtar was the god of the planet Venus. It was common practice for the statues of the gods of a captive nation to be taken away with the prisoners (43:12; 49:3; Amos 5:25; Isa. 46:1-2) reflecting the widespread notion that when a land was captured, its patron deity had been defeated by those of the conqueror. Here the priests go too. It is not certain if the 'officials' were involved in the cult, or if they were political and administrative figures, but it is clear that the opinion formers and religious leaders of the land are not exempted from the coming disaster in which the whole social structure of the land will be overthrown.

8. Moab will also be physically devastated. **The destroyer** ($<\sqrt{šādad}$, cf. v. 1) **will come against every city, and not a town shall escape.** Notice again that the identity of the destroyer is not stated. He is doing the LORD's work and it is that which is important. The destruction that is envisaged is so sweeping that it will affect every centre of population. **The valley will be ruined and the plateau destroyed** ($<\sqrt{šāmad}$, cf. v. 42)**, because**[55] **the LORD has spoken.** The valley may be the downward slope of Moab towards the Dead Sea, or more probably Moabite holdings in the Jordan valley just north of the Dead Sea (cf. Josh. 13:27). The plain is the high inland area from Arnon to Heshbon which was very fertile, before it gradually merged into desert. Their fate is sealed because what is happening has been divinely mandated.

9. Another difficult passage occurs in v. 9, where the word *ṣîṣ* occurs. Ordinarily this refers to the blossom of flowers or to the ornament on the front of the high priest's turban (Exod. 28:36), but neither of these renderings seems relevant here. The traditional approach is reflected in 'Give wings (*ṣîṣ*) to Moab, for she must go hence' (NJPS; cf. RSV, NKJV, NLT, NASB), based on the meaning 'wings' for *ṣîṣ* as in Aramaic and later Hebrew. The injunction then was a rhetorical device to emphasise that Moab needed birds' wings so swiftly would she have to depart before the invasion. A more modern possibility is reflected in

54. The kethibh *yaḥad* need not be changed. It is a less common form of *yaḥdāw*, for which the qere would substitute a third form *yaḥdāyw*.

55. *ʾăšer* is here used causally.

the NIV: **Put salt on Moab, for** (*kî*) **she will be laid waste**[56] (cf. also
NASB margin; NRSV). It has been argued on the basis of Ugaritic
evidence that *ṣîṣ* may mean 'salt', and the picture is then one based on
the ancient practice of sowing cities that were destroyed with salt
(Judg. 9:45), something that might well have been suggested to a
conqueror by the numerous salt deposits around the Dead Sea.
However, the posited Ugaritic connection is far from secure (*HALOT*
1023) and probably ought to be abandoned. A third possibility
(suggested by BDB 851 and *HALOT* 1023) is to read *ṣiyôn* in place of
ṣîṣ. This word may mean a 'road marker' (31:21) or a 'gravestone' (2
Kgs. 23:17; cf. GNB). This seems to be reflected in the LXX 'signs'
which underlies the REB rendering 'Give a warning signal to Moab'.
Her towns will become desolate, with no one to live in them.

10. Some take v. 10 as prose, and also as a later insertion, but it
certainly has poetic qualities about it. It refers to the one who will carry
out the LORD's work. He is urged to pursue his divinely appointed role
with fervour. **A curse on him who is lax in doing the LORD's work!
A curse on him who keeps his sword from bloodshed!** 'Lax'/
'laxness' (*rəmiyyâ*) has the basic meaning of 'deceit, treachery', but it
can also signify the untrustworthiness of a lazy person who exhibits a
careless attitude towards what he does. (BDB separates these concepts
by positing two roots, I 'deceit'; II 'slackness', but *HALOT* (1243)
prefers a single origin.) The LORD's work here is a matter of judgment.
Again there is no hint as to who is addressed, but it may have been
intended as a warning of how thorough the devastation of the country
was expected to be as divine judgment is called down on the head of
the conqueror if he slacks in carrying out his appointed role.

2. Unsettling the Complacent (48:11-13)

There is no doubt that this brief section comes from a time when Moab
had been untroubled by foreign invasion. It is quite possible that there
is an indirect reflection upon circumstances in Judah which were such
that this was not true there. This oracle would then fit at any time in the

---

56. There is a second difficulty in this already difficult verse. *nāṣōʿ tēṣēʿ* is
unusual in that it is the infinitive construct of *nāṣāʿ*, perhaps a by-form of *nāṣâ*
II, 'to fall in ruins', followed by the qal imperfect of another verb *yāṣāʿ*, 'to go
out'. If the second verb is repointed as *tiṣṣeh* (BHS) and it is assumed that
aleph is also written for *he* in this verb, then this could be taken as an
intensive expression of Moab's destruction. Alternatively, the first verb form
may be taken as an alternative form/error for *yāṣōʿ*, the qal infinitive absolute
of *yāṣāʿ*, which is used in the sense 'to surrender' in 1 Sam. 11:3; Isa. 36:6.

turbulent years after the death of Josiah.

11. In vv. 11-13, Jeremiah uses imagery drawn from the cultivation of vines and the production of wine to bring out the reason for Moab's downfall. **Moab has been at rest from youth.** 'Youth' refers to the period when Moab was established as a nation. This seems to point back to the time when they conquered the Emim and became an established power themselves (Deut. 2:9-12). It was not the case that from then on Moab had enjoyed complete tranquillity. The precise sense in which they had been 'at rest' is brought out later in the verse in that they had not experienced exile. To a certain extent Moab had been isolated from many of the conquering armies that swept through Palestine, by its location west of the Dead Sea, and with the desert on other side. It was also mountainous. Not that the isolation was complete. It had been conquered by Israel, and also had been tributary to the Assyrians—but despite all that it had not yet suffered the deportation that had befallen others. Such a relatively unthreatened life had engendered complacency.

Moab's situation is analysed in terms of being 'like wine' (a translator's supplement to clarify the reference). **Like wine left on its dregs, not poured from one jar to another.** Moab was renowned for her wine, so the comparison is apposite (vv. 32-33; Isa. 16:8-11). When wine was made, it was customary for it to be left to ferment and mature in underground storage where the temperature would be fairly constant, and it would then be poured from one container to another to prevent it from going harsh. Thus wine on the 'dregs' or 'lees' (sediment or particles settling at the bottom, usually in an undisturbed, unmoved container) would be a long-matured wine, but it had to be well refined (cf. Isa. 25:6). Moab had, however, been left indefinitely on its dregs, and the sediment had not been purified away (cf. Zeph. 1:12). Nations left too long to enjoy prosperity become arrogant; there is a discipline in hardship and defeat which Moab has not experienced. So what should have been of good quality has become harsh. **She**[57] **has not gone into exile**—in contrast to what has been foretold in v. 7. This explains the comparison that is being made, in that up to that time Moab had not been affected by such an upheaval. **So she tastes as she did**/'So (*kēn*) his taste remains in him', **and her aroma is unchanged.** Moab's attitude towards God's people is particularly being reflected on. It had always been hostile, and the fact that it had experienced relative immunity from the dangers of the international scene had led to an

---

57. In Hebrew, the references to Moab from v. 11 on are masculine, but the NIV retains feminines for the nation.

attitude of complacency and self-satisfaction that reinforced hostility towards Judah.

12. But that is not going to be allowed to continue much longer. **But** (*lākēn*, 'therefore') indicates the divine reaction in condemning the spiritual outlook found in Moab. **'Days are coming,' declares the LORD.** Although this phrase is frequently used in circumstances when the remote future is in view, it need not be. It indicates a divine response out of the present situation but occurring at a time unknown to the prophet (7:32). There is no doubt, however, that a time of judgment is about to come on Moab.

Many versions (BHS, NRSV, REB, NASB) treat vv. 12-13 as prose. This has led to them being thought of as prose insertions by some later editor commenting on Jeremiah's oracle. This seems unnecessary. The verses can be treated as verse (so NIV, NKJV), and the comparison made in v. 13 supports the idea of them originating before the Exile.

When I will send men who pour/'tilt' from jars, and they will pour her out. The LORD is going to send an unidentified adversary who will treat Moab as wine ready to be decanted from one vessel to another. Normally this would be a task carried out with considerable care, not only to avoid spillage, but also so as not to disturb the sediment and keep the wine as pure as possible. Those who are going to tilt the containers of Moabite wine will act with no such gentle treatment. **They will empty her jars and smash her[58] jugs.** The invading forces are going to harry the land, and the figure of smashing probably indicates breaking down the political and economic structure of the nation. Her security is going to be harshly and totally disrupted.

13. This is further brought out in the thought: **Then Moab will be ashamed of Chemosh.** 'Ashamed' (<√*bôš*) is closely related to the experience of failure—the disappointment and disillusionment which will arise because of the lack of help from these gods in which they trusted. Chemosh was the god of Moab, and the one to whom they attributed their prosperity and security. But the complete success of the invaders will expose their god's powerlessness and Moab will no longer be able to boast in him. **As the house of Israel was ashamed when they trusted in Bethel.** 'Trusted' (<√*bāṭaḥ*, cf. v. 7) draws together the experience of Moab and the northern kingdom, which experienced deportation at the hand of Assyria in 721 BC. Israel

---

58. The MT has *niblêhem*, 'their jugs', but the LXX and Aquila read 'his jugs', which is followed by the English versions.

became ashamed of Bethel and all that it stood for (cf. 1 Kgs. 12:26-33; Hos. 8:5-7), particularly the worship of the golden bull that was erected at the shrine there. It had not been capable of averting the disaster of deportation. There is also some evidence that Bethel may have been used as a name for the deity in the cult of the northern tribes. It is found as part of Jewish names in the Elephantine colony in Egypt in the fifth century BC. This verse fits more naturally into a pre-exilic context, for otherwise there would be the comparison to be made with Jerusalem and their faith in the gods they worshipped (cf. 44:17). Instead what is said is presented as a lesson for Judah. If this was true of Moab as it had been of Israel, what would be the outcome of what was now happening in Jerusalem?

3. Warriors No More (48:14-17)

The description of the impending fate of Moab reverts to the military conflict found in vv. 2-9, and also brings out that boastfulness was a characteristic of Moab.

14. The challenge is issued to Moab: **How can you say, 'We are warriors, men valiant in battle'?** (cf. 2:23; 8:8). The Moabites obviously considered themselves to have prowess in military affairs, but their boasting will be shown to be misplaced by the impending disaster.

15. Moab will be destroyed (<√šādad, cf. vv. 1, 8) **and her towns invaded.**[59] This looks forward with prophetic perfects to what is certainly going to happen, but the identity of the one who will carry out the destruction is not stated. **Her finest** ('chosen', the best, 22:7) **young men will go down in the slaughter** (cf. 50:27). Those who form the very best of her troops will be decimated in the attack. That would point to immediate defensive weakness for the land and also to future population problems. **Declares the King whose name is the LORD Almighty** is added to show the certainty of what will happen. The one who is sovereign ruler of Moab, indeed of all that is, is the

---

59. This phrase is literally, 'her towns he went up', and has been variously interpreted. For example, the NRSV offers 'The destroyer of Moab and his towns has come up', reading šōdēd as in v. 18 instead of šuddad, but the latter form is found in v. 20, is reflected in all the early versions, and Jeremiah is fond of playing on similarly sounding words. Undoubtedly 'and her towns' (wəʿārêhā) is difficult in that Moab is treated as masculine in the passage. But ʿālâ can be read with an indeterminate subject, 'one came up' referring to the enemy, and 'towns' may be an accusative of direction.

Lord of hosts, and it is he who will direct her affairs, not Chemosh whom they thought of as their king.

16. The fall of Moab is at hand shows that the timescale which had been left open by v. 12 is of very short duration. The language is reminiscent of other passages such as Deut. 32:35; Isa. 13:22; 56:1. The destruction is imminent, **her calamity will come quickly.** It had been prophesied by Balaam (Num. 24:17) and repeated by Amos 2:1-3 and Isa. 15-16. But now the Lord has decreed that there is little time left. Josephus (*Ant.* 10.9.7) records that five years after the fall of Jerusalem in the twenty-third year of his reign Nebuchadnezzar subjugated Moab, though the absence of Babylonian records for this period means that this has not been corroborated (cf. 46:13).

17. Mourn for her, all who live around her, all who know her fame is not an ironic jibe at a fallen enemy, but a command issued to underscore the poignancy of her fall. 'Mourn' is 'nod the head in mourning' (<√*nûd*, 15:5; 16:5; 18:16; 22:10; 31:18). Moab's demise is certain, and it will come soon so that her neighbours who had known her greatness should get ready to express their sympathy. 'All who know her fame'/'his name' is a reference to those who have heard of Moab by reputation rather than through personal contact. **Say, 'How broken is the mighty sceptre, how broken the glorious staff!'** Whereas *maṭṭeh*, 'sceptre', has frequent reference to power and authority, *maqqēl*, 'staff', usually does not have such overtones (1:11). Their joint use here does not so much refer to Moabite domination of other nations, which seems not to have occurred, but to her ability and power to join with others and assist them. These symbols of her power (cf. Ezek. 19:11, 12, 14; Ps. 110:2) are broken because the reality they represented will be gone. Moab's prestige will be a thing of the past, her grandeur a mere memory.

4. Judgment on Moab's Cities (48:18-25)

Verses 18-25 turn from the attitude of neighbouring countries to Moab itself, and address ten Moabite cities in various parts of the country to dramatise the extent of the disaster which will occur throughout the country when the enemy forces advance. Verse 25 indicates that the whole description is divine speech.

18. By poetically addressing the population of a specific town in Moab the Lord presents a vivid picture of the calamity that was impending on the land. **Come down from your glory and sit[60] on the**

---

60. The kethibh *yšby* is miswritten for *ûšəbî*, given in the qere.

parched ground,[61] **O inhabitants**[62] **of the Daughter of Dibon.**
'Glory' refers to their previous dignity and high status, and so 'come
down' is a matter of intense humiliation. It may be that they are to sit
as they wait as captives to learn what their fate will be. Dibon was a
major walled city of Moab, set on two hills, and located beside the
important international trade route, the King's Highway, that ran
north–south through Transjordan from Damascus to the Gulf of Aqaba
(Num. 20:17-19). The town lay four miles (6½ km) north of the River
Arnon, and thirteen miles (21 km) east of the Dead Sea. The town was
the capital of King Mesha, and it was there that the Moabite Stone was
found in 1868. Now, however, its inhabitants are pictured as defeated
and dejected. For the idiom 'daughter of' see on 4:31. **For** (*kî*) **he who
destroys** (<√*šādad*, 4:13) **Moab will come up against you and ruin
your fortified cities.** The verbs may be taken either as future or as past
(as in NASB) in that the prophet may now be urging the people of
Dibon to react in this way now, by way of dramatic anticipation of the
fate that will come upon them; alternatively he may have projected
himself in thought to the time when the devastation had already
occurred, and be speaking to the people then.

19. Stand by the road and watch, you who live in Aroer. Aroer
also lay on the King's Highway, south-east of Dibon on the north bank
of the Arnon, and had been a frontier town between Moab and the
Amorite kingdom of Sihon. But the scene that confronts its citizens is
not that of caravans making steady progress along a trade route, but of
refugees pouring down the road in headlong flight before an army. All
this has taken place so suddenly that news of the invasion and collapse
has not had time to reach Aroer before the refugees themselves do.
**Ask the man fleeing and the woman escaping, ask them, 'What has
happened?'** The mention of a man and a woman is to convey the full
extent of the catastrophe that has struck all the population (cf. Isa. 3:1).

20. The first part of v. 20 seems to be the response that is given to the
inquiry. **Moab is disgraced/**'ashamed', **for** (*kî*) **she is shattered**
(<√*ḥātat*, 1:17). The enemy has dealt a stunning blow to the northern

---

61. *baṣṣāmāʾ*, 'in thirst', is retained in the NKJV. To others the thought 'sit
in thirst' seems too paradoxical and they read *baṣṣāmēʾ*, 'on parched ground'.
However, the MT may be retained as a bold use of the abstract for the
concrete.

62. 'One (fem.) inhabiting' is, as in 46:19, a reference to those inhabiting
the town. Compare 21:13 and 22:23 for 'inhabitress' describing a town or
location. The NRSV takes the root in a specific sense to yield 'enthroned
daughter Dibon!'

part of the kingdom, and its morale has been undermined. **Wail and cry out!** is addressed by the prophet to the inhabitants of Aroer. This is the response that they are to make to the news that will reach them.[63] **Announce by the Arnon that Moab is destroyed** (<√šādad, cf. v. 18) is a plural command, either to the people of Aroer now thought of as a group, or to the refugees by the prophet. The Arnon was the chief river of Moab, rising in the mountains of Arabia and flowing into the Dead Sea.

21. Verses 21-25 are often treated as a prose insertion, but the NIV and the NKJV show how they may be treated as verse. If they are analysed as prose, this should not be taken as indicating that they are a later insertion. This is another and very effective way of making the same point of the total destruction that is about to fall on Moab, not now by using individual pictures but by a catalogue of the places that will be affected.

Judgment has come to the plateau refers to the region north of the Arnon. This was the area that had originally belonged to the Amorite kingdom of Sihon and was taken by Moab from Israel. Many of the towns listed are mentioned in Scripture as being allocated to the tribe of Reuben at the time of the Settlement.

Holon is mentioned only here. **Jahzah** (Num. 21:23) is the same place as Jahaz (Josh. 21:36), and lay near the border with the desert. **Mephaath**[64] was in the neighbourhood of Jahzah (Josh. 13:18; 21:37), lying perhaps six miles (9½ km) south of Ammon.

22-24. For **Dibon**, see v. 18, and for the location of **Nebo**, see v. 1. The name **Beth Diblathaim**[65] is found only here, but possibly refers to Almon-Diblathaim (Num. 32:46), north of Dibon. For **Kiriathaim**, see on v. 1. No other record exists of **Beth Gamul** which was perhaps situated eight miles (13 km) east of Dibon. **Beth Meon** is also known as Baal-Meon (Num. 32:38) and Beth-Baal-Meon (Josh. 13:17), and was located over nine miles (15 km) south of Heshbon and over five miles (9 km) south-west of Medeba. For **Kerioth**, see on v. 41. It was a town on the Moabite plateau, possibly another name for Ar, the ancient capital (Num. 22:36). **Bozrah** is not the town in Edom (49:13), but probably the same place as Bezer (Deut. 4:43; Josh. 20:8; 21:36). **To all the towns of Moab, far and near** refers to those on the frontiers of

---

63. The verbs of the kethibh are feminine singular *hēlîlî ûzəʿāqî*. The qere proposes to read plurals *hēlîlû ûzəʿāqû*. Either would be possible with the collective noun.

64. The kethibh (supported by the LXX) offers *môpaʿat*, the qere *mêpaʿat*.

65. For a discussion as to whether the termination is dual, see GKC §88c.

the land, and those which were more centrally situated.

25. **'Moab's horn is cut off; her arm is broken,' declares the LORD.** This sums up the dire message that is contained in the preceding catalogue. The horn of an animal was an obvious symbol of its ferocity and strength, and it is used in Scripture to refer to the power of individuals and nations (e.g. 'horn' used of Israel in Lam. 2:3). But once an animal's horns had been cut off it was powerless to resist its enemies. So here Moab has been deprived of the resources to withstand those invading her. The broken arm, powerless to grasp sceptre or sword, is another vivid picture of military defeat (Ezek. 30:21). The strength of the nation is exhausted before its aggressors.

5. The Doom of the Defiant (48:26-33)

As people view with disgust a drunkard wallowing shamefully in his vomit, so will the nations look on Moab. Once it had been a proud and boastful nation, but it will be overwhelmed and reduced to ignominy.

26. This section continues the intimation of Moab's punishment. **Make her**[66] **drunk** employs symbolism often used of the LORD's judgment coming upon people (25:15-19; cf. also 13:12-14). Drunkenness is that which causes them to reel with their faculties out of control; so too does the impact of the LORD's judgment. These words seem to be a command addressed to those who are coming as the LORD's instruments of judgment upon Moab (cf. v. 10, 21). They are to strike at Moab with such ferocity that the nation will stagger helplessly. The 'declares the LORD' of v. 25 brought the preceding section of the chapter to an end, and so does not determine who is the speaker at this point; it could be either the LORD (NIV, NKJV, NASB) or the prophet (the NRSV and REB are indeterminate). Certainly at v. 29 there is a different speaker. **For** (*kî*) **she has defied**[67] **the LORD** gives the reason for the judgment. It is the picture of an individual pulling himself up to full height to stand his ground against an adversary. Moab has had the temerity to do this with the LORD. The precise way in which this has been done is pointed out in v. 27: it was through her attitude towards Israel. But before setting that out the sentence against Moab is

---

66. The NIV continues its practice of referring to Moab personified as feminine. The Hebrew usage, which is masculine, is found in other English translations.

67. *IBHS* §27.2f. The hiphil = 'causes himself to be regarded as great', that is, 'talks big' (so here, against the LORD); the hithpoel is 'make oneself great', 'become arrogant'.

described: **Let[68] Moab wallow in her vomit.** The verb rendered 'wallow' (*sāpak*) is literally 'strike with the hand', often in a derisive fashion. It would here seem to picture the drunken man lying flat out on the ground, struggling to remove himself from his own vomit. Alternatively it might depict an individual clasping his hands to his own body as he is sick.[69] It is no wonder that it is said **let her be an object of ridicule** (*śǝḥōq*, cf. 13:13; 20:7; 25:15). What is to come upon Moab will leave it helpless, a forlorn figure only capable of eliciting the response of mockery from those who observe its plight.

27. The focus then turns to the relationship of Moab to Israel, as being the way in which she showed her opposition to the LORD. This is brought out by two rhetorical questions. **Was not[70] Israel the object of your ridicule?** The repetition of 'ridicule' from the previous verse emphasises the fairness of the sentence executed against Moab.[71] They will be treated as they had themselves treated the LORD's people (Zeph. 2:8, 10; cf. Ezek. 25:6). Furthermore, Moab's treatment of Israel, here probably the whole people viewed as belonging to the LORD, had been quite unjustified. Possibly this reflects Moab's reaction to the death of Josiah and the disasters that subsequently befell Judah. **Was she caught[72] among thieves that** (*kî*) **you shake your head in scorn whenever[73] you speak of her?** If there had been some culpable offence alleged against Judah, then the display of scorn would have been justified. This is not to betray a double standard on Jeremiah's part regarding the behaviour of his own people, whom he so often criticises. They had transgressed against the LORD, but when it came to the treatment they received from foreign nations, what was under consideration was the way Judah had behaved towards them—

68. The *waw*-consecutive after the imperative expresses the temporal or logical consequence of the action, and is equivalent to 'so' (GKC §112r).

69. The REB renders 'Let Moab overflow with his vomit' on the basis *śāpaq* II (*sāpaq* in 48:26) is 'be in abundance', whereas *śāpaq* I is 'to slap or clap'.

70. The construction of v. 27 is generally taken as a double interrogative introduced by *'im lō'* ... *'im*, though the NRSV renders these expressions as statements. If the *he* with *haśśǝḥōq* is interrogative, the force of the preceding *'im lō'* is not all that clear. The NASB has 'Now was not ... ?'

71. This is also brought out by an emphatic phrase at the end of v. 26, *gam-hû'*, 'he also', that is as well as Israel, Moab will be an object of ridicule.

72. The kethibh has a feminine form *nimṣǝ'ā*. The qere offers instead a masculine *nimṣā'*, 'he was caught/found', which agrees with the following *bô*, 'of him' in reference to Israel.

73. *middê dǝbārêkā*, 'as often as your words'. For *middê*, cf. 20:8.

and that could not be categorised as lawless or aggressive. They had not acted as robbers towards the other nations. The gesture of shaking their head (cf. 'moaning' 31:18) was probably a stylised rhythmical moving to-and-fro in grief or in mockery. It is a stronger expression than shake the head found in 18:16.

28. Moab's unjustified behaviour will bring on her judgment that they will be unable to withstand, and so the Moabites are presented with an alternative policy they should pursue. There is a change from figurative to literal language. **Abandon your towns and dwell among the rocks, you who live in Moab.** The rocky terrain would provide cover from the enemy, who would also find it difficult to mount effective large-scale operations there. They are being urged to take up the life of a fugitive (like David), because they would be unable to offer effective resistance (cf. vv. 6, 9). **Be like a dove that makes its nest at the mouth of a cave.** 'Cave' is *paḥat*, a depression or hole in the ground, cf. 'on the sides of the mouth of a gorge' (NRSV). The wild pigeons of Palestine are frequently found nesting in inaccessible spots on the heights of the rocky slopes or the sides of steeply banked rivers. If the Moabites are able to do this—is there perhaps a hint of the difficulty of following this course of action, even though it is the only one that will enable them to escape?—then they might manage to avoid the worst of the impending devastation.

29. Next, six terms are heaped up to reinforce the depiction of Moab's pride, and five of these provide an extended example of assonance which builds up a cumulative picture of the intense pride that characterises Moab as she asserts her self-sufficiency. **We have heard of Moab's pride** (*gəʾôn*)—**her overweening pride** (*gēʾeh*) **and conceit** (*gobhô*), **her pride** (*gəʾônô*) **and arrogance** (*gaʾăwātô*) **and the haughtiness** (*rûm*) **of her heart.** 'We' probably refers to the Israelites and the prophet who have heard in past revelation from God, indicating what is to follow in the extensive quotations from, or rather allusions to, Isaiah. This makes the punctuation of NIV (and also NKJV and NASB) seem somewhat improbable in that they include these words in the divine speech. Much may be said for the prophet being the speaker in vv. 26-28, he then associates the people with himself in v. 29, and then finally the indisputable divine speech of v. 30 functions to reinforce the message about Moab. Extensive use of Isa. 15–16 is made in 48:29-38; here there is development of Isa. 16:6, 'We have heard of Moab's pride—her overweening pride and conceit, her pride and her insolence—but her boasts are empty.'

30. '**I** ('myself', emphatic) **know her insolence but it is futile,**'

declares the LORD. The attitude of Moab is described as 'insolence' (<*ᶜebrâ*, 7:29), a word indicating an intense, overflowing reaction, which NKJV understands as 'wrath' (cf. NASB), but which in this context is more probably excessive self-conceit. *kēn* indicates something that is rightly expected and conforms to a known standard; so when it is negated (*lōᶜ-kēn*) it points to what is not right or sound, hence 'futile'. **Her boasts accomplish nothing.** 'Boasts' denotes what is fabricated, 'empty talk' (<√*bāda*ᶜ, 'to invent, make up, lie'; *NIDOTTE* 1:599), and 'nothing' repeats *lōᶜ-kēn* in the sense of futile. The REB favours a different clause structure: 'I know his arrogance … his boasting is false, false are his deeds' (cf. NRSV), but this is less likely.[74] Moab's bluster has nothing to back it up and will only serve to frustrate them when, self-deluded by their arrogance, their deeds are unable to match their words.

31. The speaker in vv. 31-33 seems determined as the LORD by the reference in 'I have stopped' in v. 33. Drawing on the language of Isa. 16:7-10, the attitude that is displayed is one of divine sorrow over the intransigence of the people. **Therefore** (*ᶜal-kēn*) echoes not merely the emptiness of Moab's boasting, but the whole attitude of unchanging spiritual obstinacy that has been displayed. **I wail over Moab, for all Moab I cry out.** The reference to 'all Moab' may pick up the fact that in vv. 21-25 it had been particularly the north of the country that was in view. It is now made abundantly clear that no area of the land will escape. **I moan[75] for the men[76] of Kir Haresath.** 'Moan' (<√*hāgâ*, 'to sigh') covers a broad range of sounds from the cooing of a dove (Isa. 38:14) to the praise of Yahweh (Ps. 35:28) or the growling of a lion (Isa. 31:4). Here it refers to the low, inarticulate sounds of human sorrow (cf. Ps. 115:7; Isa. 8:19; 16:7) to which the divine reaction is likened. The form of the place name is here Kir Heres (NKJV, NRSV, NJPS), but Kir Haresheth (possibly a pausal form in Isa. 16:11; 2 Kgs. 3:25) is what it is now usually called. It was the ancient capital of

---

74. 'Deeds' translates the plural verb *ᶜāśû*, 'they do', for which the subject is naturally provided by *baddayw*, 'his boasts'. It is then the case that there is a deliberate variation in the sense attached to *lōᶜ-kēn.*

75. The Hebrew is *yehgeh*, 'he will moan'. The indefinite usage may well indicate that here we have an apposite citation of a well-known popular saying rather than a textual corruption. One Hebrew manuscript and the Oriental qere support a reading with *aleph* 'I will cry', and this weaker reading is adopted in most translations and commentaries.

76. *ᶜanšê*, 'men', is found in Jeremiah instead of *ᶜăšîšê*, 'delicacies, raisin cakes', as found in Isa. 16:7 (NRSV).

Moab, seventeen miles (27 km) south of the Arnon and eleven miles
(18 km) east of the Dead Sea.

32. The variation in the rendering of the first part of v. 32 reveals the
difficulty of the Hebrew. **I weep for you, as Jazer weeps, O vines of
Sibmah!**[77] The NIV brings the Hebrew into alignment with the text of
Isa. 16:9.[78] But though Jeremiah is undoubtedly reflecting on what
Isaiah had previously said, it does not mean that he uses identical
language. There are too many variations between the passages to
suggest that, and therefore it seems better to try to do justice to the text
as it stands: 'More than ⌐my⌐ weeping over Jazer, I weep for you, O
vines of Sibmah.' Jazer was situated ten miles (16 km) north of Heshbon (Num. 21:32). Although there will be grief over what will happen
to it, it does not match the grief that is felt in the case of Sibmah, three
miles (5 km) north-west of Heshbon, and obviously an area renowned
for its vines. No doubt the intensity of grief matched the devastation
experienced in these localities.

Your branches spread as far as the sea. If 'the sea' refers to the
Dead Sea, the picture is one of the branches or tendrils (so NASB) of
Sibmah's vines spreading southwards in their luscious growth to
occupy even the less fertile area towards the Dead Sea. Keown et al.
advocate the translation, 'Your branches passed over the sea', and suggest that the reference is to the Mediterranean and the extent of exports
of Moabite wine (1995:318). **They reached as far as the sea of Jazer.**
The 'sea of Jazer' is otherwise unknown, and not readily identified
with any physical feature of the area. On the basis of two manuscripts
and the corresponding passage in Isa. 16:8, the REB and the NRSV
suggest that 'sea' has been wrongly inserted here from the previous
phrase, and simply have 'as far as Jazer'. 'Sea' is, however, used in
Hebrew of any extensive artificial stretch of water, as well as of natural
phenomena (cf. the seas of Solomon's temple, 51:36) and so what is
referred to might possibly be some irrigation pond well-known in its
day. In either event the picture is of the vines of Sibmah spreading out
in their growth northwards towards Jazer. But that was in the past.
Now it is the case that **the destroyer** (<√šādad, v. 1) **has fallen on
your ripened fruit and grapes.** Jeremiah, by using 'destroyer',

---

77. For an explanation of the noun with article, followed by Sibnah, see
GKC §127f.

78. Isa. 16:9 has *bibəkî yaʿzēr*, 'with the weeping of Jazer' (cf. NKJV). Here
the MT reads *mibbəkî yaʿzēr*, where the use of *min* indicates a comparison,
either 'more than Jazer weeps', or 'more than the weeping for Jazer', either by
others (NASB) or by the speaker (REB, NRSV).

explains the desolation of the scene described in Isa. 16:9-10. 'Fall' in
a military context denotes attack leading to death. 'Ripened
fruit'/'summer fruit' refers to produce such as figs and pomegranates
which were commonly cultivated together with vines. At the very time
when they should have been rejoicing over the bounty of the land and
the fruits of their labour the unnamed enemy will come and snatch it
from them.

**33. Joy and gladness are gone from the orchards and fields of
Moab** reflects Isa. 16:10. Normally harvest would be a time of gladness but here the picture is reversed. The devastation of the enemy's
plundering has fallen especially on the rich vineyards. 'Are gone'/
'have been gathered': there has been a harvest, but one in which the
enemy has reaped joy and gladness from the 'orchards and fields'/
'fruitful land' (*karmel*, 2:7). And behind the enemy is the controlling
hand of the LORD who has sent them. **I have stopped the flow of wine
from the presses; no one treads them with shouts of joy. Although
there are shouts, they are not shouts of joy.** 'Of joy' is a supplement
to bring out the meaning of a terse Hebrew expression which uses the
same word three times.[79] There is a play on the fact that the word can
mean both a shout of joy (25:30), and a shout in battle (51:14). The
picture of those who press the wine shouting with joy as they go about
their task has given way to another where the shouting that is heard is
now that of warfare.

6. A Jar No One Wants (48:34-39)

Verses 34-39 are treated in the NRSV, REB, and NASB as prose,
though there seem to be no great difficulties in following the NIV or
the NKJV in treating them as verse. The passage again draws on Isaiah
(particularly 15:4-6, and 16), though the sequence is often changed.
This deliberate use of an earlier prophecy brings out the continuity of
the prophetic message.

**34. The sound of their cry rises from Heshbon to Elealeh and
Jahaz, from Zoar as far as Horonaim and Eglath Shelishiyah** (cf.
Isa. 15:4-6). Some of these places have been mentioned already: Heshbon in v. 2, Zoar in v. 4, and Horonaim in v. 3. Elealeh was about two
miles (3 km) north of Heshbon. Both were built on hills and had good
views over the surrounding country. The first phrase is 'because of the
cry of Heshbon', presumably the distress and anguish is felt there first.

---

79. *hêdād hêdād lōʿ hêdād*, literally 'a shout, a shout, not a shout'.

They raise their voices as far as Elealeh,[80] which is quite close, and as far as Jahaz, which is probably the same as Jahzah in v. 21. But the grief and mourning sweeping the land stretches also from Zoar as far as Horonaim, in the south. Eglath-Shelishiyah is a well-known difficulty. There is no grammatical indication of how it should be connected with the rest of the sentence, though in the corresponding passage in Isaiah it is linked with Zoar. Literally it means the 'third heifer', and is taken as a comparison 'like a three-year old heifer' (NKJV, following LXX and Vulgate), presumably pointing to the strength of her bellowing. It is, however, found in contexts which seem to indicate that it is a place name. It might be that three places were known by the name Eglath, and 'third' is used to distinguish this one from the others. It was probably located in the south of Moab near the other cities which are mentioned in connection with it. **For** (*kî*) **even the waters of Nimrim are dried up** seems to be a reference not to the river Nimrim which flowed into the Jordan eight miles (13 km) north of the Dead Sea (Num. 32:3, 36; Josh. 14:27), but to a river flowing into the Dead Sea ten miles (16 km) from its southern end. Drought is affecting the land as well as invasion.

35. There is then an authoritative declaration that God will remove idolatrous worship totally from the land of Moab. **'In Moab I will put an end** (<√*šābat*, hiphil) **to those who make offerings[81] on the high places and burn incense to their gods,' declares the** LORD. Presumably this will be done not so much by the destruction of the people as by their experiencing deportation. There will be no one left in the land to practise idolatry.

36. Verses 36-38 continue the direct speech of the LORD, as the phrase 'I have broken' in v. 38 indicates. **So** (*'al-kēn*) introduces the first consequence of the devastation. **So my heart laments[82] for Moab like a flute;[83] it laments like a flute for the men of Kir Hareseth.** The

---

80. The NRSV renders 'Heshbon and Elealeh cry out' to bring the passage into alignment with Isa. 15:4a.

81. *ma'āleh* is a singular participle, 'one who offers/causes to go up'. So too is the following *maqṭîr*, 'one who burns incense'. The participles are being used in a generalising sense, 'anyone who', and hence the plural translations in the NIV, NRSV, [REB].

82. *hāmâ*, 'to make a noise/sound, be restless'. Metaphorical use of the word in an emotional context, close to 'lament'. Compared to resonating sound of the lyre (Isa. 16:11); here double reed pipes.

83. *ḥālîl* in post-biblical Hebrew and Jewish Aramaic means a 'flute, pipe'. Many take it to refer to a double-reed shawm, a bored flute of some sort.

Lord is not impassive in the face of the suffering of Moab; he is hurt most deeply and expresses his reaction by joining in the funeral rites. The flute, or reed-pipe, was used on occasions of joy and mourning— obviously the latter here. The first line of the verse reflects Isa. 16:11, though harp is replaced by pipe perhaps because of its association with funerals (Matt. 9:23). For Kir Hareseth, see v. 31.

The second consequence of the devastation is introduced in the same way: 'so' (*ʿal-kēn*) **the wealth they acquired**[84] **is gone.** It is not that the divine sympathy is over their lost wealth, but that there are two consequences which flow from what precedes. The language used here reflects Isa. 15:7, though there they seem able to salvage their possessions.

37. The 'for' (*kî*) with which v. 37 begins indicates that the description which follows provides the justification for the divine lament of v. 36. The scene depicts what Moab will suffer in the predicted invasion. **Every head is shaved and every beard cut off; every hand is slashed and every waist**[85] **is covered with sackcloth.** Mourning is universal in Moab (cf. Isa. 15:2-3), and the traditional funeral customs are being observed by all. 'Slashed' (<√*gādad* I 'to cut oneself') was a sign of mourning (16:6; 41:5). For 'sackcloth' see on 4:8.

38. On all the roofs in Moab and in the public squares, there is nothing but mourning. Compare Isa. 15:3. Rooftops were used for private offerings to the gods (cf. 19:13), and were also natural gathering places for family and friends. Here the expressions of grief that were evident throughout the land take place in private on the rooftops and in public in the squares, as people are overwhelmed by the catastrophe that has struck them. **'For (*kî*) I have broken Moab like a jar that no one wants,' declares the Lord.** The same imagery is used in 22:28 of Jehoiachin.

39. It is not clear who the speaker is in v. 39; quite possibly it is a comment by the prophet himself. Since the second 'how!' is a translator's supplement, it is also possible to translate, 'They shall wail: "How she is broken down!" ' (NKJV), with reference to the content of the mourning cries. **How shattered she is! How**[86] **they wail! How**

---

84. For the ellipsis with the construct see GKC §130d.

85. The MT does not have 'every' (hence it is omitted in the NKJV, NRSV and NASB), but it is attested by the Cairo Geniza, many manuscripts, the LXX and Vulgate.

86. The REB omits *hêlîlû*, 'they wail', following the recommendation of BHS as it is not found in Aquila or Symmachus.

Moab turns her back in shame! The first verb (<√*ḥātat*, 1:17) refers to how utterly devastated and disoriented Moab is as a nation. 'Turn the back' in military contexts is equivalent to retreat (Exod. 23:27; Josh. 7:8, 12), causing shame, or else to a gesture wishing to hide herself from others. **Moab has become an object of ridicule** (*śəḥōq*, v. 26), **an object of horror** (*məḥittâ*, an object of both terror and destruction; 17:17) **to all those around her** (v. 17). There is no mitigating feature expressed here as regards the catastrophe that will engulf Moab.

7. Destruction and Restoration (48:40-47)

The last section of the chapter is clearly marked by the introductory formula in v. 40, and the destruction of Moab is then further predicted in two divine sayings, followed by a brief announcement of restoration.[87] Though the presence of 'declares the LORD' at the end of vv. 43, 44, and 47 might indicate that these should be thought of as indicators marking divisions in the material, the sense of the passage and the fact that vv. 43-44 draw on one passage in Isaiah suggests the paragraphs are better taken as vv. 40-44, 45-46, 47.

40. The first of these sayings is introduced by 'for' (*kî*; NRSV, NASB, NKJV, REB). The destiny predicted of Moab in v. 39 will surely come about because the divine decree has gone forth. **This is what the LORD says: 'Look! An eagle is swooping down,[88] spreading its wings over[89] Moab.'** The NIV changes a simile, 'Look, he shall swoop down like an eagle' (so NRSV) into a metaphor, but the person referred to is not identified. It is a picture of savage, unremitting attack which presumably anticipates the invasion of Nebuchadnezzar. However, while the eagle (*nešer*; 4:13) is used elsewhere to refer to the Babylonian power (Ezek. 17:3-5), it can also be applied to Egypt (Ezek. 17:7-8). It is the ferocity, rather than the identity, of the aggressor that is crucial. The bird of prey has risen high in the sky, has located its hapless victim, and its wings are already casting a dark shadow over its quarry as it awaits the right moment to swoop down for the kill.

---

87. Verses 40-42 are omitted by the LXX except the heading in v. 40 and first half of v. 41. Verses 45 and 46 are also lacking.

88. While *hinnēh* is used to make a vivid and dramatic presentation of material, its use here is with the imperfect rather than the participle, and the NIV change of tense from the present 'is swooping' to 'will be captured' (v. 41) unnecessarily alters the time element in a unified future description.

89. *ʿel* for *ʿal*, cf. 49:22.

41. Kerioth will be captured and the strongholds taken. The two verbs are perfects of certainty, and thus properly rendered as futures. 'Strongholds' (<*məṣād*, 'an inaccessible redoubt') may refer to natural fortresses such as mountain strongholds, or to purpose built fortifications. There has been ongoing dispute over the identification of Kerioth as a town rather a common noun, 'cities' (NRSV, NLT),[90] as can be seen by the way the renderings of the text and footnote have been interchanged between editions of the NIV. The mention of Kerioth in Amos 2:2 and on the Moabite Stone favours identification of it as an important town on the Moabite plateau. It has not been positively identified and may refer to settlements round the former capital of the land. When this area falls before the enemy, all is lost, and demoralisation settles in throughout the forces of the land. **In that day the hearts of Moab's warriors of Moab will be like the heart of a woman in labour.**[91] The figure points to a sudden, and commanding experience of pain and dread. They are unable to present any opposition to the invader so overcome are they by what has gripped them. For men turned into women, see on 30:6; and for the figure of a woman in labour, see on 4:31.

42. Moab will be destroyed (<√*šāmad*, cf. v. 8) **as a nation because** (*kî*) **she defied the LORD.** The destruction 'from being a people', so as not to be a people (cf. v. 2), indicates the overthrow of Moab in a catastrophic fashion. This is linked to the attitude of self-exaltation (v. 26) which she adopted towards the LORD, as evidenced by Moab's attitude towards the LORD's people.

43-44. Verses 43 and 44 reflect Isa. 24:17-18, with 'Moab' substituted for 'earth'. **'Terror and pit and snare await you, O people/** 'inhabitant' **of Moab,' declares the LORD.** 'Terror' (*paḥad*, 'trembling', and what causes it,), 'pit' (*paḥat*, cf. v. 28), and 'trap' (*pāḥ*, a net used for snaring birds, cf. 18:22) are all based on the same consonants and build up a picture of total entrapment. This is intensified by the description of v. 44. **Whoever flees**[92] **from the terror will fall into a pit, whoever climbs out of the pit will be**

---

90. The presence of the article in *haqqərîyôt* motivates the idea of 'the cities', though the plural of *qiryâ* is not found elsewhere. The possibility has also been mooted that the singular verb is in fact a third feminine plural form, cf. GKC §44m.

91. *məṣērâ* is a hiphil participle from *ṣārar* I, a denominative use from *ṣārâ*, 'need, distress' (*HALOT* 1058), found only here and 49:22.

92. The kethibh is *hēnîs*, 'he has fled', seems to be in error for the qere *hannās*, a participle of general reference.

caught in a snare. The people are doomed, because if they escape one horror they will only fall into another. A similar figure of speech is found in Amos 5:19. This is ultimately not because of their own unwariness or incompetence. **'For** (*kî*) **I will bring upon Moab**[93] **the year of her punishment,' declares the LORD** points in Jeremianic language (4:23; 23:12) to the ultimate reason for the ineffectual endeavours of the people to extricate themselves from the impact of enemy action. It is the LORD who will ensure their destruction.

45. In v. 45 there is a reversion to Heshbon, which had been mentioned right at the start of the oracle against Moab in v. 2. This inclusion shows the whole Oracle against Moab to have a deliberate structure rather than to be a miscellaneous collection as is often alleged. The words, **In the shadow of Heshbon the fugitives stand**[94] **helpless**, at first seem to create a problem in that Heshbon was in the north of the land, and as that was the direction from which the invasion would come, it is an unlikely place to seek refuge. But this is probably intended only to refer to the start of the invasion when those from the immediate vicinity of Heshbon moved towards the city for protection. If, as seems to be the case, Heshbon was in fact Ammonite at this time (49:3), then presumably the expected refuge was in terms of some treaty arrangement between them. 'Shadow' is frequently used for protection (Pss. 17:8; 36:8; 91:1; 121:5), but that is not now forthcoming. Instead the refugees that gathered there are helpless to do anything, **for** (*kî*) **a fire has gone out from Heshbon, a blaze from the midst of**[95] **Sihon.** These words are an adaptation of an ancient ballad found in Num. 21:28, in which the fire referred to is now the anticipated military devastation that would sweep south through Moab as a result of the plotting of v. 2. Sihon was not the name of an area or city, but of the Amorite ruler of the lands north of the Arnon in the days of Moses, whose success in expanding his territory was celebrated in the ballad. His name is used here by metonymy for the territory he once ruled, and from which the future attack would be launched. **It burns the foreheads** (*pē'â*, 'side, corner', used by

93. Literally 'upon her, upon Moab', the noun anticipated by a pronoun as in 9:14; 41:3; 43:11. The LXX has 'these things' reflecting *'ellēh* rather than *'ēlêhā*.

94. Again, the time reference of the verbs has to be decided (perfect; perfect; *waw*-consecutive imperfect); they could be prophetic perfects used of future actions.

95. The MT *mibbên* is read as *mibbêt* by a few manuscripts and so the NRSV has 'from the house of Sihon', a reference to his dynasty.

metonymy for the 'brow' or 'forehead') **of Moab, the skulls of the noisy boasters.** These words are drawn from the concluding lines of Num. 24:17, part of Balaam's oracles predicting a deliverer who would arise from Israel and crush Moab. The original reference to crushing the foreheads of Moab is changed to one of burning to suit this context where fire has been mentioned, and the figure now seems to be a synecdoche in which not just part of the land ('the skull'), but the whole of it, will be destroyed by the fires of war. 'The noisy boasters'/'sons of tumult' (*šā'ôn*, 46:17) may also be a reference to the otherwise unidentified 'people of Shaon' (NJPS, NRSV margin), or more probably to 'war-loving people' (GNB; BDB 981).

46. Woe to you, O Moab! The people of Chemosh are destroyed; 'for' (*kî*) **your sons are taken into exile and your daughters into captivity.** This is again a free adaptation of Num. 21:29. 'Woe!' picks up on the beginning of the oracle in v. 1. It had already been predicted that Chemosh, their god, would be exiled (v. 7). The god that could not vindicate himself before the onslaught of the LORD will not be able to act effectively on behalf of those who entrusted themselves to him. So the people will perish, and the whole population, 'sons and daughters', will be carried off. This is how the LORD who triumphed over the gods of Egypt (Exod. 12:12) and over Dagon of the Philistines (1 Sam. 5:2-5) displays his effective power over the god of Moab.

47. 'Yet I will restore the fortunes of Moab in days to come,' declares the LORD. Moab, which has been condemned to exile (*šəbî*, v. 46) and captivity (*šibyâ*, v. 46), will have these sentences revoked at a future date when her fortunes are restored (*šûb šəbût*; see on 30:3), a phrase originally applied to the blessing to come on Israel and Judah, but extended here and in 49:6, 39 to cover other peoples also. This unexpected and unmotivated reversal seems to be an intrusion into a passage about the judgment that will descend on the land of Moab, and is often thought on that account to be a later editorial insertion. But in the Oracles against the Nations such provision is often found (for Egypt, 46:26; Ammon, 49:6; Elam 49:39). It is not just a matter of the LORD being the one who so controls the events affecting the nations that whatever measure of national prosperity is found after the disaster is also to be attributed to his direction and provision. 'In days to come'/ 'in the latter days' looks forward to a time, at present not specifically revealed, when this prediction will come true, often involving the Messianic period, though not necessarily so (cf. 12:15; 23:20). What is of significance in this oracle is the preparation found for such divine benevolence in the attitude of the LORD described in vv. 31-32.

Here ends the judgment on Moab seems to be an editorial comment at the end of a long section of material (cf. the use of colophons discussed at 51:64).

E. AGAINST AMMON (49:1-6)

The Oracle against Ammon is the first in a series of short oracles concerning other nations found in chapter 49. While there is no direct evidence regarding the date at which this oracle was first delivered, it does not seem improbable that it was at or after the Jerusalem conference of 594 BC (cf. v. 4).

1. The title, **Concerning the Ammonites**, points to a people whose territory was not so clearly defined as that of Edom or Moab to the south of them (see Map 1). Their capital city was Rabbah, which is the modern Amman. Ammonite ancestry can be traced back to Lot (Gen. 19:38), but hostility between Israel and Ammon had existed for centuries, particularly focusing on the land that Reuben and Gad had been allocated east of the Jordan. At the time Israel had captured this territory it was controlled by Sihon king of the Amorites, who had previously taken it from the Ammonites. Notwithstanding the agreement reached in Judg. 11:24, Ammon repeatedly sought to repossess it. Although at first well-disposed towards David, the Ammonites subsequently revolted and David incorporated their land into his empire (2 Sam. 10). When Tiglath-Pileser took Gilead where the tribes of Reuben and Gad had settled and led them into exile in 734/33 BC (2 Kgs. 15:29), the Ammonites were able to regain their former territory, and it is to that fact that reference is made here. With the rise of the Babylonian empire in 605 BC the Ammonites were at first loyal to Nebuchadnezzar, being used by him to harass Judah in 598 BC (2 Kgs. 24:2), but this was shortly to change and they sent a delegation to the Jerusalem conference in 594 BC (27:3). In 589 BC Nebuchadnezzar had to decide whether to move first against Rabbah or Jerusalem, because both were in rebellion against him (Ezek. 21:18-23). After the fall of Jerusalem Ammon offered shelter to refugees and their king was behind the assassination of Gedaliah (40:13; 41:15). Josephus records that they were conquered by Babylon in 582 BC (*Ant.* 10.9.7). Their territory was later invaded by Arabs and their national identity completely lost.

While Israel viewed the Edomites, Ammonites and Moabites as having a common ancestry (indeed one not dissimilar to that of Israel herself), there is no independent evidence of how these peoples viewed themselves. In the ancient Near East the unity of a nation tended to be thought of not in terms of common ancestry, but in terms of worshipping the same national god. Other oracles concerning Ammon are to be found in Amos 1:13-15; Zeph. 2:8-11; Ezek. 21:20, 28-32; 25:1-7.

This is what the LORD says, 'Has Israel no sons? Has she[96] **no heirs?'** For a brief oracle that shares many elements found elsewhere in the Oracles against the Nations, what is said about Ammon has a startlingly different introduction in the form of two questions, both of which expect a negative response, 'No; Israel *has* sons and heirs', followed by 'Why?' In this way there is brought out the problem that had to be resolved in the relationship between Ammon and Israel. When Gad had been taken into exile, they had not surrendered their rights to the land. Nevertheless the Ammonites had reoccupied what they considered to be their territory, but on the assumption that there was no one left who would ever assert a claim to occupy their ancestral property. In doing so, the Ammonites had not taken account of the LORD's promise of restoration to his people. 'Heir' involves the first occurrence of a fourfold use of the same root (*yāraš*) found in 'heirs', 'take possession' (v. 1), and 'take possession' and 'took possession' (v. 2). The repetition of the root emphasises not only the idea of who is the rightful heir of the territory, but seems to reflect back on Judg. 11:24.

In that Gad does have heirs who will return, there follows a puzzled and somewhat sad question: **Why then has Molech taken possession of Gad? Why do his people live in its towns?** This asserts the improper and transient nature of the annexation. Milcom (REB), or Molech (NKJV, NRSV), is the name of the patron deity of the Ammonites (32:35).[97] Solomon had built a shrine to this god on the Mount of Olives (1 Kgs. 11:5, 33), but it had been destroyed by Josiah (2 Kgs. 23:13). It was generally accepted in the ancient Near East that the god of a land would drive out its previous inhabitants and give it to his own worshippers, who would then serve him. This is seen from a

---

96. The NIV, here as elsewhere, personifies nations as feminine: 'Has she no heirs?' The Hebrew has a masculine *lô*, 'to him'.

97. Hebrew has *malkām*, 'their king' (perhaps = 'chief god of their pantheon'), of which the LXX Milcom, seems a variant. Molech, which uses the same three root consonants, *mlk*, is the form by which we generally know this god. By adopting the hypothesis that Oracles against the Nations were associated with a celebration of the universal sovereignty of the LORD at the Feast of Tabernacles, Jones argues that 'their king' was deliberately and ironically used rather than the name of their god (1992:510).

Canaanite perspective in the Moabite Stone, lines 33-34: 'Chemosh said to me, "Go down, fight against Hauronen." And I went down [and I fought against the town and took it], and Chemosh dwelt there in my time' (*ANET*, 321).

2. But/'therefore' (*lākēn*) begins v. 2 with a note of judgment. The LORD is going to intervene to rectify the situation. **'The days are coming,' declares the LORD, 'when I will sound the battle cry against Rabbah of the Ammonites.'** The reference is to a future event about which there is no uncertainty even though its date is not yet specified (7:32). At that time divine intervention and guidance will ensure that judgment comes upon Ammon. For 'battle cry'/'trumpet blast of war' see on 4:19; Amos 1:14. The focus of the attack will be the capital, Rabbah (the modern Amman), which lay fourteen miles (22½ km) north-east of Heshbon (v. 3). **It will become a mound of ruins, and its surrounding villages will be set on fire.** 'Surrounding villages' is literally 'her daughters'. The reference is not in the first instance to people, but to smaller settlements economically and politically dependent on the capital (Num. 21:25; Josh. 15:45; Judg. 1:27).

'Then Israel will drive out those who drove her out,' says the LORD. 'Israel shall dispossess those who dispossessed him' (NRSV). The idea is that of retribution in kind. Unless we take Jonathan Maccabeus receiving Perea (144 BC) as a reference to this region, it not known what event is here referred to.

3. It is not just the region that Ammon annexed that is affected; the devastation extends right to the heart of their own acknowledged territory. **Wail, O Heshbon, for** (*kî*) **Ai is destroyed!** The injunction to engage at present in lamentation ('wail' <√*yālal*, 4:8) is a poetic technique which brings out the certainty and the extent of the impending calamity. Heshbon is generally understood to have been part of the territory of Moab to the south, but its mention here seems to imply that it was held by the Ammonites at the period of the composition of this oracle (48:2). The boundaries between these groups were fluid. Ai (literally, 'heap of ruins') is not the site west of the Jordan (Josh. 8:28), but some otherwise unknown site in Ammonite territory. Ai is supported by MT and versions, and there are no grounds for emendation.

Cry out, O inhabitants of Rabbah!/'daughters of Rabbah' may be addressed to the people of the capital city, or to neighbouring villages as in v. 2. The people there are to engage in weeping and **put on sackcloth**, which was part of the rituals associated with mourning. Not only were they to **mourn** (<√*sāpad*, 16:4), but they were to **rush here and**

there[98] **inside the walls** (cf. 4:8). The word rendered 'walls' is used
for the walls of vineyards, fields and sheep-pens. The picture is of
them seeking cover and safety as they are scattered through the countryside. Some translations are uncertain if this describes an appropriate
accompaniment of the weeping they are called on to engage in, and so
the NRSV has 'slash yourselves with whips' as an exhibition of your
grief while the REB renders 'score your bodies with gashes'.[99]
However, the picture of bewildered people seeking not very effective
refuge wherever they could does fit in with the overall scene.

**For (*kî*) Molech will go into exile, together with his priests and
officials.** Molech, god of the Ammonites, will suffer the same fate as
Chemosh of Moab (48:7), and lose credibility as a god. Similarly the
religious and political establishment of Ammon will be deported, as
was prophesied also for Moab.

4. The reason why this end will come on Ammon is presented in terms
of pride (for 'boast', *hālal*, hithpael, cf. 4:2). **Why do you boast of
your valleys, boast of your valleys so fruitful?** has occasioned
perplexity to translators. It might well refer to the valley of the Jabbok.
'Your fruitful valley' is literally 'your flowing valley' as in NKJV, or
'your valley flows', and could refer to either people or produce. But
there is evidence from Ugaritic (cf. 21:13) that the word rendered
'valley' could have possessed a homonym meaning 'strength' or
'might' (hence 'arsenals'; REB), and that is also what lies behind the
NRSV rendering, 'Why do you boast in your strength? Your strength
is ebbing', understanding the word rendered 'flow' as used in the sense
of 'flow away'[100] (Lam. 4:9). But the traditional understanding of the
text probably still stands. Unlike its desert neighbours, Ammon
occupied a high plateau which was intersected by streams flowing into
the Jordan, and its people were proud of the fertility of these valleys.

---

98. For the unexpected hithpolel form see GKC §54b; *IBHS* §26.1.1b.

99. The REB changes *baggədērôt*, 'among the walls', to *bigdudôt*, 'with
slashes' (cf. 48:37). The NRSV seems to change *šût*, 'rove about', to *šôṭ*,
'scourge, whip', or even to find an otherwise unattested hithpolel verb.

100. The LXX (30:20) omits *zāb* completely. If the MT is a conflated text,
then Holladay's reconstruction is possible, 'of your ebbing strength' (*bə'imqēk
hazzāb*; 1989, 2:366). Holladay assumes that the *kaph* and *he* were misread as
yodh and *mem* in the paleo-Hebraic script. He follows Dahood who understands '*mq* to take the Ugaritic meaning 'strength'. 'Why boast of your
strength, your ebbing strength?' A second solution comes from Duhm who
divided *zb* so that the first letter *z* represents *zeh*, 'this' and *b* is the preposition
before '*imqēk*, 'that is, in your valley'. (*NIDOTTE* 1:1087-88).

From a theological point of view, the address to Ammon, **O unfaithful daughter**, is problematic. That such language could be used of Israel (31:22) was natural because of the covenant relationship that existed between them and the LORD, but in what way could Ammon be so addressed? It might be that it looked back to the way Ammon had formed part of David's empire, and their unfaithfulness refers to their deliberate rejection of the LORD and his people. In this their attitude was similar to that of Moab (cf. 48:7). However, the unfaithfulness referred to may not have been directly against the LORD, but may have been Ammon's political rejection of Nebuchadnezzar's rule. In becoming tributary to Babylon, Ammon would have given solemn pledges to him as suzerain, including not entering into alliances with those opposed to him. Such a commitment would have been broken when she sent envoys to the Jerusalem conference in 594 BC (27:3). Their willingness to participate in such discussions came from their arrogant reliance on their own resources. **You trust in your riches and say, 'Who will attack me?'** 'Trust in' (*bāṭaḥ bə*) almost implies they made a religion of their possessions and found security in them (cf. 48:7).

5. Ammon's misplaced confidence will become evident when the LORD initiates action against her. There is a change of focus with the words, 'Behold, I'. It is the LORD who is the ultimate power to be reckoned with. **'I will bring terror on you from all those around you,' declares the Lord, the LORD Almighty.** This is a play, using the word 'terror' (*paḥad*), on the saying 'Terror (*māgôr*) on every side' which Jeremiah uses a number of times (6:25; 20:3). Their security is ineffective against the action of the LORD who is the supreme ruler of all. For 'all those around you' compare 48:17, 39. **Every one of you will be driven away** (<√*nādaḥ*, 'to banish'; niphal 'be scattered')**, and no one will gather the fugitives** (<√*nādad* I, 'to flee, depart'). There is a switch here from 'you' being feminine to a masculine plural 'you'. Such transitions occur too often in Hebrew to be dismissed as scribal errors. The change was no doubt assisted here by the use of the idiom 'a man before him' (*'îš ləpānāyw*; 46:5; 47:3). This phrase is not considered significant by the NIV, but other translations find in it a picture of 'headlong' (NRSV) flight in any and every direction (NJPS). The picture of a disintegrating nation helpless before its foes, and with no one trying to rally the scattered and fleeing citizenry, is reinforced by the assonance between 'driven away' and 'fugitives'. The second root is also used of the fluttering of birds' wings as they scatter in fright (4:25; 9:10), and further contributes to the picture of confusion.

6. But that is not the end of the story. Again (cf. 46:26) there is a message of future hope from the LORD. **'Yet afterwards, I will restore the fortunes of the Ammonites,' declares the LORD.** 'Restore the fortunes' (30:3) extends to a foreign nation the consolation that had originally been focused on the covenant people. It is not stated when this will be realised. As with the similar passage in 48:47, there is no mention of this hopeful prospect in the LXX.

F. AGAINST EDOM (49:7-22)

One feature of the prophecy against Edom that arouses interest is the relationship between it and Obadiah's prophecy. Verses 9 and 10a resemble Obadiah 5 and 6, and vv. 14-16 resemble Obadiah 1-4. There is considerable dispute as to the date of Obadiah. It seems clear that if there is any direct literary dependence between the two, then it is Jeremiah who has borrowed from Obadiah. Modern scholarship, however, prefers the hypothesis that both are drawing on earlier prophetic material against Edom, of which there may well have been much because of the long running antagonism between the two countries. Other oracles against Edom are found at Isa. 21:11-12; 34:5-15; 63:1-6; Ezek. 25:12-14; 35:1-15; Joel 3:19; Amos 9:12, and the prophecy of Obadiah in its entirety.

The oracle consists of three parts: the inevitability of judgment (vv. 7-13); how destruction will come (vv. 14-19); and, the completion and consequences of the LORD's judgment (vv. 20-22).

1. Inevitable Doom (49:7-13)

7. As with the other Oracles against the Nations, there is an introductory title, **Concerning Edom.** Edom was a relatively isolated territory lying to the south of the Dead Sea (see Map 1). Its northern boundary was the wadi Zered which flowed into the southern tip of the Dead Sea, and formed the border with Moab to the north. The southern edge of Edomite territory varied over the years, but they generally controlled the hundred mile stretch south to the Gulf of Aqaba. To the west lay the Negev, and to the east the deserts of Arabia, while Edom itself was largely mountainous but with some fertile spots, particularly in the north. There were copper and iron mines, but most of Edom's wealth came from its control over the King's Highway, the caravan route from Aqaba to Damascus that passed through its territory.

Though the people of Edom were descended from Jacob's brother Esau (cf. v. 8), relationships between Edom and Israel had always been

strained (Num. 20:14-30; Judg. 11:17). At the time of the Exodus, the
people had been forbidden to attack Edom (Num. 14:21; Deut. 2:4),
though subsequently the land was subjugated by David (2 Sam.
8:13-14). The Edomites set up their own king in the days of Jehoram
(2 Kgs. 8:20-22) and recovered more territory in the time of Ahaz
(2 Kgs. 16:6). After a period of Assyrian hegemony, it seems likely
that Edom paid tribute to Nebuchadnezzar in 605 BC, but subsequently
joined with Ammon and Moab in plotting rebellion against him in
594 BC (27:3). However, when Judah faced the Babylonian onslaught
in the years 588–86 BC Edom did not intervene to help. Indeed, the
attitude displayed seems to have been one of gloating over the fate of
Judah (Ezek. 25:12-14; 35:15; 36:5; Ps. 137:7; Obad.; Lam. 4:21).
There is no evidence to indicate that Edom was invaded by Nebuchadnezzar, and it remained independent until Nabonidus' campaign in
552 BC which resulted in extensive destruction and the end of the
Edomite monarchy.

It is not certain when Jeremiah composed this message against
Edom, but it was probably in the years immediately prior to the fall of
Jerusalem when the Edomites distanced themselves from Jerusalem. It
is quite conceivable that they were aware of the warnings the prophet
gave, warnings which should have stirred a 'wise' people out of their
complacency, but which they ignored.

**This is what the LORD Almighty says: 'Is there no longer wis-
dom in Teman?'** The message is that of the LORD, the God of Israel,
who is in control of all that there is in the universe. The use of questions may reflect the way in which the wise traditionally spoke. Here
the LORD questions if the wisdom for which Edom was famed still
existed. Edom was traditionally associated with wisdom (Obad. 8).
Eliphaz, one of Job's friends, was from there (Job 2:11). But we are
uncertain of the basis for this reputation. Perhaps, because of the trading routes that crossed its territory, there was a mix of cultures and
information there that led to a multiperspectival assessment of
phenomena. But, whatever its origins, Edom had an undoubted reputation for knowing the answers to life's conundrums and for practical
common sense. The question therefore is ironic, suggesting as it does
that they no longer are acting in a way that corresponded to their
reputation.

Teman was the grandson of Esau (Gen. 36:11). Perhaps the term is
not used to refer to a particular city but to an area, from which it was
transferred to the country as a whole (Hab. 3:3). Although the word
têmān means 'south', it is likely that the area indicated was in the
centre of Edomite territory, though south of the Dead Sea.

The challenge of v. 7 is pressed home in two further questions: **Has counsel perished from the prudent?**[101] **Has their wisdom decayed?**[102] English versions generally agree in taking these two clauses as still under the influence of the interrogative marker in the first clause. They could, however, be taken as statements. What sort of wisdom is described here? McKane points to the wisdom of court advisers which is a wisdom of statecraft, in which 'its practitioners have to take the world as they find it and that in their approach to its complex reality they do not permit themselves the luxury of religious or ethical assumptions' (1965:48). 'The prophetic *dābār* is set against the political calculations of the *ḥᵃkāmîm* in Edom, and Yahweh, through the prophet, asserts that when the threat of judgment against Edom has been fulfilled (vv. 8ff.), it will be seen that the *ḥᵃkāmîm*, for all their pretensions, are incapable of imposing their purpose or will on the future or of contriving the security and prosperity of Edom' (McKane 1965:73). It may, however, be the case that the wisdom of Edom contained a larger traditional, popular element, and was not so court-oriented as, say, the wisdom traditions of Egypt.

8. Turn and flee,[103] **hide in deep caves, you who live in Dedan** presents a problem in that the city of Dedan (cf. 25:23) was a major trading post situated in the north-western Arabian desert, and does not seem to have ever been under Edomite control, though the phrase 'from Teman to Dedan they will fall by the sword' (Ezek. 25:13) certainly implies an Edomite presence and influence, possibly stemming from trade contacts. While the advice given may be to a community from Dedan who for commercial reasons had come to stay in Edom, to quit the land because of the impending disaster, 'live in'/'inhabitants of' Dedan suggests rather that they should not leave home to travel the caravan routes through Edom because of the hostilities there. 'Hide in deep'/'make deep to dwell' could refer to the relative height of Edom compared to the Arabian desert, to which the foreigners are urged to return as they avoid the scene of impending hostilities (cf. v. 30). **For** (*kî*) **I will bring** (a prophetic perfect)

---

101. *bānîm* could be the plural of *bēn*, 'son', but is more likely to be a qal participle from *bîn*, 'to have understanding'.

102. The root *sārah* means 'to go free, be unrestrained', and hence 'Has their wisdom been dispersed abroad?' (REB). But in post-biblical Hebrew *sārah* is 'to stink, rot'. The niphal of *sārah* is found only here.

103. The form of the verb *hopnû* is hophal, 'to be forced to turn, be made to turn'. As hophal imperatives are semantically anomalous, *IBHS* §28.5a suggests that this is an *ad hoc* creation (cf. also GKC §46a²).

disaster on Esau at the time I punish him (cf. 46:21). 'Disaster' (*ʾêd*) is a word of unknown origin, but its meaning of calamity is certain. 'Punish' (<√*pāqad*) is the action a superior thinks it appropriate to take with respect to a subordinate. The Edomites are referred to as 'Esau' from whom they were descended (Gen. 36:1).

9. Verse 9 is an adaptation of a sentiment similar to that found in Obad. 5.[104] **If grape-pickers came to you, would they not leave a few grapes?** 'You' refers to Edom, though possibly it anticipates the mention of Bozrah, the capital (v. 13), because the arrival of grape-pickers (*bōṣərîm*) would be an appropriate penalty for Bozrah (*boṣrâ*). The reference to grapes indicates that there were areas in Edom that were suitable for viniculture. It would be the practice for grape-pickers to leave gleanings (cf. 6:9) because they would not manage—either deliberately, as in Israel (Lev. 19:10; Deut. 24:21), or through oversight—to pick all the crop. Something would be left. **If thieves came during the night, would they not steal[105] only as much as they wanted?**/'destroy their sufficiency', that is, remove as much as they required, or as they wanted to. Even burglars do not ordinarily strip a property clean; they have their eyes fixed on the valuables they want, and that is what they take. But the destroyers of Edom will be insatiable (cf. Isa. 17:6).

10. This will occur because the LORD will bring judgment upon the land. **But** (*kî*) **I** (emphatic) **will strip Esau bare.** 'Will strip bare' renders a verb which the NIV identifies along with the two following verbs as prophetic perfects, whereas other versions render them by a past tense (NKJV, NRSV, NJPS). Esau is again used poetically for the people of Edom (cf. v. 8). They will be despoiled of all their resources. Jeremiah uses a stronger expression than Obadiah's 'be searched out'.[106] **I will uncover his hiding places** (<*mistār*, cf. 23:24)**, so that**

---

104. In Obad 5. the thieves are mentioned before the grape-pickers. Also in Obadiah the second line begins with a *he*-interrogative which is omitted in Jeremiah. The text can still be read as a question because they may occur in Hebrew without a formal marker (GKC §150a; *IBHS* p. 316, note 1).

105. In Obad. 5 the verb 'steal' is an imperfect from the root *gānab*, which is the ordinary word for theft. Here a perfect from the root *šāḥat*, 'to corrupt, ruin, destroy' is used.

106. Jeremiah uses the root *ḥāśap*, 'to strip off, lay bare', while Obadiah has the niphal of the root *ḥāpaś*, 'to search out, examine'; but it would be wrong to suppose that this is some confusion in copying. Jeremiah is not quoting, but using, the earlier material, and is free to modify it as it seems appropriate.

he cannot conceal himself.[107] The people will not be able to find any
haven from the invading forces, because the LORD will reveal their
refuges. **His children, relatives and neighbours will perish, and he
will be no more.** His 'relatives'/'brothers' refers to those peoples who
were related by blood to Edom, such as Horites and Simeonites. 'His
neighbours' are those with no kinship ties, such as Dedan (though
possibly they were reckoned to be descendants of Dedan a grandson of
Abraham and Keturah, Gen. 25:1-3), Thema and Buz, and they too will
be engulfed by the devastation. The Edomites will cease to exist as a
people, and there is no promise made to them regarding restoration and
prosperity.

11. However, there is some glimpse provided of possible survival.
Leave your orphans; I (emphatic) **will protect their lives**/'cause
them to live, stay alive'. **Your widows too can trust**[108] **in me.** These
words of the LORD point up the folly of Edom's false worship. The
men have gone out to battle, and will die. They are told they can leave
their families in the care of the LORD. God is presented in the Old
Testament as the one who defends orphans (Deut. 10:18; Pss. 10:14,
18; 68:5). The one whom they have rejected and whose people they
have opposed to such an extent that this calamity has come upon them
will show his love and mercy towards their dependents. Some find this
change of attitude so startling that they render the text in other ways.
For instance, the REB favours reading v. 11 as questions: 'Am I to
keep alive your fatherless children? Are your widows to depend on
me?'[109] In this way there is a mingling of pity with the sentence of
judgment.

12. Verses 12 and 13 present the reason for this impending judgment,
that it is the imposition of the punishment that is their due. Firstly,
there will be no immunity for Edom. 'For' (*kî*) **this is what the LORD
says: 'If those who do not deserve to drink the cup must drink it,**

107. Literally, 'and he will hide himself (<√*ḥābâ*, a variant form of *ḥabaʿ*),
he will not be able'.

108. *tibṭāḥû* seems to be a mixed form, where a masculine termination on a
jussive form has been used instead of the expected feminine. GKC §60a
explains the change as a pausal substitution for the normal form.

109. BHS cites evidence from the Greek versions of Symmachus and Lucian
which instead of 'he will be no more' at the end of v. 10 support a different
reading: 'There is no one who will say, Leave your orphans; I will protect their
lives.' These words would then be understood as describing Edom's abandonment by her allies.

why should you go unpunished?[110] **You will not go unpunished, but** (*kî*) **must drink it.'** What is referred to here is the cup of divine wrath (25:29). At first it might seem that those who do not deserve to drink that cup refers to Judah, the LORD's people, who have been victims of Edom. But elsewhere (25:18) Jeremiah insists that Judah does deserve to drink the cup of punishment. So the reference may be to those who will be swept up in the horrors of the coming invasion, though they had done nothing to incur that fate, but were the innocent victims of warfare in that as in every other century.

13. There could be no doubt about Edom's guilt or about the LORD's determination to punish her. **'For'** (*kî*) **'I swear by myself,'** declares the LORD, **'that Bozrah will become a ruin** (*šammâ*, 2:15) **and an object of horror** (*ḥōreb*[111]), **of reproach** (*ḥerpâ*, 6:10) **and of cursing** (*qəlālâ*); **and all its towns will be in ruins** (<*ḥorbâ*, 'site of ruins', echoing *ḥōreb*) **for ever.'** Because the LORD could not call on any higher power to witness that he would faithfully keep his promise, he would swear by himself (22:5; Isa. 45:23) or by his great name (44:26). When God spoke, it was inconceivable that such a solemn oath would not be carried into effect. Bozrah was the capital of Edom, and lay twenty-five miles (40 km) south-east of the Dead Sea (it was different from the Moabite Bozrah, 48:24), and just as its fate is determined, so all the cities of Edom will be engulfed in the disaster.

The fact that vv. 12-13 are in prose rather than poetry suggests that they originated at a different time from the earlier verses. It is, however, unnecessary to see them as a prose comment by a later redactor. The words claim to express divine revelation, and that could only have come through a prophetic intermediary, who is not to be identified as some shadowy and otherwise unknown figure, but as the prophet Jeremiah himself. He juxtaposes this other material as an appendix to the oracle to clarify and reinforce its meaning.

---

110. 'Go unpunished' is a qal infinitive absolute from *nāqâ* with a niphal form of the same verb (*IBHS* §35.2.1d). There is no formal interrogative marker in the text.

111. The NIV seems to reorder the terms of this description. Certainly the second term of the MT, 'reproach' (cf. NKJV), is translated in third place. The third term of the MT, *ḥōreb*, comes from a root meaning 'to be dry', and while primarily used of drought (cf. 50:38), it is also applied to the desolation and devastation of warfare. Either it is translated in second place with the NIV considering it here to describe the reaction of horror to witnessing such a scene, or else it is rendered first as 'ruin' and the initial term *šammâ* is moved to second place and translated 'an object of horror' as it is in v. 17.

2. Sudden Invasion (49:14-19)

The NIV has poetry throughout vv. 14-23, as does the REB except for
v. 20a, which is printed as a prose title. The NASB and NRSV treat
vv. 14-16 as poetry, and vv. 17-22 as prose.

14. The oracle reverts to poetry, and the prophet relates what message
(*šəmûʿâ*, 'a report', what is heard) had been divinely revealed to him. **I
have heard a message from the LORD: an envoy was sent to the
nations to say, 'Assemble yourselves to attack it! Rise up for
battle!'** Using material derived from Obad. 1-2, the prophet says he
has the latest news. The corresponding material in Obadiah has 'we
have heard' as the prophet associates himself with the people. This
corresponds to the consolatory note in Obadiah's message, whereas
Jeremiah is presenting the truth of judgment on all the nations that
have offended the LORD. Though an 'envoy' (*ṣîr*, 'an ambassador, a
delegation') may be a divine messenger, here it seems to be one sent
by the enemy the LORD will raise up against the land of Edom when
the call is issued to all the nations to gather for battle (<√*qābaṣ*, hithpael 'to gather together' for a common cause).

15. The LORD then speaks to Edom to show both the outcome of, and
the reason for, this turn of events. The troops are being mustered
because of the LORD's determination to act against Edom. 'For' (*kî*)
now/'look' **I will make you small among the nations, despised
among men.** Their standing among the peoples of the day is going to
be reversed. Those who had a high opinion of themselves will now be
looked down upon by all (cf. Obad. 2).

16. Edom had been deceived by her own success. **The terror you
inspire**[112] points to their success in frightening other nations so that
they would not attack her, and also by the strong defensive positions
she had. Others have found here a reference to a cult object which
causes others to shudder with horror (the form may be related to that
found in 1 Kgs. 15:13 for 'repulsive'). In that case it is Edom's
reliance on false gods that is being condemned. No Edomite deities are
named in the Old Testament, though the unspecific designation, 'the
gods of Edom', does occur (2 Chron. 25:20). Inscriptional evidence
indicates that the chief deity of the nation was Qos/Qaus.

---

112. 'The terror you inspire' treats the pronominal suffix on *tipleṣet*
(<√*pālaṣ* hithpael 'to shudder, shake') as an objective genitive. Even though
the subject which is a feminine noun has preceded the verb, the verb *hiššîʾ* is a
masculine form.

Then using words derived from Obadiah 3-4 the message continues, **and the pride** (*zādôn*, <√*zîd*, cf. 43:2) **of your heart have deceived you.** Again reference is made to the nation's presumptuous optimism and arrogance which the LORD condemns. They were sure no attack upon them would achieve any substantial success because they could withdraw into the many mountainous regions of their country where they had prepared strong defensive positions. Thus the people are described as **you who live**[113] **in the clefts of the rocks.** 'Clefts' is used to describe the habitation of the Edomites in the highlands and sandstone cliffs on the south-east edge of the Dead Sea, but these inaccessible heights will provide them with no more secure refuge in the face of divine wrath than Sodom or Gomorrah had. In 'rocks' (<*selaʿ*) there is probably a pun on the Edomite place-name Sela (2 Kgs. 14:7), a town close to the site of the later Petra, fifty miles (80 km) south of the Dead Sea. There a virtually unapproachable mountain fortress had massive water storage facilities to outlast a prolonged siege. **Who occupy the heights of the hill** may be a corresponding reference to Bozrah, which was situated on a hill. **'Though** (*kî*) **you build your nest as high as the eagle's, from there I will bring you down,' declares the LORD.** The defensive resources on which they presumptuously relied for their future security would be no match for the forces brought against them by divine intervention. Nesting implies security in 22:23. For a fine description of an eagle's eyrie, see Job 39:27-30.

17. The consequences of the assault against them are given in vv. 17-18. **Edom**[114] **will become an object of horror** (*šammâ*; cf. v. 13; 25:11, 38)**; all who pass by will be appalled** (<√*šāmēm*, 'to be desolated', 'to shudder') **and will scoff because of all its wounds** (cf. 19:8). 'Scoff' (<√*sāraq*, 'to whistle, hiss'; cf. 18:16) may relate to a sharp release of breath in horror, or it may refer to an apotropaic procedure to avert malign influences from demons supposed to inhabit the desolate site (*HALOT* 1656). The devastation that will be inflicted on Edom will shock those who witness it and cause them to shudder with fright.

18. 'As Sodom and Gomorrah were overthrown, along with their

---

113. Construct participle ending in *î* (GKC §90l) followed by a prepositional phrase.

114. Edom, though also taken as masculine, is here feminine probably because of a suppressed headword *ʿereṣ*, 'land of …', which is feminine (*IBHS* §6.4.1d; GKC §122i).

neighbouring towns,'[115] **says the LORD, 'so no one will live there; no man will dwell in it.'** 'Dwell' (*gûr*, 'to reside as a stranger') ordinarily conveys the idea of temporary residence, and is here used to intensify *yāšab*, 'to live, dwell'. There will be no permanent residents, and no one will be there on a short term basis either (cf. 49:33; 50:40). The comparison draws on the description in Gen. 19 of the fate of the cities of the plain, Sodom and Gomorrah, and the neighbouring towns of Admah and Zeboim (cf. Deut. 29:23; cf. also 50:40; Isa. 1:9; 13:19; Amos 4:11; Hos. 11:8; Zeph. 2:9). The point of the comparison is not the mode of destruction, but the extent of it. The areas involved became desolate and without inhabitant (cf. 35:6). The figure is a common one for utter destruction, but it is of peculiar relevance to Edom, in that the site of the cities of the plain was traditionally just north of their territory, at the south of the Dead Sea.

19. It is the suddenness of the destruction that is the focus in v. 19, and Jeremiah uses substantially the same language in 50:44-46 with reference to Babylon. **Like a lion coming up from Jordan's thickets to a rich pasture-land,** (*kî*) **I will chase Edom from its land**[116] **in an instant.** The thickets of Jordan were the dense reed beds on the flood plain near the river's edge where lions were found as late as the Exile (12:5). 'Rich pasture-land'/'perennial pastures' (REB, cf. NASB, NRSV) refers to an area of permanent (<*'etān* I, 'everflowing, constant') pasture rather than one of luxuriant growth. The NKJV 'the habitation of the strong' does not fit the imagery. When a lion left its lair and went stalking in such grasslands, it could unexpectedly attack unsuspecting herds and flocks. In the same way the LORD will bring enemy forces against Edom. There will be no time for considered action. In the blink of an eye[117] the people will be routed. The forces involved are not further identified (cf. 46:18; 48:20). It is more probably the enemy forces that are compared to a lion, and not the LORD himself.

115. It is not clear what the feminine singular suffix 'her neighbours' refers to.

116. Literally, 'I will cause him to run from upon her', with assimilated energic *nun* (*IBHS* §31.7.2a).

117. 'In an instant' renders the auxiliary verb *'argî'â*, a hiphil from *rāga'*, in the sense 'to do something in a hurried or speedy fashion'. BDB (921) take the verb as indicating the winking of an eye, and so transferred to describe a response that occurs just as swiftly. *HALOT* (1188) take the verb as a denominative form from *rege'*, ' a moment, an instant'. For the use of the cohortative form here, cf. GKC §108h.

The rest of the verse consists of four clauses each introduced by the word 'who?' **Who is the chosen one I will appoint for this?**/'over her?' (NKJV, cf. NRSV). 'Appoint' ($<\sqrt{p\bar{a}qad}$) is being used for the transfer of authority from a superior to a subordinate. But unlike the remaining questions the first clause does not immediately seem to be a rhetorical declaration of the supremacy of the LORD. Consequently some have suggested emendation, reflected in the NRSV footnote and the REB.[118] The NRSV rendering 'I will appoint over it whomever I choose' is grammatically possible, taking the word 'who' not in an interrogative sense, but as equivalent to 'whoever'. This also makes sense of the $k\hat{i}$, 'for', which stands before the final three questions. God is asserting that he can appoint whoever he chooses because there is no one able to resist him. It is probable that the same sense should be attached to the interrogative rendering. As it stands, the first question evokes wonder at who can possibly be selected by the LORD to carry out the devastation successfully. The focus is then turned away from his identity to the impossibility of anyone successfully impeding the work the LORD has decided on, so that the thought is that whoever is chosen and appointed will not be thwarted because no one can defy the LORD. 'For' ($k\hat{i}$) **who is like me and who can challenge me?** This is an assertion of absolute authority of the LORD, for whom no one can state a time when he should be summoned into court so that his actions may be judicially reviewed.[119] **And what[120] shepherd can stand against me?** 'Shepherd' stands here for ruler. Neither the king of Edom nor the ruler of anywhere else is able to resist what the Almighty has decreed.

This prophecy was fulfilled after 552 BC in the events of Nabonidus' reign when he invaded Edom and brought an end to its monarchy. The destruction of Edom is referred to in Mal. 1:3 as a judgment brought on Esau by the LORD: 'I have turned his mountains into wasteland and left his inheritance to the desert jackals'. However, though the Edomites in Malachi's day were contemplating rebuilding, the LORD declared he would act to demolish anything they built (Mal. 1:4). The area later came under Arab control, and the remaining Edomites seem to have been incorporated among the Jews.

118. If instead of $\hat{u}m\hat{i}$ $b\bar{a}h\hat{u}r$ $\hat{e}ley h\bar{a}$ is read $\hat{u}mibhar$ $\hat{e}ley h\bar{a}$, then the rendering 'I will choose the choicest of his rams' may be obtained.
119. 'Challenge' renders the hiphil of $y\bar{a}\hat{a}d$, 'to appoint' (a meeting), hiphil 'to summon' (to a meeting).
120. $m\hat{i}$-zeh, 'who is this that?', is used in an exclamatory question (*IBHS* §17.4.3c).

3. Complete Destruction (49:20-22)

20. So the resolution of the matter is arrived at. **Therefore** (*lākēn*)
introduces, as often, a word of doom. **Hear what the LORD has
planned against Edom, what he has purposed against those who
live in Teman.** History is not just a sequence of random events and
occurrences. It is subject to the LORD's deliberate strategy and is
structured by his planning. Teman (v. 7) here stands for the whole of
the country. The LORD's purpose is stated in two clauses, each introduced by the oath formula *ʾim-loʿ* ('certainly'; *HALOT* 60). **The young
of the flock will be dragged away;**[121] **he will completely destroy**[122]
their pasture because of them. There is to be no doubt about the
outcome. 'The little ones of the flock' are the people of the land, probably used here because of the previous reference (v. 19) to the ruler as
the shepherd. 'Pasture' is *nāweh* (33:12), occupied by the Edomites
which 'he', probably referring to the LORD, will lay waste.

21. At the sound of their fall the earth will tremble (cf. 8:16; 4:24);
their cry will resound to the Red Sea. 'Fall' points to a violent death,
especially in battle, as one nation collapses before the onslaught of
another (19:7). The impact of what happens to Edom will not be
confined to its own territory. 'Earth' is used by metonymy for its
inhabitants. The shock waves will reach afar. The 'Red Sea' renders
the Hebrew *Yam Suph*, which may also be understood as Reed Sea. In
connection with the Exodus narratives of Scripture, the identity of this
body of water is frequently taken to be in the north-east of Egypt,
along the line of what is now the Suez Canal. In this text it is easier to
understand it of the Red Sea proper, and more particularly of the Gulf
of Aqaba which lay in the southern part of Edomite territory and
included the port of Elath (2 Chron. 26:2).

22. Verse 22 employs imagery used elsewhere by Jeremiah (cf.
48:40-41) to show the ominous nature of what awaited Edom. **Look!
An eagle will soar and swoop down, spreading its wings over
Bozrah. In that day the hearts of Edom's warriors will be like the
heart of a woman in labour.** Bozrah, the capital (v. 13), is used as
equivalent to Edom. This involves the fulfilment of the prophecy of

---

121. *yishābûm ṣaʿîrê haṣṣōʿn* is difficult. 'They shall drag them away the
young of the flock.' Are the young of the flock the subject or object? Perhaps
an object without the object marker after an indefinite plural. The change to
the singular in 'he will destroy' may indicate that the subject is God rather
than his human instrument.
122. An Aramaic hiphil infinitive *yaššîm* (GKC §67y) from *šāmam*.

Num. 24:18, which was largely accomplished through Babylon. Edom was overrun by the Nabateans in the 3rd cent BC at which period many took refuge in southern Judea in the area north of Hebron known as Idumea. These people were later conquered by the Maccabees and forced to become Jews.

G. AGAINST DAMASCUS (49:23-27)

This brief message—it is the shortest of the Oracles against the Nations—concerns Damascus in Syria, and involves a number of puzzling features. It seems to be located here as part of the oracles against smaller, more distant enemies. But what occasion could have given rise to this? No specific setting is identified, or offence against God's people mentioned. Verse 26 makes it clear that this is a divine speech of judgment.

23. Concerning Damascus seems to be a general reference to the whole area of Aram (Syria). Damascus, Hamath and Arpad had been three Aramean city-states which had been overrun by Tiglath-Pileser of Assyria (Isa. 10:9; 36:19; 37:13), with Damascus itself falling in 732 BC (2 Kgs. 16:9). No doubt they enjoyed a brief period of independence as Assyrian rule declined. There is no specific allegation made against them, and while some have supposed that their inclusion here is simply a revival of earlier hostility against them, there are two incidents which are of possible relevance. These states were in the path followed by Nebuchadnezzar when he chased the Egyptians south after Carchemish, and it may be that this prophecy was fulfilled then. Another possibility is that these words were a response to Aramean involvement under Nebuchadnezzar in attacking Judah in 598/7 BC. Even though they sided with Babylon—a course Jeremiah urged—this would not exempt them from responsibility for their actions. It would then be the case that the perfects found in vv. 23-25 are to be understood as prophetic perfects setting out a future reality.

Hamath and Arpad are dismayed, for (*kî*) **they have heard bad news.** Hamath (cf. 39:5) was on the River Orontes in central Syria 133 miles (214 km) north of Damascus, and Arpad in northern Syria a further 95 miles (153 km) north. If the news of the calamity they have heard of is of the situation in Damascus as outlined in the following verses, then it would seem that the enemy through whom the LORD is working cannot be the Babylonians, as they would have attacked from the north and subdued the other two cities first. This has given rise to suggestions that the enemy is Egypt under Pharaoh Neco who moved north in 609 BC, or perhaps even Judah under Josiah at an earlier date. Lack of specific information prevents a definitive solution. However, the calamitous news they heard need not have been about Damascus; it was probably of Babylonian armies massing to attack. They are 'dismayed' (<√bôš, 'to be ashamed', 2:26; 17:13) in that their hopes of independence have been dashed by the appearance of Nebuchadnezzar.

They are disheartened (<√mûg, 'to melt away', Exod. 15:15; niphal 'to become faint-hearted') describes the discouragement that comes over them at the news. **Troubled like the restless sea** takes the reference in '⌐There is⌐ restlessness on the sea; it cannot be quiet'[123] (<√šāqaṭ, tranquil existence; cf. NKJV; see also Isa. 57:20) to be to the Arameans. Since Syria had no sea-coast in ancient times, the turbulence of the sea is being used as a metaphor to depict the anxious restlessness of the people.

24. Damascus has become feeble (<√rāpâ, cf. 6:24)**, she has turned to flee and panic has gripped her.**[124] 'Panic' (reṭeṭ) is a hapax, referring to consternation as a result of bad news. This describes the demoralisation of Damascus, which was situated sixty miles (100 km) east of the Mediterranean, in a fertile plain east of the Anti-Lebanon mountains, and at a crossroads of international trade routes. Seeing the calamity coming on the land her people attempted to escape, but were unable to muster the resources to do so. Possibly the city came under siege. **Anguish and pain have seized her,**[125] **like that of a woman in labour.** This is the comparison often used by Jeremiah to express sudden paralysis and weakness (6:24; 13:21; 50:43).

25. Why has the city of renown[126] **not been abandoned?** This is a word of anguish or taunt. At first we might have expected the cry to be

---

123. For the use of the infinitive absolute before yākōl cf. v. 10 (*IBHS* §35.5.4b, note 63; GKC §113d).

124. heḥəzîqâ is literally 'she [that is, panic] has gripped her'; but mappiq is probably to be understood in the he (perhaps omitted because of the tone retraction in pause), and so the form would be masculine with a 3 fem. sing. suffix (GKC §59g). Compare 6:24; 8:21. The suffix is ambiguous, but the sense is not. The people of Damascus are gripped by strong emotion.

125. The verb 'ăḥāzattâ is singular, with ṣārâ as subject. Reversing the two words 'ăḥāzattâ and waḥăbālîm underlies a translation such as that of the REB, 'Trembling has seized her, pangs like childbirth have gripped her'.

126. təhillâ, 'a song of praise'. It may have the extended meanings of 'praise, renown'. The qere thlt (perhaps təhillat for təhillātî, 'my praise') seems unnecessary.

'How is the famous city forsaken!' (so NRSV)[127], but the sequence of thought seems to follow on from the previous verse with its picture of their inability to summon the courage and resources to escape from their encircling foe. This is a cry of woe, 'Why has this not happened? Why did they not escape when they could, and leave a deserted city before their enemy?' **The town in which I delight** is best taken as an expression of divine sympathy over the beauty of Damascus, which was proverbial in the east. The other alternatives, that this is an expression of the prophet rather than the LORD (cf. 48:31), or that this verse is the speech of a citizen of the town, seem just to be expedients to circumvent the obvious understanding of the words. However, it may be that 'my delight' is a misunderstanding of the ending of a Hebrew word, and what we should have is simply 'the town of delight'.[128]

26. Surely renders *lākēn*, 'therefore' (cf. NKJV, NRSV), which indicates that what follows is either the consequence of their inactivity or the divine sentence that will be imposed on the city. The NIV (cf. NJPS) favours an asseverative usage here. **'Her young men will fall in the streets; all her soldiers will be silenced** ($<\sqrt{}$*dāmam* niphal, 25:37) **in that day,' declares the LORD Almighty.** The young men are the same group as the soldiers, and they fall in the streets because they have been unable to get out and wage battle in the open field. Her protectors will themselves be overcome (cf. 6:11; 9:20).

27. The picture of the devastation is completed by emphasising that it is the LORD's judgment that has fallen on the city. **I will set fire to** (11:16) **the walls of Damascus; it will consume the fortresses of Ben-Hadad.** The use of fire in siege warfare was well known. City walls would be made of whatever material was plentiful locally, but a hot fire could turn hard limestone into powder. The fire is specifically 'in the wall of Damascus' (NKJV) from where it would spread throughout the city, destroying the palaces (REB), or strongholds (NRSV)/'citadels' (*'armôn*, 6:5; 9:21) which are also referred to in Amos 1:4. Ben-Hadad seems to have been the name of a dynasty of Aramean kings, with the name occurring in 1 Kgs. 15:18 (c. 880 BC); 20:1-34; 2 Kgs. 6:24; 8:27; 13:3, 24 (c. 790 BC). Ben-Hadad, 'son of Hadad', refers to the storm god worshipped by the Arameans, equivalent to the Canaanite Baal.

---

127. This might be achieved by deleting the *lōʾ*, 'not', from the text (as in the Vulgate) or assuming it to be a corruption of an emphatic *lamedh*, 'How completely destroyed the city is!'

128. Several versions omit 'my'. The *yodh* may be an archaic genitive ending, possibly retained here in a fossilised description of Damascus.

H. AGAINST KEDAR AND HAZOR (49:28-33)

This brief poem about the desert tribes is in two strophes each of which begins with a divine summons to invaders who are to act as his instruments, 'Arise and attack' (vv. 28, 31). What is unusual in this place is that the oracle begins with a precise identification of the invader. While there is no direct evidence to show that this title was placed here by Jeremiah himself, it is equally the case that such editorial material need not automatically be assumed to come from a later hand.

28. Concerning Kedar and the kingdoms of Hazor. Kedar is well known in biblical times (cf. 2:10) as the area of desert to the east of Palestine inhabited by bedouin who were descended from Ishmael (Gen. 25:13). They lived in tents (Ps. 120:5) and unwalled villages (Isa. 42:11), and were skilled archers (Isa. 21:16-17) and sheep breeders (Isa. 60:7), who maintained trade links with Phoenicia (Ezek. 27:21). According to the Babylonian Chronicles Nebuchadnezzar defeated them in 599 BC. Hazor is more difficult to identify. It does not here refer to the major city in northern Palestine (Josh. 11:1; 12:19; 15:23, 25; 19:36), but seems rather to reflect an area (cf. v. 33) where the desert tribes were settled in villages.[129] 'Kingdoms' are not to be thought of as major powers, but a reference to relatively minor chieftains who ruled over the various desert groups.

The desert tribes often raided the settled lands around them. They are seen acting against Israel in Judg. 6:3 ('eastern peoples'), and they were also a perpetual source of trouble to the Assyrians, and after them to the Babylonians. Nebuchadnezzar mounted a punitive expedition against them in November/December 599 BC, a year before he came against Judah. This may well be the reference in the clause **which Nebuchadnezzar[130] king of Babylon attacked.**

But though Nebuchadnezzar is the outward human aggressor, his actions are controlled by the LORD and serve his purposes. We therefore hear the divine commission that has been given to Nebuchadnezzar and his forces. **This what the LORD says: 'Arise, and attack/'go up to' Kedar and destroy[131] the people of the East.'** The

---

129. *ḥāṣēr* may refer to a 'courtyard', or 'enclosure' (LXX), or else to 'a permanent unwalled settlement', 'an unfortified village' (*HALOT* 345). *ḥāṣērîm* is found in Isa. 42:11 of the small unwalled villages where Arab tribes settled.

130. The kethibh *nəbûkadreʿṣôr* is probably an erroneous form by confusion with the preceding *ḥāṣôr*, and the qere *nəbûkadreʿṣṣar* should be read here.

131. *šodədû* is an imperative, cf GKC §67cc.

command is to get involved in battle and subject them to devastation. 'People/sons of the East' is found in a variety of contexts, referring to several different groups of nomadic tribes inhabiting the desert east of Aram and in the north of Arabia. They too had been involved in raiding the fixed settlements, e.g. in association with the Midianites and the Amalekites in Judg. 6:3 (cf. also Gen. 29:1; Judg. 6:33; 8:10-11; 1 Kgs. 4:30; Ezek. 25:4, 10). These relatively insignificant peoples would also be held accountable by God.

29. While it is not clear who is to carry out the actions referred to in v. 29, it is unlikely to be the people of Kedar themselves removing their possessions to safety (as suggested by Holladay 2, 1989:383). It is more probable that this is the action of the invading army. **Their tents and their flocks will be taken; their shelters** ('tent curtains'; 4:20; 10:20) **will be carried off with all their goods and camels.** This is an inventory of the assets of such nomadic tribes; nothing else would be found. 'Shelters' is a reference to the curtains or cloths which covered the framework of their tents. They are carried off 'for themselves', appropriated by the raiding army, presumably to provide themselves with relief from the desert heat. The camels would no doubt have helped solve the problem of how to transport their booty as well as being used in fighting. **Men will shout to them, 'Terror on every side!'** The cry of calamity, which is found often in Jeremiah for a situation of disaster (cf. 6:25), may be uttered by the people themselves, or by their enemies. It is a situation that calls for urgent action to avoid all its dangers.

30. Verse 30 then contains the advice that the LORD gives to those affected. **Flee away quickly!** The phrases used suggest that every effort should be made by them to escape the impending disaster. **'Stay in deep caves, you who live in Hazor,' declares the LORD.** 'Stay in deep caves' is literally 'Make deep with respect to staying' (cf. v. 8) and could refer to going deep into the desert, as well as caves, which are perhaps unlikely places for desert dwellers to hide in. The reason assigned for this escape action is: 'for' (*kî*) **Nebuchadnezzar king of Babylon has plotted against you; he has devised a plan against you.**[132] There is no doubt about the identity of the enemy, and none either that there is a strategy in place by which he intends to rid himself

---

132. The NIV follows the qere reading *'ălêkem*, 'against you', which has the support of many manuscripts and the LXX. However, the kethibh *'ălêhem*, 'against them', may well be an instance of the frequent Hebrew idiom of change of person in circumstances that seem odd to us, and probably represents the original reading, which has been subsequently changed.

of the troublesome behaviour of these people. Nowhere else in the Oracles against the Nations is Nebuchadnezzar explicitly named. (His name is absent from the LXX at this point also.)

31. By omitting 'declares the LORD' in v. 31 because it is not in the LXX, the REB takes v. 32 as the content of Nebuchadnezzar's plan. This is improbable. The structure of the poem, in which v. 31 begins the second stanza and parallels v. 28b, requires that the plural divine commands are addressed to the Babylonians, urging them to put into operation the course of action devised by their ruler. **'Arise and attack**/'go up to' **a nation at ease** (<*šālēw*, 'prosperous, comfortably well-off'), **which lives in confidence** (*beṭaḥ*, 23:6),' **declares the LORD.** The desert tribes thought themselves exempt from the conquering action of Babylon because of the scattered nature of their settlements, and the ease with which they could move away in the face of hostile forces. They were self-confident and lacking in apprehension at the events that were taking place in the world about them. To that extent their inadequate preparations made them an easier target to attack. Moreover, it is **a nation that has neither gates nor bars.** They did not live in fortified settlements. The gates referred to are double-leaved gates which would open to allow access to the town, and would be held closed by stout bars being placed horizontally across them. Also **its people live alone** (cf. 15:17). Dwelling far from foes in inhospitable terrain, they ordinarily were able to live without fear of attack, but the isolation of these inhabitants of the desert also meant that they did not have allies to call on if they were attacked, and therefore small groups could be picked off one by one by a larger invading force. The similarity to Ezek. 38:10-11 is probably coincidental.

32. Again (cf. v. 29) the devastation that is to come will involve their possessions being taken away. **Their camels will become plunder, and their large herds will be booty.** The herds referred to here could be of cattle or of sheep and goats. The enemy will take them for themselves. But more than the enemy is involved in the devastation; it is directly willed by the LORD. **I will scatter to the winds those who are in distant places.** The phrase that is found here is difficult to translate. Either it is a reference to where the desert tribes live,[133] or it is a description of their custom, 'those who clip the hair by their foreheads' (NIV margin; cf. 9:25; 25:23). The LORD says that he **will bring disaster on them from every side** so that they will not be able to escape.

---

133. The REB is a development of the idea 'to roam the fringes of the desert'.

33. Verse 33 provides a collection of typically Jeremianic phrases to describe the devastation that will come upon the village settlements of those found in the desert region. The land which became incapable of fulfilling its proper function for its inhabitants was generally considered in the ancient world to be divinely cursed. **Hazor will become a haunt of jackals** (cf. 9:10; 10:22)**, a desolate place** (*səmāmâ*, 2:15) **for ever. No one will live there** (cf. 4:7; 46:19)**; no man will dwell in it** (cf. v. 18). What had previously been a far from hospitable environment will be laid utterly bare by Nebuchadnezzar's invasion.

I. AGAINST ELAM (49:34-39)

In this oracle Jeremiah deals with Elam the most distant of the nations from Judah. It does not seem primarily to have been included because of any dealings, hostile or otherwise, it had with Judah, but because it represents the end of the earth as far as the prophet and his contemporaries were concerned. The basic theme is that the realm of the God of all the earth extends as far as is conceivable, and that this will be demonstrated by the judgment he brings on those who act contrary to his wishes. Though the LORD is especially the God of the small nation of Judah, his sway is universal (cf. 23:23).

Elam had for centuries been an influential kingdom situated on the north-west corner of the Persian Gulf, bounded on the west by Babylonia, on the north by Media, and on the east by Persia (see Map 2). In 640 BC it was overrun with great savagery by the Assyrians under Ashurbanipal, and its capital, Susa, was sacked. With the collapse of Assyrian power after Ashurbanipal's death in 625 BC, another dynasty arose in Elam and continued to rule there until Elam was merged with Medo-Persia by Cyrus.

Elam was known to the people of Judah as one of the areas to which the northern tribes had been deported (Isa. 11:11), and it had figured in Isaiah's prophecy of the destruction of Babylon (Isa. 21:2) along with the Medes.

34. This is the word of the LORD that came to Jeremiah the prophet concerning Elam, early in the reign of Zedekiah king of Judah. For the introductory formula see on 46:1; 47:1; 14:1. For 'early in the reign of Zedekiah' see on 26:1. The Babylonian Chronicle for Nebuchadnezzar's ninth year (spring 596–spring 595 BC) describes a military campaign he waged against a king the name of whose territory can reasonably be construed as Elam (Malamat 1956:255). It may well have been just prior to this in the winter of 597 BC that this oracle was issued in which the LORD announces what is going to happen.

35. This is what the LORD Almighty says probably contains a
significant key to the theme of the oracle in the divine name used,
emphasising as it does the universal sway of the LORD, the God of
Judah. What follows is remarkable in that the focus is totally on what
he will do, all expressed in the first person. There is no word of warning or explicit condemnation addressed to Elam, nor is there any word
of exhortation to the unnamed foes who will be the instruments of the
LORD's judgment. The focus is not on the specifics of Elam's situation,
but on the supreme scope of the LORD's sovereign action in judgment
(vv. 35-38) and in restoration (v. 39). **See, I will break the bow of
Elam.** It is the LORD's prerogative to display his power by destroying
the military might in which nations boast (Ps. 46:9; Mic. 5:10-14;
Zech. 9:10). The bow was the most fragile of ancient weapons, and
could easily be broken and rendered useless (cf. Hos. 1:4-5 for breaking of bow). There is evidence to suggest that the archers of Elam were
renowned (25:25; Isa. 22:6; Ezek. 32:24), and it was probably the case
that they were what Elam trusted in to secure her position. Certainly
the archers of the Persian empire into which Elam was incorporated
formed a significant part of her military might. (Herodotus recorded
[*Hist.* 2:136] that there were three things taught to the youth of Persia:
to ride, to draw the bow, and to speak the truth.) So it is declared to be
the LORD's prerogative to display his power by destroying the might of
earthly realms (Ps. 46:9; Mic. 5:10-14; Zech. 9:10).

The mainstay of their might is more literally 'the head of their
power', that is, what was foremost in their martial resources. Such trust
in military prowess fits in with the ground of condemnation of many
other heathen nations. By implication, if their bows are destroyed, then
all other weapons of war will be too, and they will be defenceless.

**36. I will bring against Elam the four winds from the four
quarters of the heavens.** Foes will come from every direction so that
there is no possibility of escape. The figure of the four winds being
used to signify military might is found elsewhere in the Old Testament
(Zech. 6:5; Dan. 7:2; 8:8; Ezek. 37:9). The picture is of a mighty force
that will gather to overwhelm Elam no matter how much she trusted in
her archers. **I will scatter** (cf. v. 32) **them to the four winds, and
there will not be a nation where Elam's exiles**[134] **do not go.** The

---

134. The kethibh reads *'ôlām*, that is 'scattered ones of perpetuity', which
while a strong figure is not impossible, but the reading of the qere *'ēlām* is
almost universally adopted.

figure of the four winds is now used to show the devastation that will
occur in the land. The Elamites had already experienced this in part
under the Assyrians, when some of their number had been sent to
Israel (Ezra 4:9-10), just as there had also been Israelites taken to Elam
(Isa. 11:11) as part of the Assyrian policy of fragmenting the cohesion
of subject peoples and thereby reducing the threat they might pose to
their conquerors.

37. Verse 37 states the matter in plainer language. **'I will shatter**[135]
Elam before their foes, before those who seek their lives (cf. 21:7);
I will bring disaster (cf. 4:6) **upon them, even my fierce anger** (cf.
4:8),' **declares the LORD.** This incorporates a number of standard
phrases of Jeremianic vocabulary, but this is no reason to think that the
passage is the invention of a later copyist. **I will pursue them with the
sword until I have made an end of them.** The LORD will show no
mercy in the punishment he brings upon the land (9:15, 16b). He will
use nations to punish other nations (5:14-19).

38. **'I will set my throne in Elam and destroy her king and officials,' declares the LORD.** The words used are the same as those
applied to Nebuchadnezzar setting up his throne in 43:10 (cf. also
1:15). This action which was a consequence of conquest and subjugation is used to show how completely the LORD is in control of the
affairs of Elam, even though it is a far distant land.

39. But the picture is not wholly bleak. **'Yet I will restore the
fortunes**[136] **of Elam in days to come,' declares the LORD.** A similar
reversal of fortune for other peoples is also envisaged in 48:47 and
49:6. This is not to be taken as an addition made by a later editor, but a
vision granted to the prophet of the greater purpose the LORD had for
the nations, no matter how distant and unelaborated the prospect was
in his day. Perhaps what is in view here is the way in which Elam with
its capital Susa was at the heart of the Persian empire (Neh. 1:1; Dan.
8:2), but there was a further measure of fulfilment in the Elamites
mentioned as present at Pentecost in Acts 2:9, 11.

---

135. *haḥtattî* is the hiphil of *ḥātat*, (qal 'be broken to pieces'; hiphil 'to
dispirit through fear and terror'; cf. 1:17). The form is shortened for *hăḥittôtî*,
because of change of stress to the last syllable with the *waw*-consecutive
(GKC §67aa).

136. The kethibh is *'šwb 't šbyt*, whereas the qere is *'āšîb 'et-šəbût* = 49:6.
The same kethibh/qere pattern is found in 33:26, and for the noun in 29:14.
Probably the idiom allowed either the qal or the hiphil stem to be used, and
there is a noun *šəbît* as well as *šəbût*.

J. AGAINST BABYLON (50:1–51:58)

That the two chapters 50 and 51 devote almost as many verses (110) to
Babylon as the previous Oracles against the Nations had to the other
nations combined (121 verses) is indicative of the extent to which
Babylon dominated the thinking and lives of the people of Jeremiah's
day. But it would be wrong to view this division of the prophecy as
focusing solely on Babylon. There are two themes pursued here in an
interlinked fashion. One repeats what had been previously foretold—
the downfall of Babylon. Though Babylon had been divinely assigned
the role of being the LORD's destroyer of the other nations, Babylon
itself would be called to account by the LORD for her conduct and
would in turn be subject to conquest and destruction. Though used by
the LORD as his instrument of punishment, Babylon did not possess
any special exemption from divine scrutiny of her conduct. But now,
linked to the theme of Babylon's overthrow is that of the deliverance
of the LORD's people. This too testifies to the universal sovereignty of
the LORD and also to his gracious provision for his own. This is the
true climax to Jeremiah's prophecy: not just the destruction of all that
is opposed to God, but the rescue through his grace of a remnant the
LORD acknowledges as his own. Here Jeremiah is privileged to be able
to enlarge on the theme of restoration after judgment that had been
found in earlier prophets such as Amos 9:11-15 or the closing chapters
of Isaiah.

Theological Coherence
Given that these chapters predict Babylon's downfall, how can they
cohere with the message very clearly spelled out by Jeremiah that the
people should submit to Babylon? Jeremiah had predicted that the foe
from the north would come as the instrument of the LORD's judgment
on Judah, and after the events of 605 BC there was no doubt that the
foe had been identified as Babylon, and more particularly Nebuchadnezzar. He had been recognised by the LORD as his servant (25:9),
carrying out the task the LORD wished to see done. Furthermore
Jeremiah's letter to the exiles in Babylon made no secret of the fact
that their stay there would be long, and that they ought to settle down
and settle in and pray for the well-being of the city (chap. 29). Yet in
chapters 50–51 a violent end is announced for Babylon. Further, the
end of Babylon is presented as occurring only after a long time in 27:7
and 29:10, whereas it is imminent in 51:13, 24. Also, in his earlier
prophecies Jeremiah had not voiced any doubts as to the propriety of
Nebuchadnezzar's actions, whereas here Babylon is shown to have

opposed and defied the LORD (50:24, 29) and Nebuchadnezzar is personally arraigned for misconduct (51:34). The contrasting viewpoints expressed in chapters 27–29 and 50–51 have led critics to deny the authenticity of the latter. Carroll (1986:816) argues that there is an inherent contradiction in the editing of the book. It should be noted that the problem does not disappear by treating chapters 50–51 as the outcome of a later redactorial process. The perceived incompatibilities in the thought of the book remain as they were, and it would have been a very obtuse editor who was unaware of them.

But there is no need to suppose that the two strands of thought regarding Babylon are utterly incompatible. The same fact of foreign powers being used by the LORD to execute his purposes had been clearly expressed by Isaiah in relation to Assyria (Isa. 7:20; 8:7-8) and also anticipated in regard to Persia (Isa. 44:28; 45:1-6). But that did not make the Assyrians any the less accountable for what they did. The LORD pronounced his woe over the Assyria whom he had used as the rod of his anger (Isa. 10:5) and declared, 'I will punish the king of Assyria for the wilful pride of his heart and the haughty look in his eyes' (Isa. 10:12). Both the immediate policy prescription of submission to Babylon and the longer term prediction of the overthrow of Babylon may be integrated as parts of one scenario arising out of the LORD's purposes for his people. That, at the end of the day, is the abiding reality: the LORD, his jurisdiction, power and purpose.

Furthermore there is no real tension between the earlier material recorded in Jeremiah and that found in chapters 50–51. The thought of 25:12, 'But when the seventy years are fulfilled, I will punish the king of Babylon and his nation, the land of the Babylonians for their guilt', clearly anticipates the development of this later section, as does the statement of 25:26, 'the king of Sheshach will drink it also'. Already in the mention of seventy years (29:10) there is implied that after that time the captivity will come to an end, certainly leaving open the possibility that circumstances in Babylon would change then. It would be at that juncture that purchasing fields would once more become the norm in Jerusalem (32:15), again implying a situation in which Babylonian control had ended.

Historical Setting
In terms of the events of Jeremiah's life the question arises: If the negative prophecies of chapters 50–51 pre-date the fall of Jerusalem, how can we explain the favourable attitude of Nebuchadnezzar and the Babylonians to Jeremiah? Probably the intelligence reports they received were selective and filtered out what was considered politically

less relevant. Moreover, we may not simply say that in chapters 27–29 and 39–40 Jeremiah is the friend of Babylon. The prophet certainly promoted policies that recognised the immediate political supremacy of Babylon and urged acquiescence in this undoubted reality. But these circumstances had arisen only because at that moment the LORD was working through Babylon. The time would come when the ways of the LORD and of Babylon would diverge.

There are features of these poems which favour an early date for their composition. There is, for instance, the mention of Ararat (51:27), which was captured by the Medes early in the sixth century BC and ceased to be a separate entity. Similarly Minni and Ashkenaz (51:27) had been assimilated by the Medes by 590 BC. Furthermore, the mention of the Temple in 51:50 and of violence done to Jerusalem in 51:35 and 51 need not presuppose the fall of the city and the destruction of the Temple; the events of 597 BC provide sufficient background for understanding these verses. Equally, the absence of any direct mention of Cyrus points to an early setting for these oracles.

Structure of the Oracle
The structure of the prophecy requires comment. Beginning and ending as it does with references to Jeremiah (50:1 and 51:59, cf. also 51:64), it obviously is intended to be understood as coming from him. Jeremiah drew together many elements from visions given to him at various dates, but that does not mean that the end product lacks smooth development of its themes. Aitken has provided an analysis which shows that 'the composition is not a disordered and chaotic conglomerate of at best thematically related elements but rather a well-ordered complex of structurally related elements' (Aitken 1984:26). The analysis of these two chapters largely follows that of Aitken. Six main blocks of material are distinguished: 50:4-20; 50:21-32; 50:33-46; 51:1-33; 51:34-44; 51:45-53. There are also within the overall structure of the poem framing elements to be found in 50:2-3; 50:46 and 51:54-58. Finally there is a prose appendix in 51:59-64.

Fulfilment of the Oracle
Was the prophecy recorded here in fact fulfilled? When Babylon was captured by Cyrus, the city was not destroyed. Indeed, subsequent events led not to some massive overthrow of Babylon, but rather to a gradual decline. There were a number of revolts in Babylonia against Persian rule, leading to the removal of the statue of Marduk and destruction of the Esagila temple by Xerxes. Although the city enjoyed a brief recovery of its fortunes under Alexander the Great, his successors viewed it less favourably, eventually removing the population to a

new settlement nearby. Parthian occupation led to a significant fall in Babylon's prestige around 124 BC, and the city was in ruins by AD 200.

Probably because of the role Babylon played in the destruction of the Temple and the exile of the people from the land, Babylon and not Assyria became the epitome of evil in the New Testament (Rev. 14:8; 16:19; 17:5; 18:1-24). What was revealed to Jeremiah regarding its future often anticipates this eschatological world view, so that what the prophet is seeing is a vision not simply of the end of Babylon, but through that, or against that background, of the total destruction of all that opposes God and his people. A similar vision had earlier been granted to Isaiah in terms of the destruction of Edom, which is also set against a much broader background (Isa. 34).

1. Superscription and Introduction (50:1-3)

a. Superscription (50:1)

1. This is the word the LORD spoke uses a relatively rare formula of introduction (cf. 46:13). **Concerning Babylon and the land of the Babylonians**. 'And' is a translator's supplement; the second phrase is intended to define the first more closely. Babylon was a major city with a history stretching back to the third millennium BC. It was situated on the River Euphrates in what is now southern Iraq (its ruins lie fifty-five miles [88 km] south of Baghdad). It also controlled an area around it, whose extent varied with the fortunes of the various states in the region. 'The land of the Babylonians'/'Chaldeans' refers to the immediate hinterland of the city. The term 'Chaldean' goes back to the second millennium BC, and relates to a people who lived to the south of Babylon. Nabopolassar, Nebuchadnezzar's father, who seized control of Babylon in 626 BC, was a Chaldean, and so the term is used appropriately at this period to refer to the surrounding area as well. **Through** (*bəyad*, 'through the hand/agency of'; cf. 37:2) **Jeremiah the prophet**, not 'to Jeremiah', may well indicate that the message is viewed as being relayed in writing, but there is to be no doubt about the authenticity of the message the prophetic intermediary conveys.

b. Introduction (50:2-3)

Three passages may be identified as constituting a framework to this long oracle: 50:2-3; 50:46; and 51:54-58. These verses share the theme of a call to hear the news that Babylon is captured (50:2, 46), echoed by the cry of Babylon itself announcing its own doom (51:54; Aitken 1984:30-31). These brief introductory verses also foreshadow many other themes in the whole poem.

2. Announce and proclaim among the nations, lift up a banner and proclaim it; keep nothing back, but say with its six imperatives builds up a picture of vitally important news that must be publicly delivered (cf. 4:5-6; 46:14). The imperatives are all plural, indicating that these are not tasks assigned to the prophet, but that they rather are the LORD's commands through the prophet for a message to be relayed by other parties, either the exiles or the nations themselves. The news is of international significance, and those who hear it are to act as God's heralds in proclaiming the decisive event which is anticipated. 'Banner' (*nēs*, 'flag, standard; 4:6; 6:1; Isa. 13:2), represented a form of communication, whether in peace or in war. Here it does not function as a signal for battle to commence, but more probably as a rallying point where the peoples may gather to hear the vital news. The significance of the message in every aspect is underlined by the injunction to 'keep nothing back' (cf. 38:14).

But what precisely is the message? The prophet may be describing what he has been told regarding the future downfall of Babylon when the message to be proclaimed will be, 'Babylon has been captured' (NASB; cf. GNB) or 'Babylon is taken' (NKJV, NRSV, NJPS). Alternatively, the news to be broadcast now is what the LORD has revealed, namely that, **Babylon will be captured**. This and the following verbs are perfects which may be understood as describing accomplished facts of present validity, or, using the idiom of the prophetic perfect, they may be used to present the future as so certain and guaranteed that it ought to be accepted as if it had already occurred. The two imperfects at the end of v. 3, 'will lay' and 'will live', favour the NIV interpretation that what is related has not already occurred, but is what is to be confidently anticipated. For the peoples who had suffered under Babylonian hegemony it is not the agent of this overthrow that mattered but the fact of the collapse of the superpower.

The ideological underpinning of the regime will also succumb. **Bel will be put to shame, Marduk filled with terror.** 'Bel' is etymologically related to the Canaanite 'Baal', both of which come from the common Semitic root for 'ruler' or 'master'. The title was applied to various gods, but when the original Sumerian peoples of Mesopotamia were assimilated by Semitic peoples, it came to be particularly associated with the storm-god Enlil, the head of the pantheon of Nippur. Marduk (this is the Akkadian pronunciation of the word, the Hebrew pointing gives the form Merodach; 52:31) was the chief god of the Babylonian pantheon, whose symbol was the planet Jupiter. He was also venerated as a storm god, and was assigned the role of the creator

god in the Babylonian Creation Epic. With the fusion of the religions
of the area, the honorary title Bel ('lord' or 'master') was applied to
Marduk; indeed Bel seems to have been the more common title for the
head of the Babylonian pantheon. There are therefore not two gods,
but two references to the one god. No matter in what way he is viewed,
the events that have taken Babylon have shown how powerless he is.
Her images[137] **will be put to shame and her idols filled with terror**
is a personification which indicates the grave impact on the land of
defeat by the enemy. 'Idols' is an ancient word that was applied
derogatorily to heathen images. Its origin is obscure[138] but early, and
although found only here in Jeremiah, it was common in Ezekiel. It
emphasises the vanity and ineffectiveness of such worship. The day
was going to come when the whole political order of the world would
be turned upside down, and what seemed to be the abiding contours of
the international landscape would be dramatically reshaped. At that
time the religious beliefs of the empire would be exposed as without
substantive basis.

3. Verse 3 is treated by the NRSV and the NASB as prose, but it can
be and probably ought to be read as poetry (so the NIV and the
REB).[139] **For** (*kî*) introduces the reason for the revolutionary change
described in v. 2. **A nation from the north will attack her and lay**

---

137. *'āṣāb* is only found in the plural, referring to images used in foreign
worship. The collocation here of *'āṣabbîm* and *gillûlîm*, 'idols', suggests a
disdainful attempt to deny the existence of such gods and to reduce them to
mere images.

138. *gillûlîm* seems to come from a word meaning 'log' or 'roll', referring
to the wood or stone as having to be put into place. The Rabbis related the
word to droppings of dung (cf. Lev. 26:30. Deut. 29:17). It occurs 39 times in
Ezekiel. Perhaps we are meant to hear in it a reference to *'ĕlîlîm*, 'nothing', or
'ēlîm, or *'ĕlōhîm*, 'gods'.

139. The finely balanced decisions that have to be made as to what is highly
rhythmical prose and what is poetry can be seen by the variations in transla-
tions in the following verses:
NIV   vv. 2-20 poetry with the exception of the heading in v. 18;
NKJV   as NIV;
NASB   v. 2, poetry; vv. 3-5 prose; vv. 6-16 poetry; vv. 17-20, prose;
NRSV   v. 2, poetry; vv. 3-10, prose; vv. 11-16, poetry; vv. 17-20, prose;
REB   vv. 2-3, poetry; vv. 4-7, prose; vv. 8-19, poetry (except v. 18a);
         v. 20, prose;
NJPS   vv. 2-3 poetry; vv. 4-7, prose; vv. 8-16, poetry; vv. 17-19, prose;
         v. 20, poetry.

waste her land[140] arouses memories of Jeremiah's early prophecies where the threat of the foe from the north loomed over Judah (1:14; 4:6). The phrase is not precisely the same here, but it does have the same openness as the earlier expression had. The enemy is not specified, but devastation of the land of Babylon is confidently predicted. The irony for Jeremiah's hearers lies in the fact that the threat from the north that originally proved to be Babylon is now turned against Babylon, for it, in its turn, will experience invasion from the north. This time, however, the northern threat was realised in the form of the forces of Medo-Persia (cf. v. 9 and 51:27-28). For 'lay waste', see on 2:15; 48:9. **No one will live in it; both men and animals will flee away.** For 'both men and animals'/'from mankind and as far as to beast', see on 33:12; 9:9. 'Flee away'/'wander off' comes from the root *nûd*, 'to be aimless', 'shake the head' in sympathy, but that significance is unlikely here because it also applied to animals.

2. Babylon's Fall and Israel's Return (50:4-20)

OUTLINE

- a. The Restoration of Israel (50:4-7)
- b. Take the Lead in Escape (50:8-10)
- c. The Plunderer Plundered (50:11-13)
- d. No Relief for Babylon (50:14-16)
- e. The Scattered Flock (50:17-20)

There are five stanzas to the first major section of the Oracle against Babylon, with the first (vv. 4-7) and last (vv. 17-20) balancing each other, as also do the second (vv. 8-10) and fourth (vv. 14-16). Israel's return and repentance are delineated in vv. 4-5 and vv. 19-20, while her past experience is found in vv. 6-7 and vv. 17-18. The second and fourth stanzas employ the themes of the appearance of the foe and flight from Babylon. The central third stanza focuses on the theme of Babylon's doom (Aitken 1984:31-36). In this section of the oracle the interconnections between the destiny of Babylon and that of Israel are

---

140. It is difficult to interpret the imperfect *yāšît*, 'it will lay', as of anything other than a future action. This indicates that the preceding perfect *'ālâ*, 'he has come up', is to be understood as a prophetic perfect, and so similarly the perfects in v. 2.

explored, using a series of contrasts involving their present and future state. It is only through the reality of divine pardon (vv. 4, 20) that there will be a way forward for Israel from the self-inflicted disaster of the Exile. Divine forgiveness opens the way up for the people to return to their land (vv. 5, 19) because the LORD will bring an enemy against Babylon to overthrow it.

a. The Restoration of Israel (50:4-7)

4. The fact of Babylon's fall had major implications for the destiny of the LORD's people, and vv. 4-5 set out what would be involved. **'In those days, at that time,' declares the LORD, 'the people of Israel and the people of Judah together will go in tears[141] to seek the LORD their God.'** The temporal phrases (cf. v. 20; 33:15; cf. 3:16-18) look forward to the time of deliverance from exile and link it to the fall of Babylon. It is wrong to take the reference to the people of Judah as an interpolated addition. The emphasis on the future fortunes of the LORD's people frequently highlights the harmony that will prevail in place of the former tension and strife (3:18), a harmony based on a spiritual reaction to their changed situation. They are coming with tears of repentance, genuinely wishing to submit to the LORD. 'Seek the LORD' (<*bāqaš* ('et) *Yhwh*) does not occur elsewhere in Jeremiah, though 'seek me' occurs in 29:13 (cf. Hos. 3:5; 5:6; Zeph. 1:6; 2:3) and the verb 'seek' occurs in v. 20 to form an inclusion. This is an activity that is concerned with the use of recognised forms of worship. It is therefore primarily a communal reaction rather than an individual one. Nonetheless it is to be accompanied by individual repentance and genuine personal commitment. Seeking the LORD involves turning from wicked ways and worshipping him in humility, and is the response of those who have renewed their covenant pledge of loyalty to the LORD and now desire to know his will for every aspect of their living. Those who approach the LORD in such a manner are recognised by him as his own and are blessed by him.

5. They will ask the way to Zion[142] (cf. 6:16) since they have not been able to go there for a long time and so are uncertain as to how to proceed, but the emphasis is now on the fact that it is to Zion, with all

---

141. 'Going and weeping (two infinitives absolute) they will go' (cf. 41:6; and also 3:21; 31:9) expresses the repetition or continuance of the action (*IBHS* §35.3.2c). Their sorrow will characterise the whole of their journey.

142. The Massoretic accents favour reading the statements as '⌐For⌐ Zion they will ask; the way towards here ⌐is before⌐ their faces'. English translations, following the LXX, take *derek*, 'way, path', with 'ask'.

its cultic associations, that they will return (cf. also Isa. 40:3; 51:11).
And turn their faces towards it/'to here' (*hēnnâ*) indicating the
perspective of the speaker, as someone who is in Jerusalem. Turning
the face indicates deliberate action: they had been forced into exile, but
they will return voluntarily. **They will come and bind themselves**[143]
to the LORD in[144] **an everlasting covenant that will not be forgotten.** 'Bind' (<√*lāwâ* I niphal, 'to accompany, join') is most commonly
used in the niphal with positive associations of non-Israelites joining
the community of the faithful (Isa. 56:3, 6; Zech. 2:11). This takes up
the grand theme of Jeremiah's Book of Consolation, only now the
covenant that is made is described not from the point of view of the
LORD giving it, but from the people subscribing to it. Unlike the Exile
in which the people are now found, the situation that is envisaged is
one that will not come to an end. Dislocation, disruption and
disharmony will be permanently banished. This vision therefore
combines union between the two parts of the divided people with
repentance and genuine desire to restore their relationship with the
LORD in an enduring covenant bond (32:40). The question arises as to
when this will occur, and the answer may be given that it is what is
found successively over long periods which are here presented to the
prophet as fused into one. The oblique expression 'will not be
forgotten' might be simply be an expression to reinforce 'everlasting'
(cf. 20:11), or a periphrasis for divine action. However, since 'to
forget' (*šākaḥ*) is one of Jeremiah's words for condemning Israel
(2:32) and since it is repeated in the following verse, it is probably
suggested that now the people will not forget their renewed commitment to the LORD.

6. Verses 6 and 7 probe the history that lay behind the anticipated
restoration. The theme of the people's disloyalty in worshipping idols
reflects what had been said in chapter 2. There is no suggestion that
they are to be delivered from Babylonia because they are innocent
victims. Their sin is evident, and their release is therefore a tribute to
the LORD's gracious acknowledgment of them as still being his people.

---

143. *bōʾû* is an imperative, 'Come' (masc. pl.), and *wənilwû* is a third person
plural *waw*-consecutive perfect niphal. Hence the interpretation of this as
direct speech in the NKJV, 'ʟsayingʲ, "Come and let us join ourselves to the
LORD".' (cf. also the RSV). Alternatively, following the Aquila's Greek
version, the Vulgate and the Aramaic Targum the form may be read as *bāʾû*, a
(prophetic) perfect, 'they will come' (NIV, NRSV).

144. The expression may be taken as a modal accusative.

My people have been[145] **lost sheep.** For the use of 'sheep' for Israel, see 23:1 (also Isa. 53:6; Ezek. 34:5). The people were in process of being destroyed because of lack of appropriate leadership. **Their shepherds have led them astray** (a hiphil $<\sqrt{t\bar{a}\,{}^\varsigma\hat{a}}$, 'to wander off, roam') **and caused them to roam on the mountains.**[146] 'Their shepherds' are the nation's spiritual and political leaders (cf. 23:1-4). It was not just the prophets and the priests that had given poor guidance to the people; their kings were especially culpable for not enforcing the requirements of the covenant. They had even promoted abhorrent practices contrary to the divine law. The reference to the 'mountains' probably picks up the idea that they were the location of pagan worship (cf. 2:20). **They wandered over mountain and hill and forgot their own resting place.** This is more than a continuation of the shepherd imagery. Wandering over mountains and hills was what sheep had ordinarily to do in many areas of Palestine because of the sparsity of pasture. But what is in view is a spiritual pilgrimage in which the people had forgotten their proper 'resting place', the spot where animals could lie down in safety. The idea is taken up again in the next verse where the LORD is called 'their true pasture'. They went from one pagan site to another, quite forgetful of how they could truly be at rest.

7. Whoever found them devoured them. This again reflects chapter 2, where 'devour' and 'guilty' are found in 2:3. The spiritual wanderings of Israel and Judah made them vulnerable and helpless before their enemies, because they had abandoned their God and so had left themselves open to attack, their apostasy depriving them of divine protection.

What was more, the idolatry of Judah led to a situation in which others thought themselves justified in attacking them. **Their enemies said, 'We are not guilty, for they sinned against the LORD.'** 'For' renders *taḥat ʿăšer*, 'in return for the fact that', 'inasmuch as'. The heathen nations did not consider themselves in the wrong, because Israel had abandoned their God. While the recognition of their sin against the LORD is put in the mouths of their pagan adversaries as a

---

145. The kethibh *hāyâ* takes the collective 'my people' as requiring a singular verb, the qere *hāyû* takes a plural according to sense. Perhaps the plural participle *ʿōbədôt*, 'perishing, lost', which is also not in agreement with the singular *ṣōʾn*, 'flock', makes the qere more likely.

146. The kethibh is *šôbēbîm* (cf. 31:32; 49:4) not *šôbābîm*. *šôbēb* is used in the sense of Isa. 47:10, 'faithless mountains, recusant mountains'. The qere reads *šôbəbûm*, 'they made them stray on the mountains', a local accusative.

rhetorical device to emphasise the gravity of Israel's ingratitude, it need not be treated as only a figure of speech. It may well be that the Babylonians had a clearer perception of the enormity of the rebellion of the LORD's people than they had themselves. They had abandoned **their true pasture**/'pasture (*nāweh*, 10:25) of righteousness', one that matched up to the standard of all that a pasture should be. The LORD did not provide them with the unwholesome diet of pagan worship, but care and nurture that met their genuine needs (31:23). 'The habitation of justice' (NKJV) or 'of righteousness' understands the phrase as pointing to the LORD as the one in whom is contained that righteousness which is the source of Israel's salvation (Keil 1873, 2:274). **The LORD,**[147] **the hope of their fathers,** was the one who had formed the focus of their national life (cf. 14:8; 17:13; Ps. 22:3-5). 'Hope' (*miqweh*) is the attitude of confident expectation that looks to divine intervention to provide meaning and satisfaction in the future (contrast the unspecified nature of hope in 29:11; 31:17).

b. Take the Lead in Escape (50:8-10)
8. There is then another unannounced transition, from a description of Israel's rebellious conduct to an exhortation to flee from Babylon. It is the fact of their homecoming that is to take the centre of the stage. **Flee**[148] **out of Babylon; leave**[149] **the land of the Babylonians.** Whereas in other Oracles against the Nations those who are called on to flee are the citizens of the countries addressed, here the LORD addresses his people and shows them the way to safety in the dangerous times that lie ahead for Babylon. These words are reminiscent of Isa. 48:20 and 52:11 in a call to the exiles to leave. They were not under immediate pressure to flee, but in the light of impending disaster it was as well for them to act promptly and decisively. It was no longer appropriate to build houses, plant gardens and settle in (29:5-7)—that time had long passed.

And be[150] **like the goats that lead the flock.** This picks up the

---

147. The final emphatic repetition of Yahweh is omitted by the REB as an addition to the text which is not found in the LXX. BHS proposes that it be read as *hôy* and taken with the next verse. These proposals diminish the emphatic conclusion to this section.
148. *nūdû* means 'wander aimlessly' (cf. NASB). 'Flee' (NIV) seems to involve reading *nūsû*. The two words are, however, associated elsewhere.
149. The kethibh is *yēṣ'û*, 'they will leave', a sudden and not impossible transition of person. The qere has *ṣē'û*, an imperative.
150. The REB 'go out like' ignores the athnach under *ṣē'û*, and divides the verse one word earlier.

imagery of v. 6. Flocks would have consisted of sheep and goats. The he-goats provided leadership and the other animals followed. Here the picture is of the Jews (rather than just their leaders) taking the initiative and showing other captive peoples how to leave Babylon. The time for fearful submission will be past.

9. The LORD then reveals the political and military changes he will bring about to permit such an exodus to occur. **For (kî) I will stir up and bring against Babylon an alliance of great nations from the land of the north.** For 'stir up'/'arouse', compare Isa. 13:17. 'Alliance'/'assembly' (*qāhāl*) is here used of a group of persons gathered for military purposes (cf. Isa. 13:4). Like all the empires of the ancient Near East the Medo-Persian empire, which was to be the instrument used to overwhelm Babylon, was composed of many different races. Herodotus (*Hist.* 7:61-69) lists twenty-two different national contingents in the army of the Persian emperor Xerxes. It is divine judgment that is coming on Babylon through the instrumentality of unspecified northern peoples (some of whom are listed in 51:27-28). **They will take up their positions against her, and from the north/ 'from there' she will be captured. Their arrows will be like skilled**[151] **warriors who do not return empty-handed.** The Hebrew makes clear that the comparison is between the enemy's arrows and 'a skilled warrior who does not return empty-handed', that is, without success. He successfully achieves the object of his warfare.

10. That thought is continued in the next verse. **'So Babylonia will be plundered;**[152] **all who plunder her will have their fill,' declares the LORD.** The enemy forces will be able to pillage to their hearts' content. For the connection between eating and plundering, see 31:16.

c. The Plunderer Plundered (50:11-13)

11. In vv. 11-13 the LORD addresses Babylon directly. The link with v. 10 is more thematic than explicitly stated. Three times in v. 11

---

151. The Massoretic Text (followed by the Targum and the Vulgate) reads *maškîl*, a hiphil participle <√*šākal*, 'to cause to have a miscarriage or abortion'. The reading *maśkîl*, a hiphil participle <√*śākal*, 'to be skilful, successful', is found in some manuscripts and Greek texts.

152. The verb *wəhāyətâ*, 'and she will be', is feminine agreeing with *kaśdîm*, 'Chaldea'/'Babylonia', which, as the name of the country, is treated as feminine (GKC §122i). The same word is also used for the inhabitants of the land. *ləšālāl*, 'for plunder, as plunder'. *šālāl* is used for the actual items taken whereas *baz* refers rather to the act of pillaging.

'because' is found expressing the reasons for what follows in v. 12.[153]
The four imperfect verbs are translated by the NKJV as referring to
past action, e.g. 'you were glad', but this presupposes Jerusalem had
already fallen at the time this oracle was uttered. It rather seems to be
the case that the actions in the subordinate clauses refer to ongoing
future attitudes which have as their consequence what is expressed in
v. 12 using a prophetic perfect. **Because** (*kî*) **you rejoice**[154] **and**
'because' (*kî*) **are glad, you who pillage my inheritance** addresses
Babylon in her triumph over Judah. For 'rejoice' (*śāmaḥ*), see on
15:17, and for 'are glad' (*'ālaz*), see 30:16. 'Inheritance' (*naḥălâ*) is
used variously in Jeremiah (cf. 10:16). It may refer to the land as
Israel's inheritance (3:18-19; 12:14-15), or as belonging to the LORD
(2:7; 16:18; 50:11). It can also refer to the LORD himself as Israel's
inheritance (10:16; 51:19), or Israel as the LORD's inheritance (12:7-9).
It is used here for the land which is looted with dire consequences for
the people who had been settled there by the LORD. The Babylonians
have brought destruction on them, but their triumphant rejoicing will
rebound upon themselves and lead to their downfall. This thought
gives opportunity for some to indicate that this is in tension with other
parts of the Jeremiah tradition where Nebuchadnezzar comes against
the land as the LORD's servant, doing his will. The reconciliation
between the two is obviously to be found in the fact that in the one
case the LORD is overruling the actions of men for his own ends; in the
other he is bringing upon Babylon the just reward of her own wrong
conduct.

Because you frolic (<√*pûš* I, which describes an animal galloping
about or hopping and springing, and is used in Mal. 3:20 of calves let
out to pasture) **like a heifer threshing grain** introduces a picture that

153. 'Because' renders *kî*, which because of its multiple parallel usage does
not introduce the reason for what precedes it in v. 10, but what follows it. The
NRSV translates the clauses concessively, 'although', but the link is stronger
than that.
154. *tiśməḥî* in the kethibh is a feminine singular, whereas the qere and
many manuscripts read a masculine plural *tiśməḥû*. Either is possible: the first
treats Babylon as a collective (cf. 13:20); the second under the influence of the
plural 'you who plunder' and the plural suffixes in 'your mother' and 'gave
you birth' (v. 12) reads a masculine plural. The same change is made in the
three subsequent verbs also where the kethibh has feminine singular forms
(*ta'ăləzî, tāpûšî, tiṣhălî*) and the qere with substantial manuscript support
substitutes masculine plural forms, *ta'ăləzû*, 'you are glad', *tâpûšû*, 'you
frolic', and *tiṣhălû*, 'you neigh'.

has caused perplexity because it seems unlikely that threshing grain and frolicking would occur simultaneously. 'You frisk about like a heifer on the grass' (NRSV) follows the Greek[155] and presents a coherent picture of a young calf bounding about in joy. The Babylonians too rejoiced greatly when they took Jerusalem. However, 'thresh' is used to refer to the destructive action of invading armies (2 Kgs. 13:7; Mic. 4:13), and that may be intended here. **And neigh like stallions** (8:16) is also a picture of animal excitement (cf. 5:8; 47:3) which knows no bounds until it is satisfied. Babylon had acted with unrestrained, reckless abandon, acknowledging no limits to what they did in devastating countries they conquered.

12. But despite what initially will seem to be resounding success, there is a different reality awaiting them on a day of reckoning. **Your mother will be greatly ashamed** refers to the whole land by personification, or perhaps to the capital city, Babylon. 'Mother' is used much less frequently in an extended sense than 'father', though the metaphor of a mother in distress is also found in 15:9. Their joy and triumph are going to be reversed. **She who gave you birth will be disgraced** (<√ḥāpar II, 'to be dismayed'). The proud status of Babylon at the head of an empire is going to come to an end; she will be transformed into a petty state. **She will be the least of the nations—a wilderness** (used here by the NIV to render *midbār* because of the third word in the series; 2:2), **a dry land** (*ṣiyyâ*, 2:6), **a desert** (*ʿărābâ*, 2:6). A threefold figure intensifying the picture of the land—not just the city— being turned back to its natural state. The implication is that if this happens to the land, then its people have been destroyed and are unable to rectify the damage done to the irrigation systems on which Babylon's agriculture depended.

13. Because of the LORD's anger (*qeṣep*, 10:10; cf. Isa. 13:20) **she will not be inhabited** (17:5-6) **but will be completely desolate** (*šəmāmâ*, 4:17). This did not happen in 539 BC with Cyrus, and therefore the view being revealed here must have comprised more than the events of that period. **All who pass Babylon will be horrified** (<√šāmēm, cf. 18:16) **and scoff** (<√šāraq) **because of all her wounds.** For similar words in connection with Jerusalem, see 19:8. Her fortunes will be completely reversed (cf. 49:17).

---

155. The MT reads *kəʿeglâ dāšâ*, treating the form as a qal participle from *dûš*, 'to thresh, trample down'. However, the LXX suggests a text like *kəʿeglê baddešeʿ*, 'like heifers in the grass', reading a preposition and the noun *dešeʿ*, 'grass, vegetation'.

d. No Relief for Babylon (50:14-16)
14. The idea of a reversal of fortune is continued in this stanza in which the LORD speaks as the ultimate commander of the forces that will attack Babylon. He addresses his armies and urges them to act unsparingly against Babylon. No mercy is to be shown to the merciless oppressor. **Take up your positions around Babylon, all you who draw the bow** (cf. 46:9). 'Around' is 'on all sides', so that the city is hemmed in with no hope of escape. The archers may well be a reference to the lightly armed troops that were the strength of the Medo-Persian army, including Elamites whose skill in this field was renowned (49:35). **Shoot**[156] **at her! Spare**[157] **no arrows** (13:14; cf. 51:3)**, for** (*kî*) **she has sinned against the LORD.** The motive clause (not found in the LXX) shows how this is intended to be heard as much by the LORD's people, as by the enemy army. It is a graphic description of what will lie behind the enemy attack on Babylon rather than a message to which the invaders will be directly responding. Babylon's abuse of her position cannot be tolerated any longer by the LORD.

15. Shout against her on every side! continues the picture of Babylon hemmed in ('on every side' is the same word as 'around' in v. 14). The attack is successful. **She surrenders**/'has given her hand' is an idiom for 'surrender', probably from some gesture of stretching out the hand to indicate submission. Though the phrase is often used as a pledge of faithfulness (2 Kgs. 10:15; Ezek. 17:18), the meaning 'to surrender' is warranted in 1 Chron. 29:24; 2 Chron. 30:8; and Lam. 5:6. The past tenses are probably prophetic perfects in view of the preceding and following imperatives. **Her towers**[158] **fall, her walls are torn down.** For the root *hāras*, 'to tear down', see on 1:10. Here is a complete reversal of Babylon's fortunes.

This infliction comes on her **since** (*kî*) **this is the vengeance of the LORD, take vengeance on her; do to her as she has done to others.**

---

156. Only here is *yādâ* (qal) found as 'shoot' the bow, elsewhere it is the piel. A few manuscripts read the synonymous verb *yārâ* as a qal imperative *yərû*, confusion between *daleth* and *resh* being common and easily explained.

157. <√*hāmal*, 'hold back' from an expected action, often out of a sense of pity or compassion.

158. There is little doubt about the meaning of the word because of the cognate *ʿošyâ*, 'tower', found in Akkadian sources for a tower which was part of a city wall. The kethibh might be *ʿašwiyyōteyhā* as if from a noun *ʿašwît*, or it may be an error corrected in the qere to *ʿašyôteyhā* from a noun *ʿašyâ*, both nouns meaning 'tower'.

'Vengeance' (*niqmâ*; 11:20; 15:15) is perhaps too personal and
subjective a word. 'Retribution' is perhaps more accurate (cf. Num.
31:3). The LORD is calling on those who attack Babylon to play their
part in the process by which he rewards her according to what she has
done (cf. v. 28-29; 51:11). This theological statement shows that the
ultimate standard of conduct is not what empires think they can get
away with, but what the LORD mandates as right and appropriate.
There will be a correspondence between sin and punishment as in
Obad. 15, 'As you have done, it will be done to you; your deeds will
return upon your own head.' It is also similar to the expression in Lev.
24:19, 'Whatever he has done must be done to him.' So the LORD's
verdict against Babylon is that her punishment will come because of
her sin, and her punishment will be like her sin. What she had done to
other nations through siege, destruction of property, loss of life and
exile of peoples will come upon her. The LORD's retribution will be
worked out through the processes of history and by means of other
nations invading Babylon (cf. Miller 1982:129).

16. Cut off (that is, 'kill', anticipating and reversing the reference to
the reaper) **from Babylon the sower, and the reaper with his sickle
at harvest.** Babylon is not here the city but the whole area whose rich
alluvial plains were very productive. The devastation of war that she
had brought to others she will now experience. **Because of the sword
of the oppressor let everyone return**[159] **to his own people, let everyone flee to his own land.** There were more peoples than Judah alone
involved in the deportations of the day. What is seen here is a general
return from this enforced exile when the enemy forces come against
Babylon (25:38; 46:16; 50:16; Isa. 13:14b).

e. The Scattered Flock (50:17-20)
17. In vv. 17-20 the focus again moves back to the history of the
LORD's people. Previously their downfall had been explained in terms
of the deficiencies of their leadership and their consequent sin
(vv. 6-7); now they are viewed as the victims of foreign aggression.
Israel is a scattered flock that lions have chased away. The lion is
used as a figure for the great Mesopotamian empires who attacked
Israel (2:15; 4:7). Here it is probable that there is an element of irony
because the comparison is not with many sheep but with one (*śeh* is

---

159. Unlike many English translations (e.g. NKJV, NRSV) which render
this and the following imperfect as describing a predicted future, the NIV
takes the sense as jussive. This may well be correct in view of the preceding
imperative, 'cut off'.

usually a single sheep, and not a collective noun), who strangely is the
focus of attention of many lions. 'Israel is a hunted sheep driven away
by lions' (NRSV). Behind this there is the suggestion that so much
attention would not have been given to her had she not been the
LORD's people and her aggressors motivated by a more than ordinary
hostility. **The first to devour him was the king of Assyria** looks back
to Tiglath-Pileser's annexation of Israelite territory in Galilee and
Transjordan, culminating in the deportation of the ten tribes at the fall
of Samaria in 722 BC. **The last to crush his bones was Nebuchadnezzar king of Babylon.** What events are referred to here, depends on the
date of this passage. It certainly includes 605 BC and 598/97 BC, and
probably determines the date of this unit as after the fall of Jerusalem,
because the idiom of 'crushing the bones'[160] seems to indicate a more
thorough and complete destruction than the previous 'to devouring'.

18. But this is not happening without divine retribution. **Therefore**
(*lākēn*) **this is what the LORD Almighty, the God of Israel, says**
where the title 'God of Israel' points to the special relationship and
covenant bond that is the basis of the divine intervention. **I will punish
the king of Babylon and his land as I punished the king of Assyria.**
The fall of Nineveh in July/August 612 BC and the subsequent rout of
the remnant of the Assyrians in June/July 609 BC is history, and the
same fate will assuredly befall Babylon for the same reason: their
attack on the LORD's people. Both occurrences of 'punish' render the
root *pāqad*, describing the intervention of the one who is the true superior and ruler of all nations.

19. But the LORD shows that his purposes are not exhausted in the
downfall of Babylon. That will provide the occasion for the LORD as
the good shepherd of the sheep to show how he can provide for his
flock by restoring them to the enjoyment of their own pasture, picking
up the figure of Israel as sheep from v. 17. **But I will bring Israel
back to his own pasture** (*nāweh*), the place where he should have
enjoyed peace and abundant provision (23:3). **And he will graze on
Carmel and Bashan.** Carmel on the sea-coast (46:18) and Bashan on
the west of the Jordan (22:20) were noted for their lush pastures and
forests. The fact that the figures here all relate to areas which in its
closing years the northern kingdom lost to Assyria suggests that Israel

---

160. *'āṣam* is a denominative verb (*IBHS* §24.4f) used in the piel in a priva-
tive sense, indicating taking away of the substance indicated by the noun. The
sense 'break the bones' is given by BDB (1126), whereas *NIDOTTE* (3:499)
prefers 'gnaw the bones', picturing a meat-eating animal chewing on a bone
and cracking with its jaws to get at the marrow.

is being used primarily to refer to the destiny of the north only, though that obviously has implications for Judah. **His appetite** (<*nepeš*, 2:34) **will be satisfied on the hills of Ephraim and Gilead.** The territory of Ephraim formed the centre of the northern kingdom (4:15), including the plain of Jezreel. Gilead (8:22) was the central part of Israelite territory west of the Jordan (Num. 32:1; Mic. 7:14). 'Satisfied' (31:14; 46:10) refers to more than an exile's longing to return home; it takes in enjoyment of a renewed relationship with the LORD and his provision.

20. Verse 20 continues the picture of the LORD's restoration. **'In those days, at that time,' declares the LORD.** The formula, which forms an inclusion with the similar expression in v. 4 to mark the end of the section, looks forward to the Messianic era, or in Jeremiah's terms to that of the new covenant (31:34; 33:8). **Search will be made**[161] **for Israel's guilt** (<*ʿāwôn*, 2:22), **but there will be none, and for the sins** (<*ḥaṭṭāʾt*, cf. 2:35) **of Judah, but none will be found, for** (*kî*) **I will forgive** (<√*sālaḥ*, cf. 31:34; 33:8) **the remnant I spare.** For 'search', compare 35:14. The dark shadow of their guilt (cf. Ezek. 33:10-11) would be taken away. Here at the end of the section is the resolution of the problem of how there could be a future for the fallen people: divine forgiveness and divine choice. 'The remnant I spare' renders the hiphil of the verb *šāʾar* used in the sense of 'constitute as a remnant'. They are given this status not because they have survived but because they have been divinely preserved. Mere survival does not constitute 'the remnant'; it requires divine acknowledgment of their status.

3. The LORD's Work in Babylon (50:21-32)

OUTLINE

a. Broken and Shattered (50:21-25)
b. Woe To Them! (50:26-28)
c. The End of the Arrogant (50:29-32)

In this section the focus remains on how the LORD has resolved to act against the Babylonians (cf. v. 25), and the theme of Israel's future recedes into the background. The struggles and hostilities of earth are

161. In *yəbuqqaš* the root *bāqaš* is repeated from v. 4 to form an inclusion, but it is the pual that is used here impersonally and the object of the active verb is retained (GKC §121b).

determined by what the LORD wills, and he has decreed that there will
be utter destruction for Babylon (v. 21) because it has acted in defiance
of what he requires. The section explores various aspects of their
impending overthrow in three stanzas, each of which begins with a call
to battle which is then followed by a description of some aspect of
Babylon's doom. A number of verbal echoes and repetitions unify the
three stanzas: the unusual verbal root 'kill'/'put to the sword' in vv. 21
and 27; the mention of the ban/'completely destroy' in vv. 21 and 26;
the repetition of the root *pālaṭ* in vv. 28 and 29 as 'refugees' and
'escape', and of the root *pātaḥ*, 'opened', in vv. 25 and 26; and also the
synonymous terms 'remnant', 'fugitives and refugees', 'escape' in
vv. 26 and 28-29 (Aitken 1984:36-40).

a. Broken and Shattered (50:21-25)
21. A divine exhortation is issued to the enemy, the foe from the north
of vv. 3 and 9, to attack. The four verbs of command are masculine
singular imperatives, unlike the plurals that occurred previously, but
this is not sufficient to warrant the thought that the address is to Israel.
Attack the land of Merathaim and those who live in Pekod. There
are two unusual wordplays here in both of which areas of Babylonia
are used by metonymy to refer to the whole of the land. The first
involves an area between the confluence of the Tigris and the
Euphrates and the head of the Persian Gulf, known as Māt (or Nār)
Marrāti, 'land of the bitter river', presumably because of the saltiness
of the water. Merathaim is a name specially coined for this occasion
from a similar sounding Hebrew root, *mārâ*, 'to be rebellious'. The
noun is in fact a dual formation which, as well as conveying the idea of
'twofold rebellion'/'more rebellious' than others, is intended by its
similarity in formation to *miṣrayim* to remind of the other ancient
superpower of Egypt. Pekod is similar to the name of a people who
lived in south-eastern Babylonia, Puqūdu (cf. Ezek. 23:23), but the
same form is also that of a Hebrew verb conveying the ideas of punishment and doom (*pəqôd* would be an infinitive construct from *pāqad*
which describes the action of a superior, here imposing a penalty). 'The
land of Out-and-Out Rebellion and those who live in Doom' leaves no
doubt about where is intended, what their fate will be, or why.
    'Pursue,[162] **kill and completely destroy them,' declares the**

---

162. 'Pursue' in the NIV is an attempt to do justice to the problematic
'aḥărêhem, 'after them', which can hardly indicate the object of 'completely
destroy'. However, the phrase also occurs in 49:37; 48:2, 9, 15, and, following
the Targum, the NRSV takes the word as *'aḥărîtām*, 'the last of them'.

LORD. 'Kill' renders *haḥărēb*, a denominative formation from *ḥereb*, 'sword' (also found in v. 27); hence the verb means 'put to the sword'. 'Completely destroy' comes from the root *ḥāram*, 'to devote to the ban', which was a divinely required dedication of someone or something as a permanent and definitive offering. It may denote the total annihilation of a population in a war. Such total destruction had been the LORD's imposition on the cities of Canaan, and now it is to be imposed on Babylon also. When a people were solemnly devoted to divine destruction, nothing was to be left in the land (cf. 25:9; Josh. 8:26). **Do everything I have commanded you.** This presents the key to interpreting what the invading force are called on to do: they are to act under direct divine instructions. It is the LORD who controls what happens to Babylon and authorises its overthrow.

22. It is uncertain who speaks in vv. 22-25. 'I set a trap' in v. 24 (but see comments there) suggests the LORD, and so the NIV takes these verses as direct divine speech, but against this there are the third person references to the LORD at the end of v. 24 and in v. 25. Much may be said for this being a prophetic description of what the LORD has revealed to Jeremiah regarding the future of Babylon, which he expresses in the form of a lament.

There are two exclamatory phrases. **The noise of battle is in the land, the noise of great destruction!** The land is, of course, Babylonia, which is experiencing this invasion. The commands given in v. 21 are being carried out (cf. 4:6; 6:1). For 'great destruction' (*šeber*), see on 4:6 and 6:1. Again a future scene is being portrayed by means of the sounds that will accompany the action.

23. Verse 23 beings with 'how', a word often found in laments (cf. Zeph. 2:15), but here the tone is not that of sympathy, but irony. **How broken and shattered is the hammer of the whole earth!** The repeated 'how' (*'êk*) expresses a measure of grim satisfaction in what is to be seen. The hammer or sledgehammer (*paṭṭîš*) was an instrument that could break rock, and it was used as a figure for the equally destructive power of the LORD's word in 23:29. Here there is announced a staggering reversal of fortune for the empire which had brought such shattering blows upon others as it is subjected to the same destruction. The 'hammer' is a metaphor for Babylon (cf. 51:20; Isa. 14:5-6) which was God's war club to shatter the nations and destroy kingdoms, just as Assyria is represented in Isa. 10:5 as a rod and a war club. **How desolate** (*šammâ*, 2:15) **is Babylon among the nations!** What she brought on others, she now experiences herself, and it causes astonishment to the nations (cf. 51:41).

24. I set a trap for you, O Babylon may also be rendered 'you set a snare for yourself' (NRSV, REB).[163] Babylon has been trapped by the technique she had used to catch others: military power. The reversal of the fortunes of war happens so suddenly to her that she does realise it till it is over (cf. 51:8; Isa. 47:11). **And you were caught before you** (emphatic) **knew it.** 'You were caught' (<√*lākad*) echoes the theme of v. 2, 'Babylon is captured.' The Persians under Cyrus were able to enter the city unexpectedly and undetected. Herodotus (*Hist.* 1:191) relates that though the Persians had already taken other neighbouring towns and had defeated Babylonian armies on the outskirts of the city, the defending troops still felt they could withstand a lengthy siege, being well-provisioned and behind extensive defence works. However, when Cyrus diverted the Euphrates some distance upstream from Babylon, his men were able to enter the city along the river bed unopposed. **You were found and captured** (<√*tāpaś*, 'to seize'; 40:10) **because** (*kî*) **you opposed the LORD.** While this opposition is expressed here in general terms, it is more specifically identified as directed against the LORD and his people in v. 28. The bone of conten-tion between the LORD and Babylon was over who should control the destiny of the LORD's land and people. Like Egypt before her, Babylon was refusing to let God's people go (vv. 29, 33). The LORD does not absolve a nation from the consequences of its actions, even though they have been appointed by him (cf. Isa. 10:5-19). They have 'opposed'/'set themselves to engage in strife against' (*gārâ*, hithpael) the LORD, and there can be only one outcome to such a foolhardy course.

25. **The LORD has opened his arsenal and brought out the weapons of his wrath.** The LORD's treasure chest (*'ôṣār*, 'treasure' or 'treasure house, storehouse') may be used to describe natural phenomena (10:13), but here the storehouse is stocked with the arms of nations whom he summons to do his bidding against the Babylonians. For 'wrath' (*za'am*), see on 10:10; there is a link in thought back to v. 13. **For** (*kî*) **the Sovereign LORD Almighty**[164] **has work to do in the land of the Babylonians.** For 'work' (*məlā'kâ*), compare 48:10. The LORD will work through the forces he brings against Babylon,

---

163. *yāqōštî* (<√*yāqaš*, 'to lay bait/a snare') may also be read as an archaic second person feminine singular verb, which would fit in with the feminine subjects found with the other verbs of the sentence. 'For yourself' would then be a dative of advantage, with a view to receiving benefit from it.

164. The same collocation of divine names *'ădōnāy Yhwh ṣəbā'ōt* is rendered 'the Lord, the LORD Almighty' in v. 31 by the NIV.

though in the Cyrus Cylinder Cyrus attributes his easy victory to the guidance of Marduk (*ANET* 315-6).

b. Woe to them! (50:26-28)

26. In vv. 26-27 we again hear the LORD's commands (masc. pl. imperatives) to the forces he is summoning against Babylon. **Come against her from afar.**[165] The opposition is not some local revolt, but is international in its scope. **Break open her granaries;**[166] **pile her**[167] **up like heaps of grain.** Verse 26 focuses on what happens to Babylon's material wealth. Her stockpiles of food are looted. While 'heaps' may be heaps of ruins (NKJV), the word is ordinarily used of accumulations of produce. What happens to her granaries is selected to represent what happens to all the city's resources. The enemy forces are spoiling the land, but they do not carry it off. It is rather a matter of destruction: **Completely destroy her** (<√*ḥāram*, cf. v. 21). Things devoted had to be burned (Josh. 11:12-13). **And leave her no remnant!** There is to be no hope of a future reversal of Babylon's fortunes. 'Remnant' (*šəʾērît*) is usually understood of people rather than things. This would then be a transitional phrase into the thought of the following verse.

27. Kill all her young bulls to the sword; let them go down to the slaughter! The focus is now on what happens to her population. A comparison may be made with Isa. 34:6-7 where the judgment to come on Edom is depicted as slaughter of lambs, rams, and he-goats. 'Young bulls' refers to those who controlled the military and economic might of Babylon (48:15; Ps. 22:12; Isa. 34:7; Ezek. 39:18), but what happens to them represents the fate of the population at large. There is then plainer language used. **Woe** (*hôy*) **to them! For** (*kî*) **their day has come, the time for them to be punished** (<√*pāqad*). Punishment shows that the language of bulls is metaphorical. The long-suffering of the LORD has been exhausted and judgment falls on those who oppose him.

---

165. *miqqēṣ*, 'from end', is difficult. In 51:31 we find *miqqāṣeh* meaning 'from all sides', as in Gen 19:4. That may be that meaning here (NRSV; REB 'from every quarter'), or 'from the end ˻of the earth˼' (NASB: 'from the farthest border').

166. The word *maʿăbûs* is a hapax, but the root *ʿābas*, 'to fatten', is used of giving feeding to cattle and so the noun may mean 'granary' (NIV, RSV) or more generally a 'store', a place where feeding or grain is kept.

167. The reference in the pronominal suffix on *sollûhā* (for the form, see GKC §67n), 'pile her up', may be to Babylon, or to the grain.

28. In v. 28 we seem again to have the prophet's report of what has been revealed to him. **Listen to** (*qôl*, 'sound'/'noise' picking up the theme of v. 22) **the fugitives** (<√*nûs*) **and refugees** (<√*pālaṭ*) **from Babylon declaring in Zion how the LORD our God has taken vengeance, vengeance for**[168] **his temple.** The message being brought here may be linked to the situation of v. 3. Here we have the ultimate reason for the divine retribution: what had been done against the place where he had put his name, and what that signified in terms of rebellion against him. For 'vengeance' see on v. 15; 51:11. Divine retribution is a corollary of divine holiness. Since Babylon had desecrated the Temple, the earthly abode of the LORD, he displays his authority and power by punishing such lese-majesty and so reasserting his honour and rule.

c. The End of the Arrogant (50:29-32)
29. Once more the LORD exhorts unnamed adversaries to advance against Babylon. **Summon archers**[169] **against Babylon, all those who draw the bow** (cf. v. 14). Archers were extensively used in siege warfare to attack those on the city walls and to spread fire within. **Encamp** (*ḥānâ* + accusative = 'besiege'; Ps. 53:6) **all around her; let no one**[170] **escape** (<√*pālaṭ*, cf. v. 28). Again the thought is of the completeness of the destruction that will come upon her. **Repay her for her deeds; do to her as she has done.** For 'repay' (*šālēm* piel) see on 25:14 (cf. Lev. 24:19b). It is the mark of the equity of divine justice that retribution matches the crime: 'according to all she has done' (NKJV; cf. v. 15). **For** (*kî*) **she has defied the LORD, the Holy One of Israel.** 'Defied' (<√*zādâ*, 'to act defiantly'; 43:2) sums up the presumption and arrogance with which Babylon has behaved as a militaristic empire. In Jeremiah 'Holy One' (*qādôš*) as an epithet of God occurs only here and in 51:5, though it is very common in Isaiah. Possibly this indicates the extent to which the prophecies of the earlier prophet were in Jeremiah's mind at this time. The term reflects the distance between the LORD and all possible competitors. He is supreme

168. A genitive of advantage/disadvantage, where the absolute is the beneficiary of the action denoted by the construct (*IBHS* §9.5.2e).
169. 'Archers' reads the Hebrew as *rōbîm* (the participle of *rābâ*, cf. Gen. 21:20; *HALOT* 1178) rather than *rabbîm*, 'many', as in the MT (cf. NASB). The choice of pointing seems desirable in view of the parallel phrase 'all who draw the bow'.
170. The kethibh omits 'her' which is added by the qere *lāh*. It may, however, be simply added to conform to v. 26.

in power and ethically superior to all hypothetical deities. He is the eternal being who is the focus of Israel's worship, and those who set themselves up against him bring doom upon themselves.

30. The divine sentence follows. **'Therefore** (*lākēn*), **her young men will fall in the streets; all her soldiers will be silenced in that day,' declares the LORD.** This repeats 49:26, where it applied to Damascus, but without the epithet 'Almighty'/'of hosts' added to the divine name.

31. Babylon is directly addressed as the personification of arrogance (cf. 21:13-14). **'See, I am against you[171], O arrogant one!' declares the Lord, the LORD Almighty.** 'I am against you' (21:13) indicates a clash of wills which can only be resolved in favour of one party, the LORD. For 'arrogant' (*zādôn*), compare v. 29. For the combination of divine names, see v. 25. **For** (*kî*) **your day has come, the time for you to be punished** (cf. v. 27). The day will come when the LORD intervenes to settle accounts with the presumptuous rebel power of Babylon. The problem is often raised of how the LORD could here be punishing Babylon for the role she played in the fall of Jerusalem, when Jeremiah had told Zedekiah that Babylon was performing the will of God in coming against the city (37:7-10; 38:18). One must distinguish between God's overruling of man's evil intentions to work out divine purposes and the accountability of individuals and nations for their attitudes and actions.

32. The arrogant (*zādôn*, v. 31) **one will stumble and fall and no one will help her up.** Babylon is pictured as friendless and incapable of helping herself. The personification in this verse is somewhat unusual in that Babylon is treated as masculine, rather than the more common feminine (which the NIV continues). The references to 'himself' probably evoke a picture of a proud warrior lying helplessly on the ground. A similar picture had been used earlier by the prophet Amos to describe the fate of Virgin Israel left desolate on the ground (Amos 5:2). **I will kindle a fire in her towns that will consume all who are around her.** This repeats the imagery of 21:14, which referred to Jerusalem, though 'in her towns'/'his cities' replaces 'in your/its forest', though the latter is in fact found here in the LXX. 'Around her' (*səbîbōtāyw*, 'around him') forms an inclusion with

---

171. In vv. 31-32 masculine forms are used to refer to Babylon, rather than the feminines which have occurred before and which are more natural in Hebrew in the personification of a city. This may indicate that these words were first used by Jeremiah in another context in reference to Babylon and transferred by him here.

'around' (*sābîb*, v. 29), and marks the conclusion of the stanza in
which the fate of Babylon is vividly portrayed.

4. The Invincible Purpose of the LORD (50:33-46)

OUTLINE

a.   The Strong Redeemer (50:33-34)
b.   The Opposing Sword (50:35-38)
c.   Return to Desolation (50:39-40)
d.   Babylon's Helplessness (50:41-43)
e.   Earth-Shaking Collapse (50:44-46)

The third section of the poem comprises five stanzas. The first and last
stanzas mirror each other in that both are concerned with the LORD's
intention to execute his decrees against Babylon. There is also the
verbal link in *rāgaʿ*, 'to cause unrest'/'to chase', in v. 34 and v. 44. The
second and fourth stanzas focus on the agents of destruction, the sword
and those from the north respectively, with the third stanza again
expressing the pivotal theme of the total downfall of Babylon (Aitken
1984:40-44).

a. The Strong Redeemer (50:33-34)
33. The second section of the poem had largely concentrated on the
demise of Babylon, but the third section begins by restating the plight
of the LORD's people, which is an essential factor in precipitating the
collapse of the mighty empire. The beginning of the section is marked
by an introductory heading. **This is what the LORD Almighty says:
'The people of Israel are oppressed, and the people of Judah as
well.'** They are taken together (*yaḥdāw*, 'as well') in this respect.
'Oppress' (<√*ʿāšaq*) is used by Jeremiah of the internal exploitation of
the poor by the rich (7:6; 21:12; cf. 6:6; 22:17), but here it refers to the
violence of foreign powers that invaded their territory. **All her captors
hold them fast** (<√*ḥāzaq*), **refusing to let them go.** This is the
consequence of the defiance of Babylon already spoken about. The
picture is that of Egypt revisited. Before the Exodus, Pharaoh had
refused to let the people go (Exod. 7:14, 27; 9:2, 13;10:3 cf. Isa.
14:17), and now those in Babylon are acting in the same way.
34. But in the trial of strength there is no doubt about the outcome.
There is another factor to be reckoned with in the situation, and that is

the involvement of a third party, one who is introduced asyndetically to effect a decided contrast. **Yet their Redeemer is strong.** 'Strong' (*ḥāzāq*) picks up the theme of 'hold fast' in the previous verse. 'Redeemer' (<√*gāʾal*, cf. 31:11) pinpoints the motivation of the LORD in acting on behalf of the people: he acknowledges a kinship relationship with them. The kinsman-redeemer was the one whose duty it was to avenge a murder and serve as a protector (Lev. 25:25; Num. 35:21; Ruth 4:1, 8). Here the LORD presents himself as the kinsman-redeemer voluntarily committed in covenant bond to champion Israel's cause (cf. 31:11). This designation of the LORD is frequently found in Isaiah (41:14; 43:14; 44:6, 24; 47:4; 48:17; 49:2, 26; 54:5, 8; 59:20; 60:16; 63:16), but it is also used much earlier in Exodus 6:6; 15:13, and it is probably that connection that is foremost here as the LORD acts on behalf of his oppressed people to assert their rights and freedom. **The LORD Almighty is his name.** The divine designation is deliberately used to assert not only God's willingness to act on behalf of his own, but also to indicate the resources at his disposal to ensure that his actions are effective. **He will vigorously defend their cause**[172] **so that** (*ləmaʿan*, introducing a clause of purpose) **he may bring rest**[173] **to their land, but unrest to those who live in Babylon.** The LORD acts as their legal representative to plead their cause ('powerful advocate' REB). The outcome of the matter will be twofold, and the verbs are chosen to indicate the opposite impact. Though for the first verb 'bring rest' the REB has 'give distress', it is only in the qal that *rāgaʿ* means 'to shake, rouse'; the hiphil, which is the form used here, means 'to come to rest' (Deut. 28:65; Jer. 31:2. Possibly there are two roots, *HALOT* 1188). The second verb, 'bring unrest' (<√*rāgaz*, cf. 31:2), sounds very similar, and this serves to emphasise the contrasting outcomes. The extent of the rest and relief the LORD's intervention brings is specified as to 'the land' (*ʿereṣ*), though 'earth' is the rendering favoured by the NRSV and NASB. However, the focus here is not on Babylon as the universal destroyer but on her role against the LORD's people.

---

172. The statement is rendered emphatic in Hebrew not only by the use of the infinitive construct *rîb* (probably standing for the infinitive absolute *rôb*, forms which may well have become merged, *IBHS* §35.2.1b; GKC §73d, 113x.) but also by the assonance with the following words *yārîb ʿet-rîbām*, 'he will plead their plea'. The infinitive may imply not just the certainty of his pleading their cause, but also the vigour with which he pursues it.

173. For the first syllable of the hiphil infinitive with *i* rather than *a*, see GKC §53l.

b. The Opposing Sword (50:35-38)

35. This stanza consists of a series of passionate exclamations urging destruction upon Babylon with the phrase 'A sword against ...!' which occurs five (or six: see v. 38) times. Such repetition is similar to that found in 4:23-26; 5:17 and 51:20-23. Here it results in a vivid portrayal of the carnage that warfare will bring at every level of Babylonian society as a resulting of the activities of the destructive armies of the north whom the LORD has summoned and to whom he dramatically addresses these words.

'A sword against the Babylonians,' declares the LORD. This is probably a general heading, to which no verb need be added, with the thought then more fully specified, though still with no verbs in the subsequent repetitions of 'A sword against ...' This makes the imagery even more stark and arresting. **Against those who live in Babylon** that is, the city or the territory. **And against her officials and against wise men!** refers to those who at a human level provide the wisdom by which the community operates socially and politically. Their wisdom will not exempt them from the impending calamity.

36. A sword against her false prophets is a more problematic phrase. The word[174] basically means 'empty-talkers', and so can come to mean 'boasters' (cf. 48:30). But it also seems to have been used to describe religious officials in a pejorative fashion (Isa. 44:25). Perhaps there was a play on the similarly sounding title for the priests in Babylon who practised foretelling by liver inspection ('oracle priests', NASB; 'diviners', NRSV). It is not clear whether the next clause, **they will become fools**, foretells what will happen when their prophecies do not become true (so NIV; cf. 5:4), or whether it is the intended outcome of the sword being used against them, 'so that they may become fools' (NRSV; NJPS). In either case, the prophets will be seen to be an unsuitable source of counsel regarding future action because their predictions have proved false. **A sword against her warriors! They will be filled with terror.** While it is possible that the verb here (*ḥātat*, 1:17) has the more objective sense of 'be destroyed' (NRSV), an inward paralysis at the opposition they have to face seems more probable.

---

174. *baddîm* (<√*bad* V) is used of false prophets (Isa. 44:25). There seems to be a relationship with *bad* I in the sense of separation; such prophets are set apart in the sense of being outside and alienated from the LORD's calling (*NIDOTTE* 1:501). Another understanding of the word is to see it as a play on the Akkadian term *bārû*, 'diviner' (Bright 1965:355).

37. A sword against her[175] **horses and chariots and all the foreigners in her ranks!** These would have been the main elements in a typical Asiatic army of the time (46:9; Isa. 43:16; Ps. 20:8). If 'sword' signifies death by the sword, it is used in an extended sense in reference to chariots. The 'foreigners'/'mixed multitude' (*'ereb*) were the mixed rabble of mercenaries and conscripts (25:20; 46:16) who would readily become demoralised. **They will become women** (cf. 30:6; 48:41; 49:22; Nahum 3:13). They will become weak and unable to fight. **A sword against her treasures! They will be plundered.** The devastation of Babylon results in social chaos and economic collapse from the sweeping violence of the invading forces.

38. A drought (*hōreb*) **on her waters!** might also be read with certain Greek versions as 'a sword (*hereb*) against her waters!', which retain the consonants of the Hebrew but change one vowel. It is difficult to decide between the two readings. 'A sword against her waters!' is a meaningful continuation of the preceding series with 'sword' used in an extended sense of the impact of warfare on the irrigation canal system that was the basis of agriculture in Babylonia (and not some direct attack on the Tigris or the Euphrates). However, there may have been deliberately play on the word, modifying the thought into a call for drought to come on the whole area. Such an experience would be seen as an indication of extreme divine displeasure. **They will dry up** through drought or the impact of war. This is an outcome that the LORD decides on and can effect at his pleasure.

The reason given at this point for the fate expressed in the preceding lines as awaiting Babylon is not her treatment of Judah or her arrogance, but her devotion to idolatry, **for** (*kî*) **it is a land of idols** (<*pesel*, 8:19). The LORD has determined to act against such folly. In the following clause, **idols that will go mad with terror**, 'idols' is a translators' supplement. The verb is just 'they will go mad' (<√*hālal* III 'act like madmen'; cf. 25:16 and compare 46:9)[176] which may refer to the population in general as well as the idols. 'Terror'/'terrors'

---

175. The Hebrew text reads 'against his horses and his chariots', but the NIV in continuing with 'her' smooths over the gender change, which may have occurred because of the preceding reference to the masculine 'warriors' with the singular being used in a distributive sense (cf. GKC §145.l), that is, 'their horses and their chariots'.

176. The REB rendering, 'a land ... that glories in its dreaded gods', introduces a further complication by following two Hebrew manuscripts manuscripts and the versions in reading *yithallālû* (the hithpael of *hālal* II, 'to boast') for *yithōlālû* (the hithpoel of *hālal* III, 'to be mad').

(*'êmîm*) connotes intense fright, so that the whole expression is a vivid presentation of the demoralisation that will affect the land of idols. Alternatively, 'terrors' may describe the idols as entities which causes fear in those who worship them ('dreaded gods', REB; 'frightful images' *HALOT* 41), and so the clause means, 'they are besotted with their dread images' (NJPS). A translation along these lines is found in most English versions, probably because it leads more easily into the judgment uttered against the land in vv. 39-40.

c. Return to Desolation (50:39-40)
39. So (*lākēn*, 'therefore') introduces a statement of the consequences of the judgment from the LORD that will fall upon the land. The description is of a territory that has reverted to barren wilderness. **Desert creatures and hyenas will live there, and there the owl will dwell** (cf. Isa. 13:20-22). The identification of the animals involved is disputed. 'Desert creatures' (*ṣîyîm*) are obviously creatures of the *ṣiyyâ*, 'the dry area' ('drought', 2:6), but precisely which animals is uncertain, and the ancient versions are no help on the matter. The 'marmots' of the REB is mere guesswork, as is 'wildcats' (NJPS). The similarly sounding *'îyîm* ('hyenas' NIV) should indicate creatures from the sea-coasts or islands (2:10), but the combination was probably used for sound effect. The animals involved are generally supposed to be 'hyenas' or 'jackals' (NASB, REB). The GNB reflects another understanding of the words, 'Babylon will be haunted by demons and evil spirits' (cf. also Bright 1965:344), supposing that what the people worshipped will be left to roam the ruins. But the mention of an unclean bird (whether an owl, possibly a desert owl that would rest in the ruins during the day, or an ostrich, which survived as a wild species in the area until relatively recently) makes it more plausible that all three references are to the animals that will dwell in the ruins of once great and populous Babylon. **It will never again be inhabited or lived in from generation to generation** recalls the verdict of Isa. 13:20a.

40. **'As God overthrew Sodom and Gomorrah along with their neighbouring towns,' declares the LORD, 'so no one will live there; no man will dwell in it.'** This verse is the same as 49:18, and the first part is also found in Isa. 13:19. These towns suffered total annihilation, and the same will come upon Babylon. There will be no mitigation of her punishment; there will be nothing left.

d. Babylon's Helplessness (50:41-43)

In the final section of the chapter there are two passages which are also substantially found elsewhere in the prophecy. Verses 41-43 reflect 6:22-24, and vv. 44-46 apply 49:19-21, which were previously used of Edom, to Babylon. Earlier the theme had been the menace of the invaders from the north coming on Judah. Those invaders had proved to be the Babylonians. Now in a reversal of history, it is Babylon that is being menaced from still further north, by what proved to be the Persians under Cyrus. The language of the verses is adapted accordingly in Jeremiah's description of what he has had revealed to him.

41. Look! An army is coming from the north; a great nation and many kings are being stirred up from the ends of the earth. By changing 'from the land of the north' (6:22) to simply 'the north', Jeremiah is able to generalise the situation to cover what would be involved when the Medes and Persians came from there against Babylon. The addition of 'many kings' (not found in 6:22) serves the same end. Previously it had been one nation coming against Jerusalem. The 'many kings' refers to the kings of the peoples who were made covenant vassals of Cyrus, and who were part of the combined forces that came against Babylon (cf. 51:27-28). 'Many' may be used to refer to their numbers or their strength. But their presence at Babylon would not be merely a matter of human decision; the stirring up referred to would be divine.

42. They are armed with bows and spears;[177] they[178] are cruel and without mercy. They sound like the roaring sea as they ride on their horses; they come like men in battle formation to attack you, O Daughter of Babylon. The principal change in this verse is from 'Daughter of Zion' (6:23) to 'Daughter of Babylon', or 'daughter Babylon'. The emphasis is on the similar cruel and merciless fate that awaits those who had acted against Zion, so that their punishment fits their crime. There is no implication of relationship or of tenderness in the use of 'daughter' in this phrase (4:31).

43. There are more changes made to 6:24 to modify it from a statement about how the people of Jerusalem react to the forces that will

---

177. It is not clear why the NIV has varied from 'bow and spear' (6:23) to the plural here. The words are identical in both places, *qešet wəkîdōn*, both singulars used in a generic sense.

178. In 6:23 'they' (NIV) renders the singular *hû'*, which particularly refers to the nation. Here Jeremiah in fact uses the plural pronoun *hēmmâ* to refer to the many kings as well as the great nation.

come against them to a description about how the king of Babylon will react. **The king of Babylon has heard reports about them, and his hands hang limp. Anguish has gripped him, pain like that of a woman in labour.** The changes are minor and skilfully done. 'We have heard' (6:24) becomes 'the king of Babylon has heard'; 'our hands' becomes 'his hands'; and 'us' becomes 'him'. Also 'about them' reflects a singular pronominal suffix 'about him' in 6:24, but here a plural suffix 'about them'. The once proud tyrant is reduced to a pathetic and ineffective figure, unable to cope with the blows that have come upon his empire.

e. Earth-Shaking Collapse (50:44-46)

44. In the closing stanza of this section Jeremiah sets out words that pick up a theme also found in the prophecy against Edom alluded to in v. 40, which reflected 49:18. **Like a lion coming up from Jordan's thickets to a rich pastureland, I will chase Babylon from its land in an instant.**[179] **Who is the chosen one I will appoint for this? Who is like me and who can challenge me? And what shepherd can stand against me?** is changed from a prediction of what would happen to Edom to one about the future of Babylon. The pride of nations small and great will receive the same treatment from the LORD's hand. 'Edom' in 49:18 is changed to 'Babylon', but the rest is allowed to stand. The lion had previously represented Nebuchadnezzar himself; now it stands for Cyrus, though he is not named. Verses 44-46 make much clearer what is only hinted at in 'are being stirred up' in v. 41. There the reference might be to their own kings, but now the LORD is shown as superintending the nemesis that will come on Babylon.

45. Therefore (*lākēn*), **hear what the LORD has planned against Babylon, what he has purposed against the land of the Babylonians: the young of the flock will be dragged away; he will completely destroy their pasture because of them.** This is virtually identical to 49:20 except for the necessary changes from 'Edom' to 'Babylon', and 'those who live in Teman' to 'the land of the Babylonians'.[180] 'Pasture' can apply to Babylon, because of the existence of the many irrigated areas where animals were reared.

---

179. Literally, 'I will chase them from upon it' (note the verb is cohortative in form, GKC §108h). The kethibh is *ʿrwṣm*, for which the qere proposes *ʾărîṣām*, 'I will chase them'. The verb may however be *rāṣaṣ* in the sense 'to push'.

180. It is also the case that 'their pasture' in 49:20 is *nəwēhem* with the pronominal suffix, whereas here it is simply *nāweh*, 'pasture'.

46. At the sound of Babylon's capture the earth will tremble; its cry will be resound[181] **among the nations.** While this verse obviously is derived from 49:21, there are significant changes.[182] In the case of Edom the impact went to the Red Sea. Babylon, though experiencing the same downfall for her similar disdain of the LORD and his people, was a world power, and her fall has impact over a much wider area. 'Among the nations' also echoes the same phrase in v. 2.

In these words Jeremiah gave hope to a people menaced by the power of Babylon, and probably already suffering devastation and exile at her hands. The LORD would intervene to judge Judah's oppressors and to set his people free. In this Jeremiah's ministry parallels that of Ezekiel who, after the fall of Jerusalem (Ezek. 33:21), began to preach a message of restoration (Ezek. 34–48). That Jeremiah does so alluding to previous prophetic oracles and reusing earlier material may well be a matter of emphasising that all this would be worked out on the LORD's timescale. The people in their anguish no doubt wanted a speedy reversal of their fortunes, but Jeremiah is implicitly pointing out that while the Sovereign LORD does not forget what has been previously announced in his name the resolution to the prevailing upheaval is one that he will provide when he sees fit.

5. Proud Babylon Shattered (51:1-33)

OUTLINE

a.   The Winnower of the Proud (51:1-2)
b.   Destroy Completely (51:3-5)
c.   The Golden Cup (51:6-10)
d.   The Purpose of the LORD Almighty (51:11-19)
e.   The Shattering War Club (51:20-26)
f.   The Enemy Advances (51:27-33)

The longer fourth section of the Oracle against Babylon may be divided into the six stanzas outlined above. The second verse and the

---

181. Note the noun is feminine. Although the noun precedes for the sake of emphasis, the verb remains undefined in gender (GKC §145u).

182. Among these changes might be noticed the use of *tāpaś*, niphal 'to be caught/conquered' instead of *nāpal*, 'to fall' (49:21), and the use of the niphal of *rāʿaš*, 'to quake', for the qal (49:21).

last (vv. 2 and 33) share the imagery of a harvest that devastates the land, while the first and fifth stanzas have in common the use of 'destroy' (*šāḥaṭ* in vv. 1, 20 and 25), and *raʿâ* ('disaster' in v. 2 and 'wrong' in v. 24). The three middle stanzas have a similar structure which begins with a summons to battle or flight, followed by a saying regarding Israel's deliverance. This pattern is varied in the sixth stanza where the summons to battle is followed by a statement regarding Babylon's impending fall (Aitken 1984:44-50).

a. The Winnower of the Proud (51:1-2)
Jeremiah's message concerning Babylon continues with a message about the ruin that is going to come upon her through external aggression.

1. This is what the LORD says: 'See, I will stir up the spirit of a destroyer against Babylon and the people/'inhabitants' **of Leb Kamai.'** Leb Kamai is a cryptogram for Babylonia. (It is in fact an instance of athbash, explained at 25:26, formed by switching the consonants of *kśdym*, 'Chaldea/Babylonia' to *lbqmy*.) But given that Jeremiah has just openly named Babylon, it is not employed here for the sake of secrecy, because no one hearing what Jeremiah said would be in any doubt that he was prophesying the downfall and overthrow of Babylon. The term therefore is probably used because the consonantal form achieved by changing the letters of Chaldeans according to the cryptogrammatic rule could be given vowels so that it meant 'the heart of those who rise up against me' (so NASB margin). It is because of that meaning that Jeremiah employs it here to portray the citizens of Babylonia as those who dwell at the centre of those who are opposed to the LORD, with 'heart' being used to indicate the inner part or the middle of something (a rare but possible Hebrew idiom, Exod. 15:8; Ps. 46:2). Babylon is identified as the focus of rebellion against God, and it is because of this attitude and position of leadership that in later apocalyptic writings Babylon becomes the symbol for the great enemy of God (Rev. 17:5).

The LORD calls attention to the fact that he has resolved to stir up against those who oppose him 'the spirit of a destroyer' (NIV, NASB) or 'a destructive wind' (REB, NKJV). The two translations reflect different aspects of a phrase that was probably originally ambiguous, because *rûaḥ* may mean 'wind' or 'spirit'. The verb 'stir up' is not used elsewhere of the wind, but, as in 50:9 and v. 11 here (cf. also Hag. 1:14; 1 Chron. 5:56; 2 Chron. 21:16; 36:22), it is employed to refer to the LORD's unperceived action within human hearts. By working unobtrusively, he is going to bring upon the scene one who will carry out the role of being Babylon's destroyer (<√*šaḥat*, 4:7; not *šādad* as in vv. 48 and 53. The words are synonyms, though *šāḥat* may emphasise the completeness of the waste that results, while the less frequent *šādad* may point more to the violence with which it is done). But there does seem to be a play on the other meaning of *rûaḥ*, 'wind'. This note of a sudden, destructive force is taken up in the following verse in the metaphor of the destroyer coming upon Babylon like a winnowing wind.

2.   I will send foreigners to Babylon to winnow her and to devastate (<√*bāqaq* I, 'to lay waste'; 19:7) **her land.** 'Foreigners' (NIV, NASB) reflects the pointing of the Hebrew, but the same consonants may also be read as 'winnowers' (NKJV, NRSV, REB),[183] and perhaps that is more likely here. The picture may be compared to that of the hunters and fishermen in 16:16 who carry out an exhaustive search of the land. Winnowing as a metaphor for judgment (cf. 15:7) derives from the fact that as the grain was thrown into the air there was a process of separation in which the lighter chaff was blown off by the wind while the heavier kernels fell to the ground. So all that is in Babylon will be scrutinised, and whatever is considered to be of value will be appropriated by her conquerors and taken away; the city will be thoroughly looted. 'For' (*kî*) **they will oppose her on every side in the day of her disaster** (*rāʿâ*). While the NIV reads this as a restatement of what has gone before, it may well express the reason for the presumed success of the winnowers in that being found on every side there was no escape route for Babylon. Such inescapable encirclement was similar to the fate that had awaited Jerusalem (4:17).

b.   Destroy Completely (51:3-5)

This section sets out the consequences of the twofold divine resolution to 'stir up' (v. 1) and to 'send' (v. 2). As the enemy forces carry out what has been sanctioned by the LORD, complete destruction overwhelms Babylon.

3.   Verse 3 presents textual problems, which are probably resolved correctly by rendering, **Let not the archer string his bow, nor let**

---

183.   The MT has *zārîm*, 'foreigners', but the consonants may also be pointed *zōrîm*, 'winnowers'. This is the reading of Aquila, Symmachus and the Vulgate; the Septuagint while identifying the same root in 'foreigners' and 'winnow' renders it differently.

him put on his armour.[184] The words refer to Babylon's armies as being unable to react quickly enough to the threat posed by the forces that surround them. The archer has insufficient warning to step on his bow to bend it and so string it with tension for effective use. He is seen as struggling to don his armour[185]—it would not amount to much in the case of an archer. This is a mocking picture of their ineffectiveness against the army the LORD is bringing against them. The alternative reading of the text (see footnote) understands these words as addressed to the attacking armies to encourage them to a surprise attack and so prevent effective resistance (Bright 1965:346; Thompson, 1980:747). **Do not spare her young men; completely destroy her army.** These words are directly spoken to the invading forces who are to make no exceptions in their destruction of the Babylon. For 'completely destroy' (*ḥāram*), see on 50:21, 26.

4. **They will fall down**[186] **slain in Babylon, fatally wounded in her streets.** 'Fatally wounded' renders a term that indicates 'pierced through', which may indicate serious injury ('wounded', 37:10; so NRSV here) or death. After 'slain' it is obviously the latter that is the appropriate rendering here. 'In Babylon'/'in the land of the Chaldeans' views the area around the city, and then in the second part of the statement the mention of 'streets' narrows the focus to the city itself.

5. From v. 5 to v. 19 the LORD is spoken of in the third person in a prophetic recital of what has been revealed to Jeremiah in vision. **For** (*kî*) **Israel and Judah have not been forsaken by their God, the LORD Almighty.** The reason for the destruction coming upon Babylon is the covenant bond between the LORD and his people. 'Their God' is

---

184. The qere takes the words as referring to the attacking forces by twice reading *'el*, 'to, against' instead of the kethibh *'al*, 'not', which has considerable manuscript support. Adopting the qere yields a translation such as, 'Against ˩her˩ let the archer bend his bow, and lift himself up against ˩her˩ in his armour' (NKJV). The absolute use of the preposition does not favour such an interpretation. The Hebrew text also repeats the verb *ydrk*, but the Massoretes omit vowel pointing from the word to indicate that they read it only once, as do many manuscripts and the versions (cf. GKC §17b).

185. The verb *'ālâ* in the hithpael is found only here, and seems to mean 'make oneself get up' or 'try to raise oneself'. The avoidance of the ordinary word for 'dress' suggests an ironic use. The jussive form *yit'al* is used after *'al*.

186. *wənāpəlû* may be understood as a *waw*-consecutive perfect with a future sense, 'they will fall'. 'Let them fall' (REB) takes the sense as jussive continuing the sequence of the previous verse (GKC §112q,r), which is also a feasible rendering.

literally 'his God' (NASB, NKJV), probably because 'Israel and Judah' are thought of as a unit. The picture is of them not being 'left widowed' (REB)[187], that is, in a vulnerable position because they lack one who would defend them (7:6). The language looks back to the people as the LORD's bride in chapter 2. Though they have violated their marriage vows and come under his curse, he has not abandoned them. After they have been punished for their sin, there is the prospect of restoration; indeed, it is certain because the LORD has not renounced the covenant. **Though (*kî*) their land is full of guilt before[188] the Holy One of Israel.** For the idiom of the land being full, compare 23:10. 'Guilt' (*'āšām*) may signify the judicial verdict on persons whose actions are judged contrary to a standard, as well as the retribution that is consequently imposed. It is uncertain whose land is referred to as guilty. The sequence of thought seems to require that it be that of Israel and Judah, with *kî* then being translated as 'although'. Another possibility is that here we have a second reason for what has been described in the preceding verses, 'for their (i.e. the Babylonians') land is full of guilt' (cf. RSV). This would be partly because of what they have done to Israel (50:21); and partly through their idolatry (50:2, 38) which has offended the Holy One of Israel (50:29). The nations had regarded Israel as guilty (50:7), but it is Babylon which is really so.

c. The Golden Cup (51:6-10)
Again in this section there is brought out the interrelatedness of the fall of Babylon and the destiny of Israel. It is not just a matter of the exiles escaping from Babylon (v. 6); what is in prospect is their vindication as the people of the LORD (v. 10).

6. Flee from Babylon! Run for your lives!/'Save/deliver your lives (<*nepeš*, 2:34), each of you'. A similar injunction is found in 50:8; for the expression see v. 45, and compare 48:6. The people are urged to take individual action to save themselves by leaving the land of their deportation in view of its impending destruction. It is possible the words are addressed to all the subject peoples of Babylon, because of the reference 'each to his own land' in v. 9, but the principal recipients of the message are the people of God. **Do not be destroyed** (<√*dāmam* III, niphal) **because of her sins**/'guilt' (*'āwôn*). It may also

---

187. The form *'almān* may be a masculine 'widower' corresponding to the common *'almōnâ*, 'widow'. But more probably it is here used in an adjectival sense 'widowed'.

188. *min*, 'from', is used not as 'on the side of', but rather as 'on account of'.

mean 'do not be destroyed in her punishment' since the one word covers both iniquity and the punishment of it (2:22). Babylon is going to be engulfed by war because of the LORD's action against her iniquity, and the only way for the exiles to avoid being drawn into the catastrophe is to act in good time on the warning they have received. 'For' (*kî*) **it is time for the LORD's vengeance; he will pay her what she deserves.** 'Vengeance' (<√*nāqam*, 5:9) is divine vindication and God's open reinstatement of his rule (50:15, 28; Isa. 34:8). What divine forbearance has let pass with seemingly no response will now become the ground of divine action. 'What she deserves' points to the LORD's intervention as an equitable reaction to what Babylon has done (cf. vv. 24, 56; 25:14; 50:29).

7. Babylon was a gold cup in the hand of the LORD resumes imagery used in 25:15-16. The cup was the portion assigned to the guests at the feast and they, including Babylon, were made to drink of it. Now Babylon in her relation to the nations is compared with a golden cup—fitting imagery because of her wealth and riches (v. 13). But still she was a cup in the LORD's hand. He was using and controlling her actions to effect his purposes among the nations. **She made the whole earth drunk. The nations drank her wine; therefore they have now gone mad.** 'Gone mad' (<√*hālal* III, 25:16; 50:38) is the consequence of the intoxicating power of the wine which leads to confused and irrational thought and action. This was what Babylon had made the nations experience, and so the same fate is threatened against her.

8. But though Babylon was a golden cup, through the LORD's action it is going to become like a cup that is dropped. **Babylon will suddenly fall and be broken.** Three facts about her destruction are brought out. (a) The use of the prophetic perfect (*nāpəlâ*) shows that the prophet conceives of the future fall as so guaranteed by the divine revelation which has been given to him that it may be described as over and done with. (b) It is also a turn of events that will occur swiftly and unexpectedly (*pit'ōm* 'suddenly', 4:20; 6:26; 18:22; cf. 15:8; the Hebrew word is placed first for emphasis). (c) What is more, it will be a shattering blow from which recovery will be impossible—the cup that has slipped to the ground is smashed into many pieces (*šābar* piel). **Wail over her!** 'Wail' (*hêlîlû*) is probably intended to re-echo 'gone mad' (*yithōləlû*; v. 7), and to bring out the change of fortune that will occur for Babylon: the cruel conqueror has become an object of pity. These words seem to be addressed to all who are captive in Babylon and are probably not uttered in mockery. **Get balm for her pain; perhaps she**

can be healed is an expression of genuine concern at what will happen to Babylon, possibly reflecting the advice of 29:7. But even though her former victims do get balm (8:22; 46:11) to heal her wounds, there is no prediction of recovery. 'Perhaps' (ʾûlay) conveys a note of sadness because Jeremiah realises the compassionate gesture has little probability of success.

9. After the exhortation to heal Babylon, a dramatic presentation of the extent of Babylon's downfall is given by envisaging the reply of those who have been exhorted to assist her. **'We would have healed[189] Babylon, but she cannot be healed.'** They had made every reasonable endeavour as subjects of Babylon to act to defend her against her attackers and to offset her losses, but their efforts had been to no avail. The wounds of Babylon could not be healed;[190] they were divinely imposed. The speakers therefore realise that they have no option but to follow the advice given in v. 6, and so they say to one another, **Let us leave her[191] and each go to his own land.** It would seem that this speech is related on behalf of the deportees in Babylon by those from Israel/Judah in particular because of the reason they assign for their action, **for (kî) her judgment reaches to the skies, it rises as high as the clouds.** Her judgment refers to the punishment imposed on her. The language used may reflect on an enormous scale, matching therefore her crime (Num. 13:28; Deut. 1:28; Pss. 57:11; 108:5), or it may arise out of the smoke of fires kindled as the land is ransacked, though this is less likely as there is no indication of fire in context. More probably the imagery reflects the incident of the Tower of Babel where the people resolved to build a tower that reached to the heavens (Gen. 11:4). Babel transliterates the Hebrew word for Babylon, which is the Greek form of the city's name. Her punishment reflects the scale of her

---

189. The kethibh is *rpʿnw* presumably to be read as *rāpāʾnû*, 'we healed' with an irreal sense (*IBHS* §30.5.4), whereas the qere is *rippinû* (piel), 'we treated'. The kethibh is to be preferred.

190. The niphal *nirpātâ* (formed on the analogy of a final *he* verb, GKC §75qq) probably carries the nuance of potentiality, 'capable of being healed' (*IBHS* §23.3d). Another possibility is that the niphal is a 'niphal tolerativum' (*IBHS* §23.4f, g), that is, Babylon would not permit herself to be healed. If the healing was to come by the recognition of the LORD as the one true God, Babylon's inveterate hostility against the truth meant that she refused to have anything to do with acknowledging the LORD and so brought her doom on herself.

191. The form *ʿizəbûhā* is in fact imperative, but a similar form is found in v. 10, *bōʾû ûnəsappərâ*, 'come and let us relate'.

rebellion against God. Mankind's attempts to build themselves up and do great things lead through inherent sinfulness to building up judgment on a similar scale.

10. The words of v. 10 are undoubtedly those of the returning Jews. **'The LORD has vindicated us'**/'brought forth our righteousnesses', the plural term indicating the abundance of the proof provided of their righteousness. This does not indicate that the LORD has shown them to be guiltless: there is no doubt that they were guilty. 'Righteousness' may have the sense 'salvation', that is, 'the deliverance extended to us is now plain for all to see'. But most probably here the term goes further than that and refers to their proper covenant standing with the LORD, for which evident proof has been provided by his action on their behalf. While they were detained in Babylon as a just consequence of their sin, they were not openly seen as the LORD's people. Indeed, their enemies regarded them as abandoned by the LORD because of their transgression. But now that Babylon has fallen and they are going home, it can be seen that they have not been forsaken by the LORD their God (v. 5). Since their time of punishment has been completed, the LORD does not merely release them; he restores them because he is acting in terms of his covenant commitment to them. **Come, let us tell in Zion what the LORD our God has done.** They are eager to announce back home in Zion (note sacral connotations with 'temple' at the end of the next verse) the work (*maʿăśeh*) of the LORD whom they acknowledge as their God (50:25, 45; 51:29).

d. The Purpose of the LORD Almighty (51:11-19)

11. A new stanza is marked by a change of theme as we again hear words of command addressed to the attacking armies of the Medes and summoning them to battle. **Sharpen**[192] **the arrows, take up the shields!**[193] 'Take up' is literally 'fill' and may be understood as filling the shields with their bodies (cf. 2 Sam. 23:7; 2 Kgs. 9:24), or else the

---

192. Treatment of the root *bārar* is confused. *HALOT* identifies two roots, the first of which means 'to purge' or 'to keep clean'. This is the normal cultic use of the term. But it is used of arrows here and in Isa. 49:2. *HALOT* distinguishes a second root *bārar* II 'to sharpen'. Others dispute this and suggest that it means 'to polish' for smoother flight.

193. *šəlāṭîm* is in connection with shields in 2 Sam. 8:7; 2 Kgs. 11:10, which is also the traditional rendering here. However, the word is now generally related to the Akkadian *šalṭu*, 'case for bow and arrows' (*HALOT* 1522-23), hence the translation 'quiver' (NRSV, REB), which goes back to the LXX, and which is more easily related to the verb 'fill up'.

item of military equipment may be a cover for bow and arrows which
is to be filled. In any event, the commands urge them to get ready to
attack Babylon. What then follows is printed in the NRSV as prose,
and the rest of the verse is often taken as interpretative comment introduced at a later stage. If Jeremiah is responsible for the poetry at the
beginning of the verse, this part with its mention of the Medes is taken
to date from after 550 BC when Cyrus was already an active force on
the scene. But to treat what follows as an interpretative comment fails
to see that v. 12 also begins with imperatives from the LORD followed
by prophetic comment. We are therefore to read these two verses in the
same way: words of divine command are followed by prophetic
commentary on them. **The LORD has stirred up**[194] (cf. v. 1) **the kings
of the Medes, because** (*kî*) **his purpose is to destroy** (<√*šāḥat*, v. 1)
Babylon. 'Stirred up'/'roused the spirit of' refers to the LORD's ability
to direct the inner being of an individual so that he thinks and acts in a
way that furthers the divine purpose. This is an enlivening and efficacious act of God upon the human spirit (2 Chron. 36:22; Ezra 1:1, 5).

Media lay north-west of Persia with its capital at Ecbatana. The
Persian king Cyrus had Median blood through his mother, but the
plural phrase 'the kings of the Medes' does not anticipate him. Rather
'king' is used of a subordinate ruler and refers to the chieftains of the
various more or less independent tribes in north-western Iran, who had
been forced to organise themselves to counter Assyrian expansion.
Eventually they formed a recognisable kingdom under the Medes and
assisted the Babylonians to destroy Assyria, and thereby greatly
increased their territory. However, they did not remain on good terms
with the Babylonians, and Jeremiah is clearly pointing out that it is
from there that the downfall of Babylon will come. In this respect it
will be like the earlier downfall of Nineveh, in which the Medes had
played a significant role. For 'purpose' (<√*zāmam*, 'to decide'), see on
4:28. 'For' (*kî*) **the LORD will take vengeance, vengeance for his
temple.** For the thought compare 50:28. The Babylonians had
ransacked the Temple, not just for booty, but as an act of sacrilege
against the LORD (cf. Ps. 74:4-7). Though the people had put a false

---

194. I find it difficult to account for the translation of *hēʿîr* as a perfect in
this verse, whereas in the parallel prophetic commentary in v. 12 the perfects
zāmam and *ʿāśâ* are treated as prophetic perfects and rendered as futures.
Consistency would require that all are treated in the same way. The NKJV,
NASB and REB all translate as pasts, but prophetic perfects, i.e. futures, seem
preferable. Jeremiah would then be giving the people after the fall of
Jerusalem encouragement for the future.

trust in the Temple, that did not mean that its sanctity could be lightly impugned, and the LORD acts to avenge what was done to his holy Temple.

12. Lift up a banner against the walls of Babylon! Again the plural commands are heard as if addressed to the advancing forces, though the NKJV prefers to translate *'el*, 'to/against' as 'on', following the LXX which views these words as an ironic summons to defend the city. The standard that led the army into battle is to be brought right up to the walls of the city ('raise the signal' 4:6; 50:2; 51:27), probably to indicate the point at which an attack was to be launched. **Reinforce the guard!** is not used of those posted on the walls of Babylon, but is part of the siege that is undertaken (cf. 2 Sam. 11:16; REB: 'mount a strong blockade'). Nothing must be allowed to move in or out of Babylon, and the guard round the city is to keep the blockade tightly in place. **Station the watchmen** presents a similar command, while **prepare an ambush!** is used of the surrounding troops getting ready to take advantage of any sally by those besieged either to capture them or to get in behind their break-out and enter the city itself. 'For' (*kî*) **the LORD will carry out his purpose, his decree against the people of Babylon** (literally, 'the LORD both has purposed [<√*zāmam*, 'to purpose, to devise', cf. v. 11] and has done what he has spoken'; for the idiom cf. Lam. 2:17). This again gives the prophet's commentary on the significance of the commands he relays. What is coming upon Babylon is not arbitrary or the consequence of expansionist plans of the Medes but the deliberate design of the LORD. There is also no break between what the LORD purposes and what he carries out (*gam ... gam*, 'both ... and'), with prophetic perfects used to show that there is no doubt about what the LORD has planned coming to pass.

13. Babylon is now addressed. **You who live**[195] **by many waters, and are rich in treasures** locates Babylon both on the Euphrates which allowed access for traders ('many waters' is used of Euphrates in Isa. 8:7) and also surrounded by a network of irrigation canals (more than twenty named canals are known; Wiseman 1985:60) on which her agricultural prosperity depended, and which were also a significant part of her city defences. It may be that there is also here an oblique reference to the Babylonian world-view in which the earth had beneath it a great subterranean ocean, whose waters could burst forth and bring chaos. But the main thrust is the prosperity and security of the town. Her

---

195. For the kethibh/qere see 22:33. *šākan* is normally used of a temporary stay, and its use here may be ironic.

treasures ('storehouses', cf. 48:7) would have come from her conquests
of cities such as Nineveh and Jerusalem, and from the tribute paid by
the subordinate nations. Neither her natural situation nor the resources
she has amassed would avail anything. **Your end has come** seems to
recall the words of Amos 8:2, but now applied to the enemy of the
nation: Babylon's time for judgment has arrived. **The time for you to
be cut off**[196] seems to be a metaphor from weaving. The requisite
length of cloth has been prepared, and now it is going to be cut and
taken off the loom.

14. The LORD Almighty has sworn by himself ('by his *nepeš*', that
is his 'being'; cf. 6:8; Amos 6:8) underlines the serious nature of the
matter and the solemn certainty of the commitment given. **I will surely**
(*kî-ʿim*, introducing a positive oath) **fill** (a prophetic perfect) **you with
men, as with a swarm of locusts.** 'Being filled (<√*mālēʿ*, cf. v. 11,
and so the recurrence of the root here possibly indicates the end of a
section) with men' might in itself have presaged a time of prosperity.
However, these men are not her own citizens but an invading army
which is likened to locusts—a figure for the swift, destructive power of
a mighty army. Just as locusts strip the fields of everything green, so
the troops will strip Babylon bare of everything of value. **And they
will shout in triumph over you**/'sing (<√*ʿānâ* IV) a joyful song
(*hēdad*; cf. 25:30; 48:33)', like the shout of those trampling the vintage
in wine harvest. The victory they achieve over Babylon ensures that the
enemy forces will enjoy a bountiful harvest from the plunder they
amass.

15-19. Jeremiah now adds words he had used earlier in 10:12-16.
Throughout the passage God is referred to in the third person, and
continuation of inverted commas to denote divine speech as in the NIV
seems misplaced. **He made**[197] **the earth by his power; he founded
the world by his wisdom and stretched out the heavens by his
understanding. When he thunders, the waters in the heavens roar;
he makes clouds rise from the ends of the earth. He sends lightning
with the rain and brings out the wind from his storehouses. Every
man is senseless and without knowledge; every goldsmith is
shamed by his idols.** 'For' (*kî*) **his images are a fraud; they have no**

---

196. Literally, 'the cubit of your being cut off'. *beṣaʿ* as a noun can mean
'unjust gain' (hence 'the measure of your covetousness', NKJV), or it could
be a infinitive construct, 'your being cut off' <√*bāṣaʿ*, 'to cut away, break up'.
197. The participle *ʿōśeh* links back to the LORD Almighty/LORD of hosts in
v. 14 and heads a series of hymnic participles which set out the reasons for
praising him.

breath in them. They are worthless, the objects of mockery; when
their judgment comes, they will perish. He who is the Portion of
Jacob is not like these, for (*kî*) he is the Maker of all things, including the tribe[198] of his inheritance—the LORD Almighty is his name.
Previously these words had been used in 10:12-16 to contrast the
powerless of idols and the power of God, in an effort to convince his
wandering people of the folly of abandoning the LORD and seeking
help from the pagan religions of their day. Now the passage is included
as a hymn of praise which enhances the majesty and superiority of the
one who has decreed the destruction of Babylon. The impending judgment of the LORD is therefore certain, and the idol gods of Babylon
will be unable to resist his purposes. The wisdom and power of the
LORD will lead to blessing for those who acknowledge him and to
destruction of all supposed gods and also of those who trust in them.

e. The Shattering War Club (51:20-26)
The section from vv. 20-26 is an elegant poem which carefully drives
home its message by repetition. It does, however, present a number of
interpretative problems, not least of which is that of who is being
addressed. In vv. 13-14 Babylon had been addressed in the second
person feminine singular, and that mode of address is resumed at v. 27
with 'her', third feminine singular. But here 'you' in vv. 20-23 and
vv. 25-26 is masculine singular, and the 'you' of v. 24 is masculine
plural. Whoever is addressed in vv. 20-23 is not directly identified.
There are a number of possibilities. (a) It may be Babylon. This was
the view of Calvin (1850, 5:230). (b) The addressee may be the northern foe that will destroy Babylon. (c) It may be Israel that is being
called on to act as the LORD's instrument of judgment in the foretold
period of their restoration. Holladay identified the hammer as Israel,
pointing out that different words are used here and in 50:23 (1989,
2:405-7). (d) There is also the possibility that it is the prophet himself,
and that was adopted by Lundbom (1997:121), who saw Jeremiah
described here as the prophet who shattered in word and deed.
Although Jeremiah had been commissioned 'to destroy and overthrow'
(1:10), such a reference to the personal ministry of the prophet does
not fit easily into one of the Oracle against the Nations. While the role

---

198. In 10:16 'Israel' is present before 'the tribe of his inheritance'. Many
manuscripts, the Targum and the Vulgate insert it here, as well as the Greek of
the Lucianic recension. This is followed by many English translations, but on
balance it is easier to see how it was added to the text here on the basis of
10:16 than to see why it would have been omitted.

reversal involved in option (c) does fit in with the concept of retributive justice, there is little to suggest that Israel is present in this
passage, or that the description is one of a future age of restoration. It
is difficult to decide between the first two options. The section
evidently has v. 24 as a pivot, but both the preceding and the following
sections might set out the same thought: the LORD's action against
Babylon, first set out indirectly and then directly. Alternatively,
vv. 20-23 may establish Babylon's role as the LORD's instrument of
judgment, and then vv. 25-26 the LORD's judgment on her because her
actions against Zion overstepped the mark (though that thought is not
actually stated in v. 24). Despite Holladay's arguments it is on balance
easier to take vv. 20-23 as a description of what the LORD had done
and was still doing through Babylon. Babylon has already been identified as 'the hammer of the whole earth' (50:23). The image here is
similar, that of a war club.

20. You are my war club. 'War club' (*mappēṣ*, an instrument for
breaking in pieces or shattering, <√*nāpaṣ* I, 'to break', see below)
refers to a short, stout cudgel intended for use in hand-to-hand combat.
It may have had a stone or metal head fixed to a wooden shaft. **My
weapon**/'weapons' **for battle** shows how the LORD intends to use the
forces that are addressed to accomplish his purposes. Neither those
against whom the action is taken nor those who are to take the action
are specified. If it is Babylon that is addressed, then the situation is
similar to that of Isaiah's day with respect to Assyria (Isa. 10:5).
Neither great empire was aware of its role in the LORD's plans.

With you I shatter nations, with you I destroy (<√*šāḥat* hiphil,
v. 1) **kingdoms**. 'Shatter'/'break in pieces' (<√*nāpaṣ* piel, 'to smash,
break up') describes a blow that is violent and intense (cf. Exod. 15:6;
Pss. 2:9; 137:9; Hos. 10:14; 13:16). Nine times the phrase 'with you I
shatter' is repeated like the stroke of doom to emphasise the thoroughness with which the LORD's actions are carried out (cf. 49:35-38;
50:35-38). No obstacle of any sort will be able to withstand this
advance. The one variation on the use of 'shatter' occurs in 'with you I
destroy', and this is of significance in that the verb 'destroy' prepares
the way for a link with v. 25, 'O destroying mountain, you who
destroy'. Because the first clause of v. 20 has no verb in Hebrew, the
following verbs may be understood to set out a series of repeated past
(GNB) and/or present actions (as in the NIV), which would then refer
to Babylon as the instrument through which the LORD is working and
will work. Alternatively, the verbs may be taken as constituting a series
of future actions which could refer equally to Babylon or her future

destroyer.[199] It is more probably a reference to Babylon as the LORD's war club, which he is using to break thoroughly the power of the nations.

21-23. The elaboration of the detail continues in v. 21 as the shattering impact of Babylon, the LORD's war club, comes repeatedly on surrounding nations. **With you I shatter horse and rider, with you I shatter chariot and driver.**[200] The military forces of the nations are disabled. **With you I shatter man and woman, with you I shatter old man and youth, with you I shatter young man and maiden.** The middle of the poem consists of three lines looking at the population in general. Distinctions of sex or age make no difference in the matter. **With you I shatter shepherd and flock, with you I shatter farmer** (*'ikkār*, 'a farm hand', a worker who prepared the soil and looked after oxen, cf. 14:4; 31:24) **and oxen.** The catastrophes overtaking the nations are not confined to their cities, but strike at the agricultural base of the economy, workers and livestock alike. **With you I shatter governors** (<*peḥâ*, an Akkadian/Assyrian loanword for a provincial official ruling on behalf of a king) **and officials** (another Akkadian term for one commissioned or appointed, an administrator in the empire). To bring the list to a conclusion, the focus returns to the nations and kingdoms with which it began (v. 20) but now it highlights those in positions of authority in these lands. There are no exemptions from the impact of the shattering blows that Babylon brings as it imposes the LORD's judgment on the nations.

24. Verse 24 is treated by the NIV, NASB and NRSV as prose, but the REB[201] and the NKJV treat it as poetry. The problem is where to link in the phrase 'before your eyes'. **'Before your eyes I will repay Babylon and all who live in Babylonia for all the wrong they have done in Zion,' declares the LORD.** The NIV puts 'before your eyes' first in the verse to emphasise the fact that it is 'before you', presumably the LORD's people, the vindication will come. But this

---

199.   The verbs are *waw*-consecutive perfect, presumably with a future sense. This was spoken at a time when Babylon is still active in subduing nations.

200.   'Rider' and 'driver' render the same word *wərōkəbô*, 'and one riding it'. The use of *rākab* does not seem to correspond precisely to the English verb 'to ride', and it may not be necessary to repoint the second occurrence to *wərakkābô* to justify the translation 'driver'.

201.   The REB rendering 'So shall I repay …' is linked to an interpretation of the one addressed in the previous words as the destroyer to come, and not Babylon.

involves removing 'before your eyes' from its position at the end of the statement to qualify the verb 'I will repay' (for 'repay', *šillēm*, cf. 50:29; 51:6). Much may be said for the rendering 'for all their evil that they have done in Zion before your eyes' (NASB; similarly the NKJV and NRSV), which brings out the fact that there would be those who had witnessed the events of 586 BC who would also witness Babylon's downfall. This transitional verse brings out that the change in the LORD's attitude to Babylon has arisen because of what had been done in Zion (cf. 50:29).

25-26. The opening words make clear the whole orientation of the oracle: the LORD is against Babylon. What more need be said? **'I am against you, O destroying mountain, you who destroy the whole earth,' declares the LORD** refers to Babylon under the description of a mountain, presumably as an analogy for a major political power which used its towering superiority to bring destruction on a worldwide scale. 'Mountain' was certainly not intended as a physical description of Babylon which was built on an alluvial plain. The destruction envisaged is spiritual as well as material. The same description (*har-hammašḥît* <√*šāḥat*; cf. v. 1 and v. 20) is rendered 'Hill of Corruption' in 2 Kgs. 23:13 and applied to the mount of Olives as the centre of false worship which had corrupted the life of Jerusalem and Judah. Here too it seems to have overtones of false worship which was at the root of all the evils of Babylon. Even though Babylon's action was ordained by God (cf. 'I destroy' in v. 20), their conduct had been such as to bring the LORD's vengeance on them. **I will stretch out my hand against you, roll you off the cliffs, and make you a burnt-out mountain.** It does not seem that the imagery of the mountain is continued at this point, because the idea of rolling a mountain off cliffs (<*selaʿ*, 'a crag') is not meaningful. Rather the description is a vivid picture of destroying a person or an object by hurling them down a precipice. 'Burnt-out mountain' may well refer to a volcano, but Babylon's days of eruption and pouring out lava are now over. It is an extinct volcano, not constituting a threat to anyone, but destined to remain barren and desolate.

No rock will be taken from you for a cornerstone, nor any stone for a foundation. The picture is that of a city that has been so completely pulverised that it is not possible to salvage any stone from it capable of being reused. As building at Babylon was done in brick, the references to stone show that this is a general description, not a particular prophecy. When the LORD's judgment has come on Babylon, the reversal of her fortunes will not be some temporary phenomenon 'for (*kî*) **you will become desolate**/'desolations' (<*šəmāmâ*, 2:15) **for ever,' declares the LORD.** The fate of Babylon contrasts with that of Zion as foretold in Isa. 28:16.

That this did not occur when Cyrus conquered Babylon may be used as an indication of the early date of this prophecy. If it was language constructed after the event, it might well have been expected to reflect the event more closely. But that then raises questions about the veracity of the prophecy as such. One way of dealing with this is to treat the language as conventional language of downfall, applied in a general way to Babylon. However, more seems to involved than that. It is much more probable that the view given Jeremiah of the future was not limited just to the events of 539 BC and the coming of Cyrus. It encompassed the whole future of Babylon, and presented it against the background of the final judgment the LORD will bring upon all those who oppose him.

f. The Enemy Advances (51:27-33)
Once more a summons is heard to an initially unnamed group to make preparations to advance against Babylon. But now the scene is not merely one of general preparation for war; the enemy forces are envisaged as being in the outskirts of Babylon.

27. In a series of seven imperatives the LORD sets out the orders the enemy forces are to follow. **Lift up a banner in the land!** is a call for an attack (v. 12). The 'banner' was the standard that went before the army as it advanced, and here an advance is to be made into Babylonian territory. There is an alternative understanding in the REB 'Raise a standard on the earth', where the purpose of the standard is to act as a rallying point, and 'earth' is read in parallel with 'nations' in the next clause. This has something to be said for it, especially if **Blow the trumpet** (*šôpār*) **among the nations!** is viewed as an initial call to arms, rather than as a signal to the already massed troops to urge them to engage in close combat. **Prepare the nations for battle against her** employs the idiom of setting them aside to a special divine task of waging war on a divinely approved mission (<√*qādaš*; cf. 6:4; 22:17). It may also have been the case that the heathen nations had certain rites that they went through before engaging the enemy in battle, but the main reference is to the fact that this is holy war waged by the authority of the LORD against Babylon. The nations are those he has designated and stirred up for this purpose.

Summon ('cause to hear', <√*šāmaʿ*, cf. 50:29) **against her these kingdoms: Ararat, Minni and Ashkenaz.** These three kingdoms were to the north of Mesopotamia, in the general area of what is now Armenia and north-west Iran. Ararat was in the middle/east of Armenia, around the area of Lake Van; Minni lay to the west of that; and Ashkenaz describes nomad tribes from further north again, who are probably to be identified with the Scythians (a Greek name found in Herodotus). The three kingdoms are known to us from Assyrian records, as Urartu, Mannai and Išguzai respectively. Urartu was the name used for a group of peoples who had united to defend themselves against the Assyrians. They had successfully expanded into and plundered the fertile plains to their south, but with the resurgence of Assyrian power under Tiglath-Pileser III they were dislodged from the territory they had captured and their homeland was devastated. A much weakened state remained until 585 BC when it was overwhelmed by the Medes as they moved westwards. Minni was at times an ally and at times a foe of Assyria. At the battle of Carchemish (605 BC) it was on the Assyrian side, and its territory was allocated to the Medes. Ashkenaz represents a fierce and powerful people who were a dominant force in sixth century BC. It is probable that by 580–570 BC the southern part of their territory had come under Median control, and all three states subsequently fell under the domination of Persia under Cyrus around 550 BC. The kings of such subordinate states would be required to contribute soldiers to the forces of their overlord, and so the army that came against Babylon would be composed of those from the north.

Appoint a commander against her. 'Commander' (*ṭipsār*, Nah. 3:17) is based on an Akkadian word (*tupšarru*) which originally denoted a scribe who wrote on a clay tablet. In a military context it may have been applied to a recruiting officer who kept records of the various contingents in the army, or to one whose duty was to keep an inventory of the plunder. Here it seems to be applied more generally to a high-ranking officer. **Send up horses like a swarm of locusts** 'against her' (the phrase is repeated). The significance of the word rendered 'swarm' is difficult. Another understanding is 'bristling locusts' (NKJV, NRSV), a highly destructive stage of locust life during which the wings are encased on their backs in rough horny covers.

28. There are further commands issued preparatory to the final conflict. **Prepare the nations for battle against her** repeats the order in v. 27, but now those involved are characterised differently. **The kings of the Medes** is an unexpected use of the plural 'kings' (the LXX has simply 'king'), but compare v. 11. Since 'king' may designate a vassal who is the ruler of his own territory, the plural may refer to all the subordinate kings of the Median empire. For **their governors and all their officials,** see on v. 23. Indeed **all the countries they rule**[202] are to be called on to contribute to the force that will advance against Babylon.

29. In vv. 29-32 the impact of all this on Babylon is described. **The land trembles** (<√rā'aš, 4:24) **and writhes** (<√ḥûl, 4:19) presents the horror and confusion in the face of the threat of the LORD's judgment as it is worked out through the advancing enemy, and the realisation that there is nothing they can do to avert them (cf. Judg. 5:4; Nah. 1:2-6; Hab. 3:1-15). **For** (kî) **the LORD's purposes against Babylon stand,**[203] or possibly 'rise up', using the same verb as in Kamai in v. 1. Behind the military manoeuvres of the enemy there lies the far more significant reality that has to be reckoned with—the LORD's purposes (<maḥăšābâ; 18:11; 29:11). These are summarised in the expression: **to lay waste** (šammâ) **the land of Babylon, so that no one will live there** (cf. 4:7; 18:16). What Babylon had done to others (44:22; 46:19; 48:9) would now come on Babylon itself.

30. Details are then given of how Babylon's preparations for military success are put into reverse. **Babylon's warriors have stopped fighting.** Have they achieved complete success? Far from it: while it is not their death that is reported, it is their complete demoralisation as they feel overwhelmed by the enemy advance and are no longer prepared to go out against them. **They remain in their strongholds.** For 'strongholds' (<məṣād), see on 48:41. What confronts them is so threatening they are unable to organise effectively against it. **Their strength is exhausted.** 'Exhausted' (<√nāšat, 'to be dry, parched') describes a state of personal weakness (Isa. 19:5; 41:17). **They have become like women,** a comparison frequently found in Jeremiah to

---

202. There is a complex sequence of pronominal suffixes in this clause which reads 'the kings of the Medes/Media and her governors and all her officials and all the country of his rule' (cf. NKJV). The feminine suffixes refer to Media and not to the kings as 'their' (NIV and most English versions) would suggest. The masculine singular pronominal suffix may well be distributive and refer to each of the lands ruled by the subordinate kings, governors and officials.

203. The verb is singular, though its subject is plural. (The feminine singular verb probably has a collective sense, GKC §145k.) The Oriental qere corrects this lack of agreement by making the verb plural; a few manuscripts, the LXX and Syriac read a singular noun maḥšebet, 'purpose', for maḥšəbôt, 'purposes'.

describe ineffectiveness (30:6; 48:41; 49:22; 50:37). **Her dwellings are set on fire;**[204] **the bars of her gates are broken.** 'Gates' is a translators' supplement but there is no doubt that 'bars' refers to the strong poles which kept the city gates secure (49:31). Other descriptions of the utter collapse of Babylon are found at 50:30, 36, 37, 43.

31. One courier follows another/'runner to meet runner he runs' **and messenger follows messenger** reflects the system of intelligence gathering in ancient warfare. The Babylonians particularly were renowned for their efficient relay system by which contact was maintained throughout the empire, but now it is not employed to give the news of their victories but **to announce to the king of Babylon that** (*kî*) **his entire city is captured.** 'Entire' is literally 'from ͺitsͺ end'. Babylon was a city covering over a thousand acres. The king would have been living in the palace at the centre of the city. But the news echoes the prediction of 50:2, 'Babylon will be captured'. Herodotus (*Hist.* 1:191) describes the inhabitants of the centre of Babylon dancing and celebrating a holiday unaware that the Persians had already penetrated the outer defences of the city.

32. But there is not just one item of bad news; it is also the case that **the river crossings** are **seized.** The word *maʿbārâ* (<√*ʿābar* I, 'to cross over, pass through') does undoubtedly mean 'ford' elsewhere, but here probably it extends to cover bridges and ferries as well as fords across the irrigation channels and artificial ponds so extensively found in the area. In the weeks before the fall of Babylon the Persians had seized control of crossings over both the Tigris and the Euphrates, cutting off communication and supplies from the north to Babylon. **The marshes set on fire**, at first seems impossible[205], but probably it is a reference to the grass and rushes that would be found there. Beyond the inner walls circling the city (cf. v. 44), there were walls at intervals round Babylon, with a chain of fortresses and many areas of deliberately flooded swamp land as part of the city defences. Such swamps might conceal in their rushes either ambushes against approaching forces, or those who were trying to remain hidden and escape the attention of the invaders. The smoke rising from such fires would have masked enemy movements and created a sense of impending doom. It is not surprising then that it is recorded, **And the soldiers are terrified** (<√*bāhal*, the

---

204. *hiṣṣîtû* is a hiphil form from *yāṣat*, 'to set on fire', 'to set fire to'. Instead a niphal form *niṣṣətû* is read with the appropriate passive sense, 'to be burned' (*HALOT* 429).

205. The difficulty of marshes being set on fire suggested a connection with an Arabic word *ujum*, 'fortress', and this lies behind 'guard-towers' (REB).

root only occurs here in Jeremiah and refers to the startled reaction of those confronted by the unexpected) at the situation they find themselves in. On every side there is evidence of the closeness and effectiveness of the enemy, and they are unable to see the enemy clearly, let alone respond to what they are doing.

33. The reason for what will happen in Babylon is again stated. 'For' (*kî*) **this is what the LORD Almighty, the God of Israel, says: 'The Daughter of Babylon is like a threshing-floor at the time it is trampled.'**[206] 'Daughter of Babylon'/'daughter Babylon' (50:42) employs the idiom 'daughter of ...' to refer to the inhabitants of the place (4:31), possibly with overtones of beauty or delicacy (6:2), but these are now going to be set aside. It is the divine intention that determines what is to happen. Threshing floors were prepared for use by being swept clean and hollows filled and then trampled hard and flat ready for use. This was generally done in expectation of an immediate harvest. After the harvest is reaped, it is the grain (rather than the threshing-floor) that is trampled when oxen drawing a threshing sled over it. So here the description shows that Babylon's end is near because preparations have been made for processing the harvest. **The time to harvest her will soon come.** The emphasis of the original is perhaps better conveyed by 'yet a little while and ...' (NKJV, NRSV) than by 'soon' (NIV). Something momentous is anticipated when Babylon's enemies will reap the harvest of her devastation (cf. Isa. 17:5; Joel 3:13), the booty taken away from her ample treasuries.

6. Israel's Plea Answered (51:34-44)

OUTLINE

a.   The Devouring Monster (51:34-35)
b.   Israel's Vindicator (51:36-37)
c.   The Banquet of Death (51:38-40)
d.   Babylon Overthrown (51:41-43)
e.   The Punishment of Bel (51:44)

In this section of the Oracle against Babylon the five stanzas noted above may be discerned. The use of 'swallow' (*bālaʿ*) in the first and

---

206. Note the *i* in the first syllable of the hiphil infinitive construct *hidrîkāh* instead of the expected *a* (GCK §531).

last verses (vv. 34 and 44) provides an inclusion round the section. The second and fourth stanzas share the use of 'sea' in vv. 36 and 42; 'object of horror' in vv. 37, 41 and 43; and *gal*, 'heap' in v. 37 and 'waves' in v. 42. There is also the similarity between 'a place where no one lives' (v. 37) and 'a land where no one lives' (v. 43) (Aitken 1984:50-53).

a. The Devouring Monster (51:34-35)

34. In vv. 34-35 for the first time in the Oracle against Babylon we hear the voice of the people of Judah and Jerusalem as they utter their complaint against Nebuchadnezzar and his oppression. **Nebuchadnezzar king of Babylon has devoured us,**[207] that is, he has oppressed us and taken away the people from our land and its resources. 'Devoured'/'eaten' anticipates the description of Nebuchadnezzar as a serpent. **He has thrown us into confusion**. The verb is generally identified as from the root *hāmam* I, 'to bring into confusion' (Exod. 14:24; Josh. 10:10), which is used of causing panic in an enemy army with a view to defeating it. But there is also the possibility of a homonymous root meaning 'to suck dry' or 'drain out' (*HALOT* 251; *NIDOTTE* 1:1046) and this is reflected in the REB, 'he has sucked me dry' which anticipates the following idea of an empty jar. **He has made us an empty jar.** The depredations of the Babylonians had left neither people nor resources in the land; only the shell of a nation remained.

Like a serpent he has swallowed us is perhaps captured better by 'monster' as in the NRSV, NKJV or NASB, or 'dragon' in the REB, rather than 'serpent' (though see Exod. 7:9). The word *tannîn*, 'serpent', usually refers to a great sea creature (Gen. 1:21; Ps. 148:7), and so this passage may refer to a Jonah-like experience. But it is more probable that allusion is made here to the Canaanite and Babylonian cosmogonic beliefs. In their myths the world began with a battle against the forces of chaos, pictured as sea monsters. From Ps. 74:13-14 and Isa. 27:1 it appears that Leviathan was thought to be one of them. These monsters were used in Israel as symbols of the power

---

207. 'Us' on each of its five occurrences in this verse renders a pronominal suffix to the verb which the kethibh reads as plural, 'us', but for which the qere substitutes the singular 'me' (presumably a collective use). This is probably done because 'delicacies' has in fact a singular suffix 'my', and singulars are found throughout v. 35 agreeing with 'she who inhabits Zion' (singular). Most English versions follow the qere in treating all as singulars; the NIV makes all uniformly plural.

of evil and the historical opponents of the divine purpose (Isa. 51:9). There are a number of such references in this passage to Nebuchadnezzar as a great dragon and chaos monster which had come and consumed Israel. **And filled his stomach**[208] **with our delicacies**/'from my delights' (*mēʾăḏānāy*), taking away all that was choice in the land. There then is added without any connecting link, **and then has spewed us out.**[209] This may be part of the animal comparison: when it has greedily eaten too much it cannot hold it all down and has to vomit it up. But that seems to advance too far in the storyline of the interaction between Babylon and Judah, and it was not in fact Nebuchadnezzar who had to 'vomit up' Judah. Two other interpretations seem more probable. The NLT takes the asyndetic verb as an explanatory prose comment, 'he has thrown us out of our own country', which reflects Jeremiah's use of the root elsewhere in the prophecy in connection with banishment and exile (e.g. 8:3; 16:5; 24:9; 30:17). A further option reads the verb as in the Massoretic Text, 'he has rinsed me out' (RSV, NJPS), and envisages a reversion to the earlier figure of the jar; not only has it been emptied, so complete has been Nebuchadnezzar's spoliation of the land that it is like a jar washed completely clean.

35. '**May the violence** (*ḥamas*, a vicious attack on the person or property of another; 13:22) **done to our flesh be upon Babylon,**'[210] **say the inhabitants of Zion.** 'Flesh' (*šəʾēr*, a synonym of the more common *bāśār*) may relate to their bodies or it may be used in the sense of 'flesh and blood', that is, 'kinsmen' (RSV) or 'kindred' (NJPS). The parallelism with 'blood' in the following line may well favour the former. This is the curse which the Jews will pronounce on Babylon: that she be held responsible and compelled to make requital for her wrongdoing (cf. 50:10; 51:24; Ps. 137:8). '**May our blood be on those who live in Babylonia,**' **says Jerusalem.** For the idiom 'the blood of A upon B', see Lev. 20: 9, 11-13, 27. It is a call for the LORD

---

208. The word for 'stomach' refers to a second stomach of an animal and the statement that Nebuchadnezzar spewed them out suggests that God's covenant people were not completely annihilated by the enemy (*NIDOTTE* 2:728).

209. The NIV and NRSV follow the LXX and change the text to *hiddîḥānî*, from *nādaḥ*, 'to thrust out, expel', and so 'to spew out' or 'spit out' (NKJV). However, the MT *hĕdîḥānî* from *dûaḥ*, 'to wash away, push away', may stand with reference to rinsing out the empty vessel just mentioned.

210. Literally, 'my violence and my flesh upon Babylon', but the suffixes are objective genitives (GKC §135n; *IBHS* §16.4d).

to hold against the Babylonians the outrages they have committed. This is later seen as fulfilled in the destruction of the eschatological Babylon on which God avenges the blood of his servants (Rev. 6:10; 16:4-6; 19:2).

b. Israel's Vindicator (51:36-37)

36. In response to these complaints against the behaviour of Babylon and her king, the LORD says that he will act as Israel's advocate and judge. **Therefore** (*lākēn*) brings out that God speaks in response to his people's pleas, and probably also that his verdict is one of condemnation. **This is what the LORD says, 'See, I will defend your cause** (again a double use of the root *rîb*, 50:34) **and avenge you** (<√*nāqam*, 5:9).' That is, the LORD will act in court on their behalf to ensure that due retribution is paid for the injuries done to them. He will not only present their case against Babylon (2:9; 12:1; 20:12; 25:31; cf. 50:34), but will also act to ensure that action follows when judgment is given in their favour. **I will dry up her sea and make her springs dry.** 'Sea' in Hebrew can refer to any large area of water (e.g. the Nile in Isa. 18:2; 19:5; Nah. 3:8), and here it is to the Euphrates and all the irrigation canals and lakes which were fed from it, and on which Babylon's wealth and security depended. They are going to vanish away along with her 'springs'/'fountains' (<*māqôr*, 2:13), naturally occurring sources of water.

37. **Babylon will become a heap of ruins** (<*gal*; 9:11), **a haunt of jackals** (9:11), **an object of horror and scorn** (25:9), **a place where no one lives** (4:7; cf. 2:15). Such expressions have been frequently used to describe the desolation that would come upon Jerusalem, but now they are cumulated to emphasise both the certainty and the severity of the inglorious end which will overtake the great city that had so dominated the world. Babylon, like Hazor (49:33), will experience the curse of the great king.

c. The Banquet of Death (51:38-40)

38. **Her people all/'together' roar like young lions, they growl like lion cubs.** The Babylonians are compared to lions in terms of their aggression against others and their readiness to attack them. For 'roar' see on 2:15 (Amos 3:4). Perhaps this focuses not just on the general attitude of Babylon towards the nations they had conquered, but more particularly on the careless revelry that preceded the capture of the city (v. 31; Dan. 5).

39. **But while they are aroused/'in their heat'** would then describe

the glow of their exulting over the victories they have gained, or the
results of excessive celebration, 'inflamed with all their wine' (NLT).
'I shall cause their drinking bouts to end in fever' (REB) understands
the 'heat' to be that of illness, but disregards the word order of the
original. **I will set out a feast for them and make them drunk, so
that they shout with laughter.**[211] The imagery of a banquet at which
drinking plays a major part is used to present the LORD's judgment. It
will not be the sort of celebration the Babylonians had intended
because the LORD will reorganise the event. They will become so
drunk with their successes that they no longer stay alert, and so at the
very time they are congratulating themselves and basking in their
achievements, a threat will arise which they will be incapable of
responding to. The LORD will intervene in their affairs and change the
outcome to ensure that their drunken stupor ends in an eternal hang-
over. **'Then sleep for ever and not awake,' declares the LORD.**
When they least expect it, they will be taken away into eternal abandonment. Sleep is an almost universal metaphor for death. There is no
doubt a picture here of what would happen on the night Babylon was
taken (Dan. 5), but the prophecy, though remarkably fulfilled in those
events, was probably originally understood in more general terms. It is
a picture of a people so taken up with enjoying the trappings of
success, that when the judgment of God suddenly confronts them, it
sweeps them completely away.

40. The same picture is found in the following verse. **I will bring
them down like lambs to slaughter, like rams and goats.** Lions no
more! Lambs, sheep and goats are used of different classes in Israel in
Isa. 34:6 and Ezek. 39:18, and may here refer to different groups in
Babylon. 'Slaughter' (<√*ṭābah*) refers to ordinary butchering for
human consumption. The phrase depicts the unsuspecting and unresist-
ing approach of the animal that is to be slain (11:19). So too the
Babylonians will be incapable of mustering any effective opposition to
their enemies and will go helplessly to their divinely imposed doom.

d. Babylon Overthrown (51:41-43)
41. Verses 41-43 express once more the fact that Babylon will be
captured. Her destruction will be so horrendous that the whole world

---

211. 'Shout with laughter' (*yaʿălôzû* <√*ʿālaz*, 'to exult, triumph') seems to
have been read by the LXX as *yeʿulāppû* <√*ʿālap̄*, 'to fall into a swoon' (so
RSV). It is argued for this understanding that it makes better sense of the
ləmaʿan, 'so that'. They will be made so drunk that they pass out and enter
into a sleep that never ends.

will be astonished. **How Sheshach will be captured, the boast/'praise' of the whole earth seized!** Sheshach is an athbash for Babel/Babylon that has already been used (25:26; cf. v. 1). It is difficult to see that there was any need for secrecy about the identity of the subject of Jeremiah's prophecy at this point. Perhaps there were circumstances when it was dangerous to speak openly about Babylon—and certainly in any negative fashion—and the name had become common in such contexts. Its employment here is then mocking the once feared occupying power whose fortunes are going to be completely reversed. Even though Babylon had been universally praised for her power, magnificence and might, she is going to be captured/seized (<√*tāpaś*, 'to grasp'; v. 32). **What a horror Babylon will be among the nations!** 'Horror' (*šammâ*) is the word that Jeremiah has often used to describe the impact of invasion by Babylon on others. Now the tables are turned, and looking at her fate, a shudder runs through all who see the devastation that engulfs her.

42. The sea will rise over Babylon; its roaring waves will cover her. This picture of too much water is an ironic contrast to v. 36 (compare the scenes in 46:7; 47:2). It is unlikely that a literal reference is intended here, whether to the Euphrates, its irrigation canals and lakes (cf. 'many waters' in v. 13), or to an inundation from the Persian Gulf, many miles distant. For one thing the next verse speaks of a dry and desert land—so at least one of the descriptions must be metaphorical. Instead the sea is an image for the invading hordes of the enemy army inundating Babylon as they advance. 'Roaring' (*hāmôn*; 3:23) implies both abundance and noisy confusion. It is also probable that there is allusion to the beliefs that were prevalent in Babylon itself (46:7; 47:2). In its creation myth, Marduk the god of Babylon overcame the water chaos monster Tiamat, and because he had defeated her, the world as we now know it came into existence. In this context which speaks of the overthrow of the Babylonian god (cf. v. 44), it is quite likely that the imagery of the invading army as the sea conveyed the idea of the destruction of Babylon being a reversal of the created order, an overthrow of the Babylonian gods, and a return to primeval chaos.

43. The overthrow of Babylon is then expressed using a different set of imagery, not dissimilar to that found in v. 37. There had to be no doubt about the certainty of what was going to happen, no matter how improbable the collapse of the great empire might have seemed. **Her towns will be desolate** (*šammâ*, cf. v. 41), **a dry and desert land** ('land of drought', 2:6; 50:12; 'land of deserts', again see 2:6; 50:12).

It is also predicted that Babylon will become **a land where no one lives**/'a land one will not dwell in them', with 'in them' referring back to the cities, and so equivalent to 'a land in whose cities none will dwell'. It will also be a land **through which no man travels** (2:6). These are conditions that Babylon's military aggression had brought to other places, and so here the prediction is not just a matter of downfall, but of retribution.

e. The Punishment of Bel (51:44)
44. I will punish Bel in Babylon brings out the demonic background to the situation (similar to that which had prevailed in Egypt, Exod. 12:12). Babylonian policy was not just a matter of politics and human cruelty, but had arisen out of a religion and set of value beliefs that were corrupt to their core. When the city falls, the decay and emptiness of its religious pretensions are shown up. The fate of the patron god (Bel, cf. 50:2) is necessarily bound up in the fate of his devotees (cf. Isa. 46:1). Just as Nebuchadnezzar had been viewed as swallowing Judah, so Bel, representing Babylon, has swallowed the wealth of the nations (the same root is used here and in v. 34 in reference to swallowing). The reference probably goes beyond what was devoted as a gift to the gods in their temples (such as the sacred Temple vessels in Dan. 1:3) to the whole of what was plundered from the nations. But now the LORD says, **And make him spew out what he has swallowed.**[212] It is not a voluntary restoration, for God has to act to ensure the prey is disgorged. (The term used for 'make spew out' is quite different from that found in v. 34 for 'spew out'.) **The nations will no longer stream to him.** For 'stream' see on Isa. 2:2 and Mic. 4:1, where the nations are pictured as streaming to Zion which has become the centre of the world. Here it is predicted that no longer will kings and princes, tribute and traders flock to Babylon; it will be a ruin. Its power and prestige will be wrested from it. **And**[213] **the wall of Babylon will fall.** The massive fortifications round the city represented Babylon's best endeavours to guarantee her security and prestige. There were two inner defensive walls, one about twelve feet (3.7 m) wide and after a twenty-three foot (7 m) gap another immense wall twenty-one feet (6.4 m) thick, round which towers were positioned at

---

212. There is perhaps a wordplay between 'Bel' (*bēl*) and 'has swallowed' (*bil'û* <√*bālaʿ*).
213. Verses 44b-49a are not in the LXX, probably due to haplography as the scribe's eye moved from 'Babylon has fallen' to 'with respect to Babylon they fell'.

regular intervals. Once these walls were breached the city was helpless before its attackers.

7. Destruction Inevitable (51:45-53)

OUTLINE

a. Unsettled Times (51:45-46)
b. Universal Exultation (51:47-48)
c. Measure for Measure (51:49)
d. Do Not Linger! (51:50-51)
e. Inescapable Overthrow (51:52-53)

The sixth and final major section of the Oracle against Babylon consists of five stanzas, of which the first and last share the same pattern: summons to flight, exhortation, and announcement of judgment. There are links between stanzas one and four through the synonyms 'run'/'deliver oneself' in v. 45 and 'escape' in v. 50, and the mention of 'heart' in vv. 46 and 50, the latter not being obvious in the NIV. The second and fifth stanzas are linked by means of *ḥālal*, 'slain' in v. 47 and 'wounded' in v. 52, as well as the expressions 'Behold! days are coming' (lit. vv. 47 and 52), 'in all her land' (lit. vv. 47 and 52), and 'destroyers will come to her' (vv. 48 and 53). The third stanza sets out the focal theme of Babylon's judgment (Aitken 1984:53-56).

a. Unsettled Times (51:45-46)

45. In v. 45 on, the LORD speaks to his own people, whom he recognises as such. The covenant Overlord once more confers status on those he acknowledges and advises them on how to behave in the situation they find themselves. **Come out of her, my people!** (cf. 50:8; 51:6; Isa. 52:11-12). The incredible thing is that the people need to be urged to escape from their oppressor (cf. Rev. 18:4 for the city's hold upon those whose true home was elsewhere). Material conditions in Babylon were quite attractive, and many exiles had settled in there all too comfortably so that when the opportunity to leave did arise, the majority of Jews stayed behind and did not return to Judah. But remaining in Babylon was to invite assimilation into the culture of the city and to risk being involved in its final overthrow. **Run for your lives!**/'Save (plural) a man his life (*nepeš*, 2:34)', that is, 'Let each of you save his own life, or himself' (cf. v. 6). **Run from the fierce**

anger (*hărôn ʿap*, 4:8) **of the LORD.** Each is being called on to take action to escape from involvement in the catastrophe. Even though the LORD's ire is not directed at them, they will be swept away in the general calamity unless they act appropriately.

46. The focus in this verse is on the interim period before the prophecy is fulfilled. It was going to be a turbulent time, and so the people are encouraged: **Do not**[214] **lose heart or be afraid when rumours are heard in the land.** For 'rumour' see on 10:22. The vast Babylonian empire was never totally at peace. At any time one or other of its many subject peoples was liable to be restless, and outside powers were pressing in at the edges of its domains. This was true before the death of Nebuchadnezzar in 562 BC, but even more so afterwards, when in addition the situation was compounded by internal power struggles. It would have been easy on any of these occasions to have interpreted events as indicating the immediate fulfilment of Jeremiah's prophecy with the consequent temptation to become embroiled in the plotting. But that was not the way forward. The people were to await the decisive move of the LORD. Though the prophet was certain that the downfall of Babylon would come, he envisaged an initial period of recurrent crises. **One rumour comes**[215] **this year, another the next, rumours of violence in the land** (or possibly 'earth', REB) **and of ruler against ruler.** But the people are warned against too hasty optimism with the danger of consequent dejection when Babylon proved capable of dealing with and weathering such emergencies (cf. use made of language in Matt. 24:6; Mark 13:7; Luke 21:9). The people were not to become confused in the turbulent conditions that were envisaged, and which occurred after the death of Nebuchadnezzar in 562 BC, when the following seven years saw four different kings on the throne of Babylon (see Volume 1, Introduction §3.13). Even so the remains of the empire managed to hold out against increasing Persian pressure for a further seventeen years until 539 BC.

b. Universal Exultation (51:47-48)
47. *lākēn*, 'therefore', is translated **for** in the NIV. The connection seems to be that these times of unrest are precursors of the final showdown, and when the unrest occurs the people are to conclude with confidence that therefore **the time will surely come.** This employs

---

214. An independent clause introduced by *pen*, 'lest', is unique in Jeremiah. It may be taken as an introductory subordinate clause, 'Lest your heart faint when these things happen, so look days are coming.'

215. *ûbāʾ* is masculine whereas the subject is feminine (GKC §145o).

Jeremiah's phrase 'Behold! days are coming' (7:32; 30:3): it is certain, indeed it is already underway, but the precise timing of events has not been made clear to the prophet. However, there should be no doubt about the LORD's action. **When I will punish** (<*pāqad*) **the idols of Babylon.** The problem is at root spiritual because allegiance to false gods had distorted the perception of the regime and its subjects. Inevitably the LORD would scrutinise their affairs and his evaluation of their conduct would be negative. **Her whole land will be disgraced and her slain will all lie fallen within her.** This description again raises the problem of the timescale involved in that Cyrus' invasion did not bring widespread havoc. There is prophetic foreshortening throughout this description (cf. v. 52) where Babylon's downfall is presented against a backdrop of the final overthrow of the powers of evil.

48. Then heaven and earth and all that is in them will shout for joy over Babylon. Babylon's empire had been enormous, and there is introduced a new thought, that the joy at her downfall is going to be more than international: the whole cosmos will be jubilant. Creation, animate and inanimate, unites in joyful song (cf. Isa. 44:23; 49:13; 52:9; 55:12; Ps. 96:11-13). This rejoicing occurs not just because of the widespread human suffering that had been involved in her cruelty, but because at root her empire was hostile to the LORD, and the LORD's creation rejoices in his antagonists being overthrown. The reason for their joy is stated: **for** (*kî*) **out of the north destroyers will attack**[216] **her** (cf. 50:3, 9, 41). The attack would come from the north where the Persians had consolidated their control, and since it was what the LORD had decreed, it would be successful. For 'destroyers' (<√*šādad*) see also vv. 53 and 56.

The material shows such similarities to other passages, particularly those mentioned in Isaiah, that critical scholars often adjudged it to be a secondary interpolation. However, it is probable that Jeremiah was looking back to the prophecy of Isaiah and was struggling to see how it should be applied in the circumstances that had been disclosed to him. He is brought to realise how the two prophetic visions are related. What better way was there to encourage the people than by showing the relevance of the previous message of the LORD!

---

216. *yābô^c* is singular with a plural subject (GKC §145o). Sometimes it is marked by sebir [qere] suggesting reading should be *yābō^cû*, also found in some manuscripts.

c. Measure for Measure (51:49)

49. The basic thought of v. 49 is clear though the grammatical details are not (the first 'because of' has to be supplied by the NIV[217]). There is set up a correspondence between what has happened in Israel because of Babylon, and what will happen to Babylon.[218] **Babylon must fall because of Israel's slain, just as the slain in all the earth have fallen because of Babylon.** 'Slain' picks up from vv. 4 and 47. This is the retribution that the LORD will bring on her (cf. v. 35). Notice that justice demands that action is taken not only for Israel's slain but for the all the atrocities of Babylonian aggression.

d. Do Not Linger! (51:50-51)

50. Again (as in v. 45) the exhortation to flee is given. **You who have escaped from the sword, leave[219] and do not linger!** Those addressed were not among Israel's slain (v. 49) but had survived the invasion of their land and had been deported to Babylon. Now they, as exiles, are urged to return home (v. 45; 50:8). **Remember the LORD in a distant land**/'from afar' (*mērāhôq*) may also convey the thought of temporal separation: 'look back to the past'. 'Remember' is more than mental recall; it is a summons to action (2:2). They are called on to align themselves with the LORD's cause (perhaps that would have involved abandoning any Babylonian practices they might have adopted during their exile there) and to commit themselves to him and all that he has pledged himself to be to his people. **Think on Jerusalem**/'Let Jerusalem come up upon your heart/mind.' The memories of the past are to engender a renewed devotion as they consider all that the LORD had previously given to them.

51. But the response of the people as they looked back was not just to

---

217. The NIV 'because of' assumes a *lə* has fallen out of the text before *haləlê*, corresponding to the *lə* before *bābel* in the second part of the verse. The *lə* with the infinitive construct of *nāpal* is taken as an expression of what is about to, or must, occur (*IBHS* §36.2.3g; GKC §114i). An alternative rendering of the idiom is found in the NKJV, 'As Babylon ⌐has caused⌐ the slain of Israel to fall, so at Babylon the slain of all the earth shall fall', where the second clause perhaps indicates those fighting for Babylon from all the nations under her sway.

218. The correspondence is expressed in Hebrew by the repetition *gam ... gam*, 'not only ... but also'; 'both ... and'; 'as ... so'.

219. *hiləkû* for *ləkû* occurs only here, perhaps to bring out the force of the verb, whose imperative had been weakened into a general interjection, cf. GKC §69x.

former blessings, but also to the catastrophe that had overtaken them. It seems that Jeremiah gives voice to the prevailing disillusionment. **'We are disgraced** (<√*bôš*, 2:26), **for** (*kî*) **we have been insulted and shame covers our faces.'** Their experiences at the hands of the Babylonians have left them downtrodden and depressed, and they cannot entertain good hopes for the future because of the reality of their present condition. They are experiencing shame (<√*kālam*, 3:3) since what they have undergone—and still are undergoing—runs counter to what they had expected. More than personal loss of dignity and status is involved; there has been open violation of the Jerusalem sanctuary. **Because** (*kî*) **foreigners have entered the holy places of the LORD's house.** 'Foreigners/'strangers' (2:25) are not merely people who are not known; there are negative overtones of those who are hostile, political enemies. Thinking about Jerusalem does not engender hope. It merely reminds them of the success of Babylon. The plural 'holy places' denotes the various parts of the sanctuary, either the multiple holy precincts within the tabernacle (Lev. 21:23) or the Temple complex (Ps. 73:17). If the LORD had not prevented such violation of his holy place in the past, could he be relied on to reverse the situation in the future?

e. Inescapable Overthrow (51:52-53)

52. 'Therefore' (*lākēn*) at the beginning of v. 52 seems to react to this by presenting again the LORD's assurance of what the future holds. It is a measure of the spiritual traumatisation of the people that the message, which is very similar to that of vv. 47-49, has to be repeated. **'But days are coming,' declares the LORD, 'when I will punish** (<√*pāqad*; no doubt here as to who is the superior) **her idols, and throughout her land the wounded will groan.'** Again we have the phrase for the definite but unspecified future. The focus is on the idolatry of Babylon, a wider reference to the religious basis of the situation (cf. v. 44). The false religion is overthrown in the overthrow of the land. Throughout Babylonia there will be heard loud groaning from the mortally wounded (<√*ḥālal*, 'to pierce'; 'slain' v. 4), those not yet dead but fatally injured.

53. Even if (*kî*) **Babylon reaches the sky and** ('if', *kî*) **fortifies** (<√*bāṣar* III, 'to make inaccessible', perhaps connected with *bāṣar* I, 'to cut off') **her lofty stronghold** reminds one of the tower of Babel, whose builders sought to reach up to heaven with its height (Gen. 10:4; cf. also Isa. 14:12). That had been motivated by human pride and arrogance, and there still remained in Babylon the same desire to achieve greatness by human effort and to maintain it by human wisdom. But though Nebuchadnezzar had engaged in a massive build-ing and fortification programme at Babylon, it would be to no avail because the LORD had determined otherwise. **'I will send destroyers against her,' declares the LORD.** A more literal rendering, such as 'From me destroyers would come upon her' (NRSV), brings out the parallel with 'Out of the north destroyers will come to her' (v. 47). The plural 'destroyers' (<√*šādad*; cf. v. 1) implies more than one enemy (contrast 48:8, 18, 32), probably the composite forces under Cyrus, but perhaps also later aggressors.

8. The God of Retribution (51:54-58)

In this conclusion to the poem Jeremiah takes up many of the themes that had been anticipated in the introductory verses (50:2-3) and subsequently developed. Here they are again mentioned to give a vivid and emphatic finale to what the prophet has been shown of the destruc-tion that is to engulf Babylon.

54. The sound of a cry comes from Babylon, the sound of great destruction (*šeber*, 4:6) **from the land of the Babylonians!** The language is immediate and vivid. It could be an invitation to hear: 'Listen! —a cry from Babylon!' (NRSV). It is a shriek of pain and distress (for 'cry' cf. 48:3; 50:22, 46). The break-up of the land rever-berates in the prophet's ears as he presses upon his audience the certainty of what the LORD will do.

55. 'For' (*kî*) there is no doubt that **the LORD will destroy** (<√*šādad*, v. 53) **Babylon; he will silence her noisy din/**'great voice'. It is on the point of happening. Graphically Jeremiah portrays 'the great noise' of the city as it goes busily about its daily tasks being drowned out by the roar of the advancing enemy forces. **Waves ⌐of enemies⌐ will rage like great waters; the roar** (*šaʿôn*, 'tumult'; 25:31) **of their voices will resound.** What is literally 'their waves' (*gallêhem*) may refer to the advancing enemy forces, or perhaps be a further description of the noisy din of Babylon itself, cf. 'her waves' (NKJV). Probably it is intended to pick up the imagery of the enemy as the sea flooding in destructively on Babylon (v. 42).

56. This will happen 'for' (*kî*) **a destroyer will come against Babylon**, picking up the theme of 'destroyer' from v. 53, but this time in the singular. **Her warriors will be captured, and their bows will be broken.** This is a picture of abject defeat in battle, where 'bow' stands for all military hardware (49:35). **For** (*kî*) **the LORD is a God of**

retribution. Babylon's fall is not to be explained merely as the outworking of historical and political processes. It is divinely decreed and divinely controlled, and so reflects the character of the LORD, the covenant God, as *ʾēl gəmûlôt*, 'a God of retribution', one who makes payment appropriately and in full (v. 6b; Isa. 59:18). **He will repay in full** may equally convey the idea 'he shall certainly repay' (<√*šillēm*), that is, in the case of Babylon. It is also possible that the imperfect here is conveying what is characteristically true of God, 'he certainly repays', rather than just indicating what will be true of his specific treatment of Babylon.

57. There are then added words of the LORD to emphasise the point: **'I will make her officials and wise men drunk, her governors, officers and warriors as well; they will sleep for ever and not awake,' declares the King, whose name is the LORD Almighty.** It is the picture of the banquet at which those who are given the cup of destruction are made drunk and pass into oblivion (v. 39). For 'governors, officers', see on 50:35. 'The King' (48:15) emphasises the true source of authority and power, as distinct from Nebuchadnezzar and his successors. Their claims to authority and dominion are mere phantoms in comparison with the power and control of the LORD Almighty/'the LORD of hosts', who has under his sway the armies of heaven and of earth. Throughout history he is forwarding his purpose of removing every force that opposes his will and purpose. For the doom of eternal sleep, see on v. 39.

58. Verse 58 adds one final item to the description of the impending doom of the empire. **This is what the LORD Almighty says: 'Babylon's thick wall**[220] **will be** 'completely' or 'certainly' **levelled**[221] **and her high gates set on fire.** The defences of Babylon which contributed so much to her feelings of security and power will be of no avail to her in the impending onslaught (cf. v. 44). Her impressive fortifications were ordinarily a source of awe to her subject peoples. These included the nine huge gates of the inner wall, such as the Ishtar Gate—the only one to be excavated—which was 30 foot (9 m) high

---

220. The MT is literally 'the walls of thick Babylon' (*ḥōmôt bābel hārəḥābâ*) or as the REB renders it 'the walls of broad Babylon'. Many Hebrew manuscripts, the LXX and the Vulgate read a singular *ḥômat* instead of a plural form, and this reading is adopted by most English translations. 'Broad walls' (NKJV) apparently assumes that the singular adjective is a transcriptional error.

221. 'Levelled' (<√*ʿûr*, 'to lay bare') is a hithpael verb preceded by a pilpel infinitive absolute for emphasis.

with massive square towers on either side.

The peoples exhaust themselves (<√*yāgaʿ*, 'to grow weary', often associated with strain and hard work; 45:3) **for nothing, the nations' labour is only fuel for the flames.**[222] These lines reflect the thought of Hab. 2:13, 'Has not the LORD Almighty determined that the people's labour (literally, the labour of the peoples, plural) is only fuel for the fire, that the nations exhaust themselves for nothing?' There are, however, several notable differences. In Habakkuk 'the peoples' are mentioned first, and the verb *yāgaʿ* is used of them in the sense 'work till exhausted'; the 'nations' are mentioned second, and the root *yāʿap*, 'to grow weary' is used of them. This describes the tiredness caused by a physically, emotionally or spiritually draining situation. The variations between what is found in Habakkuk and what is found here are such as to suggest that neither is drawing directly on the other, but that both places reflect a saying that was well-known at the time. However, there is a reapplication of the thought regarding the futility of human endeavour from the defences of Judah against the Babylonians to Babylon's defences against the onslaught they would have to face.

9. Seraiah's Mission (51:59-64)

As an historical appendix to the Oracle against Babylon, this section adds interesting historical background—not, however, without raising a considerable number of problems at the same time. The particularity of the setting is unlike the sort of material found elsewhere in the Oracles against the Nations. But the incident reinforces the theme of the preceding chapters. It is the permanent defeat of Babylon that is the surest testimony to the sovereignty of the LORD, and this is remarkably foreshadowed and demonstrated by this episode. Seraiah and his scroll here act as counterparts to the scrolls written by his brother Baruch (chaps. 32 and 36; see also Introduction §2.6).

59. This is the message Jeremiah 'the prophet' (omitted by the NIV) **gave to/'commanded'** (with the substance of the command delayed

---

222. The NKJV rendering 'And the nations, because of the fire; and they shall be weary' reflects the curious syntax of the MT. It is generally supposed that the *waw*-consecutive perfect form *wəyāʿēpû* is a transcriptional error for an imperfect, *yiyʿāpû*. It may also be noted that *HALOT* (92) distinguishes a second root *ʿēš*, 'a trifle' both here and in Hab. 2:13, possibly originating in the thought that fire leads to worthless ashes. In that case the phrase *bədê-ʿēš* would mean 'for nought', but English translations prefer to keep the rendering 'for fire'.

until v. 61) **the staff officer Seraiah son of Neriah, the son of Mahseiah, when he went to Babylon with Zedekiah king of Judah in the fourth year of his reign.** Seraiah is given the same genealogy as Baruch (32:12), indicating he was his brother. 'Staff officer' or 'quartermaster'[223] is an army officer responsible for deciding on the quarters for the army on the move. In the present context of Zedekiah going to Babylon, presumably Seraiah would travel ahead of the group to obtain suitable accommodation. The fourth year of Zedekiah's reign (594/3 BC) is one about which we have considerable knowledge, including details about the conference in chapter 27 where five other nations came up to Jerusalem presumably to plot against Nebuchadnezzar. Nothing seems to have come of it on that occasion. Did the Babylonians find out about it? Is this Zedekiah being summoned to give an account of what he was about? Or is it him going on his own initiative to offer homage to Nebuchadnezzar and secure his own position? If Zedekiah is going to acknowledge Nebuchadnezzar's overlordship, then the whole incident contrasts the political efforts of Zedekiah with respect to Babylon and his uncertainty and indecisiveness regarding the rule of the LORD who is the real and ultimate controller of all.

Indeed, there have been those who have argued that Zedekiah did not go to Babylon as so major an event would not have gone unrecorded elsewhere in Scripture. The Septuagint translation contains surprising additions to the Hebrew text—normally it omits items found there. It reads, 'This is the message the LORD commanded Jeremiah to speak to the officer of the tribute Seraiah son of Neriah, the son of Mahseiah when he went to Babylon from Zedekiah king of Judah in the fourth year of his reign.' This changes Seraiah's post in a way which makes sense of him going to Babylon with Judah's tribute, but without the thought of Zedekiah going also. However, the absence of corroboration does not undermine the Hebrew text which presents events that are plausible in the circumstances as we know them.

60. As the Hebrew stands, Jeremiah the prophet commands Seraiah what to do and say. The details of this are not given until v. 61. First there is additional background information. **Jeremiah had written on a scroll about all the disasters that would come upon Babylon—all that had been recorded concerning Babylon.** It is emphasised that it

---

223. *śar mənûḥâ* is only found here. Taking *mənûḥâ* as meaning 'resting-place' yields the 'officer of the resting-place'/'quartermaster'. The LXX understands it as 'official over tribute', a meaning *mənûḥâ* has in 2 Kgs. 17:3-4; Hos. 10:6.

is one scroll, a single scroll (*sēper 'eḥād*), but it is unclear what the significance of this was. Is it that the message was very brief, or that despite the length of the message, it could all be contained in a single scroll? This raises the relationship between the scroll and chapters 50 and 51. Certainly 'all these words that had been recorded' refer back to the previous chapters, and that substantiates the view that in 594 BC Jeremiah at the same time as he was urging submission to Babylon was also speaking about Babylon's eventual downfall. It does leave open, however, the possibility that Jeremiah added further material to these chapters at a subsequent period.

61. He said to Seraiah, 'When you get to Babylon, see that you read all these words aloud.' 'Aloud' is an NIV supplement. At this period all reading involved vocalising the sound of the words. But was Seraiah to have an audience? Certainly the Babylonians could not have been intended, for if they heard such a message, Seraiah would have sealed his own fate. There is no suggestion that he was being sent on a suicide mission. He may have been alone or in the company of some of the exiles who were already there. It would seem, however, that the purpose of the reading was not to inform Seraiah or others of the contents of the scroll, but to symbolise the effectiveness of the word of the LORD being set loose to work in Babylon itself. This was a vivid way of demonstrating that the LORD's writ ran there also.

62. Then say, 'O LORD, you have said you will destroy (<√*kārat*, hiphil, 'to cut off') **this place, so that neither man nor animal will live in it;** 'for' or possibly 'but' (*kî*) **it will be desolate for ever.'**[224] The use of 'then' (NIV) suggests that Seraiah's statement of this summary of the message is a subsequent stage to his reading, but the 'and' used in the NASB and NRSV leaves open the question of whether or not this might have been all that was on the scroll. At any rate, the scroll presented the gist of the message that Jeremiah was proclaiming about the future of Babylon. It could be summed up in one word, 'desolations' (*šəmāmâ* plural; cf. 50:3; 51:26).

63-64. When you finish reading this scroll, tie a stone to it and throw it into the Euphrates. This describes the further action Seraiah was to carry out. A parchment scroll might have floated, and the stone was to ensure that the scroll sank in the water of the Euphrates, show-ing that neither scroll nor Babylon would ever rise again. **Then say, 'So will Babylon sink to rise no more because of the disaster I will**

---

224. Unusually the word is plural *šiməmōt*. Perhaps it is used as a plural of intensification.

bring upon her.' The plunging of the scroll into the water was symbolic of the utter destruction yet to come upon Babylon. It is improper to classify this action as magical in nature. 'This story obviously presupposes ultimately the idea of a writing filled with power, which exercised its disastrous effect in the midst of the doomed land. Such magical usages are common among more primitive people' (Lindblom 1962:119). However, this action is preceded by the reading of the word and by prayer, which sets it in the context of the will and purpose of God. It is not an attempt to coerce a supernatural response by use of some formula or action. The ways of Babylon and the LORD will ultimately diverge, and it is Babylon which will be the loser in the final analysis.

And her people will fall translates one word, which is the same as the last word in v. 58, 'and they will weary themselves' (*wəyāʿēpû*). Some see the presence of the word here as a scribal error (it is not present in the LXX) and so omit it (NRSV, REB). Otherwise it is a final element in the doom awaiting Babylon.

The words of Jeremiah end here/'Thus far the words of Jeremiah' are a significant scribal annotation to indicate that chapter 52 was added as a supplement, and is not to be attributed to Jeremiah. Such colophons were a standard device in the ancient East, added at the end of written material and not forming part of the main text (cf. 48:47). The closest Old Testament parallel is 'This concludes the prayers of David son of Jesse' (Ps. 72:20), which also names the author of the preceding material.

The words also form a suitable conclusion to the book of 'the words of Jeremiah' (1:1).[225] The story has been told from start to finish: from the boiling pot tipped over in Judah's direction (1:13-15) to the mighty empire of Babylon sunk beneath the waves.

---

225. The phrase 'The words of Jeremiah end here' is not found in the LXX, where also 1:1 reads, 'The word of God which came to Jeremiah ...'. This certainly raises the possibility of both formulations in the MT being deliberate editorial devices to form an inclusion.

XVI. A SUPPLEMENT: PROPHECY FULFILLED

(52:1-34)

OUTLINE

A. Zedekiah's Rebellion and Fate (52:1-11)
B. The Fate of Jerusalem and the People (52:12-16)
C. The Temple Vessels (52:17-23)
D. The Captivity (52:24-30)
E. Jehoiachin's Release (52:31-34)

The clear annotation in 51:64 leaves no doubt that chapter 52 has been added as a supplement to the prophecy by a later hand. Some clues as to who might have done so, and when, are provided by the relationship between this chapter and the parallel passage in 2 Kgs. 24:18–25:30. While much of this material is found there almost verbatim, there are also significant differences by way of omission, inclusion and varia- tion. For instance, the spelling of Nebuchadnezzar here is as Nebuchadrezzar which, though common in Jeremiah, is uniformly found with *n* in Kings. Additional information is included in v. 10 where mention is made that Nebuchadnezzar killed all the officials of Judah, a fact not in 2 Kgs. 25:7 (but it is recorded in 39:6); in v. 23 the details regarding the pomegranate decorations are not paralleled in 2 Kings; and in vv. 28-30 precise numbers are given for three deporta- tions from Judah, including one deportation not mentioned in 2 Kings and with the other figures differing significantly from those in Kings. On the other hand, the narrative about Gedaliah's assassination (2 Kgs. 25:22-26) is omitted here, probably because it had already been told in greater detail in chapters 40–41.

Now there is biblical precedent for material being found in a prophetic work and in the history of Kings. Much of Isa. 36–39 is paralleled, frequently verbatim, in 2 Kgs. 18:13–20:19. However, there is the noticeable difference that the writer of Kings acknowledges the presence and importance of Isaiah, whereas he is silent regarding Jeremiah (as indeed is chap. 52 as well! See also Volume 1, Introduc- tion §2.4). It would seem that the author of Kings knew of the existence of Jeremiah's prophecies, quite possibly in the form in which we now have chapters 1–51, and that either he or some other party having access to the same information as underlay Kings decided to add chapter 52 as a concluding supplement to Jeremiah's work. That this was done after the composition of the Kings narrative is indicated by the additional details 'till the day of his death' (v. 11) and especially the use of the same phrase in reference to Jehoiachin in v. 34. There is also included material that is relevant to Kings but not to Jeremiah, for instance, the notice of Zedekiah's accession (vv. 1-3), but the varia- tions are such that chapter 52 does not merely copy Kings.

Views differ as to whether Kings was written in two stages, most of the material coming from the time of Josiah with a later exilic conclu- sion, or at one time late in the exile, possibly around 550 BC. On either interpretation 2 Kgs. 25 is reckoned to have originated in Babylonia, and the same background holds for this chapter of Jeremiah. In both there is shown to be acquaintance with affairs in Babylon (vv. 31-34; 2 Kgs. 25:27-30) and Jeremiah 52 also quotes information that seems to come from official (i.e. Babylonian) records in vv. 28-30. Traditions vary as to the fate of Jeremiah and Baruch in Egypt, some state that both met their deaths there, but others imply that Baruch was brought by Nebuchadnezzar to Babylon (perhaps Josephus, *Ant.*10.9.7). If so, then it might well still be Baruch's hand that is to be detected in the addition of this chapter.

But whoever it was who added this material, can we discern what their motives were for doing so? The main intention was undoubtedly to reinforce Jeremiah's status as a prophet of the LORD. There could be no doubt that what he had foretold had come to pass, unlike the optimistic and unfounded predicts of the peace prophets. From an interpretative point of view what is most significant is that this chapter is one of the four times that events connected with the fall of Jerusalem are related in the Old Testament (also 39:1-14; 2 Kgs. 25; 2 Chron. 36:11-21; Jer. 39:1-14). The event was traumatic and epochal, defining a major change in the fortunes of the people. The chapter restates the tragedy that had befallen the city.

But presumably more was at stake in the inclusion of chapter 52 than an accurate perception of their national history, written perhaps some thirty years after the event. Jeremiah's message had also included the prospect of restoration after the seventy years of captivity. It has been argued that the inclusion of the narrative regarding Jehoiachin in 2 Kgs. 25:27-30 was the opening of a window of hope for the future of the Jews. Although it is possible to argue that the outlook of this supplementary chapter is even more gloomy than that of Kings, it too ends with the same record of Jehoiachin's release, and it may possibly have been included to indicate that there was still a way forward, but only through the outworking of divine grace.

Another interesting relationship is that between this chapter and the Septuagintal text of Jeremiah. Because the Oracles against the Nations are located earlier in the LXX, chapter 52 follows the message concerning Baruch in chapter 45 (MT), and appears even more as a later addition to the text. The LXX version of the chapter has several omissions in vv. 2-3, v. 15 and vv. 28-30. It may well be that the textual history of this supplementary chapter differs from that of the rest of the LXX. It was probably added at a later stage by some third party to update the LXX by bringing it into alignment with the Massoretic tradition in the inclusion of this material.

A. ZEDEKIAH'S REBELLION AND FATE (52:1-11)

1. The account of Zedekiah's accession and reign found in vv. 1-3 closely mirrors that of 2 Kgs. 24:18-20 (cf. also 2 Chron. 36:11-14). **Zedekiah was twenty-one years old when he became king, and he reigned in Jerusalem eleven years.** That is, he reigned from the capture of Jerusalem in March 597 BC to the fall of the city in July 586 BC. He was appointed by Babylon, and ruled under their control. **His mother's name was Hamutal[1] daughter of Jeremiah; she was from Libnah.** Zedekiah (Mattaniah, cf. 37:1) was a son of Josiah, and full brother of Jehoahaz. His mother came from Libnah which was an important town in the southern Shephelah, the low hill country between the coastal plain and the higher mountains of central Judah. Its location has not yet been definitely settled (*ABD*, 4:322).

2. He did evil in the eyes of the LORD, just as Jehoiakim had done. This presents a summary of his reign in condemnatory terms (cf. 37:1-2). His half-brother Jehoiakim had given up the reform programme of their father Josiah, and Zedekiah is evaluated as continuing the same policy, even though Zedekiah was more favourably disposed towards Jeremiah. This formula is one that is repeatedly used in Kings to assess the rulers of Judah (e.g. of Manasseh in 2 Kgs. 21:20).

3. It was because of the LORD's anger that all this happened to Jerusalem and Judah, and in the end he thrust them from his presence. The Hebrew of this verse is difficult to understand. A literal rendering might be: 'For (*kî*), upon/according to the wrath of the LORD, it was in/against Jerusalem and Judah, until he cast them from his presence.' A similar construction and thought occurs at 32:31. If the initial *kî* is translated as 'indeed' (NRSV, NJPS), what is said is that all of what went on in the city and in the land caused the LORD's anger, and he then thrust the people away. If *kî* is rendered 'for' (NKJV, NASB), then this is the reason why Zedekiah behaved in the way he did. The LORD's anger (*'ap*, 2:35) had already been roused against the city, and he left it to degenerate until the situation was reached when the only course open was to expel them from the land. This came about when Zedekiah decided to revolt against Babylon. **Now Zedekiah**

---

1. The kethibh is *ḥămîṭal*, Hamital (so LXX and Vulgate); the qere (followed by the Targum) *ḥămûṭal*, Hamutal, which is in fact the form found in 2 Kgs. 23:31 where she is named as the mother of Jehoahaz. In 2 Kgs. 24:18 the same variation between kethibh and qere is found as here.

rebelled against the king of Babylon. Zedekiah violated a solemn agreement he had entered into with Babylon and to which he had pledged himself swearing by the name of the LORD (cf. 37:1; 2 Chron. 36:13). But his initiative (and that was something for Zedekiah) did not provide the anticipated benefits. He could not free his land from Babylonian control. Indeed, because he was acting in defiance of the prophetic word of warning, his rebellion was not just against Nebuchadnezzar but against the LORD. Babylon reacted against an errant vassal, as did the LORD at the same time.

4. So in the ninth year of Zedekiah's reign, on the tenth day (not mentioned in 39:1) **of the tenth month, Nebuchadnezzar king of Babylon marched against Jerusalem with his whole army.** The anniversary of this occasion became one of the four additional fast days celebrated by the Jews at this time, the fast of the tenth month (cf. vv. 6, 12; 41:1; Zech. 8:19). There are unresolved questions relating to the chronology of this period (see Appendix, especially §11), but the most likely assumptions regarding the start of Zedekiah's reign would result in Nebuchadnezzar's advance against the city as occurring in January 588 BC when the siege commenced (further information about the start of the siege is found in Ezek. 24:2). Unlike the campaign of 597 BC, it is not certain that Nebuchadnezzar himself was present at Jerusalem. He seems to have stayed at his campaign headquarters at Riblah (v. 9). **They camped outside the city and built siege works all around it.** The siege works (*dāyēq*, 'a siege-mound'; 2 Kgs. 25:1) is apparently a technical term from this period. Its precise significance is uncertain, but Holladay (1989, 2:440) suggests a form of rampart built against the walls of the city. Assyrian remains at Lachish provide an illustration of what was probably involved (see picture in *ABD* 4:122), complemented by the Lachish reliefs from Sennacherib's palace at Nineveh.

5-6. The city was kept under siege until the eleventh year of King Zedekiah. It is at this point that divergences in chronological systems affect the text. The shorter chronology assumes a siege of eighteen months, but taking an autumn starting point for the calculation of regnal years, Zedekiah's eleventh regnal year began in autumn 587 BC, and the fourth month (months were always numbered from the spring) fell in the summer of 586 BC. The siege then lasted two and a half years—a very long period of time, but not an impossible figure. Samaria had been besieged by the Assyrians for three years (2 Kgs. 17:5), and Nebuchadnezzar's siege of Tyre lasted for thirteen years (Josephus *Ant.* 10.11.1, *Ag. Ap.* 1.21), but then it could be supplied from the sea. On the other hand Jerusalem benefited from the temporary raising of the siege when the Egyptians advanced. However, **by the ninth day of the fourth month** (that is, the 18th July 586 BC) **the famine in the city had become so severe that there was no food for the people to eat.** The anniversary of this day also became a fast day for the Jews, the fast of the fourth month (cf. v. 4; Zech. 8:19). The people are here called 'the people of the land' (1:18), and in this context it is the general population of the city that is in view and not some social group within it. Conditions in a city under siege became very harsh as food supplies dwindled (Lam. 2:12; 4:4, 9-10). The situation was exacerbated by the larger than normal population because of the numbers who took refuge within the walls from the advancing forces. In the case of Jerusalem there may have been many who left the city during the lull in the siege and it is possible some limited supplies could be brought in, so that the remainder of the populace could hold out for longer. Ezekiel envisaged the possibility of cannibalism within the city before it fell (Ezek. 5:10), and this came to pass (Lam. 2:20). He also foretold that the dire conditions inside the city through disease and famine would account for as many deaths as military action would (Ezek. 5:12), a feature also reflected in the Jeremianic triplet of 'sword, famine and plague' (14:12).

7. Then the city wall ('wall' is a translator's supplement) **was broken through, and the whole army**/'all the men of war' **fled. They**[2] **left the city at night through the gate between the two walls near the king's garden, though the Babylonians were surrounding the city.** This seems to be a condensed account of what is found in 39:4 and 2 Kgs. 25:4. The locations of the gate, the two walls and the king's garden are no longer certain. Although 39:4 implies that the Babylonian army had already penetrated the city defences before this break-out occurred, presumably from the inner city, this passage and 2 Kings are open to the interpretation that another breach was made from within the city to permit the escape of those who left. Indeed it is difficult to see how the entry made by the Babylonians would have been left so unguarded as to permit the besieged forces to flee, and so their escape was probably made from a different point in the wall. Having a detailed knowledge of the locality and of where the Babylonians were situated, it would have been dangerous but not impossible for a detachment of men to pick their way at night through the surrounding forces. No mention is made here of Zedekiah, but he is

---

2. The REB adds 'When King Zedekiah of Judah saw this, he and all his armed escort left the city by night', transferring the information from 39:4.

known to have led the escape (39:4). It is difficult to gauge how many men were involved in 'the whole army' (2 Kgs. 25:4, but the NIV translates the phrase as 'all the soldiers' in 39:4). Many contingents of men were not in the city (40:7) and others had already been killed in the fighting. It is probably better to take the phrase as referring here to Zedekiah's headquarters staff ('all his armed escort' REB).

8. They fled towards the Arabah, that is towards the Jordan valley, trying to escape to the west of the river. **But the Babylonian army pursued King Zedekiah and overtook him in the plains of Jericho. All his soldiers were separated from him and scattered** ($<\sqrt{p\hat{u}\d{s}}$, 9:16), though it is not clear whether this was because of enemy action or in the confusion of the night. There is no mention of the scattering of the troops in 39:1-10. It is possible this event is alluded to in Lam. 4:19.

9-10. And he was captured, cf. 39:5-7; 2 Kgs. 25:5-7. **He was taken to the king of Babylon at Riblah in the land of Hamath, where he pronounced sentence on him.** Riblah was south of Kadesh on the Orontes river (cf. 39:5). **There at Riblah[3] the king of Babylon slaughtered the sons of Zedekiah before his eyes; he also killed all the officials of Judah. 'All the officials' presumably refers to all those who were there; others had been left with Gedaliah.**

11. To remove one or both eyes of a runaway or troublesome slave was a common punishment in the ancient East. Here Nebuchadnezzar treats his rebellious appointee no differently. **Then he put out Zedekiah's eyes, bound him with bronze shackles** (literally, 'bronzes') **and took him to Babylon, where he put him in prison till the day of his death.** The term for 'prison' is not the usual one (cf. *mattārâ*; 32:2, 8, 12; 33:1; 37:21), but *bêt happəquddôt*, 'house of oversight/punishment' (yet another occurrence of the root *pāqad*). The LXX has 'house of the mill', and there is some evidence to suggest that there was a Mesopotamian practice to put out the eyes of captives and to employ them in grinding corn as a humiliating punishment. Keeping Zedekiah alive in this way would have provided a suitable object lesson in victory parades in Babylon. The detail about him being imprisoned is not in 39:7 or 2 Kgs. 25:7. It may be that this dates the supplement after the composition of Kings, but we have no information about the time of Zedekiah's death.

---

3. *bəriblātâ*, 'at Riblah', the *-â* of direction has lost its force here after the preposition (GKC §90e).

B. THE FATE OF JERUSALEM AND THE PEOPLE
(52:12-16)

12. Having looked at what happened to Zedekiah, the narrative now considers what happened to the city about one month after the entrance of the Babylonian forces. The Babylonian perspective of the narrative leads to the use of Babylonian dating. **On the tenth day of the fifth month, in the nineteenth year of Nebuchadnezzar king of Babylon, Nebuzaradan commander of the imperial guard, who served/'stood before' the king of Babylon,[4] came to Jerusalem.** On the rank, 'commander of the imperial guard', see on 39:9. In 2 Kgs. 25:18 it is 'on the seventh day' that is found, but it may be that the discrepancy is explained by the interval between Nebuzaradan's arrival at Jerusalem and the start of the destruction. The date is 17th August 586 BC (7th Ab), which was to become a day of fasting and mourning for the Jews (v. 4; Zech. 7:3-5; 8:19).

13. Nebuzaradan put into effect a three-part policy: destruction (vv. 13-14), deportation (v. 15) and deployment of a residual work-force (v. 16). **He set fire to the temple of the LORD, the royal palace and all the houses of Jerusalem. Every important building[5] he burned down.** By burning down every important building (presumably after the city had been extensively looted), Nebuzaradan undoubtedly started a conflagration that engulfed most, if not all, of the city. 'House' is repeated four times in Hebrew: 'the house of the LORD', 'the house of the king', 'all the houses', 'every great house'. This device stresses how completely the Babylonians wreaked destruction on Jerusalem.

14. The city was also left without any defences. **The whole Babylonian army under the commander of the imperial guard broke down** (<√*nātaṣ*; cf. 1:10; 18:7; 31:28) **all the walls around Jerusalem.** Excavations on the east of Jerusalem overlooking the Kidron valley have shown how extensive this destruction was. The

---

4. The Massoretic Text reads: 'Nebuzaradan commander of the imperial guard came to Jerusalem, he stood before the king of Babylon.' The presence of *'āmad* without *'ăšer* and the use of the perfect is unusual, and probably the verb should be repointed as a participle *'ōmēd* (GKC §155d). In 2 Kgs. 25:8, it is simply 'the servant of the king'. The LXX perfect participle suggests the repointing here.

5. The MT has *kol-bēt haggādôl*, 'every house of the great/important ₍one₎'. Hence the REB has 'every notable person's house'. The article is not found in the corresponding passage in 2 Kgs. 25:9, or the LXX and Vulgate.

Babylonians were determined that Jerusalem would never again be able to function as a focus for rebellion.

15. Further there was put into operation a policy of deportation. **Nebuzaradan the commander of the guard carried into exile some of the poorest people**[6] **and those who remained in the city, along with the rest of the craftsmen and those who had gone over to the king of Babylon.**[7] For 'gone over'/'fallen to' see on 21:9.

16. However, the land was not left without any population (40:10-12). **But Nebuzaradan** (simply 'the commander' in 2 Kgs. 25:12) **left behind the rest of the poorest people of the land to work the vineyards and fields.** 'Poorest' may suggest a low evaluation of the significance of farm workers, or it may reflect a Babylonian estimate of the worth of the community that was left in the land. Deporting the skilled elite removed a potential source of trouble for the Babylonians, and they could also be usefully employed in Babylon, but the trouble involved in transporting unskilled labourers did not make it worthwhile. The word for 'work ... fields' (<√yāgab, cf. 39:10) may suggest forced labour on estates. Holladay (1989, 2:441) suggests that it is the production of goods for export that is in view, describing the workers as those 'engaged on highly organised state-managed terraced estates producing export-quality produce, such as wine and oil.' However, it may simply have the maintenance of a viable local economy that was in view to maintain a buffer zone against Egyptian encroachment.

C. THE TEMPLE VESSELS (52:17-23)

This section (vv. 17-23) gives details about the pillaging of the Temple. Indeed the Temple, its furnishings and treasuries were subject

---

6. The Massoretic Text has often been felt to include 'some of the poorest people' by a mistaken reduplication of 'some of the poorest of the land' (v. 16). Certainly 'some of the poorest of the people and the rest of the people, those who were remaining in the city' reads awkwardly, and it does not seem as if the poorest were in fact taken into captivity. They are not listed in in 39:9 or 2 Kgs. 25:11. Also the form *ûmiddallôt*, 'and from the poorest' (seemingly feminine plural) is remarkable whereas 2 Kgs. 25:12 has the form *ûmiddallat*, a collective noun for 'poor people'.

7. The NIV inverts the order of the Hebrew which is as in the NASB 'the deserters who had deserted to the king of Babylon and the rest of the craftsmen.' The MT reads *hāʾāmôn*, 'architect, builder', whereas 2 Kgs. 25:11 has *hehāmôn*, 'the crowd', and 39:9 has *hāʿam*, 'the people'. Some have suggested changing the MT to *haʿommān*, 'the artists/craftsmen'.

to a number of depredations over the years (1 Kgs. 14:26; 15:18; 2 Kgs. 12:18; 16:8; 18:15-16; 24:13; 25:13-17), and a certain amount of detective work has to be carried out to determine what items were taken away and when. This is further complicated by the fact that when certain items were removed they were subsequently replaced. In 2 Kgs. 24:11-17 it is related that all the treasures of the Temple and palace were removed in 597 BC along with all the gold articles Solomon had made for the Temple. This seems to relate to gold and silver items held in the Temple treasuries which had been dedicated to the LORD as well as the gold plating that covered the walls of the inner chambers of the Temple. However, 27:18-22 shows that certain items still remained, possibly including replacements of some articles. Of the older artefacts it seems mainly to have been bulkier items made of bronze that were left. When the city was captured in 586 BC, these too were pillaged, being broken in pieces and carried off as scrap metal. Consequently they could not be returned later, but the gold and silver items were kept whole and restored under Cyrus after 539 BC (Ezra 1:5-11). The loss of these vessels to the Babylonians was a sign of divine wrath resting upon the community, just as their restoration by Cyrus was a sign of divine favour.

17. The looting of the Temple in vv. 17-23 is paralleled in 2 Kgs. 25:13-17. **The Babylonians broke up the bronze pillars, the movable stands and the bronze Sea that were at the temple of the LORD and they carried all the bronze[8] to Babylon.** These items were too large to carry, and so they were cut up into pieces and presumably taken off for their scrap value, rather than for the craftsmanship that had been put into them. The Temple was looted before it was burned. The pillars were called Jachin and Boaz and stood at the Temple porch (1 Kgs. 7:15-22). They were 27 feet (8.3 m) high and 18 feet (5.5 m) in diameter. The movable stands are described in 1 Kgs. 7:27-33, and had wheels so that the lavers could be taken from one place to another as required. The bronze Sea was used to hold water for the ritual purification of the priests, and was 15 feet (4½ m) in diameter and 7½ feet (2.3 m) high (1 Kgs. 7:23f). An enormous quantity of bronze was involved, and it was clearly considered sufficiently valuable to justify the cost of transporting it to Babylon.

18. They also took away the pots, shovels, wick trimmers, sprinkling bowls, dishes and all the bronze articles used in the temple service. These were all bronze implements. 'The pots' (cf. 1:13) were

---

8. 'Bronze' is lacking in the LXX and 2 Kgs. 25:13.

for cooking, or for removing fat and ashes from the altar. 'Shovels' (*yāʿîm*) were used to scrape up from the altar the refuse of the sacrifices and to put it into the pots (the corresponding verb occurs in Isa. 28:17 meaning 'sweep away'). The third item 'wick trimmers'/ 'snuffers' comes from the root *zāmar*, 'to prune'. They were a type of scissor used to trim the wicks of the lamps (1 Kgs. 7:50). The 'sprinkling bowls' (not mentioned in 2 Kgs. 25:14) would be used to dash the sacrificial blood on the altar. The 'dishes' (a plural form of a word meaning 'the palm of the hand') evidently refers to small, shallow containers, perhaps used for burning and carrying incense (hence 'spoons', NASB). 'Used in the temple service' renders a verb derived from *sārat* piel, 'to minister' especially in the rites of the Temple (cf. 33:21-22). Nothing escaped the depredations of the Babylonians; even the smallest of items was removed.

19. The commander of the imperial guard took away the basins, censers, sprinkling bowls, pots, lampstands, dishes and bowls used for drink offerings—all that were made of pure gold or silver.[9] The list in 2 Kgs. 25:15 is much shorter, mentioning only the censers and sprinkling-bowls (cf. 1 Kgs. 7:40, 45, 50). These implements were of silver and gold. In 597 BC Nebuchadnezzar had undoubtedly removed the gold articles from the Temple (2 Kgs. 24:14), but presumably substitutes had been made for them in the meantime. 'Basins' are general containers, but since they were made of gold, they were probably used in the inner sanctuary. The censers were employed for carrying hot coals to and from the altar, while sprinkling bowls (as in v. 18) were used in the application of sacrificial blood. 'Pots' (<*sîr*) were cooking pots of various sizes; only here do we learn that those in the Temple were made from silver and gold. Lampstands were used to elevate the lamps so that their light shone as widely as possible. Dishes and bowls are similar to those mentioned in the previous verse, though made of different materials. 'Bowls used for drink-offerings' draws on the Septuagint and Vulgate translation as 'winecups' to guess at the meaning of this word, *mənaqqiyâ*, 'sacrificial cups, cups for pouring' (cf. Exod. 25:29). In 1 Kgs. 7 and Exod. 25:29-39 these items were to be of gold. The fact that silver is also mentioned here reveals the impact of previous depredations.

20. The bronze from the two pillars, the Sea (literally, 'one Sea'—

---

9. Literally, 'what ˪was˩ gold, gold, and what ˪was˩ silver, silver' a distributive expression. The NIV 'pure' perhaps draws on a suggestion of GKC §123e that the phrase meant 'very fine gold/silver' (cf. 15:2).

as if from a catalogue?) **and the twelve bronze bulls under it**[10]**, and the movable stands, which King Solomon had made for the temple of the LORD, was more than**[11] **could be weighed**/without weight (2 Kgs. 25:16). These items are also mentioned in v. 17. The twelve bronze bulls, which supported the Sea, had been removed by Ahaz, possibly to send as tribute to the King of Assyria (2 Kgs. 16:17), but again they had obviously been replaced in the interval.

21. Each of the pillars was eighteen cubits high,[12] which is rendered 'twenty-seven feet' (8.1 m) by the NIV in 2 Kgs. 25:17, but that account does not include the additional information: **and twelve cubits in circumference;**[13] **each was four fingers thick, and hollow.** The circumference of twelve cubits (18 feet, 5½ m) is, however, recorded in the account of the construction of the Temple in 1 Kgs. 7:15 (and in the LXX text the thickness is mentioned there also). Four fingers would be about three inches (8 cm), which is similar to the thickness of the bronze Sea (1 Kgs. 7:26; 2 Chron. 4:5). The details of the dimensions of the pillars are given to emphasise their size and consequent worth. The description of their construction emphasises the artistic skill that had gone into their manufacture.

22. The bronze capital on top of the one pillar was five cubits high, that is, 7½ feet (2.3 m), which contrasts with the figure of three cubits (4½ feet, 1.3 m) given in 2 Kgs. 25:17, but this is probably a copyist's error in that 1 Kgs. 7:16 and 2 Chron. 3:15 support the understanding of the capital as five cubits high. The Chronicles account in fact gives the height of the pillars as 35 cubits (52½ feet, 16 m), which is improbable as the height of the Temple itself was only 30 cubits (45 feet, 13.7 m). Rather these pillars were 23 cubits (34½ feet, 10½ m) high and were set at either side of the entrance to the Temple forming a grand entry which contrasted with the plain exterior of the rest of the building but hinted at the rich decoration that was to be found within, some of which was incorporated into the pillars themselves. The one **was decorated with a network and pomegranates of**

---

10. The MT has ʿăšer taḥat hammǝkōnôt, 'which under the movable stands'. Presumably a word such as 'the sea' (hayyam) has been omitted (found in the LXX; cf. NRSV), or a pronominal suffix 'it' (as in NIV; cf. 1 Kgs 7:25-26).

11. Literally 'their bronze, all of these vessels', perhaps a combination of two texts (GKC §128d).

12. The kethibh reads the absolute, qômâ, 'height', while the qere reads with 2 Kgs. 25:17 the construct qômat. The meaning would be the same, but grammatically the preference would be for the qere.

13. Literally, 'a line of twelve cubits surrounded it'.

bronze all around. The other pillar, with its pomegranates, was similar. 'Network' (*śəbākâ*) is related to *śôbēk*, 'a tangle of branches', suggesting that the design may have represented interwoven pomegranate branches (1 Kgs. 7:17-18; 2 Chron. 4:12-13); certainly some kind of-lattice work is indicated. Pomegranates were a favourite form of decoration at the time. They were to be found on the fringe of the robe of the ephod (Exod. 28:33) and also in other non-Israelite remains, including a laver from Ras Shamra which had metal pomegranates hanging from it. The two pillars were therefore works of considerable art, and destroying them was sheer vandalism.

23. This verse is not represented in 2 Kgs. 25 at all. **There were ninety-six pomegranates on the sides;**[14] **the total number of pomegranates above the surrounding network was a hundred.** Perhaps something has been omitted and the four pomegranates that are not accounted for were located at corners.

D. THE CAPTIVITY (52:24-30)

The narrative continues, at first in vv. 24-27 paralleling that found in 2 Kgs. 25:18-21, but then where Kings goes on to note briefly Gedaliah's governorship (2 Kgs. 25:22-26), here there are introduced details of the numbers taken into exile at various times (vv. 28-30), derived from an independent source.

24. Further details are given about the fate of the inhabitants of Jerusalem, particularly those in influential positions in the priestly hierarchy and the royal administration. **The commander of the imperial guard took as prisoners Seraiah the chief priest.** There is no fixed term in the Old Testament for the high priest. Here it is 'the head priest' or 'the chief priest', *kōhēn hārō'š*. There are also listed **Zephaniah the priest next in rank** (*kōhēn hammišneh*, 'the second priest', his immediate subordinate) **and the three doorkeepers.** The priests were obviously viewed as having played a significant role in the rebellion against the Babylonians. Seraiah (a different person from others of the same name mentioned in 36:26; 40:8; 51:59) was the son of Azariah and grandson of Hilkiah (1 Chron. 6:14), the high priest involved in the finding of the scroll in Josiah's day (2 Kgs. 22:8). He himself was the grandfather of the high priest Joshua at the time of the return (Ezra 3:2), so that his

---

14. *rûḥâ*, 'to the wind', might convey the thought 'open/exposed at the sides'. Alternatively, it could be a miscopying for *rewaḥ*, 'space', that is, 'evenly spaced out'.

death did not mean the end of his family line. Indeed it was from another branch of his family that Ezra himself came. Zephaniah is mentioned in 29:24-29 and 37:3. 'Doorkeepers'/'keepers of the threshold' are not mere temple functionaries but represent the next level in the Temple hierarchy, being responsible for the good order at the sanctuary (cf. 35:4), especially on feast days.

25. **Of those still in the city, he took the officer** (*sārîs*; cf. 29:2) **in charge of the fighting men, and seven royal advisers**/'men of seeing the face of the king', that is those 'with right of access to the king' (REB) or 'men of the king's council' (NRSV). The officer in charge of the fighting men is not a specific term, but the context implies he was a high-ranking military figure. **He also took the secretary who was chief officer in charge of conscripting the people of the land and sixty of his men who were found in the city.** 'The secretary who was chief officer' was probably equivalent to Secretary of State for War (McKane 1965:22), who was responsible for levying the people for war. It is difficult to decide whether the phrase 'people of the land' (cf. v. 16; 1:17-19) here points to the chief citizenry of the land, or the common people. However, 'sixty of his men' is literally 'sixty men from the people of the land', and in this case it is improbable that the phrase refers to the ordinary people of the land. Probably both times the reference is to a privileged upper class. Carroll (1986:867) suggests 'landed gentry'.

26-27. **Nebuzaradan the commander took them all and brought them to the king of Babylon at Riblah. There at Riblah, in the land of Hamath, the king had them executed.** 'Had them executed' (NIV) renders two verbs 'struck them and had them killed', where perhaps the first verb implies that he had them beaten before their execution ('had them flogged and put to death', REB).[15] **So Judah went into captivity, away from her land.** Those left behind in Judah did not count from the perspective of this writer who accepted Jeremiah's prediction that the future of the nation lay with the good fruit to be found with the exiles in Babylon. The people had experienced the ultimate penalty for covenant treachery in that they were removed from the land which had been gifted to them by their covenant Overlord.

28-30. At this point 2 Kings discusses the governorship of Gedaliah, but as this has already been described in greater detail in Jeremiah, there is added here an account of the numbers taken captive, which serves to emphasise the desolation and depopulation that was brought

---

15. The hiphil of *nākâ* can convey both 'strike' and 'kill'.

upon the land. **This is the number of the people whom Nebuchadnezzar carried into exile: in the seventh year,**[16] **3,023 Jews; in
Nebuchadnezzar's eighteenth year, 832 people from Jerusalem; in
his twenty-third year, 745 Jews taken into exile by Nebuzaradan
the commander of the imperial guard. There were 4,600 people in
all.** 'Jews' and 'people' are both used in this summary, but possibly the
figures denominated as *nepeš*, 'people' (2:34; 43:6), would include
women and children as well. The account raises two major difficulties.

(1) The first two dates disagree with those of 2 Kgs. 24:12 and
2 Kgs. 25:8 which have 'eighth' and 'nineteenth' years respectively.
'Nineteenth' is also found in v. 12 above. One way to overcome this
(see Appendix §14) is to suggest that these figures, drawn from an
independent source, use the accession year mode of reckoning regnal
years, where the short accession year up to the following New Year
was discarded in numbering the years of a reign, whereas in the other
texts the accession year (no matter what its length) was counted in
reckoning regnal years. In this way the first deportation may be identified as occurring when Jehoiachin was taken captive, the second at the
fall of Jerusalem, and the third some five years later in 582/1 BC on
some occasion we do not otherwise know about, but which Josephus
(*Ant.* 10.9.7) suggests may have been connected with reprisals in
connection with the assassination of Gedaliah. If, however, Gedaliah's
assassination took place some years earlier, then it may just be linked
to a subsequent period of Babylonian activity in the area.

(2) But even if that reconciliation does account for the differences
in dates between the sources, it still leaves the problem of the numbers
involved. 2 Kgs. 24:14 talks of 10,000 being taken into exile in
597 BC, with a further 8,000 in total mentioned in v. 16, though possibly these are included in the earlier figure. Population guesstimates
for ancient cities are notoriously unreliable, but a figure of 15,000–
25,000 for Hezekiah's day (*ABD* 2:65) might still apply at this time, so
that a substantial deportation occurred. In comparison the figure here
of 3,023, although precise, seems too low, though it might include only
males while in 2 Kings the figures may also cover the women and
children who accompanied them. The 832 mentioned in connection
with the fall of Jerusalem in 586 BC seems small, though again that
might be accounted for in terms of the many who perished either in the
fighting or by famine. The population had been significantly

16. The variation 'seventeenth' (NASB margin) has no textual support. By
identifying the year as that when Judah felt the first impact of the final
Babylonian assault on Jerusalem, it tries to harmonise the various accounts.

diminished by the earlier deportation, but on the other hand in time of siege it would have been swollen by those seeking refuge. Even so the figure seems out of proportion to the magnitude of the event.

On balance it is more likely that the first two figures do not refer to the main deportations of 597 BC and 586 BC respectively, but to events in the preceding years. The use of the more general term 'Jews' rather than 'people from Jerusalem' in connection with the first figure could point to it being that of those captured and deported earlier than the main assault on the city. Similarly the second figure, which does relate to Jerusalem, would come from activities during the earlier part of the prolonged siege. The third figure, relating to a later deportation, again speaks of 'Jews', which fits in with the period when Jerusalem was in ruins and uninhabited. The precision of the figures suggests access to some kind of record, and their inclusion points to them being of importance to whoever composed this supplement. They certainly reinforce the sense of the overwhelming devastation that had struck the city and the land.

E. JEHOIACHIN'S RELEASE (52:31-34)

The final episode recorded in the supplement to Jeremiah fast forwards from 582 to 561 BC. These verses correspond substantially to 2 Kgs. 25:27-30, and function in the same way: to show a glimmer of hope coming from an unlikely quarter. Kaiser (1998:397) envisages Jeremiah now aged between eighty-five and ninety years of age as surviving to witness this rise in the fortunes of Jehoiachin, but this is not required by the text (see on 51:64). We do not know when or where Jeremiah died. This material has been added by another hand to end the record of Jeremiah's ministry not only with a note of the fulfilment of his prophecies of doom but also with this slight harbinger of the fulfilment of his prophecies of restoration. Indeed 'as long as he lived' (v. 34) suggests this narrative was composed some years after the events it describes, distancing it even further from Jeremiah.

31. In the thirty-seventh year of the exile of Jehoiachin king of Judah, in the year Evil-Merodach[17] became king of Babylon, he released/'raised the head of' Jehoiachin king of Judah and freed

---

17. Amel-marduk ('man of Marduk', that is, one who worships that the god Marduk; 50:2) is the Babylonian/Akkadian form of his name. The Hebrew form may be a deliberate malformation since 'Evil' (*'ĕwîl*) means 'foolish', 'stupid'.

him from prison on the twenty-fifth[18] **day of the twelfth month.**[19]
The phrase 'in the year … became king' suggests Evil-Merodach's
accession year which ran from October 562 BC–March 561 BC, so that
the date given here would be 22nd March 561 BC. Finnegan
(1998:262-4) argues that this phrase and the similar expression in
2 Kgs. 25:27 are ambiguous and might refer to Evil-Merodach's accession year or to the first full year of his reign. Finnegan prefers the latter
option so that the date would be a full year later. 'Lifted up the head
of' (that is, 'showed favour to him', an act of royal pardon, cf. Gen.
40:13) probably refers to a pardon extended to prisoners, especially
those who no longer posed any political threat, possibly in connection
with a reaffirmation of their loyalty to the new monarch.

Jehoiachin was now aged about fifty-three years. After a reign of
three months, he had been in prison for thirty-seven years, but now he
is eventually treated in a way that is in marked contrast to the earlier
treatment of Zedekiah. Jehoiachin's release would have been a token
for good to the exiles who were waiting for a similar restoration of
their fortunes and liberty.

**32. He spoke kindly to him and gave him a seat of honour higher
than those of the other kings**[20] **who were with him in Babylon.** We
do not have details of who the other kings were, but they were probably other rebellious monarchs who had been detained in Babylon.
Evil-Merodach ruled for under two years 562–560 BC, but it seems that
Jehoiachin's return to favour continued with his successor, his brother-
in-law, Nergal-šar-uṣur. Tablets found near the Ishtar Gate in Babylon
confirm that Jehoiachin was the recipient of royal bounty. Significantly
he is also described as the king of the land of Yahudi (*ANET* 308).

33-34. So Jehoiachin put aside[21] **his prison clothes and for the rest
of his life he ate regularly at the king's table.** 'Ate regularly'/'lived
as a pensioner of the king' (REB) shows that Evil-Merodach granted
more than liberty; he also provided for his well-being. **Day by day the
king of Babylon gave Jehoiachin a regular allowance** (40:5) **as long
as he lived, till the day of his death.** The context suggests that 'he'
refers to Jehoiachin, not Evil-Merodach.

---

18. In 2 Kgs. 25:27 the date is given as the 'twenty-seventh'. There has been
a clerical error in one or other of the accounts.

19. The spelling of the word varies: the kethibh has *kəlîʾ*, the qere *kəlûʿ*.

20. The kethibh has *məlākîm*, 'kings', whereas the qere, probably correctly,
adds the article, *hamməlākîm*, 'the kings'.

21. The two verbs in this verse are perfects, the first generally being
explained as an Aramaism.

But this picture of restoration is not without its darker side. 'Till the day of his death' is an addition to the text found in 2 Kgs. 25:34, and suggests that unlike the author of that material, whoever was responsible for chapter 52 knew of Jehoiachin's death. If that was so, then this addition fits in with the earlier theme of the fulfilment of Jeremiah's prophecies because he has predicted the death of Jehoiachin in Babylon (22:26). If there were any who still hoped for the restoration of the Davidic dynasty in Jehoiachin, then that expectation was now brought to an end. Even so, the final note is not one of gloom. If in so many ways Jeremiah's predictions of disaster and death can be traced out to their realisation, may there not be good grounds for expecting his predictions of consolation and restoration to be equally well grounded? The path into the future is not clearly mapped out, but there is a call for faith and confidence that there will be a reversal of their current circumstances. The opportunities that human discernment can perceive may be foreclosed; all is clearly shown to depend on the grace and favour of divine intervention.

APPENDIX: THE CHRONOLOGY OF THE PERIOD

1. The Babylonian Chronicles. The chronology of the kings of Israel and Judah has long been a source of scholarly controversy, and nowhere more so than in the period covered by the book of Jeremiah. The events of the reign of Josiah and the twenty-three years that elapsed between his death and the fall of Jerusalem are described, and often dated, in the books of Kings and Chronicles. Further chronological details are provided by references in the prophecies of Jeremiah and Ezekiel. The problem that is evident to all who study the matter is how to correlate this information in a consistent manner. That difficulty was partly intensified and partly eased by the publication of the Babylonian Chronicles. In 1923 the Chronicles for the years 616 to 609 BC were published, and this was followed in 1956 by those for the years 626–623 BC, 608–595 BC, and 556 BC (Wiseman 1956). The Chronicles attest to an on-going historiographic tradition in Mesopotamia with a keen interest in current affairs and a desire to transmit to posterity an accurate record of events. The details found in the Old Testament records reveal that a similar attitude also characterised the scribes of Israel and Judah. What was lacking was a consistent and coherent account of how they recorded the calendrical data embodied in their records.

A major advance in unlocking the chronology of Kings was provided by the publication in 1951 of *The Mysterious Numbers of the Hebrew Kings* (2nd ed. 1963; rev. ed. 1983) by Edwin Thiele, a Seventh Day Adventist scholar. By making a number of plausible assumptions[1] Thiele was able to bring order into what had previously been regarded as confusion, and he did this while respecting the

---

1. These assumptions include (1) that reigns in the northern kingdom of Israel were reckoned on a non-accession year system till the end of the reign of Jehoahaz in 798 BC and on an accession year basis thereafter till the demise of the kingdom; (2) that Judah used accession year reckoning throughout, apart from reigns from Jehoram to Joash, when Israelite influence was significant in the south; (3) that the regnal year in Israel began in the spring (Nisan, March/April) but in the autumn (Tishri, September/October) in Judah; (4) that scribes of one nation used their local system of reckoning when recording information regarding the reign of a king of the other kingdom. Thiele also assumes that there was later textual corruption of certain synchronisms in 2 Kgs. 17–18, but this is not a necessary part of his system and has been corrected by others.

approach that it is also able to reconcile data from other sources with the information found in Scripture. Thiele's approach has never been disproved, and in its comprehensiveness remains the null hypothesis against which any competing theory has to show overwhelming superiority. It is also a strength of his approach that subsequent studies (notably by McFall 1991) have been able to refine it as regards certain details without violating its basic structure. Indeed one of the main criticisms made against Thiele's approach was that it explained too much. While Thiele's hypothesis has not been definitively established, it has commended itself widely in evangelical circles because of its respect for the biblical text.

It is not possible to conclude, however, that the last word has been said on this matter. New discoveries may provide key data to resolve certain issues, and it is possible that the existing pieces of the jigsaw may yet be rearranged into a more compelling pattern. It is a stimulating piece of historical detective work to examine how the chronology is built up from the evidence, and this helps one become aware of the extent to which any reconstruction depends on a number of crucial assumptions.

2. The Reign of Jehoiachin. The Babylonian Chronicle sets one of the fixed points for all subsequent discussions of this era in that it establishes 2nd Adar of Nebuchadnezzar's seventh year as the date on which Jerusalem under Jehoiachin surrendered to Babylon (Volume 1, Introduction §3.9). Because the Babylonians (like the other peoples of Mesopotamia) attached great significance to astral and planetary phenomena, they kept accurate records of solar eclipses. Modern back-calculation of such eclipses makes it possible to anchor the pattern found in Babylonian records in terms of current Western chronology, and so Babylonian dates can be synchronised with our calendrical system, and in particular absolute dates can be established for the first twelve years of Nebuchadnezzar's reign. The month Adar was the last month of the year in the Babylonian calendar, and so it has been established that Jerusalem surrendered on 16th March 597 BC.

From there, however, assumptions have to be made. While 16th March 597 BC might seem to mark the end of Jehoiachin's reign, Ezekiel dates the Exile as beginning on the tenth day of the following month Nisan (Ezek. 40:1), so that it is possible to argue that Jehoiachin's reign did not formally end until then, that is, 22nd April. This, however, is unlikely because we know Nebuchadnezzar returned to Babylon for the important New Year celebrations associated with the month Nisan, and he is likely to have settled the substantial matter of who the next ruler of Judah was to be before he left. The actual deportation could be remitted to subordinates. So working back from 16th March, since we know that Jehoiachin's reign lasted for three months and ten days (2 Chron. 36:9), it can be reckoned as having begun on 10th December 598 BC. Because Jehoiachin's three-month reign falls between autumn and spring, his regnal dates are the same whatever calendrical system is assumed to be in use. Further, since Jehoiachin had been co-regent with his father since 608 BC as 2 Chron. 36:9 requires (McFall 1991:39), it is reasonable to assume that his succession followed immediately on the death of his father. We can thus take the date of Jehoiakim's death as being 10th December 598 BC.

Moving beyond that, however, involves making yet further assumptions. We will first look back to the period before 597 BC and then consider the date of the fall of Jerusalem.

3. When the year started. We know that Jehoiakim reigned for eleven years (2 Kgs. 23:36), and so calculating back from his death in December 598 BC, his reign commenced in 608 BC. But this raises the question of when regnal years were reckoned to begin in Judah. Scholars are agreed that there were two possible starting points for a new year, either on 1st Nisan (April/May) which meant that the year began in the spring as was the convention in Babylon, or six months later on 1st Tishri (September/October), giving an autumn year for regnal calculations.[2] An autumn start to the regnal year seems to be confirmed by the account of the eighteenth year of Josiah in 2 Kgs. 22–23 where the numerous events recorded for that year could hardly have occurred in the fortnight between the finding of the book of the law and the celebration of the Passover on 14th Nisan. A year beginning in the previous autumn yields a more realistic, though still tight, timescale. Even if the Kings narrative is treated as a summary of events that took place over some time, an autumn start to the year allows a more plausible interval for organising the Passover.

However, in Babylon the year began in the spring, and this practice was adopted in Judah in the post-exilic period. It is possible to contend that increasing Babylonian influence in the pre-exilic period led to a switch by some to the use of a spring new year. Thiele argues that the

2. One must be careful not to think of years starting on different dates as an ancient phenomenon. The complications caused by academic years, fiscal years, the business year for company accounts and the years associated with various sports all remind us that this is still a feature of life.

authors of Kings continued to use autumnal regnal years until the end
of the kingdom, but that Jeremiah and Ezekiel followed a spring
calendar (1983:183) except where in Jeremiah scribes incorporated
information from Kings in the superscriptions of various chapters. This
is a clumsy feature of Thiele's analysis and the need for it has been
disputed by scholars such as Malamat (1956; 1968) who argue that
throughout Jeremiah, with the exception of 46:2, an autumn calendar is
used. Others such as Clines (1972:9-34) argue for a spring calendar
being used in all sources throughout this period. Thiele's analysis also
seems to accept a particular view of the composition of Jeremiah that
entails considerable scribal involvement in adding material, while failing to adjust discrepancies that arose. The earlier Jeremiah was written
the less likely is it that there are two calendrical systems in use
throughout the book.

4. The Battle of Megiddo, 609 BC. But what were the circumstances under which Jehoiakim came to the throne? This brings us to
consider the tragic and disruptive period in the life of Judah in which
king Josiah died at the battle of Megiddo and was briefly succeeded by
his son, Jehoahaz, before the Egyptians placed Jehoiakim on the
throne.

Earlier scholars had been uncertain as to whether the battle of
Megiddo between Josiah and the Egyptians took place in 609 or
608 BC. However, it has become clear that the Babylonian armies were
involved in fighting on their northern frontiers in 608 BC, and as there
is no mention of any Babylonian encounter with Egyptian forces in
608 or 607 BC, the date of 609 BC is now accepted for the battle. The
Babylonian Chronicle records that in Tammuz of that year (25th June–
23rd July) the king of the remaining Assyrian forces along with a large
Egyptian army crossed the Euphrates from their base at Carchemish
and attacked a Babylonian garrison at Haran. This marked the beginning of a major Egyptian presence in Syria for several years. Assuming
that Egyptian force was the same as the one which under Pharaoh
Neco II had earlier met Josiah (2 Kgs. 23:29; 2 Chron. 35:21)[3], it
would have taken them at least a month to march the 340 miles (nearly
550 km) north from Megiddo. The Egyptian encounter with Josiah
must therefore have occurred before mid-June of that year at the very

---

3. As Horn (1967:20) points out, Neco is not mentioned in the Babylonian
Chronicles, there were already Egyptian forces in the north, and it may have
been the case that Neco's late arrival, delayed by the need to fight Josiah,
contributed to the defeat of the Egyptian forces.

latest. Josiah thus died in May or early June 609 BC in the thirty-first
year of his reign (2 Kgs. 22:1).

Josiah was succeeded by one of his younger sons, Jehoahaz, who
reigned for three months (2 Kgs. 23:31, 33). When Pharaoh Neco was
repulsed after his unsuccessful attack on Haran, he seems to have made
his base at Riblah south of Hamath, and it was to there that he
summoned Jehoahaz and deposed him (2 Kgs. 23:33). As the Egyptians are recorded as retreating from Haran in the month Elul (23rd
August–20th September), Jehoahaz's deposition must have taken place
in September or early October. His reign thus falls either in the period
May–August 609 BC or in June–September 609. If the view is taken
that the regnal year began in the spring, then spring 609 to spring 608
BC covered Josiah's thirty-first year, Jehoahaz' reign and the accession
year of Jehoiakim. If, however, the year began in the autumn, then it is
necessary to assume that Jehoahaz was not deposed until after 1st
Tishri (21st September) since it is certain that Jehoiakim began his first
regnal year in 608 BC. Malamat (1956:256; 1968:141) considered that
virtually the whole of the year autumn 609 to autumn 608 BC was
Jehoiakim's accession year. An 'accession year' was a technique used
to bring the actual years of a reign into alignment with the calendar. It
is generally agreed that Babylonian practice was to reckon regnal years
from the spring (from the month Nisan, that is, March/April) and to
adjust for any preceding period of less than twelve months by treating
it as an accession year, in effect, year zero. Thus Nebuchadnezzar
came to the throne on 7th September 605 BC, but by Babylonian reckoning his first regnal year did not commence until the new year which
started in the spring of 604 BC. A similar system seems to have been
employed in Judah at this time.

The date of the deposition of Jehoahaz and the accession of
Jehoiakim is a key unknown in the chronology of the period. If
Jehoiakim's succession took place before 1st Tishri, then it is virtually
impossible to use an autumn calendar for the events of this period.
Which calendar has preference seems to be determined by one's view
on the speed at which the Egyptian forces were capable of marching
north (Malamat 1968; Clines 1972), and therefore of when it was most
probable that Jehoiakim was installed as king. It must, however, be
noted that this was itself a somewhat indefinite event. Possibly there
was an interregnum between Jehoahaz's deposition and the announcement of Jehoiakim as his successor. There might also have been
uncertainty as to whether his reign began at the time of Neco's decree
or at the time of some subsequent ceremony in Jerusalem. All this
would ordinarily have been of little significance, but if 1st Tishri

occurred in the meantime it affected the numbering of regnal years.

5. The Battle of Carchemish, 605 BC. During 606 BC there was minor aggression between Egyptian forces and the Babylonians, culminating early in 605 BC with the Egyptian seizure of a Babylonian fort at Kimuḫu on the Euphrates north of Carchemish. In response to this the Babylonian king Nabopolassar (November 625–August 605 BC) in his final year sent the crown prince Nebuchadnezzar to deal with the Egyptian threat, and there followed a decisive battle between Babylonian and Egyptian forces at Carchemish. Now Nebuchadnezzar had left Babylon after 1st Nisan (12th April) and when news of his father's death on 8th Ab (16th August) reached him, he quickly returned to Babylon for his coronation on 1st Elul (7th September). So the battle of Carchemish must have occurred between 1st Nisan (12th April) and the middle of August. In that the Babylonian Chronicle (Wiseman 1956:67) records that after the battle Nebuchadnezzar fought the Egyptians again at Hamath, chased them out of Syria–Palestine and also established some form of control over the whole area, it seems likely that the battle itself took place around the middle of May.

6. Jeremiah 46:2. The establishment of the date of the battle of Carchemish as around May 605 BC creates a major difficulty for understanding the dates in Jeremiah as calculated using an autumn calendar. Jeremiah 46:2 states that the battle of Carchemish took place in Jehoiakim's fourth year, which on an autumn calendar was from autumn 605 to autumn 604 BC, whereas it is now established that the battle took place in the spring of 605 BC before Nabopolassar's death. It may be that there is a textual error, but there is no manuscript evidence to support such a suggestion. Horn (1967:26) suggested that the verse had been misread and that there is in fact a parenthesis in the middle of 46:2, so that the date refers not to the battle but to the issuing of the prophecy. This is implausible. A more likely suggestion is that due to the confusing circumstances in which Jehoiakim came to the throne there were different systems in use for determining his regnal years, and that in 46:2 the date derives from reckoning his fourth year to be autumn 606 to autumn 605 BC, thus including the battle of Carchemish. Such an anomalous procedure is not convincing, but it is the best option at present available if in fact an autumn calendar is used elsewhere. Of course, those advocating a spring calendar consider 46:2 to be one of the most significant features in favour of their hypothesis according to which Jehoiakim's fourth year is spring 605 to spring 604 BC, which certainly covers the period in which the battle of Carchemish occurred. However, the spring calendar is not itself without difficulties as Dan. 1:1 shows.

7. Daniel 1:1. Consideration must also be given to other Scriptures bearing upon the chronology of this period, most notably Dan. 1:1, 'In the third year of the reign of Jehoiakim king of Judah, Nebuchadnezzar king of Babylon came to Jerusalem and besieged it.' Two questions arise: Is the reference to the third year of Jehoiakim consistent with other passages? and, Does the Babylonian Chronicle allow a siege of Jerusalem as early as 605 BC?

The resolution of the matter again hinges on the question of which calendar is being used. In terms of a spring calendar, Jehoiakim's third year was from spring 606 to spring 605 BC, and so was over even before Nebuchadnezzar began to move against the Egyptians in spring 605 BC. Therefore, although it might have been supposed that the Babylonian setting and origin of the book of Daniel would have led to the use of the Babylonian system of reckoning with a spring calendar, it appears that was not the case. The third year of Jehoiakim in terms of an autumn calendar can be worked out as autumn 606 to autumn 605 BC, and this covers the events of Nebuchadnezzar's first campaign in Hatti-land. Such a use of an autumn calendar even by authors who were familiar with Mesopotamian practice is also to be found in the book of Nehemiah where he is informed of conditions in Jerusalem 'in the month of Kislev in the twentieth year' presumably of Artaxerxes I (Neh. 1:1), but makes his request to the king on the basis of that information 'in the month of Nisan in the twentieth year of King Artaxerxes' (Neh. 2:1). As Kislev fell in November/December and Nisan was in March/April, the four month delay can only be accommodated on the basis that Artaxerxes' regnal years were being reckoned on an autumnal basis beginning in Tishri (September/October); otherwise Nehemiah's request in Neh. 2:1 takes place before he is made aware of the need for it.

However, what precisely did happen in Jerusalem in the summer of 605 BC before Nebuchadnezzar returned home? There is some doubt if 'besieged' (Dan. 1:1; <√ṣûr, a by-form of ṣārar) necessarily involves more than 'show hostility to' or 'treat as an enemy', denoting action preliminary to a siege but without necessarily involving a siege itself (Wiseman 1983:23). Also, it is recorded that during his follow-up operations after Carchemish and after his defeat of the remaining Egyptian forces in Syria, Nebuchadnezzar 'conquered the whole area of the Hatti-country'.[4] He probably made his base in Riblah and directed operations from there throughout the entire area that had previously been under Egyptian control. It is possible that action was then taken against Judah, which as an Egyptian vassal would have attracted Babylonian attention. Further there is the statement in 2 Chron. 36:6 that at some point 'Nebuchadnezzar king of Babylon attacked him [Jehoiakim] and bound him with bronze shackles to take him to Babylon'. His intention might have been to parade Jehoiakim in a victory procession. It is not known if Jehoiakim was in fact taken to Babylon, and it is possible that Nebuchadnezzar's plans were changed when he received news of his father's death. Josephus' account of what happened then strongly implies that there were already prisoners from Syria–Palestine, including Jews, whom Nebuchadnezzar left behind to be brought to Babylon by others (*Ant.* 10.11.1; *Ag. Ap.* 1.19). While these prisoners could have been from a Jewish contingent in the Egyptian army, it is also possible that they included political hostages such as Daniel and his friends, taken from the upper classes in Judah to ensure good behaviour on the part of the regime.

8. Nebuchadnezzar's Subsequent Campaigns. But Nebuchadnezzar's return to take the throne in Babylon did not spell the end of his interest in Hatti-land. Indeed, the Babylonian Chronicle records that within a few months, late in 605 BC and up to January/February 604 BC, he was again active in the area. This campaign, however, cannot be correlated with the events of Dan. 1:1, for late 605 BC falls outwith Jehoiakim's third year on any reckoning.

9. The Fast of 604 BC. From May/June 604 BC until January/February 603 BC Nebuchadnezzar conducted a third campaign in the area of Syria–Palestine, capturing the Philistine city of Ashkelon in November/December 604 BC and destroying it to its foundations.

This coincides with a fast that took place in the fifth year of Jehoiakim, in the ninth month, that is Kislev (November/December 604 BC; 36:9). The date is the same for both spring and autumn calendars. Malamat argues (1968:141) that Jehoiakim's reaction shows that Judah had not yet surrendered to Babylon. More probably Jehoiakim had made formal acceptance of Babylonian overlordship,

---

4. It should be noted that Wiseman no longer favours the reading 'whole area of the Hatti-country' preferring instead to read the text as 'the whole region of Hamath', which confines Babylonian activity to the area north of Riblah (Wiseman 1983:17).

but was not yet completely subjugated. This does not seem to have happened in Nebuchadnezzar's first regnal year, for the Babylonian Chronicle simply states that after the conquest of Ashkelon the king returned home in the month Shebat (January/February).

On an autumn calendar Jehoiakim's fifth year was autumn 604–autumn 603 BC, so the fast occurred in November/December 604 BC since the months were numbered from the spring no matter when the regnal year began. The winter conditions described in 36:22 fit the dating of the event in the ninth month.

However, the calendar that is used affects calculations regarding how long Jeremiah's scroll lay unread. According to Jer. 36:1 it was written in the fourth year of Jehoiakim, which on an autumn calendar ended in the sixth month (Elul, August/September) 604 BC, so that the scroll need not have lain for more than three months. Using a spring calendar the fifth year of Jehoiakim was spring 604–spring 603 BC, so the date of the fast in the ninth month remains the same, but the scroll was written in the year ending spring 604 BC, thus increasing the delay between its being written and publicly read by a further six months, to at least nine months.

The incomplete state of the tablet regarding Nebuchadnezzar's second regnal year does not explicitly record anything regarding Jerusalem, though it does indicate that Nebuchadnezzar was active in Syria–Palestine. It is in the autumn or winter of 603 BC that Malamat (1968:142) dates the arrest of Jehoiakim and his (unrealised) exile to Babylon and the taking of part of the vessels of the house of God (2 Chron. 36:6; Dan. 1:1-2). This involves emending the text of Dan. 1:1 from 'in the third year' to 'in the sixth year'. However, these events need not be synchronised, and it is possible that in 603 BC more stringent conditions were placed upon Jehoiakim without additional hostages being required. We know that Jehoiakim was vassal to Babylon for three years (2 Kgs. 24:1). If his rebellion against Babylon was prompted by the fact that Babylon and Egypt fought to a stalemate in the winter of 601/600 BC (Nebuchadnezzar's fourth regnal year), then his rebellion may be dated in the spring of 600 BC, and his formal acceptance of Babylonian overlordship around the spring of 603 BC, but there is insufficient data to permit any great certainty about this. It may be that the Aramaic Saqqarah letter was sent from the ruler of a Philistine city requesting Pharaoh's help about this time.

Nebuchadnezzar was unable to respond directly to the Judean rebellion for two years, but in his sixth year (spring 599–spring 598 BC) Nebuchadnezzar was once more in Hatti-land, paying particular attention to the Arab tribes in the northern desert during the months

December 599 BC–February 598 BC. This accords with the statement of
2 Kgs. 24:2. It also provides a background for the statements in 35:1
and 35:11, and probably relates to the figures for the first deportation
mentioned in 52:28. The following year brings us back to the event
with which we started this survey, the capture of Jerusalem in 597 BC.

10. Jehoiachin's Deportation. Although not of great significance
in terms of the chronology of Jeremiah, it is of interest at this point to
note the difference between the Babylonian Chronicle which dates
Jerusalem as having fallen in Nebuchadnezzar's seventh year, and the
statement of 2 Kgs. 24:12 where the fall of Jerusalem and more
particularly the deportation of Jehoiachin occur in Nebuchadnezzar's
eighth year. Many different approaches have been advanced to resolve
this (Green 1982:59-62), but the simplest is that of Thiele, namely, that
in Kings the reigns of both native and foreign kings are recorded in
terms of an autumn calendar. Nebuchadnezzar's first year would then
have been from autumn 505 until autumn 504 BC in terms of the Kings
chronology, so that his eighth year from autumn 598 until autumn
597 BC would have covered the capture of Jerusalem in the spring of
597 BC.

11. Zedekiah's Reign. We must now consider the chronology of
the last king of Judah, Zedekiah. Unfortunately the Babylonian
Chronicles for the period surrounding the final siege and sack of
Jerusalem have not yet been found. As a result there are unresolved
questions regarding the date of its fall and also of the duration of the
siege preceding it. If further Babylonian records are found, they might
permit a definitive calculation, but for the present we must try to
evaluate the scriptural data as best we can.

We know that after Nebuchadnezzar took Jerusalem in Adar
597 BC, he placed Zedekiah on the throne of Judah; but did this occur
before or after the start of the following month Nisan with which the
year began on a spring calendar? This, of course, also raises the question whether Zedekiah's regnal years were calculated using a spring or
autumn calendar.

If a spring calendar was employed and Zedekiah was placed on the
throne immediately after the seizure of the city, then, after a very brief
accession year, his first year would have begun on 1st Nisan 597 BC,
and his eleventh year on 1st Nisan 587 BC. Since it is clear that Jerusalem fell in his eleventh year (2 Kgs. 25:2), it would then be captured on
29th July 587 BC and destroyed on 25th August 587 BC. The siege
began on the tenth day of the tenth month of Zedekiah's ninth year

(2 Kgs. 25:1), which is equivalent to 15th January 588 BC, and so lasted somewhat over eighteen months (a figure for the duration of the siege supported by Josephus, *Ant.* 10.7.4, 10.8.1).

Alternatively, there may have been a delay in placing Zedekiah on the throne. The exile of the Judeans began a few weeks later, 'in the spring'/'at the turn of the year' (2 Chron. 36:10), possibly on the tenth day of the following month (Ezek. 40:1). In that case Zedekiah's first full regnal year did not begin until spring 596 BC, the start of the siege would be in January 587 BC, and the fall and destruction of Jerusalem in 586 BC, after a siege of eighteen months. However, Nebuchadnezzar probably had Zedekiah installed as king before the end of the year and left it to his subordinates to carry out the deportation (Malamat 1968:145), so this scenario is unlikely.

The calculations are different on the basis of an autumn calendar. Precisely when Zedekiah came to the throne is not then so significant since the period up to Tishri (September/October) counted as his accession year, and his first regnal year was autumn 597–autumn 596 BC. His eleventh regnal year during which Jerusalem was taken and destroyed would then be autumn 587–autumn 586 BC. Jerusalem would therefore have been captured on 9th Tammuz (2 Kgs. 25:3), that is, 18th July 586 BC, and finally destroyed on 7th Ab (2 Kgs. 25:8), that is, 14th August 586 BC. However, since months are numbered from the spring no matter whether the regnal year is reckoned from spring or autumn, the tenth day of the tenth month of Zedekiah's ninth year is 15th January 588 BC whether one counts from spring or autumn 597 BC. The siege then lasted two and a half years. It is this calculation that has been adopted in writing this commentary.

12. Ezekiel's Evidence. Malamat (1968:148-150) points out the significance of what is found in Ezekiel's prophecy for evaluating the evidence regarding the chronology of this period. Ezekiel, exiled in Babylonia, employed the spring calendar used there. Malamat also considers that Ezekiel calculated events according to the years of Jehoiachin's exile, which started in spring 597 BC. (While this is not unnatural, it must also be remembered that the years of exile might have been calculated beginning with a part year, a sort of accession year, so that year 1 would start with the first official new year after the start of the exile.) So 'in the ninth year, in the tenth month on the tenth day' (Ezek. 24:1) given as the date of the start of the siege refers to 15th January 588 BC, a date which corresponds with 39:1 and 52:4 (and also 2 Kgs. 25:1), that is, the tenth month of Zedekiah's ninth year reckoned from autumn 597 BC.

Ezekiel records that news of the fall of Jerusalem reached him 'in the twelfth year of our exile, in the tenth month on the fifth day' (Ezek. 33:21), that is, 8th January 585 BC. A time lapse of five months from the burning of the city is a credible delay before the messenger arrived in Babylonia, whereas the seventeen months required by a date in 587 BC is not. Furthermore in Ezek. 40:1 the twenty-fifth year of the Exile is also dated as the fourteenth year after the fall of the city, which implies Jerusalem was destroyed eleven years after the start of the Exile, that is in the twelfth year of the captivity.

So Ezekiel presents the siege as lasting from the ninth year of the Exile to the twelfth year, and this can be reconciled with its lasting from the ninth to the eleventh years of Zedekiah's reign only on the supposition that an autumn calendar was used for calculating Zedekiah's regnal years. The siege began in January, which fell after the start of the new year on either style of calculation, but it ended in the summer after the start of a new year on a spring basis (years of exile) but before the start of the new year on an autumn basis (years of Zedekiah's reign). Accepting an autumn calendar then indicates the siege lasted two and a half years.

One factor that enabled Jerusalem to hold out for so long was the lifting of the siege through Egyptian intervention (37:5-11). By Malamat's reckoning (1968:152-153) this occurred at the end of the winter and in the spring of 587 BC, that is, a year after the start of the siege and a year and three months before its termination. In January 587 BC Egypt is described as unreliable and threatened with defeat (Ezek. 29:1-16). At the end of April 587 BC Egyptian power is portrayed as broken and their armies are being defeated (Ezek. 30:20-26). Speaking in the middle of June in the same year Ezekiel treats the defeat of the Egyptians as an accomplished fact (Ezek. 31:1-18).

13. The International Conference. In Jer. 27:3 we are told about envoys from surrounding nations who gathered in Jerusalem. In 28:1 the year is identified as the fourth year of Zedekiah. Now assuming his regnal years are counted from Tishri 597 BC, his fourth year would be autumn 594–autumn 593 BC. (If his regnal years are counted from Nisan, decisions have to be made regarding when precisely he was appointed as king. His fourth year is either spring 594–spring 593 BC, or spring 593–spring 592 BC.) The question that arises is the relationship between the holding of this conference and the fact that the Babylonian Chronicle records internal unrest in Babylonia during the tenth year of Nebuchadnezzar (spring 595–spring 594 BC) in the months Kislev and Tebet (December 595–January 594 BC). The causes of this rebellion are unknown, but the way in which Nebuchadnezzar dealt with it suggests it was political rather than military in origin (Wiseman 1985:34). The Chronicle makes clear that after suppressing the rebellion Nebuchadnezzar went once more to Syria–Palestine to receive tribute and that his army was again in the area in the following year (594/593 BC; Wiseman 1985:35). It may be that the conference was convened because reports had been received regarding Nebuchadnezzar's internal troubles, but it is difficult to trace any precise link.

14. The Three Deportations of Jeremiah 52. In 52:28-30 there is a note about three deportations from Judah: the first in Nebuchadnezzar's seventh year (v. 28) involving 3,023 Jews; the second in his eighteenth year (v. 29) involving 832 people from Jerusalem; and the third, in his twenty-third year (v. 30), affecting 745. However, in 2 Kgs. 24:14 we are told that in his eighth year Nebuchadnezzar took from Jerusalem 10,000 soldiers and craftsmen. Mention is also made in 2 Kgs. 25:11 of an unspecified deportation of people who remained in the city and those who had deserted. This took place in Nebuchadnezzar's nineteenth year.

Are the deportations of the seventh and eighteenth years to be identified with those of the eighth and nineteenth years by arguing that the years have been calculated using different calendars? But modifying the calendar does not account for the significant differences in the numbers involved. Bright (1965:369) suggested that the Jeremiah figure might represent only the men. Further, these figures are not directly associated with action against Jerusalem as the third figure makes clear in connection with the twenty-third year.

If the year is reckoned on a spring basis, then the seventh year is spring 598–spring 597 BC and covers the capture of Jerusalem in the spring of 597 BC. But the discrepancy in the numbers being deported makes it unlikely that the same event is being referred to. If an autumn calendar is employed, then Nebuchadnezzar's seventh year is autumn 599–autumn 598 BC, and it may well be that these deportees resulted from the brief campaign conducted from December 599 to February 598 BC (see §9 above). The idea of a southern foray at the same time as the main action was being taken against the Arab tribes is not improbable in view of 2 Kings 24:2. This would have been part of Nebuchadnezzar's repraisals against Jehoiakim before launching his main offensive the following year.

The second figure comes from Nebuchadnezzar's eighteenth year (autumn 588–autumn 587 BC) and relates not to the fall of the city but to persons captured in the earlier stages of the siege. The figure for the Nebuchadnezzar's twenty-third year (autumn 583–autumn 582 BC) has been related by some to reprisals after Gedaliah's assassination, but if that took place in the immediate aftermath of the fall of the city (cf. 43:1), the response seems somewhat belated, and what occurred in 582 BC may relate rather to subsequent Bablyonian activity in the area (cf. 48:1).

No other source gives these figures, but that does not mean that they are the product of exilic editing and invention. The exact numbers used point to their being derived from some official data. Green (1982:64) suggests that these minor deportations were significant to whoever brought together the material in Jeremiah 52 because they represented a vindication of the prophet's repeated warnings of divine judgment as a result of Judah's rebellious history.

WORKS CITED

Aejmelaeus, A.
1986 'Function and Interpretation of כי in Biblical Hebrew'. *JBL* 105:193-209.
Aitken, K. T.
1984 'The Oracles against Babylon in Jeremiah 50-51: Structures and Perspectives'. *TynBull* 35:25-63.
Anderson, B. W.
1978 ' "The Lord Has Created Something New": A Stylistic Study of Jer 31:15-22'. *CBQ* 40:463-478.
Archer, G. L.
1991 'The Relationship between the Septuagint Translation and the Massoretic Text in Jeremiah'. *TrinJ* 12NS:139-150.
Avigad, N.
1978 'Baruch the Scribe and Jerahmeel the King's Son'. *IEJ* 28:52–56. (reprinted *BA* 42:114–18.)
Baldwin, J.
1964 '*Ṣemaḥ* as a Technical Term in the Prophets'. *VT* 14:93-97.
Balentine, S. E.
1984 'The Prophet as Intercessor: A Reassessment'. *JBL* 103:161-173.
Barstad, H. M.
1993 'No Prophets? Recent Developments in Biblical Prophetic Research and Ancient Near Eastern Prophecy'. *JSOT* 57:39-60.
Block, D. I.
2000 *The Gods of the Nations: Studies in Ancient Near Eastern National Theology.* ETS Studies. Grand Rapids: Baker and Leicester: Apollos.
Bracke, J. M.
1985 '*šûb šᵉbût:* A Reappraisal'. *ZAW* 97:233-244.
Bright, J.
1965 *Jeremiah: Introduction, Translation and Notes.* The Anchor Bible. Garden City: Doubleday & Co.
Brown, M. L.
1995 *Israel's Divine Healer.* Studies in Old Testament Theology. Carlisle: Paternoster Press.
Brueggemann, W.
1994 ' "The Baruch Connection": Reflections on Jer. 43:1-7'. *JBL* 113:405-20.
1998 *A Commentary on Jeremiah. Exile and Homecoming.* Grand Rapids: Eerdmans. Originally, *To Pluck Up, To Tear Down: A Commentary on the Book of Jeremiah 1–25* (1988) and *To Build, To Plant: A Commentary on Jeremiah 26-52* (1991).

Calvin, J.
  1850 *Commentaries on the Book of the Prophet Jeremiah and the Lamentations.* 5 vols. Trans. J. Owen. Edinburgh: Calvin Translation Society. Original Latin 1559. Various reprints.
Carroll, R. P.
  1981 *From Chaos to Covenant: Uses of Prophecy in the Book of Jeremiah.* London: SCM Press.
  1986 *Jeremiah: A Commentary.* Old Testament Library. London: SCM Press.
Castellino, G. R.
  1980 'Observations on the Literary Structure of Some Passages in Jeremiah'. *VT* 30:398-408.
Cazelles, H.
  1984 'Zephaniah, Jeremiah, and the Scythians in Palestine' in Perdue and Kovacs (1984:129-161).
Clements, R. E.
  1981 'Jeremiah. Prophet of Hope.' *Review and Expositor* 78:345-63.
  1988 *Jeremiah.* Interpretation. Atlanta: John Knox Press.
Clines, D. J. A.
  1972 'Regnal Year Reckoning in the Last Days of the Kingdom of Judah'. *Australian Journal of Biblical Archaeology* 2:9-34.
Craigie, P. C., P. H. Kelley, and J. F. Drinkard, Jr.
  1991 *Jeremiah 1–25.* Word Biblical Commentary. Dallas: Word Books.
DeRoche, M.
  1983 'Jeremiah 2:2-3 and Israel's Love for God during the Wilderness Wanderings'. *CBQ* 45:364-375.
Diamond, A. R. P.
  1990 'Jeremiah's Confessions in the LXX and MT: A Witness to Developing Canonical Function?' *VT* 40:33-50.
Diamond, A. R. P., O'Connor, K. M., and Stulman, L. (eds.)
  1999 *Troubling Jeremiah.* Sheffield: Sheffield Academic Press.
Driver, S. R.
  1895 *A Critical and Exegetical Commentary on Deuteronomy.* ICC. Edinburgh: T. & T. Clark.
  1906 *The Book of the Prophet Jeremiah: A Revised Translation.* London: Hodder and Stoughton.
Durham, J. I.
  1970 'שָׁלוֹם and the Presence of God' in *Proclamation and Presence,* J. I. Durham and J. R. Porter (eds.). London: SCM Press.
Ellison, H. L.
  1959-1967 'The Prophecy of Jeremiah'. *Evangelical Quarterly* 31 (1959):143-51, 205-17; 32 (1960):3-14, 107-13, 212-23; 33 (1961):27-35, 148-56, 220-27; 34 (1962):16-28, 96-102, 154-

162; 35 (1963):4-14, 160-67, 196-205; 36 (1964):3-11, 92-99, 148-56; 37 (1965):21-28, 100-109, 147-54, 232-41; 38 (1966): 40-51, 158-68, 233-40; 39 (1967): 40-47, 165-72, 216-24.

Emerton, J. A.
  1981 'Notes on Some Problems in Jeremiah V 26' in Caquot, A. and Delcor, M. (eds.) *Mélanges bibliques et orientaux en l'honneur de M. Henri Cazelles.* Neukirchen-Vluyn: Neukirchener Verlag.

Finegan, J.
  1998 *Handbook of Biblical Chronology. Principles of Time Reckoning in the Ancient World and Problems of Chronology in the Bible.* rev. ed. Peabody, Mass.: Hendrickson.

Finley, T. J.
  1985 'An Evangelical Reponse to the Preaching of Amos'. *JETS* 28:411-420.

Goldingay, J.
  1984 *God's Prophet, God's Servant. A Study in Jeremiah and Isaiah 40–55.* Exeter: Paternoster Press.

Green, A. R.
  1982 'The Chronology of the Last Days of Judah: Two Apparent Discrepancies'. *JBL* 101:57-73.

Habel, N.
  1965 'The Form and Significance of the Call Narratives'. *ZAW* 77:297-323.

Harrison, R. K.
  1973 *Jeremiah and Lamentations: An Introduction and Commentary.* Tyndale Old Testament Commentaries. London: Inter-Varsity Press.

Hengstenberg, E. W.
  1856 *Christology of the Old Testament and a Commentary on the Messianic Predictions.* Trans. T. Meyer. Edinburgh: T & T Clark. 4 volumes.

Henderson, J. M.
  2002 'Who weeps in Jeremiah VIII 23 (IX 1)? Identifying Dramatic Speakers in the Poetry of Jeremiah'. *VT* 52:191-206.

Heschel, A.
  1962 *The Prophets.* New York: Harper and Row.

Hess, R. S.
  1991 'Hiphil Forms of *qwr* in Jeremiah vi 7'. *VT* 41:347-50.

Hicks, R. L.
  1983 '*Delet* and *Mᵉgillāh*. A Fresh Approach to Jeremiah xxxvi'. *VT* 33:46-66.

Hillers, D. R.
  1969 *Covenant: The History of a Biblical Idea.* Baltimore: The Johns Hopkins Press.

Hoffman, Y.
1982	'From Oracle to Prophecy: Crystallization and Disintegration of a Biblical Gattung'. *JNSL* 10:75-81.
Holladay, W. L.
1962 a 'Style, Irony and Authenticity in Jeremiah'. *JBL* 81:44-54.
1962 b 'The So-Called "Deuteronomic Gloss" in Jer. viii 19b'. *VT* 12:494-498.
1974	*Jeremiah: Spokesman Out of Time.* New York: The Pilgrim Press.
1976	*The Architecture of Jeremiah 1–20.* Lewisburg: Bucknell University Press.
1980	'The Identification of the Two Scrolls of Jeremiah'. *VT* 30:452-467.
1986	*Jeremiah I.* Hermeneia. Philadelphia: Fortress Press.
1989	*Jeremiah II.* Hermeneia. Minneapolis: Augsburg Fortress Press.
Holt, E. K.
1999	'The Potent Word of God: Remarks on the Composition of Jeremiah 37–44' in Diamond et. al. 1999:161-170.
Horn, S. H.
1967	'The Babylonian Chronicle and the Ancient Calendar of the Kingdom of Judah'. *AUSS* 5:12-27.
Jobling, D.
1978	'Jeremiah's Poem in III 1– IV 2'. *VT* 28:45-55.
Johnson, A. R.
1962	*The Cultic Prophet in Ancient Israel.* 2nd edition. Cardiff: University of Wales.
Jones, D. R.
1992	*Jeremiah.* New Century Bible Commentary. London: Marshall Pickering.
Joüon, P.
1991	*A Grammar of Biblical Hebrew.* Translated and revised by T. Muraoka. Rome: Editrice Pontificio Istituto Biblico.
Kaiser, W. C. Jr.
1998	*A History of Israel from the Bronze Age through the Jewish Wars.* Nashville: Broadman & Holman.
Keil, C. F.
1873	*The Prophecies of Jeremiah.* 2 vol. in C. F. Keil and F. Delitzsch, *Biblical Commentary on the Old Testament.* Edinburgh: T&T Clark. Vol. 1 trans. D. Patrick. Vol. 2 trans. J. Kennedy. Original German 1872. Often reprinted.
Keown, G. L., P. J. Scalise, and T. G. Smothers
1995	*Jeremiah 26–52.* Word Biblical Commentary. Dallas: Word Books.

Kidner, D.
  1973 *Psalms 1–72.* Tyndale Old Testament Commentaries. Leicester: Inter-Varsity Press.
King, P. J.
  1993 *Jeremiah: An Archaeological Companion.* Louisville, Ky: Westminster/John Knox Press.
Kline, M. G.
  1989 'Double Trouble'. *JETS* 32:171-179.
Laetsch, T.
  1952 *Jeremiah.* Bible Commentary. St Louis: Concordia.
Lee, N. C.
  1999 'Exposing a Buried Subtext in Jeremiah and Lamentations: Going After Baal and … Abel' in Diamond et al. (1999:87-122).
Lehmann, M. R.
  1969 'Biblical Oaths'. *ZAW* 81:74-92.
Lindblom, J.
  1962 *Prophecy in Ancient Israel.* Oxford: Basil Blackwell.
Longman, T., III
  1996 'Literary Approaches to Biblical Interpretation' in M. Silva (ed.) *Foundations of Contemporary Interpretation.* Leicester: Apollos. Originally 1987.
Lundbom, J. R.
  1986 'Baruch, Seraiah, and Expanded Colophons in the Book of Jeremiah'. *JSOT* 36:89-114.
  1993 *The Early Career of the Prophet Jeremiah.* Mellen Biblical Press: Lewiston, New York.
  1997 *Jeremiah: A Study in Ancient Hebrew Rhetoric.* Second Edition; originally 1975. Winona Lake: Eisenbrauns.
  1999 *Jeremiah 1–20: A New Translation with Introduction and Commentary.* The Anchor Bible. New York: Doubleday.
Mackay, J. L.
  1998 *Jonah, Micah, Nahum, Habakkuk and Zephaniah.* Fearn, Ross-shire: Christian Focus.
  2001 *Exodus.* A Mentor Commentary. Fearn, Ross-shire: Christian Focus.
Malamat, A.
  1956 'A New Record of Nebuchadrezzar's Palestinian Campaign'. *IEJ* 6:246-256.
  1968 'The Last Kings of Judah and the Fall of Jerusalem: An Historical–Chronological Study'. *IEJ* 18:137-155.

Margaliot, M.
    1980   'Jeremiah X 1-16: a re-examination'. *VT* 30:295-308.
Matthews, V. H. and D. C. Benjamin
    1993   *Social World of Ancient Israel, 1250-587 B.C.E.* Peabody,
            Mass.: Hendrickson.
McComiskey, T. E.
    1993   'Prophetic Irony in Hosea 1:4: A Study of the Collocation *pqd 'l*
            and its Implications for the Fall of Jehu's Dynasty'. *JSOT*
            58:93-101.
McConville, J. G.
    1991   'Jeremiah: Prophet and Book'. *TynBull* 42:80-95.
    1993   *Judgment and Promise: An Interpretation of the Book of
            Jeremiah.* Leicester: Apollos.
McFall, L.
    1991   'A Translation Guide to the Chronological Data in Kings and
            Chronicles'. *BibSac* 148:3-45.
McKane, W.
    1965   *Prophets and Wise Men.* Studies in Biblical Theology 44.
            London: SCM Press.
    1986   *A Critical and Exegetical Commentary on Jeremiah I. Jeremiah
            I–XXV.* Edinburgh: T & T Clark.
    1996   *A Critical and Exegetical Commentary on Jeremiah II.
            Jeremiah XXVI–LII.* Edinburgh: T & T Clark.
Miller, J. M. and J. H. Hayes
    1986   *A History of Ancient Israel and Judah.* London: SCM Press.
Miller, P. D.
    1982   'Sin and Judgment in the Prophets: A Stylistic and Theological
            Analysis'. Society of Biblical Literature Monograph Series 27.
            Chico, Calif.: Scholars Press.
Naegelsbach, C. W. E.
    1871   'The Book of the Prophet Jeremiah Theologically and Homileti-
            cally Expounded' in J. P. Lange *Commentary on the Holy
            Scriptures: Critical, Doctrinal and Homiletical.* Trans. S. R.
            Ashbury. Edinburgh: T & T Clark. German original 1868.
            Reprinted.
Negev, A. and S. Gibson
    2001   *Archaeological Encyclopedia of the Holy Land.* London and
            New York: Continuum.
Nicholson, E. W.
    1970   *Preaching to the Exiles: A Study of the Prose Tradition in the
            Book of Jeremiah.* Oxford: Oxford University Press.
    1973   *The Book of the Prophet Jeremiah, Chapters 1-25.* The
            Cambridge Bible Commentary on the New English Bible. Cam-
            bridge: Cambridge University Press.

1975   *The Book of the Prophet Jeremiah, Chapters 26-52*. The
        Cambridge Bible Commentary on the New English Bible. Cam-
        bridge: Cambridge University Press.

O'Connor, K. M.
1988   *The Confessions of Jeremiah: Their Interpretation and Role in
        Chapters 1–25*. SBL Disseration Series 94. Atlanta: Scholars
        Press.

Ortlund, R. C., Jr.
1996   *Whoredom: God's Unfaithful Wife in Biblical Theology*. New
        Studies in Biblical Theology, 2. Leicester: Apollos.

Overholt, T. W.
1970   *The Threat of Falsehood: A Study in the Theology of the Book
        of Jeremiah*. Studies in Biblical Theology, Second Series:16.
        London: SCM Press

Perdue, L. G. and B. W. Kovacs, (eds.)
1984   *A Prophet to the Nations: Essays in Jeremiah Studies*. Winona
        Lake: Eisenbrauns.

Polk, T.
1984   *The Prophetic Persona: Jeremiah and the Language of Self*.
        JSOTSup 32. Sheffield: JSOT.

Rad, G. von
1984   'The Confessions of Jeremiah' in Perdue and Kovacs
        (1984:339-48). German original, 1936.

Roberts, J. J. M.
1992   'The Motif of the Weeping God in Jeremiah and Its Background
        in the Lament Tradition of the Ancient Near East'. *Old Testa-
        ment Essays* 5:361-74.

Robinson, D. W. B.
1951   *Josiah's Reform and the Book of The Law*. London: Tyndale
        Press.

Rowley, H. H.
1950   'The Prophet Jeremiah and the Book of Deuteronomy' in
        Studies in Old Testament Prophecy (pp. 157-174), ed. H. H.
        Rowley. Edinburgh: T. & T. Clark.
1963   'The Early Prophecies of Jeremiah in their Setting' in *Men of
        God: Studies in Old Testament History and Prophecy* (pp. 133-
        168). London: Thomas Nelson and Sons. Originally *BJRL* 45
        (1962-63): 198-234. Also in Perdue and Kovacs (1984:33-61).

Skinner, J.
1922   *Prophecy and Religion: Studies in the Life of Jeremiah*. Cam-
        bridge: Cambridge University Press.

Snaith, N.
1971   'Jeremiah xxxiii 18', *VT* 21:620-22.

Southwood, C. H.
   1979   'The Spoiling of Jeremiah's Girdle'. *VT* 29:231-237.
Stalker, J.
   1895   'Jeremiah: the Man and his Message'. *The Expositor,* 5th series, 1:66-73.
Thiele, E.
   1983   *The Mysterious Numbers of the Hebrew Kings.* 3rd edition. [1st ed. 1951; rev. ed. 1983] Grand Rapids: Zondervan.
Thompson, J. A.
   1980   *The Book of Jeremiah.* New International Commentary on the Old Testament. Grand Rapids: Eerdmans.
Thomson, W. M.
   1872   *The Land and the Book; or, Biblical Illustrations drawn from The Manners and Customs, the Scenes and Scenery of the Holy Land.* London: Nelson and Sons.
Von Rad, G.
   1965   *Old Testament Theology.* Volume II. London: Oliver and Boyd.
Welch, A. C.
   1928   *Jeremiah: His Time and Work.* London: Oxford University Press.
Wilson, R. R.
   1999   'Poetry and Prose in the Book of Jeremiah', pages 413-427 of R. Chazan, W. W. Hallo, and L. H. Schiffman (eds.), *Ki Baruch Hu: Ancient Near Eastern, Biblical and Judaic Studies in Honour of Baruch A. Levine.* Winona Lake: Eisenbrauns.
Wiseman, D. J.
   1956   *Chronicles of the Chaldean Kings (625–556 B.C.) in the British Museum.* London: British Museum.
   1985   *Nebuchadrezzar and Babylon.* The Schweich Lectures of the British Academy 1983. Oxford: Oxford University Press.
Wright, C. J. H.
   1983   *Living as the People of God: The Relevance of Old Testament Ethics.* Leicester: Inter-Varsity Press.
Woudstra, M. H.
   1965   *The Ark of the Covenant from Conquest to Kingship.* Philadelphia: Presbyterian and Reformed Publishing Co.

SUBJECT INDEX

References are to volume and page number.

accession year 2:117
Ahikam 2:131-3
almond tree 1:106
altar
  horns of 1:510
Ammon 2:137, 489-94
Anathoth 1:89, 413
  purchase of field in 2:247-52
Apis 2:451
Aramaic 1:378
Ararat 2:561
ark of the covenant 1:192-4
armour 2:443
Ashdod 2:103
Ashkelon 2:103, 462-3
Ashkenaz 2:561
assaying metal 1:287-91
Assyria 1:38-41, 151
astral worship 1:326, 372
athbash 2:104, 546
audience of prophet 1:121-2
Azekah 2:291

Baal 1:139
  Baals 1:157, 162
Baalis 2:385
Babel 2:551
Babylon 2:514-581
  fall of 1:49-51
  gates of 2:577
  prayer for 2:164
  seventy years 2:96-8, 165
  wall of 2:570
Babylonian Chronicle 1:36; 2:603
Babylonians
  as fishermen and hunters 1:504
  Chaldeans 2:18
  surrender to 2:21
balm 1:347
Baruch 2:251, 314-29, 407, 430-4
Bashan 2:39

baskets of figs 2:79-86
Bel 2:518, 570
Ben Hinnom, valley of
                1:553; 2:242
Benjamin 1:266, 529
Benjamin Gate 1:561; 2:340, 352
Bethel 2:472
blue 1:377
boiling pot 1:108
bondservant 2:295
Book of Consolation 2:181
bow 2:512
Branch 2:50-1, 277
bullae 1:88; 2:251, 318, 326
burden 2:74-9

call of prophet 1:93-5
Canaanite worship 1:155, 161
cannibalism 1:556
Carchemish 2:441-2, 608-9
Carmel 2:452
chaff 1:450
Chaldeans 2:18
Chemosh 2:469, 472
chronology 2:603-16
circumcision 1:207, 367
cistern 1:145-6, 458
clay jar 1:552
colophon 1:34; 2:430
Coniah, see Jehoiachin
Confessions 1:407-9
correspondence between
  sin and judgment 1:134
counsellors, royal 1:545
counter-liturgy 1:455
courtyard of the guard 2:345
covenant
  Abrahamic 1:204
  breach of 1:474
  ceremony, cutting 2:298
  Davidic 1:301

everlasting 2:264-6
formula 1:398
lawsuit 1:124, 141
covenant
  marriage as metaphor 1:125
  new 2:233-9
  Sinai 1:396; 2:234
  Zedekiah's 2:292-9
cup 2:99
Cush 1:449; 2:351, 446

Damascus 2:505-7
Dan 1:223
daughter of my people 1:220-1
daughter of Zion 1:236
David 2:190
  throne of 2:27
day of the LORD 1:216; 2:188-9
Decalogue 1:305
Dedan 2:496
deed of purchase 2:250
Deuteronomy 1:28-30
  Deuteronomic style 1:295
death personified 1:363
deportation 1:360
Diogenes 1:239
divine assembly 2:66
divorce 1:173-5
donkey, wild 1:158
dreams 2:70-2
drought 1:420, 456-60

Ebed-Melech 2:351-4, 372-3
Edom 2:137, 494-505
Egypt 1:151; 2:440-457
  execration texts 1:557
  exiles in 2:85, 395-429
  like serpent 2:454
  Upper 2:414
Elasah 2:160
Elam 2:511-3
Elephantine 1:313; 2:250, 252,
  410, 415, 422, 473
Elnathan 2:132, 320
envoys
  to Jerusalem 2:137

Ephraim 1:223
  firstborn son 2:214
  repentance of 2:220-3
Ethiopian 1:449; 2:351
Euphrates 1:433-4
Evil-Merodach 2:599
exiles
  conditions for 1:49; 2:162-3
  future of 2:82
  in Egypt 2:85
  letter to 2:159-173
Exodus 2:206

false prophets 1:466; 2:55-59
fasting 1:464
figs 2:79-86, 170
flesh 1:513
foe from north 1:110, 209-11
freeing of slaves 2:292-4

gate of Temple 1:297-8
Gaza 2:458-9
Gedaliah 1:48, 61; 2:371,
  381-88
Gehenna 1:324
Gemariah, son of Shaphan 2:318
Gibeon 2:393
Gilead 1:347; 2:29, 447
God, see LORD
grapes
  treading 2:107
great king 2:233

Hanamel 2:248
Hananiah 2:149
harvest 1:346
Hazor 2:508-11
heart 1:78, 508, 516
Hebrew 2:293
Heliopolis 2:412
helmet 2:443
Herodotus 1:48, 210; 2:103, 446,
  459, 512, 525, 534, 561, 563
Hezekiah 1:38-9; 2:128
Hilkiah 1:89
high place 1:321

highway 2:224
Hinnom, valley 1:322
Hophra 2:15, 337, 428, 452
idols
  construction of 1:373, 376-7
  impotence of 1:374
incense 1:282, 558
intergenerational responsibility
  2:231-2, 254
international blessing 1:194
iron 1:397, 485
Isaiah
  connections with 2:183, 214, 224
Ishmael 2:382, 387-94
Israel
  nation 2:240
  the northern kingdom 1:181
  rest 2:207
Jacob 1:133, 351-2, 516; 2:191
jackals 1:356
Jazer 2:481
Jehoahaz 1:43-4, 57; 2:32-3
Jehoiachin 1:46, 59, 445; 2:42-6
  deportation of 2:80, 160
  in exile 2:599-600
  status of 2:151
Jehoiakim 1:44-6, 58-9; 2:34-9,
  130-1, 310-26
  death predicted 2:38-9, 328
Jehovah Tsidkenu 2:53, 278
Jeremiah (the book)
  composition of 1:21-8
  structure of 1:17-21
  the Two Scrolls 1:22-5
Jeremiah, style of writing
  again and again, rising early
    1:308-9
  infinitive absolute 1:126
  sword, famine and plague 1:465
  three successive questions 1:347
Jeremiah
  anguish of 1:225-6, 344-8, 381,
    444

  arrest of 2:341
  attitude to Josiah's reform
    1:54-6
  avoidance of weddings and
    funerals 1:495-9
  banned from Temple 2:315
  call 1:93-5
  calls for vindication 1:548-50
  character 1:61-5
  Confessions 1:407-9
  date of birth 1:52-3
  early years 1:51-4
  Egyptian ministry 2:409-29
  flogging of 1:561; 2:341-2
  forbidden to intercede 1:311,
    411, 472
  imprisonment of 2:342, 350
  intercession 1:387
  in hiding 2:322, 326
  letter to Babylon 2:159-173
  marriage prohibited 1:494
  name, meaning of 1:88-9
  need to repent 1:490
  northern ministry 1:56, 185
  plots against 1:413, 544, 570
  prayer of 2:252-8
  purchase of field 2:247-52
  restriction of 2:315
  shepherd 1:522
  in stocks 1:561
  surrender advocated 2:21
  taken to Egypt 2:408
  well-treated by Babylonians
    2:369-72, 377-81
  writing of scrolls 2:314, 329
Jerusalem
  attitude of people 2:25-6
  diplomatic conference 2:134-8,
    614-5
  fall of city 2:363-5
  future of 1:194, 528
  rebuilt 2:241-3
  siege by Babylon 2:245
  siege by Sennacherib 1:38

set on fire   2:368
Jew   2:251, 294
Johanan   2:382, 385-409
Jordan   1:422
Josephus   1:47, 50, 53; 2:39, 103,
          328, 431, 449, 464, 474, 489,
          586, 588, 598, 610, 613
Josiah   1:41-3; 2:36-7
  death of   1:43, 57; 2:32
  reforms of   1:171-2
Judah
  attitude to ark   1:192-3
  attitude to Law   1:338
  attitude to Temple   1:300
  deceptive behaviour   1:351, 354
  not completely destroyed   1:256
  pagan influence on   1:76-8, 372
  return prophesied   2:227
  stiff-necked   1:319
  truth absent   1:350
justice   2:28

Kedar   1:142; 2:508-9
Kimchi   1:252, 323, 333, 338,
                              396, 526
Kings
  silent regarding Jeremiah   1:30;
                                    2:585
kings,
  critique of   2:26-46
  duties of   2:23-4, 28
Kittim   1:142

Lachish   2:291
Lachish Ostraca   1:31, 47, 267;
                2:292, 337-8, 349, 358
lamp   2:96
land
  ownership of   1:365
  possession of   1:398; 2:186
Lebanon   2:30, 41-2
Leb Kamai   2:546
leopard   1:449
letter to exiles   2:159-73
Levites   2:279-82
Lie, the   1:199, 240, 300

libations   1:314
linen belt   1:433-9
LORD, the
  Almighty, of hosts   1:153
  creator   1:379
  cup of wrath   2:99-101
  father   1:178, 196-7; 2:213
  as husband   1:127-9, 190
  incomparability   1:375
  hatred of   1:425
  Holy One   2:536, 549
  husband   2:235
  king   1:375, 378
  living   1:377
  love of   2:208
  loving-kindness of   2:208
  omnipresence   2:69
  omniscience   2:69
  Redeemer   2:539
  refining   1:353
  repentance of   1:233, 537
  retribution of   1:135
  our righteousness   2:53-4
  sovereign control   1:536-8
  transcendence of   2:69
  wonders of   2:17
  vengeance   1:248
Lydia   2:446

Magor-Missabib   1:562
Manasseh   1:39-40, 477
man of God   2:302
Marduk   1:379, 2:518
Medes   2:561-2
Megiddo   2:606
Memphis   1:149; 2:414, 450
Merathaim   2:532
Messianic prophecy   1:81; 2:50-4,
                              190, 277-9
  of priest-king   2:201
Micah   2:127
Migdol   2:414, 450
Minni   2:561
Mizpah   2:380
Moab   2:137, 463-89

Moabite Stone   2:466, 469, 486, 490

Molech   1:323; 2:261, 490

Moses   1:475

mourners   1:361

nations, blessing of   1:194, 506

Nebuchadnezzar   2:442

my servant   2:94, 138, 410-1

spelling of   2:139

Nebuzaradan   2:368, 377-80, 591-2

Neco II   2:442

Negev   1:529

Nehusta   1:445 ; 2:44

Nergal-Sharezer   2:365

new covenant   1:80-1; 2:233-9

Nile   2:445

nobles   1:457

officials   2:122, 347

On   2:412

Oracles against the Nations   1:25, 2:437-440

of restoration   2:455, 488

Septuagint   2:89, 437-8

partridge   1:517

Pashhur, son of Immer   1:550

Pashhur, son of Malkijah   2:15, 347

peace   1:277

see also Zion theology

Pekod   2:532

pen   1:336

people, all the   2:121

Perath   1:437

perfect

performative   1:97

prophetic   1:82-3

Persia   2:525, 534, 543

Pharaoh's palace   2:410

Philistines   2:103, 458-63

poetic justice,

see LORD: retribution

poetry

significance of   1:30-2

poisoned water   1:341

population increase   1:192

Potsherd Gate   1:553

potter   1:534

wheel   1:534-5

priests

accuse Jeremiah   2:121

conduct of   1:264, 276-7, 545, 560

restoration of   2:217, 279

prophecy

inspiration   1:68-70

institution   1:65-7

international scope   1:104

revelation   1:67-8, 90-1

Spirit's role in   1:251

prophet   1:97

burden   2:74

call   1:93-5

intercession   1:310, 475

meaning of term   1:97

vision   1:105-6

prophets, false   1:70-1, 139-40, 251, 466-8, 545; 2:55-79

Ahab and Zedekiah   2:171-3

accuse Jeremiah   2:121

conduct of   1:275-7

peace prophesied by   1:218, 276; 2:58, 65, 344

restoration prophesied by   2:144

prose and poetry   1:30-2

Psammetichus I   2:442

Psammetichus II   2:137

purchase of field   2:247-52

purple   1:377

Queen of Heaven   1:313; 2:421

Qumran   1:34; 2:252

Rachel   2:218

rains   1:177, 260-1

Rashi   1:245, 252, 333, 422; 2:206

Rechabites   2:301

red   2:36

refining ore   1:287, 353
remember   1:487
remnant   2:211, 403, 419
repentance   1:78-9, 171, 537
reunion of Israel and Judah 1:195;
                                    2:210, 231
right of redemption   2:248
righteousness   2:28, 53-4

Sabbath   1:524-30
sacrifice   1:283, 315-7
  child   1:322-3
Samaria
  downfall of   1:310
  prophets of   2:62
  restoration of   2:210-4
Samuel   1:495
schools of the prophets   2:57
scroll   2:312
  columns of   2:324
scribes   1:336-7
Scythians   1:210-1
Septuagint   1:32-5; 2:437-8
Seraiah   2:578-80
seventy years   2:96-8, 165
shalom   1:277; 2:9
Shallum, see Jehoahaz
Shaphan   2:132
Sheba   1:282
Shemaiah   2:173-7
Shephelah   1:529
shepherd   1:191; 2:46-7, 108
Sheshach   2:104-5, 569
shield   2:443
Shiloh   1:308; 2:119
Sidon   2:103, 137
siege ramps   1:270
signet ring   2:43
sin
  forgiveness of   2:238
  intergenerational   2:232
sirocco   1:220
slave
  bondservant   2:295
snakes   1:343

Sodom and Gomorrah   2:63, 502,
                                      542
spear   1:284
stocks   1:561
symbolic action   1:432-3, 551;
                                2:136-7, 410
symbolic event   1:533
symbolic perception   1:105-6

Tabor   2:452
Tahpanhes 1:149; 2:409, 414, 450
tambourines   2:209
Tekoa   1:267
tel   2:199
Temple   1:300-1
  articles from 2:146, 150, 592-96
  courtyard   1:525; 2:117
  destruction prophesied   2:127
  door-keeper   2:303, 596
  gates   1:525
  New Gate   2:123
  prophets   2:57
  Sermon   1:295-6; 2:116-20
  side rooms   2:302
  third entrance   2:355
terror on every side   1:286
Thebes   2:456
Tophet   1:322, 555
Tyre   2:103, 137
unclean   1:452
uncreation   1:230-1
Uriah   2:129-131
Uz   2:103

Valley of Ben Hinnom   1:322
vines   2:210
Virgin Israel   1:469, 541; 2:209
visions
  almond branch   1:105-7
  basket of figs   2:81
  boiling pot   1:108-10
  types of   1:105-6
war club   2:557
weddings and funerals 1:496-500
wine, new   2:216

wineskin 1:440-2
winnowing 1:220, 479; 2:547
wise, the 1:338, 545
wonders 2:17
word of God
  burden 2:74-9
  compared to fire 1:569; 2:72
  compared to hammer 2:72
  power of prophetic 1:93-4
wormwood 1:360
yoke 2:136
  broken 2:154
  of law 1:244

Zedekiah 1:46-48, 60; 2:13-15, 54, 134-5, 143, 151, 246-7, 334-5, 586-11
  approached 2:288
  capture of 2:366-7
  deputation to Jeremiah 2:14-17, 336-7
  envoys to Babylon 2:160
  interview with Jeremiah 2:343-5, 355-61
Zephaniah (priest) 2:15-16, 174-6, 336, 596-7
Zion 1:191; 2:521
Zion theology 1:301, 466

INDEX OF PRINCIPAL SCRIPTURAL PASSAGES

Genesis
1:1-2 1:231
2:5 1:231
6:17 1:381
12:3 1:204
15:7-21 2:297
15:16 1:238
16:2 2:315
17:8 1:304
17:5 2:240
18:14 2:254
20:7 1:310
22:17 1:480

Exodus
4:10 1:98
4:22 1:196
6:7 1:317
7:1 1:97
15:26 1:199
19:5 1:73, 317
20:8 1:524
22:2 1:168
24:7 1:154
32:14 1:479
34:7 2:194
34:16 1:489

Leviticus
16:30 2:272
18:19-30 1:137
24:19 2:529
26:21-22 1:245
26:33 1:360
26:44 1:233, 471
26:45 1:473

Numbers
16:22 2:258
21:29 2:488
24:5 2:198
24:17 2:463, 488
25:10-13 2:282

Deuteronomy
4:29 2:167
4:30-31 2:167
4:32-33 1:274
5:3 1:316
5:12, 15 1:527
5:33 1:317
6:5 1:129; 2:263
8:7 1:137
10:16 1:207
15:12 2:287
15:15 2:287
17:15 2:201
18:18 1:70, 100, 111
18:22 2:154
21:18, 20 1:260
24:1-4 1:173
24:4 1:174
24:16 2:232
27:15-26 1:399
27:19 1:263; 2:28
27:26 1:397
28:13 2:200
28:16 1:470
28:25 1:477
28:26 1:324
28:48 2:156
28:49 1:222
28:49-52 1:253
28:65 2:207
29:1, 9 1:396
29:18-19 1:194
29:24 2:31
29:25-26 2:31
30:4 2:168
30:6 1:207; 2:263
30:14 2:236
30:15 2:21
30:16 1:466
32:4 1:133
32:9 1:382
32:20 1:421

32:29 1:265
32:40 2:29
32:41 1:248
33:28 2:52

1 Samuel
4:4 2:25
13:14 1:191
15:22 1:317
15:29 1:233

2 Samuel
5:6 2:25
7:14 1:301
7:16 1:301; 2:278
8:15 2:52
23:5 1:301; 2:51, 282

1 Kings
2:4 2:279
5:1 1:129
18:21 1:129
19:4 1:62

2 Kings
21:18 2:39
22:11 2:325
22:17 1:113
23:3 1:75
24:7 1:45

2 Chronicles
18:18 2:66
25:20 2:500
36:6 2:610

Nehemiah
1:1 2:609
2:1 2:609
13:18 1:524

Job
42:6 1:334

Psalms
1:1, 6 1:417
1:3 1:515

2:9	1:557	27:3	1:427	**Obadiah**	
10:11	1:421	29:13	1:418	1	1:87
11:4	1:307	31:1	1:150	1-2	2:500
11:6	2:99	37:35	1:301	3-4	2:501
25:11	1:461	44:2	1:96	5	2:497
29:11	1:277	44:28	2:94	7	2:359
31:13	1:569	45:1	2:94	15	2:529
35:7	1:219	45:11	2:54	**Jonah**	
36:10	2:208	49:1	1:96	3:4	1:71
39:1-2	1:569	53:3	1:65	**Micah**	
46:5	1:301	53:7	1:410	1:1	1:87
72:2	2:52	**Lamentations**		3:5	1:276
72:4	2:37	1:2	1:478; 2:195	3:12	2:127
77:7-9	1:15	1:11	1:49	6:2	1:231
79:6-7	1:389	1:12	1:478	**Habakkuk**	
80:13	1:426	2:13	1:557	2:13	2:578
86:11	2:263	2:14	2:79	**Zephaniah**	
88:18	1:573	5:7	2:232	1:11	1:239
94:7	1:307	**Ezekiel**		1:12	1:374
104:2	1:380	16:59-60	1:473	**Zechariah**	
118:8	1:514	17:16	2:367	4:10	1:81
132:13	1:301	18:2	2:232	**Malachi**	
132:17	2:51	18:25	2:232	1:3	2:503
135:7	1:380	24:1	2:613	2:7	1:138
145:17	1:366	33:21	2:614	————	
Proverbs		**Daniel**		**Matthew**	
2:17	1:178	1:1	2:609-10	2:16-18	2:219
3:19	1:380	**Hosea**		11:29	1:280
11:28	1:515	2:2	1:125	16:18	1:117
Ecclesiastes		2:15	1:128	26:27	1:81
3:6	2:47	3:1	1:125	26:42	1:576
10:10	2:232	4:16	2:221	28:18-20	1:116-7
12:5	1:361	10:11	2:221	**Mark**	
Isaiah		10:12	1:206	4:18-19	1:206
1:1	1:87	11:4	2:209	6:4	1:415
1:9	1:238	**Amos**		13:14	1:234
1:19-20	1:172	1:1	1:87	**Luke**	
1:28	1:520	3:12	1:101	1:35	1:97
8:11	1:566	5:16	1:361	1:78	2:51
10:3	1:253, 265	5:18	1:216	4:29	1:415
13:19	2:542	6:1	1:209		
16:6	2:479				
16:9	2:481				

15:21	1:201	**Romans**		**Ephesians**	
19:41-44	1:65	2:25, 29	1:368	3:20	2:253
19:41	1:445	3:9	1:368	**Philippians**	
22:20	1:81	4:13	2:240	1:28	1:117
John		8:29-30	1:97	**Hebrews**	
1:5	1:309	9:2	1:445	4:15-16	1:576
1:11	1:17	10:12-13	2:244	5:7	1:575
3:19	1:291	11:5	2:241	8:9	2:235
13:17	1:399	**1 Corinthians**		12:22	2:243
15:1	1:156	1:26-27	2:86	13:14	2:243
17:3	1:366	1:31	1:367	**1 Peter**	
Acts		7:26	1:494	4:17	2:106
14:17	1:473	**2 Corinthians**		**2 Peter**	
		2:15-16	1:290	1:20-21	1:67
		Galatians		**Revelation**	
		3:29	2:244	5:10	2:280
		4:26	2:243	6:10	1:419
		6:7	1:400	21:2	2:243
		6:16	2:244		

INDEX OF HEBREW WORDS

א

ʾābal 1:233
ʾaddîr 1:457
ʾāhab 2:208
ʾĕwîl 1:229
ʾāwen 1:223
ʾēzôr 1:436
ʾak 1:168, 188
ʾākēn 1:197
ʾāmar 1:197
ʾĕmet 1:203
ʾap 1:168

ב

bôʿ 1:137
bādād 1:488
bāgad 1:182
baḥan 1:287
bāṭaḥ II 1:422
beṭaḥ 2:53
bākâ 1:348
bārāʿ 2:225
bāraḥ 1:234
bôrît 1:156
bāśār 1:513; 2:258
bôš 1:160
bǝtûlâ 1:541

ג

gāʿal 2:215, 539
gēbîm 1:458
geber 1:513
gǝbîrâ 1:445
gǝbûrâ 1:375
gāzal 2:24
gālâ 2:82
gôrāl 1:451

ד

dāmâ 1:268, 341
dāmam 2:110
dîn 2:36-7
dǝrôr 2:293
dāraš 2:16

ה

hābal 2:64
hebel 1:134-5
hôy 2:34
hêkāl 1:301
hālak 1:134
hālal II 1:204, 365
hālal III 2:101
hămôn 1:380
hinnēh 1:111
hāpak 1:156

ז

zîd 2:406
zākar 1:127
zānâ 1:174
zǝʿāwâ 1:477
zaʿam 1:378
zûr 1:159, 257

ח

ḥāwâ 1:298
ḥāṭāʾ 1:169
ḥākām 1:229
ḥûl 1:226
ḥālaq 2:61
ḥēmâ 1:207
ḥāmal 1:442
ḥāmās 1:567
ḥānap 1:174
ḥesed 1:127-8
ḥāsîd 1:187
ḥōq 2:239
ḥōr 2:146
ḥāram 2:95
ḥārôn 1:215
ḥerpâ 1:487
ḥāšab 1:411
ḥātat 1:114-5

ט

ṭûbâ 1:137
ṭāmēʿ 1:137
ṭāʿab 1:137

י

yāʿaš 1:159
yādaʿ 1:96, 139
yālal 1:215
yāsar 1:164
yāṣar 1:96, 536
yāšaʿ 1:222

כ

kābôd 1:473
kābas 1:156
kî 1:83-4
kālam 1:177
kāʿas 1:314
kāpar 1:549-50
kārat bǝrît 2:298

ל

lēb, lēbāb 1:207, 508
lākēn 1:240, 252
lǝmaʿan 1:314

מ

māʿas	1:290
midbār	1:129
maḥăšābâ	1:411
māqôr	1:155
marzeaḥ	1:496
maśśāʾ	2:74-9
məšubâ	1:181
mišneh	1:505
mišpāṭ	1:203, 243, 366

נ

neʿum Yhwh	1:102, 2:73
nāʾap	1:183
nāʾaṣ	1:472
nābāʿ	2:129
nābîʿ	1:97
nēbel	1:441
nûd	1:203
nāweh	1:389
nəhî	1:363
naḥălâ	1:138
nāḥam	1:233, 537
nîr	1:206
nākâ	1:241
nēkār	1:257
nāsaʿ II	1:214
naʿar	1:99
nāpal	2:21
niplaʿôt	2:17
nepeš	1:167, 271-2
nāṣal	1:101
nēṣer	2:51
nāqâ	1:167
nāqam	1:248, 412
nēr	2:96
nešer	1:221
neter	1:156

ס

sābāl	1:229
sāgar	2:80
sôd	2:66
sāhar	1:470
sāpad	1:495
sûr	1:513
sārar	1:260
sārîs	2:352

ע

ʿābar	1:259
ʿûd	1:273
ʿāwel	1:133
ʿāwōn	1:156
ʿāzab	1:145
ʿāṭâ	2:412
ʿayin	1:145
ʿîr	1:559
ʿal-kēn	1:244
ʿôlām	2:95
ʿāmāl	1:575
ʿāqab	1:352
ʿereb	2:102
ʿărābâ	1:244
ʿāšaq	1:270, 302

פ

pādâ	2:215
pûṣ	1:360
pāḥad	1:152
pālal	1:311
pāqad	1:103, 194; 2:48
pārar	1:402, 473
pātâ	1:565-6
pitʿōm	1:228

צ

ṣedeq	2:51
ṣədāqâ	1:203, 366
ṣiyîm	2:542
ṣalmāwet	1:136-7
ṣāmaḥ	2:50
ṣîṣ	2:469-70

ק

qādaš	1:97, 129, 268, 527
qāwâ	1:462
qiṭṭēr	1:112
qəlālâ	2:86, 102
qālaʿ	1:384
qînâ	1:355, 363
qesep	1:378
qārāʿ	1:124, 227
qešer	1:401

ר

rōʿš	1:341
rāgaʿ	2:207
regaʿ	1:537
ruaḥ	1:251
rāḥap	2:59
rîb	1:124, 141
reaʿ	1:354
rāʾâ	1:112
rāʿaš	1:231
rāpāʿ	1:558

שׂ

śaʿar	1:144
śārak	1:158
śōrēq	1:155

שׁ

šûb	1:172
šābar	1:558
šeber	1:214
šādad	1:222; 2:547
šōd	1:567

ת

šāwᶜ	1:164	šəmāmâ	1:148	tāᶜab	1:137
šaḥat	1:214; 2:547	šāmaᶜ	1:397	tāpal	2:62
šālôm	1:277	šiqqûṣ	1:203	tāpaś	1:138
šāmēm	1:144	šeqer	1:199, 240, 300	tarmît	1:334
šammâ	1:148	šərîrût	1:194		

Jeremiah

A MENTOR COMMENTARY

Volume 1 : Chapters 1-20

John L. MacKay

Jeremiah
Volume 1: Chapters 1 -20
John L. Mackay

'Professor Mackay's commentary on Jeremiah is trebly welcome: first, from his earlier work on Exodus (in this series) we know that he will take the highest view of Scripture as the Word of God, and do so as one fully conversant with the wide literature available on Jeremiah. His workmanlike approach and marvellous attention to detail forbid him to take short cuts, fudge issues, or misrepresent those who take a different view from his own. Secondly, he argues cogently for Jeremiah as author of the whole, contending that the book as we have it represents written records contemporary with the prophet's preaching. He rejects the unsubstantiated idea of an ongoing 'school' of interpreters, adaptors and supplementarists of a Jeremianic 'core'. Thirdly, from the start he is concerned to handle the book of Jeremiah, not as an anthology, but as unfolding a unified message. Lovers of Hebrew will find a kindred spirit in Professor Mackay. Those without Hebrew will find a patient teacher leaving no stone unturned to make the word of God plain.'

Alec Motyer

'This eagerly awaited commentary on one of the longest and most taxing books of the Old Testament fulfils every expectation. Professor Mackay has already demonstrated his erudition and scholarship in previous commentaries, and this work is a landmark in Jeremiah studies as well as in conservative evangelical exposition of the Old Testament text. The message of Jeremiah's forty-year ministry is here firmly rooted in the Old Testament history as a message from the Lord to his ancient people; but its abiding relevance is also brought out in Professor Mackay's careful application of the material. This will quickly become an indispensable tool for anyone wishing to study and preach from the Book of Jeremiah.'

Iain D Campbell

'...a first class explanation of the prophet from a staunchly and well-argued conservative and grammatico-historical perspective. It is certain to become the first 'port of call' in my studies of the book'

Stephen Dray

John L. Mackay is Professor of Old Testament at the Free Church College, Edinburgh. He has authored another Mentor Commentary on *Exodus* (ISBN 1 85792 614 5) along with two Focus on the Bible Commentaries, one on *Jonah, Micah, Nahum, Habbakkuk and Zephaniah*(ISBN 1-85792-392-8) and the other on *Haggai, Zechariah and Malachi* (ISBN 1- 85792-067-8)

ISBN 1-85792-937-3

Christian Focus Publications
publishes books for all ages

Our mission statement –

STAYING FAITHFUL
In dependence upon God we seek to help make His infallible Word, the Bible, relevant. Our aim is to ensure that the Lord Jesus Christ is presented as the only hope to obtain forgiveness of sin, live a useful life and look forward to heaven with Him.

REACHING OUT
Christ's last command requires us to reach out to our world with His gospel. We seek to help fulfill that by publishing books that point people towards Jesus and help them develop a Christ-like maturity. We aim to equip all levels of readers for life, work, ministry and mission.

Books in our adult range are published in three imprints.

Christian Focus contains popular works including biographies, commentaries, basic doctrine and Christian living. Our children's books are also published in this imprint.

Mentor focuses on books written at a level suitable for Bible College and seminary students, pastors, and other serious readers. The imprint includes commentaries, doctrinal studies, examination of current issues and church history.

Christian Heritage contains classic writings from the past.

For a free catalogue of all our titles, please write to

Christian Focus Publications, Ltd
Geanies House, Fearn,
Ross-shire, IV20 1TW, Scotland, United Kingdom
info@christianfocus.com